Read *to* Succeed

A THEMATIC APPROACH TO ACADEMIC READING

3e

Read *to* Succeed

A THEMATIC APPROACH TO ACADEMIC READING

David Rothman
Queensborough Community College

Jilani Warsi
Queensborough Community College

PEARSON

Boston Columbus Indianapolis New York San Francisco
Amsterdam Cape Town Dubai London Madrid Milan Munich Paris Montrèal Toronto
Delhi Mexico City São Paulo Sydney Hong Kong Seoul Singapore Taipei Tokyo

Editorial Director: Eric Stano
Executive Editor: Matthew Wright
Program Manager: Eric Jorgensen
Development Editor: Anne Stameshkin
Product Marketing Manager: Jennifer Edwards
Digital Editor: Kelsey Loveday
Media Producer: Marisa Massaro
Content Specialist: Julia Pomann
Project Manager: Shannon Kobran
Project Coordination, Text Design, and Electronic Page Makeup: Lumina Datamatics
Program Design Lead: Heather Scott
Cover Art: Brian Haglwara/Getty Images
Senior Manufacturing Buyer: Roy L. Pickering, Jr.
Printer/Binder: R. R. Donnelley/Willard
Cover Printer: Lehigh-Phoenix Color/Hagerstown

Acknowledgments of third-party content appear on pages 591–595.

The Library of Congress Cataloging-in-Publication Data is available at the Library of Congress.

---

1 2 3 4 5 6 7 8 9 10—RRD—19 18 17 16

www.pearsonhighered.com

Student ISBN-10: 0-13-406446-1
Student ISBN-13: 978-0-13-406446-8
A la Carte ISBN-10: 0-13-407286-3
A la Carte ISBN-13: 978-0-13-407286-9

Contents

Chapter 9 Business: Entrepreneurship 476

Chapter 10 Political Science: American Government 540

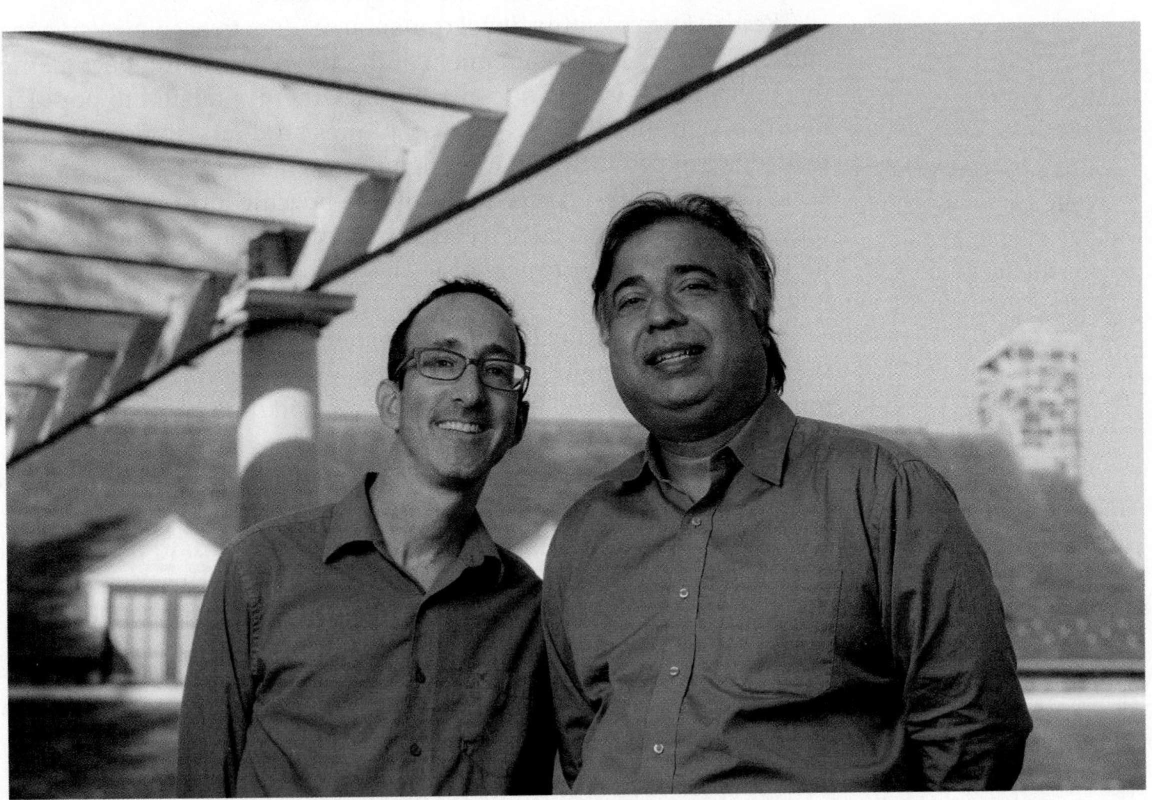

David Rothman (left) & Jilani Warsi

Preface: The Goals and Philosophy of *Read to Succeed*

Now in its third edition, *Read to Succeed* continues to engage students in academic reading through its thematic organization around academic disciplines. Our text offers an abundance of readings drawn from a variety of sources (from textbooks to blogs), provides multiple opportunities for students to build reading skills through discussion and writing, and keeps a sustained focus on vocabulary building.

Read to Succeed spurs developmental readers to become active readers and engages them in academic reading by fostering intellectual inquiry through an exploration of contemporary themes related to popular academic disciplines. When a subject piques students' interest—when the readings are provocative and engaging, when the vocabulary is made accessible through a focus on discipline-specific terminology, and when they have the opportunity to become active readers through expressing their opinion on controversial topics within a discipline—then sparks will fly.

It is our philosophy that students more successfully master key reading skills when taught in the context of engaging readings. With this in mind, we've organized *Read to Succeed* around nine academic disciplines, enabling students to build background knowledge of the major academic disciplines while honing their reading skills. To further increase their engagement with the text, the authors provide an unmatched variety of readings from sources ranging from textbooks to poetry, to blogs, to transcripts of popular online lectures. With an extensive coverage of vocabulary relevant to the academic themes and a variety of genres, *Read to Succeed* meets the needs of future academic readers.

Content Overview

Each chapter of *Read to Succeed* will take students on a journey of discovery and open their minds to new territories of knowledge and fresh ways of interacting with ideas and concepts. *Read to Succeed* is organized into ten chapters, the first providing an overview of the "reading process" and how the text is organized, and each subsequent chapter focusing on a different academic discipline. A critical reading skill focus is integrated into each chapter, so that students can master reading skills in the context of engaging readings.

Chapter 1	INTRODUCTION TO *READ TO SUCCEED*	GENERAL OVERVIEW: SKILLS, DISCIPLINES, AND HOW TO USE THIS TEXT
	Academic Discipline	**Reading Skill in Focus**
Chapter 2	EDUCATION	VOCABULARY IN CONTEXT
Chapter 3	HEALTH	MAIN IDEA AND TOPIC
Chapter 4	ENVIRONMENTAL SCIENCE	SUPPORTING DETAILS
Chapter 5	E-COMMERCE	INFERENCES
Chapter 6	CRIMINAL JUSTICE	FACT AND OPINION
Chapter 7	NURSING	PATTERNS OF ORGANIZATION
Chapter 8	PSYCHOLOGY	ARGUMENT
Chapter 9	BUSINESS	AUTHOR'S BIAS
Chapter 10	POLITICAL SCIENCE	COMBINED SKILLS

Each chapter in *Read to Succeed* contains a "Skill Focus" section that highlights key reading skills, such as main idea, patterns of organization, or argument. The authors provide instruction, practice, and application opportunities to ensure that students have had a deep focus on each reading skill before moving on to the next skill.

Throughout each chapter, the principle features are supported in a variety of ways. The culmination of the variety of features offered in *Read to Succeed* will equip students for the reading and critical thinking skills expected at the college level.

What's New in the Third Edition?

- **A NEW Chapter 1:** This introductory chapter engages students with some key reading strategies and walks them interactively through the text's goals and features.
- **MORE connections between reading and writing:** This edition integrates more writing activities and introduces a student blog feature—Writing on The Wall—which prompts students to post written responses in reaction to the text's thematic content, and to read and respond to the ideas of their classmates.
- **Over 20 NEW readings**, including memoir excerpts (from *The Other Wes Moore*), online articles ("Coping with the First year of College"), more engaging textbook excerpts ("Succeeding as a Nursing Student"), newspaper articles, ("Ocean Life Faces Mass Extinction"), and transcripts from popular online lectures (Geoffrey Canada on the Crisis in American Education), among others.
- **A NEW "Contemporary Issues in the Discipline" section in each chapter, featuring videos of lectures from professionals in the discipline:** After reading a brief contextual introduction in the text,

students are prompted to watch an online video lecture and take notes. Then they are prompted to read the speech transcript of the talk, provided in their text, before engaging in class discussions with the help of critical-thinking questions. This feature culminates by asking students to conduct mock interviews with the featured speaker.

Special Features of *Read to Succeed*

Each chapter within *Read to Succeed* contains a variety of apparatus designed to engage students and support the principle features: themes of academic disciplines, a variety of genres, extensive vocabulary support—in addition to overall reading improvement. Our goal with the chapter narratives is to take students on a journey that quite resembles the journey they will take when they encounter their 100-level content class curricula.

How *Read to Succeed* Augments Each Chapter's Academic Theme

- **Biographical Profiles** highlight well-known figures in each academic area. In every chapter, students will have the opportunity to learn about a famous figure and complete online research on another prominent person in the field.

BIOGRAPHICAL PROFILE

Oprah Winfrey

Oprah Gail Winfrey, more popularly known as Oprah, is a famous American television host, business tycoon, and philanthropist. She has received many honorary awards for her much-acclaimed internationally syndicated talk show, *The Oprah Winfrey Show*. In addition to being a popular talk show host, Winfrey is also a book critic, an Academy Award–nominated actress, and a magazine publisher. She has been ranked the wealthiest African American of the twenty-first century, the only black billionaire for three consecutive years, and the most philanthropic African American who ever lived. Some people believe that she is the most influential woman in the world.

Winfrey was born on January 29, 1954, in rural Mississippi. A child born out of wedlock and raised in a Milwaukee neighborhood, she was raped at the age of 9 and gave birth to a son at the age of 14. The son died in his infancy, and she went to live with her father in Tennessee. It was there that she landed a job in radio at the age of 19. She never looked back since then, and after working as a talk show host in Chicago for a while, she finally founded her own **production** company and became syndicated globally.

Winfrey's meteoric rise to stardom did not happen overnight. She moved to Chicago in 1983 to host a morning talk show, *AM Chicago*. After she took over the talk show, it went from last place to the

- **Debate Topics** provide instructors an option of organizing lively class debates around provocative debate questions and readings within *Read to Succeed* to stimulate student interest in each academic subject area. From our teaching experience, we know that students enjoy exploring controversial topics, and class debates are the perfect forum for the free expression of diverse opinions.

b. the study of teaching methods.
c. the review of textbooks.
d. the evaluation of student work.

Recommended Debate Topic: Should we reward good grades with money and prizes?

Your suggested debate topics:

a. ______________________

b. ______________________

c. ______________________

- **Textbook Applications** are available in every chapter and contain an extended authentic textbook reading from an introductory text. The textbook content reflects the academic discipline focus of the chapter. Students will learn how to navigate a textbook chapter and be given ample practice to check their comprehension and reading skills with questions following each textbook chapter.
- **Contemporary Issues in the Discipline:** In this new feature, students interact with a video and transcript of a lecture given by a prominent figure offering words of wisdom to a well-informed audience. Students are asked to take notes from the video presentation, which they will develop into a formal outline. They will then be asked to read the transcript and engage in a provocative discussion.
- **Chapter Recap** offers students the chance to review what they have learned over the course of each chapter. They will be asked to recycle vocabulary from the unit and reflect critically on what they have learned and on which reading was most interesting to them.

How *Read to Succeed* Engages Students with a Variety of Genres

- **A multitude of readings**—five to seven per chapter—provides opportunities for students to master key reading skills. These selections are from a variety of genres, including magazines, newspapers, textbooks, literature, blogs, and video transcripts. This third edition contains over 20 new readings, which reflect cutting-edge trends across academic fields.
- **Further Explorations** are suggested resources offered at the end of each chapter, with a list of books, movies, and websites to inspire further exploration of each academic area.

How *Read to Succeed* Develops Students' Vocabulary

- **Discipline-specific Terminology** is introduced at the beginning of every chapter—in addition to vocabulary-building activities—so that students can become familiar with key terms in the chapter's discipline. This vocabulary is recycled at the end of the chapter to deepen comprehension. In this freshly revamped, vocabulary-focused section, students will first be asked to brainstorm at least five words that are related to the given academic discipline. This is a creative way to build vocabulary through practice with associated terms. This section contains ten key words culled from the reading selections. The students' task is to find either a synonym or an antonym for these discipline-specific terms. Later, when they read the reading selections, they will have a head start on some of the text's key vocabulary terms. Studies show that one of the most effective methods of building vocabulary is through exposure to theme-based vocabulary.

- **The MyReadingLab e-text version of *Read to Succeed* includes an Academic Word List** (AWL), which contains high-frequency academic terms with which most proficient readers are familiar and can readily incorporate in speech and writing without having to look them up in the dictionary. Additionally, AWL terms are highlighted in select readings in each chapter of the print and e-texts. Students can determine each highlighted word's meaning through context or look it up in a dictionary. Their ultimate goal should not be to just memorize the words but also to use these high-frequency words in their speech and writing.
- **Marginal Definitions** define particularly challenging words or idioms in the reading selections in order to allow students to tackle reading with minimal interruption.

How *Read to Succeed* Helps Students' Overall Academic Improvement

- **Skill Focus**, available in every chapter, provides in-depth instruction for a particular reading skill. Students will work with examples and exercises to master these skills and then apply them in the context of authentic reading passages within each discipline focus.

> **SKILL FOCUS: Identifying the Main Idea and Topic**
>
> When you are asked to find the *main idea* of a sentence or a paragraph, you are really being asked to identify the most important point the author wants to convey to the reader.
>
> Imagine a friend calls you and says she is in a hurry on the way to the movies and would like you to recommend a film. You tell your friend the name of the film you think she should see, and she asks you to tell her in a sentence (there is no time to lose!) what the film is about.
>
> You say, "*Freedom Writers* is about a dedicated female teacher who inspires her underprivileged students to express themselves through writing." As you may have guessed by now, you've just offered your friend the main idea of the movie!

- **Reading with a Critical Eye** is a feature that provides students with the opportunity to observe, evaluate, and respond to the reading selections in a critical way. Each reading selection is followed by a variety of open-ended questions, allowing students to think critically about the main points.
- **NEW: Writing on The Wall:** This feature encourages students to post online responses to provocative questions related to the chapter theme and to read and respond to the ideas of their classmates. Blogging gives students writing practice, which in turn provides an opportunity for more engaged reading. It allows them time to consider and write responses carefully, and it should help make them feel more confident about class participation. These prompts encourage students to articulate their thoughts in a civil manner, to take other perspectives into consideration, and to keep an open mind as they learn.

- **From Reading to Writing** sections underscore the connections between reading and writing. Students will be prompted to transfer their academic reading skills to the task of academic writing.
- **Study Tips** are available after every chapter to help students improve their overall academic performance and to help them become more active learners. Topics include time management, skimming and scanning, and annotation and highlighting.

Using Index Cards to Study Vocabulary

Overview

As you know, one of the most challenging parts of succeeding in college is to learn new vocabulary and jargon typical of a subject. There are many techniques to build vocabulary, but here we offer you an effective technique that will help you improve your active vocabulary. For this activity, you will need index cards that are blank on one side and lined on the other.

Activity

As you come across an unfamiliar word while doing a reading assignment, write it on the blank side of the index card. On the lined side, write information related to the new word as follows. Keep in mind that you will need a good dictionary to do this exercise.

1. Look up the word in a dictionary and write how it is pronounced. Most dictionaries phonetically transcribe words, so it should not be difficult for you to write the sounds.
2. Find out what part of speech the word is and write it below. For example, write if the word is a noun, a verb, an adjective, or an adverb.
3. Write the meaning of the word.
4. Make an example sentence using the new word in context.
5. Using a dictionary, write the words that are derived from the same root. For example, the words *marine*, *maritime*, *marina*, *submarine*, and *mariner* are all derived from the same Latin root *mar*, which means sea. This way you will learn that some words are associated with each other.
6. Write at least two or three synonyms of the unfamiliar word here.
7. Finally, write at least two or three antonyms of the new word here.

Let's take a look at an index card so that you can fully understand how to **create** your own index cards for vocabulary building. We will use the word *create* for this index card exercise.

Ancillaries for Instructors

Supplement your experience using Read to Succeed with the following resources:

- Instructor's Manual for Read to Succeed, 3/e ISBN 0134072898
- Test Bank for Read to Succeed 3/e ISBN 0134064666
- MyTest Test Bank ISBN 0134064704
- Answer Key for Read to Succeed, 3/e ISBN 0134064674
- PowerPoints for Read to Succeed, 3/e ISBN 0134072855

MyReadingLab™: Improving Reading Through Personalized Learning Experiences

In an ideal world, an instructor would work with each student to help improve reading skills with consistent challenges and rewards. Without that luxury, MyReadingLab offers a way to keep students focused and accelerate their progress using comprehensive pre-assignments and a powerful, adaptive study plan.

Flexible Enough to Fit Every Course Need

MyReadingLab can be set up to fit your specific course needs, whether you seek reading support to complement what you do in class, a way to administer many sections easily, or a self-paced environment for independent study.

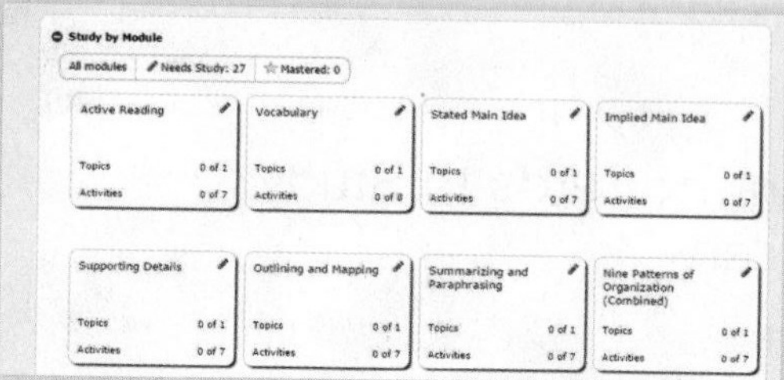

Learning in Context

In addition to distinct pre-loaded learning paths for reading/writing skills practice and reading level practice, MyReadingLab incorporates numerous activities for practice and readings from the accompanying textbook. This makes the connection between what's done in and out of the classroom more relevant to students.

NEW! Learning Tools for Student Engagement

Create an Engaging Classroom

Learning Catalytics is an interactive, student-response tool in MyReadingLab that uses students' smartphones, tablets, or laptops, allowing instructors to generate class discussion easily, guide lectures, and promote peer-to-peer learning with real-time analytics.

Build Multimedia Assignments

MediaShare allows students to easily post multimodal assignments for peer review and instructor feedback. In both face-to-face and online courses, MediaShare enriches the student learning experience by enabling contextual feedback to be provided quickly and easily.

Direct Access to MyLab

Users can link from any Learning Management System (LMS) to Pearson's MyReadingLab. Access MyLab assignments, rosters and resources, and synchronize MyLab grades with the LMS gradebook.

Visit www.myreadinglab.com for more information.

MyReadingLab for *Read to Succeed 3/e* also includes ...

- **Online versions of exercises for each reading.** In each chapter, exercises for all readings except one offer feedback; the final reading does not offer feedback and can be used as a post-test to see how students apply learned strategies and skills.
- Two online-only resources for students, **Appendix 1: Most Frequent Words of the Academic Word List by Sublist** and **Appendix 2: Discipline Guide**

Acknowledgments

We wish to acknowledge the contributions of our reviewers, who provided valuable critiques and suggestions, thus making *Read to Succeed* a much stronger book:

Janet Anthony, *Charles S. Mott Community College*

Gail Bauer, *Richland Community College*

Jaqueline A. Blackwell, *Thomas Nelson Community College*

Dale Boyle, *Community College of Rhode Island–Warwick*

Sarah Brown, *Carl Albert State College*

Darla Coffman, *Midlands Technical College*

Gina Desai, *Glendale Community College*

Ismail Hakim, *Richard J. Daley College*

Richard T. Lambdin, *Midlands Technical College*

Susan Monroe, *Housatonic Community College*

Michelle Nicholas, *Florida Keys Community College*

Mitzi Sloniger, *Norco College*

Terri Tilmon, *Richard J. Daley College*

Pat Tondini, *Midlands Technical College*

Sara Walton, *Glendale Community College*

James Willams, *Greenville Technical College*

We would like to thank Anne Stameshkin, our development editor, for her professional expertise, her valuable suggestions, and for her wit, which helped us survive the editing process. We should also thank Eric Stano, our acquisitions editor, for his sense of vision and his unbending belief in our work. We must also thank our terrific program manager, Eric Jorgensen, and our first-rate production and media teams—our project manager at Pearson, Shannon Kobran; our project manager at Lumina, Cathy Castle; our permissions editor, Barbara Ryan; our content specialist, Julia Pomann; and our media editor, Kelsey Loveday. Finally, Jilani Warsi would like to express his gratitude to Saloni, his life partner, for her patience, understanding, and encouragement throughout the writing of this book. David Rothman would like to thank his mom for teaching him the joy of reading novel after novel on the Jersey Shore.

Sincerely,
Jilani Warsi and David Rothman

INTRODUCTION TO READ TO SUCCEED

Learning Objectives

AFTER READING THIS CHAPTER, YOU SHOULD BE ABLE TO...

1. Identify the philosophy behind this text.
2. Determine what you already know about the academic disciplines featured in this text.
3. Use the reading process and predictive reading.
4. Recognize the chapter features of this text.
5. Describe the reading genres featured in Chapters 2–10.

The Philosophy of *Read to Succeed*

Objective 1: Identify the philosophy behind this text.

Welcome to the world of *Read to Succeed: A Thematic Approach to Academic Reading*!

Let's be honest. Life is short. Your time is precious and you want to reach your academic goals as smoothly and as efficiently as possible. To aid in this process, *Read to Succeed* is thematically organized so that each chapter focuses on a popular academic discipline such as psychology, business, criminal justice, and nursing. Rather than organizing chapters primarily by reading skills (such as main idea, inferences, purpose, and so on), we offer discussions of each of these skills in the context of reading about specific subjects. This text is based on the logic that reading skills evolve from the organic interplay of curiosity, critical thinking, and reflection on meaning.

In other words, the more you read, and the more engaged you are in the reading process, the more progress you will make in academic reading. Investing your energies in the academic-focused chapters of *Read to Succeed* will better prepare you for the 100-level content courses you will be taking in the near future.

Chapter Journeys

"Do the difficult things while they are easy and do the great things while they are small. A journey of a thousand miles must begin with a single step."

LAO TZU

Each chapter will take you on a journey of discovery and open your mind to new territories of knowledge and fresh ways of interacting with ideas and concepts.

EXERCISE 1.1 A Chapter Map

Figure 1-1 provides a journey map that you can apply to Chapters 2–10 of this book. Examine this map and discuss the flow of a chapter with a classmate, describing it in your own words. Consider looking over Chapter 2 as an example.

Fig. 1-1

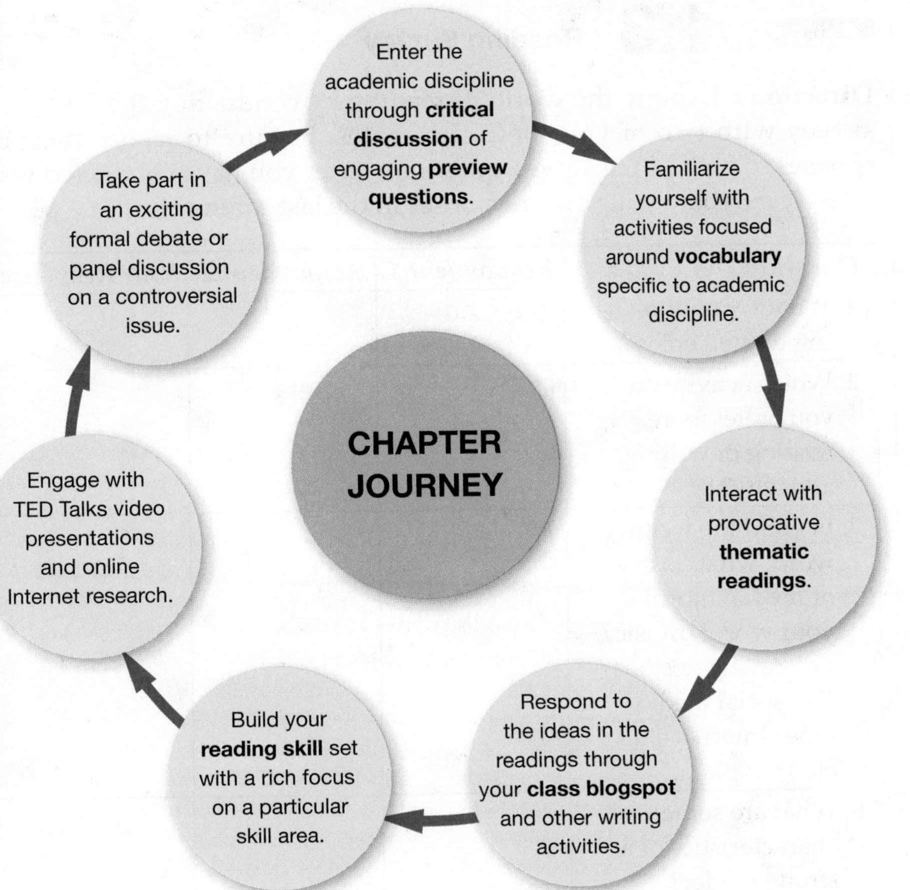

The goal of *Read to Succeed* is not to bore you with traditional skill-and-drill chapters, but to take you on memorable chapter journeys on topics that pique your interest. We want you to be able to express yourself freely in dynamic discussions and to respond to ideas in the text on your class blog.

EXERCISE 1.2 Compare Two Photos

Take a close look at these two photos, and answer the question that follows:

Can you guess what factors might explain the differences in the student's expression in the two photos?

___

EXERCISE 1.3 Reading Survey

Directions: Explore the world of reading by conducting the following survey with two of your new classmates. Be sure to record their responses to each of the survey questions. After you have conducted your interviews, share your own responses in the last column.

Question	*Respondent 1*	*Respondent 2*	*Your Responses*
1. What types of reading do you enjoy?			
2. Which activity do you prefer more, reading or writing, and why?			
3. Beyond the written word, what forms of media inform your world (music/video/ movies/art/TV/social media/other Internet sites/etc.)? Explain.			
6. What are some characteristics of a strong reader?			

EXERCISE 1.4 Free-Write Based on Interview Results

Examine your survey responses. Which responses do you find most interesting? Compare the respondents' ideas. Write for ten minutes on this topic (without stopping!).

Academic Disciplines

Objective 2: Determine what you already know about the academic disciplines featured in this text.

EXERCISE 1.5 Getting Your Feet Wet: Focus on Academic Disciplines

Directions: Take a glance at the nine disciplines listed in the following table that provide the content for the chapters in this book. Work with a partner to determine each discipline's focus and its application in the eal world, and then jot down your ideas. The first one is completed for ou as an example.

Discipline	*Focus*	*Application*	*Preference 1 to 9*
Education	*Teaching and Learning*	*Assessment Evaluation*	
Health/ Nutrition			
Environ-mental Science			
E-Com-merce			
Criminal Justice			
Nursing			
Business			
Political Science			

If you are a careful reader and pay attention to detail, you may have noticed the fourth column on the right side of the table. Consider which disciplines most pique your interest, and rate them on a scale of 1 to 9 in the right column. When you are finished, discuss your preferences with your classmates.

The Reading Process

Objective 3: Use the reading process and predictive reading.

Reading is a process and consists of applying a variety of strategies before, during, and after reading that will increase your connection to and understanding of the content. Examine Figure 1-2.

Pre-Reading and Making Predictions

Before jumping head first into a reading, it is useful to get the lay of the land in terms of the topic covered in the reading, the author's focus and purpose, and how the text is organized. The following steps can be useful in preparing for a reading assignment.

Fig. 1-2 **Steps in Reading Process**

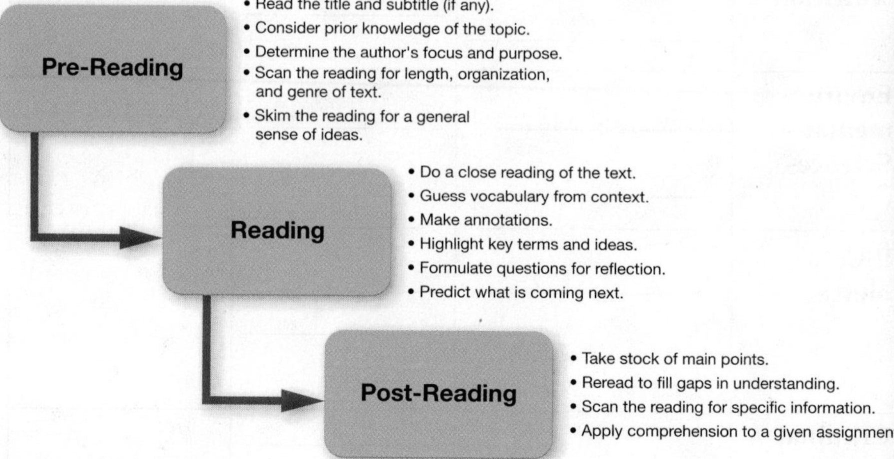

Pre-Reading
• Read the title and subtitle (if any).
• Consider prior knowledge of the topic.
• Determine the author's focus and purpose.
• Scan the reading for length, organization, and genre of text.
• Skim the reading for a general sense of ideas.
Reading
• Do a close reading of the text.
• Guess vocabulary from context.
• Make annotations.
• Highlight key terms and ideas.
• Formulate questions for reflection.
• Predict what is coming next.
Post-Reading
• Take stock of main points.
• Reread to fill gaps in understanding.
• Scan the reading for specific information.
• Apply comprehension to a given assignment.

Read the Title and Subtitle (If Any)

Many students rush into a college reading without paying attention to its title. The truth is that the title often tells you about the direction of a given reading. When you are wearing the hat of a writer, an important consideration is how your title reflects on the content of your writing. In a similar manner, good readers can often predict the author's main idea by simply reading the title. For example, if the title of a sports article is "This Time It's a She Who Is Champion," most fluent readers can surmise that the championship was traditionally won by a male, but in this case, it has been won by a female.

EXERCISE 1.6 Predicting a Reading's Main Idea from the Title

Directions: Read the following title with a partner and try to make some predictions about the main idea of the reading that follows it.

Title: There are Helpful Resources on Your Campus to Help You Succeed

Your predictions:

1. ____________________

2. ____________________

Consider Your Prior Knowledge of the Topic

Continuing with the previous example, once you understand from the title that the reading is about coping in college, it is a natural step to consider how much you know about this topic. In other words, prior knowledge of a topic can help you grasp new information on the subject in focus. Fluent readers have a vast knowledge base, which enables them to better understand a given reading. Clearly, the more you read, the better reader you will become.

EXERCISE 1.7 Building on Prior Knowledge of a Topic

Directions: Working with the title you just examined, "There are Helpful Resources on Your Campus to Help You Succeed," explore your prior knowledge of this topic and jot down a few notes on what you know about your campus's resources.

1. ______________________________

2. ______________________________

3. ______________________________

Determine the Author's Purpose

As you enter a reading, consider why the author wrote this particular piece. Some authors write to simply inform readers about a topic area. Some have the goal of persuading readers to agree with their point of view through argumentation, and others simply want to entertain readers with an amusing or dramatic narrative. Understanding an author's purpose will help you gain a general sense of the direction a reading is going. (Refer to Chapter 6 for information on the author's purpose and tone.)

Skim the Reading for Length, Organization, and Genre

Another strategy you can employ to effectively approach a new reading is to glance over the text before you read it in depth, paying attention to length, how information is organized, and the genre. For example, a poem may be divided into three stanzas and still be only half a page, whereas an excerpt from a textbook may run several pages and be organized by subtopics.

Skim the Reading to Gain a General Sense of the Ideas It Contains

Before doing a close reading of a given text, skim through it to get the gist of the whole piece: what it is about, the author's main points, and so on. As with the previous strategy, skimming is effective for familiarizing yourself with the reading to come and helps you connect the new information to what you already know, which will increase your understanding and memory of what you read.

EXERCISE 1.8 Skimming Through a Reading to Get the Lay of the Land

Directions: Skim through the following reading to answer the following general questions about the article.

1. **Genre:** ____________________
2. **How is the article organized?** ____________________
3. **Article Topic:** ____________________
4. **Main Idea:** ____________________

READING

Textbook Excerpt

There are Helpful Resources on your Campus to Help You Succeed

from *The College Experience, Compact,* 2/e, by Amy Baldwin, Brian Tietje, and Paul Stoltz

1 Now that you have a better understanding of college culture and what is expected of you, it is time to examine how your college looks. Getting to know the layout of the campus and the people who work there is important to understanding the culture and getting the help you need to support your success. A big part of being a gritty learner is proactively and creatively tapping the resources around you to fill in any gaps and to get what you need to accelerate and fortify your success both inside and outside the classroom.

For example, knowing where to go when you need to use a computer will make your ability to complete an assignment a little easier. Finding your professor's office may save you time and stress when you need to talk to him about an upcoming test. Going out of your way to take advantage of these resources can make a huge difference. The more you are on campus, the better able you will be to find people and places that will help you no matter what you need, but it will help if you take some time to study your campus so you know where to look.

Explore Your Campus

3 Find a map of your campus and study it for a few minutes. How many buildings does it have? How much parking space? How much "green" space or landscaping? Are there any unique features to your campus that make it an inviting and exciting place? Familiarizing yourself with your campus is probably the first activity you did when you enrolled in classes. If you have not taken a tour or simply walked around the campus, do so within the first few weeks of the semester. Locate the library, the student center, student parking, the bookstore, the business office, and the registrar's office—just to name a few destinations.

4 The more you know about your campus's layout, the easier it will be to find what you are looking for when you need it most. Using your map of the campus or your memory, check off in Exhibit 1.8 the types of buildings or departments within buildings that you know are present at your college.

5 If your university has more than one campus, familiarize yourself with the layout of other college property. You may have to travel to a satellite campus to take a test or to pick up materials for a class. If you have the time and the other campus is not too far away, ask for a tour. At the very least, familiarize yourself with any of the items you marked "not sure" in Exhibit 1.8.

Locate Information about Campus Resources

6 Knowing where to go to find services and people is only part of learning about your college. Another important aspect is finding and using the information that the college produces for students. College publications are a great place to find information about courses, programs, scholarships, activities, and policy changes. It is important that you regularly read these publications in order to stay up to date with what is going on.

College Catalog

7 The college catalog is an essential document during your academic career. All the information that you need to apply for financial aid, choose courses, and complete a degree is contained in the catalog. The academic calendar is usually placed at the beginning of the catalog. There you will find the dates for registering, dropping courses, and taking final exams.

8 It is important to read and keep your college catalog because if the college changes any requirements of your degree program, you will be able to follow the guidelines that were published the year you began the program. For instance, if you are working on a psychology degree and you have taken three semesters of courses so far, you will not necessarily have to adhere to new requirements that are made at a later date.

EXHIBIT 1.8 Campus Layout Checklist

Building or Area	At My College	Not Sure
Student center or union		
Library		
Bookstore		
Administration building		
Theater or auditorium		
Snack bars, food courts, and other dining facilities		
Athletic training facilities (indoor or outdoor)		
Science labs		
Computer labs		
Individual colleges and departments (such as business, psychology, engineering, and graphic communication)		
Student parking		
Benches and tables for meeting outside		
Quiet study space inside		
Disability Resource Center		
Health Center		
Cashier's Office		
Housing Office		
Registrar's Office		

Student Handbook

9 The student handbook, which provides you with specific information about student conduct, academic standards, and services, is another valuable publication. Usually, the handbook contains descriptions of career services, the bookstore, computer labs, and financial aid offices. Academic information such as terms for probation and suspension for misconduct and qualifications for making the dean's list can also be found in the student handbook. Most schools view the student handbook as a legal document that outlines what students can do in certain situations, so be sure to read it closely and keep a copy at home or in your bookbag.

College Newspaper

10 College newspapers differ from the college catalog and student handbook in that students are usually the ones who are responsible for the content. Within a college newspaper, you will find articles about upcoming events, reports on changes on the college campus, editorials on important student issues, profiles of programs, and advertisements for used books, musical performances, and anything else that students want to announce. The college newspaper is also a forum to explore controversial topics and to discuss sensitive issues.

11 Newspapers always need students to interview, write, edit, and publish. If you are interested in working for the newspaper, contact the editor or visit a journalism or composition professor.

Bulletin Boards

12 Even with the increased use of the Internet, the bulletin board is still an important way to get a message to students. Found all over campus, bulletin boards usually advertise used books, needs for roommates and part-time jobs, and upcoming campus events. Bulletin boards within academic buildings often announce study abroad opportunities, summer workshops, special events, and other types of notable activities.

It's in the Syllabus

13 Anything that professors hand out in class is a communication tool. The syllabus is one of the most important documents that you will receive in class, so be sure to read it carefully. In the syllabus you will usually find the following information:

- Instructor's name, office location, phone number, hours open to students, and email address
- Prerequisites for the course
- Course description from the catalog
- Textbook information
- Course objectives, or what you will accomplish by the time you finish the class
- Course content, or what topics will be covered throughout the semester
- Assignments and due dates
- Grading criteria
- Attendance and late-work policies
- Academic integrity statement (which also appears in the student handbook)
- Disability accommodations policy
- General policies for classroom conduct

14 The syllabus is considered a contract between the student and the instructor. This means that not only will the syllabus contain what is expected of you during class, but it will also contain what you can expect from the professor. Both of you—the student and the professor—will be bound by what is stated in the document. Reading the syllabus closely and following it regularly will keep you on top of the policies, expectations, and assignments.

15 Other essential information that is handed out in class includes directions to assignments, photocopied readings, study questions, and notes. Regard anything that is given to you by the instructor as important, even if you are told "This won't be on the test."

16 You should also consider the grades and written comments you receive as communication from your instructors. Be sure to read any comments or suggestions that are written on papers and exams, ask questions if you don't understand them or they are illegible, and save all feedback until the semester is over.

Online Resources

17 The college's website is where you can find the most current information about classes, academic programs, and contact information for professors. It is easier to update information on a website because it doesn't involve printing and distribution, so it is more likely to provide the most accurate information. College websites usually list phone numbers and email addresses of professors and deans, which makes contacting them easier.

18 In addition to general information about degrees and departments, your college's website may give you access to professors' syllabi and assignments. This provides a good opportunity to investigate what courses you want to take based on the course objectives and activities and information about the professor.

Campus Organizations

19 Campus organizations or student groups are another part of college life you will want to learn more about. Depending on how large your college is and how involved the students are, you may find a variety of student organizations and clubs in which to participate. Even if your time is limited, consider getting involved in some way, because these activities can enhance your college experience, and employers value extracurricular leadership experience when they recruit potential employees. Campus organizations include, but are not limited to, student clubs, fraternities and sororities, student government, student leadership programs, and clubs focused on certain interests (e.g., gay, lesbian, bisexual and transgendered issues; political action; community service; academic honors and distinctions; religious or spiritual development; and career exploration). Getting involved will help you transition to the college and provide immediate connections with students, faculty, and staff. You can learn about these opportunities on the university website, through on-campus club fairs and information sessions, and by asking upperclassmen about their own experiences.

20 A university is an exciting place with a wide variety of activities and experiences that can enrich your life and help you succeed. Because there are many options for how you can get involved, you'll need to gather information about them and carefully choose the best opportunities in which you'll invest time and effort. It's a common mistake among students to get excited about all these opportunities and then overcommit. This leads to avoidable disappointment and failure. As you begin your college career, carefully select only one or two extracurricular activities until you can gain experience with your academic responsibilities and determine how much capacity you have for commitments outside the classroom.

During Reading

Reading should be a pleasure, not a curse. If you make a conscious effort to focus on the task at hand, you may discover that reading can be an enjoyable experience. It may be counterproductive to discount a given reading simply because you have a preconceived notion that the subject matter is boring. You may be pleasantly surprised to find that the reading is engaging and builds on your knowledge base.

Here are some effective strategies to utilize as you read a given passage.

Do a Close Reading of the Text

Once you have taken a bird's-eye view of a reading passage, you are better prepared to read it. At this point, your goal is to obtain a deeper understanding of the full text. While many people assume that reading is a passive activity, the following active reading strategies will keep you engaged as you make your way through the text.

- **Guess vocabulary from context.** As you read, it is not realistic to look up every unfamiliar word in a dictionary. A more effective technique is to guess the meaning of new vocabulary items from the given context. Keep in mind that many words have multiple meanings, so pay attention to how a word is used in a sentence to zero in on the intended meaning. (For a detailed lesson on vocabulary in context, refer to Chapter 2, p. 37.)
- **Make annotations.** Active readers annotate a text for various reasons: sometimes they jot down the author's main points in the margin, and other times they simply make note of difficult terms and concepts. A good reader's book is usually quite marked up by the end of the semester! (For more on annotating, see Chapter 3, p. 149.)
- **Highlight key terms and ideas.** In addition to annotating, highlighting key ideas and terms is another effective reading strategy. As with annotating, a key advantage of highlighting is that it sets you up well to revisit the text at a later point, perhaps during a test review. A reader cannot be expected to simply memorize where the key points were in a given reading, and that is where highlighting comes into play. Make sure to choose a bright highlighter and remember that highlighting can be used in conjunction with annotation. (For more on highlighting, see Chapter 3, p. 148.)
- **Formulate questions for reflection.** As you make your way through a reading, frame pertinent questions in the back of your mind for further reflection. Try not to be swayed too easily by the author's arguments. Instead, ask questions that test whether the claims an author makes are valid and if there are holes in his or her arguments.
- **Predict what is coming next.** Engaged readers make predictions about the direction an author is going based on what they have already read. As you digest ideas and information, it is natural that you will wonder what is coming next. For example, if you are reading a persuasive essay about why people should quit eating meat, you may predict some of the reasons after reading just the introductory paragraph. (In each of the following chapters, you will be asked to complete a predictive activity with one of the readings.)

EXERCISE 1.9 **Making Predictions as You Read**

Directions: Read just the first paragraph of "There are Helpful Resources on your Campus to Help You Succeed." Working with a partner, make two predictions about what the author might say next.

1. ______________________________

2. ______________________________

____

Revisit your predictions after reading the entire passage to see if your predictions were right or wrong.

Post-Reading

Many students believe that once their eyes have glanced over the last paragraph of a reading, they have completed the reading assignment and fully grasped the important points. Clearly, this is a misconception. Just as with the writing process, the reading process also involves refinement and clarification of ideas. After you have read a passage, take the following steps to enhance your reading comprehension.

- **Take stock of the main points.** Before you respond to a reading either in writing or through answering reading comprehension questions, reflect on what you have just read and consider the author's main points. If you have highlighted and annotated the text, it would be a wise idea to review your work now.
- **Reread to fill in any gaps in your understanding.** Even though you have completed a reading, it is possible that you may have misunderstood certain sections of the text. This is where rereading helps fill any gaps in your understanding. You will be surprised to discover how much better you grasp a text after reading it a second time.
- **Scan the reading for specific information.** As compared with skimming, where the reader aims to get a general sense of the text, scanning involves catching particular bits and pieces of information. The goal is to zero in on content related to a given task. If a reading assignment requires you to answer multiple-choice questions, to write a brief response, or to discuss open-ended questions, scanning the text is a pertinent step toward accomplishing these tasks. (For a detailed discussion of scanning, refer to Chapter 4, p. 213.)
- **Demonstrate comprehension of a given assignment.** Throughout this text, you will be asked to complete a variety of assignments related to the chapter readings. Whether you are responding to text in summary or blog reaction form, answering multiple-choice questions, or having a brief discussion about the topics covered in the reading, you will need to rely on your reading comprehension to carry out these activities successfully. After all, the journey of reading

can be an enriching experience, but only if you fully go along for the ride. Keep your comprehension helmet on.

Previewing the Features of *Read to Succeed*

Objective 4: Recognize the chapter features of this text.

As you work through the pages of this text, it will be important for you to familiarize yourself with the features of each of the chapters. What follows is a list of these features to help you navigate the chapters smoothly.

1. **Learning Objectives:** Every chapter in this book begins with a list of specific learning objectives that outline what you are expected to learn from reading the chapter.
2. **Introduction to the Field:** The learning objectives are followed by an introduction to the academic discipline featured in the chapter. The introduction also includes a brief account of the selections you will be reading.
3. **Previewing Questions:** Four to five questions at the beginning of each chapter will ask you to think about what you already know about the field. Read these questions carefully and discuss them with your classmates at length. Once you have shared your ideas orally, you will be asked to write brief responses to two out of the five questions on "The Wall" (see below).
4. **Writing on The Wall:** This feature in the text encourages you to participate in a shared class blog, where you can write your own responses as well as read and respond to classmates' ideas. In such a forum, we encourage you to articulate your thoughts in a civil manner, to take into consideration other perspectives, and to keep an open mind as you learn. If your class does not use a blog, respond to these questions in a "Wall" of your own, a dedicated notebook or electronic file that you could easily share with classmates or your instructor.

Etiquette for Writing on The Wall

1. **Be Civil:** It is important to be civil and courteous, even to those who may have an opposing viewpoint. You can disagree in a polite manner, choosing your words carefully. As you know, words can hurt!
2. **Be Academic:** There is a big difference between texting a friend and writing an academic response to a classmate's ideas. If your writing

begins to sound like you are speaking, you are going in the wrong direction. Avoid contractions like gonna, wanna, hafta and slang, and follow punctuation rules. Take no shortcuts!

3. **Be Original:** Rather than using clichés and stating the obvious, repeating what you have heard somewhere else, or simply cutting and pasting text, express your independent thoughts. Find your academic voice!
4. **Be Factual:** It is one thing to base your opinion on evidence and another to base it on mere hearsay. As you respond to the preview questions and your classmates' ideas, resist the temptation to offer your opinion without sufficient support.
5. **Interpreting a Cartoon:** Each chapter offers a humorous cartoon related to the academic field in focus. Your job will be to examine the cartoon and figure out its deeper meaning.
6. **Discipline-specific Vocabulary:** Working with a classmate, you are asked to think of at least five words that are related to the discipline. For example, if the chapter discipline is business, would you be able to come up with five terms related to this field? Perhaps you could come up with twenty! This is a creative way to build vocabulary through practice with associated terms. This section contains ten key words culled from the readings. Your task is to find either a synonym or an antonym for these discipline-specific terms. Later, when you read the readings, you will have a head start on some of the text's key vocabulary terms. Studies show that one of the most effective methods of building vocabulary is through exposure to theme-based vocabulary.
7. **Chapter Readings:**
    - **Pre-Reading Questions** The reading is preceded by three preview questions designed to prepare you to analyze the text.
    - **Thinking About the Reading** Five open-ended questions follow the reading, and they are designed to get you to think critically about some of the issues raised in it.
    - **Reading Comprehension Check** A set of ten multiple-choice questions are included to let you check whether you understood the main points of the reading.
    - **Debatable Topic** Each chapter contains a juicy, debatable topic. Can television be blamed for people's bad behavior? Should unhealthy foods such as soda and potato chips be for sale in public school vending machines? Should juvenile offenders receive the same sentences as adults? These are just a few of the topics that will serve as subjects for class debates.
8. **Biographical Profiles:** The lives of well-known figures are highlighted in each academic area. Larry Page and Sergey Brin (founders

of Google) are featured in Chapter 5 on e-commerce. Oprah Winfrey is the focus in Chapter 9 on business. Beyond reading about these influential people, you will also have the opportunity to do research on another prominent person in each field.

9. **Reading Skill Focus:** A critical college reading skill is introduced in each chapter along with some practice exercises. Each consecutive chapter builds on the reading skills that were the focus of previous chapters.
10. **From Reading to Writing:** This feature underscores the organic connection between reading and writing. You will explore journal writing, build your summary-writing skills, and work on organizing your thoughts in outline form, among other writing foci.
11. **Careers in the Academic Discipline:** Everyone wants a good job when they graduate! In this feature, you will do online research on careers that match up with different academic disciplines.
12. **Textbook Application:** This reading is excerpted from a 100-level college-discipline-specific textbook. The purpose of this selection is to get you in the habit of reading authentic text and learning academic vocabulary. The reading is followed by ten multiple-choice questions. You will have the opportunity to listen to an audio file of the text and to practice note-taking skills.
13. **Contemporary Issues in the Discipline:** Each chapter features a TED Talk of a prominent figure offering words of wisdom to a well-informed audience. You will be asked to take notes from the video presentation, which you will develop into a formal outline. You will then be asked to read the transcript and engage in a provocative discussion with the help of a number of critical thinking questions. This activity will culminate with a mock interview with the featured speaker.
14. **Class Debates and Panel Discussions:** This feature allows you to put the ideas and knowledge you have gained on issues in a given academic field into real action! Class debates involve two teams taking opposing positions on a controversial topic. In a panel discussion, each team member plays a specific role in relation to a community issue. For example, if the issue is whether to close down all fast-food restaurants in your neighborhood, one student might play a health-food advocate while another might play a high school student who is a fast-food customer. Debates and panel discussions promise stimulating class interaction!
15. **Chapter Recap Activities:** You will have a chance to review what you have learned over the course of each chapter. This feature is divided into five challenging tasks:

    a. ***A Quick Glance*** is a 60-second express write where you are asked to share one thing you learned in each chapter.

    b. ***Summary Writing***

c. ***Internet Research on a Related Theme***
d. ***Reinforcing the Reading Skill***
e. ***Recycling Vocabulary***

16. **Further Explorations:** Once you are engaged in the readings related to a given academic discipline, your curiosity will lead you to seek additional sources of information. This feature offers you movie titles, books, and Internet sites where you can satisfy this itch!
17. **Critical Study Tips for Your Academic Success:** Tips provided after each chapter will guide you toward becoming more active learners and improving your overall academic performance. Topics include time management, skimming and scanning, and annotation and highlighting.

Guide to Genre

Objective 5: Describe the reading genres featured in Chapters 2-10.

Read to Succeed will expose you to a diversity of text genres. The word *genre* is borrowed from French, meaning type or sort. Each reading has an indication of its genre. It is critical before beginning to read a text that you are aware of both the source and genre of the text you are about to read. Embarking on a given text without knowing its genre is like turning the ignition of a transportation vehicle with no knowledge of whether you are driving a plane, a boat, or a bus!

The genre of a text offers a clear context for the reader, often determines the author's purpose for writing, and keys you in to such elements as the author's tone and bias and, perhaps more fundamentally, the kind of vocabulary that one could expect within a given genre. For example, if you are reading an *editorial* about the situation in the Middle East, you can predict that the author's goal is to persuade the reader to share his or her opinion. Thus, the author of an editorial will try to use persuasive language to achieve a certain goal. However, if you are reading a *newspaper article* on the situation in the Middle East, the author's primary purpose will usually be to report information on the topic and to expose the reader to a number of different perspectives on the issues being reported. That is not to say that newspaper articles are neutral and show no bias. This is clearly not the case. What is true is that editorials, by definition, are written with the primary purpose of expressing a viewpoint. This distinction between one genre (editorial) and another (newspaper article) is critical, and successful readers understand this. A list of all of the genres offered in *Read to Succeed* follows, with a short description of each genre type and some strategies on how best to approach these as readers.

Genres in *Read to Succeed* Readings

Newspaper/magazine/online article—This genre reports on a topic or an event and is mostly informational. Readers first must understand the general theme, context, and topic area of a news article before trying to make sense of the details. Consider how the choice of subtopics and examples given key you into the author's bias.

Newspaper editorial—These are opinion columns written with the goal of persuading the reader. Readers should first try to understand the author's general position on the topic being discussed and then try to analyze how the author goes about proving his or her argument(s).

Textbook reading—This type of genre involves discipline-specific academic content. Textbook chapters are usually assigned for given college courses. The content of a text chapter often reinforces material discussed in class, so the more active of a learner you are during your course lectures, the easier it will be to work with the textbook readings. Good highlighting skills are essential in pulling out key terms and concepts.

Memoir—A memoir is a type of autobiographical writing. It is important for readers to understand the general context when reading a memoir. Is this a famous person you are interested in learning about or someone who has had a life experience that you would like to know more about? Pay close attention to the memoirist's life perspectives and to key turning points in the memoirist's life experience and the lessons that can be learned from them.

Interview—An interview consists of a question and answer session. Often famous people or experts in a particular field are interviewed in magazines and newspapers. In *Read to Succeed,* a number of question/answer interviews serve as chapter readings. As in reading a memoir, the key to reading interviews is to try to understand the interviewed person's perspective and some of the main points he or she is trying to make.

Poetry—This particular genre is literary work often in metrical form. The key is to pay close attention to symbolic meaning and to the author's choice of words. Remember that the meaning of a poem is open to subjective interpretation.

Newspaper/magazine letters to the editor—This type of reading contains letters from newspaper readers in response to an editorial. First, make sure you have a grasp of the topic that these readers are responding to. Consider individual perspectives and how readers' viewpoints vary.

Online forum—In this genre, online readers share their opinion on a topic. Again, as is the case with letters to the editor, some knowledge of the topic/policy/article that is being discussed goes a long way. Remember also that Internet audiences are global.

Scene from a play—This genre presents the reader with an excerpt from a theater script. Remember, you are reading direct speech in this genre. Pay attention to conversational style because it often keys readers in to the characters' emotional state and how they interrelate with other characters. Notice deviations from standard language (regional dialects/slang/idiomatic expressions).

Online advice column—These are readings where experts offer their advice to Internet readers' questions. The advice columnist's language is usually coaxing and reassuring because it is their goal to guide readers through difficult situations. Focus mostly on the main points of advice offered.

Novel—These are works of fiction, extensive in length. In first entering a novel, consider the setting (time and location) and the voice of the narrator. Robert Scholes's words about reading novels are instructive:

> In considering the voices within our text, students will be encouraged to … ask who speaks it, where they come from, and what values that they share are embodied in their speech … who is speaking to us? What kind of voice is that? Does it present itself as reliable, trustworthy? How does it establish its authority? How does that voice compare to the voices of characters as they are represented? Is the narrator a character? Is the narrator the author? Do characters speak always in one voice, or in more than one? How do different characters speak to one another? The length of a novel requires prolonged engagement. One needs time to read it, time to discuss it, and time to write responses to it.

Official government document—These are often replete with legalese (legal terms) and the tone is usually authoritative. You may have to read these line by line and very carefully because the texts are written in a formal, somewhat inaccessible manner.

Blog post—The word "blog" has come to mean a range of things. It can refer to a site of its own, an offshoot or column of a larger site or publication (most magazines and newspapers feature an array of blogs), or an online journal by an individual. It might have one author or an alternating cast. And its author might be anyone from an expert in a specific field to a journalist to anyone who wants to share what he or she makes for dinner each night. It can be interactive, including comment fields and opportunities to discuss topics with the author, or it can be a "closed" space, where commentary from readers is not permitted. A good reader using critical thinking skills can distinguish between an incoherent piece of writing (often with basic grammar and spelling errors) and a well-written opinion. Just because a piece of writing appears online does not mean that a reader should accept it as an expert opinion. This does not mean that readers should devalue amateur writing. On the contrary, the beauty of most blogs is that they offer readers the opportunity to share perspectives with one another in an informal forum.

EDUCATION
American Education

Educating the mind without educating the heart is no education at all.

ARISTOTLE

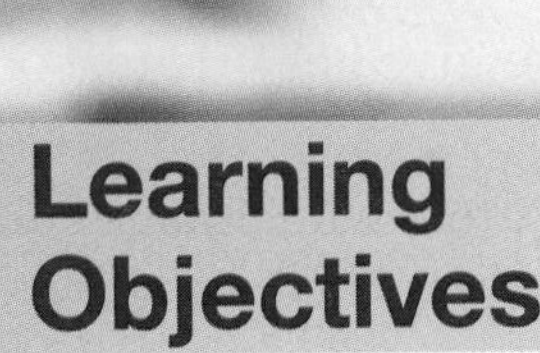

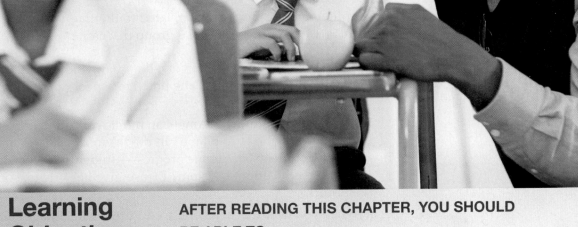

Learning Objectives

AFTER READING THIS CHAPTER, YOU SHOULD BE ABLE TO:

1. Identify contemporary issues in American education.
2. Determine meaning from context.
3. Construct a response to readings in writing.

INTRODUCTION TO THE DISCIPLINE OF EDUCATION

Teaching is one of the most challenging, demanding, and rewarding of professions. Teachers not only are expected to educate our children and provide them with an academically enriching environment, but they also play a role in students' social development. Teachers have the huge task of preparing young minds for the world ahead of them. They model collaborative learning and critical thinking, and they introduce students to the technological tools that they will need to navigate the twenty-first-century classroom and beyond. The system of American education faces many challenges in the twenty-first century. In this chapter, you will read about some of the issues that educators today must consider. Should new immigrant students be offered a bilingual curriculum? Are same-sex schools beneficial to public school students' academic achievement? What kinds of innovative teaching methods can help improve American students' low performance in the sciences and inspire more interest in scientific inquiry? Finally, how can we motivate underperforming students to work harder in their classes?

Preview Questions

The following questions are all related to the chapter focus area of education. Share your views in small group discussion.

1. Do you believe that you received a quality education at your high school? Describe some of the positive aspects and shortcomings of your high school experience.
2. Many people argue that American public education is in crisis. If you agree, then who is to blame? In other words, who is most responsible for students' academic progress—students, teachers, parents, or the state educational system? Please give specific reasons for your answer.
3. When you hear that someone is educated, what image comes to your mind about this person? In your opinion, what are some of the characteristics of an educated person?
4. In your many years of schooling, which of your teachers left the most lasting impression on you? What made this teacher so special?
5. Do you feel that you learn more when the teacher is lecturing to the class or when the teacher assigns small-group problem-solving tasks?

Writing On The Wall

After you have discussed the preview questions with your classmates, post your responses to two of them on your class blog. Review others' postings and respond to at least two of your classmates' posts that grab your interest. Remember the guidelines for blogging and commenting etiquette (see p. 15)! If your class is not using a shared blog, your instructor may ask you to record your individual or collective responses to the preview questions in another form.

EXERCISE 2.1 Interpreting a Cartoon

Discuss the cartoon shown here in small groups and answer the following questions.

"There aren't any icons to click. It's a chalk board."

1. What educational issue does this cartoon address?
2. In your opinion, what message is the cartoonist trying to convey to the reader?

Discipline-Specific Vocabulary: Understand Key Terms In Education

One of the most efficient ways to acquire an academic vocabulary is to study key terms that are thematically connected. As you begin your college-level studies, it is critical that you internalize vocabulary terms that relate to the academic disciplines that make up most 100-level content courses. For example, a student taking an Introduction to Education course should be able to apply such terms as *feedback*, *pedagogy*, and *assessment* in both spoken and written forms.

In every chapter, you will have the opportunity to interact with key terms in context.

EXERCISE 2.2 Brainstorming Vocabulary

Directions: What associated words come to mind when you think of the world of education? Work with a partner and write down as many related words as you can think of in a period of five minutes.

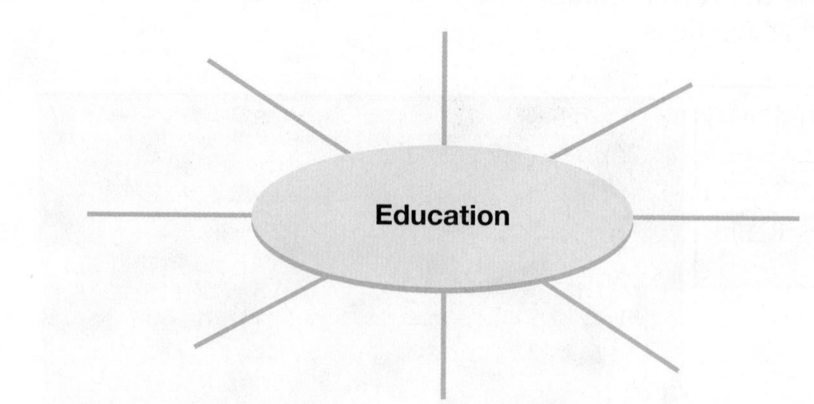

Fishing for Synonyms and Antonyms

A **synonym** is a word or phrase used to express a similar meaning to another word. An **antonym** is a word or phrase that conveys the opposite meaning of another word. Understanding how to work with synonyms and antonyms is a useful skill, especially when you are trying to paraphrase some of the key ideas contained in a reading. Clearly, you cannot simply copy the same terms you see in the text and will need to use synonyms and antonyms.

EXERCISE 2.3 Determining Synonyms and Antonyms from Context

Directions: Read the following ten (10) discipline-specific words culled from the readings in this chapter and shown in the context of the sentences in which they appeared. In the space provided after each sentence, write a synonym or antonym for the highlighted term, as directed.

Discipline-Specific Word Bank for Education

feedback	**concept**
coed	**pedagogy**
mentor	**motivation**
context	**interactive**
engage	**curriculum**

1. "'We sneak into each other's classrooms as often as we can' to watch each other teach to learn from each other and give honest **feedback**, Mulvihill says."
   A synonym for *feedback* is ____________
2. "... students of both sexes can feel like a fish out of water when they reach a **coed** college or the workplace."
   An antonym for *coed* is ____________
3. "One of the most influential **mentors** was her mother, whom Ruth Simmons watched as a child pressing fabric for hours."
   A synonym for *mentor* is ____________
4. This text provides a framework for teaching in a multicultural **context**.
   A synonym for *context* is ____________
5. "It's important to mentally **engage** students in what you're teaching."
   An antonym for *engage* is ____________
6. "On the whole, they haven't understood the basic **concepts** behind the facts."
   A synonym for *concept* is ____________
7. "Doesn't good **pedagogy** have a performance element to it?"
   A synonym for *pedagogy* is ____________
8. "That happened because of his parents, classroom teacher, paraprofessionals, and the special education teacher who kept him focused, as well as the student's own **motivation** to learn."
   An antonym for *motivation* is ____________

9. In the interview, Professor Mazur argues that students prefer an **interactive** classroom environment.

   An antonym for *interactive* is ________________

10. It would be impossible to develop a different **curriculum** for each group of students in your multicultural classroom.

    A synonym for *curriculum* is ________________

EXERCISE 2.4 Words and Definitions

Match the word in Column A with the definition in Column B. Put the letter representing the correct definition in the space preceding each term.

Column A Word		Column B Definition
1. ______	feedback	a. male and female students studying together
2. ______	engage	b. course of study
3. ______	concept	c. talk or act with each other
4. ______	curriculum	d. what inspires one to take action
5. ______	pedagogy	e. suggestions or criticism about someone's work
6. ______	mentoring	f. to actively participate
7. ______	context	g. an idea or principle
8. ______	motivation	h. principles and practices of teaching
9. ______	coed	i. advising people with less experience
10. ______	interactive	j. a situation that helps us understand its meaning

EXERCISE 2.5 Fill in the Blanks

In the following sentences, fill in the blank with a word from the terminology bank below that makes the sentence meaningful.

coed	concept	pedagogy	context	motivation
engage	feedback	curriculum	mentoring	interactive

1. Many researchers believe that learning can be optimized in a ______ setting, as opposed to a single-sex school environment.
2. Students can benefit immensely from receiving constructive ________ on their work from both instructors and peers.
3. Good readers ________ themselves in class discussions of readings.

4. Language teachers discourage their students from overly relying on the dictionary to learn unfamiliar words and recommend determining meaning from _______.
5. Many students may think that it is enough for them to memorize terms from their college lectures. Yet, if they don't understand the key __________ involved, little real learning takes place.
6. Some high school students lack the __________ to get up each morning and study hard at school.
7. The president of the local college has instituted a __________ program whereby less experienced instructors receive feedback on their teaching from their more experienced peers.
8. Most teachers are guided by their school's __________ for the particular grade they teach.
9. Many educators believe that __________ lessons are most conducive to learning.
10. When you pursue education as a major, you will learn that __________ must be informed by research.

MyReadingLab

Visit Chapter 2: Education in MyReadingLab to complete the Reading 1 activities.

READING 1

Newspaper Article

Learning and Teaching a Two-Way Calle in Boston

Pre-Reading Questions

Before reading the following article, answer these questions in pairs or small groups. Discussing the questions will help prepare you to analyze the text with relative ease.

1. What kinds of challenges do recently arrived immigrant children face in American public schools?
2. How do you think the school system can help these students to overcome the challenges that they experience?
3. Do you think children whose first language is not English benefit more from bilingual instruction than they do from English-only instruction? Explain.

Read the reading below and practice your reading comprehension with the set of ten multiple-choice questions that follow. Write predictive questions in the margin each time you see the ? symbol.

Learning and Teaching a Two-Way Calle in Boston

By Michelle Lefort, Special for *USA Today*
December 20, 2005

1 BOSTON—It's Friday at the Rafael Hernandez Two-Way Bilingual School in Roxbury and a sign on the door of the four kindergarten and first-**grade** classrooms tells students they will speak English today.

2 When they return their homework Monday, everyone will learn songs, math and science in Spanish.

3 In one of Boston's poorest neighborhoods and named for a Puerto Rican poet who addressed the isolation of migration, Rafael Hernandez School was founded in the early 1970s to serve the children of Boston's growing Puerto Rican immigrant community. After Boston's 1974 **desegregation** order, Hernandez became a two-way language school.

4 Today, the school is highly sought after, with 250 applicants for 50 kindergarten slots. Although three-quarters of the students get free or reduced-priced lunches and many start school with little language in either English or Spanish, the kindergarten/first-grade team of Martine Lebret, Naomi Mulvihill, Brenda Rosario and Jessie Auger gets them off to a successful start.

5 Of last year's 50 first-graders, 45 were reading at or above grade level; 88% were meeting or exceeding math standards.

6 But state standards are only one measure of success for the teachers, who work long hours to build an environment of respect, pride, community and continual learning.

7 Lebret and Mulvihill teach kindergarten, and Rosario and Auger teach first grade. In each classroom, about half of the students are dominant in English and half dominant in Spanish. During the 90-minute morning literacy blocks, students change classrooms to work in their dominant language. Within each grade, the teachers design parallel curricula in each language.

8 The teachers, who average 13½ years teaching experience and have numerous individual **accolades,** each have distinct styles that are both loving and demanding.

accolades
praise and approval or even a prize given to someone for his or her work

9 But it's their teamwork that makes them click. They write almost all of their materials, coordinate plans and help one another improve.

10 "We sneak into each other's classrooms as often as we can" to watch each other teach to learn from each other and give honest **feedback** Mulvihill says.

feedback
advice, criticism, and so forth about how successful or useful something is, given so that something can be improved

11 Peer critiquing can be intimidating, but the confidence they have in each other and their drive to improve helps them use criticism constructively. Their ability to learn from each other is the key, says principal Margarita Muniz. "They can listen to each other, critique each other without hard feelings."

12 "We are all different people, but we all have a desire to learn, a desire to share,"Auger explains. "We're very proud of each other."

13 They also work together to help each child meet their own goals.

14 Carlos Piedad, now 8, wanted to move from the English-dominant group to the Spanish-dominant group. Over his two years with the team, the teachers developed individual assignments, gave ideas to his parents to work with him at home and nurtured his writing skills. He made the move midway through last year, ending the year fluent in both languages.

15 Parents Javier Piedad and Patti Lautner say Carlos wasn't particularly driven. "They motivated him," Lautner says. The team didn't spend any more time working with Carlos than they did with the other students, Lautner adds. It's not unusual for any of the teachers to work 12-hour days.

16 Even though they each teach classes of 24 or 25 students, each teacher sends regular progress reports home, or makes daily calls home if the parent requests. They also host small dinner parties for families where students write and illustrate their own books.

17 In keeping with the school's **expeditionary** learning approach, the team uses class projects to teach responsibility while meeting academic standards. Former eighth-grade classes transformed an abandoned lot into a community garden. Now, kindergarteners plant the garden each spring. The following September, both the

expeditionary
refers to a long and carefully organized trip, especially to a dangerous place

first-graders and the new kindergarteners harvest plants for use in crafts such as swan gourd maracas or in making vegetable soup.

18 Learning and teaching in two languages may be doubly difficult, but also doubly rewarding.

19 Says Auger: "Learning two languages is incredibly intellectually **stimulating.**"

Michelle Lefort, "Learning and Teaching a Two-Way Calle in Boston," *USA Today*, December 20, 2005. Reprinted with permission.

Reading with a Critical Eye

In a small group, discuss the following reflection questions, which will guide you toward a deeper understanding of the reading.

1. In paragraph 4 of the article, we read, "Today, the school is highly sought after, with 250 applicants for 50 kindergarten slots." Based on the information in the reading, why is the Rafael Hernandez School so popular?
2. In paragraph 6, the author writes, "But state standards are only one measure of success for the teachers . . . ." What other measures of success do teachers value? In your opinion, how much do these state exams tell us about an elementary school student's progress in reading and math?
3. The school principal, Margarita Muniz, says (para. 11), "They can listen to each other, critique each other without hard feelings." In this quote, what is the principal trying to say?
4. Who is Carlos Piedad? What can we learn about the school from his example?
5. In the last line of the article, a first-grade teacher in the school, Jessie Auger, says, "Learning two languages is incredibly intellectually stimulating." What are the benefits of being bilingual in twenty-first-century America?

Reading Comprehension Check

In what follows and in multiple-choice questions throughout this textbook, circle the letter of the best answer.

1. What kind of school is the Rafael Hernandez School?
   a. a high school
   b. a middle school
   c. an elementary school
   d. a university
2. The term *two-way* in the third paragraph could be replaced with
   a. round-trip.
   b. bilingual.
   c. English–only.
   d. none of the above

3. In the fourth paragraph, we read, "Today, the school is highly sought after . . . ." A synonym for *sought after* is
   a. desirable.
   b. troubled.
   c. attained.
   d. discarded.
4. What becomes clear about the school profile from the information in the third and fourth paragraphs?
   a. Many of the students speak English only.
   b. Most of the students do not live in Boston.
   c. The vast majority of the students are poor.
   d. All of the students share the same first language.
5. The word *exceeding*, in the fifth paragraph, could be replaced with
   a. equal to.
   b. less than.
   c. successful.
   d. greater than.
6. It can be inferred from the seventh paragraph that
   a. students learn completely different material in each language.
   b. students cover the same material regardless of the language in which the content is given.
   c. This issue is not discussed in this paragraph.
   d. bilingual students are slower to learn.
7. In paragraph 9 we read, "They write almost all of their materials, coordinate plans and help one another improve." A synonym for the word *coordinate* is
   a. discriminate.
   b. synchronize.
   c. derive.
   d. deliver.
8. The term *peer critiquing*, as used in paragraph 11, refers to a collaboration between
   a. students and teachers.
   b. a group of students.
   c. two teachers.
   d. both teachers and their bilingual students.
9. What is Carlos's mother's main point about his teachers?
   a. They can teach in both English and Spanish.
   b. They work hard for the students.
   c. The teachers are not strict enough in America.
   d. Carlos is progressing.
10. In the final sentence of the article, one of the bilingual teachers says, "Learning two languages is incredibly intellectually *stimulating*." The word stimulating could be replaced with the word
   a. electric.
   b. contrived.
   c. exciting.
   d. enabling.

READING 2

Online Article

MyReadingLab

Visit Chapter 2: Education in MyReadingLab to complete the Reading 2 activities.

The Lowdown on Single-Sex Education

Pre-Reading Questions

Discuss these questions in groups.

1. Have you ever studied in a single-sex school? If yes, was your experience a positive one? If no, how was your coed experience?
2. Is working together with members of the opposite sex a distraction or an advantage in a high school classroom? Explain.
3. If you were given an option, would you rather study with people of the same gender, or would you prefer a coed environment?

The Lowdown on Single-Sex Education

By Hannah Boyd, Education.com (2008)

1 Not long ago single-sex schools were viewed as relics from another age, a time when boys took woodshop and girls studied home economics. Now the pendulum is swinging the other way. Legislators are considering funding single-sex public schools, and single-sex private schools are back in **vogue**. Why?

vogue
popular acceptance or favor

2 Call it Mars and Venus in the classroom. Experts say that boys and girls simply learn differently, and that ignoring inborn differences shortchanges both sexes. According to these experts, girls tend to mature faster both socially and physically, and to develop language fluency, fine motor skills, and understanding of abstract concepts before boys do. Boys gain large motor control sooner, tend to be more literal than girls, and excel at spatial relationships. Perhaps more important, boys and girls behave differently.

3 "The behavior expected (and rewarded) in the classroom—quiet, patient, orderly acceptance of facts—favors how girls approach their classes," says Michael Obel-Omia, head of Upper School at University School in Hunting Valley, Ohio, which is all male. Like many, Obel-Omia believes boys enter coed schools at a disadvantage to girls, and may be shortchanged by a one-size-fits-all program.

4 Conversely, proponents of all-girls' schools say that deep-rooted sexism cheats girls in coed programs. Studies have shown that teachers call on girls less often than boys, and girls report feeling inhibited about speaking up in class. By removing the social pressure to impress the opposite sex, the reasoning goes, girls feel free to take more risks.

5 Although long-term research is lacking, **anecdotal evidence** seems to bear this out. Girls in single-sex schools are more likely to take math, computer science, and physics classes, as well as play sports, than their peers in coed schools; boys are more likely to study art, music, drama, and foreign languages. Some evidence suggests that boys in all-boys' schools are less competitive and more cooperative, which has led some to push for single-sex public schools in low-income areas.

anecdotal evidence
an informal account, sometimes as a story or hearsay, to prove something

6 Of course, we live in a coed world, and eventually everyone has to learn to work together. "With an all-girls' school you really need to take the initiative in finding male friends," notes Katharine Krotinger, a senior at the all-female Dana Hall School in Massachusetts. Otherwise, students of both sexes can feel like a fish out of water when they reach a coed college or the workplace.

7 Only you and your child can predict whether a single-sex school will be an educational haven or a social desert. As for Krotinger, she's looking forward to starting college in the fall—on a **coed** campus.

Hannah Boyd, "The Lowdown on Single-Sex Education." Article reprinted with permission from Education.com, a Web site with thousands of articles for parents of preschool through grade 12 children, www.education.com.

Reading with a Critical Eye

In a small group, discuss the following reflection questions, which will guide you toward a deeper understanding of the reading.

1. We read in the second paragraph that many experts believe that girls tend to mature faster than boys both socially and physically. Do you believe this to be true? Explain why or why not.
2. What is Michael Obel-Omia's view on classroom expectations and gender? Do you agree with him?
3. What are some of the results of single-sex schooling described in paragraph 5? Which of these results is most surprising to you? Why?
4. How is the expression "a fish out of water" used in paragraph 6? Do you think this expression makes sense in this context? Explain.
5. After reading this article, has your opinion about single-sex schools changed? Explain.

Reading Comprehension Check

1. As used in the first sentence of the article, "Not long ago single-sex schools were viewed as relics from another age," the word *relics* could be replaced by
   a. plans.
   b. leftovers.
   c. strategies.
   d. disasters.
2. The phrase "the pendulum is swinging the other way" in the first paragraph refers to
   a. the fact that single-sex schools are now on the decline.
   b. all-boys' schools.
   c. the fact that single-sex schools are coming back into fashion.
   d. schools moving.
3. As used in paragraph 2, in the phrase "ignoring inborn differences shortchanges both sexes," the term *shortchanges* means
   a. destroys.
   b. considers.
   c. appreciates.
   d. does a disservice to.
4. Which advantage that young female students have over boys is *not* mentioned in the article?
   a. Girls mature faster.
   b. Girls develop fine-motor skills earlier.

c. Girls excel at spatial relationships.
d. Girls develop language fluency faster.

5. What is Michael Obel-Omia's main point in the third paragraph?
   a. Boys are discriminated against.
   b. Girls tend to exhibit behavior that is more suitable to classroom learning.
   c. All schools should be coed.
   d. Girls are more mature.

6. What evidence is cited about boys' performance in all-boys' schools?
   a. They don't take art classes.
   b. They are less cooperative.
   c. They are more competitive.
   d. They are less competitive and more cooperative.

7. In paragraph 6, in the sentence, "With an all-girls' school you really need to take the initiative," the phrase *take the initiative* could be replaced by
   a. invite someone.
   b. make an effort.
   c. be shy.
   d. consider all the issues.

8. The expression *fish out of water* in the second-to-last paragraph refers to
   a. how boys and girls coming from a single-sex school environment might feel when suddenly confronted with the opposite sex .
   b. how boys feel in all-boys' schools.
   c. awkward girls.
   d. students in coed schools.

9. In the sentence, "Only you and your child can predict whether a single-sex school will be an educational haven or a social desert," the term *haven* means
   a. nightmare.
   b. safe place.
   c. prison.
   d. heaven.

10. The author of the article believes that
   a. coed schools are a better choice.
   b. single-sex schools are of higher quality.
   c. both kinds of schools are nice.
   d. We do not know the author's viewpoint.

BIOGRAPHICAL PROFILE

Ruth Simmons

Dr. Ruth J. Simmons is the first African American educator ever to be president of an Ivy League institution and the first female president of Brown University. Ruth J. Simmons was born in 1945 in Grapeland, Texas. She grew up on a farm in East Texas and had a life of deprivation and hardship. Yet she recounts her life in Texas fondly. "My journey has not been all that arduous, contrary to the way that my life is often presented. I had this wonderful grounding by my parents, and then an extraordinary streak of luck."

Despite her meteoric rise to prominence in the field of education, she remains humble and grateful to her mentors who challenged, supported, and encouraged her to pursue her dreams. One of the most influential mentors was her mother, whom Ruth Simmons watched as a child pressing fabric for hours. She recalls, "I remember thinking what a horrible, horrible thing to have to do. And yet she would see a crease invisible to everyone else, and she would work on it until it disappeared." Her mother passed away when Simmons was 15 but not before teaching her the value of perseverance, a precious lesson that has stayed with her since then. Simmons studied at Dillard University and later at Wellesley College where she was inspired by President Margaret Clapp to view traditional **gender** roles in a different perspective. "That was defining for me, the notion that women didn't have to play restricted roles, that you didn't have to hold back at all," recounts Simmons. "The faculty demanded that you work up to your potential." She went on to earn a PhD at Harvard University in Romance Languages.

Simmons admits that shaking the traditional notion of gender was not easy for her. She recalled that her mother believed herself to be subservient to the interests of men. "I expected that in my relationship with men. I should pretend not to be smart. I never wanted to be valedictorian because I thought it was very important for a boy to be valedictorian." She got married at the age of 22, had two children, and is now divorced. She was the director of studies at Princeton University and rejuvenated black culture on campus by hiring prominent black **scholars** such as Cornel West, Henry Louis Gates, and Toni Morrison to teach in the Department of African American Studies.

Simmons became president of Brown University in 2001. She is known to be a pioneer. As president of Brown University, she has taken an ambitious $1.4 billion initiative known as the Campaign for Academic Enrichment to boost Brown University's academic programs. She remains dedicated to the cause of education and encourages students to succeed in their academic endeavors. "The best thing any parent can do for a child is to give your child a sense of love and support to be open to the idea that they need to learn."

Some Questions for Group Discussion

1. Simmons was inspired by her mother to persevere in her goals. Do you believe that parents influence their children to succeed in their professional careers? Explain how. Do you have a mentor or a series of mentors who have inspired you to pursue your academic goals?
2. Simmons's road to success was replete with hurdles. In what way did she have to struggle to get to a high position as an educator?
3. Simmons believes that the best thing any parent can do for a child is to give your child a sense of love and support to be open to the idea that they need to learn. What do you understand about Simmons's philosophy of education from this quote? Do you share her views? Explain.

Biographical Internet Research

Research another great figure in Education from the list below and share a biographical profile with your fellow students:

- Paulo Freire
- Jonathan Kozol
- Geoffrey Canada
- Maria Montessori
- Michelle Rhee

READING SKILL FOCUS: Determining Meaning from Context

Regardless of the academic career you are pursuing in college, you are likely to encounter discipline-specific terminology—unfamiliar words and expressions in text and lectures given by professors. It is, therefore, essential that you build a strong vocabulary to comprehend the text and to do well on standardized reading tests administered by most U.S. state colleges. You may not have a dictionary at your disposal all the time, so you will need to rely on the context to figure out the meaning of an unfamiliar word, especially when answering multiple-choice questions. Although there is no single technique that will always work, the following strategies will help you determine meaning from context without turning to a dictionary.

Parts of Speech

When you come across an unfamiliar word in a sentence, try to find out what part of speech the word is. As you know, *nouns* are names of people, objects, phenomena, and places. *Verbs*, on the other hand, are usually actions carried out by people or nature. Some examples of verbs are *admire, love,* and *destroy*. Furthermore, *adjectives* modify the nouns by describing their characteristics. *Beautiful, intelligent,* and *constructive* are all examples of adjectives. Finally, *adverbs* show the manner in which an action (the verb) is conducted. These are examples of adverbs: *skillfully, abruptly,* and *viciously*. Knowing the part of speech of the word will help you determine its meaning (see also the Parts of Speech section in Chapter 2).

EXERCISE 2.6 Identifying Parts of Speech

Read the following sentences and label nouns as N, verbs as V, adjectives as Adj, and adverbs as Adv. Be sure to write these labels right beneath the word. The first one is done for you.

1. The frustrated educator quit his job.
   Adj N V N
2. Professor Smith's students flunked the standardized reading exam.
3. New technologies have changed America's classrooms significantly.
4. The history professor grudgingly allowed the student to turn the paper in late.

Word Forms

Sometimes the roots, prefixes, and suffixes will help you arrive at the correct meaning of the word. For example, some nouns end with suffixes such as *ity, ian, ist, tion, ary,* and so forth. Verbs have suffixes such as *ate, ify, ize, en,* and so forth. Adjectives are formed by adding suffixes such as *ous, ish, less, y, ive, ful,* and so forth. Let's see how this works by looking at the verb *create.*

Verb	*Noun*	*Adjective*	*Adverb*
create	creation creator creature	creative uncreative	creatively

EXERCISE 2.7 Practice with Word Forms

Complete the table below by writing in the different forms of the provided word.

Noun	*Verb*	*Adjective*	*Adverb*
product	_______	_______	_______
_______	study	_______	_______
_______	_______	successful	_______
_______	_______	_______	critically

For more complete coverage of prefixes, roots, and suffixes, see pages 44–48 in this chapter.

Connotation

Most words have either a positive or negative connotation. Even if you do not know the meaning of the new word you have just encountered, most of the time you can tell whether it has a negative or positive feel to it. Examine the examples below of words with positive and negative connotations.

Word	*Connotation*
uplifting	positive
critical	negative
downtrend	negative
enlightening	positive
optimistic	positive

EXERCISE 2.8 Connotation

In the table below, read the words in the left column and decide whether they have a positive or negative connotation. Put a check in the appropriate box.

	Connotation	
Word	***Positive***	***Negative***
consistent	☐	☐
disruptive	☐	☐
conducive	☐	☐
commend	☐	☐
distract	☐	☐

Contextual Clues

The context in which a word occurs can also lead you to its correct meaning. Read the sentence carefully and look at the words that precede and follow the unfamiliar word. If you are reading an entire passage, read the sentences that come immediately before and after the sentence that has the word in question. These adjacent sentences will provide the context that will help you zero in on the correct meaning of the new word. Let's look at an example in a multiple-choice question to see how this works.

Example

John runs his business like a dictator, but none of his employees have the **temerity** to defy his orders.

In the sentence, the word *temerity* could be replaced by

a. calamity.
b. insincerity.
c. audacity.
d. mortality.

The following strategies will help you figure out the meaning of the word *temerity*.

Strategy 1: Identify Part of Speech

When you come across an unfamiliar word, first identify what part of speech it is. For example, is it a noun, a verb, an adjective, or an adverb? However, determining the part of speech of the word *temerity* is not going to help you in this case, because all of the four choices are nouns. This means that you will need to use another strategy to answer the question correctly.

Strategy 2: Determine the Connotation

As you learned earlier, most words have either a positive or negative connotation. Understanding the connotation of a word will give you a clue to its meaning. If you look at the context, it tells us that John is a dictator, someone who likes to order his employees and probably does not care much about how they feel. To disobey John, an employee would have to have courage, strength, and boldness, which all have positive connotations. Therefore, you can deduce that *temerity* also has a positive connotation and determine that it means (c) audacity.

Now that you have learned different strategies to determine meaning from context, let's do an exercise and apply these strategies.

EXERCISE 2.9 Practice with Determining Meaning from Context

Read the short passage below and try to determine the meaning of the highlighted words from the context.

> Students with limited proficiency are required to take **remedial** reading and writing courses. Some students are **indignant** that these courses are given a noncredit status. However, until they pass these courses, they are not **entitled** to take most classes in their major.

Word	*Part of Speech*	*Connotation*	*Your Definition*
remedial	______	______	______
indignant	______	______	______
entitled	______	______	______

PRACTICING THE SKILL: PRACTICE 1

Applying the Skill to Readings

Let's practice vocabulary in context questions with a few short readings from *Foundations of American Education*.

Read the following paragraph with a partner and try to define the highlighted words using the clue strategy. Write your definitions for the bolded words first. Then look them up in a dictionary and compare your definitions. Do the same for the rest of the readings.

Passage 1

> Assimilation is a process by which an immigrant group is **incorporated** into the **dominant** culture. The group either adopts the culture of the dominant group as its own or interacts with it in a way that **forges** a new or different culture that is shared by both groups. Members of a group experience a number of stages in this process. (p. 49)

	Your Definition	*Dictionary Definition*
1. incorporated		
2. dominant		
3. forges		

Passage 2

All people have preferred learning and teaching styles that are **embedded** in their cultural backgrounds and experiences. Until teachers learn to recognize these differences and develop a **repertoire** of different strategies for teaching subject matter, some students will be **deprived** of appropriate support in the learning process. However, making generalizations about culturally diverse learners can be dangerous. (p. 120)

	Your Definition	*Dictionary Definition*
1. embedded		
2. repertoire		
3. deprived		

Passage 3

The physical arrangement of a school into classrooms has organizational as well as instructional **implications**. For example, it is easy for teachers to be isolated in their classrooms. This geographic **isolation** contributes to their not knowing about or becoming **engaged** with issues that affect the whole school. Geographic isolation can affect the school as a whole too. The school staff might not be aware of community concerns or of what is going on in other schools across the district. Teachers and administrators must make **deliberate** efforts to learn about other parts of the education system. (p. 143)

	Your Definition	*Dictionary Definition*
1. implications		
2. isolation		
3. engaged		
4. deliberate		

Passage 4

In the past, an important and **unique** feature of education in the United States was local control, the belief that educational decisions should be made at the local level rather than at the state or national level. The **rationale** has been that people at the local level, including teachers and parents, know what is best for the students in their community. As has been described in this chapter, the **trend** over the last sixty years has been toward more federalism. The No Child Left Behind Act is the latest and heaviest centralization **initiative** by the federal government and includes many **mandates** to states, school districts, schools, and teachers. (p. 164)

	Your Definition	*Dictionary Definition*
1. unique		
2. rationale		
3. trend		
4. initiative		
5. mandates		

PRACTICE 2

More Vocabulary in Context Practice

Read the following passages and answer the multiple-choice questions that follow. Remember to use the two strategies you learned earlier to determine meaning from context.

Passage 1

A sampling of large New York City high schools showed that the schools failed to notify the state of a significant number of violent or **disruptive** episodes in the 2004–5 school year, the city comptroller announced yesterday.

The comptroller, William C. Thompson Jr., said an audit showed that the city had not ensured that all principals accurately report violence in their schools, making it difficult for the public to **assess** their safety. The audit examined an array of records in 10 schools, comparing them with computerized data sent to the state. It found, for example, that officials at Brooklyn's Boys and Girls High School informed the state of 14 cases of violence or misbehavior through a special computer system, which the state uses to **comply** with reporting obligations under the federal No Child Left Behind law.

From Elissa Gootman, "Undercount of Violence in Schools." From *The New York Times*, September 20, 2007. www.nytimes.com

1. The word *disruptive* in the first paragraph means
a. peaceful. c. unruly.
b. obedient. d. quiet.

2. The word *assess* in the second paragraph means the same as
a. ignore. c. criticize.
b. disqualify. d. evaluate.

3. As used in the last sentence of the second paragraph, the word *comply* means
a. disobey. c. allow.
b. act in accordance with. d. violate.

assage 2

A shy high school freshman, Harpal Singh Vacher, ended the school year last spring as the latest collateral damage in a citywide political **tussle**. What began as a childish argument with fellow students on May 24 ended with Harpal crouched on a bathroom floor at Newtown High School in Elmhurst, Queens, his previously unshorn hair littered on the ground around him.

In keeping with his Sikh faith, Harpal had kept his unshorn hair tucked inside a dastaar, a religious turban. The police say that his attacker, a high school senior named Umair Ahmed, had removed Harpal's turban and cut his hair to punish him for making **derogatory** comments about Mr. Ahmed's mother—comments for which Harpal had apologized. The Queens district attorney has charged Mr. Ahmed with a hate crime. The case is one of the few in which anyone has acted to stem bias-based **harassment** in city schools, though only after the damage has been done. The City Council recognized and addressed the systemic gaps in countering prejudice and intimidation in public schools years ago, when it passed the Dignity for All Students Act in 2004.

From Neha Singh and Khin Mai Aung, "A Free Ride for Bullies." From *The New York Times*, September 23, 2007.

1. As used in the first sentence, the word *tussle* means
a. gathering.
b. convention.
c. clash.
d. organization.

2. The word *derogatory* in the second sentence of the second paragraph is *opposite* in meaning to
a. insulting.
b. offensive.
c. deprecating.
d. complimentary.

3. As used in the sentence, "The case is one of the few in which anyone has acted to stem bias-based harassment in city schools, though only after the damage has been done," the word *harassment* means
a. persuasion.
b. aggravation.
c. argumentation.
d. celebration.

Passage 3

Military recruiters are frequently given free **rein** in New York City public schools and allowed into classes in violation of the school system's regulations, according to a report released yesterday by the Manhattan borough president and the New York Civil Liberties Union.

The report, based on surveys of nearly 1,000 students at 45 high schools citywide last spring, said the city's Department of Education exercised almost no **oversight** over how much access recruiters had to students at high schools.

There were recruiters who were in the classroom not to talk to students about reading, writing and arithmetic, but to talk to them about how to get a one-way ticket to Iraq and all the benefits you will **accrue** by that process, Scott M. Stringer, the Manhattan borough president, said at a news conference. This is something that must be stopped. It's outrageous, and it gives recruiters a captive audience.

1. As used in the first sentence of the first paragraph, the word *rein* means
a. coupons. c. tickets.
b. control. d. vouchers.

2. The word *oversight* in the second paragraph means
a. supervision. c. modification.
b. error. d. overpaid.

3. The word *accrue* in the third paragraph means
a. decrease. c. decline.
b. accumulate. d. forsake.

Vocabulary Development with Common Prefixes, Suffixes, and Roots

In English we can often determine the meaning of a word by looking at the sum of its parts—that is, if we have good knowledge of common prefixes, suffixes, and roots, this gives us a great advantage in figuring out the meaning of unfamiliar words.

The following tables contain common prefixes, suffixes, and roots (word bases). With a partner, try to give two examples of words that are derived from these forms. Once you get started, you will realize how many words you already have in your active vocabulary!

1. Prefixes

Prefixes are words that attach to the front (*pre* = before) of a root. Give two examples of words with the listed prefixes.

Prefixes	*Meaning*	*Example 1*	*Example 2*
a- (an-)	not, without		
anti-	against, opposite		
dis-	not, away, remove		
il-	not		
im-	not		

(Continued)

in-	not		
ir-	not		
mal-	poor, bad, evil		
mis-	wrong, bad		
non-	not		
ob- (op)	against, stopping, in the way		
un-	not		
ante-	before in time/place; in front of		
pre-	before in time or place		
post-	after in time or place		
inter-	between time or place		
sub-	below, under, lower		
under-	below, under, lower		
super-	higher, greater, larger, above		
sur-	higher, greater, larger, above		
over-	higher, greater, larger, too much		
out-	higher, greater, better		

2. Suffixes

The following suffixes are added to a root to change the form of the word. Identify the part of speech and give two examples of each suffix.

Suffix	*Meaning*	*Part of Speech*	*Example 1*	*Example 2*
-ion	act of doing			
-ish	like, similar to			
-ence	act of doing			
-ate	make or become			
-y	full of or covered with			
-ment	state of being			
-en	to make			
-ent/-ant	like, similar			
-ness	state of being			
-ly	in a way that is			
-al	related to			
-ous	full or covered with			
-ship	state of being			
-ity	state of being			
-ile (-ine)	like, similar			
-ify	make or become			

(Continued)

-ive	causing, having power			
-ic	like, similar			
-ize	make or become			

3. Roots

A root is the base of a word that can accept prefixes or suffixes. Please add the meaning of the following roots and provide examples of words containing them.

Roots	*Meaning*	*Example 1*	*Example 2*
mar-			
ped-			
sol-			
mort-			
vis-			
terr-			
path-			
dict-			
prim-			
centr-			
medi-			
equi-			
circul-			
fin-			
-meter			
-graph			

Once you have finished, check the tables that you and your partner have filled in against the completed tables below. Some of the words you came up with may be the same; some may be different.

1. Prefixes

Prefixes	*Meaning*	*Example 1*	*Example 2*
a- (an-)	not, without	atheist, amnesia	amnesty, anonymous
anti-	against, opposite	antonym, antiwar	antisocial, antidepressant
dis-	not, away, re-move	disagree, dishonest	disconnect, disrepect
il-	not	illegal, illogical	illiterate, illusion

(Continued)

im-	not	immature, impolite	imperfect, immortal
in-	not	invisible, insomnia	infinite, incomplete
ir-	not	irregular, irreligious	irresponsible, irregular
mal-	poor, bad, evil	malfunction	malpractice
mis-	wrong, bad	miscommunicate	misspell, misplace
non-	not	nonsmoker, nonstop	nonprofit, nonsense
ob- (op)	against, stopping, in the way	oppose, obstruct	obstacle
un-	not	unequal, uncover	unhealthy, uncommon
ante-	before in time/ place; in front of	ancient, antique	anticipate
pre-	before in time or place	prefix, preseason	pretest, preview
post-	after in time or place	postpone, postwar	postindustrial, posttest
inter-	between time or place	interactive	interview, international
sub-	below, under, lower	subway, subtitle	submarine, substandard
under-	below, under, lower	underground, undersea	underdeveloped, undernourished
super-	higher, greater, larger, above	superman, superstar	supermarket, superlative
sur-	higher, greater, larger, above	surpass, survive	surcharge
over-	higher, greater, larger, too much	override, overpaid	overwork, overconfident
out-	higher, greater, better	outdo, outrace	outsmart, outnumber

2. Suffixes

Suffix	*Meaning*	*Part of Speech*	*Example 1*	*Example 2*
-ion	act of doing	Noun	education	discussion
-ish	like, similar to	Adjective	sluggish	childish
-ence	act of doing	Noun	conference	audience
-ate	make or become	Verb	moderate	graduate
-y	full of or covered with	Adjective	windy	funny
-ment	state of being	Noun	encourage-ment	agreement
-en	to make	Verb	darken	lighten

(Continued)

-ent/-ant	like, similar	Adjective	dependent	pleasant
-ness	state of being	Noun	seriousness	kindness
-ly	in a way that is	Adverb	clearly	similarly
-al	related to	Adjective	dental	verbal
-ous	full or covered with	Adjective	humorous	nervous
-ship	state of being	Noun	friendship	scholar-ship
-ity	state of being	Noun	clarity	complexity
-ile (-ine)	like, similar	Adjective	fragile	juvenile
-ify	make or become	Verb	verify	magnify
-ive	causing, having power	Adjective	festive	talkative
-ic	like, similar	Adjective	Arabic	athletic
-ize	make or become	Verb	publicize	memorize

3. Roots

Roots	*Meaning*	*Example 1*	*Example 2*
mar-	of the sea	marine	maritime
ped-	foot	pedestrian	pedicure
sol-	alone	solidarity	solitude
mort-	death	mortician	mortal
vis-	to see	visual	vision
terr-	land	terrestrial	terrain
chrono-	time	synchronize	chronology
dict-	word	predict	dictionary
prim-	first, original	primordial	primitive
centr-	a point in the middle	centralize	centrifuge
medi-	enclosed	Mediterranean	medicinal
equi-	equal	equivalent	equivocate
circul-	around	circulatory	circular
fin-	last	finality	finale
-meter	measuring device	centimeter	perimeter
-graph	something written or drawn	monograph	polygraph

The next reading allows you to apply the skill of determining meaning from context.

MyReadingLab

Visit Chapter 2: Education in MyReadingLab to complete the Reading 3 activities.

READING 3

Interview

A Conversation with Eric Mazur

Pre-Reading Questions

Discuss the following questions in small groups as an introduction to the topic of the reading.

1. Many high school students believe that science classes are taught in a boring way. How was your experience with science courses in high school? Did you enjoy them? Did you like your teachers' methodology?
2. America's graduate programs in the hard sciences are filled with international students. Why do you think it is that, in general, Americans show little interest in pursuing careers in science?
3. In the interview, Professor Mazur argues that students prefer an interactive classroom environment, and that the old way of students passively listening to a lecture does not work anymore. Do you agree with Professor Mazur? Why or why not?

A Conversation with Eric Mazur Using the Beauties of Physics to Conquer Science Illiteracy

By Claudia Dreifus, the New York Times
July 17, 2007

1 CAMBRIDGE, Mass.—In the halls of academia, it is the rare senior professor who volunteers to teach basic science courses to undergraduates.

2 But Eric Mazur, the Gordon McKay Professor of Applied Physics at Harvard, is driven by a passion. He wants to end science illiteracy among the nation's college students; specifically, he strives to open them to the great beauties of physics.

3 Mazur's own Harvard course, Physics 1b, is the kind of science class that even a literature student might love—playful, engaging, something like a trip to a science museum. Indeed, Dr. Mazur, 52, is as experimental in his classroom as he is in his research laboratory.

4 "It's important to mentally **engage** students in what you're teaching," he explains. "We're way too focused on facts and rote memorization and not on learning the process of doing science."

5 **Q.** *Why do you willingly teach an introductory physics course?*

6 **A.** First, it's part of my job description. Professors are supposed to teach. The problem is how we teach, particularly how we teach science to **undergraduates**.

7 From what I've seen, students in science classrooms throughout the country depend on the rote memorization of facts. I want to change this. The students who score high do so because they've learned how to regurgitate information on tests. On the whole, they haven't understood the basic concepts behind the facts, which means they can't apply them in the laboratory. Or in life.

8 On a physics exam, the student will see a diagram and they'll classify it. Then, it's simply a matter of putting the right numbers in the right slots and, sort of, turning a crank. But this is algebra. It is not physics. When you test the students later on the concept, they can't explain what they've just done.

9 This saddens me. In my laboratory, we've made some important discoveries. Several were accidental—serendipitous. If we'd only functioned on the standard knowledge, we wouldn't have recognized what was before us.

10 **Q.** *What were these findings?*

11 **A.** Here's the biggest one: Just for the fun of it, we once put a silicon wafer into some gas we had lying around the lab. We then irradiated it with ultra-short laser pulses. What came out was a wafer as black as the blackest velvet. Until that moment, the conventional wisdom was that silicon was never black. So it certainly was possible to think of this thing as a mistake and to have tossed it away. Instead, we put it under an electron microscope where we saw that we had found a new material: 98 percent silicon, 2 percent embedded gas.

12 And today, we have a patent for this black silicon, which has important applications in communications and sensor technology.

13 **Q.** *Where were you educated?*

14 **A.** In Holland. At the University of Leiden. In my first year, we started out as 72 physics majors. By the second year, we were winnowed down to 11. Only those who could maintain themselves in rote memorization were able to continue.

15 I was one. But throughout my college years, I often thought of quitting, becoming an artist or a photographer instead. The lectures were deadening, frustrating. Only later, in graduate school, when I got into a laboratory did I see the creative part of science. It's beautiful to design an experiment.

16 **Q.** *Do you think you're better than the instructors you experienced as a student?*

17 **A.** When I first started teaching here in the 1980s, I didn't ask myself such questions. I did what everyone else did: lectures. And the feedback was **positive**. The students did well on what I considered difficult exams.

18 Around 1990, I learned of the work of David Hestenes, an Arizona State physicist studying how abysmally students in his

region did in science. He'd given hundreds of undergraduates a test in concept comprehension before and after they'd taken their physics classes. The tests showed that even with a term of instruction, their understanding hadn't improved very much.

19 I felt challenged by this. I then tested my own Harvard students similarly. We had discussed Newtonian mechanics earlier in the semester, and the students had already solved some difficult problems. Yet, when I gave them a new concept-based exam, about half had no clue as to what Newtonian mechanics were about.

20 **Q.** *Perhaps this concept-based test was flawed?*

21 **A.** No. But it was different. It measured their knowledge of physics forces in daily life. If they'd really understood Newtonian mechanics, they would have aced it. One student asked me: "How should I answer these questions? According to what you taught me? Or according to the way I usually think about these things?"

22 That was the moment I fell out of my ivory tower. It was then that I began to consider new ways of teaching.

23 **Q.** *Doesn't good* ***pedagogy*** *have a performance element to it?*

24 **A.** It does, though that doesn't necessarily translate into better learning. I used to get in front of my students and do all the science for them. I should have been showing them how to do it themselves. If they were studying the piano, I wouldn't have gone, "sit down, I'll play the piano for you."

25 **Q.** *How do you teach undergraduate physics today?*

26 **A.** I have the students read the text before the lecture. This is standard practice in the humanities, but a **heresy** in science. I don't know why. I think perhaps science professors like to present material.

heresy
beliefs or behaviors that are considered to be wrong by a particular religious, political, or social group

27 In my class, we talk about the applications of physics in everyday life. The lectures are broken up with these concept tests, where the students move into groups to work on a physics problem together. They talk, argue—they teach each other. After some discussion, they enter their answers into a computer that tabulates their collective response. From that, I can see if they've understood the topic before we move on.

28 We don't grade on a curve. Modern science is a cooperative **endeavor**.

endeavor
an attempt or effort to do something new or difficult

29 **Q.** *You permit students to take their textbooks into the final exam. Why?*

30 **A.** Life, you know, is an open book. They can bring any book they want to class. My objective is to see if they can solve a problem.

31 **Q.** *When a* ***task*** *force on teaching at Harvard gave its report this past January, its chairwoman, Theda Skocpol, cited you as one of Harvard's most innovative teachers. Have many of your colleagues since asked to observe your classes?*

32 **A.** A few. At Harvard, teaching is left to the individual professor There isn't a lot of cross-pollination. The upside is that this "every tub on its own bottom" credo has made it possible to experiment with my own classes and not get much interference.

33 Now, I've walked into science classrooms here to see what the others do. Some of it makes me burn. You know, these great, fantastic performances by energetic professors where attendance is miserable and half the students seem asleep. Toward the front of the room, you see a handful of kids furiously taking notes, while others fiddle with their laptops. "Any questions?" the professor asks. There are none.

34 **Q.** *When you teach Physics 1b, do you give "fantastic performances?"*

35 **A.** You know, I've come to think of professorial charisma as dangerous. I used to get fantastic evaluations because of charisma, not understanding. I'd have students give me high marks, but then say, physics sucks. Today, by having the students work out the physics problems with each other, the learning gets done. I've moved from being "the sage on the stage" to the guide on the side.

Claudia Dreifus, "A Conversation with Eric Mazur: Using the 'Beauties of Physics' to Conquer Science Illiteracy." From *The New York Times*, July 17, 2007. www.nytimes.com

Reading with a Critical Eye

In a small group, discuss the following reflection questions, which will guide you toward a deeper understanding of the reading.

1. What is Eric Mazur's chief goal laid out in the first part of the interview? Do you think he can reach this goal? Why or why not?
2. In paragraph 4, Professor Mazur says, "We're way too focused on facts and rote memorization and not on learning the process of doing science." Do you agree with his argument? Explain with an example from your own experience studying science.
3. Why does Eric Mazur mention the work of David Hestenes? How did learning about Hestenes change the way Mazur taught?
4. When a student says to Mazur (para. 21), "How should I answer these questions? According to what you taught me? Or according to the way I usually think about things?", it had a great impact on Mazur. Why did this student's comment wake him up?
5. What comparison does Mazur make between studying science and studying piano (para. 24)? What point is he trying to make? Do you agree with his argument? Why or why not?

Reading Comprehension Check

Read the following sentences carefully and determine the meaning of the bolded words from the context.

1. In the sentence "He wants to end science illiteracy among the nation's college students; specifically, he strives to open them to the 'great beauties of physics'," the word *strive* means
   a. to impede learning.
   b. to simplify the subject matter.
   c. to try hard to achieve something.
   d. to complicate the content.
2. In the sentence "It's important to mentally engage students in what you're teaching," the word *engage* is similar to
   a. confuse.
   b. involve.
   c. exclude.
   d. explain.
3. As used in the passage "The students who score high do so because they've learned how to regurgitate information on tests. On the whole, they haven't understood the basic concepts behind the facts, which means they can't apply them in the laboratory," the word *regurgitate* means
   a. to think deeply.
   b. to guess meaning from context.
   c. to repeat without thinking.
   d. to analyze carefully.
4. Professor Mazur says, "Until that moment, the conventional wisdom was that silicon was never black. So it certainly was possible to think of this thing as a mistake and to have tossed it away." *Conventional wisdom* in this passage means
   a. new ways of thinking.
   b. a widely held belief.
   c. nonconforming views.
   d. unique concepts and ideas.
5. In the sentence "And today, we have a patent for this black silicon, which has important applications in communications and sensor technology," the word *patent* means
   a. illegal use.
   b. contraband.
   c. counterfeit.
   d. official license.
6. As used in the following, "I did what everyone else did: lectures. And the feedback was positive. The students did well on what I considered difficult exams," the word *feedback* means
   a. rejection of someone's work.
   b. suggestion or criticism about someone's work.
   c. dismissal of a lecture.
   d. assistance with difficult exams.

7. Professor Mazur recalls, "Around 1990, I learned of the work of David Hestenes, an Arizona State physicist studying how abysmally students in his region did in science." By *abysmally,* he means
   a. performing well.
   b. passing an exam easily.
   c. performing poorly.
   d. performing successfully.
8. In the question "Perhaps this concept-based test was flawed?" the word *flawed* means
   a. impeccable.
   b. perfect.
   c. erroneous.
   d. accurate.
9. Answering a question about the concept-based test, Professor Mazur says, "It measured their knowledge of physics forces in daily life. If they'd really understood Newtonian mechanics, they would have aced it." The word *aced* in this sentence is *opposite* in meaning to
   a. excelled.
   b. get a high score.
   c. breeze through the test.
   d. flunked.
10. The interviewer asks, "Doesn't good pedagogy have a performance element to it?" The word *pedagogy* in the question is similar in meaning to
    a. the psychology of learning.
    b. the study of teaching methods.
    c. the review of textbooks.
    d. the evaluation of student work.

Recommended Debate Topic: Should we reward good grades with money and prizes?

Your suggested debate topics:

a. ______________________________

b. ______________________________

c. ______________________________

MyReadingLab

Visit Chapter 2: Education in MyReadingLab to complete the Reading 4 activities.

READING 4

Magazine Article

Should We Reward Good Grades with Money and Prizes?

Pre-Reading Questions

Discuss the following questions with a partner. If your instructor has assigned a debate activity, read the opposing viewpoints offered in the reading and consider how you can integrate some of the information into your debate preparation.

1. Can you think of some examples from life where good performance is rewarded?
2. In your opinion, what motivates a good student to do well in school?
3. Would giving money to the better students be fair to the weaker-performing ones?

Should We Reward Good Grades with Money and Prizes?

NEA Today

May 2004

1 There is a wide range of perspectives about rewarding students for good grades. There also are differences in views about what is **appropriate** for teachers to do versus what parents should do.

Margo Ungricht, seventh-grade English teacher, Lehi, Utah

2 I believe we can offer prizes, food, money, or field trips to students for good grades. I don't see the difference between offering students prizes and money for good grades and having a 3.0 dance or special assembly. A reward is a reward.

3 Most students who work hard for good grades would do it without the prizes and dances, so the prizes and money are simply an added bonus that they can choose to accept or decline.

4 Students who cheat, beg, badger, and whine for a good grade in order to earn money or prizes generally do not maintain a good grade for long. **Intrinsic values** usually have the upper hand in the end.

intrinsic values those that are basic, essential, enduring

Tennille Jones-Lewis, high school guidance counselor, Alliance, Ohio

5 Students should be rewarded for good grades. I view school for students similar to the way I view a **job** for an adult, and I believe it's

appropriate for parents to provide monetary rewards for good work and penalties for poor performance. If you are late for school, money is deducted. If you miss a day for illness, money is deducted. If your performance suffers, so will your pay. It gives students a chance to relate real-world experiences to school-related tasks.

6 This may not work for every family or for every child, but it's one of many things a parent can do.

7 My husband and I reward our eight nieces and nephews for earning good grades on their report cards. We give them $5 for each A and $3 for each B. Money is deducted for each C, D, and F. When their report cards come out, they call us immediately. They all do well in school and we want to show them we value their achievements, the same way a future employer will when they perform well in their jobs.

8 However, I don't think it is appropriate for teachers to use money as a reward. There's a fine line—a teacher giving the whole class a pizza party for a **job** well done could be appropriate, but a teacher giving money as a reward would cross the line.

Karen Barksdale, ninth-grade English teacher, Memphis, Tennessee

9 The only money and prizes a student should be given for good grades are the better money they will earn as adults and the prizes of self-esteem, pride, and commitment to attaining the highest level of their educational and intellectual development.

10 Instead of the student asking, "What will you give me for trying?" we should be asking students, "What will you be giving yourself for your future if you apply yourself?" The ultimate reward for a good education is a secure and rewarding future.

Brenda Nelson, social worker, Barrington, Illinois

11 External rewards undermine students' natural eagerness to learn. When we offer kids money and prizes, we cheapen the value of learning. We have all seen kids who become so accustomed to external rewards that the presents, candy, or money are what they want, rather than the academic achievement itself. I recently overheard a teenage girl and her father arguing about how high her grades needed to be in order to get a car, and what kind of car it would be. The conversation had everything to do with the prize and nothing to do with learning.

12 Our ultimate goal is to create citizens who make decisions for the right reasons—not because someone is **dangling** a prize in front of them.

dangling
hanging or swinging loosely

Mary Bungert, special education teacher, Topeka, Kansas

13 When students receive good grades, it is because of a team effort. The parents in most cases have worked diligently in the evenings with homework, the paraprofessionals have put in time and effort, the teachers do the same. How do we determine who made that achievement possible?

14 We had a second-grade student who knew seven sight words when he came to our school. He was on target by the end of third grade.

That happened because of his parents, classroom teacher, paraprofessionals, and the special education teacher who kept him focused, as well as the student's own motivation to learn. Who deserved a prize?

"Should We Reward Good Grades with Money and Prizes?" *NEA Today*, May 2004, p. 39. Reprinted by permission of the National Education Association.

Reading with a Critical Eye

In a small group, discuss the following reflection questions, which will guide you toward a deeper understanding of the reading.

1. What does Margo Ungricht, a seventh-grade English teacher, mean when she writes, "A reward is a reward" (para. 2)? Do you agree with her point? Explain.
2. Tennille Jones-Lewis, a high school guidance counselor, argues that school for kids is like a job is for adults (para. 5). How do you feel about this comparison? How is school unlike an adult job?
3. Karen Barksdale, a ninth-grade English teacher, writes (para. 10), "Instead of the student asking, 'What will you give me for trying?' we should be asking students, 'What will you be giving yourself for your future if you apply yourself?'" What point is she trying to make? How do you relate to her idea?
4. Brenda Nelson, a social worker, argues that "When we offer kids money and prizes, we cheapen the value of learning." What does she mean by the word *cheapen*? Do you agree with her point? Why or why not?
5. What is Mary Bungert's position on this question of whether it makes sense to give prizes to students? How does she support her opinion?

Reading Comprehension Check

Read the following sentences carefully and determine the meaning of the bolded words from the context.

1. What does Margo Ungricht mean when she writes, "A reward is a reward"?
   a. Money is the best prize.
   b. It doesn't matter whether the reward is in the form of cash or prizes.
   c. Most students do not care about rewards at all.
   d. Field trips give students the opportunity to experience something with their classmates.
2. In line 2 of Tennille Jones-Lewis's opinion, she states, ". . . and I believe it's appropriate for parents to provide monetary rewards for good work and penalties for poor performance."
   The word *appropriate* could be replaced by ___________
   a. unimportant.
   b. fraudulent.
   c. valid.
   d. irreplaceable.

3. When Karen Barksdale speaks of prizes, what kinds of prizes does she believe in?
   a. immediate money
   b. good grades
   c. self-esteem and pride
   d. developing motor skills
4. When Brenda Nelson writes, "External rewards undermine students' natural eagerness to learn," the word *undermine* means ___________
   a. enhance.
   b. display.
   c. weaken.
   d. strengthen.
5. In Mary Bungert's example about the second-grade student, who is *not* mentioned as contributing to this student's academic achievement?
   a. his parents
   b. his teacher
   c. paraprofessionals
   d. the police

From Reading to Writing: Responding to Reading Using a Reflective Journal

Overview

Occasionally your instructor will ask you to reflect on what you have read by responding to the articles in writing. This type of informal writing assignment will enable you to comment on the author's main idea in a reflective way. Simply put, this assignment is about your own opinion of the topic, analysis of a controversial issue or claim, and pertinent questions you would like to formulate/raise about the main idea. This is a great opportunity for you to express your thoughts and ideas in an informal way.

Purpose

Responding to reading in informal writing serves many purposes. It improves your critical-thinking skills, develops your fluency in the language, allows you to express emotional reactions to the original text, enables you to paraphrase and summarize the main ideas, and helps you explore your thoughts in writing. This type of assignment gets you to generate ideas with less attention paid to the mechanical aspects of writing. It goes without saying that the more you practice informal writing, the more you will learn to communicate clearly. Last but not least, keep in mind that reading and writing are active processes, and that you are actively participating in the process by responding to the articles you have discussed in class with your peers and instructor.

What You Should Write About

Your instructor may assign one of the following informal writing tasks to you:

1. Give a thoughtful response to a pertinent question raised by you or your peers.
2. Raise questions about a difficult concept or a dubious claim made by the author.
3. Present your disagreement with the author's main idea.
4. Communicate with your instructor your own ideas about the topic that was discussed in class. Remember that the burden of clarity is on the writer, so be sure to express your ideas as precisely and clearly as possible.

Length

When doing this informal writing assignment, it is important that you focus more on quality than quantity. Your instructor can easily discern between a student who has made an honest effort to produce original thoughts and someone who has copied from various sources simply to fill the space. It is important to note that your instructor will be asking you to respond to the readings quite frequently, and he or she will become familiar with your writing style. Your instructor will be able to recognize when you have produced quality work and when you have put more effort into quantity. Sometimes your instructor may indicate a length, but generally speaking, a paragraph or two is the minimum length of your response.

Writing Informally: Implications for Your Learning

The main purpose of this type of informal writing assignment is to help you improve your ability to communicate in writing. Because there is no restriction on your thoughts or the length of your response, you can consider this exercise as a casual conversation with your instructor, who will provide you with constructive feedback on content and organization. Instead of worrying about grammar mistakes, focus on generating interesting and relevant ideas. This assignment gives you an opportunity to explore your thoughts in writing and gain from the invaluable experience.

Writing Assignment: For your first informal writing exercise, you will be asked to choose one of the five viewpoints in the reading about rewarding students and then respond to it. You can explain why you agree or disagree with something the writer said or just discuss what interested you in this particular writer's ideas.

Reflection Journal: Response to a Viewpoint on Rewarding Students

Note: You may choose to use an electronic medium for your reflective journal or to write in a journal notebook. In either case, ask your instructor for feedback on your written work.

Careers in Education

When considering a college major, it is prudent to think about possible career paths.

Working in small groups, discuss careers one can pursue after obtaining an advanced degree in education. You may wish to do some research on the Internet to find other careers related to the field of education. In the space below, write down the job title and responsibilities. The first example is done for you. Be sure to share your findings with your peers.

Job Title	*Responsibilities*
1. Professor of Education	Teach education courses to undergraduate and graduate students, do teacher training for future public school teachers, publish textbooks and research papers in peer-reviewed journals, present at professional conferences.
2.	
3.	
4.	
5.	

Textbook Application

In each chapter of this book, you will read extensively from a chapter of a 100-level college course textbook. First, you will have the opportunity to listen to this Introduction to Education textbook excerpt before reading this extended passage. The ability to comprehend content-area texts is a critical ingredient in overall success in college courses. Read the following section from Part 3 of *Becoming a Teacher* and try to accurately answer the multiple-choice questions, which are labeled by the topic you have studied. You will notice that the key points in the reading are highlighted to help you navigate the passage easily.

MyReadingLab

Visit Chapter 2: Education in MyReadingLab to complete the Reading 5 activities.

READING 5

Textbook Reading

Today's Students, pp. 266–270

From *Becoming a Teacher* by Forrest W. Parkay

1 Today's teachers must be sensitive to the needs of students from different cultural backgrounds. As a teacher, you will need to communicate effectively with students from diverse populations and cultural backgrounds. You will have students from families that differ from the idealized traditional family. Some of your students may be from biracial families, adoptive families, stepfamilies, gay families, or immigrant families. According to the U.S. Census Bureau, married couples make up less than 50 percent of U.S. households in 2014, down from 71 percent in 1970. During the same period, nontraditional households increased from 29 percent in 1970 to over 50 percent (U.S. Census Bureau, April 23, 2014).

2 It would be impossible to develop a different curriculum for each group of students in your multicultural classroom – that would place under emphasis on differences among students. Instead, you can develop a curriculum that affirms all students' cultures and increases their awareness and appreciation of the rich diversity in U.S. culture.

3 This chapter looks at cultural diversity in the United States and the challenges of equalizing educational opportunity for all students. A goal for your professional development as a teacher, then, is to see cultural

diversity as an asset to be preserved and valued, not a liability. The United States has always derived strength from the diversity of its people, and all students should receive a high-quality education so that they may make their unique contributions to society.

How is Diversity Reflected in the Culture of the United States?

4 The percentage of ethnic minorities in the United States has been growing steadily since the end of World War II. Approximately 40.8 million foreign-born people, or 13 percent of the total U.S. population of 314 million, lived in the United States during 2014. More than half (53 percent) were born in Latin America and more than one-fourth (29 percent) in Asia. Most (56 percent) lived in just four states: California, New York, Texas, and Florida. Less than half (45 percent) were naturalized citizens (U.S. Census Bureau, 2014). Each year, more than 1 million immigrants obtain legal permanent resident status in the United States (U.S. Department of Homeland Security, 2013).

5 Figure 8.1 shows that more than 17 million U. S. children under age 18 had at least one foreign-born parent during 2012. The figure also shows that, nationally, more than half of immigrant children have parents from Latin American countries – Mexico, Central America and Spanish-speaking Caribbean, and South America.

6 The Center for Children of Immigrants (2013) describes the challenge of providing equal educational opportunity to the growing U.S. immigrant population, particularly undocumented children:

> It is critical that the specific needs of children and youth are considered in the ongoing immigration debate and that particular attention is paid to their education opportunities. Of the approximately 5.5 million children of immigrants in the U.S., around 1 million are undocumented. Many of these children entered the country at a young age, have been educated in American schools, and have grown up speaking English and embracing American culture.
>
> While undocumented children in grades K-12 are legally allowed to attend school, they often face challenges that their peers do not. Additionally, undocumented status becomes a significant barrier after youth leave high school. Undocumented youth who graduate from high school face significant barriers to everything typically associated with youth of that age, including driving, working, and receiving financial aid for higher education. With an estimated 65,000 undocumented students graduating from American high schools every year, this is an important issue not only for these youth, but for the entire country (p.1)

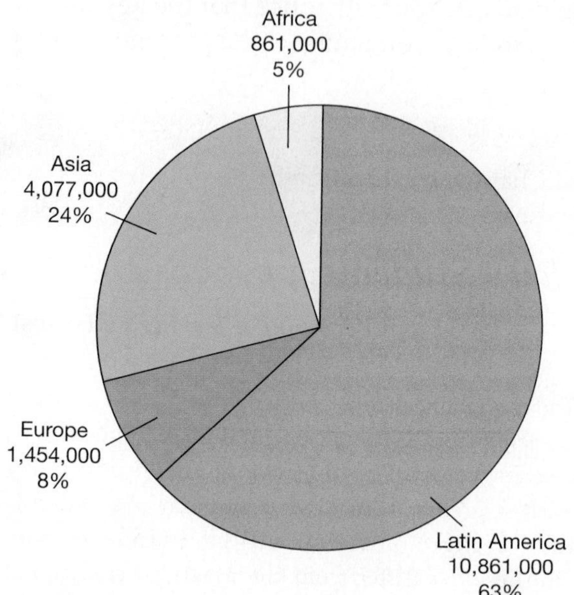

Figure 8-1 ■ Children in immigrant families by parents' region of origin, 2012

Note: The share of children under age 18 either foreign-born or who have at least one foreign-born parent with at least one parent from Latin America, Europe, Asia, or Africa.

Adapted from the U.S. Census Bureau, 2012 American Community Survey. Retrieved May 7, 2014, from http://www.census.gov/acs/www/.

7 Minorities, which made up 37 percent of the U.S. population in 2012, are projected to comprise 57 percent of the population in 2060. During that period, the total minority population would more than double, from 116.2 million to 241.3 million. The Hispanic population would increase from 53.3 million in 2012 to 128.8 million in 2060; similarly, the Asian population would more than double, from 15.9 million in 2012 to 34.4 million in 2060 (U.S. Census Bureau, December 12, 2012).

8 Increasing diversity in the United States is reflected, of course, in the nation's schools. Nearly 48 percent of public school students were considered part of a minority group during 2011, an increase of 16 percentage points from 1988 (Keaton, 2012a). Before the middle of this century, more than half of the nation's students will be minority-group members (U.S. Census Bureau, 2012). In the nation's 25 largest cities, students of color represent half or more of the student population (National Center for Education Statistics, July 2012).

9 Changes in the racial and ethnic composition of student enrollments are expanding the array of languages and cultures found in the nation's public schools. Differences in student backgrounds offer opportunities to enhance the learning environment, however, these differences also raise challenges for schools. For example, there is an increased demand for bilingual programs and teachers in many parts of the country. All but a few school districts face a critical shortage of minority teachers. And there is a need to develop curricula and strategies that address the needs and backgrounds of all students – regardless of their social class; gender; sexual orientation; or ethnic, racial, or cultural identity.

The Meaning of Culture

10 One mission of schools is to maintain the culture of the United States. But what is the U.S. culture? Is there a single culture to which everyone in the country belongs? Before answering that question, we must define the term culture. Simply put, culture is the way of life common to a group of people. It consists of the values, attitudes, and beliefs that influence their traditions and behavior. It is also a way of interacting with and looking at the world. At one time, it was believed that the United States was like a melting pot in which ethnic cultures would melt into one; however, ethnic and cultural differences have remained very much a part of life in the United States. A salad-bowl analogy captures more accurately the cultural pluralism of U.S. society. That is, the distinguishing characteristics of cultures are to be preserved rather than blended into a single culture. Or, as one columnist observed regarding the continuing increase in people of mixed-race identity in the United States: "America's melting pot isn't going to create a bland, homogenous porridge so much as a deeply flavored, spicy stew" (Stuckey, 2008).

Dimensions of Culture

11 Within the United States, cultural groups differ according to other distinguishing factors, such as religion, politics, economics, and geographic region. The regional culture of New England, for example, is quite different from that of the Southeast. Similarly, Californians are culturally different from Iowans.

12 However, everyone in the United States does share some common dimensions of culture. James Banks (2014), an authority on multicultural education, has termed this shared culture the "national macroculture." In addition to being members of the national macroculture, people in the United States are members of ethnic groups. An ethnic group is made up of individuals within a larger culture who share a self-defined racial or cultural identity and a set of beliefs, attitudes, and values. Members of an ethnic group distinguish themselves from others in the society by physical and social attributes. You should be aware also that the composition of ethnic groups can change over time, and that there is often as much variability within groups as between them. Clearly, the United States is a "culturally complex society . . . the most racially and ethnically diverse democracy in the world" (Wells, 2014, p.19–20).

Cultural Identity

13 In addition to membership in the national macroculture, each individual participates in an array of subcultures, each with its customs and beliefs. Collectively, these subcultures, determine an individual's cultural identity, an overall sense of who one is. Other possible elements that might shape a person's cultural identity include age, racial identity, exceptionalities, language, gender, sexual orientation, income level, and beliefs and values. The importance of these

elements differs among people. For some, their cultural identity is most strongly determined by their occupations; for others, it is determined by their ethnicity; and for others, by their religious beliefs.

14 Remember that your future students will have their own complex, cultural identities, which are no less valid for being different. For some of them, these identities may make them feel disconnected from the attitudes, expectations, and values conveyed by the school. You will be challenged as a teacher to understand the subtle differences in cultural identities among your students. You will need to create a learning environment that enables all students to feel connected to their school experiences.

15 Some of your students may have cultural backgrounds that are individualistic, whereas the backgrounds of others may be collectivistic. Individualistic cultures tend to emphasize the individual and his or her success and achievement. Collectivistic cultures, on the other hand, tend to emphasize group membership and a sense of "we," rather than "I" (Greenfield, 1994; Hofstede, 2001); (Rothstein-Fisch & Trumbull, 2008; Traindis, 1989). "While self-realization is the ideal with many individualistic cultures, in the collectivist model, individuals must fit into the group, and group realization is the ideal" (Waltman & Bush-Bacelis, 1995, pp. 66–67). Figure 8.2 presents a comparison of individualistic and collectivistic cultures that can be helpful in understanding how students from different cultural backgrounds view life in classrooms. Remember, though, that everyone has values and points of view that are both individualistic and collectivistic. The two types of cultures represent "general tendencies that may emerge when the members of . . . [a] culture are considered as a whole" (Markus & Kitayama, 1991, p. 225).

Individualistic Cultures *(United States, Canada, Western Europe, Australia)*	**Collectivistic Cultures** *(Many Asian, African, and South American Cultures)*
Individual uniqueness, self-determination. **Independence, self-reliance, and individual achievement.** **Self-expression.** **Individual choice.** **Equality of relationships.** **Task orientation.** **Individual well-being.** **Self-esteem.**	**Loyalty to group and family.** **Interdependence, cooperation, and group success.** **Adherence to group norms.** **Group consensus.** **Hierarchical relationships.** **Group orientation.** **Group well-being.** **Modesty.**

Figure 8-2. ■ Individualistic and collectivistic cultures: A comparison

Reading Comprehension Check

Read the following questions and circle the correct answer.

1. In the introduction to the chapter, what skill is mentioned as most important for teaching today's students?
   a. the ability to care about students and be strict at the same time
   b. the ability to communicate effectively with diverse students
   c. the ability to teach a subject competently and efficiently
   d. the ability to teach competently and be extremely serious
2. "Each year, more than 1 million immigrants **obtain** legal permanent resident status in the United States."

   In the above sentence, the word *obtain* means
   a. acquire.
   b. abandon.
   c. abdicate.
   d. relinquish.

3. According to Figure 8.1, which parents' region of origin is behind two other regions in terms of percentage?
   a. Latin America
   b. Africa
   c. Asia
   d. Europe
4. "Many of these children entered the country at a young age, have been educated in American schools, and have grown up speaking English and **embracing** American culture."

   The meaning of the word *embracing* in the above context is
   a. rejecting.
   b. denying.
   c. denouncing.
   d. accepting.
5. In the sentence, "Undocumented youth who graduate from high school face significant **barriers** to everything typically associated with youth of that age, including driving, working, and receiving financial aid for higher education," the word *barriers* is similar in meaning to
   a. gateway.
   b. obstacles.
   c. chances.
   d. exams.
6. In paragraph 8, which of the following is *not* mentioned?
   a. In 2011, 48 percent of the students were part of a minority group.
   b. In 2011, the number of students from a minority group increased 16 percent.
   c. Before 2050, more than 50 percent of students will be from minority groups.
   d. In 2011, 62 percent of the students were part of a majority group.
7. In the section The Meaning of Culture, the term *culture* is defined as
   a. how people from a particular group disregard other groups of people.
   b. how people from a specific group live life in accordance with their beliefs.
   c. how people from culturally diverse backgrounds do not mingle at all.
   d. how U.S. society forces foreign cultures to blend into a single culture.
8. Read paragraph 14 and determine the meaning of **subtle** from the context. In this context, the word *subtle* means
   a. easy to understand.
   b. easy to perceive.
   c. difficult to perceive.
   d. difficult to misunderstand.
9. Figure 8.2 shows that
   a. individualistic and collectivistic cultures are strikingly similar.
   b. individualistic and collectivistic cultures have much in common.
   c. individualistic and collectivistic cultures share the same values.
   d. individualistic and collectivistic cultures are significantly different.

10. The main idea of the chapter is that
   a. aspiring teachers should think twice before choosing teaching as a profession, because it is an extremely challenging career.
   b. a curriculum should be developed to include only specific groups of students in a multicultural classroom.
   c. the challenge for today's teachers is to provide a quality education to students of diverse cultural backgrounds.
   d. today's teachers should consider their students' diverse cultural backgrounds a serious weakness and a liability.

Contemporary Issues in the Discipline

Geoffrey Canada: Educational Reformer

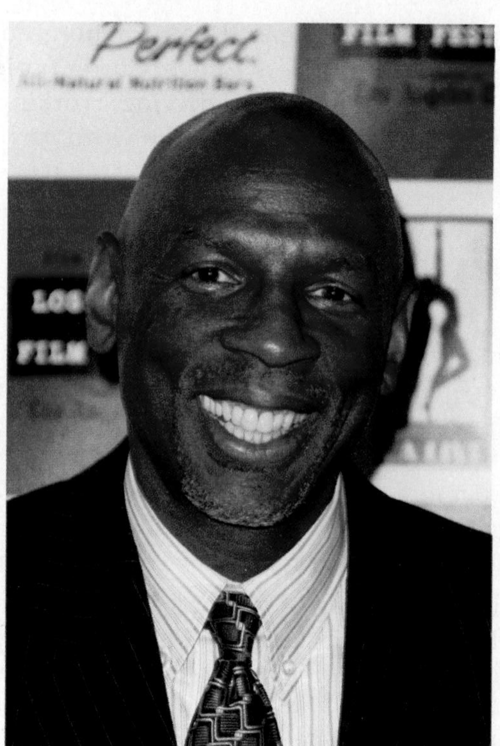

Geoffrey Canada grew up in an underserved South Bronx neighborhood. After earning a Master's in education from Harvard, Canada has devoted his life to working with kids in impoverished neighborhoods, specifically in Harlem, where he serves as the president of the Harlem Children's Zone.

Under Canada's leadership, this organization has expanded exponentially, encompassing more than 100 square blocks and serving an estimated 10,000 children, providing services from Pre-K to college planning, as well as health care.

Canada has become known nationally for his work, and in 2011, he was listed as one of *TIME* magazine's 100 most influential people.

He is the author of two books: *Fist Stick Knife Gun: A Personal History of Violence in America* and *Reaching Up for Manhood: Transforming the Lives of Boys in America*.

MyReadingLab

Visit Chapter 2: Education in MyReadingLab to complete the Reading 6 activities.

READING 6

Lecture (TED Talk)

Our Failing Schools: Enough is Enough!

Pre-Reading Activity

Before reading the following transcript of Geoffrey Canada's speech, you can watch the talk itself here: https://www.ted.com/talks/geoffrey_canada_our_failing_schools_enough_is_enough?language=en (Courtesy of TED). As you listen to the videoed presentation, take notes. (See the note-taking activity on p. 190 for some pointers.)

After reading the transcript, you will answer some open-ended questions about some of the issues Mr. Canada raises in his speech. Finally, you will formulate questions for Mr. Canada about issues pertinent to education and answer them from his perspective.

Our Failing Schools: Enough is Enough!

by Geoffrey Canada

May 2013

Transcript courtesy of TED © TED CONFERENCES, LLC

1 I'm a little nervous, because my wife Yvonne said to me, she said, "Geoff, you watch the TED Talks."

2 I said, "Yes, honey, I love TED Talks."

3 She said, "You know, they're like, really smart, talented—"

4 I said, "I know, I know." *(Laughter)*

5 She said, "They don't want, like, the angry black man." *(Laughter)*

6 So I said, "No, I'm gonna be good, Honey, I'm gonna be good. I am." But I am angry. *(Laughter)* And the last time I looked, I'm —

7 *(Applause)* So this is why I'm excited but I'm angry. This year, there are going to be millions of our children that we're going to needlessly lose, that we could—right now, we could save them all. You saw the quality of the educators who were here. Do not tell me they could not reach those kids and save them. I know they could. It is absolutely possible. Why haven't we fixed this? Those of us in education have held on to a business plan that we don't care how many millions of young people fail, we're going to continue to do the same thing that

didn't work, and nobody is getting crazy about it—right?—enough to say, "Enough is enough." So here's a business plan that simply does not make any sense.

8 You know, I grew up in the inner city, and there were kids who were failing in schools 56 years ago when I first went to school, and those schools are still lousy today, 56 years later. And you know something about a lousy school? It's not like a bottle of wine. Right? *(Laughter)* Where you say, like, '87 was like a good year, right? That's now how this thing—I mean, every single year, it's still the same approach, right? One size fits all, if you get it, fine, and if you don't, tough luck. Just tough luck. Why haven't we allowed innovation to happen? Do not tell me we can't do better than this.

9 Look, you go into a place that's failed kids for 50 years, and you say, "So what's the plan?" And they say, "We'll, we're going to do what we did last year this year." What kind of business model is that? Banks used to open and operate between 10 and 3. They operated 10 to 3. They were closed for lunch hour. Now, who can bank between 10 and 3? The unemployed. They don't need banks. They got no money in the banks. Who created that business model? Right? And it went on for decades. You know why? Because they didn't care. It wasn't about the customers. It was about bankers. They created something that worked for them. How could you go to the bank when you were at work? It didn't matter. And they don't care whether or not Geoff is upset he can't go to the bank. Go find another bank. They all operate the same way. Right? Now, one day, some crazy banker had an idea. Maybe we should keep the bank open when people come home from work. They might like that. What about a Saturday? What about introducing technology?

10 Now look, I'm a technology fan, but I have to admit to you all I'm a little old. So I was a little slow, and I did not trust technology, and when they first came out with those new contraptions, these tellers that you put in a card and they give you money, I was like, "There's no way that machine is going to count that money right. I am never using that, right?"

11 So technology has changed. Things have changed. Yet not in education. Why? Why is it that when we had rotary phones, when we were having folks being crippled by polio, that we were teaching the same way then that we're doing right now? And if you come up with a plan to change things, people consider you radical. They will say the worst things about you. I said one day, well, look, if the science says—this is science, not me—that our poorest children lose ground in the summertime—You see where they are in June and say, okay, they're there. You look at them in September, they've gone down. You say, whoo! So I heard about that in '75 when I was at the Ed School at Harvard. I said, "Oh, wow, this is an important study." Because it suggests we should do something. *(Laughter)* Every 10 years they reproduce the same study. It says exactly the same thing: Poor kids lose

ground in the summertime. The system decides you can't run schools in the summer.

12 You know, I always wonder, who makes up those rules? For years I went to—Look, I went to the Harvard Ed School. I thought I knew something. They said it was the agrarian calendar, and people had—but let me tell you why that doesn't make sense. I never got that. I never got that, because anyone knows if you farm, you don't plant crops in July and August. You plant them in the spring. So who came up with this idea? Who owns it? Why did we ever do it? Well it just turns out in the 1840s we did have, schools were open all year. They were open all year, because we had a lot of folks who had to work all day. They didn't have any place for their kids to go. It was a perfect place to have schools. So this is not something that is ordained from the education gods.

13 So why don't we? Why don't we? Because our business has refused to use science. Science. You have Bill Gates coming out and saying, "Look, this works, right? We can do this." How many places in America are going to change? None. None. Okay, yeah, there are two. All right? Yes, there'll be some place, because some folks will do the right thing. As a profession, we have to stop this. The science is clear.

14 Here's what we know. We know that the problem begins immediately. Right? This idea, zero to three. My wife, Yvonne, and I, we have four kids, three grown ones and a 15-year-old. That's a longer story. *(Laughter)* With our first kids, we did not know the science about brain development. We didn't know how critical those first three years were. We didn't know what was happening in those young brains. We didn't know the role that language, a stimulus and response, call and response, how important that was in developing those children. We know that now. What are we doing about it? Nothing. Wealthy people know. Educated people know. And their kids have an advantage. Poor people don't know, and we're not doing anything to help them at all. But we know this is critical.

15 Now, you take pre-kindergarten. We know it's important for kids. Poor kids need that experience. Nope. Lots of places, it doesn't exist. We know health services matter. You know, we provide health services and people are always fussing at me about, you know, because I'm all into accountability and data and all of that good stuff, but we do health services, and I have to raise a lot of money. People used to say when they'd come fund us, "Geoff, why do you provide these health services?" I used to make stuff up. Right? I'd say, "Well, you know a child who has cavities is not going to, uh, be able to study as well." And I had to because I had to raise the money. But now I'm older, and you know what I tell them? You know why I provide kids with those health benefits and the sports and the recreation and the arts? Because I actually like kids. I actually like kids. *(Laughter) (Applause)*

16 But when they really get pushy, people really get pushy, I say, "I do it because you do it for your kid." And you've never read a study from MIT that says giving your kid dance instruction is going to help them do algebra better, but you will give that kid dance instruction, and you will be thrilled that that kid wants to do dance instruction, and it will make your day. And why shouldn't poor kids have the same opportunity? It's the floor for these children. *(Applause)*

17 So here's the other thing. I'm a tester guy. I believe you need data, you need information, because you work at something, you think it's working, and you find out it's not working. I mean, you're educators. You work, you say, you think you've got it, great, no? And you find out they didn't get it. But here's the problem with testing. The testing that we do—we're going to have our test in New York next week—is in April. You know when we're going to get the results back? Maybe July, maybe June. And the results have great data. They'll tell you Raheem really struggled, couldn't do two-digit multiplication—so great data, but you're getting it back after school is over. And so, what do you do? You go on vacation. *(Laughter)* You come back from vacation. Now you've got all of this test data from last year. You don't look at it. Why would you look at it? You're going to go and teach this year. So how much money did we just spend on all of that? Billions and billions of dollars for data that it's too late to use. I need that data in September. I need that data in November. I need to know you're struggling, and I need to know whether or not what I did corrected that. I need to know that this week. I don't need to know that at the end of the year when it's too late.

18 Because in my older years, I've become somewhat of a clairvoyant. I can predict school scores. You take me to any school. I'm really good at inner-city schools that are struggling. And you tell me last year 48 percent of those kids were on grade level. And I say, "Okay, what's the plan, what did we do from last year to this year?" You say, "We're doing the same thing." I'm going to make a prediction. *(Laughter)* This year, somewhere between 44 and 52 percent of those kids will be on grade level. And I will be right every single time.

19 So we're spending all of this money, but we're getting what? Teachers need real information right now about what's happening to their kids. The high stakes is today, because you can do something about it.

20 So here's the other issue that I just think we've got to be concerned about. We can't stifle innovation in our business. We have to innovate. And people in our business get mad about innovation. They get angry if you do something different. If you try something new, people are always like, "Ooh, charter schools." Hey, let's try some stuff. Let's see. This stuff hasn't worked for 55 years. Let's try something different. And here's the rub. Some of it's not going to work. You know, people tell me, "Yeah, those charter schools, a lot of them don't work." A lot of them don't. They should be closed. I mean, I really believe they should be closed. But we can't confuse figuring out the

science and things not working with we shouldn't therefore do anything. Right? Because that's not the way the world works.

21 If you think about technology, imagine if that's how we thought about technology. Every time something didn't work, we just threw in the towel and said, "Let's forget it." Right? You know, they convinced me. I'm sure some of you were like me—the latest and greatest thing, the PalmPilot. They told me, "Geoff, if you get this PalmPilot you'll never need another thing." That thing lasted all of three weeks. It was over. I was so disgusted I spent my money on this thing. Did anybody stop inventing? Not a person. Not a soul. The folks went out there. They kept inventing. The fact that you have failure, that shouldn't stop you from pushing the science forward.

22 Our job as educators, there's some stuff we know that we can do. And we've got to do better. The evaluation, we have to start with kids earlier, we have to make sure that we provide the support to young people. We've got to give them all of these opportunities. So that we have to do. But this innovation issue, this idea that we've got to keep innovating until we really nail this science down is something that is absolutely critical.

23 And this is something, by the way, that I think is going to be a challenge for our entire field. America cannot wait another 50 years to get this right. We have run out of time. I don't know about a fiscal cliff, but I know there's an educational cliff that we are walking over right this very second, and if we allow folks to continue this foolishness about saying we can't afford this—So Bill Gates says it's going to cost five billion dollars. What is five billion dollars to the United States? What did we spend in Afghanistan this year? How many trillions? *(Applause)*

24 When the country cares about something, we'll spend a trillion dollars without blinking an eye. When the safety of America is threatened, we will spend any amount of money. The real safety of our nation is preparing this next generation so that they can take our place and be the leaders of the world when it comes to thinking and technology and democracy and all that stuff we care about. I dare say it's a pittance, what it would require for us to really begin to solve some of these problems.

25 So once we do that, I'll no longer be angry. *(Laughter)* So, you guys, help me get there. Thank you all very much. Thank you. *(Applause)*

26 **John Legend:** So what is the high school dropout rate at Harlem Children's Zone?

27 **Geoffrey Canada:** Well, you know, John, 100 percent of our kids graduated high school last year in my school. A hundred percent of them went to college. This year's seniors will have 100 percent graduating high school. Last I heard we had 93 percent accepted to college. We'd better get that other seven percent. So that's just how this goes. *(Applause)*

28 **JL:** So how do you stick with them after they leave high school?

29 **GC:** Well, you know, one of the bad problems we have in this country is these kids, the same kids, these same vulnerable kids, when you get them in school, they drop out in record numbers. And so we've

figured out that you've got to really design a network of support for these kids that in many ways mimics what a good parent does. They harass you, right? They call you, they say, "I want to see your grades. How'd you do on that last test? What are you talking about that you want to leave school? And you're not coming back here." So a bunch of my kids know you can't come back to Harlem because Geoff is looking for you. They're like, "I really can't come back." No. You'd better stay in school. But I'm not kidding about some of this, and it gets a little bit to the grit issue. When kids know that you refuse to let them fail, it puts a different pressure on them, and they don't give up as easy. So sometimes they don't have it inside, and they're, like, "You know, I don't want to do this, but I know my mother's going to be mad." Well, that matters to kids, and it helps get them through. We try to create a set of strategies that gets them tutoring and help and support, but also a set of encouragements that say to them, "You can do it. It is going to be hard, but we refuse to let you fail."

JL: Well, thank you Dr. Canada. Please give it up for him one more time.

(Applause)

Reading with a Critical Eye

1. When it comes to educating our children, why does Canada believe that the business plan does not make any sense? Refer to the transcript to answer the question.
2. What is Canada's purpose in using the bank example? In other words, how is the bank example relevant to the current state of education in the United States?
3. What makes Canada draw the conclusion that "our business has refused to use science"? Use specific examples to support your answer.
4. Canada tells his audience that the field of education must innovate. Why, in your opinion, does he think that "We can't stifle innovation in our business," and why do people get uncomfortable and angry when someone tries to do something innovative?

Imagined Interview: If you had the opportunity to interview Geoffrey Canada in person, what would you ask him? With a partner, compose three questions for him.

Question 1. ______________________________

Question 2. ______________________________

Question 3. ______________________________

Interview Challenge: In a group, ask one student to play Mr. Canada. This student should carefully consider Geoffrey Canada's views, outlined clearly in the TED Talk, and try to answer the questions from Canada's perspective on education.

Chapter Recap

Now that you have made it through a full chapter focusing on the field of Education, let's review the chapter reading content, skill focus, and vocabulary to gain a better understanding of what we have learned.

Recap Activity 1: A Quick Glance

In 60 seconds, answer the following two questions:

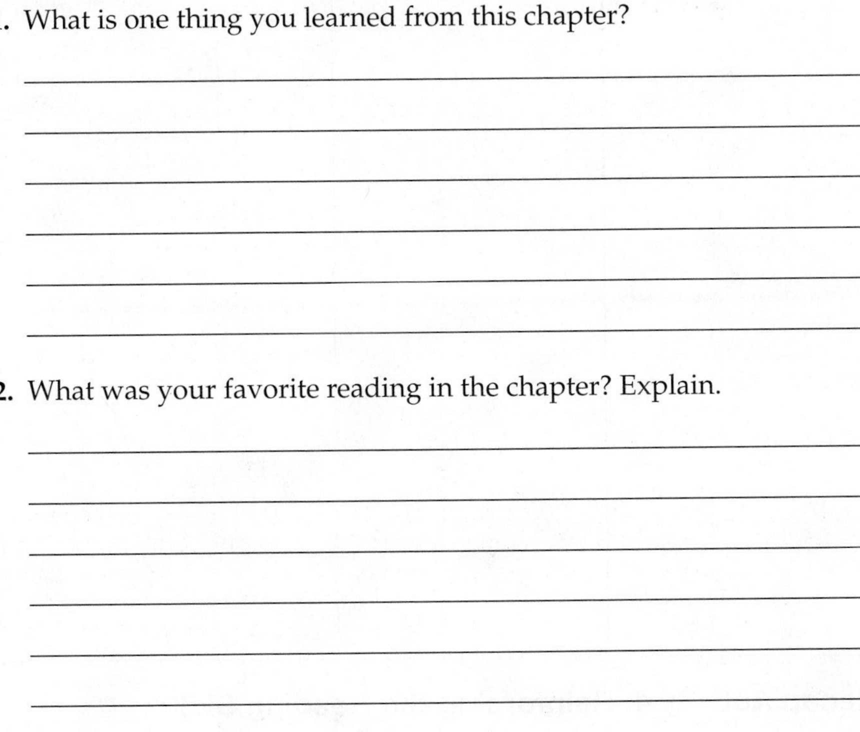

1. What is one thing you learned from this chapter?

____

____

____

____

____

____

2. What was your favorite reading in the chapter? Explain.

____

____

____

____

____

____

Now discuss what you wrote in a small group. Do not read what you wrote. Paraphrase yourself!

Recap Activity 2: Summary Writing

Choose your favorite reading from this chapter and write a summary containing the main idea and some major details. Keep in mind that the key to summary writing is to convey the author's ideas accurately, but to relay this information in your own words. Last but not least, be sure to include reminder phrases and appropriate transitions.

Recap Activity 3: Internet Research on a Theme of Interest

Think about the choice you made in Activity 2 concerning which reading in the chapter was your favorite.

What was the theme of your chosen reading?

Theme = ____

Using a search engine, such as Google, go online and locate a quality reading on the same theme as your favorite chapter reading. Write a three- to five-sentence summary of the reading that you found from your Internet research.

Title of Reading	*Article Source*	*Summary of the Reading (in your own words)*

Recap Activity 4: Reinforcing the Reading Skill

Reread the paragraph below from the chapter excerpt from *Geoffrey Canada's speech* (p. 70, para. 20). After reading, discuss it with a partner: What plan of action can be used to determine the meaning of the bolded words from the context?

> So here's the other issue that I just think we've got to be concerned about. We can't **stifle** innovation in our business. We have to **innovate**. And people in our business get mad about innovation. They get angry if you do something different. If you try something new, people are always like, "Ooh, charter schools." Hey, let's try some stuff. Let's see. This stuff hasn't worked for 55 years. Let's try something different. And here's the rub. Some of it's not going to work. You know, people tell me, "Yeah, those charter schools, a lot of them don't work." A lot of them don't. They should be closed. I mean, I really believe they should be closed. But we can't confuse figuring out the science and things not working with we shouldn't therefore do anything. Right? Because that's not the way the world works.

How do you determine the meaning of the bolded words you have just read?

Strategy 1: ____________________

Strategy 2: ____________________

Recap Activity 5: Recycling Vocabulary

With a partner, locate the following vocabulary terms, review them in context, and try to define the terms without using a dictionary. Make sure to underline the vocabulary term used in the sentence. The first example is done for you.

Word and context location	*Sentence containing the word*	*Meaning in this context*
coed p. 33, para. 3	*Obel-Omia believes boys enter* ***coed*** *schools at a disadvantage to girls.*	*mixed gender*
pedagogy p. 51, para. 23		
abysmally p. 50, para. 18		
standards p. 29 , para. 6		
undergraduate p. 49, para. 6		
shortchange p. 33, para. 3		
approach p. 33, para. 3		
stimulating p. 30, para. 19		

Further Explorations

Books

1. *Learning in Small Moments: Life in an Urban Classroom* by Daniel Meier. Practioner Inquiry Series, 1997. This book offers an introduction to urban elementary school teaching from the experience of a veteran teacher.

2. *Teaching and Learning in a Diverse World* by Patricia Ramsey. Teachers College Press, 2004. This text provides a framework for teaching in a multicultural context.
3. *Teacher Man: A Memoir* by Frank McCourt. 2005. In this memoir, McCourt recalls teaching high school English in New York City for 30 years and feeling insecure about teaching while relying on his experience growing up in Ireland to engage his students.

Movies

1. *Freedom Writers* (2007). Directed by Richard LaGravenese. This is an inspiring movie about a female high school teacher who motivates her underprivileged students to become creative writers.
2. *The Great Debaters* (2007). Directed by Denzel Washington. Denzel Washington directs and stars in this movie based on a true story about an inspiring debate team coach who transforms his African American college students with the power of his words to challenge the Harvard elite in a debate.
3. *Chalk* (2008). Directed by Mike Akel. This movie is about a group of high school teachers and how they act in classrooms and behind the scenes.

Internet Sites

1. http://wps.ablongman.com/ab_johnson_introfound_14/
   This is the companion Web site for *Foundations of American Education*, the education textbook chapter sampled in this chapter's Reading 5.
2. http://www.teachers-teachers.com/
   If you are considering pursuing teaching as a career, this Web site offers practical information about this profession.

Using Index Cards to Study Vocabulary

Overview

As you know, one of the most challenging parts of succeeding in college is to learn new vocabulary and jargon typical of a subject. There are many techniques to build vocabulary, but here we offer you an effective technique that will help you improve your active vocabulary. For this activity, you will need index cards that are blank on one side and lined on the other.

Activity

As you come across an unfamiliar word while doing a reading assignment, write it on the blank side of the index card. On the lined side, write information related to the new word as follows. Keep in mind that you will need a good dictionary to do this exercise.

1. Look up the word in a dictionary and write how it is pronounced. Most dictionaries phonetically transcribe words, so it should not be difficult for you to write the sounds.
2. Find out what part of speech the word is and write it below. For example, write if the word is a noun, a verb, an adjective, or an adverb.
3. Write the meaning of the word.
4. Make an example sentence using the new word in context.
5. Using a dictionary, write the words that are derived from the same root. For example, the words *marine*, *maritime*, *marina*, *submarine*, and *mariner* are all derived from the same Latin root *mar*, which means sea. This way you will learn that some words are associated with each other.
6. Write at least two or three synonyms of the unfamiliar word here.
7. Finally, write at least two or three antonyms of the new word here.

Let's take a look at an index card so that you can fully understand how to **create** your own index cards for vocabulary building. We will use the word *create* for this index card exercise.

Learning Implications

In order to succeed in college and later in your professional career, it is essential that you improve and continue to build your active vocabulary. Words that are part of your active vocabulary are readily available for speech and writing.

CREATE

1. Pronunciation: \krē-'āt\
2. Part of speech: verb
3. Meaning: to make something new
4. Example: The art students *created* a wonderfully colorful mural from cereal boxes.
5. Family: creator – noun   creation – noun   creationist – noun
   creationism – noun   creative – adjective   creatively – adverb
   creativity – noun   creature – noun
6. Synonyms – design, invent, devise, construct
7. Antonyms – demolish, ruin, destroy, destruct

In other words, you do not need to stop in the middle of speaking or writing and look up new words in a dictionary if your active vocabulary is expansive. At first, this exercise may seem challenging and somewhat repetitive to you, but soon you will realize that using index cards is an integral part of your active vocabulary development.

HEALTH: Nutrition

3

"You are what you eat."
VICTOR LINDLAHR

Learning Objectives

AFTER READING THIS CHAPTER, YOU SHOULD BE ABLE TO DO THE FOLLOWING …

1. Describe the fundamentals of health and nutrition.
2. Distinguish among parts of speech.
3. Use a survey to collect data.
4. Analyze graphic aids.
5. Construct an outline of a reading.
6. Devise and deliver a formal presentation.

INTRODUCTION TO THE DISCIPLINE OF HEALTH

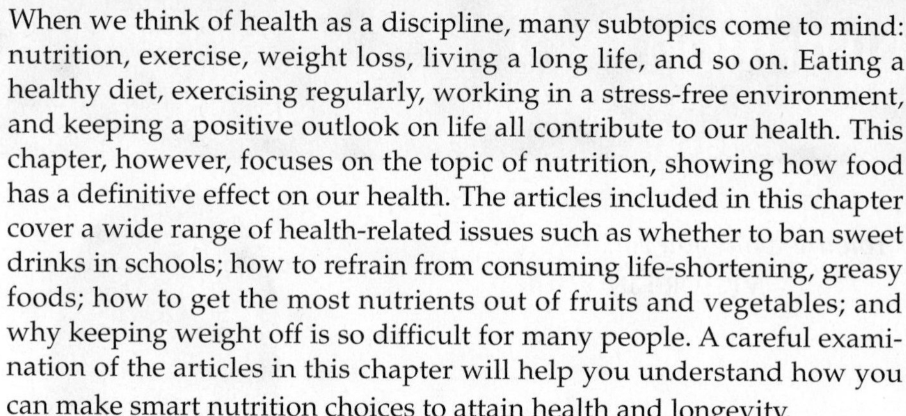

When we think of health as a discipline, many subtopics come to mind: nutrition, exercise, weight loss, living a long life, and so on. Eating a healthy diet, exercising regularly, working in a stress-free environment, and keeping a positive outlook on life all contribute to our health. This chapter, however, focuses on the topic of nutrition, showing how food has a definitive effect on our health. The articles included in this chapter cover a wide range of health-related issues such as whether to ban sweet drinks in schools; how to refrain from consuming life-shortening, greasy foods; how to get the most nutrients out of fruits and vegetables; and why keeping weight off is so difficult for many people. A careful examination of the articles in this chapter will help you understand how you can make smart nutrition choices to attain health and longevity.

Preview Questions

Working in small groups, answer the following questions. Notice that they all focus on the topic of health.

1. How would you define a "health nut" or a "health not"? What are some characteristics of these groups of people?
2. Do you know someone who is an absolute health nut or an absolute health not? Describe this person's health and nutrition habits.
3. Do you consider yourself a health nut, a health not, or someone in between?
4. Some health advocates believe that unhealthy foods should not be available in certain places. Do you think that the government should regulate our eating habits? For example, should vending machines containing soda and candy be banned from public schools?
5. Imagine you are a nutritionist, and your obese client asks you how she can lose weight and keep it off. What types of foods and exercise would you recommend to this client? Be specific.

Writing on The Wall

After you have discussed the preview questions with your classmates, post your responses to two of them on your class blog, which we refer to as The Wall. Review others' postings and respond to at least two of your classmates' posts that grab your interest. Remember the guidelines for blogging and commenting etiquette (see Chapter 1, p. 15).)! If your class is not using a shared blog, your instructor may ask you to record your individual or collective responses to the preview questions in another form.

EXERCISE 3.1 Interpreting a Cartoon

Examine the cartoon shown here, and in pairs, answer the following questions.

1. What is amusing about this cartoon?
2. In your opinion, what message is the cartoonist trying to convey to the reader?

Discipline-Specific Vocabulary: Understand Key Terms in Health

In this chapter, you will learn some key terms in the discipline of health. Your goal is to use these terms in your speech and writing. You will have the opportunity to interact with key terms in context, so study them carefully and make them part of your active vocabulary.

EXERCISE 3.2 Brainstorming Vocabulary

Directions: What associated words come to mind when you think of the discipline of health? Work with a partner and write down as many related words as you can think of in a period of five minutes.

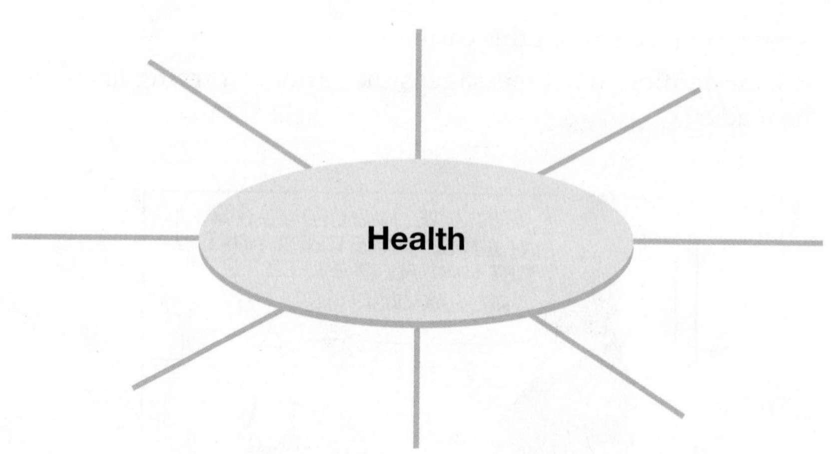

Fishing for Synonyms and Antonyms

In your written work, you will often need to use synonyms and antonyms (see Chapter 2, p. 24 to review these terms) in order to paraphrase statements or claims made by writers.

EXERCISE 3.3 Determining Synonyms and Antonyms from Context

Directions: Read the following nine (9) discipline-specific words culled from the readings in this chapter and shown in the context of the sentences in which they appeared. In the space provided after each sentence, write a synonym or antonym for the highlighted term, as directed.

Discipline-specific Word Bank for Health		
obese	environmental	lifestyle
fiber	saturated	longevity
sedentary	consumption	nutrient

1. When a researcher asked that question of a group of formerly **obese** people, 89 percent said they would prefer to lose their sight than their hard-won slimness.

   An antonym for *obese* is ____________.

2. How much sleep is necessary to maintain a healthy **lifestyle**?

   A synonym for *lifestyle* is ________________________.

3. "Many of us remove the skins from eggplant, bell peppers, peaches, apples, and nectarines while preparing recipes, but we're really just tossing away nutrients and **fiber**," says nutritionist Forberg.

   A synonym for *fiber* is ____________.

4. A careful examination of the articles in this chapter will enable you to understand how you can make smart nutrition choices to attain health and **longevity**.

   A synonym for *longevity* is ____________.

5. On the one hand, we've been told with almost religious certainty by everyone from the surgeon general on down, and we have come to believe with almost religious certainty, that obesity is caused by the excessive **consumption** of fat, and that if we eat less fat we will lose weight and live longer.

   A synonym for *consumption* is ____________.

6. In other words, is obesity genetically determined, or is it influenced by **environmental** factors?

   A synonym for *environmental* is ________________.

7. It's true that they're also high in fat, but it's the heart-healthy **monounsaturated** kind.

   An antonym for saturated is ____________.

8. Meanwhile, for reasons that are not fully understood, many people become more **sedentary** after they lose weight.

   An antonym for sedentary is ____________.

9. And recent preliminary evidence suggests that the levels of certain **nutrients**, especially vitamin C, some minerals, and some polyphenols—naturally occurring antioxidants that may help bolster the immune system—are higher in organically grown crops.
   An antonym for nutrients is ________________.

EXERCISE 3.4 Matching Terms with Definitions

Match the word in Column A with the definition in Column B. Put the letter representing the correct definition in the space preceding each term.

Column A Word		Column B Definition
1. ____	obese	a. roughage found in plants
2. ____	lifestyle	b. a substance needed to be alive
3. ____	fiber	c. significantly overweight
4. ____	longevity	d. sitting down and not moving
5. ____	consumption	e. the highest amount of substance
6. ____	environmental	f. the way people live and work
7. ____	saturated	g. using food for energy
8. ____	sedentary	h. external conditions or surroundings
9. ____	nutrient	i. long life

EXERCISE 3.5 Choosing the Right Word

In the following sentences, fill in the blank with a word from the terminology bank that makes the sentence meaningful.

obese	lifestyle	fiber	longevity	consumption
environmental	cholesterol	saturated	sedentary	nutrient

1. Many ancient societies around the world that practice internal medicine have attempted to find various ways to attain health and ______________.
2. In many underdeveloped African countries, children suffer from a severe ______________ deficiency because of a lack of agricultural produce.
3. Obesity is on the rise in the United States due to a combination of ______________ jobs, lack of exercise, and poor food habits.

4. Christina's physician warned her that if she did not make some serious dietary changes, she could not lead a healthy ____________ and would most likely die prematurely.
5. Many people who were formerly ___________ would prefer to lose their eyesight than regain their weight.
6. In addition, many people who consume a vegan diet feel that consumption of animal products wastes natural resources, contributes to ________________ damage, and is therefore morally wrong.
7. As a result of health magazines reporting findings of research conducted by nutrition scientists in the United States, the American people are gradually becoming aware of the consequences of eating foods containing large amounts of _____________ fat.
8. After the wild spread of the mad cow disease in England and other European countries, the U.S. government declared imported meat products unfit for human ________________.
9. This campaign promotes eating a variety of colorful fruits and vegetables—which are rich in vitamins, minerals, __________, and phytochemicals—each day to help reduce the risk of cancer and heart disease and slow the effects of aging.

EXERCISE 3.6 Word Form

In the table below, five discipline-specific words are provided. Working with a partner, write different forms that are associated with the words in appropriate columns. Finally, write a synonym and an antonym of the discipline-specific word. You may need to use a dictionary to complete this exercise. The first example is done for you.

Noun	*Adjective*	*Verb*	*Adverb*	*Synonym*	*Antonym*
1. harm	harmful	harm	harmfully	damage	protect
2. genes	________	________	________	________	________
3. trend	________	________	________	________	________
4. depression	________	________	________	________	________
5. ban	________	________	________	________	________

Vocabulary Development: Parts of Speech

Word Formation

For every new word you learn, there are associated forms that can strengthen your vocabulary further. Academic reading demands that you have the ability to identify different forms in different contexts. Suffixes in English have two primary functions: (1) to change the meaning of the root to which they are attached and (2) to change the part of speech of the root. The following rules show how certain words are formed in English. Keep in mind that word formation is not always entirely predictable, but that these rules apply in most cases.

Rule 1: Noun → Noun		
-hood	brotherhood	parenthood
-ship	friendship	membership
-ist	novelist	guitarist
-ism	capitalism	socialism
Rule 2: Verb → Noun		
-ment	enhancement	parchment
-er	trainer	mixer
-ation	purification	justification
Rule 3: Adjective → Noun		
-dom	freedom	boredom
-ness	madness	sadness
-ity	equality	purity
Rule 4: Adjective/Noun → Verb		
-ify	liquefy	solidify
-ize	legalize	prioritize
Rule 5: Noun → Adjective		
-y	sunny	windy
-ous	religious	famous
-ful	beautiful	faithful
-ial	collegial	official
Rule 6: Verb → Adjective		
-ive	relative	regressive
-able	believable	commendable
-ful	regretful	wishful
-ent/ant	competent	hesitant
Rule 7: Adjective → Adjective		
-ish	smallish	greenish
-ly	sickly	lonely
Rule 8: Adjective → Adverb		
-ly	politely	equally

EXERCISE 3.7 Word Formation

The following words are taken from "Fat Chance" by Emily Bazelon, an article you will read later (it starts on page 91). Practice word formation by using the above rules. Your task is to identify what part of speech the word is, write the rule that can change the meaning of the root, and write the derived form next to it. The first example is done for you. (The number in parentheses represents the reading paragraph in which the word appears.)

1. Obese (paragraph 1)
   Rule: (3) *Adjective → Noun*
   Derived Form: *obese + ity → obesity*
2. Study (paragraph 3)
   Rule: ____________________
   Derived Form: ____________________
3. Sympathy (paragraph 3)
   Rule: ____________________
   Derived Form: ____________________
4. Journal (paragraph 4)
   Rule: ____________________
   Derived Form: ____________________
5. Benefit (paragraph 5)
   Rule: ____________________
   Derived Form: ____________________
6. Explain (paragraph 6)
   Rule: ____________________
   Derived Form: ____________________
7. Insist (paragraph 7)
   Rule: ____________________
   Derived Form: ____________________
8. Biological (paragraph 8)
   Rule: ____________________
   Derived Form: ____________________
9. Anxiety (paragraph 10)
   Rule: ____________________
   Derived Form: ____________________

EXERCISE 3.8 Parts of Speech

The table below shows the different parts of speech for words from the terminology bank. The first two examples are done for you. Using a monolingual dictionary, find the derivations of the highlighted words and complete the table. Keep in mind that some words may not have multiple forms, in which case simply put an X in the appropriate box.

Noun	*Adjective*	*Verb*	*Adverb*
nutrition	nutritious	X	nutritiously
diagnosis	diagnostic	diagnose	diagnostically
genes			
	obese		
		harm	
	environmental		
		ban	
regulation			
	saturated		

In-Class Health Survey

Refer to the following questions to interview at least two classmates. Please take notes as they respond to your questions and orally report your findings.

Question	*Respondent 1*	*Respondent 2*
1. How often do you eat fast food?		
2. Do you ever cook at home, or do you usually eat out?		
3. When you are choosing what to eat, how much do you take into consideration the health value of what you are going to consume?		
4. In your opinion, what food items are the most hazardous to your health?		

Fieldwork Health Survey

Please give the survey below to people in your neighborhood, at work, or at school. (You can copy the form as many times as needed.) Tell the respondents that the survey is conducted solely for academic purposes, their participation in the survey is totally voluntary, their names will be kept confidential, they will not be contacted in the future for further interviews, and the survey should not take more than five minutes to complete. You can ask them to write brief answers to the survey questions if they prefer to do so themselves, or you can write down their oral answers to your questions. Be prepared to report the results of the survey to your class later. The survey will help you learn more about health in general.

Health Survey

1. How many glasses of water do you drink every day?

____

2. How often do you exercise every week? What types of exercise do you do? Do you lift weights, do cardiovascular exercise, or practice yoga/tai chi?

____

3. Do you cook at home? If yes, then how often and what kinds of food do you cook?

____

4. How many servings of fruits and vegetables do you eat every day?

____

5. How often do you eat fast food? When you eat out, what do you usually eat?

____

6. How often do you eat processed foods such as donuts, cheese balls, chips, crackers, and so forth?

____

7. What percentage of your daily intake consists of natural foods such as fruits, vegetables, and salads?

____

8. Do you weigh yourself regularly?

____

9. What time of day do you find yourself to be most energized? When and how often do you feel physically exhausted during the day?

____

10. What kinds of food did you eat growing up with your family members? How has your diet changed since your childhood?

____

Graphic Analysis

In this section, you are asked to interpret a graph. The graph shown here is the food pyramid that was until very recently recommended by the National Institutes for Health (NIH). Examine the content-focused graph, and with a partner answer the questions that follow.

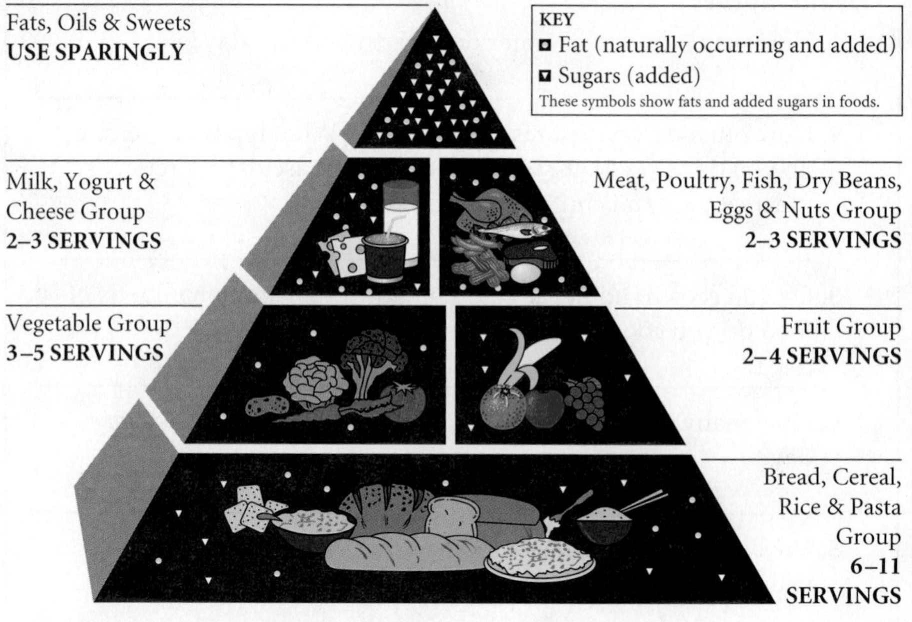

1. According to the food pyramid, what type of food should you eat the most of each day?

____

2. Why are sweets at the top of the pyramid?

____

3. What do all the food items in the second tier from the top of the pyramid have in common?

____

____

4. Which food groups have the least fat content?

____

MyReadingLab

Visit Chapter 3: Health in MyReadingLab to complete the Reading 1 activities.

READING 1

Newspaper Article

Fat Chance

Pre-Reading Questions

Before reading the following article, answer these questions in pairs or small groups. Discussing the questions will help prepare you to analyze the text with relative ease.

1. What is more important to you, your ability to see or being slim? Explain.
2. What factors result in a person being "overweight"? In other words, is obesity genetically determined, or is it influenced by environmental factors?
3. Do you believe that American society is prejudiced against overweight people? If yes, how? Do the media play a role in reinforcing negative stereotypes toward these people?

Read the article below and practice your reading comprehension with the set of ten multiple-choice questions that follow. For the first few paragraphs, remember, be an information predictor by writing questions about the text.

Fat Chance

By **Emily Bazelon[1], the** *New York Times*

May 6, 2007

1 If you had to choose, would you rather be fat or blind? When a researcher asked that question of a group of formerly **obese** people, 89 percent said they would prefer to lose their sight than their hard-won slimness. "When you're blind, people want to help you. No one wants to help you when you're fat," one explained. Ninety-one percent of the group also chose having a leg amputated over a return to obesity.

[1]Emily Bazelon is a senior editor at Slate.

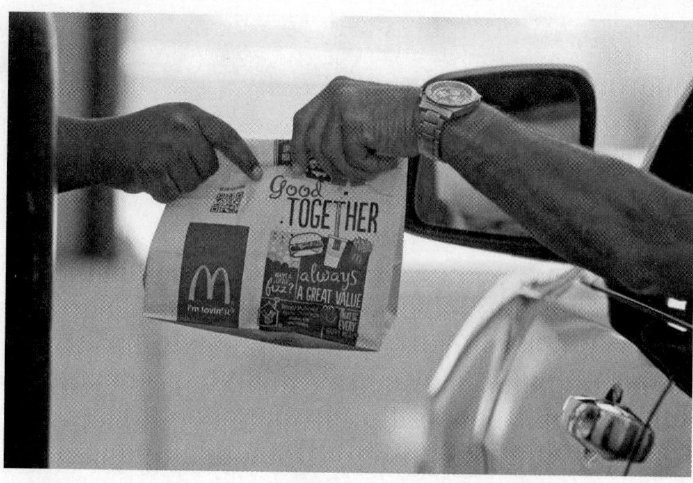

2 This is shocking. But it seems less so by the end of "Rethinking Thin," a new book about obesity by Gina Kolata, a science reporter for the *New York Times*. Kolata argues that being fat is not something people have much control over. Most people who are overweight struggle to change their shape throughout their lives, but remain stuck within a relatively narrow weight range set by their **genes**. For those determined to foil biology, strict dieting is a life sentence. "I am a fat man in a thin man's body," an MIT obesity researcher who shed his unwanted pounds years ago tells Kolata.

3 He's one of the lucky and single-minded few. Study after study, Kolata notes, has shown that for most fat people the long-term rewards of dieting are modest at best. Yet as obesity rates have skyrocketed, **exhortations** to eat right, exercise and shed pounds have gone from loud to shrill. Kolata's understandable sympathy for those caught between the ever intensifying pressure to be thin and the stubborn size of their bodies, however, leads her to flirt with an unlikely conclusion: Maybe the outcry over obesity is itself supersized, and being fat isn't really unhealthy after all.

exhortation
utterance conveying urgent advice

4 Kolata follows a two-year clinical trial at the University of Pennsylvania designed to test the low-carbohydrate, high-fat Atkins diet against a traditional low-calorie, low-fat one. Kolata wrote her book before she had the results for the trial, though a different study, published in March in the *Journal of the American Medical Association*, found that Atkins beats the low-cal diet for keeping off weight. The diet-versus-diet contest, however, isn't her real story.

?

5 Instead, she focuses on how little weight those who follow any diet usually manage to keep off. (The average participant on the Atkins diet reported in JAMA lost only 10 pounds over the course of a year.) Kolata tells the stories of four dieters in the Penn trial who are smart and likable. They had the benefit of a professionally led support group and the status of taking part in a well-financed study. They started exercising; they stopped eating mindlessly. After two years, they're a bit lighter. But none achieved the 50- to 100-pound weight loss they strove for (though one lost more than 30 pounds, 15 percent of his body weight).

6 Kolata **marshals** scientific evidence to explain why keeping weight off is so difficult. (The discovery last month of a garden-variety "fat gene" further backs her up.) Fat people have more fat cells than other people. Their metabolisms are normal but their appetites are larger—after they lose a significant amount of weight, one researcher explains, they often feel "a primal hunger" as strong as the urge a thirsty person feels to drink. Studies of twins and of adopted children show that inheritance may account for as much as 70 percent of weight variance. In one study of adopted children, 80 percent of those with two obese birth parents became obese, compared with 14 percent of those with birth parents of normal weight—and it didn't much matter what the adoptive parents fed the kids.

marshal
to arrange in proper order

7 Given such proof of the power of genetics, Kolata asks, why do we continue to insist that fat people can become thin people if they only put their minds to it?

8 She's surely right to push back against bafflement and intolerance, and her argument that we've tilted too far toward blaming fat people's bad habits for their weight is convincing. But Kolata goes so far in arguing for biological predestination that she sometimes seems to completely dismiss the other part of the fat equation—what we eat. In all likelihood, the obesity rate has doubled in the United States since 1980 for all the familiar reasons: fattening food has never been so cheap, convenient and **cunningly** marketed. "The genes that make people fat need an environment in which food is cheap and plentiful," she writes. It's in a world of giant muffins and bowls of office candy that Americans need wider movie seats and larger coffins.

cunning
crafty, done in a shrewd or sly manner

9 Kolata knows this. She touches on reasons that poor people are more likely than rich people to be overweight, all of them environmental. But she treats childhood obesity as virtually inevitable. In addition to the twin and adoption studies, she cites research showing that teaching kids to eat right in school, and serving them leaner lunches, has no effect on their weights. The researchers concluded that the intervention was too limited—the children's diets needed to

change at home as well as at school. But Kolata scoffs at the "popular solution," which is "not to question the premise but rather to increase the intensity of the intervention."

10 Given the rise in obesity, however, is it really credible to put all the blame on our genes—and ignore the gazillion-dollar food industry? And while it's useful to point out that obese people don't have higher rates of anxiety, depression or mood **disorders**, that doesn't mean these conditions are never a factor in causing obesity in those who are genetically susceptible to it. As some of the testimony of Kolata's own dieters attests, we eat not just because our appetites drive us to but because our psyches do, in search of both pleasure and relief from pain or stress. Rather than go where many authors have gone before, Kolata questions whether the current alarm over obesity is **overblown**—and whether the culture of dieting isn't itself harmful. The fat wars are less a legitimate public health campaign than a "moral panic," she suggests. In fact, she argues, some recent epidemiological studies show lower death rates for somewhat overweight people than for "so-called normal-weight people" or very thin ones.

overblown
exaggerated; done to excess

11 The data are certainly intriguing. But living longer doesn't mean that fat people are in good health along the way. In fact, they suffer from higher rates of diabetes, stroke, certain cancers and heart trouble. Kolata skirts this, because her argument is that thinness in and of itself is not a goal many people can achieve—or even an important one. She also quotes one expert who claims that "national data" do not show that Americans are in fact more sedentary than in the past. It's a surprising assertion that begs for development. Kolata ends on a quixotic note, by wondering if perhaps Americans weigh more for the same reason that we're taller on average than we were a century ago—because we're in better health. Maybe the extra pounds even help contribute to this well-being. No one has found the **smoking gun** in the mysterious fattening of America, but Kolata, following the obesity researchers Jules Hirsch and Jeff Friedman, briefly speculates whether, say, better early nutrition, vaccines or antibiotics somehow "precipitated changes in the brain's controls over weight." It's a twist on the usual evolutionary argument. The problem isn't that we evolved to store fat in times of famine and now can't handle our 24-hour, all-you-can-eat buffet of abundance. We're fat because we're changing in response to the medical **strides** we've taken.

smoking gun
definite proof of who is responsible for something bad or how something really happened

strides
advancements or progress

12 A nice idea, maybe, but one as yet unsupported by evidence. What's more persuasive is Kolata's contention that we should replace the elusive goal of thinness with the goal of better health and greater happiness. Here her argument is eminently sensible: Sure, shape up your body. But mostly, make your peace with it.

Reading with a Critical Eye

Critical thinking is a process of looking at an idea or a set of ideas from different angles. To think critically, you will need to ask and respond to a series of questions pertinent to the idea under consideration. Answering the following questions will lead you to a critical understanding of your relationship to the text. Keep in mind that you may need to refer to the text to answer these questions.

In a small group, discuss the following reflection questions, which will guide you toward a deeper understanding of the reading.

1. In the introductory paragraph, we read: "When you're blind, people want to help you. No one wants to help you when you're fat." Tell why there is such a stigma attached to obesity that no one wants to help fat people.
2. Kolata argues that people really do not have much control over being fat. Do you agree with this contention? Explain what the MIT obesity researcher meant when he said, "I am a fat man in a thin man's body."
3. In paragraph 6, Kolata explains why most people find it so difficult to keep weight off. What evidence does she provide to support her claim? Are you convinced by her explanation? Why, or why not?
4. Kolata seems to underplay the role of food in making us fat. Paragraph 10 begins by questioning her avoidance of the topic: "Given the rise in obesity, however, is it really credible to put all the blame on our genes—and ignore the gazillion-dollar food industry?" Discuss whether obesity is genetically determined or whether it is caused by America's burgeoning food industry.
5. In paragraph 11, we read, "The problem isn't that we evolved to store fat in times of famine and now can't handle our 24-hour, all-you-can-eat buffet of abundance. We're fat because we're changing in response to the medical strides we've taken." What is your opinion of this contention?

Reading Comprehension Check

1. What group of people did the researcher interview?
   a. obese
   b. overweight
   c. emaciated
   d. slim
2. Gina Kolata, a *New York Times* science reporter, argues that most people who are overweight
   a. find a way to lose weight and get slimmer.
   b. never lose any weight.
   c. usually stay around the same weight.
   d. die of an obesity-related illness.

3. What does the MIT researcher who was once obese and found a way to lose weight mean when he says, "I am a fat man in a thin man's body"?
   a. His natural condition is to be fat.
   b. He is still overweight regardless of his diet.
   c. His body was never thin.
   d. He has been taking diet pills.
4. Why does Kolata follow a two-year clinical study of popular weight-loss diets?
   a. to learn more about obesity and genetics
   b. to see if these diets really have an effect on reducing obesity
   c. to see if one particular diet is more cost-effective than another
   d. to lose weight herself
5. What did a study of adopted children show?
   a. If their birth parents were obese, they would not be obese.
   b. There was no relationship between their birth parents' obesity and their own weight.
   c. In most cases, if the birth parents of the adopted children were obese, they, too, would likely be obese.
   d. The most important factor was the weight of their adoptive parents.
6. The author's mention that "fattening food has never been so cheap, convenient and cunningly marketed" is an example of a/an ________ factor in explaining the rise in obesity.
   a. genetic
   b. auxiliary
   c. environmental
   d. obsequious
7. In paragraph 9, "But she treats childhood obesity as virtually inevitable . . .," the word *inevitable* could be replaced with
   a. preventable
   b. consistent
   c. predictable
   d. curable
8. Kolata makes the connection between Americans being much taller than a century ago with Americans also being much heavier to show
   a. the dangers of obesity.
   b. how everything changes over time.
   c. that perhaps being bigger is a sign of a more affluent, healthier society.
   d. the politics of eating.
9. In the final paragraph, the author criticizes some of Kolata's assumptions, arguing that they are not
   a. believable
   b. logical and convincing
   c. supported by evidence
   d. based on truth
10. The author concludes by agreeing with Kolata's contention that
   a. losing weight is more important than the pursuit of happiness.
   b. weight loss is an economic issue.
   c. better health and happiness should take precedence over slimness.
   d. only affluent people can be both content and thin.

MyReadingLab

Visit Chapter 3: Health in MyReadingLab to complete the Reading 2 activities.

READING 2

Newspaper Blog

How Weight Training Can Help You Keep the Weight Off

Pre-Reading Questions

In a small group of classmates, discuss the following questions.

1. The weight-loss industry in the United States is a multibillion-dollar business. Why do you think the weight-loss industry has profited so much, especially in the United States? Give specific reasons to support your answer.
2. Do you think that dieting alone can help people lose weight? If not, what types of exercise along with a healthful diet can keep the weight off? Explain.
3. What advice would you give an obese person who is trying to lose weight? In other words, what would be the most effective way for this person to lose weight and keep it off? Be specific.

How Weight Training Can Help You Keep the Weight Off

by Gretchen Reynolds

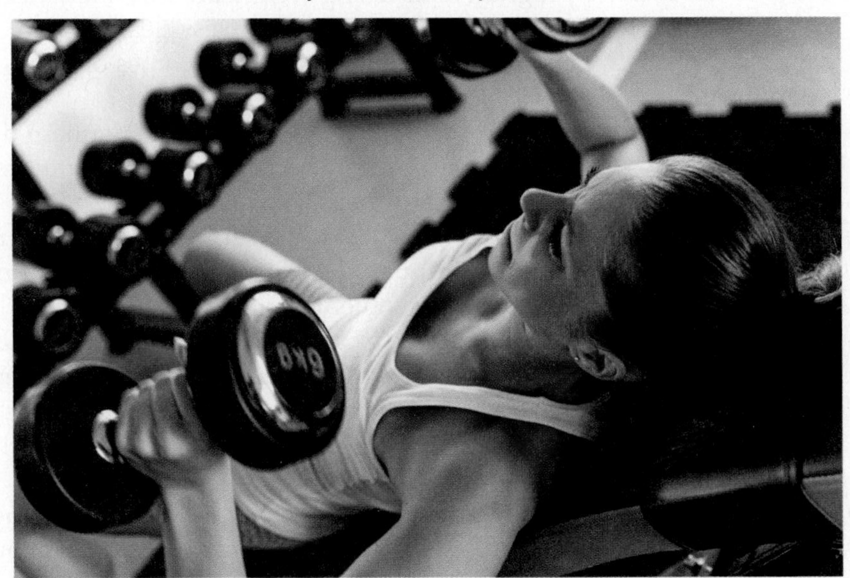

1 Exercise may help people avoid regaining weight after successful dieting, according to a new study. It shows that exercise can crucially alter the body's response to weight loss and potentially stop unwanted pounds from creeping back on.

2 The study, published this month in *Medicine & Science in Sports & Exercise*, offers rare good news about exercise and body weight. As readers of the Phys Ed column know, the relationship between the two is tangled. Multiple past studies have found that exercise alone — without food restriction — rarely reduces weight and frequently adds pounds, since many people feel hungry after workouts and overeat.

3 In general, most nutrition experts agree that to lose weight, you must reduce calories, whether you exercise or not. Take in fewer calories than your body burns and by the ineluctable laws of math, you will drop pounds.

4 Unfortunately, that same heartless math dictates that weight loss then makes it difficult to stay thin. After losing weight, your body burns fewer calories throughout the day than it did before, because you have less body mass using energy.

5 Meanwhile, for reasons that are not fully understood, many people become more sedentary after they lose weight. Studies show that non-exercise activity thermogenesis, or N.E.A.T. — a measure of how much energy people use to stand, fidget, walk to the car and otherwise move around without formally exercising — often declines substantially after weight loss, perhaps because the body thinks you are starving and directs you to stay still and conserve energy.

6 The upshot is that successful dieters typically burn fewer calories each day than they did when they were heavier, which sets them up for weight regain.

7 Enter exercise. Past studies have found that people who begin or continue an exercise program after losing weight are less likely to experience as much regain. But scientists have been less clear about how exercise protects against rebound pounds, and what types of exercise might be best.

8 So researchers at the University of Alabama at Birmingham decided to closely study the effects of exercise during that pivotal time just after someone has reached his or her goal weight.

9 They began by recruiting about 100 overweight, sedentary women, all of whom agreed to undertake a stringent diet, consisting of only 800 calories per day. The women also completed an array of baseline tests to determine their body composition, resting metabolic rate, daily levels of N.E.A.T., and walking economy, which tells scientists how easy it is for them to move around. The Alabama researchers also used an elaborate equation to establish how much time the women were moving each day.

10 Then a third of the women were asked not to exercise. Another third began a supervised aerobic exercise program, consisting of about

40 minutes of walking or jogging on a treadmill at a brisk pace three times a week. The final third started supervised upper- and lower-body weight training three times per week.

11 Each woman, whether she exercised or not, stayed on the 800-calorie daily diet until she had lost 25 pounds. At that point, she continued to follow the exercise instructions and transitioned for a month to a customized, supervised diet designed to keep her in energy balance, or at a level intended to make her neither gain nor lose weight. The scientists wished to focus more on movement patterns than eating habits.

12 What they found was that the women who did not exercise generally did not move much either. They spent fewer minutes each day in motion than they had before their weight loss. Their levels of N.E.A.T. fell significantly. Their resting metabolic rates also declined, since they weighed less. Over all they were burning considerably fewer calories each day than before they had shed the 25 pounds.

13 Meanwhile, the women who exercised had a drop-off in their resting metabolic rates after losing the weight, as expected, but much less of a slump in their everyday movements. Their levels of N.E.A.T. — the calories they burned in activities apart from exercise — declined only slightly for the exercising volunteers as a group, and some women increased how much they moved. They walked, stood, took the stairs and fidgeted more than they had before their weight loss.

14 This increase in N.E.A.T. was most common among the women who weight trained. Those who lifted weights also, interestingly, tended to have better walking economy; movement felt easier for them than it did before the weight loss. At the same time, many of the women who did not exercise showed worse movement economy, even though they now weighed less.

15 Over all, the data suggest that exercise — and, in particular, weight training — after weight loss prompts people to move more throughout the day, said Gary R. Hunter, a distinguished professor in the department of human studies at the University of Alabama at Birmingham and lead author of the study. As a result, they burn more calories and, with some discipline about food intake, should stave off weight regain.

16 This study, though, was relatively short-term and narrow, using only female volunteers and following them for only a month. Whether the results would be similar over a longer period, for men, or for those who begin exercising only after they have lost weight remains to be determined, Dr. Hunter said.

17 But even so, "It seems clear that exercise is very important if you wish to keep the weight off," he said.

Reading with a Critical Eye

In a small group, discuss the following reflection questions, which will guide you toward a deeper understanding of the reading.

1. We learn that exercise alone rarely reduces weight no matter how rigorous it may be. In your opinion, why isn't exercise sufficient to lose considerable weight? Refer to the article to answer the question.
2. Most nutrition experts believe that to lose weight people should consume fewer calories than they burn even if they do not exercise on a regular basis. Why is it, then, that this commonsense approach to weight loss is not obvious to most people? Explain.
3. According to the article, why do many people become more sedentary after losing weight? Give specific reasons for your answer.
4. Even scientists are not sure about what types of exercise are best to keep a person in shape after losing a considerable amount of weight. In your opinion, what specific exercise can help people avoid regaining weight after being on a successful diet?
5. What are the limitations of the study conducted by researchers at the University of Alabama at Birmingham? If you were to conduct the same study, what would you do differently? Be specific.

Reading Comprehension Check

1. What is the topic of the article?
   a. weight lifting
   b. weight machines
   c. weight loss
   d. weight rooms
2. The main idea of the article is that
   a. exercise can help people avoid regaining weight after eating a healthful diet.
   b. both men and women can keep the extra pounds off by exercising daily.
   c. exercise has little or no effect on weight loss no matter how rigorous it is.
   d. weight training can help people avoid regaining weight after successful dieting.

3. The study published in *Medicine & Science in Sports & Exercise* is
   a. no news.
   b. good news.
   c. rare news.
   d. bad news.
4. "So researchers at the University of Alabama at Birmingham decided to closely study the effects of exercise during that **pivotal** time just after someone has reached his or her goal weight."
   In this context, the word *pivotal* means
   a. unimportant.
   b. critical.
   c. insignificant.
   d. irrelevant.
5. According to the article, many people become more sedentary after they lose weight because
   a. they lose the desire to lose weight after losing substantial weight.
   b. the body thinks it has large amounts of energy and can burn more calories.
   c. non-exercise activity thermogenesis declines significantly after weight loss.
   d. they try other types of exercise that are inefficient and regain weight.
6. In the sentence, "Studies show that non-exercise activity thermogenesis, or N.E.A.T. — a measure of how much energy people use to stand, fidget, walk to the car and otherwise move around without formally exercising — often **declines** substantially after weight loss, perhaps because the body thinks you are starving and directs you to stay still and conserve energy," the word *declines* means
   a. deteriorates.
   b. improves.
   c. ascends.
   d. increases.
7. "The women also completed an array of baseline tests to determine their composition, resting metabolic rate, daily levels of N.E.A.T., and walking economy, which tells scientists how easy it is for them to move around." In the above sentence, the word *array* means
   a. an individual.
   b. obese people.
   c. a random test.
   d. a large group.

8. "Another third began a supervised aerobic exercise program, consisting of about 40 minutes of walking or jogging on a treadmill at a **brisk** pace three times a week."

   In the above sentence, the meaning of the word *brisk* is

   a. energetic.

   b. inactive.

   c. lifeless.

   d. languid.

9. "As a result, they burn more calories and, with some discipline about food intake, should **stave off** weight regain." In this context, *stave off* means

   a. promote.

   b. invite.

   c. repel.

   d. compel.

10. Another title for this article could be

   a. "Weight Loss and Common Sense."

   b. "Weight Loss and Weight Training."

   c. "Weight Loss and Successful Dieting."

   d. "Weight Loss and Common Behavior."

BIOGRAPHICAL PROFILE

Pierre Dukan

When Dr. Dukan's obese friend asked him for some dietary advice, he had no idea that he was about to start a revolution that would have widespread repercussions all over Europe and later in the United States. Dr. Dukan recommended that his friend eat a low-fat, protein-only diet to lose weight. He says, "'I told him to eat nothing but protein and drink only water for five days. When he came back, he asked if he could use my scales because his appeared to be broken." Dr. Dukan and his friend were both surprised to see that he had lost 10 pounds in five days. The friend was so pleased with the result that he remained on the same diet and lost another 6 pounds in the next five days.

Dr. Dukan was so amazed with the serendipitous results that he changed his area of specialization from neurology to nutrition. He spent the next 35 years doing research and perfecting his diet, which has become popularly known as the Dukan Diet. He says, "It has become clear to me over the years that calorie counting does not work—dieters' brains don't work like that."

He published a book on the Dukan Diet ten years ago in France that became the French best seller and engendered a dieting revolution of 200 Internet sites, forums, and blogs. Today, 1.5 million French women strictly follow the Dukan Diet, and celebrities such as Gisele Bündchen and Jennifer Lopez stick to the low-fat, protein-only diet. The Dukan Diet has made its way to Britain, with the publication of an English version of the famous French book. Dr. Dukan has given lectures in the United States in English with a distinct French accent.

His protein-based diet sounds similar to Atkins, but the Dukan Diet is different. When people reach their desired weight, they can get back to a life of normal eating, but they must eat only proteins every Thursday for the rest of their lives. Dr. Dukan says, "By sticking to protein one day a week, you can lose 1.5 pounds to 2 pounds instantly and, in so doing, correct any **excess** that may have occurred during the rest of the week."

The number of people living the Dukan life is increasing rapidly, and the Dukan Diet is well on its way to becoming a global phenomenon. However, there are some critics who believe that the Dukan Diet is not healthy and not sustainable.

Some Questions for Group Discussion

1. Why do you think the Dukan Diet has become so popular in Europe and the United States? In other words, what is it about the Dukan Diet that has made so many people around the world follow it religiously?
2. Discuss why scores of people put so much faith in a dietary concept created by one person. Would you change your dietary habits based on an expert's advice? Why, or why not?
3. Do you agree with the critics that the Dukan Diet is not healthy and not sustainable? Do research on the Internet to determine whether this protein-only diet is healthy and practical.

Biographical Internet Research

Find out about another prominent figure in Health and Nutrition online, selecting one from the list below, and share a biographical profile with your classmates:

- Jenny Craig
- Robert Atkins
- Bernard Jensen
- Michael Pollan
- Michio Kushi

SKILL FOCUS: Identifying the Main Idea and Topic

When you are asked to find the *main idea* of a sentence or a paragraph, you are really being asked to identify the most important point the author wants to convey to the reader.

Imagine a friend calls you and says she is in a hurry on the way to the movies and would like you to recommend a film. You tell your friend the name of the film you think she should see, and she asks you to tell her in a sentence (there is no time to lose!) what the film is about.

You say, "*Freedom Writers* is about a dedicated female teacher who inspires her underprivileged students to express themselves through writing." As you may have guessed by now, you've just offered your friend the main idea of the movie!

Main Idea versus Topic

Another way to understand the concept of *main idea* is to compare it with the idea of *topic*.

A topic is a word, name, or phrase that tells what an author is writing about. It is more *general* than a main idea.

Examine the paragraph example below.

Not too long ago, when you went to the supermarket to pick eggs, you had a choice between a few brands. But nowadays consumers are faced with a host of choices when purchasing a carton of eggs. There are eggs from cage-free chickens, organically grown eggs, and traditional farm-raised eggs.

The topic, or what general category the author is writing about in the above paragraph, would be:

Buying eggs

The main idea, however, is more specific and could be stated as:

Modern-day consumers have more choices in purchasing eggs than in the past.

So, from a comparison of the topic and the main idea, we can see that we are moving from general to more specific.

Topic	*Main Idea*
Buying eggs	Modern-day consumers have more choices in purchasing eggs than in the past.

We can see this relationship expressed on a continuum; see the one below. This can be very helpful when trying to locate the main idea in a reading.

Too general X Too specific

←→

Topic Main Idea Details/Examples

Stated Main Idea versus Implied Main Idea

Every textbook paragraph has a main idea. Sometimes the main idea is stated directly—that is, the author's most important point is stated in a sentence (for example, "Russia must do something to save its economy," or "The exact nature of the five stages of death has been disputed"). Other times, the author gives you the information needed to understand the main point without stating it directly as a single sentence. This is called an *implied main idea* because you the reader must use information contained in the paragraph to infer (reason out) the author's main point.

We will return to the key reading skill terms of *inference* and *implication* in later chapters. For now, let's practice distinguishing between topic and main idea in paragraph contexts.

PRACTICING THE SKILL

Practice 1

Identifying Topic and Main Idea

Read the following short paragraphs and practice distinguishing between topic and main idea.

Passage 1

How much sleep is necessary to maintain a healthy lifestyle? Many people say they need at least eight hours to feel refreshed in the morning. Researchers say the amount of sleep one needs depends on the individual. Some can thrive on as few as six hours of sleep, while others lag behind if they sleep fewer than eleven.

Topic	*Main Idea*

Passage 2

Swimming is one of the healthiest activities for your body. Unlike running or weight lifting, it will put little physical strain on your system. The water helps support your body and allows you to both build muscle tone and get the cardiovascular workout you need.

Topic	*Main Idea*

Passage 3

Mad cow disease is a fatal brain disorder caused by a prion, which is an abnormal form of protein. Prions influence other proteins to take on their abnormal shape, and these abnormal proteins cause brain damage. Mad cow disease is also called bovine spongiform encephalopathy (BSE). The disease eats away at a cow's brain, leaving it full of sponge-like holes. Eventually, the brain can no longer control vital life functions, and the cow literally "goes mad."

(From *Nutrition: An Applied Approach*
by Janice Thompson and Melinda Manore, p. 216)

Topic	*Main Idea*

Passage 4

A classic study done by researchers at Laval University in Quebec, Canada, shows how genetics plays a role in our responses to overeating (Bouchard et al. 1990). Twelve pairs of male identical twins volunteered to stay in a dormitory where they were supervised 24 hours a day for 120 consecutive days. Researchers measured how much energy each man needed to maintain his body weight at the beginning of the study. For 100 days, the subjects were fed 1,000 kcal more per day than they needed to maintain body weight. Daily physical activity was limited, but each person was allowed to walk outdoors for 30 minutes each day, read, watch television and videos, and play cards and video games. The research staff stayed with these men to ensure that they did not stray from the study protocol.

(From *Nutrition: An Applied Approach*, p. 395)

Topic	*Main Idea*

Practice 2

Identifying Main Idea and Topic

Let's practice identifying main idea and topic by revisiting Reading 1. Work with a partner to restate the main idea of the selected paragraphs provided below, using your own words.

Passages: Excerpts from "Fat Chance"

? **What is the main idea?**

____

____

____

1. If you had to choose, would you rather be fat or blind? When a researcher asked that question of a group of formerly obese people, 89 percent said they would prefer to lose their sight than their hard-won slimness. "When you're blind, people want to help you. No one wants to help you when you're fat," one explained. Ninety-one percent of the group also chose having a leg amputated over a return to obesity.

? **What is the topic here?**

____

2. This is shocking. But it seems less so by the end of "Rethinking Thin," a new book about obesity by Gina Kolata, a science reporter for the *New York Times*. Kolata argues that being fat is not something people have much control over. Most people who are overweight struggle to change their shape throughout their lives, but remain stuck within a relatively narrow weight range set by their genes. For those determined to foil biology, strict dieting is a life sentence. "I am a fat man in a thin man's body," an MIT obesity researcher who shed his unwanted pounds years ago tells Kolata.

3. He's one of the lucky and single-minded few. Study after study, Kolata notes, has shown that for most fat people, the long-term rewards of dieting are modest at best. Yet as obesity rates have skyrocketed, exhortations to eat right, exercise and shed pounds have gone from loud to shrill. Kolata's understandable sympathy for those caught between the ever intensifying pressure to be thin and the stubborn size of their bodies, however, leads her to flirt with an unlikely conclusion: Maybe the outcry over obesity is itself supersized, and being fat isn't really unhealthy after all.

? **What is the topic here?**

____

4. Kolata follows a two-year clinical trial at the University of Pennsylvania designed to test the low-carbohydrate, high-fat Atkins diet against a traditional low-calorie, low-fat one. Kolata wrote her book before she had the results for the trial, though a different study, published in March in the *Journal of the American Medical Association*, found that Atkins beats the low-cal diet for keeping off weight. The diet-versus-diet contest, however, isn't her real story.

? **What is the main idea?**

____

____

____

Practice 3

Identifying Stated Main Idea

In the following passages about health and nutrition from the *New York Times*, try to locate which sentence contains the *stated main idea*, and underline it. To help guide you toward recognition of the main idea sentence, consider which sentence does the following:

- States the single most important point about the topic
- Is general enough to cover all the information in the paragraph
- Is explained, focused on, and supported by the other sentences

Underline the stated main idea in each of the examples below.

Passage 1

America has become weirdly polarized on the subject of weight. On the one hand, we've been told with almost religious certainty by everyone from the surgeon general on down, and we have come to believe with almost religious certainty, that obesity is caused by the excessive consumption of fat, and that if we eat less fat we will lose weight and live longer. On the other, we have the ever-resilient message of Atkins and decades' worth of best-selling diet books, including "The Zone," "Sugar Busters" and "Protein Power" to name a few. All push some variation of what scientists would call the alternative hypothesis: it's not the fat that makes us fat, but the carbohydrates and if we eat less carbohydrates we will lose weight and live longer.

Passage 2

Americans are eating more fresh fruits and vegetables, and that is a healthy development. But a recent outbreak of hepatitis in western Pennsylvania is a reminder that in order to ensure the safety of our food supply chain, changes in our eating patterns require similar adjustments in our vigilance. Traditionally, concerns about food-borne illnesses focused on meat and poultry, foods inspected by the Department of Agriculture. Fresh produce, overseen by the Food and Drug Administration, is increasingly seen as a potential source of disease. Yet the FDA lacks the resources and policing authority of the Agriculture Department. An ever-growing reliance on imported produce compounds the challenge. The recent hepatitis outbreak was traced to one restaurant's imported green onions.

Passage 3

For decades, the beauty industry was described as—or accused of—selling "hope in a jar." Now, a marketing blitz with a budget estimated at more than $150 million in the first year will try to persuade dieters to seek hope in a pill bottle despite widespread skepticism about the grandiose promises of diet pills, plans and potions. A campaign for the drug Alli is being waged on many fronts by seven agencies. Its first-year budget is estimated at more than $150 million. The campaign, being introduced in stages by seven agencies, promotes a product from GlaxoSmithKline called Alli—pronounced, not coincidentally, like "ally," as in a helper or associate. Alli is the first weight-loss drug to be approved by the Food and Drug Administration for sale in the United States over the counter, no prescription necessary. It works by preventing the body from absorbing some of the fat one eats.

Passage 4

In the debate over whether organic food is better than conventionally raised food, advocates for organic produce say it contains fewer harmful chemicals and is better for the earth, and some claim that it is more nutritious. And recent preliminary evidence suggests that the levels of certain nutrients, especially vitamin C, some minerals and some polyphenols—naturally occurring antioxidants that may help bolster the immune system—are higher in organically grown crops. As a result of this preliminary evidence and the Agriculture Department's adoption in 2000 of standards for organic foods, the Organic Trade Association has created the nonprofit Center for Organic Education and Promotion to finance research that could verify what small-scale research may suggest: organic food may provide greater health benefits than conventional food.

From Marian Burros, "Eating Well: Is Organic Food Provably Better?" From *The New York Times*, July 16, 2003.

Passage 5

Mothers who are depressed or anxious are more likely to take their children to doctors for stomachaches and abdominal pains, a new study has concluded. The study found that mothers with the highest levels of depression were twice as likely as mothers with the lowest levels to seek medical help for abdominal pain reported by their children. The gap persisted even when the figures were adjusted to account for different levels of pain. Dr. Rona L. Levy, a psychologist at the University of Washington School of Social Work, presented the findings to a conference of the Society of Behavioral Medicine in Salt Lake City late last month.

From John O'Neil, "Vital Signs: Mental Health; Mothers' Minds and Babies' Bellies." From *The New York Times*, April 8, 2003.

Identifying the Main Idea

Sometimes the main idea of a reading passage is not directly stated, but implied. It is the reader's responsibility to read between the lines and figure out the author's implied main idea. Consider the following example.

Example

Why do so many people take dietary supplements? Many people believe they cannot consume adequate nutrients in their diet, and they take a supplement as extra nutritional insurance. Others have been advised by their healthcare provider to take a supplement due to a given health condition. There are people who believe that certain supplements can be used to treat illness or disease. There are also people who believe that supplements are necessary to enhance their physical looks or athletic performance.

(From *Nutrition: An Applied Approach*, p. 302)

After reading the passage above, you realize that the main idea is not directly stated. However, when you pay attention to the details that are offered, you will notice that all of the supporting sentences discuss the many reasons people take dietary supplements. Thus, the main idea of the passage is that *people take dietary supplements for different reasons.*

Practice 4

Identifying the Implied Main Idea

Passage 1

For most of her life, Darcy had thoroughly enjoyed good food. Her husband bragged about her being a gourmet cook. But a few weeks after learning she was pregnant, her appetite seemed to disappear. She would wander through the aisles of the grocery store with an empty cart, knowing she should be choosing nutritious foods for her growing baby but feeling unable to find a single food that appealed to her. Eventually she'd return home with a few things for her husband … and a large bag of ice.

(From *Nutrition: An Applied Approach*, p. 548)

What is the implied main idea?

____

____

Passage 2

Strong proponents of veganism state that any consumption of animal products is wrong and that feeding animal products to children is forcing them into a life of obesity, clogged arteries, and chronic diet-related diseases. In addition, many people who consume a vegan diet feel that consumption of animal products wastes natural resources and contributes to environmental damage and is therefore morally wrong. In contrast, strong antagonists of veganism emphasize that feeding a vegan diet to young children deprives them of essential nutrients that can only be found in animal products. Some people even suggest that veganism for young children is, in essence, a form of child abuse.

(From *Nutrition: An Applied Approach*, p. 482)

What is the implied main idea?

____

Passage 3

"You know I never thought I needed to take a multivitamin because I am healthy and I eat lots of different kinds of foods. But now I have learned in my nutrition course about what all these vitamins and minerals do in the body, and I'm thinking, heck, maybe I should take one just for insurance. I mean, I use up a lot of fuel playing basketball and working out. Maybe if I popped a pill every day, I'd have an easier time keeping my weight up!"

(From *Nutrition: An Applied Approach*, p. 372)

What is the implied main idea?

____

____

Recommended Debate Topic: Should unhealthy foods such as soda, high-caffeine drinks, candy, and fast food be available in public school and college campuses?

Brainstorm other debate topics related to health and nutrition with your peers, and present your ideas to your instructor for approval.

Your suggested debate topics:

a. ____

b. ____

c. ____

The following article and subsequent letter response will help prepare you for the debate activity because they examine the issue of soft drink bans in public schools. You will also receive more practice in recognizing main ideas and topics.

READING 3A

Newspaper Article

MyReadingLab

Visit Chapter 3: Health in MyReadingLab to complete the Reading 3A activities.

Bottlers Agree to a School Ban on Sweet Drinks

Pre-Reading Questions

Discuss these questions in small groups.

1. What kinds of drinks do you usually consume
   a. early in the morning?
   b. during the school/workday?
   c. in the evening?
2. What types of drinks are most readily available in vending machines at your college?
3. Do you agree with the common view that young people consume too much sugar every day?
4. If you had to reduce your sugar intake for health reasons, what food item would be most difficult for you to sacrifice? Explain.

Bottlers Agree to a School Ban on Sweet Drinks

By Marian Burros and Melanie Warner, the *New York Times*

May 4, 2006

1 The country's top three soft-drink companies announced yesterday that beginning this fall they would start removing sweetened drinks like Coke, Pepsi and iced teas from school cafeterias and vending machines in response to the growing threat of lawsuits and state legislation.

2 Under an agreement between beverage makers and health advocates, students in elementary school would be served only bottled water, low-fat and nonfat milk, and 100 percent fruit juice in servings no bigger than eight ounces. Serving sizes would increase to 10 ounces in middle school. In high school, low-calorie juice drinks, sports drinks and diet sodas would be permitted; serving sizes would be limited to 12 ounces.

3 The agreement, which includes parochial and private schools contracts, is voluntary, and the beverage industry said its school sales would not be affected because it expected to replace sugary drinks with other ones.

4 "This is a voluntary policy, but I think schools will want to follow it," said Susan K. Neely, president of the American Beverage Association. Still, about 35 million public school children would be affected by the agreement, which would apply to extended school functions like band practice but would not apply to events likely to be attended by parents, like evening plays or interscholastic sports. An additional 15 million students attend schools that operate under stricter regulations, where the guidelines would not apply.

5 Last week, for example, Connecticut banned all sodas, including diet drinks and sports drinks like Gatorade, in its schools; New York

City schools permit only low-fat milk, water and 100 percent fruit juice, which is sold under an exclusive **contract** with Snapple. Contracts between schools and bottlers would be updated under the deal, and changes would not go into effect before the next school year.

brokered
arranged and managed

6 The agreement was **brokered** by the Alliance for a Healthier Generation, a collaboration between the William J. Clinton Foundation and the American Heart Association. It is similar to an arrangement that the industry had been negotiating with a coalition of lawyers and the Center for Science in the Public Interest, an **advocacy** group that had threatened to sue if an agreement could not be reached. The terms were accepted by the three biggest soft-drink companies, Coca-Cola, PepsiCo Inc. and Cadbury Schweppes (whose products include Dr Pepper and Snapple), which together control more than 90 percent of school sales.

7 At a news conference at his office in Harlem, Mr. Clinton called the beverage industry "courageous" for agreeing to switch to lower-calorie drinks. Mr. Clinton, who has made obesity a major issue of his post-presidency agenda, was joined by Gov. Mike Huckabee of Arkansas, a vocal **proponent** of fitness.

proponent
a supporter or advocate of something

8 Later in the day, Mr. Clinton said it was more than the threat of lawsuits that spurred the agreement.

9 "We've been talking to them for months and months, and they may have liked the way we were working with them, not just singling them out," he said in a telephone interview. "I'm glad we did it without litigation and could accelerate the process."

10 It will take three years for the agreement to be put fully into effect. The industry has agreed at the end of each school year starting in 2007 to disclose the progress toward fulfilling the agreement. The new standards are expected to be in place in 75 percent of schools by the summer of 2008 and all by 2009. The success of the program depends on schools' willingness to amend existing contracts, industry representatives said. The majority of school contracts with Pepsi Bottling Group, Pepsi's largest bottler, for instance, are for three to five years, said its spokeswoman, Kelly McAndrew, who said Pepsi would encourage schools to renegotiate their contracts.

11 "We're doing our part to communicate this new policy," she said.

12 Mirroring overall beverage consumption in the United States, bottled water and sports drinks have become increasingly popular in schools in recent years. But in a survey released in August, the American Beverage Association said 45 percent of all school vending sales were sweetened soda.

accord
an agreement

13 While the soft-drink industry was negotiating the deal, it was discussing a similar **accord** with the Center for Science in the Public

Interest and a group of lawyers who had successfully sued tobacco companies.

14 Richard A. Daynard, associate dean at Northeastern University School of Law, a tobacco-lawsuit veteran, called the agreement "the first major victory for the obesity-litigation strategy."

15 "This would not have happened but for the threat of litigation," Professor Daynard said.

16 Beverage-industry officials acknowledged discussions with the lawyers but would not comment further.

17 Dr. Michael Jacobson, executive director of the Center for Science in the Public Interest, applauded the agreement, but said, "I'd like to get rid of the Gatorades and diet soft drinks completely."

18 Nutritionists and parent groups have pressured schools and the beverage industry for some time to restrict sales. Several states, including California, and some local school districts have banned soft-drink sales, and other states are considering similar crackdowns. In response, the beverage association last year announced a policy that would have cut back on the sale of certain soft drinks in schools. But critics said the plan was unenforceable.

19 Gary Ruskin, executive director of Commercial Alert, a nonprofit public-health group, said the new agreement might prove to have the same problem. Mr. Ruskin criticized it, too, because it did not address soft-drink advertising in schools and did not stop bottlers from advertising on Channel One, which is shown to seven million schoolchildren a day. Mr. Clinton said there remained "an enormous amount to be done" about childhood obesity.

single out
select from a group

20 "You can't **single out** one cause of this problem," he said. "But if an 8-year-old child took in 45 less calories per day, by the time he reached high school, he would weight 20 pounds less than he would have weighed otherwise."

MyReadingLab

Visit Chapter 3: Health in MyReadingLab to complete the Reading 3B activities.

READING 3B

A Letter of Response

My Soda, My Choice

Monday, May 15, 2006

This is a response to the article in Reading 3A.

To the Editor:

Re "Bottlers Agree to a School Ban on Sweet Drinks" (front page, May 4): As a 16-year-old high school student, I strongly object to the lobbying by state legislatures to deny students the right to buy certain soft drinks in school.

preposterous completely unreasonable or silly

1 It is **preposterous** that by the middle of my senior year, I will have the right to vote, but the state will consider me unable to make proper **lifestyle** choices. Although some lawmakers believe that they are endowed with the wisdom to make daily choices for others, I would prefer personal freedom.

Jonathan Panter
Palisades, N.Y., May 6, 2006

Reading with a Critical Eye

In a small group, discuss the following reflection questions, which will guide you toward a deeper understanding of the reading.

1. In the first paragraph, we learn that three leading soft-drink companies in the United States have agreed to remove sweetened drinks from school cafeterias and vending machines to avoid lawsuits. Tell why these companies are foregoing huge profits by removing sweetened drinks from school cafeterias when they have the money and resources to fight the lawsuits.
2. The agreement between beverage makers and health advocates to stop selling sweet drinks in school cafeterias is voluntary. In your opinion, why don't schools forbid beverage makers to sell sweetened drinks to students, knowing fully that the drinks are unhealthy for them? In fact, why are beverage makers allowed to make and market unhealthy sweetened drinks to begin with? Explain.
3. Why does Mr. Clinton call the beverage makers "courageous," and why does he think that it was more than the threat of lawsuits that forced these companies to agree to remove sweetened drinks from school cafeterias?
4. In paragraph 17, Dr. Michael Jacobson says, "I'd like to get rid of the Gatorades and diet soft drinks completely." Do you think this goal is attainable? Why, or why not?
5. Gary Ruskin, executive director of Commercial Alert, says that the new agreement between beverage makers and health advocates may have the same problem. Discuss what he means by "the same problem." In your opinion, why do the critics of the agreement believe that it is unenforceable?

Reading Comprehension Check

1. According to the article, what motivated the top three soft-drink companies to remove their sweetened drinks from vending machines?
   a. fear of bad press
   b. fear of being sued
   c. general altruism
   d. exponential sales

2. What is the topic of the article?
   a. public schools
   b. Due to increasing pressure, the top three bottlers agreed to a ban on soda in public schools.
   c. soft drinks in schools
   d. It will take three years for the ban to go into effect.
3. The agreement to replace sweetened drinks was
   a. mandatory.
   b. compulsory.
   c. voluntary.
   d. sanctioned by law.
4. What is the main idea of the article?
   a. schools and soda bans
   b. Large soda companies feared being sued.
   c. Giving in to heavy pressure, the top soda companies have agreed not to sell soft drinks in schools.
   d. Some states have stricter policies than others.
5. Find the sentence in paragraph 7 that states: "Mr. Clinton, who has made obesity a major issue of his post-presidency agenda ..." From this sentence, we can derive that Mr. Clinton focused on the obesity issue mostly
   a. before he was president.
   b. while he was president.
   c. after he was president.
   d. both b and c
6. According to the American Beverage Association, what percentage of vending machine sales were from sweetened soda?
   a. exactly half
   b. almost half
   c. about a quarter
   d. 30 percent
7. What is Mr. Clinton's idea in the last paragraph of the article?
   a. Every child must deal with obesity-related illnesses such as diabetes.
   b. A few calories less a day for a child could make a big difference in the long run.
   c. By the time an 8-year-old reaches high school, it is too late to change his drinking habits.
   d. Health is a national issue of great concern.

8. In the letter that responds to the article, who is criticized for their lobbying efforts?
   a. a 16-year-old student
   b. the school system
   c. politicians
   d. none of the above
9. What is the topic of the letter?
   a. personal freedom and soda bans
   b. teenage disagreement
   c. the value of today's soft drinks
   d. A student wants to change the regulations of the soda ban
10. The writer uses the term *personal freedom* at the end of his letter to express
    a. his outrage at the schools.
    b. his belief in the value of soft drinks.
    c. his right to choose what he wants to drink.
    d. the freedom that teenagers have.

READING 4

Online Magazine Article

MyReadingLab

Visit Chapter 3: Health in MyReadingLab to complete the Reading 4 activities.

The 9 Most Common Kitchen Mistakes Even Healthy Women Make … and Why They're Robbing Your Food of Nutrients

Pre-Reading Questions

Answer these questions in small groups.

1. How often do you (or someone in your family) go grocery shopping? Do you buy groceries in small batches for a few days, or do you purchase foods in big batches for longer durations? Give specific reasons for your answers.
2. When you go grocery shopping at a supermarket, what criteria do you use to select the food items? For example, do you consider the nutritional value of the foods you purchase? Give specific examples.
3. Do you think that most supermarkets provide the nutritional information and shelf life of the agricultural produce they sell? If not, then should the government require them to provide this information to the consumer? Explain why.

The 9 Most Common Kitchen Mistakes Even Healthy Women Make ... and Why They're Robbing Your Food of Nutrients

By Amanda Pressner
Shape.com

1 There's something empowering about **hitting** the supermarket to shop for your week's meals. Rather than putting yourself at the mercy of the local Chinese take-out restaurant or succumbing to the lure of the drive-through, you're taking dinner—and your waistline—into your own hands. "Eating out less and cooking more may be one of the most effective things you can do to keep fat and calories in check," says Cheryl Forberg, R.D., author of *Stop the Clock! Cooking*. "Plus, building your diet around produce, whole grains, beans, and lean protein practically guarantees you'll reach your recommended targets for most vitamins and minerals." But while we may be tossing the freshest, most wholesome foods into our carts, many of us are storing and preparing them in ways that rob them (and our bodies) of the very nutrients we're seeking. Nutritionists and food-safety experts point to nine typical kitchen blunders that negatively impact the quality of our diets. Fortunately, you can **sidestep** all of them easily. Follow this advice to make your next meal healthier.

hitting
going to or visiting

? **What is the main idea?**

____

____

____

____

sidestep
to avoid a difficult question or decision

Mistake #1 ***You're overloading on produce***

2 Sure, making one big grocery run at the start of the week seems like a no-fail way to get your five a day. After all, if those carrots, greens, apples, and berries are around, you'll eat more of them and therefore get more nutrients, right? Wrong. "The vitamins and minerals in fruits and vegetables begin to diminish the moment they're harvested," says Geri Brewster, R.D., a wellness consultant at Northern Westchester Hospital in Mt. Kisco, New York. That means the longer you store produce, the fewer nutrients it will contain. After about a week in the fridge, for example, spinach retains just half of its folate and around 60 percent of its lutein (an antioxidant associated with healthy eyes), concludes a study in the *Journal of Food Science.* Broccoli loses about 62 percent of its flavonoids (antioxidant compounds that help ward off cancer and heart disease) within 10 days, according to a study in the *Journal of Agricultural and Food Chemistry.* "You're better off buying smaller batches at least twice a week," says Brewster. If you can't shop every few days, pick up frozen produce. These fruits and veggies are harvested at their peak and are flash-frozen immediately. Because the produce isn't exposed to oxygen, the nutrients stay stable for a year, according to researchers at the University of California, Davis. Just be sure to avoid frozen products packed in sauces or syrups. These additions can mean extra calories from fat or sugar, and sometimes they're high in sodium as well.

? **What's the topic of this paragraph?**

____

____

Mistake #2 ***You're stashing foods in see-through containers***

3 If you're still buying your milk in clear plastic jugs, consider switching to cardboard cartons. Milk is rich in the B vitamin riboflavin; when exposed to light, a chemical reaction is kicked off that reduces the vitamin's potency, according to researchers from Ghent University in Belgium. Other nutrients, such as amino acids (the building blocks of protein) and vitamins A, C, D, and E, are also affected. And because lowfat and nonfat milk varieties are thinner than whole milk, light can penetrate them more easily. "This process, known as photooxidation, can change the flavor of the milk and create disease-causing free radicals," says Susan Duncan, Ph.D., a food scientist at Virginia Tech. Since grain products (especially whole grains) are also high in riboflavin, they too are susceptible to this breakdown of nutrients and production of free radicals. Duncan recommends avoiding the practice of storing dry goods like pasta, rice, and cereals in clear containers on your countertop. Instead, keep them in their original boxes or in **opaque** containers and stash them in your kitchen cabinets, where they'll be shielded from light.

stashing
keeping something in a safe, often secret, place

? **What's the main idea?**

____

____

____

____

____

____

opaque
not transparent or translucent

Mistake #3 ***You're too quick to cook your garlic***

4 Legend has it that these **pungent** little bulbs can ward off vampires, but science shows that if you cook them correctly, they may have the power to fight off an even more frightening villain: cancer. "Chop,

pungent
sharply affecting the organs of taste or smell

slice, or crush your cloves, then set them aside for at least 10 minutes before sautéing," says John Milner, Ph.D., chief of the nutritional science research group at the National Cancer Institute in Rockville, Maryland. "Breaking up garlic triggers an enzymatic **reaction** that releases a healthy compound called allyl sulfur; waiting to cook garlic allows enough time for the full amount of the compound to form."

? **What's the topic of this paragraph?**

____

Mistake #4 ***The only time you eat avocados is in guacamole***

5 Adding this green fruit to salads and sandwiches is an easy way to raise your nutritional bar. Avocados are exceptionally rich in folate, potassium, vitamin E, and **fiber**. It's true that they're also high in fat, but it's the heart-healthy monounsaturated kind. And half an avocado has just 153 calories. One novel way to work them into your diet is to use them as a fat substitute in baking. Many of us have been using applesauce or puréed prunes in place of butter and oil in brownie and cookie recipes for years. Researchers at Hunter College in New York City wanted to see if avocado could work in the same way without affecting the taste. They replaced half of the butter in an oatmeal cookie recipe with puréed avocado. Not only did this swap cut the total fat count by 35 percent (avocados have fewer fat grams per tablespoon than butter or oil), it also made the resulting treats softer, chewier, and less likely to crumble than cookies made according to the original recipe. If you're still wary of using such a nontraditional ingredient in sweets, try adding it to savory baked items, such as quick breads and muffins.

? **What's the main point here?**

____

____

____

Mistake #5 ***You skimp on seasonings***

skimp on
to supply inadequately

6 Herbs and spices not only enhance the flavor of your cooking without adding fat or sodium, many of these fragrant ingredients also protect you from food poisoning. After testing 20 common seasonings against five strains of bacteria (including E. coli, staphylococcus, and salmonella), researchers at the University of Hong Kong found that the higher the antioxidant value of the spice, the greater its ability to inhibit bacterial activity. Cloves, cinnamon sticks, and oregano were the most effective at fighting off these food-borne pathogens. A separate study published in the *Journal of Agricultural and Food Chemistry* shows that rosemary, thyme, nutmeg, and bay leaves are also antioxidant-rich. Of course, you can't ignore standard food-safety practices, but adding half a teaspoon of herbs or spices to salads, vegetables, and meats can give you extra peace of mind and boost your intake of disease-fighting antioxidants.

? **What's the main focus here?**

____

____

____

____

____

Mistake #6 You're a serial peeler

7 Most of the antioxidants and polyphenols in produce are located very close to the surface of the skin or in the skin itself. A study published in the journal *Nutrition Research* found that most fruit peels exhibited two to twenty-seven times more antioxidant activity than the pulp of

? **What's the main idea of this paragraph?**

____

____

____

the fruit. "Many of us remove the skins from eggplant, bell peppers, peaches, apples, and nectarines while preparing recipes, but we're really just tossing away nutrients and fiber," says nutritionist Forberg. She recommends gently scrubbing potatoes and carrots rather than removing their skin, and using a vegetable peeler or sharp knife to pare away as thin a layer as possible from fruits and veggies that must be peeled.

? What is the focus of this paragraph?

____

____

____

____

Mistake #7 ***You're simmering away vitamins and minerals***

8 Boiling may seem like a simple, no-fuss way to prepare vegetables without adding oil, but this cooking method can cause up to 90 percent of a food's nutrients to leach out, says Karen Collins, R.D., a nutrition advisor to the American Institute for Cancer Research in Washington, D.C. "Minerals like potassium and water-soluble vitamins like B and C end up getting tossed out with the water," she says. To keep these essentials from draining away during the cooking process, try steaming (use a minimal amount of water with a steamer basket), microwaving, or stir-frying. A study from the University of Essex in England showed that when certain vegetables were prepared using these techniques, most of the nutrients they contained were spared. And stir-frying scores even more points when you're cooking dark green or orange vegetables. These are rich in beta-carotene, and the oil you use in stir-frying them can increase the amount of the antioxidant you absorb by up to 63 percent, according to a study published in the journal *Molecular Nutrition & Food Research.* You don't need to use a lot of oil; even just a tablespoon will do.

? What is the topic of this paragraph?

____

____

____

Mistake #8 ***You don't wash all your produce before eating it***

9 Most of us remember to rinse plums and berries before noshing on them, but when was the last time you doused a banana, orange, cantaloupe, or mango with water? It may seem strange to wash peel-and-eat produce, but harmful bacteria lingering on the surface could be transferred to your hands or even to the inside of the fruit when you cut into it. To clean produce, simply run each piece under the tap and gently scrub. "Using your hands to rub fruits like oranges, bananas, and peaches under water is sufficient," says Ruth Frechman, R.D., a dietitian in Burbank, California, and a spokeswoman for the American Dietetic Association. When you're done, dry the items with a clean cloth or paper towel. It's important to wash your hands with soap and warm water for at least 20 seconds before and after you handle the items to further reduce the spread of bacteria. Frechman also suggests throwing out the outer leaves of greens like cabbage and lettuce before washing, as they've been handled the most and can have the highest levels of bacterial contamination.

Mistake #9 You're not pairing foods properly

10 Many of us think about getting enough iron only when we feel **lethargic** or fatigued. But we should pay attention to our iron intake every day, before symptoms occur. Our bodies absorb about 15 to 35 percent of heme iron (found in meats and seafood), but just 2 to 20 percent of non-heme iron (from beans, whole-grain cereal, tofu, and dark, leafy greens). We can maximize how much iron we take in by pairing the latter group with vitamin C-rich foods and beverages, such as citrus fruits and juices, tomatoes, hot and sweet peppers, strawberries, and melons. On the other hand, drinking tea or coffee at meals can inhibit how much iron we absorb by up to 60 percent, says Marla Reicks, R.D., a professor of nutrition at the University of Minnesota in St. Paul. That's because these beverages contain compounds called polyphenols that bind to the iron. Wait until you've completely finished your meal before putting the kettle on to boil.

lethargic
drowsy, sluggish

? **What is the topic of this paragraph?**

____

____

____

____

Reading with a Critical Eye

In a small group, discuss the following reflection questions, which will guide you toward a deeper understanding of the reading.

1. It is common sense that "Eating out less and cooking more may be one of the most effective things you can do to keep fat and calories in check." Why do you think American people tend to eat out more and cook less?
2. How is it that we buy fresh, wholesome foods from the supermarket, and they lose most of their nutrients because of the way we store and prepare them? Give specific reasons to support your answer.
3. In paragraph 3, we learn that it is harmful to store milk and whole grains in clear containers because photooxidation takes place when these containers come into contact with light. The U.S. Food and Drug Administration must be aware of this fact. Why is it then that companies are allowed to manufacture clear containers?
4. In paragraph 7, nutritionist Forberg says, "Many of us remove the skins from eggplant, bell peppers, peaches, apples, and nectarines while preparing recipes, but we're really just tossing away nutrients and fiber." Modern technology has made it possible to find information related to health and nutrition on the Internet with relative ease. Despite this, why is it that so many people could be wrong at the same time by peeling fruits and vegetables? Can you think of another example of people practicing something that flies in the face of empirical evidence? What does this pattern tell us about human nature in general? Be specific.

5. Some people believe that the emphasis on hygiene in the United States is somewhat overrated. For example, experts believe that "It's important to wash your hands with soap and warm water for at least 20 seconds before and after you handle the items to further reduce the spread of bacteria." In many countries, people do not think much of these things and handle food items without washing their hands with soap and warm water. Discuss what causes these cultural differences in people's approach to health and nutrition.

From Reading to Writing: Making an Outline

Overview

You may have noticed that the readings in this chapter are coherent and flow smoothly. The reason for this is that there are logical relationships between the main ideas and the supporting details that make those ideas clear and easy to understand. However, sometimes you may be required to read complex texts in which the ideas are not that easy to follow. *Outlining*, in this sense, is an important skill that helps the reader see how the different ideas are organized logically in the original text. One of the main purposes of outlining is to first identify how the author develops the argument by using several ideas with supporting evidence. Then, you can use your outline to discuss the ideas, elaborating on the specific topic of the text, orally and in writing.

Preparing an Outline

The first step toward preparing an outline is to write down the title and the author of the original text. The next step is to write the author's main idea, which can usually be found in the introductory paragraph. Keep in mind that an outline does not necessarily have to contain complete sentences. Your task, however, is to retain the original meaning, yet use your own words. We have provided a worksheet (see below) to make outlining a fruitful and enjoyable exercise.

As you begin the process of outlining, constantly frame these questions in the back of your mind:

- What is the author's main idea?
- What specific bits and pieces of evidence does he or she present to support the main idea?

You will need to read the entire text carefully to answer these questions. While reading the text, focus on identifying the logical connections between the different ideas and the overall structure and content.

Once you have prepared a rough outline, read it carefully, and read the original text a second time to fill in the information gaps. You will notice that during a second reading, you comprehend the text more clearly, as you search for and find the missing pieces of information. As you can see, outlining will enable you to recall information later when you discuss the reading with your peers in class and submit your outline to your instructor in written form.

Implications for Your Learning

While it is not necessary to prepare an outline of every single reading in your textbook, practicing outlining regularly will improve your ability to read, review, and discuss information related to the general and specific ideas contained in the original text. Moreover, outlining has implications for writing as well. You can prepare an outline of the main ideas you want to present in a speech or in written communication. You can also apply the skill of outlining to writing well-organized paragraphs of your own. Once you have outlined the main ideas, you can expand them in a logical and coherent manner as you write the paragraph. As you can see, there are many advantages to outlining information.

Sample Outline

Here is a sample outline of Reading 3A on page 112 as a model for your outlining practice. Notice how the major details are followed by the minor details supporting the main idea.

Title: Bottlers Agree to a School Ban on Sweet Drinks

Author: Marian Burros and Melanie Warner

The *New York Times*, May 4, 2006

Main idea: Owing to growing pressure of lawsuits and state legislation, three leading soft-drink companies have decided to eliminate sweetened drinks such as Coke and Pepsi from school cafeterias and vending machines.

I. There is an agreement between soft drink makers and health advocates.
- A. Students would be served water, nonfat milk, and 100 percent fruit juice.
- B. Serving sizes would increase to 10 ounces in middle school.
- C. The companies' profits would not be affected.
- D. This agreement is voluntary.

II. Many public school students will be affected by this agreement.
- A. The ban would be limited to some school functions.
- B. Many schools have stricter soda ban policies.
- C. Connecticut banned all soda, even Gatorade.
- D. New York allows only low-fat milk, water, and fruit juice.

III. The agreement was brokered by an alliance, a foundation, and the American Heart Association.
   A. The terms were accepted by the three largest soft-drink companies.
   B. Mr. Clinton applauded the agreement.
   C. It will be three years before the agreement is fully implemented.

IV. There has been a push in recent years by nutritionists and parent groups to limit soda sales in schools.
   A. California has already banned soft-drink sales.
   B. Owing to pressure, the beverage association has modestly cut back on soda sales.
   C. Critics argue that the agreement has not addressed the issue of marketing soda products to students on Channel One.

EXERCISE 3.9 Outlining

Now that you have looked at a sample outline, try to make an effective outline for Reading 4, "The 9 Most Common Kitchen Mistakes Even Healthy Women Make ... and Why They're Robbing Your Food of Nutrients," which begins on page 118 of this chapter. Use the worksheet below to prepare your outline. When you are finished, submit your outline to your instructor for feedback.

Outline Worksheet

Read the original text thoroughly at least once. If you are reading a lengthy selection, it is likely that the text includes many paragraphs containing several ideas. Write the title and author of the text, then the main idea, which is usually found in the introductory paragraph, followed by other ideas related to the main idea and the supporting details as follows.

Title: The 9 Most Common Kitchen Mistakes Even Healthy Women Make . . . and Why They're Robbing Your Food of Nutrients

Author: Amanda Pressner

Your name: ______________________________

Main idea: (Write the main idea of the original text in your own words here.)

____

____

I. Idea I supporting the main idea

____

____

Supporting details

A. ______________________________

____

B. ______________________________

II. Idea II supporting the main idea

____

____

____

Supporting details

A. ______________________________

____

B. ______________________________

____

C. ______________________________

____

III. Idea III supporting the main idea

____

____

Supporting details

A. ______________________________

B. ______________________________

____

IV. Idea IV supporting the main idea

____

____

Supporting details

A. ______________________________

B. ______________________________

C. ______________________________

____

If the text is really lengthy, and you find that there are more ideas expounding on the main idea, continue in the same manner and outline the information until you reach the concluding paragraph.

Self-Evaluation of Outlining

After preparing the outline, answer the following questions based on your experience. Your instructor may ask you to share your answers with your peers or to submit this self-evaluation form.

Title: ______________________________

Author: ______________________________

Your name: ______________________________

1. How did you organize the main ideas of the original text? Did you find this exercise easy, or did you find it difficult?

____

____

____

2. Did you manage to include all the main ideas and supporting details of the original text the first time? If not, what specific bits and pieces of information did you miss?

____

____

____

3. Did you read the text a second time? If you did, what additional pieces of information did you find?

____

____

____

4. Do you think this exercise helped you identify the logical relationships between the main ideas and the supporting details more easily?

____

____

____

5. Do you think outlining can help you present your ideas orally and in written form more logically and clearly?

____

____

____

Careers in Nutrition

Working in small groups, discuss careers one can pursue after obtaining an advanced degree in nutrition. You may wish to do some online research to find other careers related to the field of health and nutrition. In the space below, write down the job title and responsibilities. The first example is done for you. Be sure to share your findings with your peers.

Job Title	*Responsibilities*
1. Professor of Nutrition	Teach education courses to undergraduate and graduate students, do teacher training for future public school teachers, publish textbooks and research papers in peer-reviewed journals, present at professional conferences.
2.	
3.	
4.	
5.	

Textbook Application

Read the following section from Chapter 2 of *Nutrition: From Science to You* and try to accurately answer the multiple-choice questions. You may want to highlight key points in the reading as you navigate the passage.

MyReadingLab

Visit Chapter 3: Health in MyReadingLab to complete the Reading 5 activities.

READING 5

Textbook

Tools for Healthy Eating

Pre-Reading Questions

Before you read the chapter on healthy eating, discuss the following questions in small groups.

1. In your opinion, why is nutrition important? Do you think that proper nutrition can contribute to wellness?
2. Nutritionists believe that a healthful diet can prevent many diseases and reduce your risk for others. Do you agree with this view? Why, or why not?

3. It is important to develop a dietary plan that is nutritionally adequate. Have you ever consulted with a nutritionist to find out whether your nutrient needs are met? If you were to see a nutritionist, how would you go about finding one who is credentialed and trustworthy?
4. You receive a phone call from your mother, who is excited about a research study claiming that consuming a moderate amount of chocolate can reduce the risk of heart disease in older women. You ask your mother who funded the research study, but she does not know and asks you why it is important at all. Explain to your mother why such information is important before one takes the findings of a study for granted.

Tools for Healthy Eating

from Chapter 2 of Nutrition: From Science to You, 3/e
by Joan Salge Blake, Kathy D. Munoz, and Stella Volpe

Many Americans believe that to eat a healthful diet means giving up their favorite foods. Nothing could be further from the truth! With a little planning, you can still occasionally eat almost any food even if it contains added sugars and fat and is high in kilocalories. All it takes are the right tools to balance those higher kilocalorie foods with more nutritious choices each day.

The good news is that a number of tools are available to help you achieve a healthful, balanced, eating plan. In this chapter we will learn how to use these tools in a positive, constant manner that over time will lead to better eating habits while still enjoying those comfort foods. Let's begin with a discussion on what is healthy eating.

What Are the Key Principles of Healthy Eating?

Healthy eating means you need to **balance**, **vary**, and **moderate** your nutrient intake. As a student, you are probably familiar with these principles from other areas of your life. You balance your time between work, school, family, and friends. You engage in a variety of activities to avoid being bored, and enjoy each in moderation, as spending too much time on one activity (like working) will disrupt the amount of time you can spend on others (like studying or socializing).

A chronic imbalance of any one of these activities will affect the others. If you regularly forgo sleep in order to work extra hours at a job, sleep deprivation will affect your ability to stay awake in class, which will hamper your studies. Your unbalanced life would soon become unhealthy and unhappy. Likewise, your eating pattern must be balanced, varied, and moderate in order to be healthy. In addition, a healthy diet includes foods that are high in **nutrient density** and low in **energy density**.

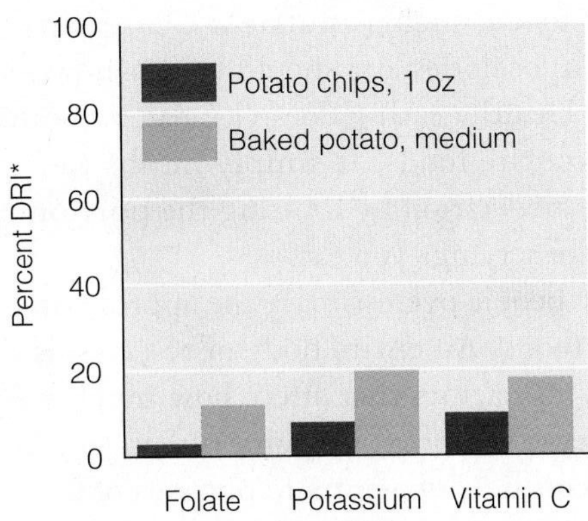

Healthy Eating Means Balance between Food Groups

A balanced diet includes healthy proportions of all nutrients and is adequate in energy. A diet that lacks balance can cause **undernutrition**. For instance, a student subsisting largely on bread, bagels, muffins, crackers, chips, and cookies might be eating too much carbohydrate and fat but too little protein, vitamins, and minerals. If the diet lacks a particular nutrient, such as protein, over time the body suffers from **malnutrition**. A meal that contains foods from the grain, vegetable, fruit, meat, and dairy groups, such as a lunch of a turkey-and-cheese sandwich with lettuce and tomato plus an apple, provides the proper proportion of foods from each of the food groups. This balancing act prevents **overnutrition** of a specific nutrient, such as fat, or too many kilocalories, which can lead to overweight and obesity. Consuming adequate amounts of all essential nutrients is key to avoiding nutrient deficiencies, and, in many cases, chronic disease.

Healthy Eating Means Consuming a Variety of Foods

Choosing a variety of foods improves the quality of the diet because the more varied the food choices, the better the chance of consuming adequate amounts of all the essential nutrients. Even within one group, the nutrient composition of foods can vary dramatically. For example, while broccoli is a good source of folate, it has less than half the vitamin A of a carrot. Similarly, if the only fruit you eat is bananas, your diet would include an excellent source of potassium, but little vitamin C. Because no single food or food group contains everything you need to be healthy, you should choose a variety of foods from within each food group and among food groups each day to achieve a healthy diet. This is the basic principle of the Fruits & Veggies – More Matters campaign developed by the Produce for Better Health Foundation and the Centers for Disease Control and Prevention. This campaign promotes eating a variety of colorful fruits and vegetables, which are rich in vitamins, minerals, fiber, and phytochemicals, each day to help reduce the risk of cancer and heart disease, and slow the effects of aging.

Healthy Eating Means Moderate Intake of All Foods

According to many Registered Dietitian Nutritionists, "there are no good or bad foods, just good or bad habits." What they mean is that all foods – even less nutritious foods – can be part of a healthy diet, as long as they are consumed in moderation. Foods such as sweets and fried or packaged snack foods should be eaten only in small amounts to avoid consuming too much sugar and fat. Eating too much of these foods can also mean taking in more energy than you need, potentially resulting in weight gain. Finally, these foods can displace more nutrient-rich choices, resulting in a diet that lacks essential nutrients. Even some healthy foods, such as nutrient-dense nuts, can be high in kilocalories and should be consumed in moderation. Healthy eating doesn't mean you can't enjoy your favourite foods. It simply means eating those foods in moderation by limiting the **portion** size and number of servings you eat.

Many people overestimate the appropriate portion sizes of foods. An entire body of research is devoted to studying factors that affect how much we put on our plates. The important point is that, in general, we tend to consume two or more portions of a given food at a given meal.

Healthy Eating Includes Nutrient-Dense Foods

Healthy eating includes not only choosing foods based on these key principles of balance, moderation, and variety, but also choosing foods that are nutrient dense. Nutrient-dense foods are high in nutrients, such as vitamins and minerals, but low in energy (kilocalories). Nutrient-dense foods provide more nutrients per kilocalories (and in each bite) than less nutrient-dense foods. Fresh fruits and vegetables, for example, are nutrient dense because they are high in B vitamins, vitamin C, minerals such as calcium and magnesium, and fiber, while usually providing fewer than 60 kilocalories per serving.

Nutrient-dense foods are also low in fat and added sugars. To illustrate this concept, compare the nutrient density of two versions of the same food: a baked potato and potato chips (Figure 2.1). Although a medium baked potato and one ounce of potato chips have about the same number of kilocalories, the baked potato provides much higher amounts of vitamins and minerals than the deep-fried chips.

Though many foods, such as broccoli and carrots, are clearly nutrient dense and other foods, such as potato chips and doughnuts, are clearly not, not all foods fit neatly into these two categories. Items such as dried fruits, nuts, peanut butter, and avocados are high in kilocalories, but they are also excellent sources of important nutrients, including polyunsaturated fatty acids, calcium, and iron. Other foods, such as whole milk or yogurt, contain the same nutrients, but higher amounts of fat and kilocalories than their nonfat or low-fat counterparts. These higher fat versions still provide significant amounts of calcium, riboflavin, vitamins A and D, and protein. Some foods, such as fruit-flavored yogurt and some fortified cereals, contain added sugars in addition to several essential nutrients. Do you think these foods can be considered nutrient dense?

In all of these scenarios, the answer is yes. Whereas nutrient dense usually means high in nutrients and low in energy, foods that are high in nutrients and high in energy can also be considered nutrient dense. The key is to be aware of the extra kilocalories and make up for them elsewhere in the diet. If you don't like skim milk and won't drink it, but do enjoy the taste of whole milk, then drinking whole milk is preferable to drinking non-calcium-containing beverages, such as soda. Just remember that unless you compensate for the extra kilocalories (by forgoing that nighttime cookie, for example), you may gain weight.

Healthy Eating Includes Low-Energy-Dense Foods

In contrast to nutrient density, energy density refers to foods that are high in energy but low in weight or volume, such as that potato chip. A serving of deep-fried chips weighs much less than a plain baked potato, but is considerably higher in fat and kilocalories. Therefore, the chip contains more energy per gram. A big, leafy green salad, on the other hand, is large in volume but low in energy density, due to its high water content.

Most high-fat foods are considered energy dense. This is because fat has 9 kilocalories per gram and is thus 2.25 times more energy dense than either carbohydrates or protein at 4 kilocalories per gram. Individuals who choose low-energy-dense foods will generally have diets that are lower in fat and higher in nutrient content.

Eating a low-energy-dense diet can sometimes be the key to weight loss. Recent studies have found that leaner individuals ate more low-energy-dense foods and fewer kilocalories, while consuming a greater volume of food, compared with their obese counterparts. Eating low-density foods means larger portions for the same number of kilocalories.

Even modest changes in dietary intake may promote and help maintain weight loss over time. One reason for this may be improved satiety and appetite control. Eating a larger volume of low-energy foods improves satiety and decreases hunger. In other words, low-energy foods will "fill you up before they fill you out."

If you are trying to maintain your current weight, or lose weight, you are probably on a limited energy budget and need to choose foods that are nutrient dense and low in kilocalories.

Many Resources Are Available for Planning a Healthy Diet

Do you think all this advice for planning a healthy diet is hard to keep straight? If so, you're not alone. Fortunately, there are several tools that can help you avoid both under- and overnutrition, including:

- The Dietary Reference Intakes (DRIs), which provide recommendations regarding your nutrient needs
- The Dietary Guidelines for Americans, which provide broad dietary and lifestyle advice
- MyPlate, part of the ChooseMyPlate.gov Web-based initative, which is designed to help you eat healthfully and implement the recommendations in the DRIs and the advice in the Dietary Guidelines
- The exchange system, which groups foods according to their macronutrient content, thus making it easier to plan meals
- The Nutrition Fact panel on food labels, which contains the Daily Values, and which can help you decide which foods to buy

Together, these tools help you plan a balanced, moderate, and varied diet that meets your nutrient and health needs.

Reading Comprehension Check

Read the following questions and circle the correct answer. Try to eliminate the three wrong answers first before choosing the correct answer.

1. As described at the beginning of the chapter, healthy eating means our food must be
   a. balanced, varied, and abnormal.
   b. balanced, varied, and temperate.
   c. balanced, varied, and immoderate.
   d. balanced, varied, and extreme.

2. "You engage in a variety of activities to avoid being bored, and enjoy each in **moderation**, as spending too much time on one activity (like working) will disrupt the amount of time you can spend on others (like studying or socializing)."

   In this sentence, the word *moderation* means
   a. excess.
   b. extreme.
   c. avoidance.
   d. restraint.

3. "If you regularly forgo sleep in order to work extra hours at a job, sleep deprivation will affect your ability to stay awake in class, which will **hamper** your studies."

   The meaning of the word *hamper* in the above context is
   a. encourage.
   b. facilitate.
   c. hinder.
   d. further.

4. In the section, Healthy Eating Means Balance between Food Groups, the example of a student mostly eating carbohydrates is given to show that
   a. a balanced diet consists of mostly carbohydrates.
   b. carbohydrates are a substitute for protein and minerals.
   c. carbohydrates replace vitamins and minerals.
   d. a diet lacking a particular nutrient can cause malnutrition.

5. Read the section Healthy Eating Means Balance between Food Groups. It explains that
   a. undernutrition can help us consume all essential nutrients.
   b. overnutrition can cause weight gain and obesity.
   c. overnutrition is key to avoiding obesity and chronic disease.
   d. malnutrition occurs when we consume all essential nutrients.

6. Read Healthy Eating Means Consuming a Variety of Foods. The main idea of the passage is that
   a. a healthy diet contains different types of foods with all the essential nutrients.
   b. a single food group contains everything one needs to be healthy.
   c. a healthy diet is made up of only protein and carbohydrates lacking vitamins.
   d. bananas must be included in every meal for potassium and Vitamin C.

7. "What they mean is that all foods – even less nutritious foods – can be part of a healthy diet, as long as they are **consumed** in moderation."

   In the sentence above, the word *consumed* means
   a. produced.
   b. grown.
   c. eaten.
   d. digested.

8. "Just remember that unless you compensate for the extra kilocalories (by **forgoing** that nighttime cookie, for example), you may gain weight."

   The meaning of the word *forgoing* in the above context is
   a. consuming.
   b. sacrificing.
   c. embracing.
   d. managing.

9. Read the section Healthy Eating Includes Low-Energy-Dense Foods. We learn that
   a. low-energy-dense foods are lower in fat and lower in nutrients.
   b. low-energy-dense foods are higher in fat and lower in nutrients.
   c. low-energy-dense foods are higher in fat and higher in nutrients.
   d. low-energy-dense foods are lower in fat and higher in nutrients.
10. MyPlate is a resource that can help people
   a. identify the nutritional contents of pre-packaged foods.
   b. plan their meals based on a pyramid system of food types.
   c. make healthy choices about food, based on recommendations in the DRIs.
   d. identify local restaurants that serve low-energy-dense foods.

Contemporary Issues in the Discipline

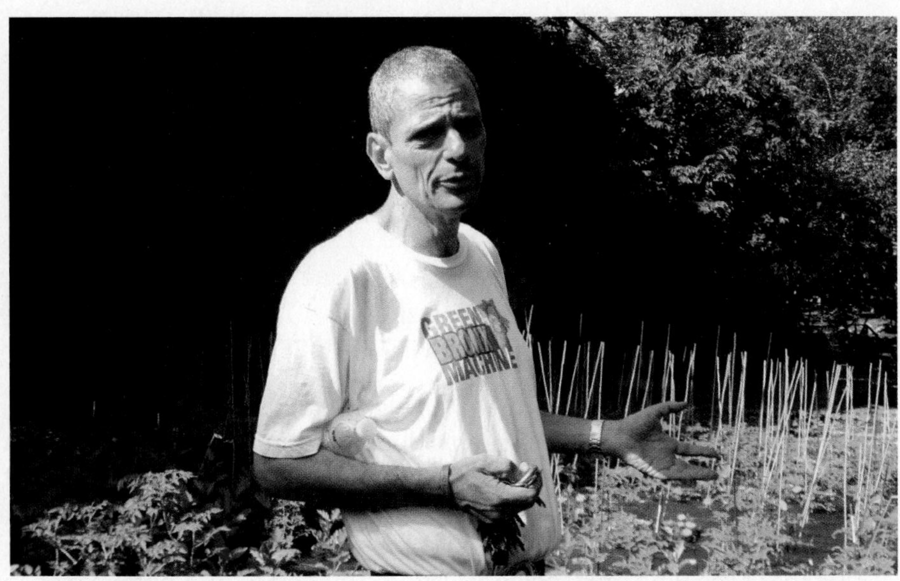

Stephen Ritz is a teacher/administrator who works with students and community members in the South Bronx to help rebuild and better their neighborhoods, in part through growing over 25,000 pounds of vegetables in the Bronx. In his classroom, students benefit from one of his projects, the first indoor edible wall in NYC. This wall yields enough produce to provide 450 students with healthy meals. Additionally, his students gain experience growing and distributing produce.

READING 6

Lecture (TED Talk)

MyReadingLab

Visit Chapter 3: Health in MyReadingLab to complete the Reading 6 activities.

A Teacher Growing Green in the South Bronx

Pre-Reading Activity

1. Before reading the following transcript of Stephen Ritz's speech, you can watch the talk itself here: https://www.ted.com/talks/stephen_ritz_a_teacher_growing_green_in_the_south_bronx?language=en (Courtesy of TED). As you listen to the videoed presentation, take notes. (See the note-taking activity in Chapter 4, p. 190 for some pointers.)
2. After reading the transcript, you will answer some open-ended questions about some of the issues raised in the speech. Finally, you will formulate questions for Mr. Ritz about issues pertinent to education and answer them from his perspective.

A Teacher Growing Green in the South Bronx

by Stephen Ritz
February 2012
Transcript courtesy of TED © TED CONFERENCES, LLC

Good afternoon. I am not a farmer. *(Laughter)*

1 I'm not. I'm a parent, I'm a resident and I'm a teacher. And this is my world. And along the way I've started noticing — I'm on my third generation of kids — that they're getting bigger. They're getting sicker. In addition to these complexities, I just learned that 70 percent of the kids that I see who are labeled learning disabled would not have been had they had proper prenatal nutrition.

2 The realities of my community are simple. They look like this. Kids should not have to grow up and look at things like this. And as jobs continue to leave my community, and energy continues to come in, be exported in, it's no wonder that really some people refer to the South Bronx as a desert. But I'm the oldest sixth grader you'll ever meet, so I get up every day with this tremendous amount of enthusiasm that I'm hoping to share with you all today. And with that note, I come to you with this belief that kids should not have to leave their communities to live, learn and earn in a better one.

3 So I'm here to tell you a story about me and this wall that I met outside, which I'm now bringing inside. And it starts with three people. The crazy teacher — that's me on the left, I dress up pretty, thank you, my wife, I love you for getting a good suit — my passionate borough

president and a guy named George Irwin from Green Living Technologies who helped me with my class and helped me get involved with this patented technology. But it all starts with seeds in classrooms, in my place, which looks like this. And I'm here today hoping that my reach will exceed my grasp. And that's really what this is all about.

4 And it starts with incredible kids like this, who come early and stay late. All of my kids are either IEP or ELL learners, most come with a lot of handicaps, most are homeless and many are in foster care. Almost all of my kids live below poverty. But with those seeds, from day one, we are growing in my classroom, and this is what it looks like in my classroom. And you see how attentive these kids are to these seeds. And then you notice that those seeds become farms across the Bronx that look like this.

5 But again, I am not a farmer. I'm a teacher. And I don't like weeding, and I don't like backbreaking labor. So I wanted to figure out how I could get this kind of success into something small, like this, and bring it into my classroom so that handicapped kids could do it, kids who didn't want to be outside could do it, and everyone could have access. So I called George Irwin, and what do you know? He came to my class and we built an indoor edible wall. And what we do is we partner it with authentic learning experiences, private-based learning. And lo and behold, we gave birth to the first edible wall in New York City.

6 So if you're hungry, get up and eat. You can do it right now. My kids play cow all the time. Okay? But we were just getting started, the kids loved the technology, so we called up George and we said, "We gotta learn more!" Now, Mayor Bloomberg, thank you very much, we no longer need work permits, which comes with slices and bonded contractors — we're available for you.

7 We decided to go to Boston. And my kids, from the poorest congressional district in America, became the first to install a green wall, designed by a computer, with real-live learning tools, 21 stories up — if you're going to go visit it, it's on top of the John Hancock building. But closer to home, we started installing these walls in schools that look like this with lighting like that, real LED stuff, 21st-century technology. And what do you know? We made 21st century money, and that was groundbreaking. Wow!

8 This is my harvest, people. And what do you do with this food? You cook it! And those are my heirloom students making heirloom sauce, with plastic forks, and we get it into the cafeteria, and we grow stuff and we feed our teachers. And that is the youngest nationally certified workforce in America with our Bronx Borough President.

9 And what'd we do then? Well, I met nice people like you, and they invited us to the Hamptons. So I call this "from South Bronx to Southampton." And we started putting in roofs that look like this, and we came in from destitute neighborhoods to start building landscape like this, wow! People noticed. And so we got invited back this past summer, and we actually moved into the Hamptons, paid 3,500 dollars a week for a house, and we learned how to surf. And when you can

do stuff like this — These are my kids putting in this technology, and when you can build a roof that looks like that on a house that looks like that with sedum that looks like this, this is the new green graffiti.

10 So, you may wonder what does a wall like this really do for kids besides changing landscapes and mindsets? Okay, I'm going to tell you what it does. It gets me to meet incredible contractors like this Jim Ellenberger from Ellenberger Services. And this is where it becomes true triple bottom line. Because Jim realized that these kids, my future farmers, really had the skills he needed to build affordable housing for New Yorkers, right in their own neighborhood. And this is what my kids are doing, making living wage.

11 Now, if you're like me, you live in a building, there are seven guys out of work looking to manage a million dollars. I don't have it. But if you need a toilet fixed or, you know, some shelving, I gotta wait six months for an appointment with someone who drives a much nicer car than me. That's the beauty of this economy. But my kids are now licensed and bonded in trade. And that's my first student to open up, the first in his family to have a bank account. This immigrant student is the first one in his family to use an ATM. And this is the true triple bottom line, because we can take neighborhoods that were abandoned and destitute and turn them into something like this with interiors like this.

12 Wow! People noticed. And notice they did. So CNN called, and we were delighted to have them come to our farmer's market. And then when Rockefeller Center said, NBC, could you put this thing up on the walls? We were delighted. But this, I show you, when kids from the poorest congressional district in America can build a 30-foot by 15-foot wall, design it, plant it and install it in the heart of New York City, that's a true "sí se puede" moment. Really scholastic, if you ask me.

13 But this is not a Getty image. That's a picture I took of my Bronx Borough President, addressing my kids in his house, not the jailhouse, making them feel a part of it. That's our State Senator Gustavo Rivera and Bob Bieder, coming to my classroom to make my kids feel important. And when the Bronx Borough President shows up and the State Senator comes to our class, believe you me, the Bronx can change attitudes now. We are poised, ready, willing and able to export our talent and diversity in ways we've never even imagined. And when the local senator gets on the scale in public and says he's got to lose weight, so do I! And I tell you what, I'm doing it and so are the kids.

14 Okay? And then celebrities started. Produce Pete can't believe what we grow. Lorna Sass came and donated books. Okay? We're feeding seniors. And when we realized that we were growing for food justice in the South Bronx, so did the international community. And my kids in the South Bronx were repped in the first international green roof conference. And that's just great.

15 Except what about locally? Well, we met this woman, Avis Richards, with the Ground Up Campaign. Unbelievable! Through her, my kids, the most disenfranchised and marginalized, were able to roll

out 100 gardens to New York City public schools. That's triple bottom line! Okay?

16 A year ago today, I was invited to the New York Academy of Medicine. I thought this concept of designing a strong and healthy New York made sense, especially when the resources were free. So thank you all and I love them. They introduced me to the New York City Strategic Alliance for Health, again, free resources, don't waste them. And what do you know? Six months later, my school and my kids were awarded the first ever high school award of excellence for creating a healthy school environment. The greenest class in New York City. But more importantly is my kids learned to get, they learned to give. And we took the money that we made from our farmer's market, and started buying gifts for the homeless and for needy around the world. So we started giving back. And that's when I realized that the greening of America starts first with the pockets, then with the heart and then with the mind.

17 So we were onto something, and we're still onto something. And thank God Trinity Wall Street noticed, because they gave us the birth of Green Bronx Machine. We're 3,000 strong right now. And what does it really do? It teaches kids to re-vision their communities, so when they grow up in places like this, they can imagine it like this. And my kids, trained and certified — Ma, you get the tax abatement. Thank you, Mayor Bloomberg — can take communities that look like this and convert them into things that look like that, and that to me, people, is another true "sí se puede" moment.

18 Now, how does it start? It starts in schools. No more little Knicks and little Nets. Group by broccoli, group by your favorite vegetable, something you can aspire to. Okay? And these are my future farmers of America, growing up in Brook Park on 141st Street, the most migrant community in America. When tenacious little ones learn how to garden like this, it's no wonder we get fruit like that. And I love it! And so do they. And we're building teepees in neighborhoods that were burning down. And that's a true "sí se puede" moment. And again, Brook Park feeds hundreds of people without a food stamp or a fingerprint. The poorest congressional district in America, the most migratory community in America, we can do this. Bissel Gardens is cranking out food in epic proportions, moving kids into an economy they never imagined.

19 Now, somewhere over the rainbow, my friends, is the South Bronx of America. And we're doing it. How does it start? Well, look at Jose's attention to detail. Thank God Omar knows that carrots come from the ground, and not aisle 9 at the supermarket or through a bulletproof window or through a piece of styrofoam. And when Henry knows that green is good, so do I. And when you expand their palates, you expand their vocabulary. And most importantly, when you put big kids together with little kids, you get the big fat white guy out of the middle, which is cool, and you create this kind of accountability amongst peers, which is incredible.

20 God, I'm going to run out of time, so I've gotta keep it moving. But this is my weekly paycheck for kids; that's our green graffiti. This is what we're doing. And behold the glory and bounty that is Bronx County. Nothing thrills me more than to see kids pollinating plants instead of each other. I gotta tell you, I'm a protective parent. But those kids are the kids who are now putting pumpkin patches on top of trains. We're also designing coin ponds for the rich and affluent. We're also becoming children of the corn, creating farms in the middle of Fordham Road for awareness and window bottles out of garbage.

21 Now I don't expect every kid to be a farmer, but I expect you to read about it, write about it, blog about it, offer outstanding customer service. I expect them to be engaged, and man, are they! So that's my incredible classroom, that's the food. Where does it go? Zero miles to plate, right down into the cafeteria. Or more importantly, to local shelters, where most of our kids are getting one to two meals a day. And we're stepping it up. No Air Jordans were ever ruined on my farm. And in his day, a million dollar gardens and incredible installations.

22 Let me tell you something, people. This is a beautiful moment. Black field, brown field, toxic waste field, battlefield — we're proving in the Bronx that you can grow anywhere, on cement. And we take orders for flowers. I'm putting the bake sale to shame. We take orders now. I'm booking for the spring. And these were all grown from seeds. We're learning everything. And again, when you can take kids from backgrounds as diverse as this to do something as special as this, we're really creating a moment.

23 Now, you may ask about these kids. Forty percent attendance to 93 percent attendance. All start overage and under-credit. They are now, my first cohort is all in college, earning a living wage. The rest are scheduled to graduate this June. Happy kids, happy families, happy colleagues. Amazed people. The glory and bounty that is Bronx County.

24 Let's talk about mint. Where is my mint? I grow seven kinds of mint in my class. Mojitos, anybody? I'll be at Telepan later. But, understand this is my intellectual Viagra. Ladies and gentlemen, I gotta move quick, but understand this: The borough that gave us baggy pants and funky fresh beats is becoming home to the organic ones. My green [unclear] 25,000 pounds of vegetables, I'm growing organic citizens, engaged kids. So help us go from this to this. Self-sustaining entities, 18 months return on investment, plus we're paying people living wage and health benefits, while feeding people for pennies on the dollar.

25 Martin Luther King said that people need to be uplifted with dignity. So here in New York, I urge you, my fellow Americans, to help us make America great again. It's simple. Share your passion. It's real easy. Go see these two videos, please. One got us invited to the White House, one's a recent incarnation.

26 And most importantly, get the biggest bully out of schools. This has got to go tomorrow. People, you can all do that. Keep kids out of

stores that look like this. Make them a healthy plate, especially if you can pick it off the wall in your own classroom — delicioso! Model good behavior. Get them to a green cart. Big kids love strawberries and bananas. Teach them entrepreneurship. Thank God for GrowNYC. Let them cook. Great lunch today, let them do culinary things. But most importantly, just love them. Nothing works like unconditional love.

27 So, my good friend Kermit said it's not easy being green. It's not. I come from a place where kids can buy 35 flavors of blunt wrap at any day of the moment, where ice cream freezers are filled with slushy malt liquor. Okay? My dear friend Majora Carter once told me, we have everything to gain and nothing to lose. So here, and at a time when we've gone from the audacity to hope to hope for some audacity, I urge you to do something. I urge you to do something.

28 Right now, we're all tadpoles, but I urge you to become a big frog and take that big, green leap. I don't care if you're on the left, on the right, up the middle, wherever. Join me. Use — I've got a lot of energy. Help me use it. We can do something here. And along the way, please take time to smell the flowers, especially if you and your students grew them.

29 I'm Steve Ritz, this is Green Bronx Machine. I've got to say thank you to my wife and family, for my kids, thank you for coming every day, and for my colleagues, believing and supporting me. We are growing our way into a new economy. Thank you, God bless you and enjoy the day. I'm Steve Ritz.
Sí se puede! *(Applause)*

Reading with a Critical Eye

1. Stephen Ritz begins his speech by claiming, "70 percent of the kids that I see who are labeled learning disabled would not have been had they had proper prenatal nutrition." Discuss the relation between prenatal nutrition and intelligence. Refer to the transcripts of the speech to answer the question.
2. Ritz believes that children should not have to leave their communities to live, learn, and earn in a better one. Why do you think children are forced to leave their communities?
3. How do you like the idea of Ritz's students learning in school and earning at the same time? Do you think that making money at such a young age can be a distraction to their education?
4. Ritz says, "But more importantly is my kids learned to get, they learned to give. And we took the money that we made from our farmer's market, and started buying gifts for the homeless and for needy around the world. So we started giving back. And that's when I realized that the greening of America starts first with the pockets, then with the heart and then with the mind." Discuss what he means by that.

Imagined Interview: If you had the opportunity to interview Stephen Ritz in person, what would you ask him? With a partner, compose three questions for him.

Question 1. ______________________________

Question 2. ______________________________

Question 3. ______________________________

Interview Challenge: In a group, ask one student to play Mr. Ritz. This student should carefully consider Stephen Ritz's views, outlined clearly in the TED Talk, and try to answer the questions from Mr. Ritz's perspective on education.

Chapter Recap

Now that you have made it through a full chapter focusing on the field of health and nutrition, let's review the chapter reading content, skill focus, and vocabulary to gain a better understanding of what you have learned.

Recap Activity 1: A Quick Glance

In 60 seconds, write brief answers to the following two questions. You may wish to share your answers with your classmates or with your instructor.

1. What is one thing you learned from this chapter?

____

____

____

____

____

2. What is one thing you found difficult?

____

____

____

____

____

Now discuss what you wrote in a small group. Do not read what you wrote. Paraphrase yourself!

Recap Activity 2: Summary Writing

Choose your favorite reading from this chapter and write a summary containing the main idea and some major details. Keep in mind that the key to summary writing is to convey the author's ideas accurately, but to relay this information in your own words. Last but not least, be sure to include reminder phrases and appropriate transitions.

Recap Activity 3: Online Research on a Theme of Interest

Think about the choice you just made in Recap Activity 2 concerning which reading in the chapter was your favorite.
What was the theme of your chosen reading? Theme = ______________
Using a search engine such as Google or Bing, go online and locate a quality reading on the same theme as your favorite chapter reading. Write a three- to five-sentence summary of the reading that you found from your Internet research. Be sure to include the author's most important points in your summary.

Title of Reading	*Article Source*	*Summary of the Reading (in your own words)*

Recap Activity 4: Reinforcing the Skill

Working with a partner, read the following paragraph. Then discuss what strategies can be used to identify the topic and determine the main idea. Keep in mind that you are not being asked to identify the topic and find the main idea of the passage. Instead, your task is to employ strategies that can help you find the topic and the main idea. In other words, when you read a passage, tell how you can find out what the topic and the author's main idea are.

> Wellness can be defined in many ways. Traditionally considered simply the absence of disease, wellness has been redefined as we have learned more about our bodies and what it means to live a healthful lifestyle. Wellness is now considered to be a multidimensional process, one that includes physical, emotional, social, occupational, and spiritual health. Wellness is not an endpoint in our lives, but is an active process we work on every day.

What strategies can you use to identify the topic and determine the main idea of the passage?

Strategy 1: ______________________________

Strategy 2: ______________________________

Recap Activity 5: Recycling Vocabulary

With a partner, locate the following discipline-specific vocabulary items, review them in context, and try to define the terms without using a dictionary. The first example is done for you.

Word and Context Location	*Sentence Containing the Word*	*Meaning in This Context*
dieting, p. 149, para. 2	He published a book on the Dukan Diet ten years ago in France that became the French best seller and engendered a **dieting** revolution of 200 Internet sites, forums, and blogs.	a limitation on the amount of food a person eats to reduce weight
sedentary, p. 94, para. 11	She also quotes one expert who claims that "national data" do not show that Americans are, in fact, more **sedentary** than in the past.	______________________________ ______________________________

obesity, p. 91, para. 1	No one wants to help you when you're fat," one explained. Ninety-one percent of the group also chose having a leg amputated over a return to **obesity**.	______________
saturated, p. 85, example 7	The American people are gradually becoming aware of the consequences of eating foods containing large amounts of **saturated** fat.	______________ ______________
cholesterol, p. 151, bullet 3	It may reduce the risk of heart disease by delaying or blocking the absorption of dietary **cholesterol** into the bloodstream.	______________ ______________
longevity, p. 80, introduction	A careful examination of the articles in this chapter will enable you to understand how you can make smart nutrition choices to attain health and **longevity**.	______________
consumption, p. 107, Practice 1	Obesity is caused by the excessive **consumption** of fat.	______________
nutrients, p. 146, Practice 1	But while we may be tossing the freshest, most wholesome foods into our carts, many of us are storing and preparing them in ways that rob them (and our bodies) of the very **nutrients** we're seeking.	______________

Recap Activity 6: Reviewing Question Types for Standardized Testing: Finding the Main Idea versus Identifying the Topic

As you learned in the previous chapter, it is important for you to be able to identify the different types of questions that are offered on standardized reading exams. In this section, you will have an opportunity to examine the various ways in which main idea questions are asked. On standardized reading exams, it is easy to confuse questions that focus on the main idea with questions that ask for the topic of a reading. Students often answer a "main idea" question with a multiple-choice option that offers the "topic," and vice versa. Pay attention to the relationship between the questions given and the answer choices offered.

Review the sample questions that focus on *finding the main idea and identifying the topic of the passage.* Pay attention to how each question is worded.

You are being asked to find the main idea of the passage when the question is worded in the following ways:

- The author's main point is that . . .
- The principal idea of the passage is . . .
- Which of the following best expresses the main point of the entire passage?
- Which of the following best expresses the main idea of the second paragraph?

You are being asked to identify the topic of a passage when the test question begins as follows:

- The best title for the selection is . . .
- The passage discusses . . .
- The passage focuses mainly on . . .
- This passage is about . . .
- This passage concerns . . .
- The problem the author is discussing in this passage is . . .
- The author is explaining the nature of . . .

Practice: With a partner, read the following passage and practice with *main idea* and *identifying topic* questions.

There's something empowering about **hitting** the supermarket to shop for your week's meals. Rather than putting yourself at the mercy of the local Chinese take-out restaurant or succumbing to the lure of the drive-through, you're taking dinner—and your waistline—into your own hands. "Eating out less and cooking more may be one of the most effective things you can do to keep fat and calories in check," says Cheryl Forberg, R.D., author of *Stop the Clock! Cooking.* "Plus, building your diet around produce, whole grains, beans, and lean protein practically guarantees you'll reach your recommended targets for most vitamins and minerals." But while we may be tossing the freshest, most wholesome foods into our carts, many of us are storing and preparing them in ways that rob them (and our bodies) of the very nutrients we're seeking. Nutritionists and food-safety experts point to nine typical kitchen blunders that negatively **impact** the quality of our diets. Fortunately, you can **sidestep** all of them easily. Follow this advice to make your next meal healthier.

1. The best title for the passage is ______________________________.
2. The author's main point is that ______________________________ ______________________________.

Further Explorations

Books

1. *Fast Food Nation: The Dark Side of the All-American Meal* (2005) by Eric Schlosser. Harper Perennial. This nonfiction exposé of the fast-food industry is both informative and shocking. Schlosser investigates how America's voracious appetite for quick and cheap fast food has led to unhealthy eating habits.
2. *Foods that Heal* (1988) by Bernard Jensen. Avery, 2nd revised edition. In this book, Dr. Bernard Jensen provides a list of therapeutic foods that one should eat to remain healthy and live a long life.

Movies

1. *Supersize Me* (2004). A filmmaker conducts an experiment in which he eats only McDonald's food for a whole month only to find out that his health has deteriorated drastically.
2. *Fat, Sick, and Nearly Dead* (2011). This is a documentary made by Australian Joe Cross, who went on a strict juice diet for 60 days to lose weight and stop medication for a debilitating disease.

Internet Sites

1. www.nutrition.gov
   This is the U.S. federal guide offering access to all government Web sites with reliable and accurate information on nutrition and dietary guidance.
2. www.sne.org
   Society for Nutrition Education (SNE). Go to this site for further information about the Society for Nutrition Education and its goals to educate individuals, communities, and professionals about nutrition education and to influence policy makers about nutrition, food, and health.

Study TIP

Active Reading: Highlighting and Annotating Relevant Text

Highlighting

There are a number of productive ways to interact with text. We have already discussed the role of outlining. Active readers can also incorporate the critical skills of highlighting and annotation to improve their ability to comprehend reading material.

Overview

Highlighting key terms and concepts in a reading passage with a brightly colored highlighter serves a number of purposes. First, it motivates the reader to seek out the most relevant points in a given section of a text upon first read (a very similar skill to note taking when listening to a lecture!). Second, when exam time approaches, highlighted text will guide you toward the key terms and concepts that you need to review.

Some hints about highlighting:

- Highlight main ideas, not minor points.
- Highlight key terms that connect to important concepts.
- Highlight points that you feel would be helpful to remember upon review.

Challenge Activity

Let's read the biographical profile of Dr. Pierre Dukan, a famous French nutritionist, below. Using a highlighter, try to highlight the key points in the text.

Biographical Profile: Dr. Pierre Dukan

When Dr. Dukan's obese friend asked him for some dietary advice, he had no idea that he was about to start a revolution that would have widespread repercussions all over Europe and later in the United States. Dr. Dukan recommended that his friend eat a low-fat, protein-only diet to lose weight. He says, "'I told him to eat nothing but protein and drink only water for five days. When he came back, he asked if he could use my scales because his appeared to be broken." Dr. Dukan and his friend were both surprised to see that he had lost 10 pounds in five days. The friend was so pleased with the result that he remained on the same diet and lost another 6 pounds in the next five days.

Dr. Dukan was so amazed with the serendipitous results that he changed his area of specialization from neurology to nutrition. He spent the next 35 years doing research and perfecting his diet, which has become popularly known as the Dukan Diet. He says, "It has become clear to me over the years that calorie counting does not work—dieters' brains don't work like that."

He published a book on the Dukan Diet ten years ago in France, which became the French best seller and engendered a dieting revolution of 200 Internet sites, forums, and blogs. Today, 1.5 million French women strictly follow the Dukan Diet, and celebrities such as Gisele Bündchen and Jennifer Lopez stick to the low-fat, protein-only diet. The Dukan Diet has made its way to Britain, with the publication of an English version of the famous French book. Dr. Dukan has given lectures in the United States in English with a distinct French accent.

His protein-based diet sounds similar to Atkins, but the Dukan Diet is different. When people reach their desired weight, they can get back to a life of normal eating, but they must eat only proteins every Thursday for the rest of their lives. Dr. Dukan says, "By sticking to protein one day a week, you can lose 1.5 pounds to 2 pounds instantly and, in so doing, correct any excess that may have occurred during the rest of the week." The number of people living the Dukan life is increasing rapidly, and the Dukan Diet is well on its way to becoming a global phenomenon. However, there are some critics who believe that the Dukan Diet is not healthy and not sustainable.

Compare what you highlighted with a colleague, and discuss your choices.

Learning Implications

The more you interact with a text, the more connected you will feel to the ideas and information contained within it. Highlighting provides a visual aid for a later review of a text and gives the reader an opportunity to distinguish between major and minor points offered in a reading. This is especially helpful with high-level reading that is hard to comprehend. Highlighting is a way of breaking a text down into comprehensible points.

Annotating

Overview

Reading is often thought of as a passive activity whereby the reader simply reads sentences in silence. Contrary to popular belief, reading is actually a complex process, and active readers are fully aware of the fact that they must use their writing skills while reading. Annotating your textbook is an effective way to respond to what you are reading. Annotating involves adding notes to the text, explaining difficult concepts, and commenting on controversial issues for future reference. As you read your textbook, write notes in the margin of the textbook, underline main ideas and supporting details, circle unfamiliar vocabulary items, and put a question mark next to a statement you find confusing. As you get used to making annotations, you will notice that your attention, concentration, and reading comprehension have improved significantly. Annotating a text enables you to revisit the reading and understand the main idea and key concepts and review the material with relative ease.

There are various ways to annotate a text. Here are a few techniques, but you can create your own techniques to mark your textbook for clarification and further reflection.

- Use a marker to highlight the main ideas, key concepts, numbered items, definitions, and examples. You may use different colors for different purposes. For example, you may use a blue marker for the main idea and a green marker for vocabulary.
- You also may underline terms and their definitions.
- Put a question mark next to a difficult sentence, an unfamiliar word, or a confusing passage. You can always go back to the passage later. The question mark will remind you that you had difficulty understanding something.
- Highlight key concepts with an asterisk or a check mark.
- If the author has used the process analysis pattern of organization, use numbers to denote the steps in a process.
- As you read the text, write questions in the margin for further analysis. These recall questions will help you comprehend the material.
- As mentioned previously, reading is an active process. Unlike watching TV, where you do not need to get involved, active reading requires your involvement. Feel free to disagree with the author and write your thoughts in the margin. When you get used to annotating a text, you will reap the many rewards of active reading.
- Finally, if you are reading a long selection, write a summary including the main idea and a few major details.

Example of an Annotated Text

What follows is a passage from a nutrition textbook for college students. Notice how the text has been annotated. Keep in mind that there is no single way of annotating a text. Depending on what works best for you, you may develop your own technique of annotating a text.

Fiber Helps Us Stay Healthy

What is fiber?

What are some of the digestive and chronic diseases?

Although we cannot digest fiber, it is still an important substance in our diet. Research indicates that it helps us stay healthy and may prevent many digestive and **chronic** diseases. The potential benefits of fiber consumption include the following:

1

chronic: lasting for a long time

- May **reduce the risk of colon cancer**. While there is still some controversy surrounding this issue, many researchers believe that fiber binds cancer-causing substances and speeds their elimination from the colon. However, recent studies of colon cancer and fiber have shown that their relationship is not as strong as previously thought.

- Helps **prevent hemorrhoids, constipation, and other intestinal problems** by keeping our stool moist and soft. Fiber gives gut muscles "something to push on" and makes it easier to eliminate stools. 2

How does fiber consumption help us?

- Reduces the risk of **diverticulosis**, a condition that is caused in part by trying to eliminate small, hard stools. This increased pressure weakens intestinal walls, causing them to **bulge** outward and form pockets, which become infected and **inflamed**. This is a painful condition that must be treated with antibiotics or surgery. 3

bulge: a protruding part or swelling

inflamed: causing pain, redness, and swelling because of an infection

- May **reduce the risk of heart disease** by delaying or blocking the absorption of dietary **cholesterol** into the bloodstream. Fiber also contributes small fatty acids that may lower the amount of low-density lipoprotein (or LDL) to healthful levels in our bodies. 4
- May **enhance weight loss** because eating a high-fiber diet causes a person to feel more full. Fiber absorbs water, expands in our intestine, and slows the movement of food through the upper part of the digestive tract. People who eat a fiber-rich diet tend to eat fewer fatty and sugary foods. 5
- May **lower the risk of type 2 diabetes**. In slowing digestion, fiber also slows the release of glucose into the blood. It thereby improves the body's regulation of insulin production and blood glucose levels. 6

Challenge Activity

Read *Tools for Healthy Eating* on p. 130, and annotate the text. Use the techniques mentioned above, or refer to the annotated text above, or create your own techniques to mark the text. Underline or circle main ideas and unfamiliar words, write in the margin, place question marks next to something you do not understand, and write open-ended questions about the content. You can discuss these questions with your peers and instructor to understand the story more clearly.

Learning Implications

As you annotate a text, you interact with the material. Furthermore, you take a multisensory approach to reading—kinesthetic and visual learning. Annotating your textbook will help you improve your attention, concentration, and reading comprehension. Keep annotating the text, and you will gradually develop a consistent marking system, which will become an effective study aid for you.

ENVIRONMENTAL SCIENCE: Climate Change

"America has not led but fled on the issue of global warming."

JOHN KERRY

Learning Objectives

AFTER READING THIS CHAPTER, YOU SHOULD BE ABLE TO...

1. Analyze the issue of global warming
2. Recognize supporting details within a paragraph
3. Differentiate major details from minor details
4. Construct effective notes from a lecture

INTRODUCTION TO THE DISCIPLINE OF ENVIRONMENTAL SCIENCE

Environmental science is the study of interactions among physical, chemical, and biological components of the environment. Environmental scientists use their knowledge of the physical makeup and history of the earth to protect the environment. A major focus in the field is on locating energy resources, predicting geologic hazards, and providing environmental site assessments and advice in such areas as indoor air quality and hazardous waste cleanup. The great scale and complexity of environmental problems are creating a growing need for scientists with rigorous, interdisciplinary training in environmental science. Many environmental scientists work at consulting firms, helping businesses and government agencies comply with environmental policy. They are usually hired to solve problems. There are environment-related jobs in industry, environmental protection agencies, local/central government, media, international organizations, and environmental consultancy. The opportunities are endless. Environmental science graduates could be managing tropical rainforests, monitoring coral reef biodiversity, or practicing environmental law. This chapter focuses primarily on one of the greatest challenges facing not only environmental scientists but all of us who inhabit the earth: global warming. You will read about some of the devastating effects of global warming on our ecosystem and those it will cause in the future. This chapter will also explore some ways in which we can all play a role in conserving energy. The role of the government in placing stricter controls on energy consumption is a critical question and one that serves as this chapter's subject for debate.

Preview Questions

The following questions are all related to the chapter focus area of environmental science. Share your views in small group discussion.

1. Do you feel that summers and winters are usually warmer than they used to be during your childhood? If so, then what do you think is causing the climate change?
2. Scientists studying climate change believe that human activities are dangerously warming the earth. Do you agree with their view that global warming is caused by humans, or do you believe that human activities have absolutely no impact on global warming? If you agree with the scientists, describe specific human activities that might be warming the earth. If you don't agree, why?
3. Climate scientists have found evidence that greenhouse gas emissions, including carbon dioxide, methane, and nitrous oxide, are caused by human activities, mainly the burning of fossil fuels.

Discuss effective ways of reducing greenhouse gas emissions that have driven climate change recently.

4. A report of the Intergovernmental Panel on Climate Change (IPCC) concludes that further climate change is inevitable, and that the earth's future depends on how humans treat it. Is it the government's responsibility to make people aware of how their activities are harming the earth? If so, how can the government best educate citizens to become more environmentally friendly?
5. Most environmental scientists are concerned that the continued depletion of earth's natural resources and the destruction of biodiversity, its flora and fauna, are caused by human activities. In your opinion, what can people do to ensure that most forms of life, including plants and animals, are respected and preserved?

Writing on The Wall

After you have discussed the preview questions with your classmates, post your responses to two of them on your class blog, which we refer to as The Wall. Review others' postings and respond to at least two of your classmates' posts that grab your interest. Remember the guidelines for blogging and commenting etiquette (see Chapter 1, p. 15). If your class is not using a shared blog, your instructor may ask you to record your individual or collective responses to the preview questions in another form.

EXERCISE 4.1 Interpreting a Cartoon

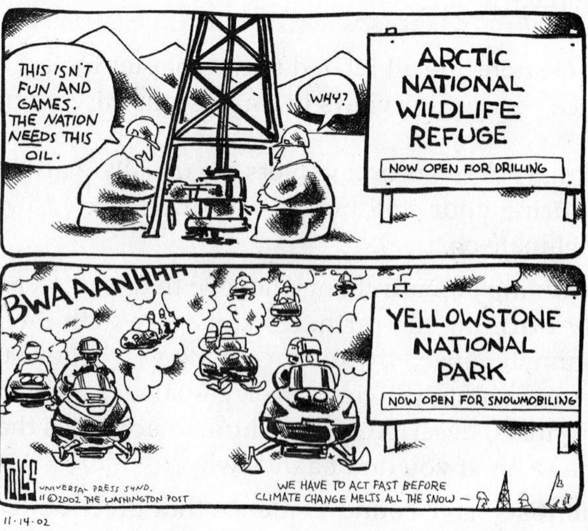

Examine the cartoon shown here, and in pairs, answer the following questions.

1. What is amusing about this cartoon?
2. In your opinion, what message is the cartoonist trying to convey to the reader?

Discipline-specific Vocabulary: Understand Key Terms in Environmental Science

One of the most efficient ways to acquire an academic vocabulary is to study key terms that are thematically connected. As you begin your college-level studies, it is critical that you internalize vocabulary terms that relate to the academic disciplines that make up most 100-level content courses. For example, a student taking an Introduction to Environmental Science course should be able to apply such terms as *deforestation*, *depletion*, and *biodiversity* in both spoken and written forms.

EXERCISE 4.2 Brainstorming Vocabulary

What associated words come to mind when you think of the world of environmental science? Work with a partner and write down as many related words as you can think of in a period of five minutes.

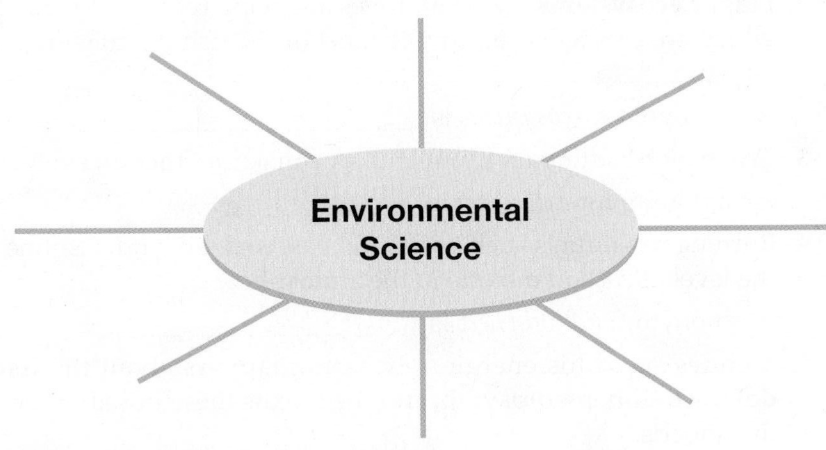

Fishing for Synonyms and Antonyms

In your written work, you will often need to use synonyms and antonyms (see Chapter 2, p. 24 to review these terms) in order to paraphrase statements or claims made by writers.

EXERCISE 4.3 Determining Synonyms and Antonyms from Context

Directions: Read the following ten (10) discipline-specific words culled from the readings in this chapter and shown in the context of the sentences in which they appeared. In the space provided after each sentence, write a synonym or antonym for the highlighted term, as directed.

Discipline-specific Word Bank for Environmental Science

species	**sustain**
ecosystems	**toxic**
extinction	**emissions**
atmosphere	**preserve**
deforestation	**erode**

1. "It's much harder for researchers to judge the well-being of a **species** living under water."

   A synonym for *species* is ______________________________.
2. Fragile **ecosystems** like mangroves are being replaced by fish farms, which are projected to provide most of the fish we consume within 20 years.

   A synonym for *ecosystems* is ___________________________.
3. "We may be sitting on a precipice of a major **extinction** event."

   An antonym for *extinction* is _______________.
4. Burning fossil fuels such as natural gas, coal, oil, and gasoline raises the level of carbon dioxide in the **atmosphere**.

   A synonym for *atmosphere* is _______________________.
5. Mendes spent his energies educating tappers about the issues of **deforestation**, road paving, and the threats these posed to their own livelihoods.

   An antonym for *deforestation* is _______________.
6. Primitive peoples were **sustained** solely by the energy flowing from the sun.

   A synonym for *sustained* is _______________________.

7. You give me **toxic** canals
   I give you a butterfly
   An antonym for *toxic is* _______________.
8. At the same time, carbon **emissions** are altering the chemistry of seawater.
   An antonym for *emissions* is _______________.
9. He fought to **preserve** the Amazon rainforest.
   A synonym for *preserve* is _______________.
10. If the nutrients are released to the soil by burning the natural vegetation, the heavy year-round rainfall quickly dissolves and **erodes** them.
   A synonym for *erode* is _______________.

EXERCISE 4.4 Matching Terms with Definitions

Match the word in Column A with the definition in Column B. Put the letter representing the correct definition in the space preceding each word.

Column A	Column B
Word	**Definition**
1. _____ species	a. slowly destroying the surface through the wind or rain
2. _____ ecosystems	b. to keep alive or in existence
3. _____ atmosphere	c. something that is discharged
4. _____ deforestation	d. gaseous envelope surrounding the earth
5. _____ extinction	e. having the effect of a poison
6. _____ sustain	f. group of interconnected elements, formed by the interaction of a community of organisms with their environment
7. _____ toxic	g. death of a species
8. _____ emissions	h. the act of cutting down trees
9. _____ preserve	i. the major subdivision of a genus or subgenus, regarded as the basic category of biological classification
10. _____ erode	j. to bear the weight of

EXERCISE 4.5 Choosing the Right Word

In the following sentences, fill in the blank with a word from the terminology bank that makes the sentence grammatically correct and meaningful.

deforestation	toxic	preserve	sustain	atmosphere
erode	species	emissions	ecosystems	extinction

1. The southern coastline has been gradually ____________ because of the torrid waves of the sea, making the foundations of several beach houses weaker.
2. Many ____________ chemicals are polluting our air.
3. One goal of many environmentally friendly policy makers is to cut ____________ drastically in new cars and trucks.
4. Due to the combined effects of human action and climate change, a number of animal species are nearing ____________.
5. Industrial factories spew pollutants into the ____________.
6. The goal of many environmental activists is to do everything they can to help ____________ the earth's natural beauty and plentiful resources.
7. Scientists are searching for renewable energy sources, which are less damaging to the earth's ____________.
8. Some environmental scientists claim that the earth cannot ____________ the damage caused by human activity.
9. Large-scale illegal ____________ in the Amazon has been increasing at an alarming rate, causing the Brazilian government to take strict measures to protect the natural habitat of wildlife.
10. Many plant ____________ will not survive a 10-degree increase in average temperature.

In-Class Survey: Personal Connection to Environmental Issues

Refer to the following questions to interview at least two classmates. Please take notes on a separate piece of paper as they respond to your questions, and orally report your findings.

Question	*Respondent 1*	*Respondent 2*
1. How would you describe the air quality in your neighborhood? If it is not very clean, what is causing the air pollution?		
2. How often do you recycle the paper, glass, and plastic products that you use? What kinds of items do you recycle? Which ones do you dispose of?		
3. Considering your neighborhood, in what ways do you see people act that are harmful to the environment?		

MyReadingLab

Visit Chapter 4: Environmental Science in MyReadingLab to complete the Reading 1 activities.

READING 1

Newspaper Article

Ocean Life Faces Mass Extinction, Broad Study Says

Pre-Reading Questions

Before reading the following article, answer these questions in pairs or small groups. Discussing the questions will help prepare you to analyze the text with relative ease.

1. How will the potential extinction of all ocean species affect our lives? In other words, how will our lives change if there is nothing living in our seas?
2. In what ways are humans harming the world's oceans? Give specific examples.
3. What can be done to limit the human-caused damage to ocean life?

Read this selection. Write predictive questions in the margin of the reading. Then practice your reading comprehension with the multiple-choice questions that follow under the heading **Reading Comprehension Check**.

Ocean Life Faces Mass Extinction, Broad Study Says

By **Carl Zimmer,** *New York Times*
January 15, 2015

1 A team of scientists, in a groundbreaking analysis of data from hundreds of sources, has concluded that humans are on the verge of causing unprecedented damage to the oceans and the animals living in them. "We may be sitting on a **precipice** of a major extinction event," said Douglas J. McCauley, an ecologist at the University of California, Santa Barbara, and an author of the new research, which was published on Thursday in the journal Science.

2 But there is still time to avert catastrophe, Dr. McCauley and his colleagues also found. Compared with the continents, the oceans are mostly intact, still wild enough to bounce back to ecological health. "We're lucky in many ways," said Malin L. Pinsky, a marine biologist at Rutgers University and another author of the new report. "The impacts are accelerating, but they're not so bad that we can't reverse them."

3 Scientific assessments of the oceans' health are dogged by uncertainty: It's much harder for researchers to judge the well-being of a **species** living underwater, over thousands of miles, than to track the health of a species on land. And changes that scientists observe in particular ocean **ecosystems** may not reflect trends across the planet. Dr. Pinsky, Dr. McCauley and their colleagues sought a clearer picture of the oceans' health by pulling together data from an enormous range of sources, from discoveries in the fossil record to statistics on modern container shipping, fish catches and seabed mining. While many of the findings already existed, they had never been juxtaposed in such a way.

4 A number of experts said the result was a remarkable synthesis, along with a nuanced and encouraging prognosis. "I see this as a call for action to close the gap between conservation on land and in the sea," said Loren McClenachan of Colby College, who was not involved in the study.

5 There are clear signs already that humans are harming the oceans to a remarkable degree, the scientists found. Some ocean species are certainly overharvested, but even greater damage results from large-scale habitat loss, which is likely to accelerate as technology advances the human footprint, the scientists reported. Coral reefs, for example, have declined by 40 percent worldwide, partly as a result of climate-change-driven warming.

6 Some fish are migrating to cooler waters already. Black sea bass, once most common off the coast of Virginia, have moved up to New Jersey. Less fortunate species may not be able to find new ranges. At the same time, carbon emissions are altering the chemistry of seawater, making it more acidic. "If you cranked up the aquarium heater and dumped some acid in the water, your fish would not be very happy," Dr. Pinsky said. "In effect, that's what we're doing to the oceans."

7 Fragile ecosystems like mangroves are being replaced by fish farms, which are projected to provide most of the fish we consume within 20 years. Bottom trawlers scraping large nets across the sea floor have already affected 20 million square miles of ocean, turning

parts of the continental shelf to rubble. Whales may no longer be widely hunted, the analysis noted, but they are now colliding more often as the number of container ships rises.

8 Mining operations, too, are poised to transform the ocean. Contracts for seabed mining now cover 460,000 square miles underwater, the researchers found, up from zero in 2000. Seabed mining has the potential to tear up unique ecosystems and introduce pollution into the deep sea.

9 The oceans are so vast that their ecosystems may seem impervious to change. But Dr. McClenachan warned that the fossil record shows that global disasters have wrecked the seas before. "Marine species are not immune to extinction on a large scale," she said. Until now, the seas largely have been spared the carnage visited on terrestrial species, the new analysis also found.

10 The fossil record indicates that a number of large animal species became **extinct** as humans arrived on continents and islands. For example, the moa, a giant bird that once lived on New Zealand, was wiped out by arriving Polynesians in the 1300s, probably within a century. But it was only after 1800, with the Industrial Revolution, that extinctions on land really accelerated. Humans began to alter the habitat that wildlife depended on, wiping out forests for timber, plowing under prairie for farmland, and laying down roads and railroads across continents. Species began going extinct at a much faster pace. Over the past five centuries, researchers have recorded 514 animal extinctions on land. But the authors of the new study found that documented extinctions are far rarer in the ocean.

11 Before 1500, a few species of seabirds are known to have vanished. Since then, scientists have documented only 15 ocean extinctions, including animals such as the Caribbean monk seal and the Steller's sea cow. While these figures are likely underestimates, Dr. McCauley said that the difference was nonetheless revealing. "Fundamentally, we're a terrestrial predator," he said. "It's hard for an ape to drive something in the ocean extinct." Many marine species that have become extinct or are endangered depend on land—seabirds that nest on cliffs, for example, or sea turtles that lay eggs on beaches.

12 Still, there is time for humans to halt the damage, Dr. McCauley said, with effective programs limiting the exploitation of the oceans. The tiger may not be salvageable in the wild—but the tiger shark may well be, he said. "There are a lot of tools we can use," he said. "We better pick them up and use them seriously."

13 Dr. McCauley and his colleagues argue that limiting the industrialization of the oceans to some regions could allow threatened species to recover in other ones. "I fervently believe that our best partner in saving the ocean is the ocean itself," said Stephen R. Palumbi of Stanford University, an author of the new study. The scientists also argued that these reserves had to be designed with climate change in mind, so that species escaping high temperatures or low pH would be

able to find refuge. "It's creating a hopscotch pattern up and down the coasts to help these species adapt," Dr. Pinsky said.

14 Ultimately, Dr. Palumbi warned, slowing extinctions in the oceans will mean cutting back on carbon emissions, not just adapting to them. "If by the end of the century we're not off the business-as-usual curve we are now, I honestly feel there's not much hope for normal ecosystems in the ocean," he said. "But in the meantime, we do have a chance to do what we can. We have a couple decades more than we thought we had, so let's please not waste it."

Reading with a Critical Eye

In a small group, discuss the following reflection questions, which will guide you toward a deeper understanding of the reading.

1. In paragraph 1, Douglas J. McCauley, an ecologist, says, "We may be sitting on a precipice of a major extinction event." What message is McCauley trying to get across? What evidence backs up his claim?
____
____
____

2. What methods did Dr. Pinsky and Dr. McCauley's team employ in getting a clearer picture of the oceans' health? _______________
____
____

3. In paragraph 8, we learn that mining operations are causing great damage to the deep seas. What benefits do we derive from deep-sea mining? In your opinion, are these benefits worth the costs? Explain._
____

4. According to the article (para. 10), animal extinctions on land accelerated after 1800, but ocean extinctions were rare. Why do you think that terrestrial animals were traditionally more threatened than sea creatures? _______________
____

5. Explain the last quote of the article (para. 14). "We have a couple decades more than we thought we had, so let's please not waste it."
____

Reading Comprehension Check

1. The main idea of the article is that
   a. human activity affects only terrestrial animals.
   b. ocean damage caused by human activities is threatening many ocean species.
   c. polar bears and penguins have been the most threatened.
   d. damage to the ocean is ignored by mining interests.

2. According to Loren McClenachan (para. 4), it is time to close the gap between
   a. the conservation of land and sea.
   b. extinct and living creatures.
   c. global efforts and local efforts to save the oceans.
   d. temperatures on land and in the sea.

3. "At the same time, carbon emissions are **altering** the chemistry of seawater, making it more acidic" (para. 6). The word *altering* could be replaced by
   a. effective.
   b. desiccating.
   c. changing.
   d. maintaining.

4. "The scientists also argued that these reserves had to be designed with climate change in mind, so that species escaping high temperatures or low pH would be able to find **refuge**." A synonym for the word *refuge* is
   a. danger.
   b. food.
   c. safe haven.
   d. enemy territory.

5. The Caribbean monk seal and the Steller's sea cow are mentioned as
   a. ocean animals that have been saved from extinction.
   b. examples of sea creatures that are now extinct.
   c. safe havens for animals.
   d. animal species that have done damage to the ocean floors.

6. "If you cranked up the aquarium heater and dumped some acid in the water, your fish would not be very happy," Dr. Pinsky said. "In effect, that's what we're doing to the oceans." What is Dr. Pinsky's main point in the above statement?
   a. Recent human activity is threatening ocean sea life.
   b. Fish have adapted to acid dumping in their habitat.
   c. Fish are generally not a contented species.
   d. If we do not stop dumping acid in our seas, the climate change will be prounounced.

7. "The tiger may not be **salvageable** in the wild—but the tiger shark may well be" (para. 12). The word *salvageable* could be replaced by ______________
   a. abandoned.
   b. deplorable.
   c. able to be rescued.
   d. extinct.

8. "I fervently believe that our best partner in saving the ocean is the ocean itself" (para. 13). Which of the following best paraphrases Stephen R. Palumbi's statement?
   a. The ocean has many partners including humans and other animal species.
   b. Food supply is limited across the ocean.
   c. Threatened species can recover in other ocean regions.
   d. There is no hope for the future of the world's oceans.

9. "Marine species are not **immune** to extinction on a large scale" (para 9). A synonym for the word *immune* in the above sentence is ______________.
   a. endangered.
   b. protected.
   c. escaped.
   d. destructive.
10. The author of this article would most likely agree that
    a. There is still plenty of time to find solutions to the long-term effects of ocean dumping.
    b. Only professionals working in the field of conservation biology should be concerned about the devastation of ocean species.
    c. It is far too costly to invest in ocean conservation.
    d. A large-scale effort of ocean conservation is absolutely necessary.

READING 2

Newspaper Article

MyReadingLab

Visit Chapter 4: Environmental Science in MyReadingLab to complete the Reading 2 activities.

To Fight Global Warming, Some Hang a Clothesline

Pre-Reading Questions

Answer the following questions in small groups.

1. Have you ever hung laundry outside to dry? Do you think there are any advantages to doing this instead of throwing your clothes in a dryer?
2. Is the latest, up-to-date technology always better than what we used in the past? For example, do you think modern-day cell phones are an improvement over rotary phones? Consider other technologies.
3. Would you be willing to sacrifice your state-of-the-art premium dryer for the sake of a cleaner environment? Explain.

To Fight Global Warming, Some Hang a Clothesline

By Kathleen A. Hughes, *New York Times*
April 12, 2007

1 As a child, I helped my mother hang laundry in our backyard in Tamaqua, Pa., a small coal mining town. My job was handing up the clothespins. When everything was dry, I helped her fold the sheets in a series of moves that resembled ballroom dancing.

2 The clothes and linens always smelled so fresh. Everything about the laundry was fun. My brother and I played hide-and-seek in the rows of billowing white sheets.

3 I remember this as I'm studying energy-saving tips from Al Gore, who says that when you have time, you should use a clothesline to dry your clothes instead of the dryer.

4 A clothesline. It **strikes me** that I haven't seen one since 1991, when I moved to Rolling Hills, Calif., a gated community about an hour south of Los Angeles. There are rolling hills, ranch houses, sweeping views of the ocean and rocky cliffs—plenty of room—but not a single visible clothesline.

strikes me
to come to the realization/to understand

5 I decide **to rig** a clothesline as an experiment. My mother died many years ago and the idea of hanging laundry with my own daughter, Isabel, who is 13 and always busy at the computer, is oddly appealing. I'm also hoping to use less energy and to reduce our monthly electric bills, which hit the absurdly high level of $1,120 last summer.

to rig
to arrange something so that it will do something in a particular way

6 That simple decision to hang a clothesline, however, catapults me into the laundry underground. Clotheslines are banned or restricted by many of the roughly 300,000 homeowners' associations that set rules for some 60 million people. When I called to ask, our Rolling Hills Community Association told me that my laundry had to be completely hidden in an enclosure approved by its board of directors.

7 I briefly considered hanging our laundry in the front yard, just to see what would happen, but my family vetoed this idea. Instead, I settled on stringing two lines in a corner of the backyard, a spot not visible to neighbors or officials. I'm supposed to submit a site plan of our property and a photograph of my laundry enclosure. But I don't have an enclosure, unless the hedge qualifies.

8 Looking for fellow clothesline fans, I came across the Web **site** of Alexander Lee, a lawyer and 32-year-old clothesline activist in Concord, N.H. In 1995 Mr. Lee founded Project Laundry List, a non-profit organization, as a way to champion "the right to dry." His Web site, laundrylist.org, is an encyclopedia on the energy advantages of hanging laundry.

9 Mr. Lee sponsors an annual National Hanging Out Day on April 19. He plans to string a clothesline at the State House in Concord, N.H., this Saturday as part of a Step It Up 2007 rally on climate change, where he will hang T-shirts and sheets with the slogan "Hang Your Pants. Stop the Plants."

10 Inspired, I moved forward with my project without submitting the **site** plan and photograph for approval. My daughter agreed to help me hang the first load.

11 "It looks beautiful," she said when we stepped back. "It looks like we care about the earth."

12 The experiment was off to a good start. The first load dried in less than three hours. The clothes smelled like fresh air and wind. As we took them down, the birds were chirping and the sun was shining.

13 But there was a downside. "The towels are like sandpaper," said my husband, Dan, after stepping out of the shower.

14 Not only that. Heading outside to the clothesline and hanging each load takes about 7 minutes—6 minutes and 30 seconds longer than it takes to stuff everything into the dryer.

15 As the months rolled by, no one from the community association complained. Of course, since the clotheslines are in a lowered corner of the backyard surrounded by hedges, they cannot be seen from the street, the neighbors' houses or even our own house. But the rope lines started to sag, allowing the sheets and heavy wet towels to drag in the dirt. The wooden clothespins soon became weathered and fell apart.

16 Meanwhile, my daughter lost interest after the first load, **dashing my hope** of recreating the happy times I spent hanging clothes with my own mother.

dashing my hope erasing hope

17 I briefly gave up—the dryer was so much easier—but then tried again. I bought stronger lines, plastic instead of rope, and switched to plastic clothespins. I also learned that tossing the clothes in the dryer for just a few minutes after they have dried on the line makes them softer.

18 Everyone now seems happy enough with the fresh smelling laundry, which is just slightly stiff. Of course, I still haven't asked our local board of directors for approval. If they object, I could be forced to take my laundry down or build an enclosure, an inconvenient confrontation I'm simply avoiding. In the meantime, our electric bill has dropped to $576 in March from its high last summer, reflecting a series of efforts to cut energy. (That's still too high, so we're about to try fluorescent bulbs.)

19 There were more than 88 million dryers in the country in 2005, the latest count, according to the Association of Home Appliance Manufacturers. If all Americans line-dried for just half a year, it would save 3.3% of the country's total residential output of carbon dioxide, experts say.

20 "It's a huge waste of energy to tumble dry your clothes," said Tom Arnold, chief environmental officer of TerraPass, a San Francisco company that sells carbon offsets, which aim to reduce **greenhouse gases** to compensate for one's activities. "It's one of the simplest things to do to help with global warming."

greenhouse gases those, especially carbon dioxide or methane, that trap heat above the earth and cause the greenhouse effect

21 The laundry underground is a mixed group. It includes the frugal, people without dryers, and people from countries where hanging laundry is part of the culture. Many people hang a few delicate items. Tim Eames, a British designer who lives in Los Angeles, does not own a dryer. "The thought of getting a machine to do something as simple as drying my laundry is totally inconceivable," he said.

22 For those in colder climates, going without a dryer can be a challenge. Tom Stokes, a global warming activist in Stockbridge, Mass., managed to fit six clotheslines in a large downstairs bathroom, and he now hangs all of his laundry there in the winter. "It's relatively easy in the summer. It takes more determination to string up a line and hang laundry year round," he says.

23 Indeed, Annalisa Parent, a photographer who grew up in New Hampshire, said that when she was a child, her family hung all their laundry outside, even in the snow. Her father, an engineer, built a one-of-a-kind clothesline with an arched roof above it. She recalls standing her frozen jeans on the furnace to thaw them before school and wishing that her family could be like the families with dryers.

24 Now, at 32, she still doesn't own a dryer. She hangs all of her laundry inside her town house in South Burlington, Vt. Ms. Parent says she was inspired to see "the beauty in a clothesline" by Mr. Lee, a friend from college. She has taken more than 500 photographs of clotheslines and her work, featured on his Web site, shows clotheslines by the sea, clotheslines in Romania and even close-ups of clothespins.

25 In Hollywood movies, however, clotheslines often appear in scenes depicting dire poverty. Jennifer Williams, a set decorator, says she hung clotheslines to help convey that in the films "Angela's Ashes," "Children of Men" and "Pearl Harbor."

26 That image could limit the comeback of the clothesline. "People see laundry as an ugly flag of poverty," said Mr. Lee. "It's a reminder to some people of where they grew up." For me, that was Tamaqua, Pa., where my father worked for a company that made explosives for the mines. Clotheslines are still popular in Tamaqua, where the average home price is $64,400. Linda Yulanavage, head of the local Chamber of Commerce, says more than half of the town's 11,000 residents use clotheslines because they like the smell of fresh air in their laundry and because it saves energy. "People see it as a normal, everyday thing to see clothes hanging on the line," she says. "It gives a homey, close neighborhood feeling."

27 I completely agree, although I seem to have the only clothesline in Rolling Hills. Maybe others will join. Meanwhile, my **carbon footprint** is shrinking and our clothes smell like the great outdoors.

carbon footprint the amount of harmful carbon dioxide that a person, company, industry, etc. produces when doing normal activities, such as driving a car, heating a building, or producing goods

Reading with a Critical Eye

In a small group, discuss the following reflection questions, which will guide you toward a deeper understanding of the reading.

1. What is the author's first memory of hanging clothing outside? How can a strong first memory affect the way you feel about a particular subject?
2. In paragraph 4, the author explains that she hasn't seen one clothesline in the sixteen years she had been living in Southern California. Why do you think this was the case?

3. Why does the author include the detail, in paragraph 5, that her daughter Isabel is "always busy on the computer"?
4. How does the author connect with a fellow clothesline fan? What does the author learn about Alexander Lee?
5. In the end, how does the author's daughter react to her mother's clothes-hanging adventure (para. 16)? Do you think hanging clothes out to dry will come back into fashion for your generation? Explain.

Reading Comprehension Check

1. What does the author compare ballroom dancing with?
   a. hanging the laundry
   b. her movements folding sheets
   c. her mother's footsteps
   d. the feeling of her backyard
2. The word *billow* in the second paragraph ("My brother and I played hide-and-seek in the rows of *billowing* white sheets.") could be replaced by
   a. dirty.
   b. endless.
   c. fluttering.
   d. descending.
3. What is the main idea of paragraph 4?
   a. Hanging clothes is fashionable.
   b. The author misses hanging clothes.
   c. There are no clotheslines in the author's gated community.
   d. The author thinks hanging clothes is fresher than using a machine.
4. Which reason is *not* given for why the author wanted to try using a clothesline?
   a. It could save her money.
   b. It could save energy.
   c. She wanted to show off to her neighbors.
   d. She is sentimental about sharing her mother's tradition with her daughter.
5. In the first sentence of paragraph 6, "That simple decision to hang a clothesline, however, *catapults* me into the laundry underground," a synonym for the word *catapults* could be
   a. considers.
   b. deceives.
   c. hurls.
   d. promotes.
6. What is Alexander Lee's relation to the author?
   a. He is her brother.
   b. He is her leader.
   c. He is against her plan.
   d. He is an inspiration for her to hang her clothes out to dry.
7. What is the main point made by Tom Arnold, chief environmental officer of TerraPass?
   a. Using a clothesline is an easy way to help the environment.
   b. Using a clothesline is the main solution to global warming.

c. It's fine to use a dryer when you really need to.
d. A lot of what we do wastes energy.

8. The word *inconceivable,* as used in paragraph 21 in the sentence "The thought of getting a machine to do something as simple as drying my laundry is totally inconceivable," could be replaced by
a. realistic. c. thoughtless.
b. unimaginable. d. durable.

9. According to the author, how are clotheslines depicted in Hollywood movies?
a. as inconvenient c. as attractive
b. as a sign of poverty d. as environmentally sensitive

10. In the last paragraph, the author completely agrees with which of the following statements?
a. Hanging laundry is worth the effort.
b. Hanging laundry is an ugly flag of poverty.
c. Hanging clothes makes her neighborhood feel more like home.
d. There are advantages and disadvantages to hanging laundry.

BIOGRAPHICAL PROFILE

Chico Mendes

Francisco Alves Mendes Filho Cena, better known as Chico Mendes, was a Brazilian environmentalist, a rubber tapper, and a trade union leader. He fought to **preserve** the Amazon rainforest and became internationally famous when he was murdered at the age of 44 by an enemy of his movement.

Mendes followed a path set by generations of his family. He made his living harvesting sap from rubber trees. As a child, he also supported himself and his family by gathering and selling nuts and fruit from the rainforest. As he grew up, Mendes witnessed the depletion of the rainforest as many Brazilians, attempting to make large short-term profits, chopped down vast sections of trees in an effort to convert forest lands to cattle pastures.

The first meeting of Mendes's union, the National Council of Rubber Tappers, was held in the capital, Brasilia, in 1985, and rubber tappers from all over Brazil came. Many of these rural peasants had never been outside their local area before. Mendes spent his energies educating tappers about the issues of deforestation, road paving, and the threats these posed to their own livelihoods. The meeting gained the attention of the international environmental movement and the media.

In 1987, Mendes flew to India in an attempt to convince the Inter-American Development Bank that a huge road project they were planning to build in his area would end in disaster. Mendes urged the organization to focus on protecting the forest and the livelihoods of its inhabitants. He triumphed, with the project first being postponed, and then renegotiated under more environmentally friendly conditions. He won two international environmental awards for this action.

On the evening of December 22, 1988, exactly one week after his 44th birthday, Chico Mendes was assassinated by gunshot at his home. Thanks in part to the international media attention surrounding the murder, the Chico Mendes Extractive Reserve was created in the area where he lived. There are more than 20 such preserves now, along the same lines as Mendes had proposed, covering more than eight million acres. His memory is preserved in the powerful "save the Brazilian rainforest movement" that still struggles forward today.

At first, I thought I was fighting to save rubber trees, then I thought I was fighting to save the Amazon rainforest. Now I realize I am fighting for humanity.
—Chico Mendes

(continued)

BIOGRAPHICAL PROFILE *(continued)*

Some Questions for Group Discussion

1. Read Mendes's quote at the end of the reading. What is his main point?
2. Mendes is a symbol to many of the little guy who takes on the big guy and wins. What do you think were the secrets of his success?
3. If there is money to be made, both large international corporations and small local farmers will continue to contribute to the destruction of the Amazon rainforest. Is the death of the rainforest inevitable, or can it be saved?

Biographical Internet Research

Research another great figure in Environmental Studies, taken from the list below, and share a biographical profile with your fellow students:

- Rachel Carson
- Jane Goodall
- John James Audubon
- Lisa Jackson
- Al Gore

SKILL FOCUS: Identifying Supporting Details

Supporting details are a key element in a reading passage because they provide additional information to explain, illustrate, or prove the main idea of a particular paragraph. Supporting details answer the questions readers naturally formulate as they interact with a given text. Imagine you are reading a textbook paragraph and the first sentence is "When winter arrives, the Alaskan grizzly must adapt to this harsh, new environment." Clearly, this is the main point of the paragraph. The reader then predicts how the paragraph will follow—in other words, what supporting details the paragraph will consist of—by formulating questions.

Main idea: *When winter arrives, the Alaskan grizzly must adapt to this harsh, new environment.*

Questions: How/In what particular ways does the Alaskan grizzly adapt to winter?

What are some characteristics of a harsh Alaskan winter?

Following through with the full paragraph, the reader's questions are answered.

When winter arrives, the Alaskan grizzly must adapt to this harsh, new environment. Temperatures in the Alaskan plains often dip to –30° F and winds can be very strong. The grizzly adapts first through bodily change, putting on as many as one hundred extra pounds through a heavy autumn eating season. In the heart of the winter, grizzlies hibernate to maintain a healthy body temperature.

Types of Supporting Details

Supporting details most often come in the form of:

- Characteristics (Three characteristics of gene mutation are ...)
- Steps (First, the kangaroo emerges from its hiding place. Then, it ...)
- Examples (Another example of dyslexic behavior is ...)
- Reasons (These religions are often in conflict because ...)
- Results (A consequence of this action is that the night owl ...)
- Descriptions (Sharp, rocky coasts contrast with the smooth blue Aegean Sea.)
- Dates (The battles that occurred in the winter of 1943 and summer of 1944 were critical.)
- Places (Some cities with high rates of violence include Washington, Miami, and Detroit.)
- Names (Such leaders as Franklin, Washington, and Hamilton are most remembered from this period.)
- Statistics (Americans consume nearly a quarter of the world's energy supply.)

Let's practice predicting supporting details by trying to formulate questions from main idea sentences related to our chapter theme.

EXERCISE 4.6 Predicting Supporting Details

Work with a partner to formulate who/what/why/where/how questions about the main ideas offered. The first one has been done for you.

1. **Main Idea:** The president's proposal to drill for oil in Alaska has been defeated by Congress.

   Questions: **a.** Why did Congress reject the president's proposal?
   b. What prompted the president to offer this proposal?
   c. What were the exact details of the drill-for-oil project?

2. **Main Idea:** A basic law of thermodynamics is that energy is never completely efficient.

   Questions: **a.** ______________________________
   b. ______________________________

3. **Main Idea:** In the 1940s, the properties of the new insecticide DDT seemed close to miraculous.

Questions: a. ______________________________

b. ______________________________

c. ______________________________

____

4. **Main Idea:** Chains of carbon atoms form the framework of all organic molecules, the building blocks of life.

Questions: a. ______________________________

b. ______________________________

5. **Main Idea:** Many of the environmental problems that plague modern society have resulted from human interference in ecosystem function.

Questions: a. ______________________________

b. ______________________________

c. ______________________________

d. ______________________________

6. **Main Idea:** Many scientists believe that global warming is already affecting our ecosystem.

Questions: a. ______________________________

____

b. ______________________________

c. ______________________________

____

Major and Minor Details

Read the following example paragraph and highlight the main idea.

> Tap water is not without its problems. In 2005, the nonprofit Environmental Working Group (EWG) tested municipal water in 42 states and detected some 260 contaminants in public water supplies. Of those, 141 were unregulated chemicals for which public health officials have no safety standards, much less methods for removing them. Even the more controlled contaminants pose a safety threat.

Supporting details are used by a writer to explain, illustrate, or prove a **main idea** of a particular paragraph. So, for example, in the above passage, if the main focus of the paragraph is spelled out in the first sentence (*"Tap water is not without its problems"*), a **supporting detail** could explain *how* we know that tap water can have problems.

Supporting Detail: *In 2005, the nonprofit Environmental Working Group (EWG) tested municipal water in 42 states and detected some 260 contaminants in public water supplies.*

This kind of detail is known as a **major detail** because it directly supports the **main idea**.

The paragraph continues by explaining more about the **major detail** (What do we know about these contaminants?).

"Of those, 141 were unregulated chemicals for which public health officials have no safety standards, much less methods for removing them."

The above sentence represents the first **minor detail** because minor details explain and support **major details**. This is followed by another **minor detail**:

Even the more controlled contaminants pose a safety threat.

This relationship between **main point** and **major and minor details** is diagrammed below.

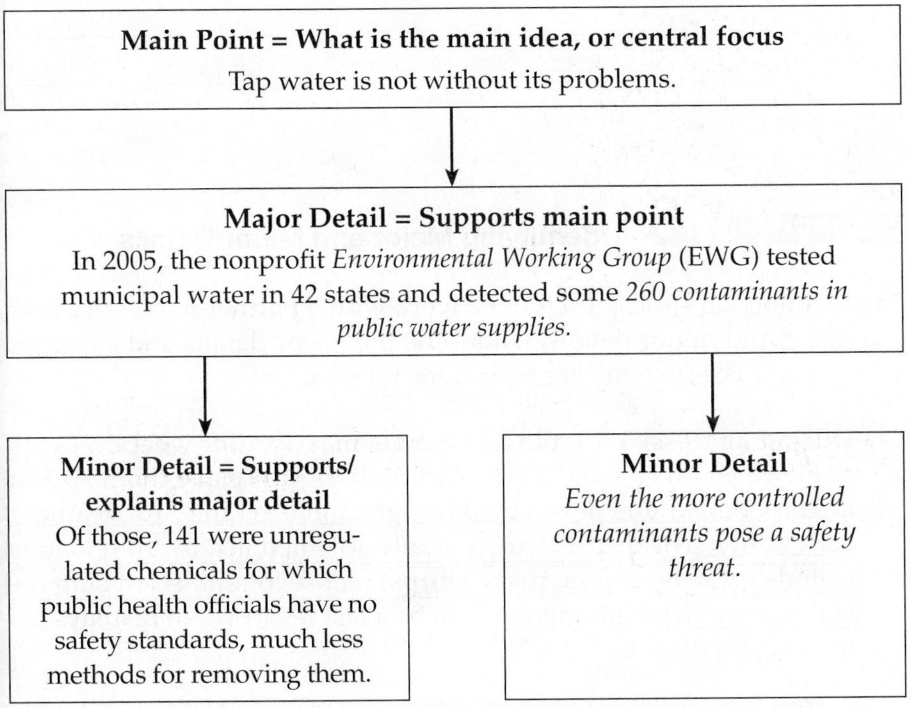

Main Point = What is the main idea, or central focus
Tap water is not without its problems.

↓

Major Detail = Supports main point
In 2005, the nonprofit *Environmental Working Group* (EWG) tested municipal water in 42 states and detected some 260 *contaminants in public water supplies.*

↓ ↓

Minor Detail = Supports/ explains major detail	**Minor Detail**
Of those, 141 were unregulated chemicals for which public health officials have no safety standards, much less methods for removing them.	*Even the more controlled contaminants pose a safety threat.*

EXERCISE 4.7 Predicting Supporting Details

With a partner, imagine some logical details that follow from the main point and the major detail offered below. Turn the questions you might have into statements, providing the minor details in the table below.

Main Point
The rising price of gasoline has caused the government to look for renewable sources of energy.

Major Detail
These renewable sources of energy may pose some risks to the environment.

Minor Detail	Minor Detail
________________	________________
________________	________________
________________	________________

EXERCISE 4.8 Identifying Major and Minor Details

In the following short paragraphs, work with a partner to identify both the major and minor details. Underline the major details and circle the minor ones. The first one has been done for you.

1. During aggressive displays, animals may exhibit weapons such as claws and fangs and they often do things to make them appear larger. Competitors often stand upright and erect their fur, feathers, ears, or fins. The displays are typically accompanied by intimidating sounds (growls, croaks, roars, chirps) whose loudness can help decide the winner. Fighting tends to be a last resort when displays fail to resolve a dispute.

2. In addition to observing natural selection in the wild, scientists have also devised numerous experiments that confirm the action of natural selection. For example, one group of evolutionary biologists

released small groups of *Anolis sagrei* lizards onto fourteen small Bahamian islands that were previously uninhabited by lizards. The original lizards came from a population on Staniel Cay, an island with tall vegetation, including plenty of trees. In contrast, the islands to which the small colonial groups were introduced had few or no trees and were covered mainly with small shrubs and other low-growing plants.

(From *Biology: Life on Earth*, p. 291)

3. The scientific name of an organism is formed from the two smallest categories, the genus and the species. Each genus includes a group of closely related species, and each species within a genus includes populations of organisms that can potentially interbreed under natural conditions. Thus, the genus *Sialia* (bluebirds) includes the eastern bluebird (*Sialia sialis*), the western bluebird (*Sialia mexicana*), and the mountain bluebird (*Sialia currucoides*)—very similar birds that normally do not interbreed.

(From *Biology: Life on Earth*, p. 358)

4. Chemical reactions fall into two categories. In exergonic reactions, the re-actant molecules have more energy than do the product molecules, so the reaction releases energy. In endergonic reactions, the reactants have less energy than do the products, so the reaction requires an input of energy. Exergonic reactions can occur spontaneously; but all reactions, including exergonic ones, require an initial input of energy to overcome electrical repulsions between reactant molecules.

(From *Biology: Life on Earth*, p. 114)

5. Paleontologists (scientists who study fossils) have cataloged the extinction of approximately 70 percent of all living species by the disappearance of their fossils at the end of the Cretaceous Period. In sites from around the globe, researchers have found a thin layer of clay deposited around 65 million years ago; the clay has about 30 times the typical levels of a rare element called iridium, which is found in high concentrations in some meteorites.

(From *Biology: Life on Earth*, p. 130)

EXERCISE 4.9 More Practice with Supporting Details

The following excerpts are taken from an introductory biology text. Read the following paragraphs carefully and answer the multiple-choice questions that follow, by circling the letter of the correct answer. Remember to apply the skills you learned earlier to identify the major and minor details supporting the main idea.

Passage 1

Biodiversity refers to the total number of species within an ecosystem and the resulting complexity of interactions among them; in short, it defines the biological "richness" of an ecosystem. Rain forests have the highest biodiversity of any ecosystem on Earth. Although rain forests cover only 6% of Earth's total land area, ecologists estimate that they are home to between 5 million and 8 million species, representing half to two-thirds of the world's total. For example, a recent survey of a 2.5 acre site in the upper Amazon basin revealed 283 different species of trees, most of which were represented by a single individual. In a 3-square-mile (about 5-square-kilometer) tract of rain forest in Peru, scientists counted more than 1300 butterfly species and 600 bird species. For comparison, the entire U.S. is home to only 400 butterfly and 700 bird species.

(From *Biology: Life on Earth*, p. 588)

1. The main idea of the passage is
   a. there are 400 butterflies and 700 birds in the United States.
   b. the Amazon basin has 283 tree species.
   c. the rich flora and fauna of an ecosystem is called biodiversity.
   d. rainforests have approximately 8 million species.

2. The first major detail presented in the passage is which of the following?
   a. A survey of a large area in the Amazon basin was recently conducted.
   b. Rainforests cover 6% of Earth's land area.
   c. Scientists found 1300 butterflies and 600 birds in Peru.
   d. The highest biodiversity is found in the rainforests.

3. Which of the following is a minor detail?
   a. Biodiversity refers to the complex interactions between plants and animals in an ecosystem.
   b. Biodiversity is a term used to define the richness of an ecosystem.
   c. The Amazon basin has 283 different species of trees.
   d. Rainforests have the highest biodiversity of an ecosystem.

Passage 2

Because of infertile soil and heavy rains, agriculture is risky and destructive in rain forests. If the trees are carried away for lumber, few nutrients remain to support crops. If the nutrients are released to the soil by burning the natural vegetation, the heavy year-round rainfall quickly dissolves and **erodes** them away, leaving the soil depleted after only a few seasons of cultivation. The exposed soil, which is rich in iron and aluminum, then takes on an impenetrable, bricklike quality as it bakes in the tropical sun. As a result, secondary succession on cleared rain-forest land is slow; even small forest cuttings take about 70 years to regenerate. Despite their unsuitability for agriculture, rain forests are being felled for lumber or burned down for ranching or farming at an alarming rate. The demand for biofuels (fuels produced from biomass, including palm and soybean oil) is driving rapid destruction of rain forests to grow these crops. Estimates of rain-forest destruction range up to 65,000 square miles (42 million acres, or about 170,000 square kilometers) per year, or about 1.3 acres each second. In recent years Brazil alone has lost about 10,000 square miles (6000 square kilometers) annually. For comparison, the state of Connecticut occupies about 5000 square miles.

(From *Biology: Life on Earth*, pp. 589–590)

1. Which of the following is the main idea of the passage?
a. Agriculture can thrive in rainforests.
b. Heavy rains have caused a boom in Brazil's agricultural growth.
c. Rain forests are unsuitable for agriculture.
d. Infertile soil helps the natural vegetation to grow rapidly.

2. According to the passage, which of the following statements is not true?
a. Deforestation deprives the soil of its rich nutrients.
b. Heavy rains deplete the soil.
c. Humans' cutting down rain forests for lumber and farming is a cause for concern.
d. Brazil has lost approximately 10,000 square miles of rain forests annually.

3. According to the passage, biofuels
a. have sparked an interest in protecting rain forests.
b. are not in demand at all.
c. have saved 42 million acres of rain forests.
d. have accelerated deforestation.

Passage 3

Although they are as diverse as terrestrial ecosystems, aquatic ecosystems share three general features. First, because water is slower to heat and cool than air, temperatures in aquatic ecosystems are more moderate than those in terrestrial ecosystems. Second, water absorbs light; even in very clear water, below 650 feet (200 meters) little light is left to power photosynthesis. Suspended sediment (nonliving particles carried by moving water) or microorganisms greatly reduce light penetration. Finally, nutrients in aquatic ecosystems tend to be concentrated near the bottom sediments, so where nutrients are highest, the light levels are lowest. Of the four requirements for life, aquatic ecosystems provide abundant water and appropriate temperatures. Thus, the availability of energy and nutrients largely determines the quantity of life and the distribution of life in aquatic ecosystems.

(From *Biology: Life on Earth*, p. 598)

1. Which of the following sentences best states the main idea of the passage?
   a. Terrestrial ecosystems are incredibly diverse.
   b. Energy and nutrients influence the quantity of life in aquatic ecosystems.
   c. Three characteristics distinguish aquatic ecosystems from terrestrial ecosystems.
   d. Water absorbs light in clear water.
2. The first major detail is
   a. the diversity of terrestrial ecosystems.
   b. three general features of aquatic ecosystems.
   c. that water is slower to heat.
   d. that aquatic ecosystems have lower temperatures than terrestrial ecosystems do.
3. The second major detail discussed by the author is that
   a. aquatic ecosystems have insufficient light for photosynthesis.
   b. aquatic ecosystems have moderate temperatures.
   c. there are four requirements for life in aquatic ecosystems.
   d. water is cooler than air.
4. The third major detail that the author discusses is
   a. microorganisms greatly reduce light penetration.
   b. photosynthesis does not occur in aquatic ecosystems.
   c. aquatic ecosystems contain nutrients near the bottom.
   d. aquatic ecosystems provide plenty of water and appropriate temperatures.
5. Which of the following is not a major detail?
   a. Aquatic ecosystems have three general features.
   b. It is difficult to power photosynthesis in aquatic ecosystems.
   c. Nutrients are found near the bottom sediments in aquatic ecosystems.
   d. Nonliving particles reduce light penetration.

The next reading allows you to apply the skills you have just learned.

READING 3

Online Article

MyReadingLab

Visit Chapter 4: Environmental Science in MyReadingLab to complete the Reading 3 activities.

Climate Change: What You Can Do at Home

Pre-Reading Questions

1. What are five things you can do at home to reduce climate change?
2. Do you ever leave the lights on when you leave your home? What about the air conditioning? Why do you think so many people (perhaps not yourself) waste energy every day?
3. Why do humans tend not to think about the future and the preservation of our natural resources for future generations?

Climate Change: What You Can Do at Home

By **The Environmental Protection Agency (EPA)**

The water you save every year by purchasing a new ENERGY STAR qualified clothes washer instead of a new non-qualified model is enough to do 300 loads of laundry.

Making a few small changes in your home and yard can reduce greenhouse gases and save you money. Explore our list of 10 simple steps you can take to reduce greenhouse gas emissions:

1. Change five lights

Replace your five most frequently used light fixtures or the light bulbs in them with ENERGY STAR® qualified products and you will help the environment while saving $70 a year on energy bills. ENERGY STAR lighting provides bright, warm light; generates 75% less heat; uses about 75% less energy than standard lighting; and lasts from 10 to 50 times longer.

2. Look for ENERGY STAR

When buying new products for your home, look for EPA's ENERGY STAR label to help you make the most energy-efficient decision. You can find the ENERGY STAR label on more than 60 kinds of products, including appliances, lighting, heating and cooling equipment, electronics, and office equipment. Over their lifetime, products in your home that have earned the ENERGY STAR label can reduce greenhouse gas emissions by about 130,000 pounds and save you $11,000 on energy bills.

3. Heat and cool smartly

Heating and cooling accounts for almost half your energy bill—about $1,000 a year! There is a lot you can do to drive down this cost. Simple steps like changing air filters regularly, properly using a programmable thermostat, and having your heating and cooling equipment maintained annually by a licensed contractor can save energy and increase comfort, while helping to protect the environment. Depending on where you live, you can cut your annual energy bill by more than $200 by replacing your old heating and cooling equipment with ENERGY STAR-qualified equipment.

4. Seal and insulate your home

Reduce air leaks and stop drafts by using caulk, weather stripping, and insulation to seal your home's envelope and add more insulation to your attic to block out heat and cold. A knowledgeable homeowner or skilled contractor can save up to 20% on heating and cooling costs and significantly enhance home comfort with comprehensive sealing and insulating measures.

5. Reduce, reuse, recycle

Reducing, reusing, and recycling in your home helps conserve energy and reduces pollution and greenhouse gas emissions from resource extraction, manufacturing, and disposal. If there is a recycling program in your community, recycle your newspapers, beverage containers, paper, and other goods. Also, composting your food and yard waste reduces the amount of garbage that you send to landfills and reduces greenhouse gas emissions. Visit EPA's Individual Waste Reduction Model (iWARM) to learn about the energy benefits of recycling, rather than landfilling, common waste products.

6. Use water efficiently

It takes lots of energy to pump, treat, and heat water, so saving water reduces greenhouse gas emissions. Saving water around the home is simple. Three percent of the nation's energy is used to pump and treat water so conserving water conserves energy that reduces greenhouse gas pollution. Reduce the amount of waste you generate and the water you consume whenever possible. Pursue simple water-saving actions such as not letting the water run while shaving or brushing teeth and save money while conserving water by using products with the WaterSense label. Did you know a leaky toilet can waste 200 gallons of water per day? Repair all toilet and faucet leaks right away. Running your dishwasher only with a full load can save 100 pounds of carbon dioxide and $40 per year. Be smart when irrigating your lawn or landscape. Only water when needed, and do it during the coolest part of the day; early morning is best. See EPA's WaterSense site for more water saving tips.

7. Be green in your yard

Composting your food and yard waste reduces the amount of garbage that you send to landfills and reduces greenhouse gas emissions. EPA's GreenScapes program provides tips on how to improve your lawn or garden while also helping the environment.

8. Purchase green power

Power your home by purchasing green power. Green power is environmentally friendly electricity that is generated from renewable energy sources such as wind and the sun. There are two ways to use green power: You can buy green power, or you can modify your house to generate your own green power. Buying green power is easy. It offers a number of environmental and economic benefits over conventional electricity, including lower greenhouse gas emissions, and it helps increase clean energy supply. There are a number of steps you can take to create a greener home, including installing solar panels and researching incentives for renewable energy in your state.

9. Calculate your household's carbon footprint

Use EPA's Household Carbon Footprint Calculator to estimate your household greenhouse gas emissions resulting from energy use, transportation, and waste disposal. This tool helps you understand where your emissions come from and identify ways to reduce them.

10. Spread the word

Tell family and friends that energy efficiency is good for their homes and good for the environment because it lowers greenhouse gas emissions and air pollution. Tell five people and together we can help our homes help us all.

Reading with a Critical Eye

In a small group, discuss the following reflection questions, which will guide you toward a deeper understanding of the reading.

1. Examine the list. In your view, which of the items on the list would involve the greatest sacrifice on your part? Which would involve the least sacrifice? Explain.
2. Thinking about item #1 on the list, why do you think many Americans are reluctant to move away from traditional light bulb usage even though ENERGY STAR lighting is cheaper and generates less heat?
3. Item #6 focuses on Americans wasting too much water every day. What are the disadvantages, if any, of wasting water during showers and brushing teeth and for washing clothes?
4. The last item suggests that it would be helpful to encourage others to conserve energy. How do you think your close friends and family would react if you gave them this advice? Explain.
5. Reviewing the list of ten items again, are there any other things we can do to help the environment that are missing from the list? Explain.

Reading Comprehension Check

1. In item #2, we read: "When buying new products for your home, look for EPA's ENERGY STAR label to help you make the most energy-efficient decision." This is an example of:
   a. a main idea.
   b. a topic.
   c. a major detail.
   d. a theme.
2. "Running your dishwasher only with a full load can save 100 pounds of carbon dioxide and $40 per year." This detail supports which main point?
   a. Buy energy-efficient products.
   b. Saving water reduces greenhouse emissions.
   c. Use less heat and air conditioning.
   d. Encourage others to conserve energy.
3. Which is a supporting detail for the idea of changing light bulbs?
   a. You will help the environment while saving $70 a year on energy bills.
   b. People need to think twice before keeping all the lights on in their homes.

c. ENERGY STAR lighting uses about 75% less energy than standard lighting and lasts from 10 to 50 times longer.
d. both a and c

4. Which is an example of a supporting detail for "Heat and Cool Smartly"?
a. It is also a good idea to turn off the water when you are not using it.
b. Avoid products that come with excess packaging.
c. You can save more than $200 by using ENERGY STAR –qualified equipment for heating and cooling.
d. Do your laundry every other week.

5. Examine #2: "Look for ENERGY STAR." Which sentence is an example of a minor detail?
a. ENERGY STAR products can reduce greenhouse emissions by 130,000 pounds and save $11,000 on energy bills.
b. When buying products for your home, look for the ENERGY STAR label.
c. Make the most energy-efficient decision.
d. Contact the Environmental Protection Agency to learn about ENERGY STAR lighting.

Recommended Debate Topic: Should the government place stricter controls on energy consumption?

Brainstorm other debate topics related to global warming with your peers, and present your ideas to your instructor for approval.

Your suggested debate topics:

a. ______________________________

b. ______________________________

c. ______________________________

The following article will help prepare you for the debate activity by offering a counterargument to the more popular environmentalist position.

READING 4

Newspaper Editorial

MyReadingLab

Visit Chapter 4: Environmental Science in MyReadingLab to complete the Reading 4 activities.

My Nobel Moment

Pre-Reading Questions

Discuss these with a small group of classmates.

1. It is never easy to defend a position/idea that goes against what most people believe. Why is it important for someone to do so? What type of person is willing to argue against the majority view?

2. If global warming is a myth, how else can glacial meltdowns, animal extinctions, and rising temperatures be explained?
3. Some critics argue that the government has denied the phenomenon of global warming and finds experts to side with their view mostly because they don't want to pay the high cost of remedying the problem. Would you agree that past governments have played the role of "naysayer" on global warming for economic reasons, or might there be another explanation?

My Nobel Moment

By John R. Christy, ***Wall Street Journal***
November 1, 2007

John Christy is director of the Earth System Science Center at the University of Alabama in Huntsville, a participant in the UN's Intergovernmental Panel on Climate Change, and corecipient of the 2007 Nobel Peace Prize.

1 I've had a lot of fun recently with my tiny (and unofficial) slice of the 2007 Nobel Peace Prize awarded to the Intergovernmental Panel on Climate Change (IPCC). But, though I was one of thousands of IPCC participants, I don't think I will add "0.0001 Nobel Laureate" to my resume.

2 Both halves of the award honor promoting the message that Earth's temperature is rising due to human-based **emissions** of **greenhouse gases**. The Nobel committee praises Mr. Gore and the IPCC for alerting us to a **potential catastrophe** and for spurring us to a carbonless economy.

catastrophe
a sudden and widespread disaster

smoking gun
definite proof of who is responsible for something bad or how something really happened

mortals
relating to humankind

3 I'm sure the majority (but not all) of my IPCC colleagues cringe when I say this, but I see neither the developing catastrophe nor the **smoking gun** proving that human activity is to blame for most of the warming we see. Rather, I see a reliance on climate models (useful but never "proof") and the coincidence that changes in carbon dioxide and global temperatures have loose similarity over time.

4 There are some of us who remain so humbled by the task of measuring and understanding the extraordinarily complex climate system that we are skeptical of our ability to know what it is doing and why. As we build climate data sets from scratch and look into the guts of the climate system, however, we don't find the alarmist theory matching observations. (The National Oceanic and Atmospheric Administration satellite data we analyze at the University of Alabama in Huntsville does show modest warming—around 2.5 degrees Fahrenheit per century, if current warming trends of 0.25 degrees per decade continue.)

5 It is my turn to cringe when I hear overstated confidence from those who describe the projected evolution of global weather patterns over the next 100 years, especially when I consider how difficult it is to accurately predict that system's behavior over the next five days.

6 Mother Nature simply operates at a level of complexity that is, at this point, beyond the mastery of mere **mortals** (such as scientists) and the tools available to us. As my high-school physics teacher admonished us in those we-shall-conquer-the-world-with-a-slide-rule days, "Begin all of your scientific pronouncements with 'At our present level of ignorance, we think we know …' "

7 I haven't seen that type of climate humility lately. Rather I see jump-to-conclusions advocates and, unfortunately, some scientists who see in every weather anomaly the specter of a global-warming apocalypse. Explaining each successive phenomenon as a result of human action gives them comfort and an easy answer.

8 Others of us scratch our heads and try to understand the real causes behind what we see. We discount the possibility that *everything* is caused by human actions, because everything we've seen the climate do has happened before. Sea levels rise and fall continually. The Arctic ice cap has shrunk before. One millennium there are hippos swimming in the Thames, and a geological blink later there is an ice bridge linking Asia and North America.

9 One of the challenges in studying global climate is keeping a global perspective, especially when much of the research focuses on data gathered from spots around the globe. Often observations from one **region** get more attention than equally valid data from another.

10 The recent CNN report "Planet in Peril," for instance, spent considerable time discussing shrinking Arctic sea ice cover. CNN did *not* note that winter sea ice around Antarctica last month set a record maximum (yes, maximum) for coverage since aerial measurements started.

11 Then there is the challenge of translating global trends to local climate. For instance, hasn't global warming led to the five-year drought and fires in the U.S. Southwest?

12 Not necessarily.

13 There has been a drought, but **it would be a stretch** to link this drought to carbon dioxide. If you look at the 1,000-year climate record for the western U.S. you will see not five-year but 50-year-long droughts. The 12th and 13th centuries were particularly dry. The inconvenient truth is that the last century has been fairly benign in the American West. A return to the region's long-term "normal" climate would present huge challenges for urban planners.

it would be a stretch
it is probably not true, a logical leap

14 Without a doubt, atmospheric carbon dioxide is increasing due primarily to carbon-based energy production (with its undisputed benefits to humanity) and many people ardently believe we must "do something" about its alleged consequence, global warming. This might seem like a legitimate concern given the potential disasters that are announced almost daily, so I've looked at a couple of ways in which humans might reduce CO_2 emissions and their impact on temperatures.

15 California and some Northeastern states have decided to force their residents to buy cars that average 43 miles-per-gallon within the next decade. Even if you applied this law to the entire world, the net effect would reduce projected warming by about 0.05 degrees Fahrenheit by 2100, an amount so minuscule as to be undetectable. Global temperatures vary more than that from day to day.

16 Suppose you are very serious about **making a dent** in carbon emissions and could replace about 10% of the world's energy sources with non-CO_2-emitting nuclear power by 2020—roughly equivalent to halving U.S. emissions. Based on IPCC-like projections, the required 1,000 new nuclear power plants would slow the warming by about 0.2176 degrees Fahrenheit per century. It's a dent.

making a dent
having a modest effect

17 But what is the economic and human price, and what is it worth given the scientific uncertainty?

18 My experience as a missionary teacher in Africa opened my eyes to this simple fact: Without access to energy, life is brutal and short. The uncertain impacts of global warming far in the future must be weighed against disasters at our doorsteps today. Bjorn Lomborg's Copenhagen Consensus 2004, a cost-benefit analysis of health issues by leading economists (including three Nobelists), calculated that spending on health issues such as micronutrients for children, HIV/AIDS and water purification has benefits 50 to 200 times those of attempting to marginally limit "global warming."

19 Given the scientific uncertainty and our relative impotence regarding climate change, the moral imperative here seems clear to me.

Reading with a Critical Eye

In a small group, discuss the following reflection questions, which will guide you toward a deeper understanding of the reading.

1. In the fourth paragraph, Christy stresses one of his key points when he writes: "There are some of us who remain so humbled by the task of measuring and understanding the extraordinarily complex climate system that we are skeptical of our ability to know what it is doing and why." What is Christy trying to say here? Paraphrase his idea.
2. Analyze the following quotation from paragraph 6: "Mother Nature simply operates at a level of complexity that is, at this point, beyond the mastery of mere mortals (such as scientists) and the tools available to us."
3. What point is Christy making in quoting his high school teacher in paragraph 6? Do you agree with this philosophy? Explain.
4. In paragraph 8, what argument is Christy backing up in offering supporting details concerning the sea levels rising and falling, and the Arctic ice cap having shrunk before?
5. What did Christy learn about life from his missionary work in Africa? Do you agree with his idea? Explain.

Reading Comprehension Check

1. In the third paragraph, Christy argues that there is no evidence that
   a. humans are to blame for climate change.
   b. human life existed for as long as most scientists say.
   c. animal species are dying.
   d. Al Gore deserved an award.
2. Christy uses the example of how difficult it is to predict climate change over the next five days to prove
   a. that global warming has ample evidence on its side.
   b. how much more difficult it is to predict climate change over the next one hundred years.
   c. that most scientists haven't considered the patterns of climate change.
   d. both a and b
3. Christy mentions his high school physics teacher
   a. to show how wrong teachers can be.
   b. to illustrate the effects of global warming.
   c. as an example of someone who took a humble approach to scientific knowledge.
   d. as someone he learned a lot from.

4. Christy argues that many scientists
   a. are quick to jump to conclusions.
   b. look for easy answers to a complex problem.
   c. are not well educated.
   d. both a and b
5. Arctic ice caps shrinking and sea levels rising and falling are offered as examples of
   a. crises that need immediate attention.
   b. climate dipping.
   c. phenomena that have happened before.
   d. evidence of global warming.
6. Christy cites a maximum level of winter sea ice around Antarctica to make the point that
   a. the media ignores important evidence in the global warming story.
   b. global warming does not get enough media coverage.
   c. polar bears are in peril.
   d. none of the above
7. Christy argues that California's and some Northeastern states' forcing people to drive cars with high gas mileage
   a. will make a big difference in slowing global warming.
   b. will have little effect on climate change.
   c. makes a lot of sense.
   d. both b and c
8. Christy mentions his missionary teaching experience in Africa to make the point that
   a. limiting access to energy is important.
   b. access to energy makes a big difference in people's lives.
   c. we have to put climate control over the daily concerns of the earth's people.
   d. none of the above
9. Micronutrients for children, HIV/AIDS, and water purification are given as examples of
   a. life-threats due to global warming.
   b. exaggerated concerns.
   c. global concerns which are more important than climate control.
   d. UN issues.
10. What is the main idea of this editorial?
    a. Scientists should not exaggerate both the existence and the human causation of global warming.
    b. Global warming is a completely made-up phenomenon.
    c. Climate change needs our immediate attention.
    d. If we study the facts, we can see that climate change is happening faster than we expected.

READING 5

Poetry

MyReadingLab

Visit Chapter 4: Environmental Science in MyReadingLab to complete the Reading 5 activities.

"Meltwater" and "Give and Take"—Two Environmental Poems

Read the following poems and practice with the *identifying supporting details*–type questions that follow each of the poems.

Meltwater

***By* Maggie Butt, from *Feeling the Pressure: Poetry and Science of Climate Change*, ed. Paul Munden. Berne, Switzerland: British Council, 2008.**

my time is coming, smell it on the wind
watch raindrops winnowing down glass
touch ice-cube to your lips and tongue
feel the cool chemistry of meltwater.
see me submerge fields and swallow crops
spill out of wells to infiltrate your graves

raising the dead; firm ground will swamp
to ooze and squelch and slip, mud-symphony.
hear gurgles, trickles, runnels in your sleep
reach for the drifting flotsam of your dreams.
sweep river-sludge and sewage from the rug
swell my boundaries with your salt tears;
heave seas, wide breaths to rear up hills
waves come to claim their lost inheritance
listen to the future: rain-rocked, lake-like
nothing divides the waters from the waters.

Give and Take

***By* Roger McGough, from *Feeling the Pressure: Poetry and Science of Climate Change*, ed. Paul Munden.**

I give you clean air
You give me poisonous gas
I give you mountains
You give me quarries
I give you pure snow
You give me acid rain
I give you spring fountains

You give me toxic canals
I give you a butterfly
You give me a plastic bottle
I give you a blackbird
You give me a stealth bomber
I give you abundance
You give me waste
I give you one last chance
You give me excuse after excuse after excuse.

Reading with a Critical Eye

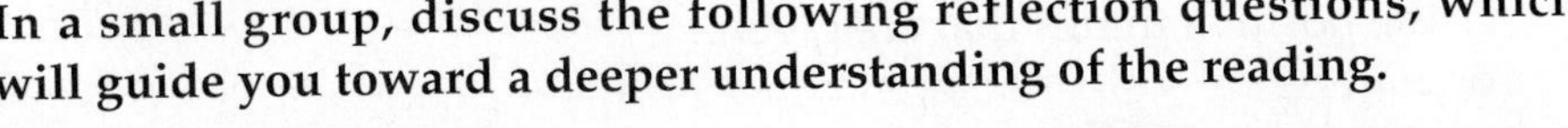

In a small group, discuss the following reflection questions, which will guide you toward a deeper understanding of the reading.

1. What kind of mood is set from the first line of the poem "Meltwater" ("my time is coming, smell it on the wind")? How does this line make you feel?
2. In the second stanza, what action is the poet describing with the lines "firm ground will swamp to ooze and squelch and slip, mud-symphony"?
3. What images in the poem point to the consequences of a deepening water crisis? Point out a few lines.
4. Explain the last line of the poem "Give and Take": "You give me excuse after excuse after excuse."
5. Which of the two poems did you appreciate more? Discuss your choice.

Reading Comprehension Check

Meltwater

1. *Lips and tongue* are mentioned
   a. as raindrops.
   b. as what you touch a melting ice cube with.
   c. to compare with the wind.
   d. as coolers.
2. The words *spill, ooze, slip,* and *trickles* all refer to what natural resource?
   a. wind
   b. the sea
   c. water
   d. the air

3. *Sweep river-sludge and sewage* and *waves come to claim their lost inheritance* offer promises of
   a. a global water crisis.
   b. a better world.
   c. a shortage.
   d. a balanced state.

Give and Take

4. Plastic bottles, acid rain, and toxic canals are mentioned to contrast
   a. negative things.
   b. both positive and negative things.
   c. the positive things that are given.
   d. water.
5. What evidence do we have of the giver's patience?
   a. the offering of spring fountains
   b. the offer of a last chance
   c. The giver shows no patience.
   d. butterflies and abundance

From Reading to Writing: Taking Notes

Overview

In the previous chapter, you learned how to prepare an outline of a full-length article or essay. In this chapter, you will focus on developing note-taking skills. In most mainstream courses in college, your instructor is likely to give a lecture on a specific topic. Depending on the subject of the course, he or she also may invite an expert from a discipline, a government official, the president of a nonprofit organization, or a celebrity to deliver a lecture. (Sometimes your instructor may play an audio lecture and ask you to take specific notes for an activity or brief assignment afterward.)

It will be important for you to listen to the speaker carefully and write down the main idea and supporting details (including both major and minor details) quickly. You will need to rely solely on your listening ability and, of course, knowledge of the subject matter to take good, useful notes. Remember that unlike an audio lecture, which can be rewound and played again for further clarification, you only have one opportunity to listen to the speaker carefully and obtain information in the form of notes. It is, therefore, important that you pay attention to the speaker's main idea and relevant, supporting examples. Imagine that you are attending an important meeting where main ideas are only offered once, and participants usually do not repeat their points unless they are asked for clarification. Paying close attention to the lecture while taking brief notes quickly will enable you to understand the general idea of the content and some of the key concepts.

How to Take Notes

The lecturer will most likely be speaking at a fast pace, and it will not be possible for you to write complete sentences. If you try to write down everything, you will have a great deal of difficulty keeping up with the lecturer. The following note-taking tips will help you gather as much information as possible while listening to the lecturer.

1. Ask questions

As the lecturer speaks and you take brief notes, search for answers to the following questions: How? Why? What? Where? When? Who? Framing questions such as "What is the main focus of this lecture?", "Who introduced this concept?", "When did this event happen?", and "Where did this event/incident take place?" will help you understand the lecturer's movement of thoughts and follow the main idea and supporting details easily.

2. Use abbreviations and symbols

In listening to a lecture, your primary goal is to capture the main idea and supporting details. However, you may realize that sometimes a certain word is difficult to spell. To keep up with the lecturer, it is recommended that you use abbreviations and symbols to catch the main idea. If, for instance, the lecturer mentions, "The polar bear has become an endangered species," then you only need to write "p bear," and "in danger." Keep in mind that as you take notes you will also be taking mental notes, and that you can always revisit your notes to recall information. When you reflect on your notes, you will remember that by "p bear," you meant "polar bear." As mentioned previously, writing complete sentences will make the note-taking task more difficult. Simply look for the main ideas and supporting details while taking notes. The following table shows a few abbreviations and symbols that will help you note the content of a lecture easily. Keep in mind that this is not an exhaustive list, and that you can always create your own symbols as you try to understand the lecture.

Abbreviations	*Symbols*
EPA = Environmental Protection Agency	+ = growth, surplus, increase, progress
CO_2 = carbon dioxide	– = reduce, deduction, decrease
UN = United Nations	= = equal, similar to something
US = United States	$ = income, salary, money, revenue, profit, sales, dollar
KP = Kyoto Protocol	% = percent, percentage, approximate
IPCC = Intergovernmental Panel on Climate Change	# = number of people, countries, etc.
RH = Rolling Hills	& = and, extra, in addition
CA = California	

(continued)

Abbreviations	*Symbols*
AHAM = Association of Home Appliance Manufacturers GG = greenhouse gases	< = smaller than, shorter than, less than > = larger than, greater than

Why Take Notes?

After reflecting on your notes, you will realize that you understand the content of the lecture more clearly, compared to when you heard it the first time. You may want to compare your notes with those of your classmates and fill in any information gaps. By sharing your notes with your classmates and answering their questions, you will focus in on the information that the lecturer presented. As you develop your note-taking skills, you will also improve your reading and listening ability. In fact, your note-taking skills have implications for your ability to write well-organized essays as well. Before you begin to write an essay, you can brainstorm main ideas and supporting details, making specific notes. You will then be able to write coherent paragraphs. It is clear that taking good, brief notes is important to improving reading, writing, listening, and speaking skills.

Note-Taking Exercise

You will soon listen to a TED Talk presentation by Majora Carter, an environmental activist. As you listen to the lecture, use the following worksheet to take specific notes following the instructions outlined in the above lesson.

Note-Taking Worksheet

If you feel you need more space to take effective notes, do not hesitate to use your notebook for this exercise.

Title: ______________________________

Main Idea: ______________________________

____

____

1st Major Detail: ______________________________

____

____

Minor Detail: ______________________________

____

____

2nd Major Detail: ______________________________

____

____

Minor Detail: ____

____

____

3rd Major Detail: ____

____

____

Minor Detail: ____

____

4th Major Detail: ____

____

____

Minor Detail: ____

____

____

5th Major Detail: ____

____

____

Minor Detail: ____

____

____

6th Major Detail: ____

____

____

Minor Detail: ____

____

____

Careers in Environmental Science

Working in small groups, discuss careers one can pursue after obtaining an advanced degree in Environmental Science. You may wish to do some research on the Internet to find other careers related to the field of Environmental Science. In the space below, write down the job title and responsibilities. The first example is done for you. Be sure to share your findings with your peers.

Job Title	*Responsibilities*
1. Environmental Engineer	Watershed management; waste water treatment plant inspection and design; upholding federal environmental law.
2.	
3.	
4.	
5.	

Textbook Application

The following reading is taken from an introductory book on Environmental Science. You will notice that the language used in the excerpt is a bit more challenging than what you encountered in the previous readings. Read the chapter excerpt carefully and answer the multiple-choice questions accurately.

READING 6

Textbook Reading

MyReadingLab

Visit Chapter 4: Environmental Science in MyReadingLab to complete the Reading 6 activities.

How Do Ecosystems Work?

(Excerpt from *Biology: Life on Earth*)

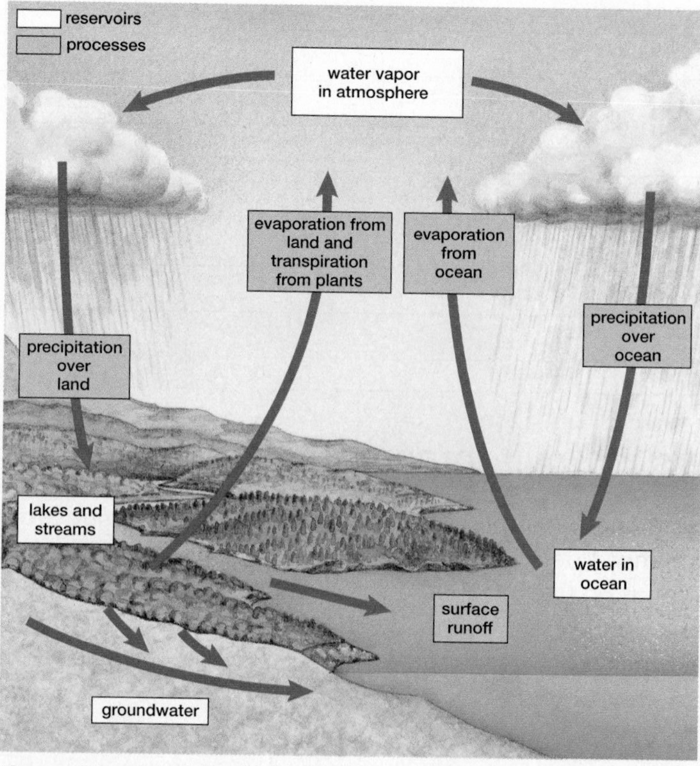

Figure 4.7. ■ The hydrologic cycle.

Most Water Remains Chemically Unchanged During the Hydrologic Cycle

The water **cycle,** or **hydrologic** cycle (Fig. 4.7), differs from most other nutrient cycles in that most water remains in the form of water throughout the cycle and is not used in the synthesis of new molecules. The major reservoir of water is the ocean, which covers about three-quarters of Earth's surface and contains more than 97% of Earth's water. Another 2% is trapped in ice, leaving only 1% as liquid fresh water. The hydrologic cycle is driven by solar energy, which evaporates water, and by gravity, which draws it back to Earth in the form of **precipitation** (rain, snow, sleet, and dew). Most evaporation occurs from the oceans, and much water returns directly to them as precipitation. Water falling on land takes various paths. Some is evaporated from the soil, lakes, and streams. A portion runs off the land back to the oceans, and a small amount enters underground reservoirs. Because the bodies of living things are roughly 70% water, some of the water in the hydrologic cycle enters the living communities of ecosystems. It is absorbed by the roots of plants; much of this water is evaporated back to the atmosphere from plants' leaves. A small amount is combined with carbon dioxide during photosynthesis to produce high-energy molecules. Eventually these molecules are broken down during cellular respiration, releasing water back to the environment. Consumers get water from their food or by drinking.

LACK OF ACCESS TO WATER FOR IRRIGATION AND DRINKING IS A GROWING HUMAN PROBLEM

As the human population has grown, fresh water has become scarce in many regions of the world. Additionally, contaminated, untreated drinking water is a **major** problem in developing countries, where over 1 billion people drink it. Impure water spreads diseases that kill millions of children each year. In both Africa and India, where water contamination poses significant threats, people are starting to use sunlight to kill disease-causing organisms. They place water in plastic bottles and shake them to increase the oxygen levels in the water. Then they put the bottles in a sunny spot, allowing the combination of oxygen, warmth, and ultraviolet (UV) light to **create** free radicals that kill bacteria. With no **technology** other than plastic bottles, these people are generating safe drinking water.

Currently, about 10% of the world's food is grown on cropland irrigated with water drawn from aquifers, which are natural underground reservoirs. Unfortunately, in many areas of the world including China, India, Northern Africa, and the midwestern United States, this groundwater is being "mined" for agriculture; that is, it is **removed** faster than it is replenished. Parts of the High Plains aquifer, which extends from the Texas Panhandle north to South Dakota, have been depleted by about 50%. In India, two-thirds of crops are grown using underground water for irrigation, draining aquifers far faster than they are being replenished. One promising solution is to devise ways of trapping the heavy monsoon rains, whose water usually pours into rivers and **eventually** into the ocean. People of a village in India have found that by digging a **series** of holding ponds, they can capture rainwater that would formerly run off. Their system allows the water to percolate down into the soil and helps replenish the underground water supplies. During the dry season, the people can then tap these supplies for irrigation.

28.4 WHAT CAUSES "ACID RAIN"?

Many of the environmental problems that plague modern society have resulted from human interference in ecosystem **function.** Primitive peoples were sustained **solely** by the energy flowing from the sun, and they produced wastes that were readily taken back into the nutrient cycles. But as the population grew and **technology** increased, humans began to act more and more independently of these natural processes. The **Industrial Revolution,** which began in earnest in the mid-nineteenth century, resulted in a tremendous increase in our **reliance** on **energy** from fossil fuels (rather than from sunlight) for heat, light, transportation, industry, and agriculture. In mining and transporting these fuels, we have exposed ecosystems to a variety of substances that are foreign and often toxic to them (Fig. 4.8). In the following sections, we describe two environmental problems of global proportion that are primarily a direct result of human reliance on fossil fuels: acid deposition and global warming.

Figure 4.8. ■ A natural substance out of place. This bald eagle was killed by an oil spill off the coast of Alaska.

Overloading the Sulfur and Nitrogen Cycles Causes Acid Deposition

Although volcanoes, hot springs, and decomposer organisms all **release** sulfur dioxide, human industrial activities, primarily burning fossil fuels in which sulfur is trapped, account for about 75% of the sulfur dioxide emissions worldwide. This is far more than natural ecosystems can absorb and recycle. The nitrogen **cycle** is also being overwhelmed. Although natural processes such as the activity of nitrogen-fixing bacteria and decomposer organisms, fires, and lightning produce nitrogen oxides and ammonia, about 60% of the nitrogen that is **available** to Earth's ecosystems now results from human activities. Burning of fossil fuels combines atmospheric nitrogen with oxygen, producing most of the emissions of nitrogen oxides. On farms, ammonia and nitrate are often supplied by **chemical** fertilizers produced by using the **energy** in fossil fuels to convert atmospheric nitrogen into **compounds** that plants can use.

Excess production of nitrogen oxides and sulfur dioxide was **identified** in the late 1960s as the cause of a growing environmental threat: **acid rain**, more accurately called **acid deposition**. When combined with water vapor in the atmosphere, nitrogen oxides and sulfur dioxide are **converted** to nitric acid and sulfuric acid, respectively. Days later, and often hundreds of miles from the **source**, these acids fall to Earth with rainwater, eating away at statues and buildings (Fig. 4.9), damaging trees and crops, and rendering lakes lifeless. Sulfuric acid may form particles that visibly cloud the air, even under dry conditions. In the U.S., the Northeast, Mid-Atlantic, Upper Midwest, and West regions, as well as the state of Florida, are the most vulnerable, because the rocks and soils that predominate there are less able to buffer acids.

Acid Deposition Damages Life in Lakes and Forests

In the Adirondack Mountains, acid rain has made about 25% of all the lakes and ponds too acidic to support fish. But by the time the fish die, much of the food web that sustains them has been destroyed. Clams, snails, crayfish, and insect larvae die first, then

Figure 4.9. ■ Acid deposition is corrosive. This limestone statue at Rheims Cathedral in France is being dissolved by acid deposition.

amphibians, and finally fish. The result is a crystal-clear lake, beautiful but dead. The **impact** is not limited to aquatic organisms. Acid rain also interferes with the growth and yield of many farm crops by leaching out essential nutrients such as calcium and potassium and killing decomposer microorganisms, thus preventing the return of nutrients to the soil. Plants, poisoned and deprived of nutrients, become weak and vulnerable to infection and insect attack. High in the Green Mountains of Vermont, scientists have witnessed the death of about half of the red spruce and beech trees and one-third of the sugar maples since 1965. The snow, rain, and heavy fog that commonly cloak these eastern mountaintops are highly acidic. At a **monitoring** station atop Mount Mitchell in North Carolina, the pH of fog has been recorded at 2.9Ñ more acidic than vinegar (Fig. 4.10).

Acid deposition increases the exposure of organisms to toxic metals, including aluminum, mercury, lead, and cadmium, which are far more soluble in acidified water than in water of neutral pH. Aluminum dissolved from rock may inhibit plant growth and kill fish. The tap water in some households has been found to be dangerously contaminated with lead dissolved by acidic water from lead solder in old pipes. Fish in acidified water often have dangerous levels of mercury in their bodies, because mercury is subject to biological magnification as it is passes through trophic levels.

Figure 4.10. ■ Acid deposition can destroy forests. Acid rain and fog have destroyed this forest atop Mount Mitchell in North Carolina.

Reading Comprehension Check

Statistical Analysis

1. What percentage of the earth's surface does the ocean cover?
   a. 97%
   b. half
   c. about 75%
   d. none of the above

   Question Type ____________________
2. Examine Figure 4.7 — The Hydrologic Cycle. Where is the water vapor in the air two steps down the chart?
   a. over the ocean as precipitation
   b. groundwater
   c. in the ocean
   d. on land

   Question Type ____________________
3. Read the section "Lack of Access for Water Irrigation and Drinking Is Growing Human Problem." What are *aquifers*?
   a. man-made water holes
   b. natural underground reservoirs
   c. cropland irrigation
   d. depleted soil

   Question Type ____________________

4. What is causing problems in some parts of the world for groundwater?
a. It is being mined for agriculture.
b. It doesn't rain enough.
c. Only 10% of the world's food is grown in the correct way.
d. It is being polluted.
Question Type ____________________

5. Read the section "What Causes Acid Rain?" *Primitive peoples* are mentioned to illustrate
a. the technological progress humans have made over time.
b. that they are to blame for our current environmental problems.
c. that earlier in human history people produced only natural wastes.
d. the concept of nutrient cycles.
Question Type ____________________

6. The Industrial Revolution is mentioned to illustrate
a. early human activity.
b. that this period was one of great environmental protections.
c. how much richer the world is now than it was in the past.
d. that this period saw a big growth in our dependence on energy.
Question Type ____________________

7. Read the section "Overloading the Sulfur and Nitrogen Cycles Causes Acid Decomposition." Which is *not* mentioned as a negative effect of acid rain?
a. tree and crop damage
b. lifeless lakes
c. the death of whole human populations
d. damage to statues and buildings
Question Type ____________________

8. Read the section "Acid Deposition Damages Life in Lakes and Forests." In the sentence "Acid rain also interferes with the growth and yield of many farm crops by leaching out essential nutrients such as … ", the term *leaching out* could be replaced with
a. destroying.
b. adding.
c. identifying.
d. complementing.
Question Type ____________________

9. How does acid rain prevent the return of nutrients to the soil?
a. It kills decomposer microorganisms.
b. It adds calcium and potassium to farm crops.
c. It gives rise to tree growth.
d. It takes away nutrients such as zinc.
Question Type ____________________

10. What topics are covered in this textbook reading?
   a. Acid rain needs scientists' attention and must be remedied.
   b. groundwater and nutrients
   c. acid rain and water quality
   d. environmental science
   Question Type ____________________

Contemporary Issues in the Discipline

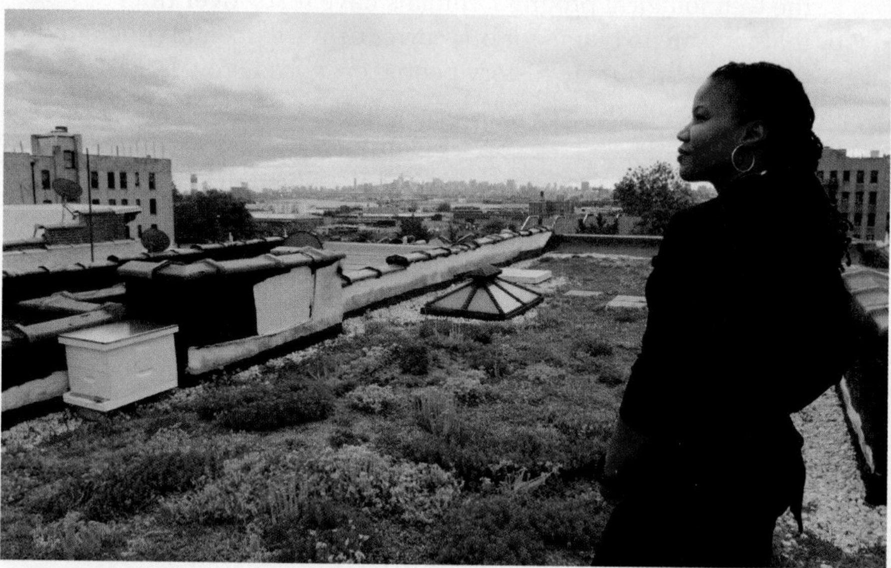

City planner, environmental activist, and entrepreneur **Majora Carter** has a motto: "Green the ghetto!" For most of the 00s, she served as the executive director of Sustainable South Bronx, where she raised federal funds to create a greenway on the South Bronx's waterfront, creating both green space and jobs, and where she secured support to establish Hunts Point Riverside Park—the borough's first open-waterfront park in 60 years. Now she has established her own company, the Majora Carter Group, which helps communities from New Orleans to Detroit—as well as universities—to adopt more eco-friendly practices.

READING 7

Lecture (TED Talk)

MyReadingLab

Visit Chapter 4: Environmental Science in MyReadingLab to complete the Reading 7 activities.

Greening the Ghetto

Pre-Reading Activity

Before reading the following transcript of Majora Carter's speech, you can watch the talk itself here: https://www.ted.com/talks/majora_carter_s_tale_of_urban_renewal (Courtesy of TED).

As you listen to the videoed presentation, take notes. (See the note-taking activity on p. 190 for some pointers.)

After reading the transcript, you will answer some open-ended questions about some of the issues raised in the speech. Finally, you will formulate questions for Ms. Carter about issues pertinent to environmental science and answer them from her perspective.

Greening the Ghetto

by Majora Carter, February 2006

1 If you're here today—and I'm very happy that you are—you've all heard about how sustainable development will save us from ourselves. However, when we're not at TED, we are often told that a real sustainability policy agenda is just not feasible, especially in large, urban areas like New York City. And that's because most people with decision-making powers, in both the public and the private sector, really don't feel as though they're in danger.

2 The reason why I'm here today, in part, is because of a dog: an abandoned puppy I found back in the rain, back in 1998. She turned out to be a much bigger dog than I'd anticipated. When she came into my life, we were fighting against a huge waste facility planned for the East River waterfront, despite the fact that our small part of New York City already handled more than 40 percent of the entire city's commercial waste: a sewage treatment pelletizing plant, a sewage sludge plant, four power plants, the world's largest food distribution center, as well as other industries that bring more than 60,000 diesel truck trips to the area each week. The area also has one of the lowest ratios of parks to people in the city.

3 So when I was contacted by the Parks Department about a $10,000 seed grant initiative to help develop waterfront projects, I thought they were really well-meaning, but a bit naive. I'd lived in this area all my life, and you could not get to the river because of all the lovely facilities that I'd mentioned earlier. Then, while jogging with my dog one morning, she pulled me into what I thought was just another illegal dump. There were weeds and piles of garbage and other stuff that I won't mention here, but she kept dragging me—and lo and behold, at the end of that lot was the river. I knew that this forgotten little street-end, abandoned like the dog that brought me there, was worth saving. And I knew it would grow to become the proud beginnings of the community-led revitalization of the new South Bronx.

4 And just like my new dog, it was an idea that got bigger than I'd imagined. We garnered much support along the way. And the Hunts Point Riverside Park became the first waterfront park that the South Bronx had had in more than 60 years. We leveraged that $10,000 seed grant more than 300 times into a $3 million park.

5 And, in the fall, I'm actually going to—I exchange marriage vows with my beloved. Thank you very much. That's him pressing my buttons back there, which he does all the time. *(Laughter) (Applause)*

6 But those of us living in environmental justice communities are the canary in the coalmine. We feel the problems right now, and have for some time. Environmental justice, for those of you who may not be familiar with the term, goes something like this: no community should be saddled with more environmental burdens and less environmental benefits than any other.

7 Unfortunately, race and class are extremely reliable indicators as to where one might find the good stuff, like parks and trees, and where one might find the bad stuff, like power plants and waste facilities. As a black person in America, I am twice as likely as a white person to live in an area where air pollution poses the greatest risk to my health. I am five times more likely to live within walking distance of a power plant or chemical facility—which I do. These land-use decisions created the hostile conditions that lead to problems like obesity, diabetes and asthma. Why would someone leave their home to go for a brisk walk in a toxic neighborhood? Our 27 percent obesity rate is high, even for this country, and diabetes comes with it. One out of four South Bronx children has asthma. Our asthma hospitalization rate is seven times higher than the national average. These impacts are coming everyone's way. And we all pay dearly for solid waste costs, health problems associated with pollution and more odiously, the cost of imprisoning our young black and Latino men, who possess untold amounts of untapped potential. 50 percent of our residents live at or below the poverty line. 25 percent of us are unemployed. Low-income citizens often use emergency room visits as primary care. This comes at a high cost to taxpayers and produces no proportional benefits. Poor people are not only still poor; they are still unhealthy.

8 Fortunately, there are many people like me who are striving for solutions that won't compromise the lives of low-income communities of color in the short term, and won't destroy us all in the long term. None of us want that, and we all have that in common. So what else do we have in common?

9 Well, first of all, we're all incredibly good-looking—*(Laughter)*—graduated high school, college, post-graduate degrees, traveled to interesting places, didn't have kids in your early teens, financially stable, never been imprisoned. OK. Good. *(Laughter)*

10 But, besides being a black woman, I am different from most of you in some other ways. I watched nearly half of the buildings in my neighborhood burn down. My big brother Lenny fought in Vietnam, only to be gunned down a few blocks from our home. Jesus. I grew up with a crack house across the street. Yeah, I'm a poor black child from the ghetto. These things make me different from you.

But the things we have in common set me apart from most of the people in my community, and I am in between these two worlds, with enough of my heart to fight for justice in the other.

11 So how did things get so different for us? In the late '40s, my dad—a Pullman porter, son of a slave—bought a house in the Hunts Point section of the South Bronx, and a few years later he married my mom. At the time, the community was a mostly white, working-class neighborhood. My dad was not alone. And as others like him pursued their own version of the American dream, white flight became common in the South Bronx and in many cities around the country. Red-lining was used by banks, wherein certain sections of the city, including ours, were deemed off-limits to any sort of investment. Many landlords believed it was more profitable to torch their buildings and collect insurance money rather than to sell under those conditions—dead or injured former tenants notwithstanding.

12 Hunts Point was formerly a walk-to-work community, but now residents had neither work nor home to walk to. A national highway construction boom was added to our problems. In New York State, Robert Moses spearheaded an aggressive highway expansion campaign. One of its primary goals was to make it easier for residents of wealthy communities in Westchester County to go to Manhattan. The South Bronx, which lies in between, did not stand a chance. Residents were often given less than a month's notice before their buildings were razed. 600,000 people were displaced. The common perception was that only pimps and pushers and prostitutes were from the South Bronx. And if you are told from your earliest days that nothing good is going to come from your community, that is bad and ugly, how could it not reflect on you? So now, my family's property was worthless, save for that it was our home and all we had. And luckily for me, that home and the love inside of it, along with help from teachers, mentors and friends along the way, was enough.

13 Now, why is this story important? Because from a planning perspective, economic degradation begets environmental degradation, which begets social degradation. The disinvestment that began in the 1960s set the stage for all the environmental injustices that were to come. Antiquated zoning and land-use regulations are still used to this day to continue putting polluting facilities in my neighborhood. Are these factors taken into consideration when land-use policy is decided? What costs are associated with these decisions? And who pays? Who profits? Does anything justify what the local community goes through? This was "planning"—in quotes—that did not have our best interests in mind.

14 Once we realized that, we decided it was time to do our own planning. That small park I told you about earlier was the first stage of building a greenway movement in the South Bronx. I wrote a one-and-a-quarter-million dollar federal transportation grant to design the plan

for a waterfront esplanade with dedicated on-street bike paths. Physical improvements help inform public policy regarding traffic safety, the placement of the waste and other facilities, which, if done properly, don't compromise a community's quality of life. They provide opportunities to be more physically active, as well as local economic development. Think bike shops, juice stands. We secured 20 million dollars to build first-phase projects. This is Lafayette Avenue—and as redesigned by Matthews-Nielsen landscape architects. And once this path is constructed, it'll connect the South Bronx with more than 400 acres of Randall's Island Park. Right now we're separated by about 25 feet of water, but this link will change that.

15 As we nurture the natural environment, its abundance will give us back even more. We run a project called the Bronx Ecological Stewardship Training, which provides job training in the fields of ecological restorations, so that folks from our community have the skills to compete for these well-paying jobs. Little by little, we're seeding the area with green collar jobs—then the people that have both a financial and personal stake in their environment. The Sheridan Expressway is an underutilized relic of the Robert Moses era, built with no regard for the neighborhoods that were divided by it. Even during rush hour, it goes virtually unused. The community created an alternative transportation plan that allows for the removal of the highway. We have the opportunity now to bring together all the stakeholders to re-envision how this 28 acres can be better utilized for parkland, affordable housing and local economic development.

16 We also built the city's—New York City's first green and cool roof demonstration project on top of our offices. Cool roofs are highly reflective surfaces that don't absorb solar heat and pass it on to the building or atmosphere. Green roofs are soil and living plants. Both can be used instead of petroleum-based roofing materials that absorb heat, contribute to urban "heat island" effect and degrade under the sun, which we in turn breathe. Green roofs also retain up to 75 percent of rainfall, so they reduce a city's need to fund costly end-of-pipe solutions—which, incidentally, are often located in environmental justice communities like mine. And they provide habitats for our little friends! So—*(Laughter)*—so cool! Anyway, the demonstration project is a springboard for our own green roof installation business, bringing jobs and sustainable economic activity to the South Bronx. *(Laughter) (Applause)* I like that, too.

17 Anyway, I know Chris told us not to do pitches up here, but since I have all of your attention: we need investors. End of pitch. It's better to ask for forgiveness than permission. Anyway—*(Laughter) (Applause)*

18 OK. Katrina. Prior to Katrina, the South Bronx and New Orleans' Ninth Ward had a lot in common. Both were largely populated by poor people of color, both hotbeds of cultural innovation: think hip-hop and jazz. Both are waterfront communities that host both industries and

residents in close proximity of one another. In the post-Katrina era, we have still more in common. We're at best ignored and maligned and abused, at worst, by negligent regulatory agencies, pernicious zoning and lax governmental accountability. Neither the destruction of the Ninth Ward nor the South Bronx was inevitable. But we have emerged with valuable lessons about how to dig ourselves out. We are more than simply national symbols of urban blight. Or problems to be solved by empty campaign promises of presidents come and gone. Now will we let the Gulf Coast languish for a decade or two like the South Bronx did? Or will we take proactive steps and learn from the homegrown resource of grassroots activists that have been born of desperation in communities like mine?

19 Now listen, I do not expect individuals, corporations or government to make the world a better place because it is right or moral. This presentation today only represents some of what I've been through, like a tiny little bit. You've no clue. But I'll tell you later if you want to know. But—I know it's the bottom line, or one's perception of it, that motivates people in the end. I'm interested in what I like to call the "triple bottom line" that sustainable development can produce. Developments that have the potential to create positive returns for all concerned: the developers, government and the community where these projects go up. At present, that's not happening in New York City. And we are operating with a comprehensive urban planning deficit. A parade of government subsidies is going to propose big-box and stadium developments in the South Bronx, but there is scant coordination between city agencies on how to deal with the cumulative effects of increased traffic, pollution, solid waste and the impacts on open space. And their approaches to local economic and job development are so lame it's not even funny. Because on top of that, the world's richest sports team is replacing the House That Ruth Built by destroying two well-loved community parks. Now, we'll have even less than that stat I told you about earlier. And although less than 25 percent of South Bronx residents own cars, these projects include thousands of new parking spaces, yet zip in terms of mass public transit. Now, what's missing from the larger debate is a comprehensive cost-benefit analysis between not fixing an unhealthy, environmentally challenged community, versus incorporating structural, sustainable changes. My agency is working closely with Columbia University and others to shine a light on these issues.

20 Now let's get this straight. I am not anti-development. Ours is a city, not a wilderness preserve. And I've embraced my inner capitalist. You probably all have it, and if you haven't, you need to. *(Laughter)* So I don't have a problem with developers making money. There's enough precedent out there to show that a sustainable, community-friendly development can still make a fortune. Fellow TEDsters Bill McDonough and Amory Lovins—both heroes of mine by the way—have shown that you can actually do that. I do have a problem with developments that

hyper-exploit politically vulnerable communities for profit. That it continues is a shame upon us all, because we are all responsible for the future that we create. But one of the things I do to remind myself of greater possibilities is to learn from visionaries in other cities. This is my version of globalization.

21 Let's take Bogota. Poor, Latino, surrounded by runaway gun violence and drug trafficking: a reputation not unlike that of the South Bronx. However, this city was blessed in the late 1990s with a highly influential mayor named Enrique Penalosa. He looked at the demographics. Few Bogatanos own cars, yet a huge portion of the city's resources was dedicated to serving them. If you're a mayor, you can do something about that. His administration narrowed key municipal thoroughfares from five lanes to three, outlawed parking on those streets, expanded pedestrian walkways and bike lanes, created public plazas, created one of the most efficient bus mass-transit systems in the entire world. For his brilliant efforts, he was nearly impeached. But as people began to see that they were being put first on issues reflecting their day-to-day lives, incredible things happened. People stopped littering; crime rates dropped—because the streets were alive with people. His administration attacked several typical urban problems at one time, and on a third-world budget at that. We have no excuse in this country. I'm sorry. But the bottom line is: their people-first agenda was not meant to penalize those who could actually afford cars, but rather to provide opportunities for all Bogatanos to participate in the city's resurgence. That development should not come at the expense of the majority of the population is still considered a radical idea here in the US. But Bogota's example has the power to change that.

22 You, however, are blessed with the gift of influence. That's why you're here and why you value the information we exchange. Use your influence in support of comprehensive sustainable change everywhere. Don't just talk about it at TED. This is a nationwide policy agenda I'm trying to build, and as you all know, politics are personal. Help me make green the new black. Help me make sustainability sexy. Make it a part of your dinner and cocktail conversations. Help me fight for environmental and economic justice. Support investments with a triple-bottom-line return. Help me democratize sustainability by bringing everyone to the table and insisting that comprehensive planning can be addressed everywhere. Oh good, glad I have a little more time!

23 Listen—when I spoke to Mr. Gore the other day after breakfast, I asked him how environmental justice activists were going to be included in his new marketing strategy. His response was a grant program. I don't think he understood that I wasn't asking for funding. I was making him an offer. *(Applause)*

24 What troubled me was that this top-down approach is still around. Now, don't get me wrong, we need money. *(Laughter)* But grassroots groups are needed at the table during the decision-making process. Of the 90 percent of the energy that Mr. Gore reminded us that we waste every day, don't add wasting our energy, intelligence and hard-earned experience to that count. *(Applause)*

25 I have come from so far to meet you like this. Please don't waste me. By working together, we can become one of those small, rapidly growing groups of individuals who actually have the audacity and courage to believe that we actually can change the world. We might have come to this conference from very, very different stations in life, but believe me, we all share one incredibly powerful thing: we have nothing to lose and everything to gain. Ciao bellos! *(Applause)*

Reading with a Critical Eye

In a small group, discuss the following reflection questions, which will guide you toward a deeper understanding of the reading.

1. At the beginning of her speech, Ms. Carter says, "The reason why I'm here today, in part, is because of a dog: an abandoned puppy." What is the connection between this puppy and Ms. Carter's mission? ______________________

2. What is Ms. Carter's mantra about environmental justice? Do you agree with her definition? Why or why not? ______________________

3. What statistics does Ms. Carter offer to prove the point that race is a reliable indicator of environmental injustice? ______________________

4. What are "green roofs" and "cool roofs"? What environmental advantages do they offer? ______________________

5. Is Ms. Carter completely anti-development? ______________________

Imagined Interview: If you had the opportunity to interview Majora Carter in person, what would you ask her? With a partner, compose three questions for her.

Question 1. ______________________________

Question 2. ______________________________

Question 3. ______________________________

Interview Challenge: In a group, ask one student to play Ms. Carter. This student should carefully consider Majora Carter's views, outlined clearly in the TED Talk, and try to answer the questions from Carter's perspective on education.

Chapter Recap

Now that you have made it through a full chapter focusing on the field of Environmental Science, let's review the chapter reading content, skill focus, and vocabulary to gain a better understanding of what we have learned.

Recap Activity 1: A Quick Glance

In 60 seconds, answer the following two questions:

1. What is one thing you learned from this chapter?

____
____
____
____
____
____

2. What was your favorite reading in the chapter? Explain.

____
____
____
____
____
____

Now discuss what you wrote in a small group. Do not read what you wrote. Paraphrase yourself!

Recap Activity 2: Summary Writing

Choose your favorite reading from this chapter and write a summary containing the main idea and some major details. Keep in mind that the key to summary writing is to convey the author's ideas accurately, but to relay this information in your own words. Last but not least, be sure to include reminder phrases and appropriate transitions.

Recap Activity 3: Internet Research on a Theme of Interest

Think about the choice you just made in Activity 2 concerning which reading in the chapter was your favorite.

What was the theme of your chosen reading?

Theme = ______________________________

Using a search engine, such as Google, go online and locate a quality reading on the same theme as your favorite chapter reading. Write a three- to five-sentence summary of the reading that you found from your Internet research.

Title of Reading	*Article Source*	*Summary of the Reading (in your own words)*

Recap Activity 4: Reinforcing the Skill

Reread the paragraph below from the biographical profile of Chico Mendes (p. 169). After reading, discuss with a partner: What plan of action can be used to best identify supporting details?

The first meeting of Mendes's union, the National Council of Rubber Tappers, was held in the capital, Brasilia, in 1985 and rubber tappers from all over Brazil came. Many of these rural peasants had never been outside their local area before. Mendes spent his energies educating tappers about the issues of deforestation, road paving, and the threats these posed to their own livelihoods. The meeting gained the attention of the international environmental movement and the media.

____

How do you identify major and minor supporting details from what you have just read?

Strategy 1: ____

Strategy 2: ____

Recap Activity 5: Recycling Vocabulary

With a partner, locate the following vocabulary terms, review them in context, and try to define the terms without using a dictionary. The first example is done for you.

Word and context location	*Sentence containing the word*	*Meaning in this context*
species p. 161, para. 10	The fossil record indicates that a number of large animal **species** became extinct as humans arrived on continents and islands.	Biological classification; the major subdivision of a genus or subgenus
preserve p. 169, par. 1	"He fought to **preserve** the Amazon rain-forest …"	___________________
emissions p. 160, par. 6	At the same time, carbon **emissions** are altering the chemistry of seawater.	___________________
sustained p. 195, par. 4	Primitive peoples were **sustained** solely by the energy flowing from the sun.	___________________
deforestation p. 169, par. 3	Mendes spent his energies educating tappers about the issues of **deforestation**, road paving, and the threats these posed to their own livelihoods.	___________________
atmosphere p. 156, question 4	Burning fossil fuels such as natural gas, coal, oil and gasoline raises the level of carbon dioxide in the **atmosphere**.	___________________ ___________________
extinction p. 160, par. 1	"We may be sitting on a precipice of a major **extinction** event."	___________________
ecosystems p. 160, par. 7	Fragile **ecosystems** like mangroves are being replaced by fish farms, which are projected to provide most of the fish we consume within 20 years."	___________________ ___________________ ___________________ ___________________

Further Explorations

Books

1. *Cool It: The Skeptical Environmentalist's Guide to Global Warming* by Bjørn Lomborg. Vintage 2010. Lomborg's book on global warming is ideal for anyone who is interested in learning about the phenomenon from an objective perspective. As a political scientist and economist, he offers feasible solutions to the real problems of global warming in this book.
2. *An Inconvenient Truth: The Planetary Emergency of Global Warming and What We Can Do About It* by Al Gore. In his book on global warming, Al Gore makes a clear call to action and urges the American people to take a proactive role in reducing CO_2 emissions to make the earth a cleaner and healthier planet for generations to come.

Movies

1. *An Inconvenient Truth* (2006). This informative documentary highlights the urgency of acting now to reduce the effects of global warming lest we face the consequences of harmful human activities. Using concrete examples and information, Gore inspires viewers to protect the living planet by being environmentally friendly.
2. *Earth on Fire* (2014). A one-hour Australian special that focuses on mega fires and fires in general as they relate to our forests and ecosystem.

Internet Sites

1. www.epa.gov
   This is the U.S. Environmental Protection Agency's official site. Here you can find up-to-date information on such environmental topics as recycling and acid rain. You can also interact with the site by submitting letters stating your viewpoint on a particular issue.
2. www.niehs.nih.gov
   The National Institute of Environmental Health Sciences' Web site. This site explores the relationship between the environment and health concerns such as lead poisoning, asthma, and breast cancer.

Study TIP

Skimming and Scanning

Overview

Skimming and *scanning* are two reading techniques that enable you to read a passage quickly and determine the main idea and specific bits and pieces of information without having to read the function words such as prepositions, articles, conjunctions, and so forth. First, we will look at the technique of skimming. Then, we will discuss how scanning can help you find specific information.

Skimming

When you skim a passage, you read it quickly to find out what the main idea is. Your goal is to understand the main idea of the passage without reading every single word. As mentioned above, while skimming, skip the function words such as prepositions (*to, into, on, at*), articles (*a, an, the*), and conjunctions (*so, but, yet, and*), and pay attention to the content words such as nouns (*government, policy, citizens, law*), verbs (*approve, penalize, allow*), adjectives (*mandatory, strict, legitimate*), and adverbs (*temporarily, permanently, momentarily*). You will notice that function words are not that important, and that content words carry the meaning. When you skim, follow these steps to determine the main idea:

1. Skim the introductory paragraph quickly without reading every single word. Usually, the main idea is found in the first paragraph. Sometimes, the main idea may not be in the first paragraph, in which case you will need to skim the first two paragraphs. Keep in mind, however, that in some cases the main idea is offered in the final paragraph of a text.
2. While skimming, pay attention to the content words such as nouns and verbs. These will give you a clue as to the main idea of the entire passage.
3. Go all the way to the last paragraph and read it quickly. Most authors usually summarize the main ideas in the last paragraph.
4. Focus on some key words as you skim, and find the main idea. Keep in mind that skimming will help you get a general sense of what the reading is about. It will not help you find specific details. For that purpose, you will need to use another reading technique called scanning, but let's first focus on skimming.

Challenge Activity: Skimming

Use skimming as a reading technique to find the main idea of the following passage. Read the passage carefully, delete the function words such as articles, prepositions, and conjunctions, and underline the main idea. Keep in mind that when you skim, you need to read slowly and carefully.

Yes, a mighty change is coming. With temperatures warming, snow evaporating and portions of the Alps melting away, forecasts suggest we're looking ahead to a tourism revolution. Warming weather is shrinking prospects at most low- and even mid-altitude ski resorts, from the Rockies to the Pyrenees, while increasingly violent weather is destabilizing traditional beach paradises from the Mediterranean to Southeast Asia and the Caribbean. "[Global warming] will have important consequences on the whole tourism chain, from the choice of destination to transportation and accommodation," says Jürgen Bachmann, of the Association of French Tour Operators. Hordes of northern European tourists may descend on Spain's Costa del Sol as long as the average August temperature sticks around 35 degrees Celsius, but if it rises to 40 degrees they might just shift toward the country's more temperate Basque coastline. Ski resorts that increasingly rely on snow cannons still need cold enough temperatures to use them. Indeed, weather-dependent destinations are increasingly facing a harsh Darwinian choice: adapt to the new climate realities or disappear.

Scanning

Unlike skimming, which is used to find the main idea, scanning is used to find specific details. Try to focus on the content words such as nouns, verbs, adjectives, and adverbs, and find the specific bits and pieces of information you need to answer a question about the passage. Take the following steps to scan a passage:

1. First, read the title and subtitle of the passage. Then read the sections and subheadings, if any, to focus your search for specific details.
2. As you scan the passage, constantly ask yourself questions you need to answer. For example, ask *who* if you are looking for names, *where* if you need to know the place where something happened such as a meeting or an accident, *what* if you want to know what actually happened, *when* if your focus is the time of an event or an incidence, and *why* if you are looking for reasons.
3. Keep scanning and look for specific words that answer the above questions.
4. Stop scanning and read the passage slowly to understand the context better. You will notice that most of your questions were answered through scanning.

The following questions will help you scan a passage and find the answers. Keep in mind that these are just a few questions to help you scan with relative ease and success. You can most certainly create your own questions to scan. Remember that the questions you ask will depend on the context, so some of these questions may not be relevant to the reading.

1. Why did something (an event, incident, accident, natural calamity) happen?
2. How does something (passing an exam, writing a good essay) happen?
3. How much time or money is involved in this process?
4. Which of the two options/topics/decisions is more appropriate?
5. When does something (a semester, a sports event, a political event) happen?
6. How often does something (an event, a publication, a grant or scholarship, an award) happen?
7. Where did/does this (an important political meeting, an international event, a violent crime) happen?
8. Who did/does this (a criminal, a teaching assistant, director of a foundation, an author, a university professor)?

Challenge Activity: Scanning

Now use scanning as a reading technique to look for supporting details. When you read the following passage, ask some of the questions listed above. Depending on the topic of the passage, you may have to ask a different set of questions. Once again, skip the function words such as the articles, prepositions, and conjunctions, and focus on the content words such as nouns, verbs, adjectives, and adverbs. After you read the passage, try to answer the questions that follow.

> In November 2014, President Barack Obama and President Xi Jinping stood together in Beijing to make a historic U.S.-China Joint Announcement on Climate Change, emphasizing their <u>personal commitment to a successful climate agreement</u> in Paris and marking a new era of multilateral climate diplomacy as well as a new pillar in their bilateral relationship. On the occasion of President Xi's State Visit to Washington, D.C., the two Presidents reaffirm their shared conviction that <u>climate change is one of the greatest threats facing humanity and that their two countries have a critical role to play in addressing it</u>. The two Presidents also reaffirm their determination to move ahead decisively to <u>implement domestic climate policies</u>, to strengthen bilateral coordination and cooperation, and to promote sustainable development and the transition to green, low-carbon, and climate-resilient economies.

Advancing Domestic Climate Action

The United States and China are committed to achieving their respective post-2020 actions as announced in last November's Joint Announcement.

Since that time, both countries have taken key steps toward implementation and are committing to continue intensifying efforts, which will substantially promote global investment in low-carbon technologies and solutions.

(The White House, Office of the Press Secretary, "U.S.-China Joint Presidential Statement on Climate Change," US.gov, September 25, 2015)

Did you understand the passage completely? Scan the passage a second time and answer the following questions:

1. What did Barack Obama and the Chinese president, Xi Jinping, stress at their meeting? ______________________________

____

____

2. What are some examples of domestic climate change policy goals that both leaders agreed to pursue? ______________________________

____

____

____

3. According to the article, what kind of global investment would both leaders make an effort to promote? ______________________________

____

____

E-COMMERCE
Internet Marketing

5

"The internet is becoming the town square for the global village of tomorrow."

BILL GA

Learning Objectives

AFTER READING THIS CHAPTER, YOU SHOULD BE ABLE TO ...

1. Recognize the fundamentals of e-commerce.
2. Describe the future of Internet marketing.
3. Determine inferences based on facts.
4. List details to arrive at a logical conclusion.
5. Compose an email to your professor.

INTRODUCTION TO THE DISCIPLINE OF E-COMMERCE

Electronic commerce, most commonly known as **e-commerce**, focuses on the buying and selling of products and services over the Internet and other computer networks. Since the advent of the Internet, both small and large businesses have made their presence known in the virtual world. The cost of online marketing is rather inexpensive, so more and more businesses brand their products and services online, reaching out to potential customers worldwide. It is beyond the scope of this chapter to cover everything related to e-commerce. Instead, it focuses on an e-commerce subtopic: Internet marketing.

This chapter will introduce you to the various approaches businesses use to sell their products on the Internet. The readings cover topics such as ordering food online, gender differences in Internet use, and the popularity of Internet marketing in China. It is our hope that after completing this chapter, you will better understand how e-commerce facilitates the payment aspects of online business transactions.

Preview Questions

1. How often do you purchase products and services online? What types of items do you usually buy online? Has your online shopping experience mostly been positive? If not, explain the drawbacks of e-commerce.
2. Do you know anyone who has ever been a victim of online identity theft? If yes, describe the incident and its resolution. Discuss ways of preventing identity theft on the Internet.
3. Do you believe that e-commerce is breaking down international boundaries and creating a truly global village? If so, does everyone benefit from doing business in cyberspace? Who are the losers in this virtual enterprise?
4. In your opinion, what types of action can the government take to protect traditional businesses from their inevitable decline in the wake of aggressive Internet marketing?
5. Internet usage is growing exponentially in China and India. Approximately 900 million people use the Internet together in the two countries. How does this surge in Internet usage affect Western corporations doing business in China and India online? In other words, do you think Western corporations will continue to have a monopoly in emergent markets such as China and India, or do you think developed countries will face stiff competition from local corporations?

Writing on The Wall

After you have discussed the preview questions with your classmates, post your responses to two of them on your class blog, which we call The Wall. Review others' postings and respond to at least two of your classmates' posts that grab your interest. Remember the guidelines for blogging and commenting etiquette (see Chapter 1, p. 15)! If your class is not using a shared blog, your instructor may ask you to record your individual or collective responses to the preview questions in another form.

EXERCISE 5.1 Interpreting a Cartoon

Examine the cartoon shown here and, in pairs, answer the following questions.

1. What is amusing about this cartoon?
2. In your opinion, what is the cartoonist's message?

Discipline-specific Vocabulary: Understand Key Terms in Internet Marketing

As you did in the previous chapter, you will learn some key terms in the discipline of Internet marketing in this chapter. Your goal is to use these terms in your speech and writing. You will have the opportunity to interact with key terms in context, so study them carefully and make them part of your active vocabulary.

EXERCISE 5.2 Brainstorming Vocabulary

Directions: What associated words come to mind when you think of Internet marketing? Work with a partner and write down as many related words as you can think of in a period of five minutes.

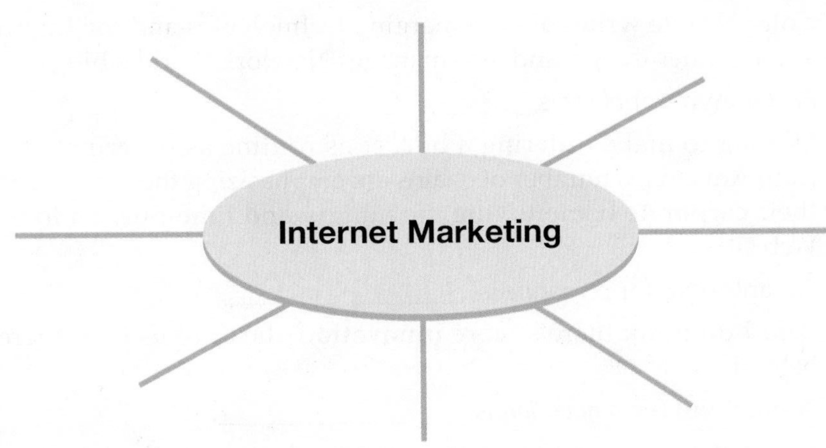

Fishing for Synonyms and Antonyms

In your written work, you will often need to use synonyms and antonyms (see Chapter 2, p. 24 to review these terms) in order to paraphrase statements or claims made by writers.

EXERCISE 5.3 Determining Synonyms and Antonyms from Context

Directions: Read the following ten (10) discipline-specific words culled from the readings in this chapter; most are shown in the context of the sentences in which they appeared. In the space provided after each sentence, write a synonym or antonym for the highlighted terms, as directed.

Discipline-specific Word Bank for Internet Marketing

copyright **cyberspace** **online**
blogs **forecasts** **globally**
corporate **access**
innovation **track**

1. All works in this text are used by permission; these works are protected by the **Copyright** Laws of the United States.

   A synonym for **copyright** is ________.
2. Colin Neagle writes about emerging technologies and the Internet, among other things, and also manages Network World's **blogs**.

   A synonym for *blogs* is __________.
3. Hoping to make ordering a burger as routine as ordering a book from Amazon, a number of chains are emphasizing the dot-com after their **corporate** name to lure the hungry and time-pressed to their Web sites.

   An antonym for *corporate* is ________________.
4. And I do think there's more **innovation** ahead of us than there is behind us.

   A synonym for *innovation* is ________________.
5. For that reason, perhaps no group understands the benefits of new ordering methods better than college students, who grew up zooming through **cyberspace**.

   A synonym for *cyberspace* is __________.
6. Goldman Sachs **forecasts** that the Chinese economy will overtake that of the United States by about 2040.

   A synonym for *forecasts* is ________.
7. The report highlights some of the ongoing work to improve **access** to Internet services for women. An antonym for *access* is ________.
8. Internet applications enable you to **track** and measure successful integrated campaigns.

   An antonym for *track* is _____.
9. About 13 percent of Americans placed **online** food orders from a restaurant last year, according to the National Restaurant Association, up from about 10 percent in 2004.

   A synonym for *online* is ________.
10. Some major tech companies have already moved forward with plans to expand the Internet **globally**.

    An antonym for *globally* is ________.

EXERCISE 5.4 Matching Terms with Definitions

Match the word in Column A with the definition in Column B. Put the letter representing the correct definition in the space preceding each term.

Column A **Word**	**Column B** **Definition**
1. _____ globally	a. personal Web sites to share activities and opinions
2. _____ forecast	b. a path
3. _____ corporate	c. the legal right to publish or broadcast
4. _____ cyberspace	d. to follow progress or development
5. _____ blogs	e. world wide
6. _____ innovation	f. shared by members of a group
7. _____ track	g. saying what will happen in the future
8. _____ copyright	h. an imaginary space where electronic messages exist
9. _____ online	i. the act of introducing new ideas or methods
10. _____ access	j. connected to the Internet

EXERCISE 5.5 Choosing the Right Word

In the following sentences, fill in the blank with a word from the terminology bank that makes the sentence grammatical and meaningful.

blogs	innnovation	copyright	corporate	cyberspace
forecast	online	access	track	globally

1. __________ has become an extremely busy information highway where people using computers, phones, tablets, and other devices exchange electronic messages.
2. The government has announced that it will grant free online ______ to government business records that were formally blocked from public view.

3. One advantage of the publishing house conducting more of their business online is that they can market their products ________, as the Internet is open to users world wide.
4. Many tech companies have an impressive history of figuring out how to copy others' ideas, but these companies are often short on ________.
5. Internet marketing experts ________ that the number of people buying goods and services from the Internet will continue to grow exponentially in the future.
6. It is the CEO and Board of Directors' ________ responsibility to ensure that business transactions on their Web site are carried out in a secure manner.
7. Unlike the traditional brick-and-mortar businesses, most small businesses nowadays offer their products and services ______.
8. ______ have become a popular forum where people share their activities, opinions, and travel experiences with others.
9. Most online businesses use software programs to _____ the number and demographics of consumers visiting their Web sites.
10. A group of British singers has sued an online business selling its music without its knowledge and consent for ________ infringement.

READING 1

Newspaper Article

MyReadingLab

Visit Chapter 5: E-Commerce in MyReadingLab to complete the Reading 1 activities.

www.FriesWithThat?.com

Pre-Reading Questions

Before you read the following reading, get into small groups of three or four and discuss these questions.

1. Have you ever ordered your lunch or dinner online? If not, explain why. If you have, share what prompted you to place your food order online instead of ordering your food by phone and driving to a restaurant to pick it up.
2. Do you think more and more people will eventually be ordering food online? Discuss the factors that will change the ways in which people purchase commercial food.
3. In your opinion, as online food businesses gain popularity, what role should government regulatory agencies play to ensure that the food items sold online are safe for consumption?

Read the following article and answer the multiple-choice questions that follow it. Try to be an "information predictor" for the first part of the reading.

www.FriesWithThat?.com

By Stephanie Rosenbloom, the *New York Times*
August 5, 2007

1 Who has never been put on hold while trying to order pizza, hot wings or moo shu pork? Who has never opened a delivery bag and discovered a Coke instead of a Diet Coke, or that the brown rice is as white as the napkins the restaurant neglected to include?

2 "I hate calling up to order food," said Lewis Friedman, a Manhattan real estate broker. "It **throws me over the edge.** They put you on hold. They get the order wrong. It's always **a crap shoot**."

3 But all that changed last month when he saw a sign in the window of Lenny's, a chain of sandwich shops in Manhattan, encouraging customers to place orders online. Mr. Friedman returned to his office, logged on and, at long last, felt in control of his gustatory future.

4 "I'm **in the driver's seat**," he said. "I can click that I use skim milk. I can click that I like light skim milk. I can click for Equal as opposed to Sweet'N Low or Splenda."

5 The comedian Jim Gaffigan has teased Americans about how fast they want their food. "That's why we really love those value meals,"

?

throws me over the edge
something that really annoys

a crap shoot
left up to chance; up against the odds

in the driver's seat
to be in a controlling position

? ____________________

he said. "You just have to say a number: 'Two!' Soon you won't have to speak. It will just be a noise. 'Ennnghhh!'"

6 Mr. Gaffigan must **have a crystal ball**. Small and large chains, even individual restaurants, are now enabling customers to order without speaking: They can order online before pulling into a drive-through; they can text-message an order, and soon, they will be able to experience one-click ordering on their cell phones, for pickup or delivery. Push a button, and a hoagie is on the way.

have a crystal ball
have a means of predicting the future

7 The restaurant industry is investing in such technology to woo the thousands of consumers like Mr. Friedman who fly through life with their thumbs on their BlackBerrys.

8 Hoping to make ordering a burger as routine as ordering a book from Amazon, a number of chains are emphasizing the dot-com after their corporate name to lure the hungry and time-pressed to their Web sites.

9 As for all those supposed concerns about unhealthy eating and the retreat from home cooking—who are we fooling? The average American 18 and older buys a snack or a meal from a restaurant five times a week on average, according to a 2006 survey by the National Restaurant Association. More people eat at their desks and in their cars. And children are weaned on drive-through, pickup and delivery.

10 The biggest regret Americans seem to have about fast food is that it isn't snappier: A survey last year by QSR magazine, a restaurant industry publication, found that 68 percent of people are willing to wait no more than five minutes in a drive-through line. And in an age where everything from sneakers to cars is customizable, people think they should be able to get exactly what they want, when they want it.

? ____________________

11 "It has really, really exploded in the past year or two," said J. Patrick Doyle, the executive vice president of Team USA, the name Domino's Pizza uses for its corporately owned locations. "I predict pizza will be one of the top 10 items purchased online within the next 12 to 24 months."

12 Though online ordering has been around at some locations for about five years, most people still call in or wait in lines to place their orders. About 13 percent of Americans placed online food orders from a restaurant last year, according to the National Restaurant Association, up from about 10 percent in 2004.

13 But Philip DeSorbo Jr., a project leader for the retail **technology** department at Subway, which has nearly 28,000 restaurants in 87 countries, said these days many people would rather send an e-mail message than leave a voice mail message. "I think online will eventually surpass picking up the phone," he said.

14 Igniting the trend are consumers like Mr. Friedman, who may seem like the **finicky** protagonist of Dr. Seuss's "Green Eggs and Ham," but who is just your average **multitasking**, high-speed wireless American.

finicky
liking only a few kinds of food, clothes, music, and so forth; difficult to please

multitasking
doing several things all at once

15 Now each weekday morning he places an online order with Lenny's. Soon an iced coffee and an Atkin's Special (egg whites, turkey, onion, tomato, roasted red pepper) are made to his typed specifications and delivered to the reception desk.

16 "I'm saving time," said Mr. Friedman, who orders breakfast and lunch online. "I'm so adept at it now that I can actually do business on the phone while I'm placing my food order."

17 People like him see advantages to online and text ordering. It is faster; there is no being placed on hold or inadvertently hung up on; and you need not ask about the specials or explain that the jalapenos should be on the side. It is more accurate; you type in the order and delivery address yourself. There is no need for cash. Favorite orders and credit card information can be saved so re-ordering is a matter of a few mouse clicks. A delivery can be scheduled days in advance. And thanks to **electronic** menus, there is more drawer space in the kitchen.

18 Yet as recently as 2001, Jim Kargman, the president of QuikOrder, a company that provides the technology for online ordering, found some fast food chains reluctant to adopt online ordering. "Now it's basically become mainstream," said Mr. Kargman, whose clients now include Pizza Hut and Domino's.

19 Industry executives have found that those inclined to use online or text ordering are less defined by race or age than by whether or not they have access to high-speed Internet connections.

20 Online orders on corporate Web sites or sites like SeamlessWeb.com, an aggregate site for restaurant ordering, come from working parents in search of no-fuss family dinners, ravenous college students and professionals working overtime.

21 "The heavy user for fast food is the heavy user for computers and hand-held devices," said David Palmer, a restaurant analyst for UBS, the financial services company.

22 For that reason, perhaps no group understands the benefits of new ordering methods better than college students, who grew up zooming through **cyberspace**. In response to student demand for a way to text food orders to restaurants in between classes, Campusfood.com, an online network of restaurants available on more than 300 campuses, began offering text and SMS message ordering in April. The first big push for the service will be this fall.

23 "It's exactly like sending a regular text message like I do with my friends all the time," said Rebecca Minsky, 21, a junior at Cornell University who has been using Campusfood.com since her freshman year. When she leaves the gym she texts her order; by the time she arrives home, dinner is ready.

24 In fact, Ms. Minsky used Campusfood.com so often that she ended up interning for the company this summer.

25 "What they like is it's really on their own terms," said Jim Ensign, the vice president for marketing communications for Papa John's International.

26 The advantages for restaurants include fewer phone calls to answer, higher sales prices (the average pizza sale is $2 to $5 higher than over the phone, said Mr. Kargman of QuikOrder), and access to the e-mail addresses of thousands of customers.

27 What is good for the industry, though, is not necessarily good for the consumer. "I'm sure it will be popular among the heavy users of fast food who will be encouraged to eat even more of it," said Marion Nestle, a professor of nutrition, food studies and public health at New York University and the author of "Food Politics: How the Food Industry Influences Nutrition and Health" and "What to Eat." "And that's too bad," she said, "because there are healthier eating options, obviously."

28 Still, she said, the industry is giving people what they want: "How clever of them to take advantage of that kind of technology." Ms. Nestle also pointed out that consumer interest in these new ways of ordering is an intriguing commentary on class, as it shows how **reluctant** people are to speak with fast food workers—often teenagers and immigrants with accents.

reluctant
unwilling, disinclined

29 Pizza is the nation's most delivered food category, Mr. Kargman said, so it is not surprising that the world's three largest pizza chains (Pizza Hut, Domino's and Papa John's) are at the forefront of electronic ordering. Nationwide, nearly 30 online orders on average are placed every minute at Pizza Hut, and the company said in June that its online ordering business grew six fold in the last three years.

30 The major national pizza chains have about 41 percent of the pizza–restaurant business, according to the Associated Press.

31 "This is one way among many that the chains are trying to grow within this mature market," said Mr. Palmer of UBS. "Other ways include offering breakfast, staying open later, introducing premium items, or credit card payment capability, offering wi-fi."

32 "I only order online," said Andy Claude, 31, who works in the investment industry in San Diego and who has been ordering from Papa John's for about five years. "When you order on the phone, sometimes you say 'extra cheese' or 'half pepperoni' and it doesn't always come that way."

33 Pizza, however, is not the only cuisine that has gone **digital.** A little more than a year ago, Chipotle, the Mexican chain, began offering online ordering, which it calls DSL (Don't Stand in Line). In the first six months of this year it did 350,000 transactions online, up from 250,000 in the first half of last year, said Chris Arnold, a spokesman.

34 About three months ago, an Outback Steakhouse on West 23rd Street in Manhattan began offering curbside take away, said Chris Eldridge, the proprietor. Customers place an order online and type in

the make and color of their car. When they pull up to the restaurant, their food is carried out to them.

35 Of course there are consumers who have ordered online only to have their food never arrive or arrive with fixings they won't so much as poke at. Nonetheless, industry professionals generally agree that online orders are more accurate.

36 Restaurants like Subway and Papa John's are experimenting with **text** messaging. At the National Restaurant Association show in May, Mr. Kargman of QuikOrder announced that he had acquired patented technology called FavOrder that will allow customers to place orders on Web sites and **via** cellphones and PDAs with a single click. Cellphone one-click ordering will be available to the public later this year.

37 "The reality of it is, there's a lot of us that are resistant to change," said Tom Santor, a spokesman for Donatos Pizza, a chain with 176 restaurants in the United States. "But guess what? It ain't doing us any good. This train has done left the station."

38 People like Alison Striansе of Brooklyn are riding it into the future.

39 "I'm hooked on Delivery.com," she said, which she uses to order lunch. "You literally don't have to leave your desk."

40 When she learned about the Web site from a friend a few weeks ago she looked at him and thought: "You've changed my life."

Reading with a Critical Eye

1. In the first paragraph, we learn that it is a hassle to order commercial food by phone, and that restaurants almost always get the order wrong. Despite this, most people continue to call up for food. Instead of cooking at home, why do you think most people prefer to buy restaurant food?
2. The comedian Jim Gaffigan is critical of the American consumer when he says, "That's why we really love those value meals. You just have to say a number: 'Two!' Soon you won't have to speak. It will just be a noise. 'Ennnghhh!'" In your opinion, what is Gaffigan implying?
3. According to the article, "The average American 18 and older buys a snack or a meal from a restaurant five times a week on average, according to a 2006 **survey** by the National Restaurant Association. More people eat at their desks and in their cars. And children are weaned on drive-through, pickup and delivery." Discuss what has caused this retreat from home cooking and whether or not the growing trend toward commercial food is healthy for the human race.

4. In paragraph 18, we read that "Yet as recently as 2001, Jim Kargman, the president of QuikOrder, a company that provides the technology for online ordering, found some fast food chains reluctant to adopt online ordering." Despite the fact that ordering commercial food online has become so popular, why do you think some restaurants are reluctant to provide this service? Give specific examples to support your answer.
5. In paragraph 27, Marion Nestle, professor of nutrition, reminds us that even though much healthier options are available to us, we choose to eat unhealthy foods. In paragraph 37, Tom Santor tells us, "The reality of it is, there's a lot of us that are resistant to change." Tell why humans continue to do what is unhealthy for them and resist change. Be specific.

Reading Comprehension Check

1. As used in the sentence in paragraph 3, "Mr. Friedman returned to the office, logged on and, at long last, felt in control of his gustatory future," the word *gustatory* means
   a. the art of cooking.
   b. a gust of wind.
   c. related to eating.
   d. buying food online.
2. A Manhattan real estate broker, Lewis Friedman's main point about ordering food online is that
   a. he prefers calling up restaurants to order food.
   b. restaurant Web sites offer unhealthy food.
   c. it is inconvenient to order food from a computer.
   d. he is completely in control of what he wants to eat.
3. In making fun of the American people, the comedian Jim Gaffigan's main point in paragraph 5 is that
   a. they do not mind waiting for hours to have their food delivered.
   b. the restaurant industry's push for online food will not become popular.
   c. they prefer convenience to quality.
   d. they are overly conscious about healthy food.
4. In the sentence, "The restaurant industry is investing in such technology to *woo* the thousands of consumers like Mr. Friedman who fly through life with their thumbs on their BlackBerrys" (para. 7), the word *woo* could be replaced with
   a. solicit.
   b. distract.
   c. discourage.
   d. sanction.
5. Americans eighteen and older buying commercial food at least five times a week is offered as an example of
   a. Americans' tendency to prefer homemade food.
   b. Americans clamoring for healthier eating options.
   c. fewer Americans eating while commuting to work.
   d. Americans withdrawing from homemade food.

6. Thirteen percent of Americans purchasing food from restaurant Web sites is mentioned to support the point that
   a. the number of people placing online food orders has decreased.
   b. most people still purchase food the conventional way.
   c. those who purchase food online are dissatisfied with the quality.
   d. those who purchase food online are satisfied with the quality.
7. The main idea of the article is that
   a. most people eat while commuting to work or at their desks.
   b. it is much easier to order food by phone than it is to purchase it online.
   c. pizza is the most popular food item purchased online.
   d. the restaurant industry is capitalizing on the American people's tendency to want food fast.
8. In the sentence in paragraph 19, "Industry executives have found that those inclined to use online or text ordering are less defined by race or age than by whether or not they have access to high-speed Internet connections," the word *inclined* means
   a. feeling repelled.
   b. disenchanted.
   c. having tendency.
   d. not in favor of (using).
9. A professor of nutrition, food studies, and public health at New York University, Ms. Marion Nestle's main point about restaurant Web sites becoming popular among fast food users is that
   a. consumers will gain health and longevity from purchasing food online.
   b. restaurant Web sites are extremely good for the consumer.
   c. the popularity of online food purchases is good for the restaurant industry.
   d. consumers do not have many healthier options left.
10. What advantage is mentioned to ordering food online?
   a. The food is more delicious and healthier.
   b. The food is inexpensive.
   c. The service is accurate.
   d. Side dishes are free.

MyReadingLab

Visit Chapter 5: E-Commerce in MyReadingLab to complete the Reading 2 activities.

READING 2

Online Magazine Article

UN Report Highlights Massive Internet Gender Gap

Pre-Reading Questions

Discuss the following questions in small groups before reading the article.

1. If you are female, how often and for what purposes do you use the Internet? If you are male, what prompts you to navigate the Internet? Discuss if there are gender differences in Internet usage and give specific examples to support your answer.

2. Do you think men outnumber women in terms of browsing the Internet, or do you think the number of men and women surfing the Internet is equal? Give specific reasons for your answer.
3. According to the results of a study sponsored by Intel, Inc., women are behind men in terms of using the Internet in many countries. In your opinion, why is it that women lag in Internet adoption in several countries in the developing world? Be specific.

UN Report Highlights Massive Internet Gender Gap

By **Colin Neagle,** ***Network World*****, September 24, 2013**

1 Globally, men have a much easier time accessing the Internet than women, according to a new report issued by the United Nations' Broadband Commission Working Group.

2 The report estimates that more than 200 million more men have access to the Internet than women, particularly in countries where Internet access is relatively new and still difficult to come by. Citing statistics from the ITU World Telecommunications/ICT Indicators database, the report says 41% of men worldwide are connected to the Internet, compared to 37% of women. In what is defined as the

"developed world," or countries with wide-reaching access to the Internet, 80% of men are online, compared to 74% of women. In the "developing world," those figures drop to 33% of all men and just 29% of women.

3 In the developing world, the report claims that 16% fewer women use the Internet than men, whereas just 2% fewer women are online in the developed world.

4 The gender gap in Internet services is particularly noticeable in major Arab countries, according to the report. Statistics from the Arab Advisors Group showed that higher percentages of men in Saudi Arabia, Morocco and Jordan use ecommerce services than women. In Egypt, Jordan, Kuwait, Lebanon, Morocco, Saudi Arabia, and the United Arab Emirates, no fewer than 62% of men use smartphones. Among those same countries, Morocco's 38% of females using smartphones is the highest rate, according to the report.

5 Several factors contribute to the online gender gap. Specifically, the report mentions the online harassment and threats frequently aimed towards women. In July, Caroline Criado-Perez, the journalist heading up the campaign to make British author Jane Austen the face of England's £10 note, was bombarded with abusive comments and rape threats via Twitter. On Facebook, sexism had become such a pervasive issue that earlier this year the company announced "(https://www.facebook.com/notes/facebook-safety/controversial-harmful-and-hateful-speech-on-facebook/574430655911054) new efforts to crack down specifically on content that "targets women with images and content that threatens or incites gender-based violence or hate."

6 Similarly, the report also cites studies showing "some early indications that cyberbullying might vary by gender," and research indicating discrepancies in representations of men and women in popular culture.

7 By working through these issues and facilitating Internet access, the UN predicts that a larger presence of women online could have a drastic global economic impact.

8 "The World Bank (2009) estimates that every 10% increase in access to broadband results in 1.38% growth in Gross Domestic Product (GDP) for developing countries," the report says. "Bringing women online can boost GDP – Intel (2013) estimates that bringing 600 million additional women and girls online could boost global GDP by up to US$13-18 billion."

9 The report highlights some of the ongoing work to improve access to Internet services for women, which focuses primarily on putting Internet-enabled mobile phones in their hands. However, it also calls for new policies to make Internet access more affordable and easier to use, while making the content more localized and relevant for new users in developing markets.

10 Closing the Internet gender gap also poses many new business opportunities. A report by the GSMA/Cherie Blair Foundation for Women, which was cited in the UN's document, says the mobile industry is

missing out on 300 million users and $13 billion in revenues, as women worldwide are an estimated 21% less likely to own a mobile phone.

11 Some major tech companies have already moved forward with plans to expand the Internet globally, most notably with Internet.org, the nonprofit organization run by Facebook, Qualcomm, Samsung, Ericsson, Nokia, Opera and MediaTek. Last week, the group released a document with a rough outline of the technology that could help accomplish its goal, which included a Facebook app for feature phones called "Facebook for Every Phone."

12 Colin Neagle writes about emerging technologies and the Internet, among other things, and also manages Network World's blogs.

Reading with a Critical Eye

1. The article begins with a statement that "men have a much easier time accessing the Internet than women." Why do you think women are still lagging in Internet adoption since its inception in the late 1980s? Give specific reasons to support your answer.
2. We learn from the article that more men than women access the Internet in countries where Internet access is not common. Discuss why more men are able to access the Internet in countries where surfing the Web is relatively new.
3. Paragraph 3 states, "In the developing world, the report claims that 16% fewer women use the Internet than men, whereas just 2% fewer women are online in the developed world." In your opinion, what factors may cause the greater gender disparity in Internet use in the developing world as compared to the developed world? You may discuss this question with your male and female peers in a wider context. Make sure that you provide specific examples to make your point clear.
4. The UN predicts that "a larger presence of women online could have a drastic global economic impact." Discuss how this is possible.
5. We learn from the article that it is in the best interest of tech companies to bridge the Internet gender gap. Discuss how these corporations can expand the Internet globally and how they stand to gain from such an endeavor. Be specific.

Reading Comprehension Check

1. As used in the sentence, "The report estimates that more than 200 million more men have **access** to the Internet than women … ," the word *access* means
   a. depart.
   b. exit.
   c. entry.
   d. leave.

2. In the sentence, "On Facebook, **sexism** had become such a pervasive issue that earlier this year the company announced (https://www.facebook.com/notes/facebook-safety/controversial-harmful-and-hateful-speech-on-facebook/574430655911054) new efforts to crack down specifically on content that "targets women with images and content that threatens or incites gender-based violence or hate," the word *sexism* means
   a. discrimination based on a person's gender.
   b. discrimination based on a person's nationality.
   c. discrimination based on a person's sexuality.
   d. discrimination based on a person's Internet use.
3. In the sentence, "Similarly, the report also cites studies showing 'some early indications that cyberbullying might vary by gender,' and research indicating **discrepancies** in representations of men and women in popular culture," the word *discrepancies* can be defined as
   a. the state of being consistent.
   b. the state of being accurate.
   c. the state of being acceptable.
   d. the state of being inconsistent.
4. Which of the following sentences is the best statement of the main idea of the article?
   a. American men outnumber American women in terms of browsing the Internet.
   b. The number of women surfing the Internet far exceeds that of men worldwide.
   c. Men outnumber women in terms of accessing the Internet worldwide.
   d. The number of male and female Internet users globally is almost equal nowadays.
5. The UN report cites statistics from the ITU World Telecommunications/ICT Indicators database to support the fact that
   a. the gender gap in Internet usage is more noticeable in the developing world.
   b. the gender gap in Internet usage is more noticeable in the developed world.
   c. the gender gap in Internet usage is nonexistent in the developing world.
   d. the gender gap in Internet usage is more pervasive in the developed world.
6. According to the UN report, the gap between men and women using smartphones in major Arab countries is the narrowest in
   a. Saudi Arabia.
   b. the United Arab Emirates.
   c. Morocco.
   d. Lebanon.
7. "Several factors contribute to the online gender gap. Specifically, the report mentions the online harassment and threats frequently aimed towards women. In July, Caroline Criado-Perez, the journalist

heading up the campaign to make British author Jane Austen the face of England's £10 note, was bombarded with abusive comments and rape threats via Twitter. On Facebook, sexism had become such a pervasive issue that earlier this year the company announced (https://www.facebook.com/notes/facebook-safety/controversial-harmful-and-hateful-speech-on-facebook/574430655911054) new efforts to crack down specifically on content that 'targets women with images and content that threatens or incites gender-based violence or hate.'

It can be inferred from the above passage that

a. men are more likely to be threatened by religious websites.
b. men are harassed and threatened by women online.
c. both men and women are harassed by each other online.
d. women are more likely to be harassed by men online.

8. "The World Bank (2009) estimates that every 10% increase in access to broadband results in 1.38% growth in Gross Domestic Product (GDP) for developing countries," the report says. "Bringing women online can boost GDP – Intel (2013) estimates that bringing 600 million additional women and girls online could boost global GDP by up to US$13-18 billion."

Based on the above passage, a logical conclusion can be drawn that

a. women would usually get special discounts from websites that men do not.
b. women would pay for Internet access and spend money shopping online.
c. men would compete with women and spend more money shopping online.
d. men would not contribute to global GDP by canceling their Internet service.

9. According to the article, Internet access for women can be made attractive by making it

a. simply economical.
b. economical and exclusive.
c. economical and relevant.
d. economical and expensive.

10. Which of the following statements explains why it is worthwhile for major technology companies to expand the Internet globally?

a. It is a losing proposition for companies like Facebook and Samsung.
b. Women around the world will stay away from the Internet out of fear.
c. Technology companies will learn about the reasons for the Internet gender gap.
d. It would result in increased revenues generated by new subscribers worldwide.

BIOGRAPHICAL PROFILE

Larry Page and Sergey Brin

While pursuing his PhD in computer science at Stanford University, Larry Page met Sergey Brin, a Russian immigrant who was also pursuing a PhD in computer science there, and together they founded the Google search engine in 1998. Since then, Google has become the largest search engine in the world, highly frequented by Internet surfers looking for various Web sites. Both Larry Page and Sergey Brin have suspended their doctoral studies indefinitely while they are both working at Google.

Larry Page was born on March 26, 1973, in Lansing, Michigan, into a family of educators. His father, Dr. Carl Victor Page, was a professor of computer science at Michigan State University, and his mother, Gloria Page, taught computer programming at the same university. Sergey Brin was born on August 21, 1973, in Moscow in the Soviet Union. Like Larry Page, Sergey Brin also grew up in an educational environment. His father, Michael Brin, taught mathematics at the University of Maryland, and his mother was an economist.

Before Sergey Brin met Larry Page at Stanford University, he had written several papers on data mining and pattern extraction. He coauthored a seminal paper with Larry Page, entitled "The Anatomy of a Large-Scale Hypertextual Web Search Engine." Their paper has become the tenth most widely read scientific article at Stanford University.

Larry Page and Sergey Brin are currently tied as the twenty-fourth richest person in the world with a net worth of $19.8 billion each. Larry Page and Sergey Brin recently purchased a Qantas Boeing 767 for business and personal purposes. Both of them appeared on the list of the 50 most important people on the Internet by *PC World* in 2006. Prior to that, they were named "Persons of the Week" by ABC *World News Tonight* in 2004. In 2005, Sergey Brin was considered to be one of the "Young Global Leaders" by the World Economic Forum. Larry Page became the CEO of Google in January 2011.

Page is heavily invested in Tesla Motors, a company that is designing the Tesla Roadster, a battery electric vehicle. Sergey Brin drives a Toyota Prius, a hybrid car that uses both gasoline and electrical energy.

Some Questions for Group Discussion

1. Do you think that Larry Page and Sergey Brin's tremendous success had something to do with the fact that both of their parents were educators? In other words, do highly educated parents determine and influence their children's financial success? Support your answer with specific examples.
2. The parents of Larry Page and Sergey Brin were university professors, not business icons. What do you think motivated Larry Page and Sergey Brin to become world leaders in the area of Internet marketing?
3. Larry Page has invested in a company that is developing a battery electric vehicle. His partner, Sergey Brin, who is tied with Larry Page as the world's twenty-fourth richest individual, drives a Toyota Prius while he can easily afford the most expensive cars in the world. Discuss why you think Larry Page and Sergey Brin have gone "green."

Biographical Internet Research

Research another leader in Internet Marketing from the list below, and share his or her biographical profile with your peers. Discuss what set them apart from others in the business world.

- Jeff Bezos
- Pierre Omidyar
- Michael Dell
- Meg Whitman
- Jerry Yang

SKILL FOCUS: Making Inferences

When good readers make an *inference*, they draw logical conclusions based on facts. It is important to remember that the reader must avoid inferring on the basis of opinion, because sometimes authors present information that is not clearly stated. In other words, information is implied, so the reader has to examine facts and details closely to make a conclusion that is factual and logical.

Look at the following sample exercise to understand clearly that inferences must be based on facts.

Example

When people ask me what I do for a living, and I tell them that I am a linguist, they respond with a blank stare.

What can you infer from the above statement?

a. Linguists are extremely popular nowadays.

b. Linguistics can be a rewarding career.

c. Most people are not familiar with the field of linguistics.

d. Linguists are in great demand.

If you read the sentence carefully, you will notice that Choice (a) is exactly the opposite. If linguists were that popular, then people would not give the author "a blank stare." So, Choice (a) is not correct. Choice (b) is also incorrect, because if linguistics were such a rewarding career, then most people would be aware of the discipline. Choice (c) is a logical conclusion because most people respond to the author with "a blank stare," not knowing what a linguist does for a living. Choice (c), therefore, is the correct answer. In contrast, Choice (d) cannot be true either because the sentence does not give the impression that linguists are, indeed, in demand. An effective technique to make correct inferences on a multiple-choice test is to determine how many statements are false. Think about the question as if the choices were true/false questions. Read the four choices carefully, and then reread the passage to determine which statements are false. If you focus on the facts and clues presented in the passage, you will notice that there is always only one statement that is true, so it is the correct conclusion. The following example will make this point clear. Read the sentence carefully and answer the question that follows.

Example

Shakespeare wasn't far from truth when he wrote, "The first thing we do, let's kill all the lawyers." *(Henry VI)*

It can be inferred from the above statement that

a. Shakespeare killed many lawyers.

b. the author murdered several lawyers.

c. the author is not too fond of lawyers.

d. the author is seriously considering killing all the lawyers.

Choice (a) is not true, because the above sentence is taken from Shakespeare's famous play *Henry VI,* in which a character says this line. It does not mean that Shakespeare himself killed many lawyers. We know that the author agrees with Shakespeare's statement, but we do not know if he murdered several lawyers. Choice (b), therefore, is not correct. The author writes, "Shakespeare wasn't far from truth . . . [supporting the statement that all the lawyers should be killed]." Choice (c) says that the author is not too fond of lawyers. We can make this inference correctly on the basis of the statement. It is reasonable and logical to infer that the author most probably dislikes lawyers. Otherwise, he would not agree with Shakespeare. Choice (c) is the correct answer. Choice (d) is false because the author simply affirms that Shakespeare was right in condemning all the lawyers. The statement does not indicate that the author is actually planning to kill all the lawyers.

When making inferences, think like a detective, read the main idea, and look at the details closely. It is important that you abstain from forming your own opinion of the topic and that you focus on what is stated. By relying on the facts and details in the passage, you will arrive at a logical conclusion.

Let's look at another example to understand how inferences are made. Read the brief passage below and answer the question, paying close attention to the facts to arrive at a logical conclusion.

Example

Jennifer entered the house. Upon hearing the door, Jimbo, the dog, snarled, thinking it was an intruder. However, when Jimbo saw Jennifer, he rolled over, wagging his tail.

A logical conclusion drawn from this passage is

a. Jennifer is Jimbo's veterinarian.

b. Jennifer is Jimbo's owner.

c. Jimbo is Jennifer's Seeing Eye dog.

d. Jimbo knows Jennifer.

Now read each of the choices carefully and determine which statement is true and which one is false.

There is nothing in the passage that leads us to conclude that Jennifer is a veterinarian. The passage does not give us any information about Jennifer's profession. Choice (a), therefore, is not a logical conclusion. (False) Choice (b) is not a correct conclusion either, because we cannot find anything in the passage that establishes the fact that Jennifer is indeed Jimbo's owner. The passage begins with "Jennifer entered the house," not "Jennifer entered her house." It is probably true that Jimbo lives in the house, but we cannot tell if Jennifer owns the house.

(False) Is there any information in the passage that supports the idea that Jennifer is blind? Seeing Eye dogs are usually owned by people who are blind. We do not know if Jennifer is blind, so we cannot say Choice (c) is true. (False) What we do know from the passage is that Jimbo rolled over after seeing Jennifer. It is unusual for a dog to roll on its back, asking a stranger to scratch its tummy, but Jimbo does that to Jennifer. This is the only piece of fact that is presented in the above passage, and the information is implied that Jimbo wants Jennifer to rub his stomach. We can safely conclude that Choice (d) is the correct inference. (True)

PRACTICING THE SKILL

Practice 1: Making Inferences

Practice making inferences by reading the following passages with a classmate and arrive at a logical conclusion based on the facts. Underline the sentence, or sentences, that clue you in to the correct answer.

Passage 1

> Many sites exist primarily to inform and influence target audiences favorably about the owner of the site. Such sites typically emphasize a firm or organization's mission, size, scope, services, revenue, profitability, stock market success, industry relationship, and so forth—in much the same way as an annual financial report would. In fact, much of what you find on corporate identity sites is there to influence Wall Street, stockholders, and investors, and to instill a sense of pride among company employees.
>
> (Barbara G. Cox and William Koelzer, from *Internet Marketing*. Upper Saddle River: Pearson Prentice Hall, 2004, p. 5)

It can be inferred from this passage that

- **a.** the primary purpose of corporate identity sites is marketing.
- **b.** company employees are frustrated with the corporate identity sites.
- **c.** owners of the sites are proud of their employees.
- **d.** there is no difference between the sites and an annual financial report.

Passage 2

> Similar to corporate identity sites, product or service information sites emphasize positioning products or services more than selling them. Some of these sites are posted by businesses that really do intend to sell their products directly, but haven't mastered the Internet marketing elements they need to use to accomplish that goal. These sites are akin to product brochures. They may give the business telephone number and perhaps the e-mail address, but they do not provide the

interactive tools that are central to the Web's capacity for direct selling. These information-oriented Web sites reflect a product focus, but usually do not communicate urgency or establish a two-way information exchange with site visitors.

(From *Internet Marketing*, p. 6)

It can be inferred from this passage that

a. information-oriented Web sites are not interested in selling their products.

b. these sites are primarily concerned with the owner's identity.

c. information-oriented Web sites do not provide their contact information.

d. some businesses providing information-oriented sites have poor Internet marketing skills.

Passage 3

Online banking was among the earliest and most successful Web-based services. Not only can users get information about bank offices and hours and locations, types of accounts, rates, terms, and other bank products but they can also access their account information; transfer funds; pay bills; plan a reinvestment, retirement, or home loan refinance; and communicate with the bank. Investors can learn about bank assets and liabilities, stability, size, and investments.

(From *Internet Marketing*, p. 8)

We can conclude from this passage that

a. online banking is not successful nowadays.

b. customers shy away from online banking because of the hidden charges.

c. customers can access many useful pieces of information about their bank accounts from their homes.

d. customers must attend a series of workshops before using online banking.

Passage 4

News and entertainment sites are usually tied to another media, such as television, films, magazines, or newspapers. Cnn.com, tvguide.com, Hollywood.com, usatoday.com, and austindailyherald.com are all examples. These sites keep visitors returning day after day for updates and current information, as well as for customer service regarding subscription, delivery, or other services. What do they gain by providing all this information? Increased ratings, circulation, and physical sales—which, in turn, help increase advertising sales.

(From *Internet Marketing*, p. 8)

A correct conclusion drawn from the above passage is that

a. news and entertainment sites provide useless information.

b. these sites work independently of other media sources such as TV and films.

c. visitors are satisfied with the information and services news and entertainment sites provide.

d. providing information and services causes advertising sales to plummet.

Passage 5

Some large stores and manufacturers are finding ways to personalize their Web sites. These sites usually encourage visitors to sign in or register for something or otherwise provide a name or nickname that the site can use when the visitor returns in the future. Amazon.com, for example, displays "Welcome back, [visitor name]." The entry page has "New books for [visitor name]" based on searches or purchases the visitor made on previous visits.

(From *Internet Marketing*, p. 8)

It can be inferred from the above passage that

a. some manufacturers want to prevent potential customers from visiting their Web sites.

b. some large stores are writing their customers' names on signboards.

c. most people appreciate it when they are addressed by their names.

d. many Web sites offer their customers free cookies when they sign in.

The next reading allows you to apply the skills you have just learned. Now that you have read brief passages and have drawn logical conclusions, let's practice reading full-length articles to make inferences based on facts and details.

Recommended Debate Topic: Should all companies be allowed to advertise online, or should the government regulate the types of businesses that are permitted to do Internet marketing?

Brainstorm some controversial topics related to e-commerce with your classmates and instructor for the debate activity.

Your suggested debate topics:

a. ______________________________

b. ______________________________

c. ______________________________

MyReadingLab

Visit Chapter 5: E-Commerce in MyReadingLab to complete the Reading 3 activities.

READING 3

Newspaper Article

Got a Search Engine Question? Ask Mr. Sullivan

Pre-Reading Questions

Before you read the following article, discuss these questions in small groups and share your answers with your classmates.

1. Do you use search engines such as Google, Yahoo!, and Bing? If yes, which search engine do you usually use to find information on the Internet? How does your favorite search engine compare with others?
2. What kind of information do you search for on the Internet? In your opinion, how reliable and accurate is the information search engines provide to Internet users?
3. Some critics think that search engines tend to be invasive because they make people's personal information accessible to the public. Do you think the government should protect people's privacy and mandate what kind of information is made available to Internet users?

Got a Search Engine Question? Ask Mr. Sullivan

By Jefferson Graham, *USA Today*

August 1, 2006

1 SALISBURY, England—Google's Matt Cutts considers Danny Sullivan's Search Engine Watch website "must reading." To Yahoo's Tim Mayer, it's simply the "most authoritative source on search."

2 His readers would naturally assume that Sullivan, the self-described "world-renowned search authority," is the ultimate Silicon Valley insider. He is. But he does it all some 4,000 miles away—near here, in the remote little village of Chitterne, about four hours southwest of London.

3 When the world he writes about arrives at work in Silicon Valley, Sullivan has just finished dinner with his wife and two boys. He then retires to his den, parks himself in front of three computer monitors and spends the remaining evening hours trying to decipher the mystery of how online search engines rank listings.

4 "That he can do what he does from so far away is just wild," says Cutts, a Google engineer who is a regular on Sullivan's online podcasts.

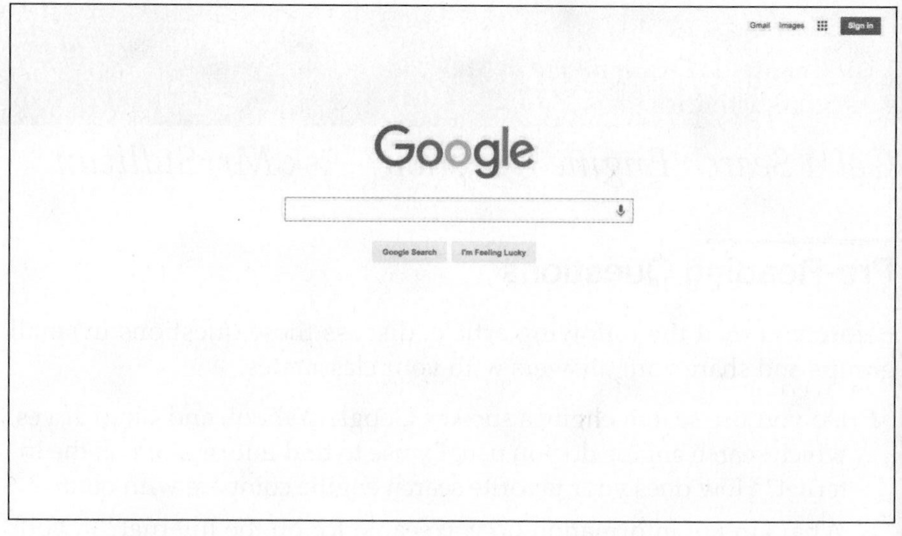

5 The website takes up much of Sullivan's time. But his biggest income producer is the Search Engine Strategies conference (SES), which he stages six times a year. The next one opens in Silicon Valley's San Jose, Calif., on Monday. The conferences attract 1,500 to 6,000 attendees who pay nearly $2,000 each to hear tips about how to get websites to the top of search queries.

6 Sullivan's conferences attract some of the search industry's biggest players. Next week's features an address by Google CEO Eric Schmidt. Past sessions attracted IAC/InterActive CEO Barry Diller, Yahoo co-founder Jerry Yang and Google founders Sergey Brin and Larry Page.

7 SES is attended by owners of small and large businesses, their employees and independent operators who call themselves search engine optimizers. SEOs work with companies to make their websites more likely to be found on Google and rival Yahoo.

8 Sullivan says SES attracts executives in newly created positions for vice presidents of search at companies such as Coca-Cola, Citigroup and *The New York Times.*

9 For smaller ventures, the type of information discussed at SES is "life or death" advice, says Rand Fishkin, CEO of SEOmoz.org, a Seattle SEO firm.

10 "If I'm a small company and get five inquiries a day from people who found me in search engines, suddenly I am lifted out of obscurity and in the prime real estate for this new way of advertising," he says.

11 The search advertising market—those little text ads published near search listings—is one of the fastest-growing areas of advertising. It's expected to grow to $26 billion in 2010 from $17.4 billion this year, according to market tracker Forrester Research.

Falling into a new industry

12 Sullivan, 40, says he shares common roots with employees at Google and Yahoo, even though he works thousands of miles away. He recalled his life over a lunch of soup and crisps (potato chips) at a small pub on a tiny, lush country lane with lots of sheep and barely enough room for one car.

13 He was born and raised in Newport Beach, Calif. After graduating from the University of California, Irvine, he spent a year in England, where he was hired by the BBC to type articles for reporters.

14 He met his future wife, Lorna, at the BBC. They married and moved back to California, where Sullivan worked at the *Los Angeles Times* and *The Orange County Register* in their graphics departments.

15 Then search came into his life. At the time, a friend had put up a website and couldn't make sense of how to be found in search listings. Sullivan tried to help him and was so successful, he went to work with his friend helping others with their sites.

16 Meanwhile, Lorna missed home, and Sullivan agreed to leave California behind for this village near her family. Chitterne is so small that it got high-speed Internet access only last year.

17 While trying to figure out what to do for a job in England, he posted a Web page with tips for how to rise to the top of search engine results. Response was so great, he decided to turn his Web page into an online resource. That was in 1996. "And I've never looked back since," Sullivan says.

18 Within a year, he sold his website for an undisclosed price to MecklerMedia (now Jupitermedia), which kept him on as an independent contractor and expanded into trade shows. The business was sold again this year to Incisive Media for $43 million.

19 Sullivan is still a contractor, but he profits from the trade shows, based on attendance.

20 Yahoo's Mayer, a product manager in the search division, remembers attending Sullivan's earliest shows, when just a few hundred came. These days, "It's just insane," he says. "I'm always amazed at how many people now attend. It just shows how many people are making their living through search engine advertising."

21 On top of the ticket prices, the conferences also attract other fees from sponsorships and exhibitions, starting at about $5,000.

22 Rory Brown, who oversees the show as managing director for Incisive, says Sullivan has nothing to do with that side of the business. The separation between editorial and business "is carefully guarded," Brown says. Sullivan has completely free rein "to program the conference however he wishes."

23 Sullivan says he likes it this way. "I would hate having to call Google and ask them to sponsor the show. It would be too much of a conflict."

24 Sullivan says he has no regrets about selling Search Engine Watch before companies such as Google and Yahoo became household names and started generating billions of dollars in revenue.

25 "The sale did not make me a millionaire, but it helped me into a new house, and I've done well by the site and conference since," he says.

No Illusions About Fame

26 He may not have a **fortune,** but in his own little world, "Danny is the rock star of our industry," says Brown, who sells him that way to potential attendees of shows.

27 Sullivan holds well-attended Q&A sessions, where he takes questions from the audience for several hours.

28 But he **harbors no illusions** about how large his **niche** fame actually is.

29 "Sure, you can **get swamped** at the show," he says. "A lot of people want to talk to you. But then I'll stand next to Matt Cutts, and he'll get masses of people **vying for** his attention."

30 Sullivan calls this fame within a small group of people. "Here in England, where people ask what I do, and I tell them about search marketing, they respond with **a blank stare**. That says it all."

Reading with a Critical Eye

1. How does Sullivan manage to remain the world-renowned search authority without physically residing in Silicon Valley? Discuss how he keeps himself abreast of the search engines in the United States from a remote village in England.
2. Paragraph 7 states, "SES is attended by owners of small and large businesses, their employees and independent operators who call themselves search engine optimizers." Why do you think these professionals pay as much as $2,000 to attend Sullivan's Search Engine Strategies conference?
3. After trying many jobs in the United States, Sullivan carved a niche for himself serendipitously by helping a friend get his Web site found in search listings. The rest is history. Tell how it is possible for some people to find the meaning of their lives almost accidentally.
4. In paragraph 24, we read, "Sullivan says he has no regrets about selling Search Engine Watch before companies such as Google and Yahoo became household names and started generating billions of dollars in revenue." Discuss why Sullivan does not regret missing a great opportunity to become a multimillionaire.
5. Paragraph 30 reads, "Sullivan calls this fame within a small group of people. 'Here in England, where people ask what I do, and I tell them about search marketing, they respond with a blank stare. That says it all.'" What does the English people's response to Sullivan tell us about the field of search marketing in general?

Reading Comprehension Check

1. "Google's Matt Cutts considers Danny Sullivan's Search Engine Watch website 'must reading.' To Yahoo's Tim Mayer, it's simply the 'most authoritative source on search.'"

   Which of the following conclusions can be drawn from the passage?

   a. Danny Sullivan's Web site is specifically designed for students enrolled in remedial reading courses.
   b. His Web site is authoritarian.
   c. Yahoo!'s Tim Mayer has formed a strategic alliance with Danny Sullivan.
   d. The information the Search Engine Watch Web site provides is reliable.

2. "His readers would naturally assume that Sullivan, the self-described 'world-renowned search authority,' is the ultimate Silicon Valley insider. He is. But he does it all some 4,000 miles away—near here, in the remote little village of Chitterne, about four hours southwest of London."

   According to the passage, which of the conclusions *cannot* be true?

   a. Danny Sullivan is a Silicon Valley insider.
   b. Sullivan flies 4,000 miles to his office in Silicon Valley, California, from London to meet with his clients.
   c. Sullivan does most of his work in a little-known village in England.
   d. He describes himself as the "world-renowned search authority."

3. What can be inferred from the following statement?

   "The [SES] conferences attract 1,500 to 6,000 attendees who pay nearly $2,000 each to hear tips about how to get websites to the top of search queries."

   a. Attendees do not find the SES conferences worth their while.
   b. Sullivan's Search Engine Watch Web site is not a profitable enterprise.
   c. These attendees believe that the information they receive at the conferences will help them make their Web sites more accessible to the Internet users.
   d. The SES conferences are a losing proposition.

4. What does the following statement suggest about smaller businesses?

   "'If I'm a small company and get five inquiries a day from people who found me in search engines, suddenly I am lifted out of obscurity and in the prime real estate for this new way of advertising,' he says."

   a. People have difficulty finding smaller businesses on the Internet.
   b. Most search engines usually ignore smaller companies.
   c. Smaller companies largely depend on search engines to be recognized by potential customers.
   d. People find smaller businesses without using search engines.

5. "The search advertising market—those little text ads published near search listings—is one of the fastest-growing areas of advertising. It's expected to grow to $26 billion in 2010 from $17.4 billion this year, according to market tracker Forrester Research."

   Which of the following inferences can be made from this projection?

   a. Forrester Research believes that the search advertising market will continue to decline in the coming years.
   b. The market for Internet advertising will most likely shrink rapidly.
   c. The market tracker company thinks that the search advertising market will grow exponentially in the future.
   d. Forrester Research's projection cannot be trusted.

6. "Meanwhile, Lorna missed home, and Sullivan agreed to leave California behind for this village near her family. Chitterne is so small that it got high-speed Internet access only last year."

   A logical conclusion drawn from this passage is that

   a. Sullivan left California because he was not getting along with his clients in Silicon Valley.
   b. Sullivan cares about Lorna's feelings.
   c. Sullivan and Lorna did not have a comfortable house in California.
   d. Sullivan moved to Chitterne because of high-speed Internet access.

7. Which of the conclusions listed below can be drawn from the following statement?

   "While trying to figure out what to do for a job in England, he posted a Web page with tips for how to rise to the top of search engine results. Response was so great, he decided to turn his Web page into an online resource."

   a. Sullivan's tips on search engine results were poorly received.
   b. Sullivan's tips on search engine results were well received.
   c. Sullivan got most of his ideas for his Web page from his wife.
   d. Most smaller businesses could care less about search engine results.

8. "Within a year, he sold his website for an undisclosed price to MecklerMedia (now Jupitermedia), which kept him on as an independent contractor and expanded into trade shows."

   It can be inferred from the passage that MecklerMedia maintained its business relation with Sullivan because

   a. it incurred huge losses after buying his Web site.
   b. it paid a very small amount of money to Sullivan for his Web site.
   c. the company thought it could use Sullivan's expertise to generate revenue.
   d. Sullivan resisted the idea of the company's expansion into trade shows.

9. "Sullivan says he has no regrets about selling Search Engine Watch before companies such as Google and Yahoo became household names and started generating billions of dollars in revenue."

   Based on this passage, we can conclude that

   a. Sullivan has second thoughts about selling his popular Web site.
   b. Sullivan wishes he had not sold Search Engine Watch.
   c. Sullivan is satisfied with his decision to sell Search Engine Watch.
   d. Sullivan wonders if his Web site could have generated billions of dollars in revenue.

10. "Sullivan calls this fame within a small group of people. 'Here in England, where people ask what I do, and I tell them about search marketing, they respond with a blank stare. That says it all.' "

    It can be inferred from Mr. Sullivan's statement that

    a. he is extremely popular in England.
    b. most people in England are not aware of what Mr. Sullivan does for a living.
    c. he is the rock star of the search marketing industry in England.
    d. Mr. Sullivan has reached the status of a cult figure in England.

From Reading to Writing: How to Compose an Email to a Professor

Experts in the field of education believe that those students who keep in touch with their professors perform more successfully in courses than those who do not. As a college student, you will need to communicate with your professor effectively when you have questions about homework assignments and other course requirements. It may be worth your while to email your professor, as it has become a dominant form of communication in academic contexts, and most professors usually check their email 3 – 4 times a day.

When you email your professor, adhere to certain rules about composing an email.

Here are some things to keep in mind regarding e-mail etiquette:

1. Indicate your purpose in the subject line.

If you are emailing your professor about a summary or a reflection paper, in the subject field, say, "My summary," or "My reflection paper". This way, your professor, the recipient of the message, will know what your email is about.

2. Begin with a salutation.

Before you write your email to your professor, say, "Hi/Hello Professor Feedback:". Then hit the enter key on the keyboard twice and begin your message with:

- I hope this finds you well.
- I hope that things are going well for you.
- I trust you are doing well.
- I hope this finds you in good health and high spirits.
- I hope you are enjoying the long weekend.

When you say these things, you are basically making small talk with your professor before getting to the point. You need to maintain a professional tone throughout the email message, so it is important that you avoid beginning your email with:

- What's up!
- Hey there,
- Hey professor,
- How goes it!
- How is it going?
- What's goin' on?

3. Pay attention to language.

In your email message, follow spelling, grammar, and punctuation rules. If your language is sloppy, your professor may get irritated and misinterpret your intended meaning. Before you send the email to your professor, proofread your message carefully and correct any spelling and grammar errors you may have made.

4. Keep your messages brief.

Most professors teach, do research, write papers and present at national conferences, so they have very busy schedules. Try to keep your email message brief and to the point. It may be a good idea to focus on one subject per message.

5. Sign off properly.

After you write the email message, it is important that you sign off properly. There are various ways of doing it:

- Yours truly,
- Your student,
- Sincerely,
- Best regards,
- Warm regards,
- Respectfully,

Do not say, "take care," "see you later," "later", "take it easy", "bye", "ciao for now", etc. After all, you are communicating with your professor, so a certain level of formality is appropriate.

6. Provide your contact information.

If you are emailing your professor about an urgent matter, and you need her or him to reply immediately, include a signature that has your contact information, including your student ID and phone numbers. Make sure that you write your name at the end of the message. In any given semester, professors teach many students, and they may not recognize who you are unless you write your name.

When to *Not* Send an Email

While it is true that college professors and students often exchange emails, do not use email to avoid an uncomfortable situation or to cover up a mistake. It is best to have face-to-face communication with your professor to resolve issues effectively.

Sample Email

Read the following sample email for your reference and practice:

Dear Professor Grade,

I hope this finds you well.

This is Garry Kaplan from your advanced reading class. I am sorry for missing class last Thursday. I had a family emergency that I needed to attend to, and it kept me from attending your class.

I asked my classmates about the homework assignments, and they told me that we have to write a summary of the article we read on Tuesday. I think I know how to summarize the original text, but I am not sure if I am allowed to express my opinion in a summary. I am going to write the summary this weekend, so I thought I should ask you.

I greatly appreciate your prompt response and look forward to seeing you at class next week.

Regards,

Garry Kaplan
Advanced Reading 121
Section K13A
Student ID: 12034765
C: 917 564 8454

EXERCISE 5.7 Writing a Formal Email

Write an email to your professor about a genuine concern you may have about your performance as a student. You may be worried about a particular homework assignment, your course grade, overall performance, or difficult course content. As you compose your email to your professor, adhere to the above-mentioned rules and keep your email message succinct and to the point. Make sure that your tone is polite, your language concise, and your purpose clearly stated.

Textbook Application

The following reading is taken from an introductory book on Internet marketing. The purpose of this reading exercise is to give you an opportunity to practice reading authentic text and apply what you have learned. Read the chapter excerpt carefully and answer the multiple-choice questions that follow.

MyReadingLab

Visit Chapter 5: E-Commerce in MyReadingLab to complete the Reading 4 activities.

READING 4

Textbook Reading

Emerging Markets

Pre-Reading Questions

Before you read the chapter on Internet Marketing, discuss the following questions in small groups.

1. As more and more people become comfortable buying products and services online around the world, which countries do you think will be most profitable for Internet marketing businesses? Think of the countries that are experiencing strong economic growth and give reasons to support your answer.
2. Western corporations have benefitted tremendously from outsourcing processes and operations in India. U.S. companies, such as IBM, Hewlett Packard, and Microsoft, have made massive investments in India to outsource their technology services. In your opinion, what other countries can become a hotspot for outsourcing? Again, think of strong economic growth in developing countries to answer the question.
3. It is imperative that countries provide reliable Internet access to attract foreign businesses. In your opinion, which countries offer reliable Internet access? Discuss why countries where Internet penetration is not easy have not realized that reliable Internet access is fundamental to economic growth.
4. In developed countries such as the United States and Japan, online sales growth is slowing down or in decline. What is the reason for the decline in sales in developed markets, and what do you think Internet businesses need to do to compete with their archrivals? Be specific.

Emerging Markets

By **Lara Fawzy & Lucas Dworski**
from Chapter 1 of *Emerging Business Online: Global Markets and the Power of B2B Internet Marekting*

Why These Markets Are Significant

1 One defining factor of an Emergent Market (EM) is that it is experiencing strong economic growth. This was certainly the case of the nations mentioned so far in the chapter, at least until the current global recession. These markets are even more significant now, however, because of the economic slowdown in *developed* markets.

2 Many of these numbers have historically been considered high risk. Some have even had sanctions applied against them, including embargos and otherwise restricted trade. A number of megashifts in the global economy have caused these markets to become more stable and open to trade. As corporations reengineered their operations through global outsourcing and new market development, they also imported into "client" EM nations advanced expertise in finance and business processes. Global intermediaries such as the International Monetary Fund (IMF) became more sophisticated in advising EM nations on economic management. As China and India drove economic supergrowth during this time, they also generated secondary waves of demand and market activity for less-developed nations.

3 Although, the less-developed world has been impacted by the global recession, "there is no doubt that there is still huge growth potential in emerging markets," said Paul Mountford, president Cisco emerging markets in 2009, "to the point where we probably will not be able to call some of them emerging anymore in a few years' time."

4 The Internet has removed travel and time boundaries by allowing trade among markets in real time. The global reach of the Internet may be the most significant transformative development since the industrial age. As infrastructure and telephony bring Internet penetration to billions more of the world's people over the next few years, the EM phenomenon will be exponential. The Internet will become the major platform that allows the free flow of business activity, leveraged by applications and tools such as websites, video applications, and databases. Therefore, EMs will only become easier to access and to do business with.

5 EMs are also able to leapfrog developed economies in terms of Internet technology because they do not have legacy infrastructure. Service providers, such as mobile companies, are investing in

powerful devices and high-speed mobile networks such as 3G, and faster connected mobile broadband led by consumer demand.

The West and Outsourcing

1 As mentioned previously, EMs received massive economic stimulus through foreign direct investment as Western corporations outsourced processes and operations. The role of India and its technology services industries as the major example of outsourcing economics is well known. Egypt is also fast becoming a hotspot for outsourcing.

2 The past ten years have been exciting times for Egypt. The list of multinationals outsourcing to Egypt has been growing at an unprecedented rate (e.g., Microsoft, IBM, Vodafone, Oracle, and Hewlett-Packard). The government has been wooing industry investment for years and has made outsourcing a key foreign investment attracter, while leveraging key advantages such as languages and proximity to Europe and North America.

3 Turkey also has high-skilled, low-cost labor and a well-educated pool (as have many countries in the CEE region). China is renowned for manufacturing outsourcing. Outsourcing has stimulated local markets in EMs by creating jobs, wealth, and making these countries part of the global economy.

Future Superpowers

1 Investment in these countries has huge potential for high returns and high reward. The initial hype about EMs has subsided during the global recession, but that has allowed us to instead focus on their long and steady growth. These economies are resource rich. Resources include gold, petroleum, diamonds, and other natural resources. A lot of these EMs have enormous populations and a growing middle class. Some EM nations are predicted to become future superpowers, powerful enough to influence the global economy and other sociopolitical realities.

2 According to the Financial Times, "China overtook Germany to become the world's third-largest economy in 2007 after the Chinese authorities revised upward the figures for growth during that year." China surpassed Germany in terms of gross domestic product (GDP), just behind Japan and the United States." Goldman Sachs forecasts that the Chinese economy will overtake that of the United States by about 2040.

3 The ebocube can help your business reach all these markets at the click of a button, and can help you to develop your B2B relations in EM regions/nations.

Internet Penetration: Fundamental to the ebocube Model

1 Through the Internet, almost any business can reach their targets in these markets, directly and economically, no matter the size or location of the business. In terms of the ebocube model, reliable Internet

access in a particular market is a prerequisite for launching successful integrated Internet campaigns. The Internet works as a response mechanism for customers and vendors and transfers data back into your company databases. Internet applications enable you to track and measure successful integrated campaigns. Therefore, reliable Internet access and service is a major consideration when deciding in which market to implement ebocube. Internet or web-based tools are also used for planning, executing, and reporting through ebocube. In addition, partners may execute campaigns on your behalf, and ebocube can be used by companies in those areas.

2 Over the past ten years, Internet penetration has grown rapidly in developing economies as a result of continued government and service provider investment and direct investment by technology companies. Technology is also improving, facilitating the implementation of the Internet. For example, from 2000 to 2009, the MEA region had the highest percentage increase in the number of Internet users (a world-leading 2,196% gain). This was followed by the LatAM region, which increased its web users by 883%. More mature Internet markets such as Asia are up 545%; considering the size of the population rates and investment are set to increase in line with global demand as the Internet becomes more of a pivotal role in business and consumer lives.

3 The adoption of mobile broadband is also likely to continue in EMs. Global mobile operators with experience in developing markets are introducing their bundled data services into these regions.

Emerging on Emerging

1 Global competition is intensifying as EM countries build trade relationships with other less-developed markets and meet demand in their own domestic markets. For developed countries, the time window to get a business foothold in some of these markets may begin to close over the next decade. Internet marketing and ebocube can give you quick entry to market in terms of raising brand awareness, generating interest, and creating sales leads. As nations, including Russia and China, expand global market reach, competition will intensify in the near future.

2 These statistics relate to country Internet penetration rates as a whole, including the usage increase rates for consumers and businesses. In some markets, Internet penetration rates may be lower in rural areas. However, they are likely to be higher in business areas because the Internet is a prerequisite for many companies to compete globally.

3 Many EMs have also witnessed significant investment in mobile broadband telephony. Following on this trend will be an increase in web applications, communications innovations, and collaborative tools and ways of working.

4 In July 2009, the company SEACOM announced that its submarine fiber-optic cable system linking south and east Africa to global networks via India and Europe was up and running. That system creates unprecedented opportunities. After all, government, business leaders, and citizens can now use the network to compete globally,

foster economic growth, and raise living standards across the continent. The move heralds the advent of affordable, high-quality broadband capacity and experience in East African economies.

Mobile Phones

1 The ecbocube model also shows you how to plan, execute, track, measure, and learn from mobile Internet, email, and SMS marketing. All of this marketing is measurable. The ebocube model shows marketers what to measure and how to measure it.

2 Currently, fast-growing opportunities to market via mobile phone include SMS marketing, multimedia messaging (MMS), push email, and mobile web. The general population of China has access to mobile web, and so you can leverage this in the way that you market in a B2B context, because consumer habits carry over to the workplace.

3 A profound influence in the mobile world and mobile web is the iPhone 3G and its large touchscreen and browsing capability. Not only can you download content, you can also create and use applications. The iPhone 3G is being sold in EMs, and now the iPad has been introduced and promises even more possibilities.

4 Internet usage via mobile phones will see a massive surge driven by growth in EMs. China's Internet penetration via mobile phone is set to grow. And some predict that India will have the fastest growing mobile Internet population, doubling by 2013. The number of mobile devices will increase accordingly.

5 Internet-connected mobile phones are reshaping the way people go about their personal and business lives, offering new opportunities to marketers and a new way to reach prospective customers in EMs.

Smartphones

1 As mobile broadband infrastructure and coverage expands, smartphone adoption will also grow, allowing marketers new opportunities. Businesses in these areas are ramping up use of smartphones such as iPhones, BlackBerrys and Nokias. Smartphones enable business users, as well as consumers, to be connected on the move to mobile web, with email delivered to their phones or to other web applications. The Apple iPad is also popular in emerging markets. The aggressive promotion of smartphones and wider portfolios is creating this growth. Many EM nations are younger demographically, and young people are more willing to adopt the latest technologies and think in wireless and digital terms. These also allow B2B marketers new opportunities.

Developed Markets: Maturity and Decline

1 Developed markets can be described as mature, which means for a lot of sectors growth in sales is slowing down or in decline. Demand is slowing down, and competition is intense. Customers are more sophisticated in their needs. A slowdown in growth is also compounded

by the recession in developed markets. Naturally, in a mature market, smaller and less-dominant firms are squeezed out of the market. In this current recession, however, we have also seen large global companies collapse.

2 Traditionally, strategies for selling in mature markets, depending on the service or product, rely on the following:

- Cost cutting
- Producing innovation in the market (line extensions)
- Repeat purchases from existing customers

3 As competition continues to intensify, companies need to innovate with new value propositions, price promotion, and sophisticated marketing to grab attention and sell. The years 2010, 2011, and beyond are the time to market and to sell to EMs. While the developed economies experience a historically devastating recession during this period, emerging economies are leading indicators of recovery. Figure 5.9 shows the life cycle of emerging and developed markets seen through classic market-cycle theory.

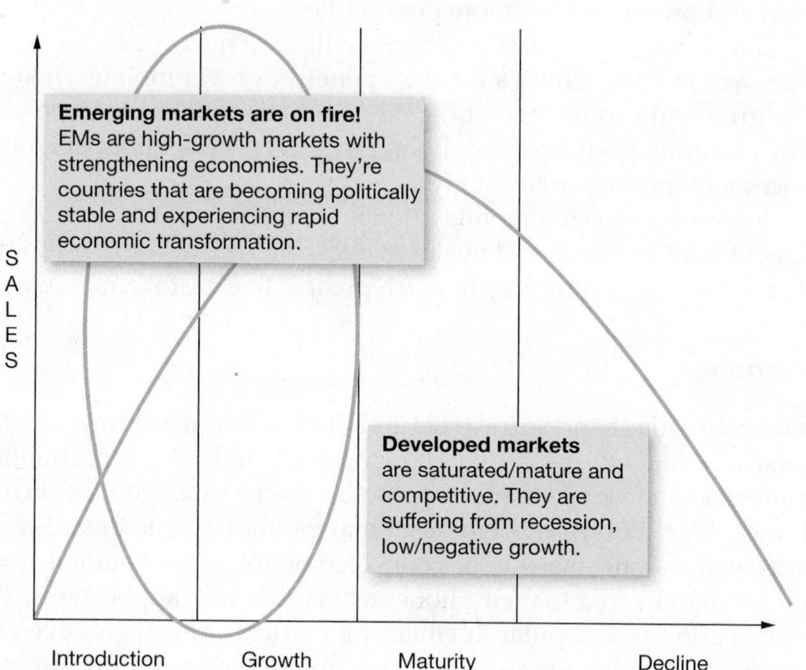

EM Strategies

1 EMs promise growth, but businesses may face challenges in terms of education and adoption of products/services. For instance, local businesses might know nothing of your products/services/brands. There is also a risk that your products/services will not be adopted. Your strategy in these markets must, therefore, differ from your strategy to developed markets. The ebocube offers a well-tested sales and marketing strategy.

Reading Comprehension Check

Read the following questions and circle the correct answer. As you answer the questions, try to eliminate the three wrong answers first before choosing the correct answer.

1. In the sentence, "Some have even had **sanctions** applied against them, including embargos and otherwise restricted trade," a synonym for the word *sanctions* is
   a. aids. c. favors.
   b. orders. d. grants.
2. As used in the sentence, "As China and India drove economic supergrowth during this time, they also **generated** secondary waves of demand and market activity for less-developed nations," an antonym for the word *generated* is
   a. caused. c. produced.
   b. created. d. restricted.
3. What is the main point of the following passage?
   "One defining factor of an Emergent Market (EM) is that it is experiencing strong economic growth. This was certainly the case of the nations mentioned so far in the chapter, at least until the current global recession. These markets are even more significant now, however, because of the economic slowdown in *developed* markets."
   a. Emerging markets are experiencing exponential economic growth.
   b. Emerging markets were insignificant until the global recession.
   c. Emerging markets are significant because the global economy is slowing down.
   d. Emerging markets are causing a slowdown in developed markets.
4. "Although, the less-developed world has been impacted by the global recession, 'there is no doubt that there is still huge growth potential in emerging markets,' said Paul Mountford, president Cisco emerging markets in 2009, 'to the point where we probably will not be able to call some of them emerging anymore in a few years' time.'"
   It can be inferred from the above passage that
   a. some of these emerging markets will experience a slowdown in economic growth eventually.
   b. all of these emerging markets will continue to experience explosive economic growth.
   c. the economy of the less-developed countries will be more affected by the global recession.
   d. some less-developed countries had the opportunity to experience economic growth in 2009.
5. "As mentioned previously, EMs received massive economic stimulus through foreign direct investment as Western corporations outsourced processes and operations. The role of India and its technology

services industries as the major example of outsourcing economics is well known. Egypt is also fast becoming a hotspot for outsourcing."

Which of the following conclusions can be drawn from the above statement?

a. Western corporations are only interested in outsourcing to India and Egypt.
b. India is interested in outsourcing to Western countries for cheap labor.
c. Egypt is interested in outsourcing to Western corporations for cheap labor.
d. Western corporations will continue to outsource to other countries in the future.

6. "Investment in these countries has huge potential for high returns and high reward. The initial hype about EMs has subsided during the global recession, but that has allowed us to instead focus on their long and steady growth. These economies are resource rich. Resources include gold, petroleum, diamonds, and other natural resources. A lot of these EMs have enormous populations and a growing middle class. Some EM nations are predicted to become future superpowers, powerful enough to influence the global economy and other sociopolitical realities."

The main point of the above passage is that

a. some EMs have resources that include gold, petroleum, diamonds and natural gas.
b. China's economy will grow exponentially and overtake that of the United States.
c. some EM nations may become superpowers such as the United States and China over time.
d. the United States and China will continue to be the only two superpowers of the world.

7. "Through the Internet, almost any business can reach their targets in these markets, directly and economically, no matter the size or location of the business. In terms of the ebocube model, reliable Internet access in a particular market is a prerequisite for launching successful integrated Internet campaigns. The Internet works as a response mechanism for customers and vendors and transfers data back into your company databases. Internet applications enable you to track and measure successful integrated campaigns. Therefore, reliable Internet access and service is a major consideration when deciding in which market to implement ebocube."

It can be concluded from the statement that

a. businesses can thrive in EMs without reliable Internet access.
b. businesses can suffer in EMs without reliable Internet access.
c. unreliable Internet access is a prerequisite for launching business.
d. emerging markets will continue to grow without reliable Internet access.

8. "For example, from 2000 to 2009, the MEA region had the highest percentage increase in the number of Internet users (a world-leading 2,196% gain). This was followed by the LatAM region, which increased its web users by 883%. More mature Internet markets such as Asia are up 545%."

   The above examples are offered to support the idea that

   a. the number of Internet users declined around the world from 2000 to 2009.
   b. Internet use grew rapidly in Asian countries only from 2000 to 2009.
   c. the number of Web users increased rapidly around the world from 2000 to 2009.
   d. the number of Internet users remained the same from 2000 to 2009.

9. "Global competition is intensifying as EM countries build trade relationships with other less-developed markets and meet demand in their own domestic markets. For developed countries, the time window to get a business foothold in some of these markets may begin to close over the next decade. Internet marketing and ebocube can give you quick entry to market in terms of raising brand awareness, generating interest, and creating sales leads. As nations, including Russia and China, expand global market reach, competition will intensify in the near future."

   Which of the following conclusions can be drawn from the above passage?

   a. EM countries will give stiff competition to developed countries in 10 years.
   b. EM countries will be extremely profitable for developed countries in 10 years.
   c. Developed countries will stop raising brand awareness in EM countries in 10 years.
   d. Less-developed countries will directly compete with developed countries in 10 years.

10. "Internet usage via mobile phones will see a massive surge driven by growth in EMs. China's Internet penetration via mobile phone is set to grow. And some predict that India will have the fastest growing mobile Internet population, doubling by 2013. The number of mobile devices will increase accordingly."

    Based on the information presented in the above passage, which of the following *cannot* be a true statement?

    a. Smartphone manufacturers will benefit from the surge in Internet usage in EMs.
    b. The iPhone will exploit the massive surge in Internet usage via mobile phones in EMs.
    c. Most smartphone manufacturers will compete with each other in China and India.
    d. The iPhone will face less competition from other smartphone manufacturers.

READING 5

Newspaper Article

MyReadingLab

Visit Chapter 5: E-Commerce in MyReadingLab to complete the Reading 5 activities.

Baidu CEO Robin Li Becomes China's Richest Man

Pre-Reading Questions

Before you read the following article, discuss these questions in small groups and share your answers with your classmates.

1. Which search engine do you often use, and why? In your opinion, what makes a search engine extremely popular among Internet users? Be specific.
2. The growth of Internet users in China has been explosive in recent years. Approximately 400 million people, mostly young, use the Internet in China frequently. What do you think has caused this explosive growth of Internet use in China?
3. Baidu, a popular Chinese search engine, has forced Google, an American search engine behemoth, to exit the Chinese market. Discuss why a Chinese corporation would be motivated to compete with an American corporation. Use specific examples to support your answer.

Baidu CEO Robin Li Becomes China's Richest Man

By **Jimmy Chuang**
March 11, 2011

1 Baidu's CEO Robin Li has come into the **spotlight** after Forbes listed him as the world's 95th and China's richest man for this year on March 10.

assets
the items detailed on a balance sheet

2 Li's **assets** were estimated to be worth US$9.4 billion, followed by Apple's CEO Steve Jobs's US$8.3 billion, Google's CEO Eric Schmidt's US$7 billion, Taiwan's HTC Chairwoman Cher Wang's US$6.8 billion, Fubon Group Chairman Tsai Wan-tsai's US$6.3 billion.

3 Want Want Group Chairman Tsai Eng-meng checked in with US$5.2 billion, which made him Taiwan's fourth richest man and the world's 196th.

tycoon
a businessperson of great wealth and power

4 Hong Kong's business **tycoon** Li Ka-shing was ranked the top rich man in Hong Kong and the world's 11th with his assets of US$26 billion.

5 Li, a Chinese-American, was born in Yangquan, Shanxi Province, on Nov. 17, 1968. He spent most of his childhood in Yangquan while both of his parents were factory workers. He is also the only boy and the second youngest among five children of his parents.

6 Li was admitted to Yangquan First High School after achieving the second highest grades in the entrance exam. He began to show his interests in computer since high school, when he participated in numerous programming competitions in Yangquan.

7 In 1987, Li attended the National Higher Education Entrance Exam and achieved the top grade among all examinees in Yangquan. He was admitted to Peking University, one of China's top universities, to continue his college education and received a bachelor's degree in information management.

8 In 1991, Li continued his graduate education at State University of New York-Buffalo (SUNY-Buffalo) and planned to go all the way for a doctoral degree. He later received his master's in computer science in 1994 after he decided to discontinue his PhD program.

9 In 1994, Li began his first job by joining IDD Information Services, a New Jersey division of Dow Jones and Company, where he helped develop a software program for the online edition of the Wall Street Journal. Li stayed there until 1997.

10 In 1996, Li developed the RankDex site-scoring algorithm for search engines results page ranking for IDD. He also received a US patent for his work and later took advantage of the same technology for Baidu's search engine.

11 Li met his wife Ma Dongmin at a ball-dancing occasion during his study at SUNY-Buffalo. He said that they decided to get married after six months and had their first baby girl in 2000.

12 Between 1997 and 1999, Li worked as a staff engineer for Infoseek, a pioneer Internet search engine company.

13 Li established Baidu in 1999 and turned the company into the largest Chinese search engine within nine years, with over 70% market share, and the third largest independent search engine in the world. In 2005, Baidu completed its successful IPO on NASDAQ, and in 2007 became the first Chinese company to be included in the NASDAQ-100 Index.

14 Li said that "technology changing people's lives" is his dream, and being challenged by one of his professors at SUNY-Buffalo was the ignition for him to "do something."

15 "I decided to do something in the Internet industry to change foreigners' views of China," Li said.

16 Li's remarks referred to a conversation with one of his professors when he was studying at SUNY-Buffalo.

17 "He was not very satisfied with my answers so he challenged me by saying, 'You are from China? Well, do you have computers there?' " Li said. "That was **humiliating** to my country and I decided to prove him wrong by returning to China and establishing a new Chinese competitor for US companies."

humiliating lowering the pride, self-respect, or dignity of a person

18 Li's efforts resulted in his company earning a 137% increase net profit last year.

19 At his company's first IPO, Li was told and suggested to start with a lower price, which Li decided to ignore.

20 "They said 'China' means low quality so we shall start with a lower price to attract more investors. Well, I said, Baidu is a developing company. The earlier you own its shares, the more you will end up with," Li said.

21 Baidu's share price rose 353.85% the first day it was listed.

Reading with a Critical Eye

1. What is the author's purpose in mentioning some of the richest people of the world at the beginning of the article? In other words, what do some of the richest people in the United States and Hong Kong have to do with China's richest man?
2. The article mentions that Robin Li was the second-youngest among five children of his parents. Why is it that only he became the richest man of China and that his siblings lagged behind?
3. We learn that Robin Li's parents were factory workers, which means that he was not born with a silver spoon. What do you think motivated him to become an entrepreneur and start his own business in China?
4. Robin Li was interested in computers from an early stage in his life. His interest in programming took him from China to the United States, where he pursued an advanced degree in computer science at the State University of New York (SUNY). Tell how one carves a niche for oneself by turning one's love of a particular field into a professional career.
5. Robin Li established Baidu in 1999 and made it China's largest search engine in nine years. Baidu has continued to grow exponentially since then, boasting millions of Chinese Internet users. What are the key elements of Robin Li's tremendous success?

Reading Comprehension Check

1. "Li's assets were estimated to be worth US$9.4 billion, followed by Apple's CEO Steve Jobs's US$8.3 billion, Google's CEO Eric Schmidt's US$7 billion, Taiwan's HTC Chairwoman Cher Wang's US$6.8 billion, Fubon Group Chairman Tsai Wan-tsai's US$6.3 billion."

In the above sentence, the word *estimated* means
a. to form an approximate calculation.
b. to form an incorrect calculation.
c. to make an erroneous judgment.
d. to form an incorrect opinion.

2. "Baidu's CEO Robin Li has come into the spotlight after Forbes listed him as the world's 95th and China's richest man for this year on March 10."

It can be inferred from the above statement that
a. it is ominous for an entrepreneur to be featured in *Forbes*.
b. only Internet users pay attention to *Forbes*.
c. *Forbes* must be a respectable business magazine.
d. Robin Li is CEO of *Forbes* as well.

3. "Li was admitted to Yangquan First High School after achieving the second highest grades in the entrance exam."

The word *achieving* in the above context means
a. flunking.
b. obtaining.
c. missing.
d. calculating.

4. "He began to show his interests in computer since high school, when he participated in numerous programming competitions in Yangquan."

In the above context, the word *numerous* means
a. existing in small quantity.
b. very poor in quality.
c. existing in great quantity.
d. very few in quantity.

5. "In 1987, Li attended the National Higher Education Entrance Exam and achieved the top grade among all examinees in Yangquan. He was admitted to Peking University, one of China's top universities, to continue his college education and received a bachelor's degree in information management."

A logical conclusion that can be drawn from the above passage is that
a. Peking University has an open admission policy.
b. all students from Yangquan are admitted to Peking University.
c. Peking University only offers a bachelor's degree in information management.
d. only high-performing students are admitted to Peking University.

6. "In 1991, Li continued his graduate education at State University of New York-Buffalo (SUNY-Buffalo) and planned to go all the way for a doctoral degree. He later received his master's in computer science in 1994 after he decided to discontinue his PhD program."

Based on the passage, which of the following conclusions is logical?
a. State University of New York does not offer a doctoral degree.
b. Robin Li lost his interest in computer science.

c. An opportunity presented itself to Robin Li, prompting him to discontinue his PhD program.
d. His professor forced him to quit the PhD program.

7. "In 1996, Li developed the RankDex site-scoring algorithm for search engines results page ranking for IDD. He also received a US patent for his work and later took advantage of the same technology for Baidu's search engine."

It can be inferred from the above passage that
a. when he applied for the U.S. patent, Robin Li had Baidu's search engine in mind.
b. Robin Li established Baidu in China in 1996.
c. Robin Li took advantage of IDD.
d. Robin Li was confused about the technology for Baidu's search engine.

8. "Baidu completed its successful IPO on NASDAQ, and in 2007 became the first Chinese company to be included in the NASDAQ-100 Index."

The term *IPO* stands for
a. Italian Painting Organization.
b. Intelligence Protection Officer.
c. International Police Office.
d. Initial Public Offering.

9. "Li established Baidu in 1999 and turned the company into the largest Chinese search engine within nine years, with over 70% market share, and the third largest independent search engine in the world."

It can be concluded from the above passage that
a. Baidu had many competitors in China in 1999.
b. Baidu surpassed its major Chinese competitors by 2008.
c. Google asked Li to establish Baidu in China in 1999.
d. Baidu became the third largest independent search engine in the world in 1999.

10. Li's remarks referred to a conversation with one of his professors when he was studying at SUNY-Buffalo. "He was not very satisfied with my answers so he challenged me by saying, 'You are from China? Well, do you have computers there?' " Li said. "That was humiliating to my country and I decided to prove him wrong by returning to China and establishing a new Chinese competitor for US companies."

It can be inferred from the above passage that
a. the American professor admired Robin Li and China.
b. Robin Li despised his American professor.
c. the American professor had a low opinion of China.
d. the American professor had traveled to China several times.

Contemporary Issues in the Discipline

Jeff Bezos has rewritten the e-commerce rulebook. The founder and CEO of Amazon.com, he expanded an online bookstore into a multi-billion dollar company that sells nearly anything to nearly anyone, and helping launch an age of online shopping. Amazon transformed how people think about shopping, and its success inspired countless other retailers to choose digital storefronts. Amazon now sells nearly every kind of product imaginable, including the world's first widely adopted e-reader, the Kindle, and it produces its own original content as a publisher and producer (of shows like *Alpha House* and *Transparent*).

MyReadingLab

Visit Chapter 5: E-Commerce in MyReadingLab to complete the Reading 6 activities.

READING 6

Lecture (TED Talk)

The Electricity Metaphor for the Web's Future

Before reading the following transcript of Jeff Bezos's speech, you can watch the talk itself here: https://www.ted.com/talks/jeff_bezos_on_the_next_web_innovation?language=en (Courtesy of TED).

As you listen to the videoed presentation, take notes. (See the note-taking activity on p. 190 for some pointers.) After reading the transcript, you will answer some open-ended questions about some of the issues raised in the speech. Finally, you will formulate questions for Mr. Bezos about issues pertinent to e-commerce and answer them from his perspective.

The Electricity Metaphor for the Web's Future

By Jeff Bezos, February 2003 Transcript courtesy of TED © TED CONFERENCES, LLC

1 When you think about resilience and technology it's actually much easier. You're going to see some other speakers today, I already know, who are going to talk about breaking-bones stuff, and, of course, with technology it never is. So it's very easy, comparatively speaking, to be resilient. I think that, if we look at what happened on the Internet, with such an incredible last half a dozen years, that it's hard to even get the right analogy for it. A lot of how we decide, how we're supposed to react to things and what we're supposed to expect about the future depends on how we bucket things and how we categorize them.

2 And so I think the tempting analogy for the boom-bust that we just went through with the Internet is a gold rush. It's easy to think of this analogy as very different from some of the other things you might pick. For one thing, both were very real. In 1849, in that Gold Rush, they took over $700 million worth of gold out of California. It was very real. The Internet was also very real. This is a real way for humans to communicate with each other. It's a big deal. Huge boom. Huge boom. Huge bust. Huge bust. You keep going, and both things are lots of hype. I don't have to remind you of all the hype that was involved with the Internet—like GetRich.com.

3 But you had the same thing with the Gold Rush. "Gold. Gold. Gold." Sixty-eight rich men on the Steamer Portland. Stacks of yellow metal. Some have 5,000. Many have more. A few bring out 100,000 dollars each. People would get very excited about this when they read these articles. "The Eldorado of the United States of America: the discovery of inexhaustible gold mines in California." And the parallels between the Gold Rush and the Internet Rush continue very strongly. So many people left what they were doing. And what would happen is—and the Gold Rush went on for years.

4 People on the East Coast in 1849, when they first started to get the news, they thought, "Ah, this isn't real." But they keep hearing about people getting rich, and then in 1850 they still hear that. And they think it's not real. By about 1852, they're thinking, "Am I the stupidest person on Earth by not rushing to California?" And they start to decide they are. These are community affairs, by the way. Local communities on the East Coast would get together and whole teams of 10, 20 people would caravan across the United States, and they would form companies. These were typically not solitary efforts. But no matter what, if you were a lawyer or a banker, people dropped what they were doing, no matter what skill set they had, to go pan for gold.

5 This guy on the left, Dr. Richard Beverley Cole, he lived in Philadelphia and he took the Panama route. They would take a ship down to Panama, across the isthmus, and then take another ship north. This guy, Dr. Toland, went by covered wagon to California.

This has its parallels, too. Doctors leaving their practices. These are both very successful—a physician in one case, a surgeon in the other. Same thing happened on the Internet. You get DrKoop.com.

(Laughter)

6 In the Gold Rush, people literally jumped ship. The San Francisco harbor was clogged with 600 ships at the peak because the ships would get there and the crews would abandon to go search for gold. So there were literally 600 captains and 600 ships. They turned the ships into hotels, because they couldn't sail them anywhere. You had dotcom fever. And you had gold fever. And you saw some of the excesses that the dotcom fever created and the same thing happened. The fort in San Francisco at the time had about 1,300 soldiers. Half of them deserted to go look for gold. And they wouldn't let the other half out to go look for the first half because they were afraid they wouldn't come back.

(Laughter)

7 And one of the soldiers wrote home, and this is the sentence that he put: "The struggle between right and six dollars a month and wrong and 75 dollars a day is a rather severe one." They had bad burn rate in the Gold Rush. A very bad burn rate. This is actually from the Klondike Gold Rush. This is the White Pass Trail. They loaded up their mules and their horses. And they didn't plan right. And they didn't know how far they would really have to go, and they overloaded the horses with hundreds and hundreds of pounds of stuff. In fact it was so bad that most of the horses died before they could get where they were going. It got renamed the "Dead Horse Trail."

8 And the Canadian Minister of the Interior wrote this at the time: "Thousands of pack horses lie dead along the way, sometimes in bunches under the cliffs, with pack saddles and packs where they've fallen from the rock above, sometimes in tangled masses, filling the mud holes and furnishing the only footing for our poor pack animals on the march, often, I regret to say, exhausted, but still alive, a fact we were unaware of, until after the miserable wretches turned beneath the hooves of our cavalcade. The eyeless sockets of the pack animals everywhere account for the myriads of ravens along the road. The inhumanity which this trail has been witness to, the heartbreak and suffering which so many have undergone, cannot be imagined. They certainly cannot be described."

9 And you know, without the smell that would have accompanied that, we had the same thing on the Internet: very bad burn rate calculations. I'll just play one of these and you'll remember it. This is a commercial that was played on the Super Bowl in the year 2000.

10 (Video): Bride #1: You said you had a large selection of invitations. Clerk: But we do. Bride #2: Then why does she have my invitation? Announcer: What may be a little thing to some . . . Bride #3: You are mine, little man. Announcer: Could be a really big deal to you. Husband #1: Is that your wife? Husband #2: Not for another 15 minutes. Announcer: After all, it's your special day. OurBeginning.com. Life's an event. Announce it to the world.

Jeff Bezos: It's very difficult to figure out what that ad is for. *(Laughter)*

11 But they spent three and a half million dollars in the 2000 Super Bowl to air that ad, even though, at the time, they only had a million dollars in annual revenue. Now, here's where our analogy with the Gold Rush starts to diverge, and I think rather severely. And that is, in a gold rush, when it's over, it's over. Here's this guy: "There are many men in Dawson at the present time who feel keenly disappointed. They've come thousands of miles on a perilous trip, risked life, health and property, spent months of the most arduous labor a man can perform and at length with expectations raised to the highest pitch have reached the coveted goal only to discover the fact that there is nothing here for them."

12 And that was, of course, the very common story. Because when you take out that last piece of gold—and they did incredibly quickly. I mean, if you look at the 1849 Gold Rush—the entire American river region, within two years—every stone had been turned. And after that, only big companies who used more sophisticated mining technologies started to take gold out of there. So there's a much better analogy that allows you to be incredibly optimistic and that analogy is the electric industry. And there are a lot of similarities between the Internet and the electric industry. With the electric industry you actually have to—one of them is that they're both sort of thin, horizontal, enabling layers that go across lots of different industries. It's not a specific thing.

13 But electricity is also very, very broad, so you have to sort of narrow it down. You know, it can be used as an incredible means of transmitting power. It's an incredible means of coordinating, in a very fine-grained way, information flows. There's a bunch of things that are interesting about electricity. And the part of the electric revolution that I want to focus on is sort of the golden age of appliances. The killer app that got the world ready for appliances was the light bulb. So the light bulb is what wired the world. And they weren't thinking about appliances when they wired the world. They were really thinking about—they weren't putting electricity into the home; they were putting lighting into the home. And, but it really—it got the electricity. It took a long time.

14 This was a huge—as you would expect—a huge capital build out. All the streets had to be torn up. This is work going on down in lower Manhattan where they built some of the first electric power generating stations. And they're tearing up all the streets. The Edison Electric Company, which became Edison General Electric, which became General Electric, paid for all of this digging up of the streets. It was incredibly expensive. But that is not the—and that's not the part that's really most similar to the Web. Because, remember, the Web got to stand on top of all this heavy infrastructure that had been put in place because of the long-distance phone network. So all of the cabling and all of the heavy infrastructure—I'm going back now to,

sort of, the explosive part of the Web in 1994, when it was growing 2,300 percent a year. How could it grow at 2,300 percent a year in 1994 when people weren't really investing in the Web? Well, it was because that heavy infrastructure had already been laid down.

15 So the light bulb laid down the heavy infrastructure, and then home appliances started coming into being. And this was huge. The first one was the electric fan—this was the 1890 electric fan. And the appliances, the golden age of appliances really lasted—it depends how you want to measure it—but it's anywhere from 40 to 60 years. It goes on a long time. It starts about 1890. And the electric fan was a big success. The electric iron, also very big. By the way, this is the beginning of the asbestos lawsuit.

(Laughter)

16 There's asbestos under that handle there. This is the first vacuum cleaner, the 1905 Skinner Vacuum, from the Hoover Company. And this one weighed 92 pounds and took two people to operate and cost a quarter of a car. So it wasn't a big seller. This was truly, truly an early-adopter product—*(Laughter)* the 1905 Skinner Vacuum. But three years later, by 1908, it weighed 40 pounds. Now, not all these things were highly successful.

(Laughter)

17 This is the electric tie press, which never really did catch on. People, I guess, decided that they would not wrinkle their ties. These never really caught on either: the electric shoe warmer and drier. Never a big seller. This came in, like, six different colors.

(Laughter)

18 I don't know why. But I thought, you know, sometimes it's just not the right time for an invention; maybe it's time to give this one another shot. So I thought we could build a Super Bowl ad for this. We'd need the right partner. And I thought that really—*(Laughter)* I thought that would really work, to give that another shot. Now, the toaster was huge because they used to make toast on open fires, and it took a lot of time and attention. I want to point out one thing. This is—you guys know what this is. They hadn't invented the electric socket yet. So this was—remember, they didn't wire the houses for electricity. They wired them for lighting. So your—your appliances would plug in. They would—each room typically had a light bulb socket at the top. And you'd plug it in there.

19 In fact, if you've seen the Carousel of Progress at Disney World, you've seen this. Here are the cables coming up into this light fixture. All the appliances plug in there. And you would just unscrew your light bulb if you wanted to plug in an appliance. The next thing that really was a big, big deal was the washing machine. Now, this was an object of much envy and lust. Everybody wanted one of these electric washing machines. On the left-hand side, this was the soapy water. And there's a rotor there—that this motor is spinning. And it would clean your clothes. This is the clean rinse-water. So you'd take the clothes out of here, put them in here, and then you'd run the clothes

through this electric ringer. And this was a big deal. You'd keep this on your porch. It was a little bit messy and kind of a pain. And you'd run a long cord into the house where you could screw it into your light socket.

(Laughter)

20 And that's actually kind of an important point in my presentation, because they hadn't invented the off switch. That was to come much later—the off switch on appliances—because it didn't make any sense. I mean, you didn't want this thing clogging up a light socket. So you know, when you were done with it, you unscrewed it. That's what you did. You didn't turn it off. And as I said before, they hadn't invented the electric outlet either, so the washing machine was a particularly dangerous device. And there are—when you research this, there are gruesome descriptions of people getting their hair and clothes caught in these devices. And they couldn't yank the cord out because it was screwed into a light socket inside the house.

(Laughter)

21 And there was no off switch, so it wasn't very good. And you might think that that was incredibly stupid of our ancestors to be plugging things into a light socket like this. But, you know, before I get too far into condemning our ancestors, I thought I'd show you: this is my conference room. This is a total kludge, if you ask me. First of all, this got installed upside down. This light socket—(Laughter) and so the cord keeps falling out, so I taped it in.

(Laughter)

22 This is supposed—don't even get me started. But that's not the worst one. This is what it looks like under my desk. I took this picture just two days ago. So we really haven't progressed that much since 1908.

(Laughter)

23 It's a total, total mess. And, you know, we think it's getting better, but have you tried to install 802.11 yourself?

(Laughter)

24 I challenge you to try. It's very hard. I know Ph.D.s in Computer Science—this process has brought them to tears, absolute tears. (Laughter) And that's assuming you already have DSL in your house. Try to get DSL installed in your house. The engineers who do it everyday can't do it. They have to—typically, they come three times. And one friend of mine was telling me a story: not only did they get there and have to wait, but then the engineers, when they finally did get there, for the third time, they had to call somebody. And they were really happy that the guy had a speakerphone because then they had to wait on hold for an hour to talk to somebody to give them an access code after they got there. So we're not—we're pretty kludge-y ourselves.

25 By the way, DSL is a kludge. I mean, this is a twisted pair of copper that was never designed for the purpose it's being put to—you

know it's the whole thing—we're very, very primitive. And that's kind of the point. Because, you know, resilience—if you think of it in terms of the Gold Rush, then you'd be pretty depressed right now because the last nugget of gold would be gone. But the good thing is, with innovation, there isn't a last nugget. Every new thing creates two new questions and two new opportunities.

26 And if you believe that, then you believe that where we are—this is what I think—I believe that where we are with the incredible kludge—and I haven't even talked about user interfaces on the Web—but there's so much kludge, so much terrible stuff—we are at the 1908 Hurley washing machine stage with the Internet. That's where we are. We don't get our hair caught in it, but that's the level of primitiveness of where we are. We're in 1908.

27 And if you believe that, then stuff like this doesn't bother you. This is 1996: "All the negatives add up to making the online experience not worth the trouble." 1998: "Amazon.toast." In 1999: "Amazon.bomb." My mom hates this picture.

(Laughter)

28 She—but you know, if you really do believe that it's the very, very beginning, if you believe it's the 1908 Hurley washing machine, then you're incredibly optimistic. And I do think that that's where we are. And I do think there's more innovation ahead of us than there is behind us. And in 1917, Sears—I want to get this exactly right. This was the advertisement that they ran in 1917. It says: "Use your electricity for more than light." And I think that's where we are. We're very, very early. Thank you very much.

Reading with a Critical Eye

1. At the beginning of his speech, Bezos opines, "A lot of how we decide, how we're supposed to react to things and what we're supposed to expect about the future depends on how we bucket things and how we categorize them." Discuss what he means by that in reference to technology and the Internet.
2. Why does Bezos think that people communicating with each other in real time on the Internet is a big deal? Be specific.
3. What is Bezos's point in using the Gold Rush analogy? In other words, why does he compare the bad burn rate in the Gold Rush and the bad burn rate during the early days of the Internet? Discuss what Bezos wants us to learn from the two mistakes.
4. Despite the advancements in science and technology, Bezos believes that we are still very, very early, and that "there's more innovation ahead of us than there is behind us." In your opinion, what kinds of innovation are awaiting us? Use specific examples to support your answer.

Imagined Interview: If you had the opportunity to interview Jeff Bezos in person, what would you ask him? With a partner, compose three questions for him.

Question 1. ______________________________

Question 2. ______________________________

Question 3. ______________________________

Interview Challenge: In a group, ask one student to play Mr. Bezos. This student should carefully consider Jeff Bezos's views, outlined clearly in the TED Talk, and try to answer the questions from Mr. Bezos's perspective on education.

Chapter Recap

Now that you have made it through a full chapter focusing on Internet marketing, let's review the chapter's reading content, skill focus, and vocabulary to gain a better understanding of what we have learned.

Recap Activity 1: A Quick Glance

In 60 seconds, write brief answers to the following two questions. You may wish to share your answers with your classmates or with your instructor.

1. What is one thing you learned from this chapter?

____

____

____

____

____

____

2. What was your favorite reading in the chapter? Explain.

____

____

____

____

____

____

Now discuss what you wrote in a small group. Do not read what you wrote. Paraphrase yourself!

Recap Activity 2: Summary Writing

Choose your favorite reading from this chapter and write a summary containing the main idea and some major details. Keep in mind that the key to summary writing is to convey the author's ideas accurately, but to relay this information in your own words. Last but not least, be sure to include reminder phrases and appropriate transitions. Which reading in this chapter did you find the most interesting, and why?

Recap Activity 3: Internet Research on a Theme of Interest

Think about the choice you just made in Activity 2 concerning which reading in the chapter was your favorite.

What was the theme of your chosen reading?

Theme = ____

Using a search engine such as Google or Bing, go online and locate a quality reading on the same theme as your favorite chapter reading. Write a three- to five-sentence summary of the reading that you found from your Internet research. Be sure to include the author's most important points in your summary.

Title of Reading	*Article Source*	*Summary of the Reading (in your own words)*

Recap Activity 4: Reinforcing the Skill

Working with a partner, read the following paragraph. Then discuss what strategies can be used to make an inference. Remember that you are not being asked to make an inference based on facts. Instead, your task is to discuss with your peer the strategies that you can employ to make an inference. That is, discuss how you will approach making an inference based on the passage below.

> A good memo need not be a Pulitzer Prize winner, but it does need to be clear, brief, relevant. LBJ got along poorly with his science adviser, Donald Hornig, because Hornig's memos, according to a White House staffer, "were terribly long and complicated. The President couldn't read through a page or two and understand what Don wanted him to do, so he'd send it out to us and ask us what it was all about. Then we'd put a short cover-memo on top of it and send it back in. The President got mad as hell at long memos that didn't make any sense."

____

What strategies can you use to make a correct inference from the passage above?

Strategy 1: ______________________________________

Strategy 2: ______________________________________

Recap Activity 5: Recycling Vocabulary

With a partner, locate the following discipline-specific vocabulary items, review them in context, and try to define the terms without using a dictionary. The first example is done for you.

Word and context location	*Sentence containing the word*	*Meaning in this context*
forecast p. 253, par. 2	Goldman Sachs forecasts that the Chinese economy will overtake that of the United States by about 2040.	to predict a future condition
gustatory p. 223, par. 3	Mr. Friedman returned to his office, logged on and, at long last, felt in control of his **gustatory** future.	______________
emphasize p. 224, par. 8	Hoping to make ordering a burger as routine as ordering a book from Amazon, a number of chains are **emphasizing** the dot-com after their corporate name to lure the hungry and time-pressed to their Web sites.	______________ ______________
accessing p. 230, par. 1	Globally, men have a much easier time **accessing** the Internet than women, according to a new report issued by the United Nations Broadband Commission Working Group.	______________ ______________
ecommerce p. 231, par. 4	Statistics from the Arab Advisors Group showed that higher percentages of men in Saudi Arabia, Morocco and Jordan use **ecommerce** services than women.	______________ ______________

Word and context location	*Sentence containing the word*	*Meaning in this context*
authoritative p. 241, par. 1	Google's Matt Cutts considers Danny Sullivan's Search Engine Watch website "must reading." To Yahoo's Tim Mayer, it's simply the "most **authoritative** source on search."	______________ ______________
undisclosed p. 243, par. 18	Within a year, he sold his website for an **undisclosed** price to MecklerMedia (now Jupitermedia), which kept him on as an independent contractor and expanded into trade shows.	______________ ______________
fortune p. 244, par. 26	He may not have a **fortune**, but in his own little world, "Danny is the rock star of our industry," says Brown, who sells him that way to potential attendees of shows.	______________ ______________
spotlight p. 260, par. 1	Baidu's CEO Robin Li has come into the **spotlight** after Forbes listed him as the world's 95th and China's richest man for this year on March 10.	______________ ______________
ignition p. 261, par. 14	Li said that "technology changing people's lives" is his dream, and being challenged by one of his professors at SUNY-Buffalo was the **ignition** for him to "do something."	______________ ______________

Further Explorations

Books

1. *One Click: Jeff Bezos and the Rise of Amazon.com (2012)* by Richard L. Brandt. Portfolio. Richard Brandt, an award-winning journalist, tells the true story of Jeff Bezos and his empire Amazon.com with meticulous research and pithy commentary.
2. *Don't Make Me Think: A Common Sense Approach to Web Usability* (2005) by Steve Krug. New Riders Press. In this book, Krug uses humor and excellent examples to prove that most Web sites are designed to reduce the user's cognitive load and make Web usability a pleasant experience.

Movies

1. *The Social Network* (2010). This Hollywood movie is based on the true story of how Mark Zuckerberg created a social networking site that became known as Facebook.
2. *Terms and Conditions May Apply* (2013). This movie reveals what American corporations are legally taking from Internet users without their knowledge and consent and shows the consequences of clicking "I accept."

Internet Sites

1. www.networksolutions.com
   This site provides useful tools and information on how to start a business online. If you are interested in starting your own e-commerce Web site, this is a good place for you to start.
2. www.commerce.gov/egov/index.htm
   This is the official Web site of the Department of Commerce, where you can find pertinent information about conducting business on the Internet. You can also apply for fishing permits and export licenses here.

Communicating with the Professor: Making an Appointment

Overview

Many students usually do not take advantage of the opportunity to meet with the professor individually. Most professors keep office hours specifically for the purpose of answering questions students may have about the course or particular assignments. In the meeting with the professor, students can ask clarification questions about their progress in the course, express concerns regarding an assignment, and even ask for help with a difficult reading. Students are expected to set up an appointment with the professor before showing up at her or his door.

Implications for Learning

Professors appreciate students who play a proactive role in their learning. By making an appointment with the professor to discuss class material or more general concerns, you are demonstrating to the professor that you are genuinely interested in your academic growth. Another implication is that in the real world you will be expected to make appointments with your colleagues and superiors, so setting up one-on-one conferences with your professors will give you a head start with this valuable skill.

Challenge Activity: Making an Appointment

Review some of your recent class reading assignments and consider which of the readings was the most difficult for you to fully understand. Look through the reading and highlight a few areas that are still confusing to you. Make an appointment with your professor following the guidelines laid out in your course syllabus. Bring the course reading you found challenging with you and discuss the text with your professor.

CRIMINAL JUSTICE
Criminal Investigation

"It is better that ten guilty persons escape, than that one innocent suffer."

SIR WILLIAM BLACKSTONE

Learning Objectives

AFTER READING THIS CHAPTER, YOU SHOULD BE ABLE TO ...

1. Analyze issues in criminal justice.
2. Differentiate between facts and opinions.
3. Argue persuasively in writing.
4. Demonstrate time management.

INTRODUCTION TO THE FIELD OF CRIMINAL JUSTICE

Criminal justice professionals provide vitally important services to society. They help fellow citizens and enjoy a sense of pride as they protect them from harm and give them peace of mind. The growing emphasis on homeland security has created an unprecedented demand for criminal justice professionals. At the same time, there is a growing distrust of the police force, who many see as discriminatory in practice and who are often viewed in relation to the many recent high-profile cases of police brutality.

Criminal justice as an academic area has evolved since its beginnings in the 1920s. Scientific research has become a major element in the increasing professionalization of criminal justice, and there is a strong call for the application in the justice field of evidence-based practices—that is, crime-fighting strategies that have been scientifically tested and that are based on social science research.

This chapter will primarily focus on issues related to criminal investigation. How has DNA evidence exposed some wrongful **convictions**? What is the role of citizen videos in uncovering police misconduct? How can our criminal justice system best deal with mentally ill criminals? These provocative questions, which are explored in the readings, engage the reader and provide a framework for thinking critically about criminal justice.

Preview Questions

1. Do you generally believe in America's criminal justice system? Do you believe the system is fair? Explain. Do you have a positive view of the police force? Why, or why not?
2. In your opinion, should the death penalty be legal? If yes, for what types of crimes should it be administered? Would abolishing the death penalty make America less safe? Explain.
3. Have you read or heard about a case where DNA samples provided incriminating evidence against a suspect? Describe the case.
4. Do you believe that DNA testing completely eliminates the possibility of innocent people being wrongly convicted of a crime? If yes, explain how this type of evidence reduces the margin of error.
5. In your opinion, is it a good idea for members of a community to form their own neighborhood-watch policing units? Why, or why not?

Writing on The Wall

After you have discussed the preview questions with your classmates, post your responses to two of them on your class blog, which we refer to as The Wall. Review others' postings and respond to at least two of your classmates' posts that grab your interest. Remember the guidelines for blogging and commenting etiquette (see p. 15)! If your class is not using a shared blog, your instructor may ask you to record your individual or collective responses to the preview questions in another form.

EXERCISE 6.1 Interpreting a Cartoon

Examine the cartoon and, in pairs, answer the following questions.

1. What is amusing about this cartoon?
2. In your opinion, what message is the cartoonist trying to convey to the reader?

"For the last time! No more DNA evidence!!"

Discipline-specific Vocabulary: Understand Key Terms in Criminal Justice

One of the most efficient ways to acquire academic vocabulary is to study key terms that are thematically connected. As you begin your college-level studies, it is critical that you internalize vocabulary terms that relate to the academic disciplines that make up most 100-level content courses. For example, a student taking an Introduction to Criminal Justice course should be able to apply such terms as *prosecute*, *plaintiff*, and *evidence* in both spoken and written forms.

EXERCISE 6.2 Brainstorming Vocabulary

Directions: What associated words come to mind when you think of the world of criminal justice? Work with a partner and write down as many related words as you can think of in a period of five minutes.

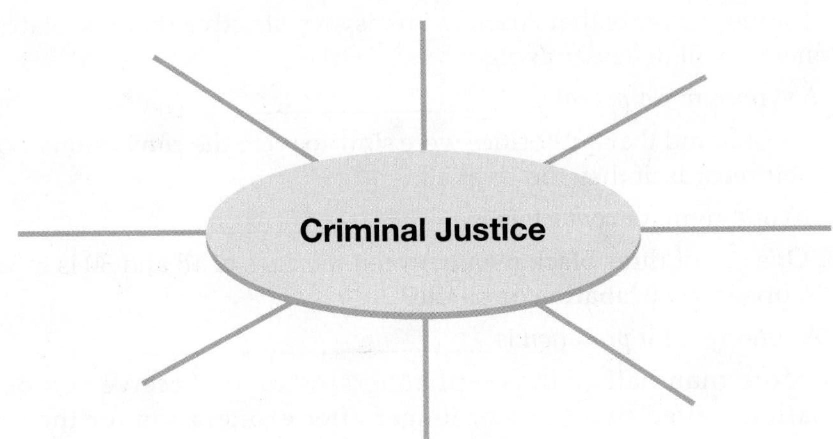

Fishing for Synonyms and Antonyms

In your written work, you will often need to use synonyms and antonyms (see p. 24 to review these terms) in order to paraphrase statements or claims made by writers.

EXERCISE 6.3 Determining Synonyms and Antonyms from Context

Directions: Read the following ten (10) discipline-specific words culled from the readings in this chapter and shown in the context of the sentences in which they appeared. In the space provided after each sentence, write a synonym or antonym for the highlighted term, as directed.

Discipline-specific Word Bank for Criminal Justice

acquittal	defendant
appeal	incarceration
conviction	evidence
probation	detained
exoneration	prosecution

1. "It is the first time the court has dealt with a direct constitutional challenge to the insanity defense since lawmakers around the country imposed new restrictions following John Hinckley's **acquittal** by reason of insanity in the 1981 shooting of President Reagan.
   A synonym for *acquittal* is ____________________.
2. "In his **appeal** to the U.S. Supreme Court, defense attorney David Goldberg asserts that Arizona law is so restrictive that it violates a mentally ill defendant's right to a fair trial."
   A synonym for *appeal* is ____________________.
3. "Most found that authorities were slow to wipe the **convictions** from their records, if they did so at all."
   An antonym for *conviction* is ____________________.
4. "One out of three black men between the ages of 18 and 30 is in jail, in prison, on **probation** or parole."
   A synonym for *probation* is ____________________.
5. "More than half of those [prisoners] who did receive compensation waited two years or longer after **exoneration** for the first payment."
   An antonym for *exoneration* is ____________________.
6. "Arizona law is so restrictive that it violates a mentally ill **defendant**'s right to a fair trial."
   An antonym for *defendant is* ____________________.
7. "The United States now has the highest rate of **incarceration** in the world."
   A synonym for *incarceration* is ____________________.
8. "The Supreme Court could establish a more specific definition of legal insanity or allow for broader discretion in determining when **evidence** of mental illness may be considered at trial."
   A synonym for *evidence* is ____________________.
9. "Why was he not immediately told why he was being **detained**?"
   An antonym for *detained* is ____________________.
10. "But authorities decided to postpone **prosecution** until Eric turned 18 later in the year."
    A synonym for *prosecution* is ____________________.

EXERCISE 6.4 Matching Terms with Definitions

Match the word in Column A with the definition in Column B. Put the letter representing the correct definition in the space preceding each term.

Column A		Column B
Word		**Definition**
1. ____	acquittal	a. a declaration that a person is guilty of an offense
2. ____	evidence	b. the person accused of a criminal offense
3. ____	conviction	c. the act of clearing someone of guilt
4. ____	prosecution	d. kept under restraint or custody
5. ____	detained	e. the release of an offender from detention, subject to a period of good behavior or supervision
6. ____	appeal	f. the body of officials who carry on legal proceedings against a person
7. ____	defendant	g. the state of being released
8. ____	exoneration	h. the act of being put in prison
9. ____	incarceration	i. anything useful to a judge or jury in deciding the facts of a case
10. ____	probation	j. an application to a higher court for a decision to be reversed

EXERCISE 6.5 Choosing the Right Word

In the following sentences, fill in the blank with a word from the terminology bank that makes the sentence grammatically correct and meaningful.

probation	appeal	detained	acquittal	evidence
defendant	incarceration	prosecution	conviction	exoneration

1. The two men faced ______________ after getting caught robbing a convenience store.
2. The accused criminal was ______________ under lock and key until his trial period.
3. The ______________ decided to take the stand and give his own testimony.
4. A 62-year-old man held in prison for 21 years was ______________ based on DNA evidence.
5. The verdict was "guilty," but his lawyers said they would ______________ the case.
6. Inconsistent evidence resulted in the defendant's ______________.
7. The case was dropped for lack of ______________.

8. Mr. Doogans was given early release and put on __________ for a period of five years.
9. The ______________ rested their case against the accused by cross-examining his wife.
10. Although they had two star witnesses, the prosecution was unable to win a ____________.

In-Class Survey: Criminal Justice Issues

Refer to the following questions to interview at least two classmates. Please take notes as they respond to your questions, and orally report your findings. Use a separate piece of paper if you need it.

Question	*Respondent 1*	*Respondent 2*
1. Do you think the death penalty should be legal in the United States?		
2. On a scale from 1 to 10, with 10 being the most effective, how effective a job do the police do in keeping our streets safe?		
3. Should juvenile offenders receive the same sentences for their crimes as adults do, or should they be given a second chance and given a lighter sentence? Give reasons for your position.		
4. If you had a high-level position in the field of criminal justice, what is one policy you would institute or change to make your city/town a safer place in which to live?		

Fieldwork Questionnaire

Please give the following survey to three people in your neighborhood, at work, or at school. Tell the respondents that the survey is conducted solely for academic purposes. You can either have them write brief answers to the survey questions if they prefer, or you can write down their answers as they respond to your questions orally. Be prepared to report the results of the survey to your class later. The survey will help you learn more about societal attitudes concerning criminal justice issues.

You can make two more photocopies of the survey so you will be able to question three respondents.

1. Using a 5-point scale with 1 representing "very low confidence" and 5 representing "very high confidence," how much confidence do you have in the following public services in your state?
   a. The public school system ____________
   b. The healthcare system ____________
   c. The welfare system ____________
   d. The criminal justice system ____________
2. Use the same 5-point scale with 1 representing "very low confidence" and 5 representing "very high confidence." How much confidence do you have in the criminal justice system's response to victims of crime? ____________
3. Using the same scale, how much confidence do you have in the following parts of the criminal justice system?
   a. The police ____________
   b. The courts ____________
   c. The corrections system ____________
4. Thinking about the police in your neighborhood, using the same scale, how confident are you in the police's ability to do each of the following?
   a. Prevent crimes from happening ____________
   b. Detect and arrest criminals ____________
5. Thinking about the courts in your city, how confident are you in the courts' ability to do each of the following?
   a. Determine if someone is guilty ____________
   b. Impose fair sentences ____________
6. Thinking about the prison system in your state, how confident are you in its ability to do each of the following?
   a. Keep prisoners from escaping ____________
   b. Rehabilitate prisoners so they do not commit another offense ____________
7. Using the same scale, how important do you think it is that the criminal justice system takes into consideration the fact that juvenile offenders are less mature than adults? ____________
8. Over the last five years, do you think that the overall crime rate in your city has gone up, stayed about the same, or decreased? ____________
9. What about property crimes such as residential break-ins and commercial theft? Do you think that over the last five years, the rate of these crimes in your city has gone up, stayed about the same, or decreased? ____________

10. When thinking about your own neighborhood compared to other neighborhoods in your city, do you think it is safer, about average, or less safe? _____________

The 2007 National Justice Survey: Tackling Crime and Public Confidence, Adaptation of *Appendix A - Questionnaire*, http://www.justice.gc.ca/eng/pi/rs/rep-rap/2007/rr07_4/a.html; Department of Justice Canada, 2007. Reproduced with the permission of the Minister of Public Works and Government Services Canada, 2011.

CSI: You Solve the Case!

We all love to play amateur detective. In this activity, you and a small group of classmates will be asked to use your deductive reasoning skills in examining the "facts" of a crime-scene investigation (CSI) case and making judgments about the criminal suspects. There has been a murder in Beverly Hills, California. After examining all of the presented facts, the list of leading suspects, and their stated **alibis**, your group's job is to decide who is most likely to be the guilty party on a scale from "most likely" to "least likely."

Facts at the Crime Scene

Fact 1: At 10:42 PM, **Pierre Emerson III** was found dead, lying face up by the side of his outdoor swimming pool in Beverly Hills. He was found by his maid, **Ms. Johnstone**, who immediately called the Los Angeles Police Department (LAPD).

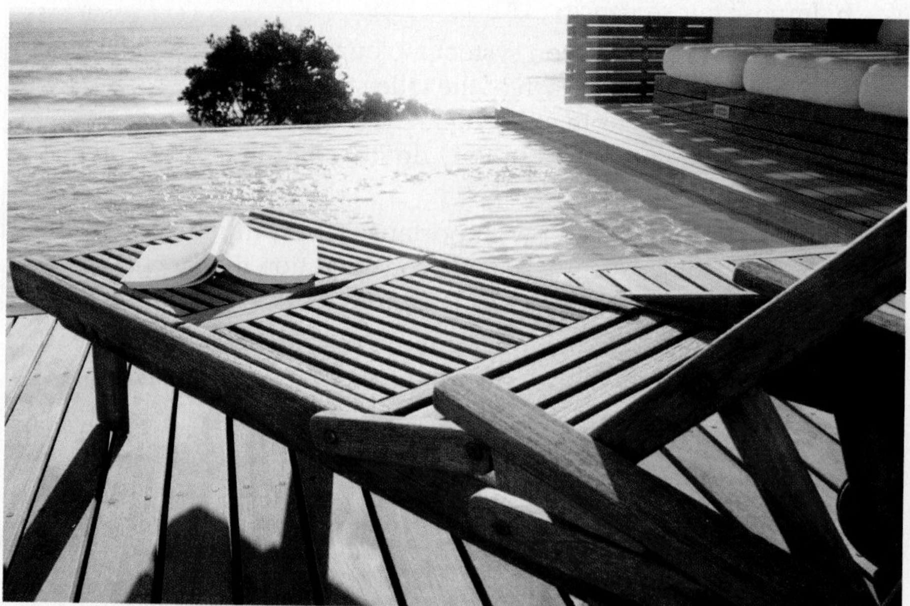

Fact 2: At 11:20 PM, a police investigator determined that the cause of death was poisoning. A half-full glass of red wine with some kind of poison inside was located near a small table inches away from the victim.

Fact 3: At 11:30 PM, the only witness, the maid, **Ms. Johnstone**, was interviewed for 40 minutes. She reported:

a. **Mr. Emerson** had seemed out of sorts all evening.

b. His lover, **Ms. Podly**, had left the premises in a limo only forty (40) to fifty (50) minutes before he was found dead.

c. He had received several threatening phone calls from **Mr. Samatini**, **Ms. Podly's** ex-husband: two this evening and a few the night before.

d. He also had received two faxes, one last week and one yesterday, from his business partner, **Mr. Lloyd**, pleading with him to agree to sign a document that would permit **Mr. Lloyd** to enjoy 100 percent control over business decisions regarding real estate.

e. **Mr. Emerson's** ex-wife, **Samantha**, had stopped by around 8 PM to pick up some items she had left behind. **Ms. Johnstone** heard the two arguing about something to do with money before **Samantha** left around 9 PM, slamming the door behind her.

The Five Possible Suspects

- **Miss Gwendolyn Podly**, his lover, 32, a connoisseur of fine wines. Fast-paced, eccentric, and a bit unstable, she had been secretly seeing **Mr. Emerson** for years while she was married. Her ex-husband had recently learned of this.
- **Ms. Johnstone**, his maid, 51. Reliable, yet had had a hard time adjusting to her life in the Emerson estate without **Mrs. Emerson**. She is the best friend of **Mrs. Emerson**.
- **Mr. Samatini, Ms. Podly's** ex-husband, 42. A well-built former wrestler. He had suspected his wife was seeing **Mr. Emerson**. He had recently learned that, in fact, his ex had been having an affair with **Mr. Emerson** for years.
- **Ms. Samantha Emerson**, his ex-wife, 38. A former model, she left **Mr. Emerson** because of his infidelities. She is attached to a high-living lifestyle and felt that upon their separation she deserved more from **Mr. Emerson's** estate.
- **Mr. Jonathan Lloyd**, his business partner, 57. He had worked together in business with **Mr. Emerson** for over 15 years. While their business empire had grown, **Mr. Lloyd** was feeling more and more trapped in this partnership, unable to make any important decisions

on his own. He had recently been approached secretly to work on a big real estate deal.

Testimony Offered by the Five Leading Suspects During Police Questioning

Suspect 1: Miss Gwendolyn Podly, his lover: "Well, it all seems so foggy now. I left his place in a hurry, this is true, but that was only because I was exhausted and needed to go to my place to catch up on my sleep. I loved this man with all of my heart, and was planning to one day get married to him."

Suspect 2: Ms. Johnstone, his maid: "Like I said earlier, one minute he was reading the stock pages and the next he was face up on his back by the side of the pool. Yes, I was disappointed when things fell apart with his lovely wife, but I remained a loyal and faithful servant to him to the end."

Suspect 3: Mr. Samatini, Ms. Podly's ex-husband: "I was absolutely infuriated to learn what I had suspected all along was true, that my wife and now ex-wife was seeing him. But I am a gentle guy, you can ask anybody. I wouldn't hurt a soul. That night, I was at the gym working out until way after midnight."

Suspect 4: Ms. Samantha Emerson, his ex-wife: "I stopped by and we had the same fight we always had, about money, money, money. If I had only known I would never see him again after that, I would have been nicer. He was a sweet man, but he certainly had his faults. He would never listen to my side of the story."

Suspect 5: Mr. Jonathan Lloyd, his business partner: "Yes, it is true that I was anxiously awaiting his reply to my urgent faxes, and that without his signature my deal couldn't go forward. I have already confessed that some of the information in the document was fraudulent, in that I misinformed him about the details of this big deal. But why would I kill him if I needed his signature? Anyway, as you know, I was out of town on vacation in Hawaii with my kids that evening."

Verdict Time

Now that you have read the facts about the case, it is time to discuss with your group who most likely murdered Pierre Emerson III on a warm night in Beverly Hills. Discuss the case and write the names on the spectrum below.

Most likely Possible Least likely

Defend Your Choices: List the factors as to why each suspect was given their "level of possible guilt" rating. *Note:* There is no one solution (except in the files of the LAPD). The fun is in comparing the results of your findings with another group!

MyReadingLab

Visit Chapter 6: Criminal Justice in MyReadingLab to complete the Reading 1 activities.

READING 1

Newspaper Article

Free and Uneasy: A Long Road Back After Exoneration, and Justice Is Slow to Make Amends

Pre-Reading Questions

Answer the three questions below with a partner.

1. Should **exonerated** prisoners who had been kept in jail for many years receive financial compensation? What level of compensation would be fair?
2. What kinds of obstacles do ex-prisoners face getting reestablished in the world outside the prison walls?
3. In your opinion, what steps can the government take to help exonerated prisoners become productive members of society?

exonerated officially cleared of blame and therefore not guilty

Before reading the entire article and answering the comprehension questions that follow, ask your own questions about the first part of the article.

Janet Roberts and Elizabeth Stanton, "Free and Uneasy: A Long Road Back After Exoneration, and Justice Is Slow to Make Amends." From *The New York Times*, November 25, 2007.

Free and Uneasy: A Long Road Back After Exoneration, and Justice Is Slow to Make Amends

By **Janet Roberts and Elizabeth Stanton,** **the *New York Times***

November 25, 2007

?

1 Christopher Ochoa graduated from law school five years out of prison and started his own practice in Madison, Wis. He has a girlfriend and is looking to buy a house.

2 Michael Anthony Williams, who entered prison as a 16-year-old boy and left more than two years ago as a 40-year-old man, has lived in a homeless shelter and had a series of jobs, none lasting more than six months.

?

3 Gene Bibbins worked a series of temporary factory jobs, got engaged, but fell into drug addiction. Four and a half years after walking out of the Louisiana State Penitentiary at Angola, he landed in jail in East Baton Rouge, accused of cocaine possession and battery.

4 The stories are not unusual for men who have spent many years in prison. What makes these three men different is that there are serious questions about whether they should have been in prison in the first place.

incarcerated
put in a prison or kept there

5 The men are among the more than 200 prisoners exonerated since 1989 by DNA evidence—almost all of whom had been **incarcerated** for murder or rape. Their varied experiences are typical of what the *New York Times* found in one of the most extensive looks to date at what happens to those exonerated inmates after they leave prison.

6 The Times worked from a list of DNA-exonerated prisoners kept by the Innocence Project—widely regarded as the most thorough

record of DNA exonerations. The Times then gathered extensive information on 137 of those whose convictions had been overturned, interviewing 115.

? ______

7 The findings show that most of them have struggled to keep jobs, pay for health care, rebuild family ties and shed the psychological effects of years of questionable or wrongful imprisonment.

8 Typically, testing of blood or semen from the crime scene revealed DNA pointing to another perpetrator. The authorities in some of the cases have continued to insist they convicted the right men, and have even fought efforts by some of them to sue for money.

9 About one-third of them, like Mr. Ochoa, found ways to get a stable footing in the world. But about one-sixth of them, like Mr. Bibbins, found themselves back in prison or suffering from drug or alcohol addiction.

10 About half, like Mr. Williams, had experiences somewhere between those extremes, drifting from job to job and leaning on their family, lawyers or friends for housing and other support.

11 And in many cases the justice system has been slow **to make amends.**

to make amends
to forgive, to resolve a conflict

12 The Times researched the compensation claims of all 206 people known by the Innocence Project to have been exonerated through DNA evidence as of August 2007. At least 79—nearly 40 percent—got no money for their years in prison. Half of those have federal lawsuits or state claims pending. More than half of those who did receive compensation waited two years or longer after **exoneration** for the first payment.

13 Few of those who were interviewed received any government services after their release. Indeed, despite being imprisoned for an average of 12 years, they typically left prison with less help—prerelease counseling, job training, substance-abuse treatment, housing assistance and other services—than some states offer to paroled prisoners.

14 "It's ridiculous," said Vincent Moto, exonerated in 1996 of a rape conviction after serving almost nine years in Pennsylvania. "They have programs for drug dealers who get out of prison. They have programs for people who really do commit crimes. People get out and go in halfway houses and have all kinds of support. There are housing programs for them, job placement for them. But for the innocent, they have nothing."

15 The Times's findings are limited to those exonerated inmates the newspaper reached and do not represent the experiences of exonerated prisoners everywhere.

16 Most of the 137 exonerated inmates researched by the Times entered prison in their teens or 20s, and they stayed there while some of their peers on the outside settled on careers, married, started families, bought homes and began saving for retirement. They emerged many years behind, and it has been difficult **to catch up**.

to catch up
to come from behind and gain equal footing; to overtake someone or something moving

17 To be sure, many in the group were already at a disadvantage when they entered prison. More than half had not finished high school. Only half could recall holding a job for more than a year. Some admitted to abusing drugs or alcohol or running with the wrong crowd.

18 But dozens of them had been leading lives of stability and accomplishment. More than 50 had held a job for more than two years in fields as varied as nursing, mail delivery, welding, fishing, sales and the military. Five had college degrees, and 20 others had completed some college or trade school.

19 Still, many of those were as unlucky as the most modestly educated when it came to finding work after their release. Most found that authorities were slow to wipe the convictions from their records, if they did so at all. Even newspaper articles about their exonerations seemed somehow to have had a negative effect in the public's mind.

stigma
a mark of shame and disgrace

walking around with a scarlet letter
carrying around blame

20 "Any time that anyone has been in prison, even if you are exonerated, there is still a **stigma** about you, and you are **walking around with a scarlet letter**," said Ken Wyniemko, who spent more than nine years behind bars in Michigan after a rape conviction.

21 Before his conviction, he managed a bowling alley. After his release in 2003, he spent two fruitless years job hunting, and he estimates he applied for at least 100 jobs. Today, he lives off money he received in a legal settlement with Clinton Township in Macomb County, Mich.

22 Many of the jobs the newly released found proved short-lived, often lasting no more than a year. A few ex-prisoners like Kevin Green, who went from bingo caller to utility crew supervisor, changed jobs to advance their careers, but most drifted from job to job with little gain in status or salary.

23 Ryan Matthews, with a fiancée and 2-year-old to support, lost a series of jobs after he was exonerated from Louisiana's death row. He lost a shipyard job after his employer saw a news report about his exoneration on television.

24 Short of suing, few received substantial compensation from the government.

hodgepodge
a lot of things put together with no order or arrangement

litigate
to engage in legal proceedings

25 Given the **hodgepodge** of state compensation laws, an exonerated prisoner's chances of receiving any significant sum depend on the state where he was convicted and whether he can find a lawyer willing to **litigate** a difficult case. One man who served three years in California sued and won $7.9 million. Another, who had served 16 and a half years in Texas, filed a compensation claim and received $27,850.

26 President Bush and Congress moved in 2004 to improve the compensation the wrongly convicted received, adopting legislation that increased payments for people exonerated of federal crimes to $50,000 per year of imprisonment, and $100,000 per year in death penalty cases. The legislation included a clause encouraging states to follow suit, at least for wrongly convicted prisoners who had been on death row.

27 Lawyers and others involved with helping the exonerated have **seized on** that recommendation in pushing for improved compensation laws nationwide. But their efforts have gained little.

seized on resorted to a method, plan, etc., in desperation

28 Only one state—Vermont—has adopted a compensation law since the bill passed. Twenty-one other states and the District of Columbia already had procedures for compensating the exonerated; half cap awards below $50,000 per year of **incarceration**.

29 Of the 124 prisoners exonerated through DNA and known to have received compensation, 55 got at least $50,000 for each year in prison. And most of them sued in federal court, claiming their civil rights had been violated by overzealous police officers, crime lab specialists or prosecutors. Lawyers say such cases are very difficult to win.

30 Twenty-five were convicted in states that provide no compensation and have collected nothing. Among them is Mr. Moto, who said he struggled this summer to raise his 10-year-old daughter on $623 a month in disability payments.

31 "You give no compensation to none of those guys who were wrongfully incarcerated and proved their innocence?" he said in an interview. "How can you say we believe in justice?"

Reading with a Critical Eye

In a small group, discuss the following reflection questions, which will guide you toward a deeper understanding of the reading.

1. In paragraph 5, we learn that more than 200 prisoners have been exonerated of their crimes since 1989 by DNA evidence. Does this number surprise you? Describe your reaction to learning about these innocent people mistakenly jailed.
2. In paragraphs 9 and 10, what do we learn about the lives of ex-prisoners after they have been released?
3. Vincent Moto is one of the exonerated prisoners discussed in the article. What point does Moto make in paragraph 14? Do you agree with him? Why, or why not?
4. Explain the following quotation by Ken Wyniemko, a man who spent nine years behind bars on inaccurate rape charges. "Any time that anyone has been in prison, even if you are exonerated, there is still a stigma about you, and you are walking around with a scarlet letter" (para. 20).
5. What do we learn about exonerated prisoners and financial compensation in paragraph 29? What is your personal view on the issue of compensation?

Reading Comprehension Check

1. What do the three men profiled in the beginning of the article have in common?
a. They are all prisoners.
b. Each of them has been exonerated for a crime based on DNA evidence.
c. They are all repeat offenders.
d. They are still on probation.

2. The *New York Times* investigation into these cases included
a. police detective work.
b. research and surveying.
c. only interviews.
d. both research and interviews.

3. The expression "stable footing in the world" in paragraph 9 could be replaced by
a. a desire to be mobile.
b. balanced feet.
c. a healthy reintegration into society.
d. a dangerous path.

4. According to the investigation, what percentage of those who were exonerated found their way to a stable life afterward?
a. about half
b. about one-third
c. one in six
d. none of them

5. What is exonerated prisoner Vincent Moto's main point in paragraph 14?
a. The government should stop offering services to those who have actually committed crimes.
b. Innocent prisoners should receive some special services that others do not receive.
c. Truly guilty prisoners receive better services upon release than do innocent ones.
d. none of the above

6. What do we learn about the lives of these exonerated prisoners before they were wrongfully convicted?
a. More than half had not finished high school.
b. Some had issues with drug and alcohol abuse.
c. Half had had problems holding a job.
d. all of the above

7. The case of one exonerated prisoner, Ken Wyniemko, is offered to illustrate
a. that the road to a successful life is never far off.
b. how difficult it is for many ex-prisoners to find a steady job after prison.

c. that if you struggle hard enough, you can reach your goal.
d. the role of the government in supporting ex-prisoners.

8. According to the article, an exonerated prisoner's chances of receiving fair compensation depend on
a. the state in which he or she was convicted.
b. his or her legal representation.
c. the judge.
d. both a and b

9. How much compensation did Vincent Moto receive for his wrongful conviction?
a. $623 a month in payments
b. none
c. His case is still pending.
d. This information is not offered.

10. What was the author's purpose in writing this article?
a. to convince the reader that all exonerated prisoners deserve just compensation
b. to argue that whether or not an exonerated prisoner should receive compensation depends on the case
c. to report on the findings of a newspaper's investigation of exonerated prisoners
d. to entertain

MyReadingLab
Visit Chapter 6: Criminal Justice in MyReadingLab to complete the Reading 2 activities.

READING 2
Newspaper Article

Schizophrenic Teen Looks for Justice After Murder

Pre-Reading Questions

Discuss these questions in small groups.

1. If a convicted murderer's lawyer successfully makes the case that his or her client is "insane," should the killer serve time, or should they be placed in a mental hospital? Explain.
2. Do you think that claiming the "insanity defense" is taking advantage of a loophole in our criminal justice system? Are there other excuses to justify a violent crime? Explain.
3. In your view, how can law enforcement officials monitor mentally unstable members of society who could potentially pose a threat to the general public? What would be a good strategy?

Schizophrenic Teen Looks for Justice After Murder

By Pauline Arrillaga, the Associated Press[1]

April 16, 2006

nudged
to push gently to gain attention

1 FLAGSTAFF, Ariz.—The phone roused Terry Clark from sleep. "Flagstaff Police Department," a voice announced, asking to speak with Mr. Clark. Terry **nudged** Dave and handed over the receiver. "My son's truck?" she heard her husband say. "Gentry?"

2 Gentry was the oldest of their three children. Had he been in a wreck? Terry crawled from bed and headed for the front door to see if her son's Toyota pickup was in the drive. She stepped out onto the porch, then stopped dead in her tracks.

3 In the dim glow of dawn, she could see that Gentry's truck was gone. Where it should have been, men in helmets stood clutching guns aimed at Terry's head. "Get against the garage!" one shouted.

4 At first, investigators told Terry only that a policeman had been shot.

5 She would hear a name, officer Jeff Moritz, and discover he was called to their neighborhood after residents reported a pickup circling, blaring loud music. The policeman had pulled the truck over and called in the license plate, then radioed dispatch once more: "999. I've been hit. 999. I've been hit."

6 The pickup—her son's pickup—sat abandoned next to the sidewalk where, Terry soon learned, the police officer had died.

7 She realized then that her son was the prime suspect. Not Gentry, who had been at home in bed.

8 Her middle son. Eric. The one who had been a star football player and a good student with dreams.

9 The one who just two months earlier called his own mother and father aliens.

10 The victim of the June 21, 2000, shooting was the only police officer ever killed in the line of duty in this mountain community north of Phoenix. He was a caring cop who cut firewood for the handicapped, a husband and father with one young son and a second on the way.

descended
to move from a higher to a lower place

delusion
the act of believing in something false

schizophrenia
characterized by illogical patterns of thinking

11 The accused was a 17-year-old high school senior who had a history of marijuana use and had been arrested two months earlier for drunken driving and drug possession after police found two dozen hits of LSD in his car.

12 A portrait emerged of a drug-crazed teen. But as the facts slowly surfaced, so did a different picture of Eric Michael Clark—that of a decent boy who had **descended** into a world of **delusion**, the terrifying existence that is **schizophrenia**.

13 It took three years for Eric Clark to be found competent to stand trial and participate in his defense. When the case proceeded, his

[1] Pauline Arrillaga, "Schizophrenic Teen Looks for Justice After Murder," April 16, 2006.

attorneys pushed for a verdict of "guilty except insane," meaning incarceration in a **psychiatric** facility. Instead, a judge found him guilty of first-degree, intentional murder and sentenced him to life in prison.

psychiatric
related to prevention of mental and emotional disorder

14 On Wednesday, the U.S. Supreme Court is to take up the case of Clark v. Arizona and the issue of just how difficult states can make it for criminal **defendants** to prove **insanity**.

insanity
mental illness

15 It is the first time the court has dealt with a direct constitutional challenge to the insanity defense since lawmakers around the country imposed new restrictions following John Hinckley's **acquittal** by reason of insanity in the 1981 shooting of President Reagan.

16 The issue is determining under what circumstances **absolution** of a criminal act is warranted.

absolution
the act of pardoning guilt or blame

17 "There are some cases," says Richard Bonnie, director of the Institute of Law, Psychiatry and Public Policy at the University of Virginia, "where a person was so mentally disturbed at the time of the offense that it would be inhumane and morally objectionable to convict and punish them."

18 Terry Clark wonders, now, when it all started.

19 Did it begin with Eric's fear of drinking tap water? It was December 1998, and a house fire forced the family to live temporarily in an apartment. Eric, then 16, worried about lead poisoning and would only drink bottled water.

20 Was that the first clue?

21 Always low-key, Eric then began to grow moody—exploding one minute, **sobbing** the next.

sobbing
crying uncontrollably

22 Was that illness or teen angst?

23 A varsity running back at Flagstaff High, Eric dreamed of becoming a professional athlete. Then he lost interest in sports.

24 Terry, a school nurse, had seen her share of troubled kids. She wondered if Eric was on something, but she had had him drug-tested before and the results were negative. Was it depression? Anger management? The pieces didn't fit into one neat puzzle, and Eric's behavior grew more bizarre.

25 On June 21, 1999, Terry and Dave had their son admitted to a mental health center. He had abandoned his car in a road, called a police officer rude and then **reeled on** his father, using the f-word. At the center, Eric tested positive for marijuana. But doctors thought his behavior perhaps stemmed from pre-schizophrenia. With no mental illness on either side of the family, Terry pushed that idea aside.

reeled on
spoke in a loud and disrespectful manner

26 The family attended counseling sessions, and Eric seemed to improve. He promised Terry he would quit using drugs and continue seeing a therapist. She had him discharged after only three days.

27 "He's getting better," Terry convinced herself.

28 He got worse.

29 That fall, Eric quit school. He became obsessed with Y2K and charged $1,700 worth of survival gear on his dad's debit card. When Jan. 1, 2000, came and went, Eric was thrilled and went back to school.

30 "He's getting better," Terry thought again—until Eric started mentioning "them."

31 "They're after me," he would tell his mother.

32 That April, in the midst of conversation, Eric referred to his mother and father as aliens.

33 "If you'd go get some tools," he told them matter-of-factly, "I'd show you."

prosecution the act of taking legal action

34 Terry was relieved when, that same month, Eric was arrested on drunken driving and drug charges. She thought that would lead to help. But authorities decided to postpone **prosecution** until Eric turned 18 later in the year.

35 She and Dave searched for counselors, but Eric refused to go. Terry left messages at treatment facilities that were never returned.

36 On June 19, 2000, Eric called his mother an alien again.

37 "How would you like to be me," he said, "and never know who your real mother is?"

38 The next day, Eric seemed better, and he, Terry and Dave went to a movie together. Afterward, Eric asked if he could stay to watch another film. He hugged his folks and said goodbye.

surmise conclude

39 Investigators **surmise** that sometime after 1:30 A.M. on June 21, 2000, Eric made his way home, sneaked into his brother Gentry's bedroom, took his keys and left in Gentry's truck.

40 What happened after that, and why, no one can know for certain. Eric's never talked about it. At the 2003 trial, prosecutors and defense attorneys presented different scenarios.

41 Both sides, and their mental health experts, agreed that Eric suffered from paranoid schizophrenia and was mentally ill.

42 But legal insanity is another matter. Arizona law spells out its qualified use as a defense.

43 "A person may be found guilty except insane if, at the time of the commission of the criminal act, the person was afflicted with a mental disease or defect of such severity that the person did not know the criminal act was wrong," the law states.

disdain to treat with contempt

44 The prosecutor, Assistant Attorney General David Powell, argued Eric did know. One witness testified that weeks before the shooting, Eric mouthed off about his **disdain** for cops and wanting to shoot them. Powell's theory was Eric lured Moritz to the scene by playing loud music until residents reported him.

45 "He wanted to kill an officer that day," Powell said at trial. "And he did."

46 Defense attorneys insisted Eric's psychosis was so severe he was incapable of hatching such a plan. They noted that after the shooting, Eric called his parents from jail and explained that Flagstaff was a "platinum city" inhabited by 50,000 aliens. He told them, "The only thing that will stop aliens are bullets."

prohibited not allowed

47 In his appeal to the U.S. Supreme Court, defense attorney David Goldberg asserts that Arizona law is so restrictive that it violates a mentally ill defendant's right to a fair trial. For one, he says, Arizona law **prohibited** the trial court from considering Eric's mental illness in weighing whether he intentionally killed a police officer.

48 Goldberg also contends that the right-wrong test is too narrow in determining legal insanity. Eric might have known that killing was wrong in the abstract, Goldberg says, but if he believed Moritz was an alien, "he didn't understand the nature of what he was doing."

49 The Supreme Court could establish a more specific definition of legal insanity or allow for broader **discretion** in determining when evidence of mental illness may be considered at trial.

discretion
the ability to decide responsibly

50 Its decision also could mean a retrial for Eric Clark, something the Moritz family would see as unjust.

51 "To say, gee if you're mentally ill you can be forgiven for murdering somebody, you're giving a license to kill to millions of people," says the victim's father, Dan Moritz.

52 Terry Clark says she doesn't want her son to get "off." She only wants him to get the psychiatric care he needs.

53 "Eric didn't choose to be mentally ill. It chose him," she says. "He shouldn't be punished for it."

Reading with a Critical Eye

In a small group, discuss the following reflection questions, which will guide you toward a deeper understanding of the reading.

1. What made Terry Clark stop "dead in her tracks" (para. 2)?
2. How is the police officer who was killed described as a person?
3. "There are some cases," according to Richard Bonnie, director of the **Institute** of Law, Psychiatry and Public **Policy** at the University of Virginia (para. 17), "where a person was so mentally disturbed at the time of the offense that it would be inhumane and morally objectionable to convict and punish them." Do you agree with his statement? Explain.
4. In paragraph 24, how does the fact that Eric's mom is also a school nurse perhaps influence and inform her understanding of the situation?
5. What was the Supreme Court's role in this story? Do you think such decisions should be handled by the courts? If not, who should decide on cases like this?

Reading Comprehension Check

1. What is the topic of the reading?
   a. Juvenile offenders should not be tried as adults
   b. the case of a schizophrenic teen who shot a police officer to death
   c. guns and teenagers
   d. a mother's fear that a police officer had shot her son
2. Which was *not* something Terry learned about the situation described in the beginning of this article?
   a. A police officer had been shot.
   b. Neighbors had reported loud music playing.

c. The policeman had pulled her son's truck over.
d. Her son had lots of drugs in the truck.

3. What made this case a surprising one?
a. In this community, a police officer had never been shot and killed.
b. The accused did not have a criminal record.
c. The accused was schizophrenic.
d. both a and c

4. What kind of verdict did Eric Clark's lawyers plead for?
a. Their client was innocent.
b. Their client was guilty.
c. Their client was guilty, but insane.
d. Their client was only a juvenile.

5. The word *absolution* in the sentence "The issue is determining under what circumstances **absolution** of a criminal act is warranted" (para. 16), could be replaced by
a. conviction.
b. forgiveness.
c. resentment.
d. delay.

6. What position does Richard Bonnie take on the issue of the insanity defense?
a. He is against it.
b. He is neutral.
c. He supports it in some cases.
d. He doesn't take a position.

7. The question in paragraph 20, "Was that the first clue?" refers to
a. evidence that Eric Clark had major psychological problems.
b. his mother's first signs of instability.
c. the police investigation.
d. none of the above

8. The word *bizarre* in the phrase, "Eric's behavior grew more bizarre" (para. 24), means
a. refined.
b. uncontrolled.
c. marketable.
d. strange.

9. Which detail does *not* support the idea that Eric's condition was improving?
a. He attended counseling sessions with his family.
b. He promised his mother he would quit using drugs.
c. He quit school.
d. both b and c

10. What is the main idea of the article?
a. Eric Clark's criminal behavior, which stunned his mother, was related to a schizophrenic condition.
b. We cannot judge criminal behavior when it is connected to a mental condition.
c. Schizophrenia is a serious mental disorder.
d. none of the above

BIOGRAPHICAL PROFILE

Eric Holder, Jr.

Eric Holder, Jr. served as Attorney General of the United States from 2009 to 2015 and was the first African American to hold the position. Holder previously served as a judge of the Superior Court of the District of Columbia, as a United States Attorney, and as Deputy Attorney General of the United States.

Eric H. Holder, Jr. was born in the Bronx, New York, in 1951, to parents with roots in Barbados. His mother was a telephone operator and his father was a real estate broker. He attended public school until the age of 10, but upon entering the fourth grade, he was selected to participate in a program for intellectually advanced students. In 1969, he entered Columbia College, where he played freshman basketball and was co-captain of his team. During his college years, he also spent Saturday mornings mentoring local kids, and became active in civil rights. He earned a Bachelor of Arts degree in American History in 1973, and three years later graduated with a law degree from Columbia Law School.

After graduating from law school, Holder joined the U.S. Justice Department's new Public Integrity Section and served there from 1976 to 1988. In 1988, he was appointed to serve as a judge of the Superior Court of the District of Columbia. Holder stepped down from the bench in 1993 to accept an appointment as United States Attorney for the District of Columbia from President Bill Clinton.

Holder took a political step in 2007 when he joined then-United States Senator Barack Obama's presidential campaign as a senior legal advisor. He served on Obama's vice presidential selection committee. On December 1, 2008, Obama announced that Holder would be his nominee for Attorney General. He was approved by the Senate Judiciary Committee two months later.

As U.S. attorney general, Holder has been in the political spotlight on numerous occasions. He gave a well-known speech on race relations in February 2009, in which he called the United States "a nation of cowards" on racial issues. "Though race-related issues continue to occupy a significant portion of our political discussion and though there remain many **unresolved** racial issues in this nation, we average Americans simply do not talk enough with each other about race," he said. The speech was controversial, with some agreeing with Holder's comments and others sharply criticizing them.

Holder has been an outspoken supporter of gun control. When interviewed about weapons regulations during a news conference to announce the arrest of Mexican drug cartel members, Holder stated that the Obama administration would seek to re-institute the expired Assault Weapons Ban.

Holder most wants to be remembered for his record on civil rights: refusing to defend a law that defined marriage as between one man and one woman; suing North Carolina and Texas over voting restrictions that disproportionately affect minorities and the elderly; and launching 20 investigations of abuses by local police departments. Holder also pressured Congress to reduce prison sentences for nonviolent drug crimes.

Holder is married to Dr. Sharon Malone, an obstetrician; the couple have three children. Holder has been involved with various mentoring programs for inner-city youths.

Some Questions for Group Discussion

1. In paragraph 5, we read about a speech Holder made in which he called America "a nation of cowards" on race relations. What do you think Holder meant by this? Do you agree with his idea? Explain.
2. In 2010, Holder argued that Arizona's tough immigration laws could lead to "racial profiling." Why might Holder hold such a view?
3. Considering Holder's biography, what factors may have influenced his rise to the top of his field?

Biographical Internet Research

Find out about another historical figure in Criminal Justice online, selecting a name from the list below, and share a biographical profile with your classmates:

- Johnnie Cochran
- The Zodiac Killer
- Troy Davis
- Janet Reno

SKILL FOCUS: Fact and Opinion

In many instances, the question of whether a sentence is made up of facts or opinions may seem clear-cut. Example 1 and Example 2 below are cases in point.

Example 1

Fact: Criminal suspects who are found innocent are released.

Example 2

Opinion: I believe that all suspects should receive a harsh interrogation.

Example 1 is a recognized truth and an observable fact. Example 2 is a judgment and a clear statement of opinion.

So why spend our valuable time on this Skill Focus area?

The answer is that the line between fact and opinion can get tricky in particular contexts, as seen in Example 3 and Example 4 below.

Example 3

The lawyer stated that it would be in the best interests of the court to delay the trial.

Example 4

California is a very tolerant state in the area of prisoner rights.

What may seem like an opinion (the lawyer's viewpoint) in Example 3 is actually a fact because the sentence simply reports that the lawyer made a statement. What may seem like a fact in Example 4 (a piece of information about California) is an opinion because a judgment is made about California's prison system's level of tolerance concerning prisoner rights.

Facts

"Don't trust half of what you hear, and less of what you read."

While this statement might seem overly skeptical, good readers think critically about what they read and do not trust claims that are not well supported. Just because you see it in print, it doesn't mean that it is true!

A **fact** is a provable claim—that is, a statement that is verifiable.

Example

The Florida police force has doubled in the last ten years.

This is a *stated fact*. It may or may not be true, but is provable. Stated facts can go in two directions. If the above fact is shown to be true about the number of members in the Florida police force, then it is a *substantiated fact* because it has been fact-checked and supported. If the information can be disproved, then it is a *false statement of fact* (see the diagram).

				Substantiated fact
Stated Fact	→	Verifying process	→	OR
				False statement of fact

Opinions

An *opinion* is a personal belief or judgment that is not provable.

Examples

1. The Florida police force is doing a very effective job.
2. The Florida police don't know what they are talking about.

It is important to make the distinction between *well-supported opinions* based on plausible evidence and valid reasons, and *poorly supported opinions* that seem to contradict known facts. That is to say that a *set of facts* can be used to support, or back up, an opinion.

EXERCISE 6.6 Finding Support

What types of facts might support the opinion in Example 1 above? Make a short list with a partner.

Opinion: The Florida police force is doing a very effective job.

Supporting facts:

a. ______________________________

b. ______________________________

c. ______________________________

EXERCISE 6.7 Identifying Fact and Opinion

How can you tell when you are reading a fact rather than an opinion? Consider the author's purpose in writing the piece you are reading. Is the author simply providing information about a topic or trying to persuade the reader about a particular argument or set of arguments? Compare the two paragraphs below on random police searches.

Passage 1

Random police searches on highway checkpoints and in subway entrances have increased in the last few years. In New York City, especially, the random checking of bags and other personal belongings has become commonplace. Police officials have developed a number of methods to conduct these searches working with X-ray technology and at times, police dogs.

Passage 2

Random police searches violate our privacy rights. Americans are not accustomed to this type of harassment. This really is a clear violation of police power. It is time that we speak up and put an end to this practice.

How does the author's purpose differ from Passage 1 to Passage 2? Which paragraph is more factual? Which is more opinion-based?

Of course, not all readings are purely fact (Passage 1) or purely opinion (Passage 2). It is often the case that an author uses a set of facts to back up an opinion. Read Passage 3, and underline any sentences that offer an opinion.

Consider the opinion put forth by the writer. What facts are used to support this viewpoint?

Passage 3

Police searches are justifiable in some cases. A few years ago, a man was searched in front of the Washington metro because he was carrying a very large bag that looked suspicious to a transit worker. It was found that the bag contained the makings of small explosives.

Signs of an Author's Point of View

Certain words and phrases signal that a judgment, belief, or interpretation is being offered by the author.

Presentation of Opinion: Signal Phrases

In my opinion
One possibility is
Maybe it is the case
I believe/I think
This suggests
In my view
It seems likely
One idea is that

Look for descriptive adjectives that specify value judgments.

Presentation of Opinion: Descriptive Words

effective
useful
successful
nicer
dishonest
stimulating
boring
best
worst
greater
better
wasteful
impressive
disastrous

Pay attention to key words that express uncertainty, such as the list below.

might
seem
doubt
perhaps
maybe

Considering the Type of Text You're Reading

Texts that are fact-based include the following:

- News reports in the form of magazine or newspaper articles are mostly factual (even though these facts are not always substantiated, and bias plays a role in which "facts" get reported).
- Textbook readings are predominantly fact-focused because the purpose is to inform.
- Statistical data is factual (because numerical claims are verifiable).

Texts that are opinion-based include the following:

- Newspaper or magazine editorials (editorials are, by definition, someone's opinion on an issue).
- Letters from readers to newspapers and magazines. These are usually readers' responses to articles they read.
- Internet blogs. Members of a Web-based discussion group share their opinions.
- Quoted speech within newspaper and magazine articles often offers a diversity of perspectives on the topic featured in the article. The journalistic tone may be neutral, but interviewed sources share their viewpoints. An example of this follows:

Steve Webb, who has been working in drug enforcement for 28 years in the Miami area, says, "We need to be stricter with drug offense sentencing if we are going to solve this problem."

PRACTICING THE SKILL: IDENTIFYING OPINIONS, EVALUATING THEIR USE

Practice 1

In the following short paragraphs, underline sentences that contain an opinion. Discuss with a partner what kind of factual support is offered, if any, to back up the opinion. What kind of factual evidence not given could support the view(s) of the writer?

Passage 1

One of these private groups is American Border Patrol. Its efforts have included rounding up illegal immigrants and turning them over to law enforcement. The group's director says his group has done nothing wrong. "Our borders are unprotected and the United States border patrol is derelict in its duty."

(Excerpted from Sharon Smith, "Who's Illegal?—Shooting to Kill on the Border," www.counterpunch.org, May 23, 2006)

Factual support for offered opinion (If not given, what kind of factual details would support such a view?)

____

____

____

Passage 2

Dear editors,

I read the article last week in your newspaper about using DNA evidence to overturn criminal sentences. I completely disagree with the writer and find this level of dependence on science to solve our criminal cases quite dangerous. Yes, it is true that DNA evidence is a useful tool in identifying criminal suspects, yet to give up on hundreds of years of time-tested crime-solving methods would be a big mistake.

Factual support for offered opinion (If not given, what kind of factual details would support such a view?)

___

___

___

Passage 3

Now some in law enforcement are calling for a national registry of every American's DNA profile, against which police could instantly compare crime scene specimens. Advocates say the system would dissuade many would-be criminals and help capture the rest. "This is the single best way to catch bad guys and keep them off the street," said a lawyer with a Washington firm.

(Rick Weiss, "Push for DNA Registry Could Affect All," The Washington Post, *June 4, 2006)*

Factual support for offered opinion (If not given, what kind of factual details would support such a view?)

___

___

Passage 4

Random searches in mass transit areas do not violate Americans' privacy rights. Extensive steps were taken to notify the public about the searches. There have been a number of efforts by terrorist groups to do damage to the U.S. infrastructure. Americans are willing to cooperate in this national effort.

Factual support for offered opinion (If not given, what kind of factual details would support such a view?)

___

___

___

Passage 5

As long as the prevalent attitude of financially irresponsible parents is that the government needs to subsidize their family dreams, reforms in our public assistance system are necessary. Reducing federal assistance will undoubtedly cause hardships for those families mired in poverty, but it would certainly rescue future children and parents from a great deal of misery and would make our streets far safer than they are.

(Excerpted from Joe Cordill, "Parents Share Blame for Crime Stats," Letter to the Editor, July 2006)

Factual support for offered opinion (If not given, what kind of factual details would support such a view?)

____

Passage 6

Many inmates are seeking changes in prison regulations or state laws in an effort to be able to use the Internet to do research or communicate with the outside world. A MySpace spokesperson said that the site is reviewing profiles posted on behalf of inmates. The mother of a police officer killed during a robbery spoke against prisoners having MySpace access. "This kind of thing dishonors Aubrey [her son]." "What should happen on death row is that these people should sit behind a locked door. . . ."

(Excerpted from Kevin Johnson, "Inmates Go to Court to Seek Right to Use Internet," USA Today, November 23, 2006)

Factual support for offered opinion (If not given, what kind of factual details would support such a view?)

____

As you approach the following reading, apply the skills you have just learned.

Nonfiction (Book Excerpt)

MyReadingLab

Visit Chapter 6: Criminal Justice in MyReadingLab to complete the Reading 3 activities.

The Other Wes Moore

Pre-Reading Questions

Work with a partner by first discussing some pre-reading questions.

1. If you were born to a different family and had worse luck than you have had so far in this life, how might your fate have turned out differently? Use your imagination, and explain your beliefs.
2. Which factor plays a larger role in determining how you develop as a person: family influence or peer influence? Explain your choice.

Excerpt from *The Other Wes Moore*

By Wes Moore, 2011

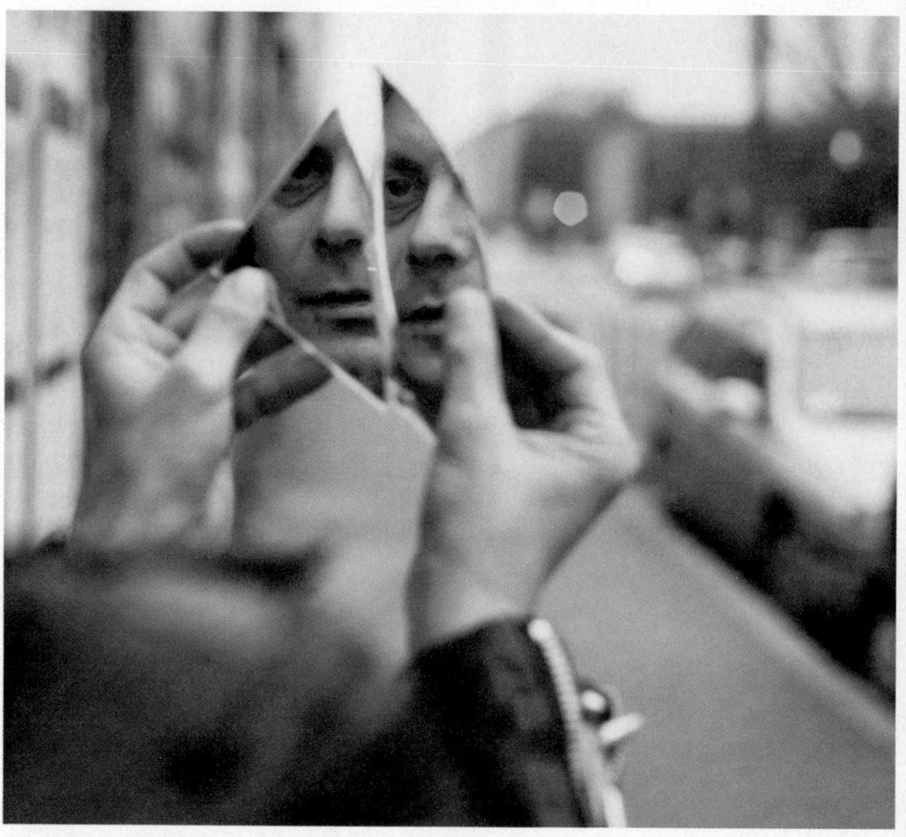

1 This is the story of two boys living in Baltimore with similar histories and an identical name: Wes Moore. One of us is free and has experienced things that he never even knew to dream about as a kid. The other will spend every day until his death behind bars for an armed robbery that left a police officer and father of five dead. The chilling truth is that his story could have been mine. The tragedy is that my story could have been his. Our stories are obviously specific to our two lives, but I hope they will illuminate the crucial inflection points in every life, the sudden moments of decision where our paths diverge and our fates are sealed. It's unsettling to know how little separates each of us from another life altogether.

2 In late 2000, the Baltimore Sun published a short article with the headline, "Local Graduate Named Rhodes Scholar." It was about me. As a senior at John Hopkins University, I received one of the most prestigious academic awards for students in the world. That fall I was moving to England to attend Oxford University on a full scholarship.

3 But that story had less of an impact on me than another series of articles in the Sun, about an incident that happened just months

before, a precisely planned jewelry store robbery gone terribly wrong. The store's security guard—an off-duty police officer named Bruce Prothero—was shot and killed after he pursued the armed men into the store's parking lot. A massive and highly publicized manhunt for the perpetrators ensued. Twelve days later it ended when the last two suspects were apprehended in a house in Philadelphia by a daunting phalanx of police and federal agents. The articles indicated that the shooter, Richard Antonio Moore, would likely receive the death penalty. The sentence would be similarly severe for his younger brother, who was also arrested and charged. In an eerie coincidence, the younger brother's name was the same as mine.

4 Two years after I returned from Oxford, I was still thinking about the story. I couldn't let it go. If you'd asked me why, I couldn't have told you exactly. I was struck by the superficial similarities between us, of course: we'd grown up at the same time, on the same streets, with the same name. But so what? I didn't think of myself as a superstitious or conspiratorial person, the kind who'd obsess over a coincidence until it yielded meaning. But there were nights when I'd wake up in the small hours and finding myself thinking of the other Wes Moore, conjuring his image as best I could, a man my age lying on a cot in a prison cell, burdened by regret, trying to sleep through another night surrounded by the walls he'd escape only at death. Sometimes in my imaginings, his face was mine.

5 There's a line at the opening of John Edgar Wideman's brilliant *Brothers and Keepers* about the day he found out that his own brother was on the run from the police for an armed robbery: "The distance I'd put between my brother's world and mine suddenly collapsed... . Wherever he was, running for his life, he carried part of me with him." But I didn't even know the other Wes Moore. Why did I feel this connection with him, why did I feel like he " carried part of me with him" in that prison cell? I worried that I was just being melodramatic or narcissistic. But still, I couldn't shake it.

6 Finally, one day, I wrote him a simple letter introducing myself and explaining how I'd come to learn about his story. I struggled to explain the purpose of my letter and posed a series of naïve questions that had been running through my mind: *Who are you? Do you see your brother? How do you feel about him? How did this happen?* As soon as I mailed the letter, the crazy randomness of it all came flooding in on me. I was sure that I'd made a mistake, that I'd been self-indulgent and presumptuous and insulting, and that I'd never hear back from him.

7 A month later, I was surprised to find an envelope in my mailbox stamped with a postcard from the Jessup Correctional Institution in Maryland. He had written back.

"Greetings, Good Brother," the letter started.

I send salutations of peace and prayers and blessings and guidance to you for

Posing these questions, which I'm going to answer, Inshallah. With that, I will

Begin with the first question posed…

8 This was the start of our correspondence, which has now gone on for years. At the beginning of our exchange of letters—which was later expanded by face-to-face visits at the prison—I was surprised to find just how much we did have in common, aside from our names, and how much our narratives intersected before they fatefully diverged. Learning the details of his story helped me understand my own life and choices, and I like to think that my story helped him understand his own a little more. But the real discovery was that our two stories together helped me to untangle some of the larger stories of our generation of young men, boys who came of age during a chaotic and violent time and emerged to succeed and fail in unprecedented ways. After a few visits, without realizing it, I started working on this project in my mind, trying to figure out what lessons our stories could offer to the next wave of young men who found themselves at the same crossroads we'd encountered and unsure which path to follow.

9 Perhaps the most surprising thing I discovered was that through the stories we volleyed back and forth in letter and over the metal divider of the prison's visiting room, Wes and I had indeed, as Wideman wrote, "collapsed the distance" between our worlds. We definitely have our disagreements—and Wes, it should never be forgotten, is in prison for his participation in a heinous crime. But even the worst decisions we make don't necessarily remove us from the circle of humanity. Wes's desire to participate in this book as a way to help others learn from his story and choose a different path is proof of that.

10 To write this book, I conducted hundreds of hours of interviews with Wes and his friends and family, as well as my friends and family. The stories you will read are rendered from my own memory and the best memories of those we grew up with, lived with, and learned from. I engaged in extensive historical research and interviewed teachers and drug dealers, police officers and lawyers, to make sure I got the facts—and the feel—right. Some names have been changed to protect people's identities and the quiet lives they now choose to lead. A few characters are composites. But all of the stories are painstakingly real.

11 It is my sincere hope that this book does not come across as self-congratulatory or self-exculpatory. Most important, it is not meant in any way to provide excuses for the events of that fateful day, February 7th, 2000. Let me be clear. The only victims that day were Sergeant Bruce Prothero and his family. Rather, this book will use our two lives as a way of thinking about choices and accountability, not

just for each of us as individuals, but for all of us as a society. This book is meant to show how, for those of us who live in the most precarious places in this country, our destinies can be determined by a single stumble down the wrong path, or a tentative step down the right one.

This is our story.

Reading with a Critical Eye

In a small group, discuss the following reflection questions, which will guide you toward a deeper understanding of the reading.

1. Paraphrase the ideas in the following two sentences, taken from the first paragraph of the reading. "The chilling truth is that his story could have been mine. The tragedy is that my story could have been his."
2. How does Wes Moore learn about "the other Wes Moore's" crime? How does this information affect him?
3. Paraphrase the quote Moore includes from the distinguished writer, John Edgar Wideman: "The distance I'd put between my brother's world and mine suddenly collapsed … Wherever he was, running for his life, he carried part of me with him."
4. How did Wes Moore manage to compile enough information to write a full-length book on this subject?
5. How does Wes Moore show his sensitivity to the shooting victim's family in the last paragraph?

Reading Comprehension Check

1. "…the sudden moments of decision where our paths **diverge** and our fates are sealed" (para. 1). An antonym for the term *diverge* is
   a. go a different direction.
   b. converge.
   c. lift up.
   d. pander to.
2. "As a senior at John Hopkins University, I received one of the most prestigious academic awards for students in the world."
   The above sentence is
   a. a statement of fact.
   b. an opinion.
   c. a mix of fact and opinion.
   d. neither fact nor opinion.
3. "But even the worst decisions we make don't necessarily remove us from the circle of humanity" (para. 9).
   The above sentence is
   a. a statement of fact.
   b. an opinion.
   c. a mix of fact and opinion.
   d. neither fact nor opinion.

4. "This book is meant to show how, for those of us who live in the most **precarious** places in this country, our destinies can be determined by a single stumble down the wrong path..." (para. 11).

   In the above sentence, the word *precarious* could be replaced by
   a. safe.
   b. stimulating.
   c. dangerous.
   d. evident.

5. What is one of the key themes Moore is trying to emphasize in this introduction to his book?
   a. Life is unfair for everyone.
   b. Drugs and poverty kill.
   c. Racism is the cause of many of our problems.
   d. The distance between life success and life failure is not as far as it seems.

6. We can infer that the author Wes Moore would agree with the following statement:
   a. We have no control over our destinies.
   b. The boys who grew up on the dangerous streets of Baltimore during the time he was a child faced an uphill battle in life.
   c. The other Wes Moore cannot be blamed for the murder he was involved with.
   d. Everyone has the same chance in life.

7. How did the other Wes Moore respond when the author wrote to him in prison?
   a. He wrote a letter back answering the questions that the author sent him.
   b. He sent an e-mail reply with words of peace.
   c. He did not respond for over a year.
   d. He was hesitant to share personal information with this stranger.

8. "But the real discovery was that our two stories together helped me to untangle some of the larger stories of our generation of young men, boys who came of age during a **chaotic** and violent time and emerged to succeed and fail in unprecedented ways."

   In the above sentence, the word *chaotic* could be replaced by
   a. organized.
   b. consecutive.
   c. disordered.
   d. benevolent.

9. When Moore writes, "Wes's desire to participate in this book as a way to help others learn from his story and choose a different path is proof of that," what is he referring to?
   a. this deep connection these two men have because of their shared name
   b. a sense of panic and disorder in our lives
   c. The other Wes Moore is not guilty in any way.
   d. the idea that even the worst decisions we make don't necessarily take away our sense of humanity

10. "This was the start of our correspondence, which has now gone on for years." The previous sentence is
    a. statement of fact.
    b. an opinion.
    c. a mix of fact and opinion.
    d. neither fact nor opinion.

MyReadingLab

Visit Chapter 6: Criminal Justice in MyReadingLab to complete the Reading 4 activities.

READING 4

Newspaper Editorial

Library Visit, Then Held at Gunpoint: At Yale, the Police Detained My Son

Pre-Reading Questions

Work with a partner by first discussing some pre-reading questions, and then focus on applying the skill of distinguishing between fact and opinion in relation to the article.

1. The following story is about a black college student wrongly stopped for a crime he had nothing to do with. In your opinion, is racial profiling ever justified? Be specific in your response.
2. Do you think the police have the right to use force under certain circumstances? Explain.

Library Visit, Then Held at Gunpoint: At Yale, the Police Detained My Son

By Charles Blow, The New York Times
January 26, 2015

1 Saturday evening, I got a call that no parent wants to get. It was my son calling from college — he's a third-year student at Yale. He had been accosted by a campus police officer, at gunpoint!

2 This is how my son remembers it:

3 He left for the library around 5:45 p.m. to check the status of a book he had requested. The book hadn't arrived yet, but since he was there he put in a request for some multimedia equipment for a project he was working on.

4 Then he left to walk back to his dorm room. He says he saw an officer "jogging" toward the entrance of another building across the grounds from the building he'd just left.

5 Then this:

6 "I did not pay him any mind, and continued to walk back towards my room. I looked behind me, and noticed that the police officer was following me. He spoke into his shoulder-mounted radio and said, 'I got him.'

7 "I faced forward again, presuming that the officer was not talking to me. I then heard him say, 'Hey, turn around!' — which I did.

8 "The officer raised his gun at me, and told me to get on the ground.

9 "At this point, I stopped looking directly at the officer, and looked down towards the pavement. I dropped to my knees first, with my hands raised, then laid down on my stomach.

10 "The officer asked me what my name was. I gave him my name.

11 "The officer asked me what school I went to. I told him Yale University.

12 "At this point, the officer told me to get up."

13 The officer gave his name, then asked my son to "give him a call the next day."

14 My son continued:

15 "I got up slowly, and continued to walk back to my room. I was scared. My legs were shaking slightly. After a few more paces, the officer said, 'Hey, my man. Can you step off to the side?' I did."

16 The officer asked him to turn around so he could see the back of his jacket. He asked his name again, then, finally, asked to see my son's ID. My son produced his school ID from his wallet.

17 The officer asked more questions, and my son answered. All the while the officer was relaying this information to someone over his radio.

18 My son heard someone on the radio say back to the officer "something to the effect of: 'Keep him there until we get this sorted out.' " The officer told my son that an incident report would be filed, and then he walked away.

19 A female officer approached. My son recalled, "I told her that an officer had just stopped me and pointed his gun at me, and that I wanted to know what this was all about." She explained students had called about a burglary suspect who fit my son's description.

20 That suspect was apparently later arrested in the area.

21 When I spoke to my son, he was shaken up. I, however, was fuming.

22 Now, don't get me wrong: If indeed my son matched the description of a suspect, I would have had no problem with him being questioned appropriately. School is his community, his home away from home, and he would have appreciated reasonable efforts to keep it safe. The stop is not the problem; the method of the stop is the problem.

23 Why was a gun drawn first? Why was he not immediately told why he was being detained? Why not ask for ID first?

24 What if my son had panicked under the stress, having never had a gun pointed at him before, and made what the officer considered a "suspicious" movement? Had I come close to losing him? Triggers cannot be unpulled. Bullets cannot be called back.

25 My son was unarmed, possessed no plunder, obeyed all instructions, answered all questions, did not attempt to flee or resist in any way.

26 This is the scenario I have always dreaded: my son at the wrong end of a gun barrel, face down on the concrete. I had always dreaded the moment that we would share stories about encounters with the police in which our lives hung in the balance, intergenerational stories of joining the inglorious "club."

27 When that moment came, I was exceedingly happy I had talked to him about how to conduct himself if a situation like this ever occurred. Yet I was brewing with sadness and anger that he had to use that advice.

28 I am reminded of what I have always known, but what some would choose to deny: that there is no way to work your way out — earn your way out — of this sort of crisis. In these moments, what you've done matters less than how you look.

29 There is no amount of respectability that can bend a gun's barrel. All of our boys are bound together.

30 The dean of Yale College and the campus police chief have apologized and promised an internal investigation, and I appreciate that. But the scars cannot be unmade. My son will always carry the memory of the day he left his college library and an officer trained a gun on him.

Reading with a Critical Eye

In a small group, discuss the following reflection questions, which will guide you toward a deeper understanding of the reading.

1. What tone does the author set for this piece of writing at the beginning of the editorial?
2. According to the female police officer, why had the author's son been suspected of a crime?
3. Paraphrase the following sentence from the text. "I had always dreaded the moment that we would share stories about encounters with the police in which our lives hung in the balance, intergenerational stories of joining the inglorious 'club.'
4. What questions does the author consider about the choices the police made in handling the situation with his son?
5. What is your opinion of the situation the author so vividly describes? Did the police act appropriately? Is the author's anger justified?

Reading Comprehension Check

1. "I faced forward again, **presuming** that the officer was not talking to me." The term *presuming* could be replaced with
   a. hiding.
   b. providing.
   c. pandering.
   d. believing.

2. "There is no amount of respectability that can bend a gun's barrel."
   The above sentence is
   a. a statement of fact.
   b. an opinion.
   c. a mix of fact and opinion.
   d. neither fact nor opinion.
3. Which fact is *not* mentioned by the author about his son's choices on the evening of the incident?
   a. He was wearing nice clothing.
   b. His son was unarmed.
   c. He did not attempt to run away.
   d. He obeyed all instructions.
4. "The stop is not the problem; the method of the stop is the problem."
   The above quotation is
   a. a statement of fact.
   b. a mix of fact and opinion.
   c. an opinion.
   d. evidence of wrongdoing.
5. What is the main point of the last paragraph of the editorial?
   a. Although apologies have been made, scars still remain.
   b. All's well that ends well.
   c. The author may sue the police department.
   d. His son was physically scarred during the incident.
6. "There is no amount of respectability that can bend a gun's barrel."
   Paraphrase the above sentence from the reading.
   a. Guns don't kill.
   b. Guns are blind to whom they are aimed at.
   c. If you have no respect, you might get shot.
   d. Gun violence is useless.
7. "When that moment came, I was **exceedingly** happy I had talked to him about how to conduct himself if a situation like this ever occurred."
   The term *exceedingly* could be replaced with
   a. mildly.
   b. off-putting.
   c. remarkably.
   d. evidently.
8. "The dean of Yale College and the campus police chief have apologized and promised an internal investigation, and I appreciate that."
   The above sentence is
   a. a statement of fact.
   b. a mix of fact and opinion.
   c. an opinion.
   d. evidence of wrongdoing.
9. Blow writes, "Yet I was brewing with sadness and anger that he had to use that advice." What can we infer about Blow's feeling?
   a. He is upset that his son had to be on alert not to upset a cop.
   b. He wants his son to be independent.
   c. He dislikes police rhetoric.
   d. He is confused about his inner feelings.
10. What can you predict will happen at Yale as a result of this unfortunate event?
   a. The police staff will be fired.
   b. nothing
   c. His son will drop out of this college.
   d. An investigation will lead to more careful police practices.

Recommended Debate Topic: Should juvenile offenders receive the same prison sentences as adults?

Brainstorm other debate topics related to Criminal Justice with your peers, and present your ideas to your instructor for approval.

DEBATABLE TOPIC

Collaboration

Your suggested debate topics:

a. ______________________________

b. ______________________________

c. ______________________________

From Reading to Writing: Persuasive Writing

Whether you are writing an argumentative essay on a controversial topic or composing a letter in response to a newspaper or magazine article that you have read, your intended goal is to persuade your audience that your opinion is credible and warrants respect.

Many of the skills used in a debate are critical to strong persuasive writing.

Keys to Writing Persuasively

- Support your arguments/opinions with relevant, detailed *facts*. Make use of readings with which you have worked and any research you have done.
- Be aware of your *intended audience*. Imagine that your audience holds the opposite view. It is your job to change their mind!
- Be organized. Present your argument(s) clearly, followed by specific, supporting details.
- Use language that is forceful and convincing (do not be shy or indirect!).

An Example of Persuasive Writing

Context: This letter was written in response to an editorial supporting random police searches.

> Dear Editors,
>
> I read the editorial published in last Tuesday's paper on random police searches in the subway. I absolutely disagree that police should be given the power to demand that we open up our purses and other personal belongings to them. This is America and we are not accustomed to compromising our right to privacy. I can understand the police stopping someone if they have a reasonable suspicion—for example, if someone enters a subway station with a strange-looking item or if this person is acting in

a peculiar manner. But for the majority of us law-abiding citizens, it is a great insult to be stopped and forced to display our personal items. The writer makes the argument that for the purpose of national security, we have to compromise our personal freedoms. Once we begin to compromise and our freedoms are taken away, we will no longer be living in the land of the free.

EXERCISE 6.8 Identifying Techniques in Persuasive Writing

With a partner, discuss whether or not the above letter is convincing (regardless of whether you agree with the writer). Then answer the following question together. Try to identify three techniques.

What techniques does the writer use to persuade his or her audience?

1. ______________________________
2. ______________________________
____
3. ______________________________

Focus on Oral Argumentation

Have you ever been in a situation where you felt strongly about an idea and the person with whom you were interacting disagreed? We all have! How can we convince others that our way makes sense?

Practice role-playing with a partner. Alternating from 1–6, try to convince your partner of one of the following. (Try to speak without pausing for a whole minute!)

1. You deserve a raise at work (imagine you are speaking to your boss).
2. The speed limit should be raised by 10 mph.
3. High schools should hold regular classes in the summer.
4. College tuition should be free for all students.
5. Riding a bike to work is better than driving.
6. Women are more intelligent than men (or vice versa).

Trying to convince others using logical argumentation can be fun! Now, let's translate our oral persuasive powers into quality persuasive writing.

WRITING on The Wall: Practice in Persuasive Writing

Write a persuasive paragraph in reaction to Charles Blow's editorial on page 313. Share your feelings on the content and perspective of the editorial in a letter to Mr. Blow beginning "Dear Mr. Blow," and ending with your signature. Then share your letter to Mr. Blow with your classmates or on your class's blog space. Once you have posted your letter, read your classmates' responses and post your reaction to two of them.

Careers in Criminal Justice

Working in small groups, discuss careers one can pursue after obtaining a degree in criminal justice. You may wish to do some online research to find other careers related to the field of criminal justice. In the space below, write down the job title and responsibilities. The first example is done for you. Be sure to share your findings with your peers.

Job Title	*Responsibilities*
1. Professor of Forensic Science	Doing research in forensic science involving DNA testing; lecturing to students studying forensics; consultant on criminal cases.
2.	
3.	
4.	
5.	

Textbook Application

Read the following reading from the first chapter of a college text, *Criminal Justice Today,* and apply the skills learned in this chapter. When you finish reading, try to correctly answer the multiple-choice questions that follow. Once again, it may be helpful to highlight key points in the reading as you work with the passage.

READING 5

Textbook Reading

MyReadingLab

Visit Chapter 6: Criminal Justice in MyReadingLab to complete the Reading 5 activities.

from Chapter 1 of *Criminal Justice Today*

by Frank Schmalleger

1 On December 14th, 2012, 20-year-old Adam Lanza, a socially awkward young man, went on a shooting rampage at Sandy Hook Elemantary School in Newtown, Connecticut. In a matter of minutes, Lanza had shot to death 20 kindergarten students, four teachers, a principal, and the school's psychologist. The shooting spree ended when Lanza turned one of his three guns on himself. Before the massacre, Lanza shot his mother to death at the home they shared only minutes from school. The horrific shooting was covered by media services for days, and reignited an intense national debate about gun control.

2 Although the Newtown shooting stood out as especially horrific because it ended so many innocent young lives, it is but one of a number of random mass shootings in the United States in recent years. In 2012 alone, there were 12 other random mass killings, including a July attack by a lone gunman, James Holmes, in an Aurora, Colorado, movie theatre where 12 people were killed and another 58 injured during a midnight showing of the movie, *The Dark Knight Rises*.

3 Experts tell us that the number of random mass shootings is on the increase. According to the Wall Street Journal, there were "18 random mass shootings in the 1980s, 54 in the 1990s, and 87 in the 2000s." The Journal's emphasis was on random shootings, but a 2013 USA Today report on mass killings found that the number of all mass killings since 2006—including those in which some of the victims were known to the killers—totalled 146, and that 900 lives were lost in such incidents. The Federal Bureau of Investigation (FBI) defines a mass killing as an incident in which at least four people lost their lives.

4 A fair question would be to ask why the number of such random incidents is increasing. After the Newtown shooting, investigators learned that Lanza had created a huge spread-sheet listing the identities of previous mass killers—including details about the crime, the number of people killed, the weapons used, locations of the shootings, and so on. A senior investigator involved in gathering evidence at Lanza's home told a police audience that Lanza appeared to be trying to "win" the record for the most killed, and that he may have been planning the attack for years.

5 Questions about Lanza's mental health were quickly raised following the Sandy Hook shootings by former friends and family members who knew him to be a painfully shy, reclusive and socially isolated individual. Holmes, the Colorado shooter, met with at least three mental health professionals prior to the movie theatre shooting, and CBS news reports that the fact "adds to the picture of Holmes being clearly on [psychiatrists'] radar in the time period leading up to the shooting."

6 Once we understand that guns, social disengagement, and certain forms of mental health can prove to be a dangerous combination, it is important to ask whether something can be done to predict and prevent episodes of random mass violence. Yet the answer may not be as simple as gun control. Lanza and Holmes were known to have serious mental health problems, yet they were able to live freely in society, to arm themselves without alarming authorities, and to attack unprotected and innocent people in what should have been safe public places. As this chapter will later explain in some detail, American society is built upon a delicate balance between the demand for personal freedoms and the need for public safety. It is within the cracks that appear within the social and legal fabric that is woven from the attempt to achieve balance between these two contrasting goals that crimes like random mass shootings emerge.

7 A dozen years before the mass shooting described here, a very different kind of criminal event thrust itself on American society and our justice system with the September 11th, 2001 terrorist attacks that targeted New York City's World Trade Center and the Pentagon. Those attacks, including one on an airliner that crashed in the Pennsylvania countryside, left nearly 3,000 dead and caused billions of dollars in property damage. They have since been classified as the most destructive criminal activity ever perpetrated on US soil. The resulting 'war on terrrorism' changed the face of world politics and ushered in a new era in American society. Before the attacks, most Americans lived relatively secure lives, largely unfettered by fear of random personal attack. The attacks of 9/11, however, share something in common with the mass shootings of recent years. Following the 9/11 attacks, a heated debate took place between those wanting to enforce powerful crime prevention and security measures and others seeking to preserve the individual rights and freedoms that have long been characteristics of American life. This issue, which is also central to recent efforts to reduce the number of random mass killings, continues to feed TV talk shows, newspaper editorials, and Web logs (blogs) nationwide. It asks Americans to determine which rights, freedoms and conveniences (if any) they are willing to sacrifice to increase personal and public safety.

Reading Comprehension Check

Fact versus Opinion

1. Examine the first sentence of this reading passage, "On December 14th, 2012, 20-year-old Adam Lanza, a socially awkward young man, went on a shooting rampage at Sandy Hook Elementary School in Newtown, Connecticut." This sentence
   a. expresses an opinion.
   b. is false.
   c. is a statement of fact.
   d. is both a fact and an opinion.

   Question Type ________________
2. Which factor did the newspaper, *USA Today*, report on?
   a. the number of all killings
   b. the number of mass killings since 2006
   c. the number of mass killings in each decade
   d. none of the above

   Question Type ________________
3. Which statistical information is *not* offered in the text?
   a. the number of mass killing since 2006
   b. the number of mass killings in each decade, from the 1980s to the 2000s
   c. the ratio of women killed compared to that of men
   d. the number of people who died due to the 9/11 attacks

   Question Type ________________

4. According to the author, what may have been Adam Lanza's motivation to commit mass murder?
   a. He may have wanted to break the record for killing the most people ever.
   b. He may have been jealous of a guy in his class.
   c. He may have hated this school for how they had treated him earlier.
   d. none of the above

   Question Type __________

5. The word *reclusive* in the sentence, "Questions about Lanza's mental health were quickly raised following the Sandy Hook shootings by former friends and family members who knew him to be a painfully shy, **reclusive** and socially isolated individual" (para. 5), could be replaced by
   a. exclusive.
   b. withdrawn.
   c. social.
   d. meandering.

   Question Type __________

6. Beyond gun control, what factor does the author point to as one on which to focus in preventing mass killings?
   a. propaganda
   b. poverty
   c. the use of drugs and alcohol
   d. mental health issues

   Question Type __________

7. The word *fabric* in the sentence, "It is within the cracks that appear within the social and legal **fabric** that is woven from the attempt to achieve balance between these two contrasting goals that crimes like random mass shootings emerge," (para. 6) could be replaced by
   a. wool.
   b. psychology.
   c. framework.
   d. distance.

   Question Type __________

8. What connection does the author make between the aftermath of general mass shootings in America and that of the 9/11 terrorist attacks?
   a. the issue of location of mass crimes
   b. the tension between public safety and individual rights in relation to these events
   c. the relationship between international and domestic threats
   d. the lack of funding for world-class security systems

   Question Type __________

9. Which media source is *not* mentioned in the reading as a place where the issue of individual freedom versus public safety is under discussion?
   a. in Hollywood movies
   b. on TV talk shows
   c. on blogs
   d. in newspaper editorials

   Question Type ________

10. "The resulting 'war on terrorism' changed the face of world politics and ushered in a new era in American society" (para. 7).

    This is a statement of
    a. fact.
    b. opinion.
    c. neither.
    d. a mix of fact and opinion.

    Question Type ____________

Contemporary Issues in the Discipline

Bryan Stevenson, an award-winning public-interest lawyer, fights poverty and unjust sentencing as the Founder and Executive Director of the Equal Justice Initiative (EJI). EJI is dedicated to defending the safety of prisoners, exonerating innocent or excessively sentenced prisoners, and protecting the rights of children 17 and under to avoid life-without-parole sentencing.

READING 6

Lecture (TED Talk)

Contemporary Issues in the Discipline

MyReadingLab

Visit Chapter 6: Criminal Justice in MyReadingLab to complete the Reading 6 activities.

We Need to Talk About an Injustice

Pre-Reading Activity

Before reading the following transcript of Bryan Stevenson's speech, you can watch the speech itself here: http://www.ted.com/talks/bryan_stevenson_we_need_to_talk_about_an_injustice?language=en (Courtesy of TED). As you listen to the videoed presentation, take notes. (See the note-taking activity on p. 190 for some pointers.) After reading the transcript, you will answer some open-ended questions about some of the issues raised in the speech. Finally, you will formulate questions for Mr. Stevenson about issues pertinent to criminal justice and answer them from his perspective.

We Need to Talk About an Injustice

***By* Bryan Stevenson March 2012 Transcript courtesy of TED © TED Conferences, LLC**

1 Well this is a really extraordinary honor for me. I spend most of my time in jails, in prisons, on death row. I spend most of my time in very low-income communities in the projects and places where there's a great deal of hopelessness. And being here at TED and seeing the stimulation, hearing it, has been very, very energizing to me. And one of the things that's emerged in my short time here is that TED has an identity. And you can actually say things here that have impacts around the world. And sometimes when it comes through TED, it has meaning and power that it doesn't have when it doesn't.

2 And I mention that because I think identity is really important. And we've had some fantastic presentations. And I think what we've learned is that, if you're a teacher your words can be meaningful, but if you're a compassionate teacher, they can be especially meaningful. If you're a doctor you can do some good things, but if you're a caring doctor you can do some other things. And so I want to talk about the power of identity. And I didn't learn about this actually practicing law and doing the work that I do. I actually learned about this from my grandmother.

3 I grew up in a house that was the traditional African-American home that was dominated by a matriarch, and that matriarch was my grandmother. She was tough, she was strong, she was powerful. She was the end of every argument in our family. She was the beginning of a lot of arguments in our family. She was the daughter of people who were actually enslaved. Her parents were born in slavery in Virginia in the 1840's. She was born in the 1880's and the experience of slavery very much shaped the way she saw the world.

4 And my grandmother was tough, but she was also loving. When I would see her as a little boy, she'd come up to me and she'd give me these hugs. And she'd squeeze me so tight I could barely breathe and then she'd let me go. And an hour or two later, if I saw her, she'd come over to me and she'd say, "Bryan, do you still feel me hugging you?" And if I said, "No," she'd assault me again, and if I said, "Yes," she'd leave me alone. And she just had this quality that you always wanted to be near her. And the only challenge was that she had 10 children. My mom was the youngest of her 10 kids. And sometimes when I would go and spend time with her, it would be difficult to get her time and attention. My cousins would be running around everywhere.

5 And I remember, when I was about eight or nine years old, waking up one morning, going into the living room, and all of my cousins were running around. And my grandmother was sitting across the room staring at me. And at first I thought we were playing a game. And I would look at her and I'd smile, but she was very serious. And after about 15 or 20 minutes of this, she got up and she came across the room and she took me by the hand and she said, "Come on, Bryan. You and I are going to have a talk." And I remember this just like it happened yesterday. I never will forget it.

6 She took me out back and she said, "Bryan, I'm going to tell you something, but you don't tell anybody what I tell you." I said, "Okay, Mama." She said, "Now you make sure you don't do that." I said, "Sure." Then she sat me down and she looked at me and she said, "I want you to know I've been watching you." And she said, "I think you're special." She said, "I think you can do anything you want to do." I will never forget it.

7 And then she said, "I just need you to promise me three things, Bryan." I said, "Okay, Mama." She said, "The first thing I want you to promise me is that you'll always love your mom." She said, "That's my baby girl, and you have to promise me now you'll always take care of her." Well I adored my mom, so I said, "Yes, Mama. I'll do that." Then she said, "The second thing I want you to promise me is that you'll always do the right thing even when the right thing is the hard thing." And I thought about it and I said, "Yes, Mama. I'll do that." Then finally she said, "The third thing I want you to promise me is that you'll never drink alcohol." *(Laughter)* Well I was nine years old, so I said, "Yes, Mama. I'll do that."

8 I grew up in the country in the rural South, and I have a brother a year older than me and a sister a year younger. When I was about 14 or 15, one day my brother came home and he had this six-pack of beer — I don't know where he got it — and he grabbed me and my sister and we went out in the woods. And we were kind of just out there doing the stuff we crazily did. And he had a sip of this beer and he gave some to my sister and she had some, and they offered it to me. I said, "No, no, no. That's okay. You all go ahead. I'm not going to have any beer." My brother said, "Come on. We're doing this today; you always do what we do. I had some, your sister had some. Have some beer." I said, "No, I don't feel right about that. Y'all go ahead. Y'all go ahead." And then my brother started staring at me. He said, "What's wrong with you? Have some beer." Then he looked at me real hard and he said, "Oh, I hope you're not still hung up on that conversation Mama had with you." *(Laughter)* I said, "Well, what are you talking about?" He said, "Oh, Mama tells all the grandkids that they're special." *(Laughter)* I was devastated. *(Laughter)*

9 And I'm going to admit something to you. I'm going to tell you something I probably shouldn't. I know this might be broadcast broadly. But I'm 52 years old, and I'm going to admit to you that I've never had a drop of alcohol. *(Applause)* I don't say that because I think that's virtuous; I say that because there is power in identity. When we create the right kind of identity, we can say things to the world around us that they don't actually believe makes sense. We can get them to do things that they don't think they can do. When I thought about my grandmother, of course she would think all her grandkids were special. My grandfather was in prison during prohibition. My male uncles died of alcohol-related diseases. And these were the things she thought we needed to commit to.

10 Well I've been trying to say something about our criminal justice system. This country is very different today than it was 40 years ago. In 1972, there were 300,000 people in jails and prisons. Today, there are 2.3 million. The United States now has the highest rate of incarceration in the world. We have seven million people on probation and parole. And mass incarceration, in my judgment, has fundamentally changed our world. In poor communities, in communities of color there is this despair, there is this hopelessness, that is being shaped by these outcomes. One out of three black men between the ages of 18 and 30 is in jail, in prison, on probation or parole. In urban communities across this country — Los Angeles, Philadelphia, Baltimore, Washington — 50 to 60 percent of all young men of color are in jail or prison or on probation or parole.

11 Our system isn't just being shaped in these ways that seem to be distorting around race, they're also distorted by poverty. We have a system of justice in this country that treats you much better if you're rich and guilty than if you're poor and innocent. Wealth, not

culpability, shapes outcomes. And yet, we seem to be very comfortable. The politics of fear and anger have made us believe that these are problems that are not our problems. We've been disconnected.

12 It's interesting to me. We're looking at some very interesting developments in our work. My state of Alabama, like a number of states, actually permanently disenfranchises you if you have a criminal conviction. Right now in Alabama 34 percent of the black male population has permanently lost the right to vote. We're actually projecting in another 10 years the level of disenfranchisement will be as high as it's been since prior to the passage of the Voting Rights Act. And there is this stunning silence.

13 I represent children. A lot of my clients are very young. The United States is the only country in the world where we sentence 13-year-old children to die in prison. We have life imprisonment without parole for kids in this country. And we're actually doing some litigation. The only country in the world.

14 I represent people on death row. It's interesting, this question of the death penalty. In many ways, we've been taught to think that the real question is, do people deserve to die for the crimes they've committed? And that's a very sensible question. But there's another way of thinking about where we are in our identity. The other way of thinking about it is not, do people deserve to die for the crimes they commit, but do we deserve to kill? I mean, it's fascinating.

15 Death penalty in America is defined by error. For every nine people who have been executed, we've actually identified one innocent person who's been exonerated and released from death row. A kind of astonishing error rate — one out of nine people innocent. I mean, it's fascinating. In aviation, we would never let people fly on airplanes if for every nine planes that took off one would crash. But somehow we can insulate ourselves from this problem. It's not our problem. It's not our burden. It's not our struggle.

16 I talk a lot about these issues. I talk about race and this question of whether we deserve to kill. And it's interesting, when I teach my students about African-American history, I tell them about slavery. I tell them about terrorism, the era that began at the end of reconstruction that went on to World War II. We don't really know very much about it. But for African-Americans in this country, that was an era defined by terror. In many communities, people had to worry about being lynched. They had to worry about being bombed. It was the threat of terror that shaped their lives. And these older people come up to me now and they say, "Mr. Stevenson, you give talks, you make speeches, you tell people to stop saying we're dealing with terrorism for the first time in our nation's history after 9/11." They tell me to say, "No, tell them that we grew up with that." And that era of terrorism, of course, was followed by segregation and decades of racial subordination and apartheid.

18 I was giving some lectures in Germany about the death penalty. It was fascinating because one of the scholars stood up after the presentation and said, "Well you know it's deeply troubling to hear what you're talking about." He said, "We don't have the death penalty in Germany. And of course, we can never have the death penalty in Germany." And the room got very quiet, and this woman said, "There's no way, with our history, we could ever engage in the systematic killing of human beings. It would be unconscionable for us to, in an intentional and deliberate way, set about executing people." And I thought about that. What would it feel like to be living in a world where the nation state of Germany was executing people, especially if they were disproportionately Jewish? I couldn't bear it. It would be unconscionable.

19 And yet, in this country, in the states of the Old South, we execute people — where you're 11 times more likely to get the death penalty if the victim is white than if the victim is black, 22 times more likely to get it if the defendant is black and the victim is white — in the very states where there are buried in the ground the bodies of people who were lynched. And yet, there is this disconnect.

20 Well I believe that our identity is at risk. That when we actually don't care about these difficult things, the positive and wonderful things are nonetheless implicated. We love innovation. We love technology. We love creativity. We love entertainment. But ultimately, those realities are shadowed by suffering, abuse, degradation, marginalization. And for me, it becomes necessary to integrate the two. Because ultimately we are talking about a need to be more hopeful, more committed, more dedicated to the basic challenges of living in a complex world. And for me that means spending time thinking and talking about the poor, the disadvantaged, those who will never get to TED. But thinking about them in a way that is integrated in our own lives.

21 You know ultimately, we all have to believe things we haven't seen. We do. As rational as we are, as committed to intellect as we are. Innovation, creativity, development comes not from the ideas in our mind alone. They come from the ideas in our mind that are also fueled by some conviction in our heart. And it's that mind-heart connection that I believe compels us to not just be attentive to all the bright and dazzly things, but also the dark and difficult things. Vaclav Havel, the great Czech leader, talked about this. He said, "When we were in Eastern Europe and dealing with oppression, we wanted all kinds of things, but mostly what we needed was hope, an orientation of the spirit, a willingness to sometimes be in hopeless places and be a witness."

22 Well that orientation of the spirit is very much at the core of what I believe even TED communities have to be engaged in. There is no disconnect around technology and design that will allow us to be fully human until we pay attention to suffering, to poverty, to exclusion, to

unfairness, to injustice. Now I will warn you that this kind of identity is a much more challenging identity than ones that don't pay attention to this. It will get to you.

23 I had the great privilege, when I was a young lawyer, of meeting Rosa Parks. And Ms. Parks used to come back to Montgomery every now and then, and she would get together with two of her dearest friends, these older women, Johnnie Carr who was the organizer of the Montgomery bus boycott—amazing African-American woman—and Virginia Durr, a white woman, whose husband, Clifford Durr, represented Dr. King. And these women would get together and just talk.

24 And every now and then Ms. Carr would call me, and she'd say, "Bryan, Ms. Parks is coming to town. We're going to get together and talk. Do you want to come over and listen?" And I'd say, "Yes, Ma'am, I do." And she'd say, "Well what are you going to do when you get here?" I said, "I'm going to listen." And I'd go over there and I would, I would just listen. It would be so energizing and so empowering.

25 And one time I was over there listening to these women talk, and after a couple of hours Ms. Parks turned to me and she said, "Now Bryan, tell me what the Equal Justice Initiative is. Tell me what you're trying to do." And I began giving her my rap. I said, "Well we're trying to challenge injustice. We're trying to help people who have been wrongly convicted. We're trying to confront bias and discrimination in the administration of criminal justice. We're trying to end life without parole sentences for children. We're trying to do something about the death penalty. We're trying to reduce the prison population. We're trying to end mass incarceration."

26 I gave her my whole rap, and when I finished she looked at me and she said, "Mmm mmm mmm." She said, "That's going to make you tired, tired, tired." (*Laughter*) And that's when Ms. Carr leaned forward, she put her finger in my face, she said, "That's why you've got to be brave, brave, brave."

27 And I actually believe that the TED community needs to be more courageous. We need to find ways to embrace these challenges, these problems, the suffering. Because ultimately, our humanity depends on everyone's humanity. I've learned very simple things doing the work that I do. It's just taught me very simple things. I've come to understand and to believe that each of us is more than the worst thing we've ever done. I believe that for every person on the planet. I think if somebody tells a lie, they're not just a liar. I think if somebody takes something that doesn't belong to them, they're not just a thief. I think even if you kill someone, you're not just a killer. And because of that there's this basic human dignity that must be respected by law. I also believe that in many parts of this country, and certainly in many parts of this globe, that the opposite of poverty is not wealth. I don't believe that. I actually think, in too many places, the opposite of poverty is justice.

28 And finally, I believe that, despite the fact that it is so dramatic and so beautiful and so inspiring and so stimulating, we will ultimately not be judged by our technology, we won't be judged by our design, we won't be judged by our intellect and reason. Ultimately, you judge the character of a society, not by how they treat their rich and the powerful and the privileged, but by how they treat the poor, the condemned, the incarcerated. Because it's in that nexus that we actually begin to understand truly profound things about who we are.

29 I sometimes get out of balance. I'll end with this story. I sometimes push too hard. I do get tired, as we all do. Sometimes those ideas get ahead of our thinking in ways that are important. And I've been representing these kids who have been sentenced to do these very harsh sentences. And I go to the jail and I see my client who's 13 and 14, and he's been certified to stand trial as an adult. I start thinking, well, how did that happen? How can a judge turn you into something that you're not? And the judge has certified him as an adult, but I see this kid.

30 And I was up too late one night and I starting thinking, well gosh, if the judge can turn you into something that you're not, the judge must have magic power. Yeah, Bryan, the judge has some magic power. You should ask for some of that. And because I was up too late, wasn't thinking real straight, I started working on a motion. And I had a client who was 14 years old, a young, poor black kid. And I started working on this motion, and the head of the motion was: "Motion to try my poor, 14-year-old black male client like a privileged, white 75-year-old corporate executive." *(Applause)*

31 And I put in my motion that there was prosecutorial misconduct and police misconduct and judicial misconduct. There was a crazy line in there about how there's no conduct in this county, it's all misconduct. And the next morning, I woke up and I thought, now did I dream that crazy motion, or did I actually write it? And to my horror, not only had I written it, but I had sent it to court. *(Applause)*

32 A couple months went by, and I had just forgotten all about it. And I finally decided, oh gosh, I've got to go to the court and do this crazy case. And I got into my car and I was feeling really overwhelmed—overwhelmed. And I got in my car and I went to this courthouse. And I was thinking, this is going to be so difficult, so painful. And I finally got out of the car and I started walking up to the courthouse.

33 And as I was walking up the steps of this courthouse, there was an older black man who was the janitor in this courthouse. When this man saw me, he came over to me and he said, "Who are you?" I said, "I'm a lawyer." He said, "You're a lawyer?" I said, "Yes, sir." And this man came over to me and he hugged me. And he whispered in my ear. He said, "I'm so proud of you." And I have to tell you, it was energizing. It connected deeply with something in me about identity,

about the capacity of every person to contribute to a community, to a perspective that is hopeful.

34 Well I went into the courtroom. And as soon as I walked inside, the judge saw me coming in. He said, "Mr. Stevenson, did you write this crazy motion?" I said, "Yes, sir. I did." And we started arguing. And people started coming in because they were just outraged. I had written these crazy things. And police officers were coming in and assistant prosecutors and clerk workers. And before I knew it, the courtroom was filled with people angry that we were talking about race, that we were talking about poverty, that we were talking about inequality.

35 And out of the corner of my eye, I could see this janitor pacing back and forth. And he kept looking through the window, and he could hear all of this holler. He kept pacing back and forth. And finally, this older black man with this very worried look on his face came into the courtroom and sat down behind me, almost at counsel table. About 10 minutes later the judge said we would take a break. And during the break there was a deputy sheriff who was offended that the janitor had come into court. And this deputy jumped up and he ran over to this older black man. He said, "Jimmy, what are you doing in this courtroom?" And this older black man stood up and he looked at that deputy and he looked at me and he said, "I came into this courtroom to tell this young man, keep your eyes on the prize, hold on."

36 I've come to TED because I believe that many of you understand that the moral arc of the universe is long, but it bends toward justice. That we cannot be full evolved human beings until we care about human rights and basic dignity. That all of our survival is tied to the survival of everyone. That our visions of technology and design and entertainment and creativity have to be married with visions of humanity, compassion and justice. And more than anything, for those of you who share that, I've simply come to tell you to keep your eyes on the prize, hold on.

37 Thank you very much. *(Applause)*

38 **Chris Anderson:** So you heard and saw an obvious desire by this audience, this community, to help you on your way and to do something on this issue. Other than writing a check, what could we do?

39 **BS:** Well there are opportunities all around us. If you live in the state of California, for example, there's a referendum coming up this spring where actually there's going to be an effort to redirect some of the money we spend on the politics of punishment. For example, here in California we're going to spend one billion dollars on the death penalty in the next five years -- one billion dollars. And yet, 46 percent of all homicide cases don't result in arrest. 56 percent of all rape cases don't result. So there's an opportunity to change that. And this referendum would propose having those dollars go to law enforcement and safety. And I think that opportunity exists all around us.

40 **CA:** There's been this huge decline in crime in America over the last three decades. And part of the narrative of that is sometimes that it's about increased incarceration rates. What would you say to someone who believed that?

41 **BS:** Well actually the violent crime rate has remained relatively stable. The great increase in mass incarceration in this country wasn't really in violent crime categories. It was this misguided war on drugs. That's where the dramatic increases have come in our prison population. And we got carried away with the rhetoric of punishment. And so we have three strikes laws that put people in prison forever for stealing a bicycle, for low-level property crimes, rather than making them give those resources back to the people who they victimized. I believe we need to do more to help people who are victimized by crime, not do less. And I think our current punishment philosophy does nothing for no one. And I think that's the orientation that we have to change. *(Applause)*

42 **CA:** Bryan, you've struck a massive chord here. You're an inspiring person. Thank you so much for coming to TED. Thank you. *(Applause)*

Reading with a Critical Eye

In a small group, discuss the following reflection questions, which will guide you toward a deeper understanding of the reading.

1. What message is Mr. Stevenson trying to convey with his examples of teachers and doctors in the second paragraph?
2. How does Mr. Stevenson describe his grandmother's background and character? In what ways did she influence him?
3. Why is Mr. Stevenson proud that he has never touched a drop of alcohol?
4. Mr. Stevenson offers a number of statistics pertaining to America's prison population in paragraph 10. Which of the statistics is most surprising to you? Why?
5. What does Mr. Stevenson say about the death penalty in America? How does he compare its practice with flying airplanes? What is your reaction to his position on this issue?

Imagined Interview: If you had the opportunity to interview Bryan Stevenson in person, what would you ask him? With a partner, compose three questions for him.

Question 1. ____________________

Question 2. ____________________

Question 3. ____________________

Interview Challenge: In a group, ask one student to play Mr. Stevenson. This student should carefully consider Bryan Stevenson's views, outlined clearly in the TED Talk, and try to answer the questions from Stevenson's perspective on criminal justice.

Chapter Recap

After reading this full chapter focusing on the field of criminal justice, let's review the chapter reading content, skill focus, and vocabulary to gain a better understanding of what we have learned.

Recap Activity 1: A Quick Glance

In 60 seconds, answer the following two questions:

1. What is one thing you learned from this chapter?

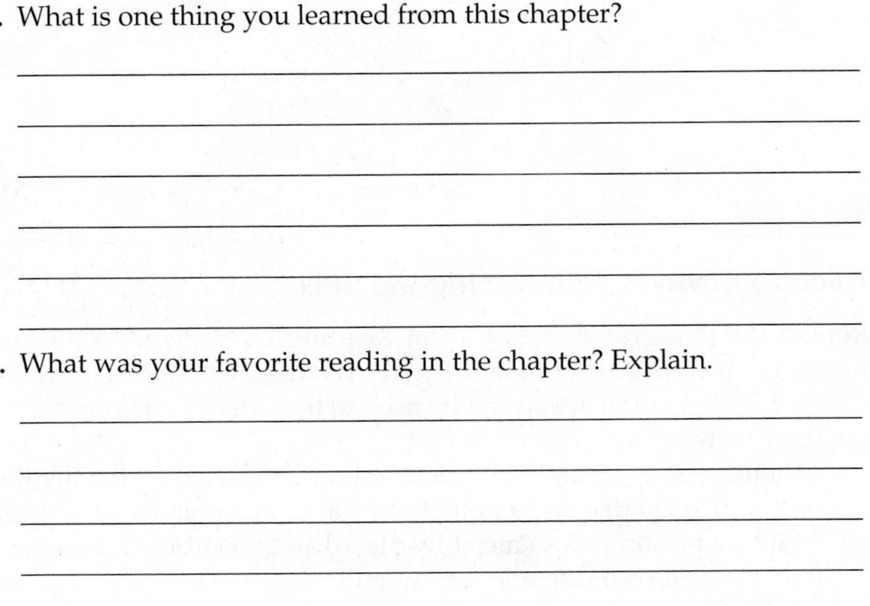

2. What was your favorite reading in the chapter? Explain.

Now discuss what you wrote in a small group. Do not read what you wrote. Paraphrase yourself!

Recap Activity 2: Summary Writing

Choose your favorite reading from this chapter and write a summary containing the main idea and some major details. Keep in mind that the key to summary writing is to convey the author's ideas accurately, but to relay this information in your own words. Last but not least, be sure to include reminder phrases and appropriate transitions.

Recap Activity 3: Internet Research on a Theme of Interest

Think about the choice you just made in Activity 2 concerning which reading in the chapter was your favorite.

What was the theme of your chosen reading?

Theme = ______________________________

Using a search engine, such as Google, go online and locate a quality reading on the same theme as your favorite chapter reading. Write a three- to five-sentence summary of the reading that you found from your Internet research.

Title of Reading	*Article Source*	*Summary of the Reading (in your own words)*

Recap Activity 4: Reinforcing the Skill

Reread the paragraphs below from Reading 2: "Schizophrenic Teen Looks for Justice After Murder." After reading, discuss them with a partner: What plan of action can be used to best identify opinions in the reading? How can you identify facts?

> "There are some cases," says Richard Bonnie, director of the **Institute** of Law, Psychiatry and Public **Policy** at the University of Virginia, "where a person was so mentally disturbed at the time of the offense that it would be inhumane and morally objectionable to convict and punish them."
>
> Terry Clark wonders, now, when it all started.
>
> Did it begin with Eric's fear of drinking tap water? It was December 1998, and a house fire forced the family to live temporarily in an apartment. Eric, then 16, worried about lead poisoning and would only drink bottled water.

How can you clearly identify both facts and opinions in the passage you have just read?

Strategy 1: ______________________________

Strategy 2: ______________________________

Recap Activity 5: Recycling Vocabulary

With a partner, locate the following vocabulary terms, review them in context, and try to define the terms without using a dictionary. The first example is done for you.

Word and context location	*Sentence containing the word*	*Meaning in this context*
circumstances p. 297, para. 16	The issue is determining under what **circumstances** absolution of a criminal act is warranted.	a condition that affects a situation
overzealous p. 293, para. 29	And most of them sued in federal court, claiming their civil rights had been violated by **overzealous** police officers… .	______
exoneration p. 292, para. 23	He lost a shipyard job after his employer saw a news report about his **exoneration** on television.	______
inhumane p. 297 para. 17	"… where a person was so mentally disturbed at the time of the offense that it would be **inhumane** and morally objectionable to convict and punish them."	______
defendant p.298, para. 47	… defense attorney David Goldberg asserts that Arizona law is so restrictive that it violates a mentally ill **defendant's** right to a fair trial.	______
nominee p. 301, para. 4	On December 1, 2008, Obama announced that Holder would be his **nominee** for Attorney General.	______
evidence p. 320, para. 4	A senior investigator involved in gathering **evidence** at Lanza's home told a police audience that Lanza appeared to be trying to "win" the record for the most killed,	______
rampage p. 320, para. 1	On December 14th, 2012, 20-year-old Adam Lanza, a socially awkward young man, went on a shooting **rampage** at Sandy Hook Elemantary School in Newtown, Connecticut	______
testimony p. 288, You Solve the Case	**Testimony** Offered by the Five Leading Suspects During Police Questioning	______
random p. 320, para. 3	Experts tell us that the number of **random** mass shootings is on the increase.	______

Further Explorations

Books

1. *The Appeal* by John Grisham. New York: Random House, 2008. A large company dumps chemicals in a rural community. An altruistic scrappy attorney fights back.
2. *Voices of Women and the Criminal Justice System* by Katherine Stuart van Wormer and Clemens Bartollas. Boston: Allyn and Bacon, 2007. This book is made up of 19 stories. Some are from female offenders; others are from female law enforcers.
3. *Careers in Criminal Justice* by W. Richard Stephens. New York: Pearson, 2001. An array of job opportunities in the field of Criminal Justice are explored.

Movies/Plays

1. *Michael Clayton* (2007). Directed by Tony Gilroy. Middle-aged lawyer Michael Clayton (George Clooney) is a "fixer" who clears up complex or dirty cases on behalf of corporate clients.
2. *The Verdict* (1982). Directed by Sidney Lumet. A lawyer sees the chance to salvage his career and self-respect by taking a medical malpractice case to trial rather than settling.
3. *Broken on All Sides: Race, Mass Incarceration and New Visions for Criminal Justice in the U.S.* (2012). This documentary project began as a way to explore, educate about, and advocate change around the overcrowding in the Philadelphia jail system. It has come to focus on mass incarceration across the nation.

Internet Sites

1. www.innocenceproject.org
   The Innocence Project is a national litigation and public policy organization dedicated to exonerating wrongfully convicted people through DNA testing.
2. www.ncjrs.gov
   The National Criminal Justice Reference Service is a very informative reference site. Explore such categories as crime prevention, corrections, the justice system, and victims.
3. www.oyez.org/tour/
   Take a virtual tour of the U.S. Supreme Court via the multimedia Oyez Project.

Time Management

Overview

Our lives are all very busy. Many students have work responsibilities, are involved in extracurricular activities, and have family responsibilities at home. With only 24 hours in a day, when can we find sufficient time in our schedules to sit and read assigned class readings carefully, without rushing? This is an important question to consider; the quality of reading that you do in your courses is one of the major keys to your overall success in college.

The challenge is to understand the reality of your weekly life schedule in advance, and to find pockets of time you can dedicate to working on your course readings.

Discuss these questions about reading and time management with a few of your classmates.

1. Take a quick glance at the textbook excerpt that you just read on pages 320–21 and the comprehension questions that follow. About how much time did it take you to do a careful reading of that excerpt from *Criminal Justice Today* and to answer the questions? Do you think by focusing more on the reading task, you could complete a reading of this length more quickly? Or, perhaps would it help you to not rush to get a better understanding of what you are reading?
2. What time of day is the best time for you to read: early morning, in the afternoon, or late at night? Where do you like to do your reading?
3. Do you feel that "time issues" make it difficult for you to successfully complete your class readings? Explain.

Challenge Activity

Tonight, take a little time to fill out the following My Week schedule, making sure to fill in all of your known daily responsibilities. Where do you have a pocket of time when you can anticipate spending time with class readings? (Consider where you will be at these times, and whether the environment will be conducive to focused reading.) Write "Course Reading Time" in these open slots in your schedule. When you are finished, tally up how many hours you slotted for course readings. Consider that researchers recommend that for every hour spent in the classroom, you should allot at least two hours for class reading.

My Week							
Time	*M*	*T*	*W*	*TH*	*F*	*Sat*	*Sun*
6 AM							
7 AM							
8 AM							
9 AM							
10 AM							
11 AM							
12 PM							
1 PM							
2 PM							
3 PM							
4 PM							
5 PM							
6 PM							
7 PM							
8 PM							
9 PM							
10 PM							
11 PM							
12 AM							
1 AM							
2 AM							
3 AM							
4 AM							
5 AM							

Anticipated Hours Dedicated to Doing College Reading = ______________

Learning Implications

Successful students manage their time effectively. If you build quality blocks of study/reading time into your weekly schedule, you will not find yourself rushing through course material and showing up for class unprepared. Instead, you will be well prepared for class discussions and for any pop quizzes that your instructor may give you.

LIFE SCIENCE
Nursing

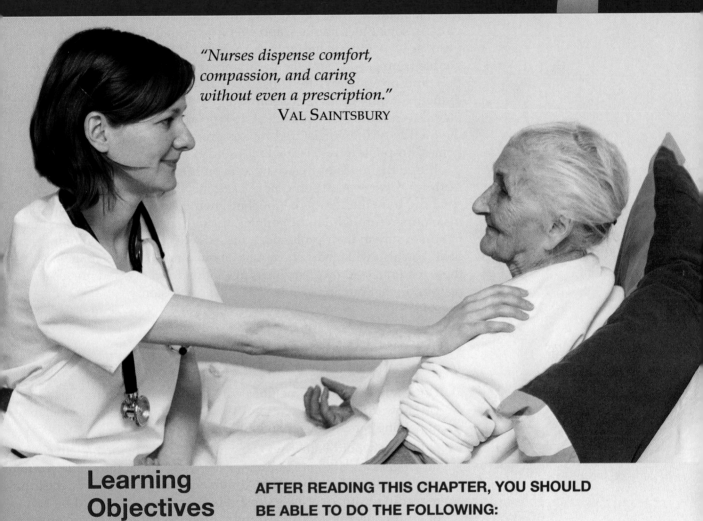

"Nurses dispense comfort, compassion, and caring without even a prescription."
VAL SAINTSBURY

Learning Objectives

AFTER READING THIS CHAPTER, YOU SHOULD BE ABLE TO DO THE FOLLOWING:

1. Identify fundamentals about the field of modern-day nursing.
2. Recognize the challenges of caring for America's sick.
3. Identify different patterns of text organization.
4. Construct a summary of an original text.

INTRODUCTION TO THE DISCIPLINE OF NURSING

With the increasing shortage of nurses in major hospitals throughout the United States, nursing has become a highly sought-after profession. Typically, women pursued nursing as a career, but now even men are gradually realizing that nursing could be financially rewarding for them and bring job satisfaction. As you know, nurses provide care for sick individuals, sometimes families, and even communities. A registered nurse's purpose is to educate individuals on how to lead a healthy life, prevent people from getting sick, help patients regain health and proper function, and provide care for those who are terminally ill and gradually dying. Not only do nurses administer medication to their patients but they also encourage sick individuals to keep a positive attitude and enhance the quality of life. Registered nurses provide care for their patients in homes, hospitals, physicians' clinics, and extended-care facilities.

While the focus of this chapter is on the discipline of nursing, the readings cover several subtopics. These include junior nursing students recalling how their patients touched their lives, recruiters looking for male nurses throughout the country, treating impaired nurses and helping them stay in their profession, and how to succeed as a nursing student. You also will read a short story about a nurse in this chapter. All of these readings will give you an appreciation for registered nurses and a realization that nursing is indeed a noble profession.

Preview Questions

1. Do you have a family member who needs in-home nursing care? If yes, how do you and your family members cope with the challenge of helping care for this individual? Be specific.
2. How long would you be willing to house and care for a relative who no longer can take care of him- or herself? How comfortable would you be allowing a professional nurse to manage critical decisions regarding your relative's lifestyle choices? What would be some of your concerns about trusting a nurse? What percentage of your monthly income would you allocate for subsidizing this relative's nursing expenses?
3. The average life expectancy of Americans has increased significantly due to the many advances in medical technology. How many years do you think the twenty-first-century American citizen can live self-sufficiently in relatively good health? At what age do you believe a senior citizen typically becomes a liability to society? Explain.
4. Senior citizens living into their eighties, nineties, and beyond pose a great challenge to the nursing profession. In what ways can the field of Nursing rise to the occasion and meet the growing needs of

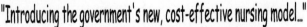

America's aging population? Discuss the role the government can play in producing sufficient Nursing graduates to deal with this demographic change.

Writing on The Wall

After you have discussed the preview questions with your classmates, post your responses to two of them on your class blog, which we refer to as The Wall. Review others' postings and respond to at least two of your classmates' posts that grab your interest. Remember the guidelines for blogging and commenting etiquette (see p. 15)! If your class is not using a shared blog, your instructor may ask you to record your individual or collective responses to the preview questions in another form.

EXERCISE 7.1 Interpreting a Cartoon

SLY
"Introducing the government's new, cost-effective nursing model..."

Working in pairs, examine the cartoon shown here and answer the following questions.

1. What is so amusing about this cartoon?
2. In your opinion, what is the cartoonist's intended message to the reader?

Discipline-specific Vocabulary: Understand Key Terms in Nursing

As you work your way through this chapter, you will learn some key terms in the discipline of nursing. Your goal is to use these terms in your speech and writing. You will have the opportunity to interact with key terms in context, so study them carefully and make them part of your active vocabulary.

EXERCISE 7.2 Brainstorming Vocabulary

Directions: What associated words come to mind when you think of the discipline of nursing? Work with a partner and write down as many related words as you can think of in a period of five minutes.

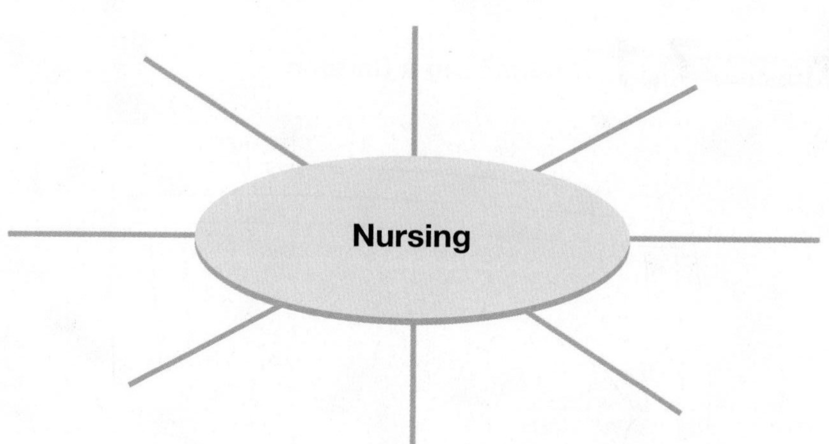

Fishing for Synonyms and Antonyms

In your written work, you will often need to use synonyms and antonyms (see p. 24 to review these terms) in order to paraphrase statements or claims made by writers.

EXERCISE 7.3 Determining Synonyms and Antonyms from Context

Directions: Read the following ten (10) discipline-specific words culled from the readings in this chapter and shown in the context of the sentences in which they appeared. In the space provided after each sentence, write a synonym or antonym for the highlighted terms, as directed.

Discipline-specific Word Bank for Nursing

oncology	**patient**	**emergency**	**chemotherapy**
clinical	**humanistic**	**trauma**	**profession**
critical	**diagnosis**		

1. Dickson leads a team of nurses and other professionals who offer **oncology** patients opportunities to participate in clinical trials and then works with these patients to coordinate their care.

   A synonym for *oncology* is _______.

2. "We aim to provide patient-centered care, so I tell the nurses that we are to engage our patients in a partnership and a dialogue and that we should be a conduit through which **patients** can bring their concerns."

   An antonym for *patient* is _______.

3. A client who is undergoing cancer **chemotherapy** says to the nurse, "This is no way to live."

   A synonym for *chemotherapy* is ______________.

4. Dickson leads a team of nurses and other professionals who offer oncology patients opportunities to participate in **clinical** trials and then works with these patients to coordinate their care.

   A synonym for *clinical* is ________.

5. How comfortable would you be allowing a professional nurse to manage **critical** decisions regarding your relative's lifestyle choices?

   An antonym for the word *critical* is ______.

6. If you had asked Mr. Van Rensselaer in 2004 if he thought he would trade in life in Margaritaville for scenes from "The Wire"—treating gunshot wounds, drug overdoses and unmanaged diabetes in one of the city's busiest **emergency** rooms—he might have assumed you had been to one too many of his wine-tasting events.

   A synonym for *emergency* is _______.

7. Women naturally make better nurses than men because they are genetically preprogrammed to do **humanistic** kinds of work.

   An antonym for *humanistic* is ________.

8. Baltimore's gritty Levindale section is a world apart from Ponce Inlet, Fla., the upscale barrier island where Rich Van Rensselaer owned a boutique liquor store and shop before becoming a **trauma** nurse in the ER.

   A synonym for *trauma* in this context is ________________________.

9. But poised for enormous growth and in the midst of sea change, the **profession** is moving to raise its educational profile.

   A synonym for *profession* is _____.

10. She notes that nurses should be aware of potential barriers to communication such as illiteracy or the patient experiencing stress from learning of a new **diagnosis**.

    A synonym for *diagnosis* is ________.

EXERCISE 7.4 Matching Terms with Their Definitions

Match the word in Column A with the definition in Column B. Put the letter representing the correct definition in the space preceding each term.

Column A			Column B
Word			**Definition**
1.	_____	critical	a. a serious situation requiring immediate action
2.	_____	humanistic	b. the branch of medical science dealing with tumors
3.	_____	patient	c. the treatment of cancer with chemical substances
4.	_____	profession	d. serious and dangerous
5.	_____	clinical	e. the act of identifying a disease or illness
6.	_____	trauma	f. solving human problems with kindness
7.	_____	chemotherapy	g. related to the examination and treatment of patients
8.	_____	emergency	h. an individual under medical care
9.	_____	diagnosis	i. a job that requires special training
10.	_____	oncology	j. a serious injury to a person's body

EXERCISE 7.5 Choosing the Right Word

In the following sentences, fill in each blank with a word from the terminology bank that makes the sentence grammatical and meaningful.

chemotherapy	clinical	diagnosis	critical	emergency
humanistic	oncology	trial	profession	patient

1. When he suspected his son might have a malignant tumor, he went online and read all he could about ________.
2. The patient was brought into the hospital in such a _____ condition that no one thought she would survive the gunshot injury.
3. The clinical _____ of a new drug has shown promising results.

4. Joan has lost all of her hair as a result of __________. Her doctor thinks that treating her cancer with chemical substances has been effective.
5. Experienced nurses know the importance of communicating with the _______ clearly and effectively.
6. Male nurses have proven that just like female nurses, they can have feelings for their patients and do _________ kinds of work.
7. With gender roles changing in society, the _________ of nursing has become attractive to men as well.
8. _________ research focuses on the examination and treatment of patients and their illnesses.
9. Cynthia's _________ showed that she had brain tumor and needed surgery immediately.
10. In an _________, sometimes the head nurse has to make crucial decisions to save the patient's life, especially if the doctor is not immediately available.

MyReadingLab

Visit Chapter 7: Life Science in MyReadingLab to complete the Reading 1 activities.

READING 1

Online Journal

Engaging Patients in Dialogue: A Partnership

Pre-Reading Questions

Before you read the following reading, get into small groups of three or four and discuss these questions based on your personal experience.

1. Have you ever encountered a nurse who treated you, your best friend, or one of your family members? Discuss how this nurse communicated with you or the patient. Do you think the nurse communicated with you pleasantly and effectively? Share your experience with your peers.
2. In your opinion, how important is it for a nurse to communicate with the patient clearly? Give specific examples to support your answer.
3. What are the disadvantages of hiring a nurse who is knowledgeable but lacks excellent communication skills? Discuss the consequences of poor communication between nurse and patient.

Read the following article and answer the multiple-choice questions that follow. Write questions you may have about the text in the space provided alongside the first paragraphs.

Engaging Patients in Dialogue: A Partnership

By Megan M. Krischke, Contributor
August 26, 2011

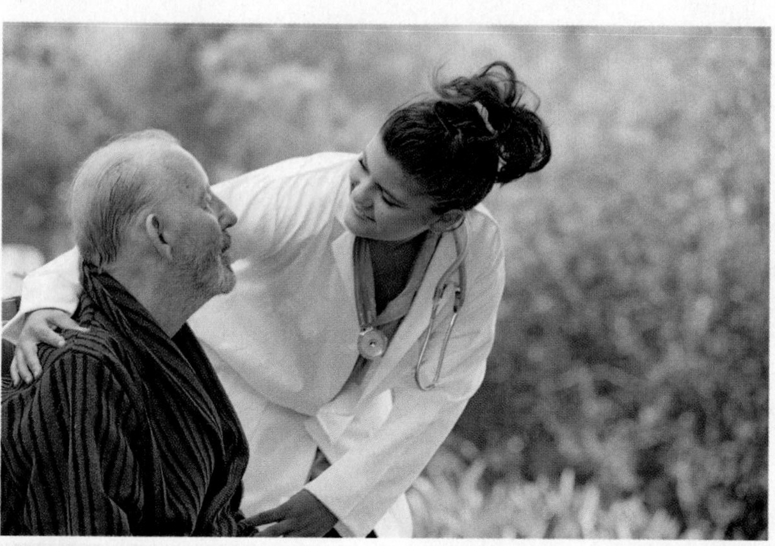

cornerstone
the main foundation to develop something

conduit
a means of communication

voluntary
done by free choice

1 "Communicating clearly with patients is a **cornerstone** to providing safe, quality and effective care," remarked Fé Ermitaño, RN, BSN, project manager for the patient experience at Virginia Mason Medical Center (VMMC) in Seattle. "We aim to provide patient-centered care, so I tell the nurses that we are to engage our patients in a partnership and a dialogue and that we should be a **conduit** through which patients can bring their concerns."

2 Clear communication with patients is of utmost importance to Erica Dickson, RN, BSN, CCRP, **oncology** research manager for Poudre Valley Health Systems (PVHS) in Fort Collins, Colo. Dickson leads a team of nurses and other professionals who offer oncology patients opportunities to participate in **clinical** trials and then works with these patients to **coordinate** their care.

3 "My job is to make sure patients have the time and the information to make their decision. 'No' is as good an answer as 'yes'," explained Dickson. "Often patients tend to take anything the doctor says as **prescriptive**. So if a doctor informs a patient that there is a clinical trial that could be a good option for them, what the patient may be hearing is the **physician** saying that they should participate in the trial. The nurse's job is to start a new conversation; to say this is a choice and it is totally voluntary."

4 She notes that nurses should be aware of potential barriers to communication such as illiteracy or the **patient** experiencing stress from learning of a new **diagnosis.**

5 "We need to be aware that reading isn't always a helpful way for a patient to receive information," Dickson said.

6 Ermitaño adds that the pressure of having more to do than time to do it and issues related to cultural diversity can also complicate a nurse's ability to communicate clearly.

7 "When working with a patient of another culture, or even if a nurse just senses his or her communication is not being well received, I encourage nurses to try to mirror the emotions and behavior of the patient. If a patient isn't making eye contact, there may be a cultural reason for that," she remarked. "Nurses who work with a diverse population could consider seeking out diversity training."

8 She also warns against using medical **jargon** when speaking to, or even around, patients.

9 "When they don't understand the lingo, not only is our ability to communicate limited, patients can also feel **alienated**. Early in my career a physician was discussing with me the patient's condition and within ear shot of that patient used the acronym SOB to refer to shortness of breath. The patient, however, thought the physician was insulting him," related Ermitaño. "This very sweet patient was hurt that the physician saw him in such a poor light."

jargon
the language particular to a profession

alienated
to make unfriendly or indifferent

10 "I consider it a sign that we are communicating well when the patient is able to state back to us the fundamental information about the study in which we are inviting them to participate," stated Dickson. "I also see a patient's willingness to ask questions as a sign that they are comfortable relating to the nurse and that they are engaged in the conversation."

11 Ermitaño also sees active listening and asking patients to say in their own words what you have just explained as key communication techniques, as well as paying attention to physical clues such as eye contact and nodding. She adds that it can help to declare your intention; to tell a patient why you are asking them a particular question

because it builds trust and gives them a better understanding of what kind of information you seeking.

12 "If I'm not making progress with the patient I try to go back and say, 'I don't think we are communicating clearly. Is there something I'm not doing or explaining well?' and have the patient direct me on what kinds of communication are helpful for him or her," she explained. "At VMMC, patients wear yellow slippers, so we talk about putting yourself in their yellow slippers. When a nurse puts his or herself into the patients' yellow slippers it is easier to overcome any communication barriers."

13 "Patients need to feel from us that they are really our focus when we are with them. Nurses need to multitask, but they shouldn't do it while they are with patients," stated Dickson. "Also, whenever we can, we should offer patients choices. I don't think patients have as many choices as we might assume. Just approaching and asking if it is a good time for a blood draw is a positive way to interact with a patient."

Reading with a Critical Eye

1. The article begins with the statement, "Communicating clearly with patients is a cornerstone to providing safe, quality and effective care." Discuss the significance of this statement for the field of nursing.
2. Using specific examples, discuss why nurses should communicate with their patients clearly and effectively. Similarly, tell why it is important for the patient to communicate clearly with the nurse.
3. Why does Dickson assert that "'No' is as good an answer as 'yes'"? Think of a medical scenario where 'no' is as good as 'yes.'
4. Ermitaño asserts that, "issues related to cultural diversity can also complicate a nurse's ability to communicate clearly." Explain what she means.
5. While Dickson admits that nurses need to multitask, why does she believe that nurses should not do it when they are with patients? Explain with specific examples.

Reading Comprehension Check

1. As used in the sentence, "We aim to provide patient-centered care, so I tell the nurses that we are to engage our patients in a partnership and a dialogue and that we should be a conduit through which patients can bring their concerns," the word *engage* means
   a. to bore someone.
   b. to not pay attention.
   c. to lose the attention of.
   d. to draw the attention of.

2. In the sentence, "Dickson leads a team of nurses and other professionals who offer oncology patients opportunities to participate in clinical trials and then works with these patients to coordinate their care," a synonym of *coordinate* is
   a. organize.
   b. complicate.
   c. prolong.
   d. discharge.
3. In the sentence, "Ermitaño adds that the pressure of having more to do than time to do it and issues related to cultural diversity can also complicate a nurse's ability to communicate clearly," the word *complicate* is opposite in meaning to
   a. elaborate.
   b. simplify.
   c. intricate.
   d. perplex.
4. The main idea of this article is that
   a. nurses with poor communication skills must not be hired.
   b. nurses need to communicate with their patients clearly to provide effective care.
   c. nurses must learn at least one foreign language to provide care to patients who speak a language other than English.
   d. nurses are required to translate from foreign languages into English so that they can understand patients' concerns.
5. In discussing the importance of clear communication with the patients, Dickson's main point is that
   a. patients should be able to make decisions that are in their best interest.
   b. patients should blindly follow whatever the doctor prescribes.
   c. patients must be intimidated by the nurse's inability to communicate clearly.
   d. patients do not know much about medical science, so it is not necessary to help them make the best decision.
6. The doctor informing a patient that a clinical trial is an option is offered as an example to support the idea that
   a. the nurse must convince the patient to participate in a clinical trial.
   b. the best option for a cancer patient is to participate in a clinical trial.
   c. patients may consider whatever the doctor suggests as prescriptive.
   d. the doctor may have poor communication skills and confuse the patient.
7. The example of the physician using the acronym SOB within earshot of the patient is mentioned to support the point that
   a. patients are so stupid that they will not understand medical jargon.
   b. only nurses should use medical jargon when speaking to the patients.
   c. physicians should refrain from using medical jargon when speaking to the patients.
   d. most patients are usually mentally deranged, so they will not understand medical jargon.

8. "When working with a patient of another culture, or even if a nurse just senses his or her communication is not being well received, I encourage nurses to try to mirror the emotions and behavior of the patient. If a patient isn't making eye contact, there may be a cultural reason for that," she remarked. "Nurses who work with a diverse population could consider seeking out diversity training." It can be inferred from the passage that
   a. those patients who do not make eye contact are upset with the nurse.
   b. nurses should look in the mirror before communicating with the patient.
   c. nurses must force the patient to make direct eye contact with them.
   d. meaning may be lost or misinterpreted in intercultural communication.
9. "We need to be aware that reading isn't always a helpful way for a patient to receive information," Dickson said. Which of the following conclusions can be drawn from Dickson's statement?
   a. Reading can only be helpful if the patient is a compulsive reader.
   b. Patients may not understand the message if the nurse reads information to them.
   c. Most patients under a nurse's care are poor listeners.
   d. Most nurses are illiterate and do not know how to read information correctly.
10. The overall tone of the article is
   a. neutral.
   b. sarcastic.
   c. inspirational.
   d. shocking.

READING 2

Newspaper Article

MyReadingLab

Visit Chapter 7: Life Science in MyReadingLab to complete the Reading 2 activities.

45, Male and Now a Nurse

Pre-Reading Questions

Discuss the following questions in small groups before reading the article.

1. When you hear the word *nurse*, what kind of image do you conjure up? Describe a nurse's physical appearance to your peers.
2. Do you truly believe that only women are capable of providing patient care as a nurse? If you do, discuss why male nurses may not be as efficient and caring as female nurses.

3. Despite a severe nursing shortage in the country, the idea that men also can pursue nursing as a rewarding career has been slow to catch on. In your opinion, what role do you think the government and educational institutions can play in encouraging men to pursue nursing as a profession?

45, Male and Now a Nurse

By Cecilia Capuzzi Simonnov, *The New York Times*
November 5, 2010

1 Baltimore's gritty Levindale section is a world apart from Ponce Inlet, Fla., the upscale barrier island where Rich Van Rensselaer owned a boutique liquor store and coffee shop before becoming a trauma nurse. If you had asked Mr. Van Rensselaer in 2004 if he thought he would trade in life in Margaritaville for scenes from "The Wire"—treating gunshot wounds, drug overdoses and unmanaged diabetes in one of the city's busiest emergency rooms—he might have assumed you had been to one too many of his wine-tasting events.

2 "Never in a million years," he says, laughing, as he walks the halls of Sinai Hospital, showing off his workplace.

3 Actually, it took six years: last May, Mr. Van Rensselaer, 45, graduated from the University of Maryland with a master's in clinical nurse leadership. His professional leap may seem far-reaching, but in some ways his choice is not so surprising.

4 Like many who come to nursing as a second profession, Mr. Van Rensselaer was motivated after caring for a loved one through an illness—in his case, his mother, who battled thyroid cancer and whom he nursed at her home in the final three months of her life. "It was rewarding," he says. "It was important for my mother to die at home. Working with hospice nurses allowed me to do that for her. And I realized, 'I can do this.' "

5 Nursing is one of the most popular and accepting professions for career changers, due in part to a shortage that's gone on for decades. Nearly 40 percent of students studying to become registered nurses are over age 30, and candidates who already have four-year degrees, like Mr. Van Rensselaer, are highly prized.

6 To attract students from other disciplines, nursing schools are putting new emphasis on second bachelor's degrees that can be completed in about a year and are introducing master's degrees meant to bring non-nurses into the profession. Half of R.N.s hold just an associate's degree or a hospital diploma.

7 Leaders in the field have long debated the need for a bachelor's in nursing. Legislation is pending in four states, including New York and New Jersey, that would require newly licensed registered nurses to hold a B.S.N. within 10 years. Few anticipate passage of such bills (a North Dakota law was revoked in 2003 shortly after being enacted, such was the dissent).

8 But poised for enormous growth and in the midst of sea change, the profession is moving to raise its educational profile. More advanced degree holders are needed in the pipeline to help stave off a shortage of faculty, especially as teachers age out, says Kathy Kaufman, senior research scientist at the National League for Nursing.

9 Furthermore, the health system has become more complex, and nurses today need the skills to take on added patient care and management responsibilities, and pick up the slack in family practice and primary care—less lucrative areas that are no longer popular with medical students. Some procedures and care are moving out of hospitals and into physicians' offices, community health centers, schools, and even CVS and Target. Nurses are running many of these operations and striking out on their own, starting clinics or home health care businesses.

10 With an opportunity for management and research, and salaries that mirror the premium that the medical field now places on the work—established nurses in the New York area earn an average of $70,000—it's no wonder that nursing is moving past its low-prestige image. The female-dominated profession is also fast shedding its negative male-nurse stereotype (think Gaylord Focker in "Meet the Parents").

11 Though men make up just 6 percent of the profession, they represent nearly 14 percent of the current nursing-student population. One of Mr. Van Rensselaer's biggest challenges was convincing his father that nursing was a career for a middle-age man. "His image of nursing was women in little white caps."

12 Eventually, his father came around. "When I talked with him about what the work was really about—keeping people alive—he understood."

13 Mr. Van Rensselaer was one of seven male students in his class of 50 at the University of Maryland, which has one of the largest nursing schools in the country.

14 Three years ago, the university closed its accelerated bachelor's program for non-nurse college graduates and instituted the leadership master's instead. The American Association of Colleges of Nursing developed the leadership curriculum to address patient safety issues, like keeping infections at bay or administering the correct medications. Students are trained in hospital management, research and patient care based on medical evidence, not just what is picked up on hospital rotation. Some 109 schools offer the curriculum, and of the master's degrees for non-nurses, almost half are in clinical nurse leadership.

15 Training can be intense, and there is still the actual nature of the work: nursing involves the most intimate of human interactions and is not for the faint of heart. Mr. Van Rensselaer knew that and took his transition slowly.

16 When his mother's cancer was diagnosed, in 2004, Mr. Van Rensselaer was already bored with his business—a specialty wine and liquor store, with a coffee shop up front that catered to tourists and a year-round population of 2,200.

17 During his mother's illness, Florida experienced three hurricanes, and the stormy weather became a metaphor for his life as he traveled between his hometown of Baltimore and Florida. On her death he sold the business and decided to explore nursing.

18 Wisely, he got his feet wet before plunging in. He became certified as a medical assistant through a community college program. This qualified him to work at an urgent care office where he could perform administrative and clinical duties like taking medical histories and recording vital signs. Mr. Van Rensselaer liked the work, especially the patient contact, and he began to take "dreaded" science prerequisites, with an eye toward a degree in nursing. He hadn't taken serious academic courses since graduating from Flagler College in St. Augustine, Fla., with a degree in business 18 years earlier. "My biggest fear going in was, 'Can I mentally do this?'" he says. He aced his classes.

19 When his wife, a pharmaceutical sales representative, was offered a job in Baltimore, they moved back, and he opted for Maryland's master's degree. The 16-month program was exhausting, and left almost no time for a personal life. The concentrated lineup of courses included pathopharmacology; children, family and geriatric nursing; psychiatric and trauma nursing; community nursing; and digital management of patient care. He completed 220 clinical hours and 90 hours applying evidence-based practice to a patient care problem—his was on alternative solutions to pain management.

20 Students have to maintain at least a 3.0 average to stay in the program; many, he says, dropped back to an expanded curriculum (it can be completed over 21 and 23 months as well). Mr. Van Rensselaer did more than survive the punishing pace. His 3.7 G.P.A. qualified him for a $10,000 scholarship from Sinai Hospital. In exchange, he committed to work at the hospital for three years.

21 At Sinai on his day off, in the week between finals and graduation, Mr. Van Rensselaer looks relieved. "I don't even know how to explain how grueling it was," he says. "I got into a rut mentally with my business, but I've been running a marathon in my mind for the last 16 months, and I'm thinking differently now."

Reading with a Critical Eye

1. In your opinion, why do men usually resist the idea of pursuing a career in nursing? Give specific reasons to support your answer.
2. When Mr. Van Rensselaer owned a liquor store and coffee shop in Baltimore in 2004, "Never in a million years," did he think he would become a male nurse. Discuss what made him change his mind about pursuing nursing as a career. Refer to the text to answer this question.
3. Rather than dispelling some of the myths about gender roles in society, why do you think the media continues to perpetuate them? Be specific.

4. The article mentions that nursing is not for the faint of heart. In your opinion, what qualities are most needed for a rewarding career in nursing?
5. Nursing is a rewarding career both professionally and financially. Why, in your opinion, do you think there continues to be a shortage of nurses across the country?

Reading Comprehension Check

1. As used in the sentence, "If you had asked Mr. Van Rensselaer in 2004 if he thought he would **trade** in life in Margaritaville for scenes from 'The Wire'—treating gunshot wounds, drug overdoses and unmanaged diabetes in one of the city's busiest emergency rooms—he might have assumed you had been to one too many of his wine-tasting events," the word *trade* means
   a. to exchange.
   b. to pursue.
   c. to withdraw.
   d. to consider.
2. In the sentence, "His professional **leap** may seem far-reaching, but in some ways his choice is not so surprising," the word *leap* most nearly means
   a. decline.
   b. defeat.
   c. victory.
   d. jump.
3. "Like many who come to nursing as a second profession, Mr. Van Rensselaer was **motivated** after caring for a loved one through an illness—in his case, his mother, who battled thyroid cancer and whom he nursed at her home in the final three months of her life."

   The word *motivated* in the above sentence can be replaced with
   a. dejected.
   b. disappointed.
   c. inspired.
   d. delighted.
4. Which of the following sentences is the best statement of the main idea of the article?
   a. Male nurses are usually not as competent as their female counterparts.
   b. Most hospitals are seriously considering hiring female nurses from overseas.
   c. The nursing industry is making conscious efforts to recruit men as nurses.
   d. Recruiters are not interested in hiring men for nursing jobs.
5. Mr. Van Rensselaer's example is offered to support the idea that
   a. the nursing industry is adamant about hiring only female nurses.
   b. the nursing industry will shy away from recruiting male nurses.

c. nursing is a losing proposition for men.
d. nursing could be a financially rewarding career for men.

6. The example of nurses making an average of $70,000 a year is used to support the fact that
   a. in general, nurses are poorly compensated.
   b. a nursing career can provide financial stability.
   c. there is no job stability in the nursing industry.
   d. only male nurses can make as much as $100,000 a year.
7. "To attract students from other disciplines, nursing schools are putting new emphasis on second bachelor's degrees that can be completed in about a year and are introducing master's degrees meant to bring non-nurses into the profession."
   A logical conclusion that can be drawn from the above statement is that
   a. the demand for registered nurses is dwindling.
   b. some healthcare operations have a huge surplus.
   c. nurses are in great demand.
   d. the number of registered nurses far exceeds the number of jobs available.
8. "Though men make up just 6 percent of the profession, they represent nearly 14 percent of the current nursing-student population."
   It can be inferred from the passage that
   a. men will outnumber women in the nursing profession in the future.
   b. women will continue to dominate men in the nursing profession.
   c. most nursing programs will not be able to produce enough nursing graduates in the future to meet the demand.
   d. more men than women will study to become a registered nurse.
9. "The female-dominated profession is also fast shedding its negative male-nurse stereotype (think Gaylord Focker in 'Meet the Parents')."
   It can be inferred from the above passage that
   a. the idea of men becoming nurses is slowly gaining acceptance.
   b. the nursing profession prefers to have female nurses.
   c. the nursing profession looks down on male nurses.
   d. the nursing profession discourages men to become a nurse.
10. "Training can be intense, and there is still the actual nature of the work: nursing involves the most intimate of human interactions and is not for the faint of heart." Based on this statement, which of the following is a logical conclusion?
    a. Training to become a nurse can be easily accomplished.
    b. People who faint at the sight of blood are good candidates for nursing.
    c. Students with a heart condition are suitable for the profession.
    d. Studying to become a nurse is an extremely challenging task.

BIOGRAPHICAL PROFILE

Florence Nightingale (1820–1910)

Florence Nightingale's valuable contributions to nursing can be determined by the fact that her work at the Nightingale School of Nursing still continues, that one of the buildings in the School of Nursing and Midwifery at the University of Southampton is named after her, and that International Nurses Day is celebrated on her birthday every year.

Florence Nightingale was born into a rich, British family on May 12, 1820, in Florence, Grand Duchy of Tuscany. She experienced a Christian divine calling in 1837, which inspired her to become a nurse. Instead of becoming a wife and mother, which was very common in those days, she chose to become a nurse despite her parents' discouragement and devoted her entire life to caring for the poor and sick.

Her most notable contribution was caring for the injured soldiers during the Crimean War in 1854. Her tireless efforts to improve the standards of healthcare for the wounded earned her the title "Lady with the Lamp." She committed herself to reforming hospitals and **implementing** public health policies throughout England. Her famous work, *Notes on Nursing: What It Is, and What It Is Not,* is still used as a reference in most nursing schools throughout the world.

After her return from Crimea, she received an honorarium of £4,500 from an English public officer. She used the amount to found the Nightingale Training School for Nurses in 1860. Throughout her career, Nightingale fervidly believed that nursing schools should give students a solid background in science to understand the theoretical implications for health care. She believed that learning was perpetual, and therefore her students should never stop learning. She once wrote to her nursing students, "[Nursing] is a field of which one may safely say: there is no end in what we may be learning everyday." Graduates of the Nightingale Training School for Nurses traveled to other countries to work in hospitals and train other nurses.

Nightingale's vision of nursing, which included promoting health and wellness among the sick and preventing sickness, has become a cornerstone of most nursing schools. Although she died on August 13, 1910, in Park Lane, London, England, her legacy lives on. Four hospitals in Turkey are named after Florence Nightingale: F. N. Hastanesi in Sisli, Metropolitan F. N. Hastanesi in Gayrettepe, Kiziltoprak F. N. Hastanesi in Kadiköy, and Avrupa F. N. Hastanesi in Mecidiyeköy. The Agostino Gemelli Medical Center in Rome named its wireless computer system "Bedside Florence" to honor Florence Nightingale. Many nursing foundations in the world are named after Florence Nightingale. There is Nightingale Research Foundation in Canada, which studies chronic fatigue syndrome. Last but not least, when doctors and nurses fall in love with their patients, the phenomenon is called the "Florence Nightingale Effect."

Some Questions for Group Discussion

1. Florence Nightingale was born into a wealthy British family in Italy. Although discouraged by her parents, she decided to become a nurse and remained committed to nursing until her death. Discuss what inspired her to become a nurse and care for others.
2. After caring for the wounded during the Crimean War, Florence Nightingale received a handsome honorarium. Instead of spending the honorarium on herself, she used the money to open a nursing school. Under what conditions would you be willing to use a cash prize for others? Explain.
3. Recent advancements in science and technology have made it possible for us to communicate with strangers in distant countries, find ways to prolong life, and treat people with diseases that were incurable in the past, yet we sometimes seem incapable of finding empathy in our hearts. In your opinion, what can be done to eradicate poverty, sickness, and hunger from the world once and for all?

Biographical Internet Research

Do research on the Internet and find humanitarians who have dedicated their lives to tending to the needs of the poor and sick. Select one from the list below and be prepared to share a biographical profile with your classmates. Discuss what inspired this person to care for others.

- Clara Barton
- Margaret Sanger
- Dorothea Lynde Dix
- Helen Fairchild
- Walt Whitman

SKILL FOCUS: Patterns of Organization

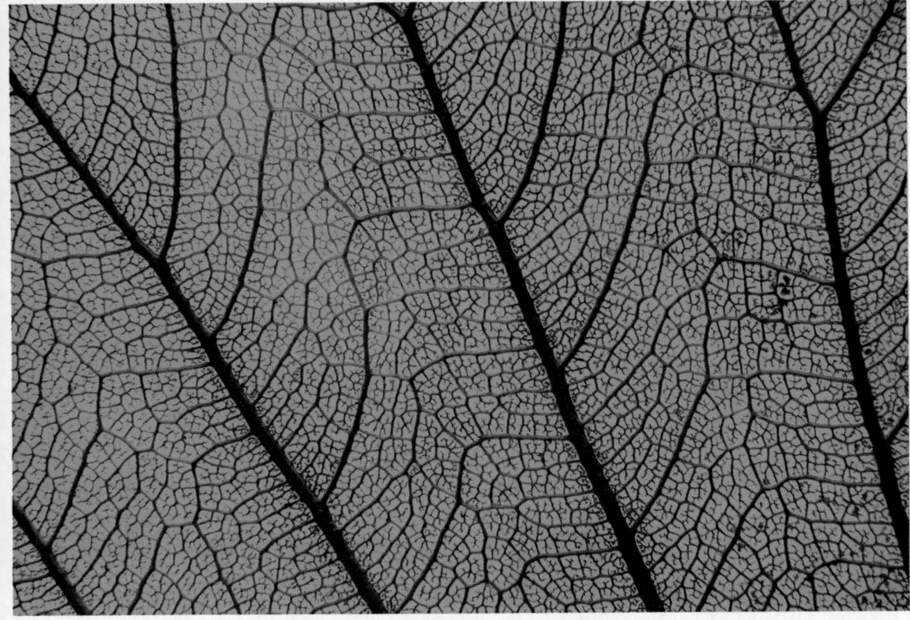

Most authors use different *patterns of organization* to get their meaning across to the reader. As a reader, you should familiarize yourself with how an author has structured his or her text so you can understand the author's main idea and the supporting details. Recognizing the main idea and the author's purpose can help you determine the specific pattern of organization.

Identifying a Pattern of Organization

To identify the overall pattern of organization, make sure that you do the following:

- Recognize the topic and the main idea.
- Identify the details supporting the main idea.
- Know the author's purpose.
- Familiarize yourself with the transitional phrases for each pattern.
- Understand how the ideas are related to each other.

Although there are several different patterns of organization, this section will first introduce the six most commonly used organizational patterns in textbooks. You will have the opportunity to practice each of the patterns as we examine them. You then will be introduced to some other organizational patterns.

Commonly Used Organizational Patterns

The six most commonly used patterns in textbooks are the following:

- Definition
- Illustration/example

- Comparison and contrast
- Cause and effect
- Classification
- Chronological order

Definition

In this organizational pattern, the author uses a term and provides examples to define it; sometimes more than one term is introduced. The definition organizational pattern is used in most technical textbooks in areas of study such as biology, nursing, and chemistry. Authors use this pattern of organization to introduce a term and help the reader understand how the term is different from others. Consider the following passage.

Example

segregation the practice of keeping people of different races or religions apart and making them live, work, or study separately

discrimination the practice of treating one person or group of people differently from another in an unfair way

Segregation (physical separation of housing and services based on race) and **discrimination** (unfair and unequal treatment or access to services based on race, culture, or other bias) have permeated the global community. Although the United States has moved beyond segregation in many areas, there are still inequalities based on lack of access to equal health care. Discrimination, as it relates to health services, can involve more than just race or ethnicity. The nurse must also guard against unequal treatment related to an individual's gender, sexual orientation, or legal status. If a client feels that the nurse is being judgmental because of his or her differences, the therapeutic relationship is compromised.

(*Roberta Pavy Ramont and Dee Niedringhaus,* Fundamental Nursing Care, *2nd ed., Upper Saddle River, NJ: Pearson Prentice Hall, 2008,* p. 19)

The following table shows how the author uses the definition organizational pattern to introduce two terms in the above passage.

Term	*Definition*
Segregation	Physical separation of housing and services based on race
Discrimination	Unfair and unequal treatment or access to services based on race, culture, or other bias

Notice how the two terms reappear in the passage to reinforce the concepts of segregation and discrimination based on race. When you read passages that use the definition organizational pattern, ask what terms are being defined. Identifying the terms will help you understand the author's purpose as well. Now that you have seen one example of the definition organizational pattern, let's do an exercise to make sure you understand how authors use this thought pattern.

PRACTICING THE SKILL: DEFINITION

Read the following passages, identify the term(s), and define them.

Passage 1

For more than 30 years, nursing has been concerned with the cultural differences among clients. In the early years, culture was equated with ethnicity. Ethnicity was identified by a code on the client's chart or on the addressograph plate. As the profession became aware of the need to provide for the client holistically, the words cultural awareness (knowing about the similarities and differences among cultures) crept into the professional vocabulary. The goal of cultural awareness was to end prejudice and discrimination. In fact, though, awareness often resulted in a focus on differences, without providing the nurse with the tools to meet the culturally related needs of the client.

(*Fundamental Nursing Care*, p. 17)

TERM: ______________________________

DEFINITION: ______________________________

Passage 2

One pitfall in communicating with a person from a different culture is ethnocentrism. Ethnocentrism means interpreting the beliefs and behavior of others in terms of one's own cultural values and traditions. It assumes that one's own culture is superior. It is difficult to avoid the tendency toward ethnocentrism. Nurses, though, must be extra diligent to avoid stereotypes (oversimplified conceptions, opinions, or beliefs about some aspects of a group of people). Individuals vary greatly within any ethnic group, just as children vary within one family. The nurse must look for ways to care for each client as a unique person, regardless of category.

(*Fundamental Nursing Care*, p. 17)

TERM: ______________________________

DEFINITION: ______________________________

____

TERM: ______________________________

DEFINITION: ______________________________

____

Passage 3

Intercultural communication occurs when members of two or more cultures exchange messages in a manner that is influenced by their different cultural perspectives (Adler et al., 1998). Communication is interrelated with all other domains. It includes verbal communication (dialects, the context in which language is used, etc.) and nonverbal communication. Clients may communicate quite differently with family and close friends than with unfamiliar healthcare professionals.

(*Fundamental Nursing Care*, p. 19)

TERM: ______________________________

DEFINITION: ______________________________

____

Illustration/Example

When we do not understand a complex phenomenon, an abstract concept, or a difficult term, we often ask, "Can you give me an example?" Research in artificial intelligence shows that we retain information rather easily when we are given appropriate examples of a key concept. Successful teachers are aware of this aspect of human nature and use the illustration/example organizational pattern to introduce the main idea or a key concept to the student. Examples are especially helpful when the subject matter is unfamiliar to the reader. Let's look at the following paragraph to understand the illustration/example pattern of organization clearly.

Example

Fidelity means to be faithful to agreements and promises. By virtue of their standing as professional caregivers, nurses have responsibilities to clients, employers, the government, and society, as well as to themselves. Nurses often make promises such as "I'll be right back with your pain medication," "You'll be all right," or "I'll find out for you." Clients take such promises seriously, and so should nurses.

(*Fundamental Nursing Care*, p. 39)

MAIN IDEA: ______________________________

EXAMPLES: ______________________________

____

PRACTICING THE SKILL: ILLUSTRATION/EXAMPLE

Read the following passages carefully, underline the main idea, and write the examples the author provides to support the main idea.

Passage 1

Autonomy refers to the right to make one's own decisions. Nurses who follow this principle recognize that each client is unique, has the right to be what that person is, and has the right to choose personal goals.

Honoring the principles of autonomy means that the nurse respects a client's right to make decisions even when those choices seem not to be in the client's best interest. It also means treating others with consideration. In a health-care setting, this principle is violated, for example, when a nurse disregards a client's report of the severity of his or her pain.

(*Fundamental Nursing Care*, p. 39)

MAIN IDEA: ______________________________

EXAMPLES: ______________________________

____

Passage 2

Values are freely chosen, enduring beliefs or attitudes about the worth of a person, object, idea, or action. Values are important because they influence decisions and actions. Values are often taken for granted. In the same way that people are not aware of their breathing, they usually do not think about their values; they simply accept them and act on them. The word *values* usually brings to mind things such as honesty, fairness, friendship, safety, or family unity. Of course, not all values are moral values. For example, some people hold money, work, power, and politics as values in their lives.

(*Fundamental Nursing Care*, pp. 37–38)

MAIN IDEA: ____

____

EXAMPLES: ____

____

Passage 3

Nonmaleficence is duty to do no harm. Although this would seem to be a simple principle to follow, in reality it is complex. Harm can mean intentional harm, risk of harm, and unintentional harm. In nursing, intentional harm is never acceptable. However, the risk of harm is not always clear. A client may be at risk of harm during a nursing intervention that is intended to be helpful. For example, a client may react adversely to a medication, and caregivers may or may not always agree on the degree to which a risk is morally permissible.

(*Fundamental Nursing Care*, p. 39)

MAIN IDEA: ____

EXAMPLES:

1. ____

2. ____

Comparison and Contrast

When authors want to show how two things are similar (comparison) or different (contrast), they use the comparison and contrast organizational pattern. When comparing the two things or objects, the author focuses on their similar features. When contrasting the two objects, the author focuses on their different characteristics. Depending on the purpose, the author may focus only on the similarities between the two objects or on the differences between them, or the author may focus on both the similarities and differences between them. Let's look at an example to understand the comparison and contrast organizational pattern clearly.

consumer
someone who buys or uses goods and services

patient
someone who is getting medical treatment

client
someone who pays a person or organization for a service

Example

The "customers" we serve in nursing today are sometimes called consumers, sometimes patients, and sometimes clients. A **consumer** is an individual, a group of people, or a community that uses a service or commodity. People who use healthcare products or services are consumers of health care. A **patient** is a person who is waiting for or undergoing medical treatment and care. The word *patient* comes from a Latin word meaning "to suffer" or "to bear." Traditionally, the person receiving health care has been called a patient. People become patients when they seek assistance because of illness. Some nurses believe that the word *patient* implies passive acceptance of the decisions and care of health professionals. Because nurses interact with family, friends, and healthy people as well as those who are ill, nurses increasingly refer to recipients of health care as clients.

A **client** is a person who engages the advice or services of someone who is qualified to provide the service. Therefore, a client is a collaborator, a person who is also responsible for his or her own health. The health status of a client is the responsibility of the individual in collaboration with health professionals. (*Fundamental Nursing Care,* p. 9)

As the passage describes, the general category of people being served in nursing are called "customers." However, there are three types of "customers," namely "consumers," "patients," and "clients." The table below shows the similarities and differences between them.

Customers	*Similarities (comparison)*	*Differences (contrast)*
Consumers	People who are served by nurses	■ Consumers use healthcare products and services.
Patients	People who are served by nurses	■ Patients receive medical treatment and care.
Clients	People who are served by nurses	■ Clients receive advice from experts and are responsible for their own health.

Now that you understand the comparison and contrast organizational pattern, do the following exercise:

PRACTICING THE SKILL: COMPARISON AND CONTRAST

Read the following passages and point out the similarities and differences between the two things being compared and contrasted.

Passage 1

Women are not the sole providers of nursing services. The first nursing school in the world was started in India in about 250 B.C.

Only men were considered to be "pure" enough to fulfill the role of nurse at that time. In Jesus's parable in the New Testament, the good Samaritan paid an innkeeper to provide care for the injured man. Paying a man to provide nursing care was fairly common. During the Crusades, several orders of knights provided nursing care to their sick and injured comrades and also built hospitals. The organization and management of their hospitals set a standard for the administration of hospitals throughout Europe at that time. St. Camillus de Lellis started out as a soldier and later turned to nursing. He started the sign of the Red Cross and developed the first ambulance service… .

In 1876, only three years after the first U.S. nurse received her diploma from New England Hospital for Women and Children, the Alexian brothers opened their first hospital in the United States and a school to educate men in nursing.

During the years from the Civil War to the Korean War, men were not permitted to serve as nurses in the military. Today, men have resumed their historical place in the profession. As the history of nursing continues to be written, men and women will work side by side.

(*Fundamental Nursing Care*, pp. 8–9)

1. What is being compared and contrasted?

____

2. *What* is the similarity between male and female nurses?

____

3. What are the differences between male and female nurses?

____

____

____

____

____

____

____

Passage 2

One of the first questions that should be asked in any healthcare situation is "What language do you normally use to communicate?" Even though a client may understand English in a casual conversation, he or she may not be able to communicate on the technical level required during a health interview. Healthcare workers need to be aware of the dominant language of an area, as well as problems that may be caused by particular dialects. Clients from Mexico may speak 1 of more than 50 dialects. People from the Philippines may speak 1 of 87. The dialect may pose a communication barrier even if a nurse speaks the same language. Dialect differences increase the difficulty of obtaining accurate information.

Many times much more is learned from what is not said than from what is said. Nonverbal communication is vital to communicating with clients, but here cultural variations can have a big impact. For example, in Western cultures, people are expected to make eye contact during communication. In other cultures, Asian specifically, making eye contact is a demonstration of lack of respect.

Touch can convey much, but again, cultures differ on what they permit and accept. It is important for the nurse to be aware of the client's reaction to touch. During the first contact with a client, the nurse should ask permission to touch the client. When performing a procedure that involves touch, the nurse should fully explain the procedure before touching the client.

Facial expressions and hand gestures also have different meanings from one culture to another. For example, individuals of Jewish, Hispanic, and Italian heritage rarely smile because showing one's teeth can be viewed as a sign of aggression. A therapeutic relationship can be promoted or hampered by the nurse's understanding of transcultural communication.

(*Fundamental Nursing Care*, p. 19)

1. What is being compared and contrasted?

____

2. What is the comparison?

____

3. What is the contrast?

____

____

____

____

Passage 3

Effective communication among health professionals is vital to the quality of client care. Generally, health personnel communicate through discussion, reports, and records. A *discussion* is an informal conversation between two or more healthcare personnel to identify a problem or establish strategies to resolve a problem. A report is an oral, written, or computer-based communication intended to convey information to others. For example, nurses always report on clients at the end of a work shift. A record is a written or computer-based collection of data. The process of making an entry on a client record is called *recording*, charting, or documenting. A clinical record, also called a *chart* or *client record*, is the formal, legal document that provides evidence of a client's care. Although healthcare organizations use different systems and forms for documentation, all client records contain similar information.

(*Fundamental Nursing Care*, p. 85)

1. What is being compared and contrasted?

____

2. What is the comparison between a report and a record?

____

3. What is the contrast between a report and a record?

____

Cause and Effect

Authors use the cause and effect organizational pattern to demonstrate a causal relation between an event and its impact. Sometimes one cause can have only one effect. Other times, one cause can have several effects. Likewise, multiple causes can have only one effect, and sometimes several causes can have several effects. Look at the diagrams to understand the different types of causal relations between events and their impact.

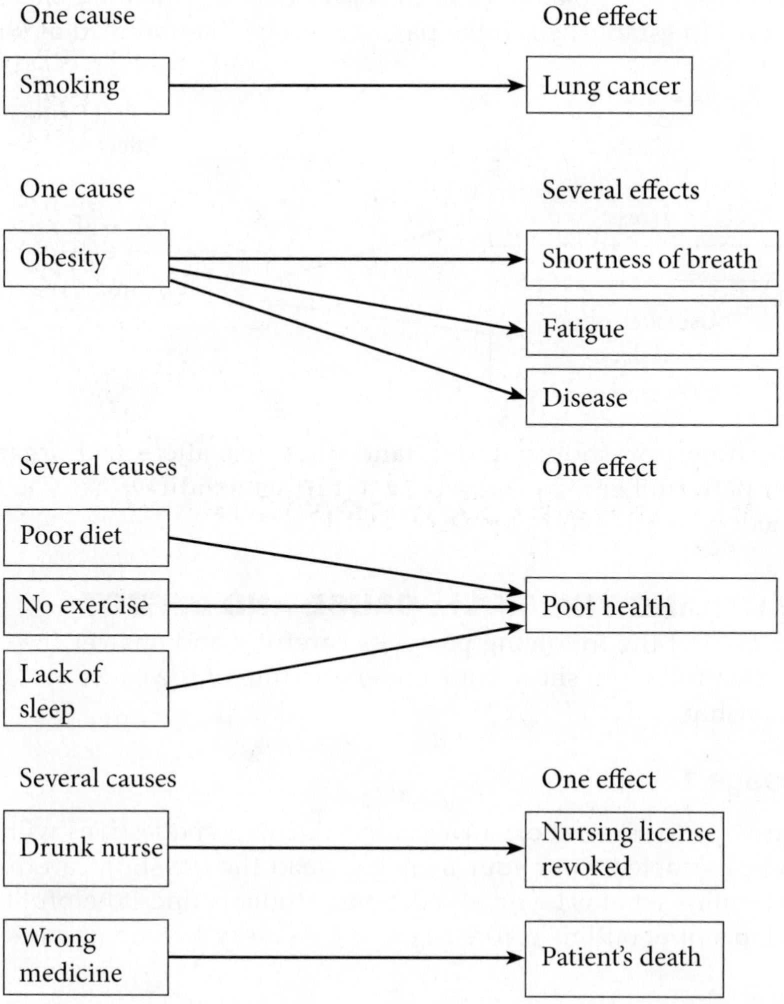

As you can see, the cause and effect relation is quite complex. You need to read a passage carefully and determine exactly what is causing what effects. The following example will help you understand the cause and effect organizational pattern.

Example

The term "impaired nurse" refers to a nurse whose practice has been negatively affected because of chemical abuse, specifically the use of alcohol and drugs. Chemical dependence in healthcare workers has become a problem because of the high levels of stress involved in many healthcare settings and the easy access to addictive drugs. Substance abuse is the most common reason for actions against nurses' licenses. Between 10% and 15% of nurses are estimated to be chemically impaired. This is about the same percentage as in the general population. Employers must have sound policies and procedures for identifying situations that involve a possibly impaired nurse. Intervention in such situations is important to protect clients and to get treatment for the impaired nurse quickly.

(*Fundamental Nursing Care*, p. 37)

This passage explains the term *impaired nurse*. The cause and effect relationship established in the passage can be diagrammed as shown here.

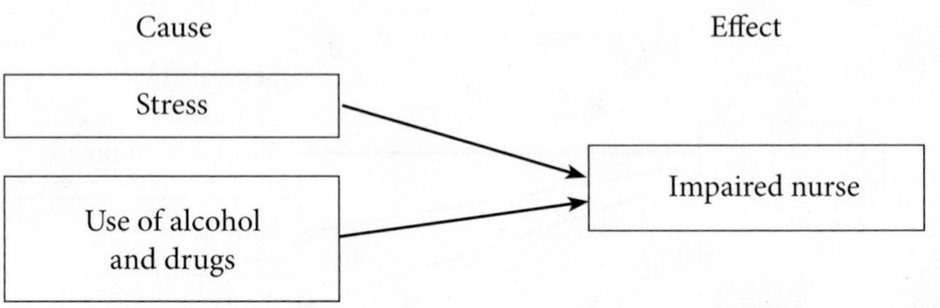

By now, you should understand the cause and effect organizational pattern. Let's do an exercise to further solidify what you have learned.

PRACTICING THE SKILL: CAUSE AND EFFECT

Read each of the following passages carefully and answer the questions that follow to show your understanding of the cause and effect relationship.

Passage 1

Answers to essay, short-answer, and calculation questions will need to be extracted from your memory. Read the question carefully to determine what is being asked. Some students find it helpful to develop a brief outline before beginning an essay question. Check with the instructor to see if this can be written on the test paper or if you are permitted to use an additional sheet. The outline can help you organize your thoughts and can serve as a checkpoint that all important information was included. Usually, a number of key introductory words appear in essay questions. Look for these words, and do only what is required of you. Many low grades are caused by ignoring these key words.

Calculation questions are particularly troubling for many students who have convinced themselves that they cannot do math. Although math may be difficult, it is a necessary skill for a nurse. With extra practice, calculations are possible to learn. Several methods are used to do calculations.

It is important to show your work on calculations. If you are unable to arrive at the correct answer, your instructor can review your work, and will be able to tell you where you went wrong. Memorizing formulas and frequently used conversions will make calculations on tests and in the clinical area much easier.

(*Fundamental Nursing Care*, p. 6)

1. What are the causes of answering successfully?

____

____

____

____

____

2. What are the effects?

____

Passage 2

Good communication is also important because customer service has become an important part of health care. Health care is a service industry, and clients are increasingly aware consumers. Clients frequently research their disease and the available treatments. When they come for a consultation, they expect to be given all the appropriate information. If information is not given to their satisfaction, they may look elsewhere for care. They may change doctors or refuse to allow a particular healthcare professional to administer treatment to them. Taking time to communicate effectively on first contact is not wasting time. In fact, it may save time, because corrections will not have to be made. Further, a well-informed client is likely to be more willing to participate in the treatment plan than one who is not well informed.

(*Fundamental Nursing Care*, p. 20)

Based on the information provided in this passage, make a list of the causes and their effects under each column in the table below.

Cause	*Effect*

Passage 3

Cultural diversity affects care of the client in pain. The influx of minorities from other countries is predicted to continue, along with the growth of the proportion of minorities within the United States. This changing population means that we as healthcare providers must learn how to respond to pain in a wide range of clients. Cultural background affects pain perception. Cultural background has long been recognized as having a major influence on how one perceives and reacts to painful situations. Pain has both personal and cultural meanings. Although clients from two different cultures may experience a similar condition or surgical procedure, their pain response may differ dramatically. An understanding of pain from a cultural perspective is vital if healthcare providers are to respond to clients in a helpful manner.

(*Fundamental Nursing Care*, p. 23)

1. What are the causes?

2. What are the effects?

Classification

Authors use the classification organizational pattern to put ideas into categories according to their characteristics. These characteristics are chosen on the basis of their similarities. For example, a Nursing textbook may describe the different types of drugs by their function and the reaction expected in a patient. An effective way to understand a Nursing textbook that uses the classification organizational pattern is to determine how the topic is divided. If you can notice how the different characteristics are categorized, you are more likely to remember the important parts of the topic. Read the following paragraph and pay special attention to how the topic is divided into different categories.

Example

To break down the barriers among cultures, there was a movement toward cultural sensitivity (being aware of the needs and feelings of your own culture and of other cultures). Since the 1990s, a new term has been added. The profession has been talking about cultural competence—a set of practical skills, knowledge, and attitudes that must encompass the following elements:

1. Awareness and acceptance of differences
2. Awareness of one's own cultural values
3. Understanding of the dynamics of difference
4. Development of cultural knowledge
5. Ability to adapt practice skills to fit the cultural context of the client

Now it is time to take the next step past competency to culturally proficient care. For culturally proficient nurses, the five components of cultural care will be second nature. Care for clients will include consideration of their physical, psychological, emotional, spiritual, and cultural components.

(*Fundamental Nursing Care,* p. 17)

As you can see, the topic of the passage is cultural competence, which has five categories according to their characteristics. Notice that all of these categories are chosen on the basis of their similarities—that is, they are a set of practical skills necessary for a nurse to be culturally competent.

Now that you understand how writers use the classification organizational pattern, do the following exercise. Look for the main categories; some of these may have subtopics.

PRACTICING THE SKILL: CLASSIFICATION

Read the following passages carefully. Then find the topic of each passage and the different categories into which the topic is divided.

Passage 1

Nurses learn general concepts about transcultural nursing and specific facts about various cultures so that we can provide ethical and effective care to all our clients. We must understand how ideas from other cultures agree with or differ from our own. We must be sensitive to issues of race, gender, sexual orientation, social class, and economic situation in our everyday work. A cultural assessment has four basic elements. These data can be collected by the LPN/LVN.

1. The cultural identity of the client. How does the client identify himself or herself culturally? Does the client feel closer to the native culture or to the host culture? What is the client's language preference?
2. The cultural factors related to the client's psychosocial environment. What stressors are there in the local environment? What role does religion play in the individual's life? What kind of support system does the client have?
3. The cultural elements of the relationship between the healthcare provider and the client. What kind of experiences has the client had with healthcare providers, either now or in the past? (The nurse should also consider what differences exist between the provider's and the client's culture and social status. These differences are important in communicating and in negotiating an appropriate relationship.)
4. The cultural explanation of the client's illness. What is the client's cultural explanation of the illness? What idioms does the client use to describe it? (For example, the client may say she is suffering from *ataque de nervios*—an attack of the nerves. This is a syndrome in Hispanic cultures that closely resembles anxiety and depressive disorders.) Is there a name or category used by the client's family or community to identify the condition? In order for care to be client centered, no matter what culture the client is, the nurse has to elicit specific information from the client and use it to organize strategies for care.

When performing the cultural assessment, the nurse needs to consider many of the cultural domains that were mentioned earlier.

(*Fundamental Nursing Care*, pp. 21–22)

1. What is the topic?

____

2. How many categories is the topic divided into? _____ What are they?

1. ____

2. ____

3. ____

4. ____

Passage 2

Larry Purnell and B. J. Paulanka (1998) developed a model for cultural competence that describes 12 domains of culture. This assessment tool identifies ethnocultural attributes of an individual, family, or group. The following box provides a list of these domains.

Twelve Domains of Culture

1. Overview, inhabited localities, and topography
2. Communication
3. Family roles and organization
4. Workforce issues
5. Biocultural ecology
6. High-risk health behaviors
7. Nutrition
8. Pregnancy and childbearing practices
9. Death rituals
10. Spirituality
11. Healthcare practices
12. Healthcare practitioners

In everyday practice as a practical or vocational nurse, you will need to be aware of these domains. You will develop knowledge of different cultures, especially those in the area where you live and work. This should include becoming familiar with the part of the world where those cultures were established and the heritage of the people. It is also important for you to realize that individuals within a particular culture may have characteristics that don't "fit" their group. It is important not to generalize and stereotype a member of a group (Purnell & Paulanka, 1998).

(Fundamental Nursing Care, p. 18)

1. What is the topic of the passage? ______________________
2. The topic is divided into 12 parts. What are they?

1. ______________	7. ______________
2. ______________	8. ______________
3. ______________	9. ______________
4. ______________	10. ______________
5. ______________	11. ______________
6. ______________	12. ______________

Passage 3

Responses to pain culturally have been divided into two categories: *stoic* and *emotive*. Stoic clients are less expressive of their pain and tend to "grin and bear it." They tend to withdraw socially. Emotive clients are more likely to verbalize their expressions of pain. They desire people around to react to their pain and assist them with their suffering. Expressive clients often come from Hispanic, Middle Eastern, and Mediterranean backgrounds. Stoic clients often come from Northern European and Asian backgrounds. However, ethnicity alone does not predict accurately how a person will respond to pain. Some individuals tolerate even the most severe pain with little more than a clenched jaw and frequently refuse pain medication.

(*Fundamental Nursing Care*, p. 23)

1. What is the topic? ________________
2. What are the categories? ________________

Chronological Order

In the chronological order organizational pattern, information is arranged in the order in which the event occurred. Chronological order also is known as time order. When you read a passage that uses the chronological order organizational pattern, pay special attention to the order in which the information is presented. Remember that the chronological pattern of organization is concerned with the sequence of events that occur over time or steps that need to be taken in sequence. Let's read the following passage to understand this type of organizational pattern.

Example

The study of transcultural nursing began in the 1950s, when Dr. Madeleine Leininger noted differences in culture among clients and nurses. As she studied cultural differences, she realized that health and illness are influenced by culture.

Events in the History of Cultural Care

1974 Transcultural Nursing Society was established as the official organization of transcultural nursing.

1991 Dr. Leininger published theory of cultural care diversity and universality

2000 The U.S. Department of Health and Human Services (USDHHS) stated, "Healthy People 2010 is firmly dedicated to the principle that—regardless of age, gender, race or ethnicity,

> income, education, geographical location, disability and sexual orientation—every person in every community across the nation deserves equal access to comprehensive, culturally competent, community-based health care systems that are committed to serving the needs of the individual and promoting community health." (USDHHS, 2000)

Dr. Leininger's work encouraged a broader awareness of cultural issues and led to the study of culture within the nursing curriculum.

(*Fundamental Nursing Care,* p. 17)

You will notice that the topic of the passage is transcultural nursing, and the box clearly shows how the study of culture within the nursing curriculum developed from 1974 to 2000. As mentioned earlier, authors use the chronological order organizational pattern when they want to show the sequence of events in reference to time. It is time for you to practice recognizing the chronological order pattern of organization, and the following exercise will help you do that.

PRACTICING THE SKILL: CHRONOLOGICAL ORDER

Read the following passages, identify the topic of each of the passages, and make a list of the events described in the passage.

Passage 1

The first training for practical nurses was at the Young Women's Christian Association (YWCA) in New York City in 1892. The following year this became the Ballard School. The program of study was 3 months long, and the participants studied special techniques for caring for the sick as well as a variety of homemaking techniques. Much of the care during this time was done in the client's home, making the licensed practical nurse (LPN) a home health or visiting nurse. Eleven years later, a second school, the Thompson Practical Nursing School, was established.

In 1914, the state legislature in Mississippi passed the first laws governing the practice of practical nurses. Other states were slow to follow. By 1940, only six states had passed such laws. In 1955, the state board test pool of the NLN Education Committee established the procedures for testing graduates of approved practical/vocational education programs in all states. Graduates who passed the examination became LPNs or, in California and Texas, licensed vocational nurses (LVNs). Each state set its own passing score.

Today, a graduate of an approved LPN/LVN training program is eligible to take the National Council Licensure Examination for Practical Nursing (NCLEX-PN).

(*Fundamental Nursing Care,* p. 9)

1. What is the topic of the passage?

___

2. What sequence of events is presented?

1. ___
2. ___
3. ___
4. ___

___

5. ___

Passage 2

The procedures provided in this book give you some of the basic skills you will need to provide excellent client care. Procedures should always begin with an initial set of actions that ensure a safe, efficient, and caring environment. These actions will become second nature to you as you continue your nursing training. Icons will be used to represent this initial set of actions at the start of each procedure. In some instances, an action may be optional. However, most are not. The icons are a reminder to do these basic, important interventions in nursing care:

1. Check the physician's order.
2. Gather the necessary equipment.
3. Introduce yourself to the client.
4. Identify the client (check the client's wristband against the chart).
5. Provide privacy as needed (close the curtain).
6. Explain the procedure.
7. Wash your hands. Hand hygiene is the single most effective way to prevent disease transmission.
8. Don gloves as needed.

(*Fundamental Nursing Care*, p. 76)

1. What is the topic of the passage?

___

2. How many steps need to be taken to provide good client care?

___

Passage 3

Health professionals frequently report about a client by telephone. Nurses inform physicians about a change in a client's condition; a radiologist reports the results of an x-ray study; a nurse may confer with a nurse on another unit about a transferred client. The nurse receiving a telephone report should document the date and time, the name of the person giving the information, and what information was received, and should sign the notation. For example:

[date] [time] GL Messina, laboratory technician, reported by telephone that Mrs. Sara Ames's hematocrit was 39/100mL. _____________ Barbara Ireland, LPN

If there is any doubt about the information given over the telephone, the person receiving the information should repeat it back to the sender to ensure accuracy.

(*Fundamental Nursing Care*, p. 98)

1. What is the topic of the passage?

____

2. What steps are presented in the passage to receive a telephone report accurately?

____

____

____

____

____

These are the six most commonly used patterns of organization you will likely encounter in college textbooks. Identifying these patterns will help you understand the author's purpose, key concepts, and relevant bits and pieces of information.

Other Useful Patterns of Organization

In addition to the patterns just studied, there are others you may find in your reading and test taking. These include the following:

- Process
- Listing (addition)
- Statement and clarification
- Spatial order

Process

This type of organizational pattern arranges information to describe how a process occurs. The process pattern of organization is almost the same as chronological order. The only difference is that instead of describing the order in which the *events occurred over a period of time*, the author describes the order in which *different steps occur in a process*. For example, the author may describe how to give an injection to a patient or give directions for installing medical equipment. Read the following paragraph to understand how the author uses the process pattern of organization.

Example

Injections into muscle tissue (IM injections) are absorbed more quickly than subcutaneous injections because of the greater blood supply to the body muscles. Muscles can also take a larger volume of fluid without discomfort than subcutaneous tissues can, although the amount varies somewhat, depending on muscle size, muscle condition, and the site used. An adult with well-developed muscles can usually safely tolerate up to 4 mL of medication in the gluteus medius and gluteus maximus muscles. A major consideration in the administration of IM injections is the selection of a safe site located away from large blood vessels, nerves, and bone. Several body sites can be used for IM injections. See procedure 29-3A for administering IM injections.

Part A: Intramuscular Injection

Interventions

1. Check the medication order for accuracy.
2. Prepare the medication from the vial or ampule.
3. Identify the client, and assist the client to a comfortable position.
4. Select, locate, and clean the site.
5. Prepare the syringe for injection.
6. Inject the medication using a Z-track technique.
7. Withdraw the needle and then release hand that has been holding skin laterally.
8. Dispose of supplies appropriately.
9. Document all relevant information.
10. Assess effectiveness of the medication at the time it is expected to act.

(*Fundamental Nursing Care*, p. 657)

Notice how the author describes the process of giving IM injections step by step. A registered nurse can easily follow the steps and administer IM injections to patients.

PRACTICING THE SKILL: PROCESS

Read the following passages carefully to understand the process pattern of organization fully and answer the questions that follow.

Passage 1

Administering Oral Medications

Tablets or Capsules

- Pour the required number into the bottle cap, and then transfer the medication to the disposable cup without touching the tablets. Usually, all tablets or capsules to be given to the client are placed in the same cup.
- Keep narcotics and medications that require specific assessments, such as pulse measurements, respiratory rate or depth, or blood pressure, separate from the others.

- Break scored tablets as needed to obtain the correct dosage. Use a file or cutting device if necessary. Discard unused tablet pieces according to agency policy.
- If the client has difficulty swallowing, crush the tablets to a fine powder with a pill crusher or between two medication cups or spoons. Mix the powder with a small amount of soft food (e.g., custard, applesauce). Note: Check with pharmacy before crushing tablets.
- Place packaged unit-dose capsules or tablets directly into the medicine cup. Do not remove the wrapper until at the bedside.

(*Fundamental Nursing Care*, pp. 650–651)

1. What is the topic of the passage?

____

2. What process is explained in the above passage?

____

3. How many steps are involved in administering oral medications to a patient?

____

Passage 2

Liquid Medication

- Thoroughly mix the medication before pouring. Discard any mixed medication changed in appearance.
- Remove the cap and place it upside down on the countertop.
- Hold the bottle so the label is next to your palm, and pour the medication away from the label.
- Hold the medication cap at eye level and fill it to the desired level, using the bottom of the meniscus (crescent-shaped upper surface of a column of liquid) to align with the container scale.
- Before capping the bottle, wipe the lip with a paper towel.
- When giving small amounts of liquids (e.g., less than 5 mL), prepare the medication in a sterile syringe without the needle.
- Keep unit-dose liquids in their package and open them at the bedside.

(*Fundamental Nursing Care*, p. 651)

1. What is the topic of the passage?

____

2. What process is explained in the above passage?

____

3. How many steps are described in the above passage?

____

Passage 3

Mixing Medication from Two Vials

- Withdraw a volume of air equal to the total volume of medications to be withdrawn from vials A and B.
- Inject a volume of air equal to the volume of medication to be withdrawn into vial A.
- Withdraw the needle from vial A and inject the remaining air into vial B.

  or

  Draw up the volume of air equal to the amount of solution to be drawn from vial B and inject into vial B. Leaving the needle in the vial, invert vial B and withdraw the prescribed amount of medication.
- Withdraw the required amount of medication from vial B. The same needle is used to inject air into and withdraw medication from the second vial.
- Using a newly attached sterile needle, withdraw the required amount of medication from vial A. If using a syringe with a fused needle, withdraw the medication from vial A. The syringe now contains a mixture of medications from vials A and B.

(*Fundamental Nursing Care*, p. 656)

1. What is the topic of the passage?

____

2. What process is explained in the above passage?

____

3. How many steps does a registered nurse have to go through to mix medication from two vials?

____

Listing (or Addition)

This pattern of organization arranges information in a list in no particular order. Unlike process or chronological order, there is no specific order in which information is arranged. For example, the author may show the different ways that computers are used in the field of medicine. Keep in mind that the listing pattern of organization uses transitional words such as *in addition*, *also*, and *furthermore*.

Example

Studying Effectively

It is easy to stare at a page of text and feel that you have "spent time" studying when, in fact, you may have understood very little. When you have a block of time set aside to study, make sure you use it wisely. For hints about what is most important in the text, look at the Learning Outcomes at the beginning of each chapter… . Another technique to employ when studying is outlining. Some students find it helpful to outline the chapter after reading it. Under the main ideas, they organize the concepts and the information that supports those ideas… . Study questions at the end of the chapter and/or in student workbooks are another way to help you pull out the most important information in a chapter… . Take advantage of all available tools. Use a computer at school or at home to access the Companion Website… . Studying with another person or group of three or four people can be helpful in processing information and discussing ideas.

(*Fundamental Nursing Care,* p. 3)

If you take a closer look at the passage, you will notice that the topic is how to study a textbook effectively. The authors suggest several ways to read a textbook—such as time management, preparing an outline, and studying with a partner or a small group. It should be noted that there is no particular order in which the different ways to read should occur. In other words, a good reader may prepare an outline and study with a partner and vice versa.

PRACTICING THE SKILL: LISTING

Read the following passages carefully, paying attention to transition words such as *in addition, also, furthermore,* and so forth, and answer the questions that follow.

Passage 1

For purposes of education and research, most agencies allow student and graduate health professionals access to client records. The records are used in client conferences, clinics, rounds, and written papers or client studies. The student is bound by a strict ethical code to hold all information in confidence. It is the responsibility of the student and health professionals to protect the client's privacy by not using a name or any statements in the notations that would identify the client. Additionally, it is very important for staff and students to maintain confidentiality with worksheets and assignment sheets. Caution must be used to ensure that papers are not left where visitors and clients may see them.

(*Fundamental Nursing Care,* p. 90)

1. What is the topic of the passage?

 ____

2. What is the general idea of the passage?

 ____

3. How is this passage an example of the listing pattern of organization?

 ____

 ____

Passage 2

Computers make care planning and documentation relatively easy. In most facilities, nurses record nursing actions and client responses by choosing from standardized lists of care and intervention using a touch screen. The nurse can also type narrative information into the computer for further explanation or to note exceptions. Some computer programs produce a flow sheet with expected outcomes and nursing interventions. The nurse chooses the appropriate interventions for the specific client and initials them, indicating they were implemented. Others use the problem-oriented format, producing a problem list in priority order. The nurse then selects the appropriate nursing diagnoses, expected outcomes, and nursing interventions by using a light pen on the screen. The nurse uses the keyboard to type in additional information.

(*Fundamental Nursing Care*, p. 97)

1. What is the topic of the passage?

____

2. What is the main idea of the passage?

____

3. What transition words are used for the listing pattern of organization?

____

Passage 3

The variety of healthcare services hospitals provide usually depends on their size and location. The large urban hospitals usually have inpatient beds, emergency services, diagnostic facilities, ambulatory surgery centers, pharmacy services, intensive and coronary care services, and multiple outpatient services provided by clinics. Some large hospitals have other specialized services such as spinal cord injury and burn units, oncology services, and infusion and dialysis units. In addition, some hospitals have substance abuse treatment units and health promotion units. Small rural hospitals often are limited to inpatient beds, radiology and laboratory services, and basic emergency services. The number of services a rural hospital provides is usually directly related to its size and its distance from an urban center.

(*Fundamental Nursing Care*, p. 111)

1. What is the topic of the passage?

____

2. What is the main idea of the passage?

____

____

3. At least three major details are provided to support the main idea. What are they?

1. ______________________________

____

2. ____
____

3. ____
____

Statement and Clarification

Using a statement and clarification pattern of organization, the author first presents a general idea and then expounds on it to help the reader understand the idea. An example of this type of pattern of organization may be a Nursing text in which a statement of fact is made and discussion is provided to make that statement clear. Let's look at an example to understand the statement and clarification pattern of organization more clearly.

Example

Personal space is the distance people prefer in interactions with others. It is a natural protective instinct for people to maintain a certain amount of space immediately around them. The amount of personal space varies with individuals and cultures. When someone who wants to communicate steps too close, the receiver automatically steps back a pace or two. When providing nursing care, the nurse may need to invade a client's personal space. It is important to be aware of this and to warn the client when this will occur.

(*Fundamental Nursing Care*, p. 228)

Notice how the author begins the passage with a statement about people's preference for personal space. Then the statement is followed by a brief discussion of how personal space varies from culture to culture.

PRACTICING THE SKILL: STATEMENT AND CLARIFICATION

Now that you understand how authors use the statement and clarification pattern of organization, read the following passages and answer the questions that follow.

Passage 1

From an early age, females and males communicate differently. Girls tend to use language to seek confirmation, minimize differences, and establish intimacy. Boys use language to establish independence and negotiate status within a group. These differences can continue into adulthood so that the same communication may be interpreted differently by a man and a woman. Many studies have found that men and women communicate differently in both content and process of communication. There is evidence to suggest that more effective communication occurs when the care provider and the client are of the same gender.

(*Fundamental Nursing Care*, p. 228)

1. What is the topic of the passage?

____

2. What general statement is made about the topic?

____

3. How is this point made clear to the reader?

____

____

____

Passage 2

The ways people walk and carry themselves are often reliable indicators of self-concept, current mood, and health. The posture of people when they are sitting or lying can also indicate feelings or mood. The nurse can validate the interpretation of the behavior by asking, for example, "You look like it really hurts you to move. I'm wondering how your pain is and if you might need something to make you more comfortable?"

No part of the body is as expressive as the face. Facial expressions can convey surprise, fear, anger, disgust, happiness, and sadness. When the message is not clear, it is important to get feedback to be sure what the person intends.

Nurses need to be aware of their own facial expressions and what they are communicating to others. Clients are quick to notice the nurse's expression, particularly when they feel unsure or uncomfortable. It is impossible to control all facial expression. However, the nurse should learn to control expressions such as fear or disgust.

(*Fundamental Nursing Care*, pp. 229–230)

1. What is the topic of the passage?

____

2. What general statement is made about the topic?

____

3. How is this point made clear to the reader?

____

____

____

____

Passage 3

Fear is an emotion or feeling of apprehension aroused by impending danger, pain, or other perceived threat. People may fear something that has already occurred, a current threat, or something they believe will happen. The fear may or may not be based in reality. For example, beginning nursing students may fear their first experience in a client care setting. They may be worried that clients will not want to be cared for by students or that they might inadvertently harm the clients. The nursing students' feelings of fear are real and will probably elicit a stress response. However, the instructor arranges the students' first client assignment so that the students' feared outcomes are unlikely to occur.

(*Fundamental Nursing Care*, p. 292)

1. What is the topic of the passage?

____

2. What general statement is made about the topic?

____

3. How is this point made clear to the reader?

____

____

Spatial Order

Spatial order arranges details according to their location in space. An example of this pattern of organization is a layout of an operating room or an Intensive Care Unit (ICU). To help the reader visualize a person, thing, place, or space, the author uses descriptive language to create a vivid image. The author may choose to describe the place or space from the north to the south, from top to bottom, from bottom to top, or from inside to outside. Consider the following example to understand the spatial order pattern of organization more clearly.

Example

An inclinometer (Scoliometer) measures distortions of the torso. The client is asked to bend over, with arms dangling and palms pressed together, until a curve can be observed in the thoracic area (the upper back). The Scoliometer is placed on the back and used to measure the apex (the highest point) of the curve. The client is then asked to continue bending until the curve in the lower back can be seen; the apex of this curve is then measured.

(*Fundamental Nursing Care*, p. 838)

Notice that words such as *the upper back*, *on the back*, and *the highest point* are used to create an image of the client's location in space. With the help of these words, the reader can almost see the client bending over and the Scoliometer placed on the back.

PRACTICING THE SKILL: SPATIAL ORDER

Now practice reading passages that use the spatial order pattern of organization. Then answer the questions that follow each of the passages.

Passage 1

Assist the client to the examination table. Place in a comfortable position supporting injured extremity. In order for the splint to be applied properly, the client must be seated or lying down. Supporting the extremity can lessen the pain. Pad the inside of the splint and check for proper fit on the extremity. Fasten the Velcro strap, or wrap splint and extremity, evenly and snug enough to provide support but not enough to impede circulation of the limb, with an elastic bandage and fasten with clips or tape. Instruct the client to keep the extremity elevated and apply ice. Elevating the extremity above the level of the heart and applying ice aid in decreasing swelling. Apply a sling for an arm splint. The sling will help the client support the injured arm and keep it elevated.

(*Fundamental Nursing Care*, p. 856)

1. What is the topic of the passage?

____

2. What transitional or descriptive phrases are used to signal how the client is arranged in space?

____

Passage 2

When the body is aligned, organs are properly supported. This allows them to function at their best, while also maintaining balance. The line of gravity is an imaginary vertical line drawn through the body's center of gravity. The center of gravity is the point at which all of the body's mass is centered and the base of support (the foundation on which the body rests) achieves balance. In humans, the usual line of gravity is drawn from the top of the head, down between the shoulders, through the trunk slightly anterior to the sacrum, and between the weight-bearing joints (hips, knees) and base of support (feet). In the upright position, the center of gravity occurs in the pelvis approximately midway between the umbilicus and the symphysis pubis. When standing, an adult must center body weight symmetrically along the line of gravity to maintain stability. Greater stability and balance are achieved in the sitting or supine position because a chair or bed provides a wider base of support with a lower center of gravity. When the body is well aligned, there is little strain on the joints, muscles, tendons, or ligaments.

(*Fundamental Nursing Care*, p. 751)

1. What is the topic of the passage?

____

2. Write down a few transitional or descriptive phrases that are used to signal how space is arranged.

____

____

Passage 3

Using Canes

Hold the cane with the hand on the stronger side of the body to provide maximum support and appropriate body alignment when walking. Position the tip of a standard cane (and the nearest tip of other canes) about 15 cm (6 in.) to the side and 15 cm (6 in.) in front of the near foot, so that the elbow is slightly flexed. Move the cane forward about 30 cm (1 ft), or a distance that is comfortable while the body weight is borne by both legs. Then move the affected (weak) leg forward to the cane while the weight is borne by the cane and stronger leg. Next, move the unaffected (stronger) leg forward ahead of the cane and weak leg while the weight is borne by the cane and weak leg. Repeat the steps. This pattern of moving provides at least two points of support on the floor at all times. Move the cane and weak leg forward at the same time, while the weight is borne by the stronger leg. Move the stronger leg forward, while the weight is borne by the cane and the weak leg.

(*Fundamental Nursing Care,* p. 756)

1. What is the topic of the passage?

____

2. Write down a few transitional or descriptive phrases that are used to signal how space is arranged.

____

____

____

Each of the organizational patterns contains transitional phrases that will help you recognize its characteristics. See a table of organizational patterns and transitional phrases in Appendix 4 for further examples.

Applying the Skill

Now that you have practiced identifying different types of organizational patterns, let's practice reading full-length articles to recognize these patterns.

Recommended Debate Topic: Women naturally make better nurses than men because they are genetically preprogrammed to do humanistic kinds of work.

Discuss debatable topics concerning nursing with your classmates and instructor for the debate activity.

Your suggested debate topics:

a. ____

b. ____

c. ____

READING 3

Online Article

MyReadingLab

Visit Chapter 7: Life Science in MyReadingLab to complete the Reading 3 activities.

New Approach Addresses Substance Abuse Among Nurses

Pre-Reading Questions

1. Nurses take a vow to provide care for patients who may have substance abuse and addiction problems. Why do you think some of them might have the same problems?
2. If a healthcare provider or a nursing school finds out that a nurse or a nursing student is taking drugs, should it punish the nurse by terminating his or her employment? In the case of a nursing student, should the school expel him or her? Why, or why not?
3. In your opinion, how can healthcare providers help impaired nurses so that they may stay in the profession? Give specific examples to support your answer.

New Approach Addresses Substance Abuse Among Nurses

By Rick Nauert, PhD, Senior News Editor
Reviewed by John M. Grohol, PsyD,

on January 27, 2011

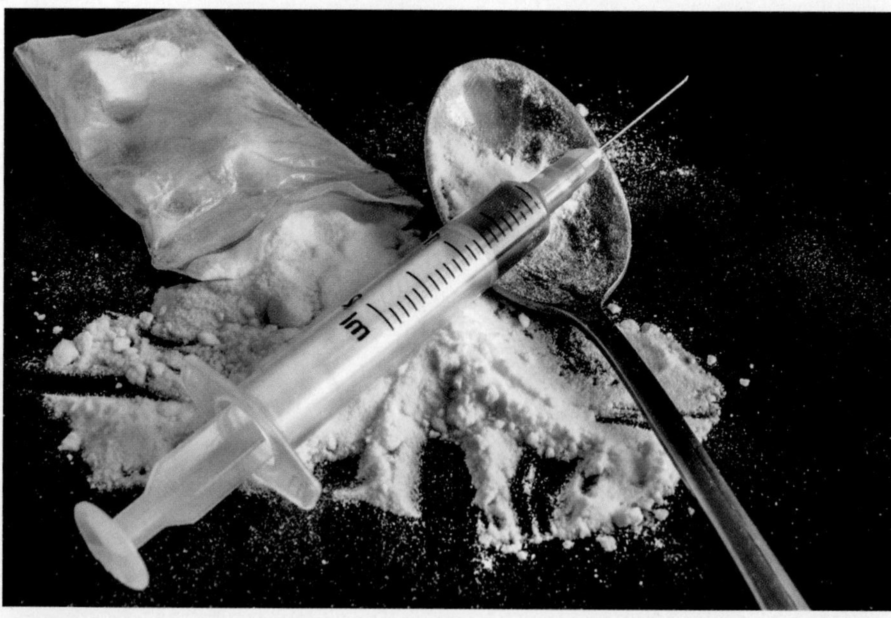

1 New research suggests as many as ten to 20 percent of nurses and nursing students may have substance abuse and **addiction** problems, this even as a severe nursing shortage threatens medical care delivery across the globe.

2 Experts say the key to **tackling** this thorny issue—and protecting public safety—is support and treatment, not punishment.

3 Researchers have recommended six key points that could be built into alternative-to-dismissal (ATD) strategies after reviewing the latest research and professional guidance from countries such as the USA, Canada, New Zealand, Australia and the UK.

4 They believe that ATD programs provide greater patient safety, as they enable managers to remove nurses from the work environment quickly, unlike traditional disciplinary procedures that can take months, if not years. ATD programs also provide non-judgmental support and treatment that encourages nurses to seek help and improve their chances of staying in the profession.

5 That is the key message in a paper in the February issue of the *Journal of Clinical Nursing*.

6 "Addiction among nurses has been recognized by professionals in the field for over a hundred years," said lead author Todd Monroe, Ph.D., from the Vanderbilt University School of Nursing. "While research consistently reports incidence rates of 10 to 15 percent, some studies suggest that this could be as high as 20 percent."

7 Monroe said doctors and nurses are "only human" and face the same problems as anyone else.

8 "The fact that they work in a highly stressful environment with easy access to powerful drugs can expose them to an increased risk of substance misuse and abuse," he said. "They are expected to show compassion when caring for patients who are alcohol and/or drug dependent and they should extend the same **compassion** to colleagues struggling with chemical dependency, which is an illness."

9 Research suggests that ATD programs help many nurses recover from addiction, reduce the chance of dismissal and return to work under strict monitoring guidelines, with random substance checks, support and meetings with managers and regulators.

10 ATD programs can also lead to a 75 percent reduction in practical problems, like obtaining **liability** health insurance after disciplinary action, and they usually help nurses to re-enter the workforce.

11 "ATD programs appear to be the best way to protect patients and retain nurses at a time when the profession is facing serious shortages of experienced professionals," said Monroe.

12 The review covers nearly three decades of research papers and professional guidance from nursing regulators and brings together a number of previous studies by Monroe on substance abuse policies in the nursing profession.

13 "We believe that the incidence of substance abuse among nurses, and especially nursing students, is both under-researched and under-reported, partly because it is considered taboo among many health-care providers and nursing school faculty and staff," he said.

14 "Poor or ineffective policies that mandate **punitive** action are more likely to endanger the public, as they make it more difficult for impaired nurses or students to seek help.

15 "That is why we support ATD strategies that motivate individuals to voluntarily seek assistance for their dependency or encourage colleagues to urge them to seek the help they need."

16 Monroe teamed up with Dr. Heidi Kenaga, a research analyst, to come up with six key points that they believe should be incorporated into ATD programs developed by regulators, educators and health care faculties:

1. Promoting open communication by discussing substance abuse in healthcare and nursing education settings;
2. Encouraging an atmosphere where people feel they can report problems confidentially;
3. Providing information about the signs and symptoms of impairment;
4. Conducting **mock** interventions to help people feel less fearful or uncomfortable about approaching a colleague or fellow student about suspected chemical dependency;
5. Inviting ATD experts to speak to hospital or school administrators;
6. Participating in scholarly forums about addiction among healthcare providers.

17 "We believe that these key points will help to transform perceptions of substance abuse among nurses, so that they are seen as a medical disorder requiring treatment, rather than a moral failing," Monroe said.

18 He noted that there is a long history of substance abuse in the medical profession and that ignoring the problem may perpetuate "fear, anxiety, poor outcomes for the nurses and risks for the people they care for.

19 "Providing early intervention and assistance is essential to help nurses and nursing students to recover from an addictive disorder. And providing a **confidential**, non-punitive atmosphere of support may well be a life-saving step for nurses and those in their care."

Reading with a Critical Eye

1. The article mentions that perhaps 20 percent of nurses and nursing students have addiction problems. Why do you think nurses and nursing students have substance abuse problems despite the fact that nursing is in great demand across the globe?
2. Do you agree with the experts that nurses who have substance abuse problems should not be punished? Why, or why not?

3. Nurses provide care to patients who are alcohol and drug dependent. Yet, some of them end up taking drugs themselves. How do we explain this paradox? Give your answer in reference to the article.
4. Monroe says, "The fact that they work in a highly stressful environment with easy access to powerful drugs can expose them to an increased risk of substance misuse and abuse." Do you think nurses can use this fact as an excuse for substance abuse?
5. Monroe notes that the incidence of substance abuse among nurses and nursing students is underreported. In your opinion, why don't healthcare providers and nursing schools report chemical dependency?

Reading Comprehension Check

1. The main idea of the article is that
   a. approximately 20 percent of nurses and nursing students have substance abuse and drug problems.
   b. healthcare providers must fire nurses who have substance abuse and drug problems.
   c. experts have found a way to address substance abuse and drug problems some nurses and nursing students may have.
   d. nurses take drugs because their jobs are stressful.
2. "Experts say the key to tackling this thorny issue—and protecting public safety—is support and treatment, not punishment."

   What is the pattern of organization shown in the above paragraph?
   a. chronological order
   b. classification
   c. cause and effect
   d. definition
3. "Researchers have recommended six key points that could be built into alternative-to-dismissal (ATD) strategies after reviewing the latest research and professional guidance from countries such as the USA, Canada, New Zealand, Australia and the UK."

   The overall pattern of organization of this passage is
   a. comparison and contrast.
   b. cause and effect.
   c. classification.
   d. listing.
4. "They believe that ATD programs provide greater patient safety, as they enable managers to remove nurses from the work environment quickly, unlike traditional disciplinary procedures that can take months, if not years."

   What is the pattern of organization shown in the above passage?
   a. cause and effect
   b. comparison and contrast
   c. classification
   d. chronological order

5. "The fact that they work in a highly stressful environment with easy access to powerful drugs can expose them to an increased risk of substance misuse and abuse," he said.

   The overall pattern of organization here is
   a. cause and effect.
   b. spatial order.
   c. classification.
   d. definition.

6. "They are expected to show compassion when caring for patients who are alcohol and/or drug dependent and they should extend the same compassion to colleagues struggling with chemical dependency, which is an illness."

   The above passage is organized by
   a. classifying the different ways to improve patient care.
   b. listing the important functions of patient care, safety, and outcomes.
   c. providing a definition of a technical term.
   d. clarifying an explanation of patient care.

7. "Research suggests that ATD programs help many nurses recover from addiction, reduce the chance of dismissal and return to work under strict monitoring guidelines, with random substance checks, support and meetings with managers and regulators."

   The author's overall pattern of organization
   a. contrasts the difference between ATD programs and research.
   b. lists the changes in the nurses' behavior after treatment.
   c. shows a causal relation between ATD programs and nurses' performance after treatment.
   d. summarizes the importance of ATD programs.

8. "ATD programs can also lead to a 75 percent reduction in practical problems, like obtaining liability health insurance after disciplinary action, and they usually help nurses to re-enter the workforce."

   The focus on ATD programs and impaired nurses shows what pattern of organization?
   a. compare and contrast
   b. listing
   c. chronological order
   d. cause and effect

9. "The review covers nearly three decades of research papers and professional guidance from nursing regulators and brings together a number of previous studies by Monroe on substance abuse policies in the nursing profession."

   The pattern of organization is
   a. cause and effect.
   b. spatial order.
   c. chronological order.
   d. definition.

10. "Monroe teamed up with Dr. Heidi Kenaga, a research analyst, to come up with six key points that they believe should be incorporated into ATD programs developed by regulators, educators and health care faculties:

    1. Promoting open communication by discussing substance abuse in healthcare and nursing education settings;

2. Encouraging an atmosphere where people feel they can report problems confidentially;
3. Providing information about the signs and symptoms of impairment;
4. Conducting mock interventions to help people feel less fearful or uncomfortable about approaching a colleague or fellow student about suspected chemical dependency;
5. Inviting ATD experts to speak to hospital or school administrators;
6. Participating in scholarly forums about addiction among health-care providers."

What is the overall pattern of organization of the above passage?

a. chronological order
b. cause and effect
c. listing
d. comparison and contrast

From Reading to Writing: Writing a Summary

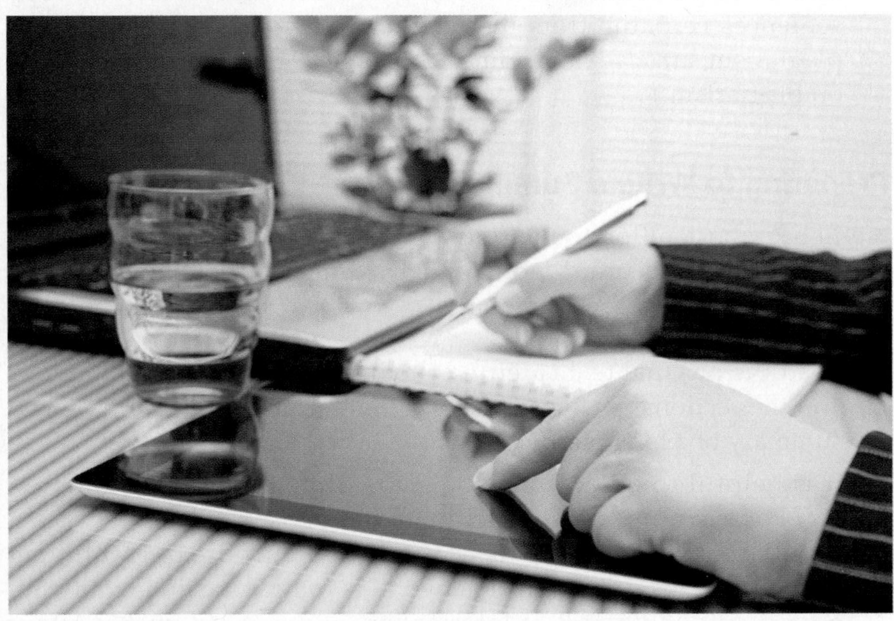

Overview

As a college student, you may be familiar with *summary writing*. Professors often ask students to summarize a specific reading, a short story, a newspaper article, or a lecture. Depending on the purpose of the writing assignment, they may ask you to write a short summary including the main idea and a few supporting details or a long summary including the main idea, key concepts, and more details. In college, summary writing could be part of a standardized reading test, or it could be an integral part of your preparation for a final exam. It is, therefore, important for you to learn how to write a concise and accurate summary of the original text.

Three Important Characteristics of a Summary

If you have written a summary, you probably know that it is difficult to restate the author's ideas in your own words. Remember that a well-written, objective summary has three important characteristics:

1. An objective summary must restate the original text accurately without altering or modifying the meaning.
2. A good summary should include only the relevant aspects of the original text. In other words, it is unnecessary to include the main point of each and every paragraph of the source in the summary.
3. The summary should be written in your own words. The trick is to change the language significantly without changing the main idea and supporting details presented in the original text. Think of yourself as an objective information processor. Your task as a summary writer is to simply present the main idea of the original source in your own language. Using your own words in writing a summary is important because you demonstrate to the reader that you have understood the original text correctly. If you copy sentences verbatim from the original text, you may be accused of plagiarism, an academic crime. (See page 394 for more information on plagiarism.)

Preparing to Write a Summary

It will be important for you to fully understand the original text so that you can write an accurate and objective summary. The following steps will help you write a good summary:

1. Read the original text carefully, paying attention to the main idea and the sections. This is particularly important if you are writing a summary of a long piece.
2. It is helpful to determine what type of text you are summarizing. For example, are you writing a summary of a research paper, a short story, or a newspaper article? The purpose of identifying the genre of the original text is twofold: you can easily identify important bits and pieces of information, and you can improve your reading skills.
3. Read the original text a second time, highlighting, underlining, or circling (whatever helps you) important pieces of information.
4. In one sentence, write down the main point of each section. Be careful to use your own words, retaining the original idea.
5. Make a list of the details that support the main idea. You may not need to include minor details such as specific examples in your summary.
6. Follow steps 1 through 5 a second time, revising, adding, or deleting information as you deem necessary.

Acknowledging the Source

Most novice summary writers usually forget to mention the source of the original text, giving the reader the impression that they are presenting their own ideas in a summary. To avoid this grave error, make sure that you mention the original source and the main idea in the first sentence of your summary, making it explicit to the reader that you are simply restating someone else's ideas without expressing your opinion. Keep in mind that at no point in the summary should you use the word *I* or express your viewpoint. Let's look at a few examples of how a summary should begin. Notice how the source is followed by the main idea.

> According to Fromkin (2007), male nurses **are** as qualified (main idea) ...
>
> In her article "Is Nursing a Noble Profession?" Smith (2006) **argues** that nursing is not necessarily (main idea) ...
>
> Seliger and Sridhar (2008) **suggest** that registered nurses in the United States (main idea) ...
>
> Hawkins (2005) **asserts/maintains** that nursing programs in the United States are not doing (main idea) ...

Notice the use of the simple present tense (highlighted) in each of the sentences.

Using Reporting Verbs

Good summary writers use a wide range of reporting verbs when referring to the original text. This is especially important if your summary is rather long. You need to remind the reader frequently that you are simply paraphrasing an author's ideas without expressing your opinion. Your task is to always remain objective and use reporting verbs, leaving no confusion in the reader's mind that you are stating your own ideas in the summary.

Here are some of the frequently used reporting verbs in a summary. Use them appropriately because they serve the purpose of your summary assignment.

Frequently Used Reporting Verbs

argue	develop	maintain	recommend
assert	discuss	note	report
claim	emphasize	observe	show
contend	examine	point out	state
demonstrate	explain	propose	study
describe	find	provide	suggest

Reminding the Reader

As mentioned previously, if your task is to write a longer summary, frequently remind the reader that, as a summary writer, you are only restating ideas presented in an original source. Your goal is to make it clear to the reader that you are not expressing your own views. You may want to remind the reader at frequent intervals that you are paraphrasing an original idea by saying:

- The author goes on to say that …
- The author further states that …
- Summer states/maintains/argues that …
- Smalley concludes that …
- Johnson believes that …

If you are writing a long summary, it is recommended that you mention the author's name at least three times: at the beginning, in the middle, and at the end of your summary.

Inserting Transition Words

When you provide additional information to the reader, be sure to use transition words. They serve as signposts, signaling to the reader that you are about to present another idea.

Some Transition Words

additionally	further	in addition	more important
also	furthermore	in fact	moreover

Avoiding Plagiarism

The term *plagiarism* is derived from the Latin word *plagiare*, which means "to kidnap." It is a writer's conscious and deliberate attempt to steal someone else's ideas and present them as his or her own. In essence, plagiarism is akin to kidnapping someone's baby and claiming that the kidnapper is the baby's biological parent. Since the baby is too young to dispute the claim, most people would usually believe that the kidnapper is indeed the mother or father of the baby.

Some cultures may be relatively tolerant of plagiarism, but plagiarism is considered to be a serious academic crime in North American educational institutions. The idea is based on the assumption that the original idea is the intellectual property of the author. It is also considered disrespectful and dishonest to borrow and use the works of distinguished authors without their consent and knowledge. A student found guilty of plagiarism can be expelled from a college or university and may find it difficult to pursue an academic career. It is, therefore, imperative that you always refer to the original source in a summary and avoid plagiarism.

Paraphrasing

When we paraphrase, we use our own words to express something that somebody has written or said. The purpose of paraphrasing is to make it easier for the reader to understand the original statement. Paraphrasing some of the sentences from the original source may be successful sometimes, but excessive paraphrasing in summary writing may give the reader the wrong impression that you do not quite understand the original work. Another reason you should avoid paraphrasing frequently in a summary is that the summary may be too close to the original text and you may be accused of plagiarism.

If you are not comfortable or confident about your ability to paraphrase, it might be worth your while to read the original source carefully, highlight the important points, and rewrite what you have understood in your own words without referring to the original. Rewriting the main points will help you write the summary accurately and in your own words.

When you write a summary of the original source, follow these steps:

1. Resist the temptation to use phrases and sentences from the original text, and always use your own words to write the summary. You may sometimes include the technical terms used in the original source.
2. Be sure to include the main idea and sufficient supporting details to make the summary clear to the reader.
3. Do not paraphrase excessively.
4. Do not lose sight of the content of the original text.
5. Use transition words to make the sentences flow smoothly. A summary without transition words can be choppy and difficult to understand.

EXERCISE 7.6 Evaluating Summaries

Reread "New Approach Addresses Substance Abuse Among Nurses" by Rick Nauert on page 386 carefully. Then read the four summaries below and decide which of the summaries is the most accurate and objective. For each of the summaries, write at least a couple of sentences, explaining its strengths and weaknesses.

Summaries

1. New research suggests as many as 10 to 20 percent of nurses and nursing students may have substance abuse and addiction problems, this even as a severe nursing shortage threatens medical care delivery across the globe. Experts say the key to tackling this thorny issue—and protecting public safety—is support and treatment, not punishment. Researchers have recommended six key points that could be built into alternative-to-dismissal (ATD) strategies after reviewing the latest research and professional guidance from countries such as the USA, Canada, New Zealand, Australia and the UK.

Your comments:

2. I really enjoyed reading Rick Nauert's article about RNs and nursing students having substance abuse and addiction problems. To tell the truth, I was not aware that there were impaired nurses who needed treatment for substance abuse to stay in the profession. In general, I agree with Nauert's assessment that impaired nurses need support and treatment, not punishment. However, I disagree with his statement that these nurses should be on probation after they return to work. In my opinion, impaired nurses may not feel comfortable working in a hostile environment where they are being monitored constantly.

Your comments:

3. In "New Approach Addresses Substance Abuse Among Nurses," Nauert mentions researchers who have recommended six alternative-to-dismissal (ATD) strategies to help nurses and nursing students who have substance abuse and addiction problems receive treatment and stay in the profession. Nauert refers to research indicating that these nurses need support and treatment, not punishment. The author concludes that early intervention is necessary because ignoring the problem of substance abuse can only aggravate the issue.

Your comments:

4. Research suggests that nurses and nursing students with substance abuse and addiction problems should be provided support and treatment. Instead of punishment, these nurses and nursing students should be dealt with compassionately. It is crucially important that substance abuse is recognized at an early stage. Once it is established that registered nurses have addiction problems, the issue must be considered seriously. It is dangerous to avoid the issue once it comes to light because impaired nurses may not be able to care for the patients properly. In this sense, it is important to treat the issue confidentially and help the nurses overcome the addiction in an effective manner.

Your comments:

____

____

____

____

____

____

____

Discuss the four summaries with your classmates and find out whether they agree or disagree with your assessment.

Summary Writing Assignment

You have read the guidelines on writing a summary. You have seen examples of both good and bad summaries. It is time for you now to practice writing a summary. Reread "45, Male and Now a Nurse" by Cecilia Capuzzi Simonnov on page 354, and write a concise and accurate summary, using your own words. Adhere to the guidelines as you write the summary. Swap summaries with a classmate for feedback.

Textbook Application

Read the following chapter from an introductory textbook on Nursing. The purpose of this reading exercise is to give you an opportunity to practice reading authentic text. Read the chapter carefully and answer the multiple-choice questions that follow.

MyReadingLab

Visit Chapter 7: Life Science in MyReadingLab to complete the Reading 4 activities.

READING 4

Textbook Reading

Succeeding as a Nursing Student

From *Fundamental Nursing Care by Roberta Pavy Ramont and Dee Niedringhaus*[1]

1 Welcome to a career in nursing. You have made an excellent choice for a future helping others to regain or maintain health and function. Nursing is full of rewards and challenges while you are a student and also after you graduate. This text is designed to help you recognize and overcome those challenges as well as to appreciate the rewards.

2 LPN/LVN training programs can be found in many different types of schools. In some states, they are part of high schools. In others, they are

[1] From Roberta Pavy Ramont and Dee Niedringhaus, *Fundamental Nursing Care,* 2nd Edition, pp. 3–13, © 2008. Printed and electronically reproduced by permission of Pearson Education, Inc., Upper Saddle River, New Jersey.

in community college settings, vocational training centers, or private schools.

3 The length of the program is dictated by the governing nursing board in each state. Some programs can be completed in about 9 months. Others take up to 2 years. Some are full-time day programs; others are part time in the evenings and/or on weekends.

4 People with a variety of backgrounds enter the nursing profession. Your classmates may represent a variety of life experiences, educational backgrounds, and ethnic/cultural influences. You can learn a great deal by collaborating with fellow students during your course of study. The ages of LPN/LVN students within a class may range from young adult to near retirement. Motives may also vary. Students may be realizing a lifelong dream to become a nurse or making a career change.

5 It may have been a long time since you studied a subject that really mattered to you, or you may have recently been in school and studied with serious commitment. In either case, here are some academic "survival skills" to help you in your vocational/practical nursing course of study.

Reading This Textbook

6 Begin by reading the preface and other material in the front of the book. Become familiar with how the book is organized and any special features that will make your reading and studying easier. Review the table of contents and look over the appendices. By spending a few minutes becoming familiar with the book, you will be ready to use your book when the first reading assignment is given. The textbook is a great stand-alone reference, as well as a source for clarifying lecture material.

7 Read textbook assignments before the class in which the material will be covered. Reading beforehand will help you organize your thoughts, and help you spell and define words that may be used in a lecture. Although many students use highlighter pens while reading, it is much better to save the highlighter for reviewing lectures notes or marking the location of answers to the chapter's study questions (Porter, L.).

Studying Effectively

8 It is easy to stare at a page of text and feel that you have "spent time" studying when, in fact, you may have understood very little. When you have a block of time set aside to study, make sure you use it wisely. For hints about what is most important in the text, look at the Learning Outcomes at the beginning of each chapter. These objectives guide you in discovering the information you need to obtain from the chapter as you read and study. When an objective states "Identify three strategies to use when … ," go to the text, find all three strategies, and write them down. As you study, review those three strategies and when you would use them.

9 Another technique to employ when studying is outlining. Some students find it helpful to outline the chapter after reading it. Under the main ideas, they organize the concepts and the information that supports those ideas. You can easily do this by using the main headings in the chapter as outline headings, then listing two or three main ideas from the paragraphs beneath those headings.

10 Study questions at the end of the chapter and/or in student workbooks are another way to help you pull out the most important information in a chapter. First, try to answer the questions from what you have read and understood. If you are unable to answer them correctly or at all, look up the information within the chapter to find the correct answer. This will help you remember the information better than simply looking up each answer. Some students find it helpful to make up their own study questions; they anticipate what instructors might ask by using information from class notes.

11 Take advantage of all available tools. Use a computer at school or at home to access the Companion Website (www.prenhall.com/ramont) or the student CD for this text. These tools provide additional questions and case studies to bring the information to life and to prepare you for future practice. The website and CD also supply links to the Internet to help you with your school projects and research.

12 Studying with another person or group of three or four people can be helpful in processing information and discussing ideas. To be successful, the groups must be well organized. Study groups are discussed further in the next section.

Managing Time

13 The "average" practical/vocational nursing student is far from average. Proposing one time management template that would work for everyone is impossible. Still, being organized

and having a plan will help you work within your time limits. Learning to manage your time is a skill that will benefit you during the nursing program and also in your career and in life.

14 Learning how to be a good student may be the most important lesson during the first few weeks of your nursing program. Study skills will support you throughout your student days and as you prepare for exams. The time taken to perfect these skills will be hours well spent. See Figure 1-1 ■ for a sample time management schedule.

15 The following suggestions for time management may be useful:

- Obtain a blank calendar or planner for the entire year.
- Fill in holidays, vacations, medical or dental appointments, class times, and clinical days as soon as you know them.
- Add due dates, tests, homework, and projects as they are assigned.
- Schedule study time by writing it on your calendar or planner.
- Schedule personal time for relaxation and being with other people.

16 Group study time can be very useful when you participate regularly. Learn to plan your group study time, just as you would plan other parts of your day. Stay focused on content, and resist the urge to talk about things that are not study material. Bring four or five questions with you to discuss with the group. This can be especially helpful if you are having difficulty understanding certain concepts.

17 It is a good idea to break a study session down into segments. For example, a 2-hour session might include 30 minutes of lecture note review, 20 minutes of shared questions and answers, a 10-minute break, 30 minutes of quizzing, and 30 minutes of review of class objectives. This plan gives focus to the study time. The change in activities also helps to sustain people's interest and energy levels.

Taking Tests

ANSWERING MULTIPLE-CHOICE QUESTIONS

18 Most tests given in nursing programs will be objective, multiple-choice tests. These are the same types of questions used on the NCLEX-PN® exam.

Sample Time Management Schedule

	Monday	Tuesday	Wednesday	Thursday	Friday	Saturday	Sunday
0600	Sleep	Sleep	Sleep	Shower/dress	Shower/dress	Shower/dress	Sleep
0700	Shower/dress	Shower/dress	Shower/dress	Clinical	Clinical	Work	Sleep
0800	Class	Class	Class				Shower/dress
0900							Breakfast
1000							Church
1100							
1200	Lunch	Lunch	Lunch	Lunch	Lunch	Lunch	
1300	Class	Class					
1400		Library	Group project				Dinner with family
1500							
1600							
1700	Dinner	Dinner	Dinner	Dinner	Dinner	Dinner	
1800						Movie	
1900	Study group	Study	Study	Study			Laundry
2000							Study
2100			Personal time	Personal time			
2200	Personal time	Personal time	Sleep	Sleep	Personal time		Personal time
2300	Sleep	Sleep	Sleep	Sleep	Sleep		Sleep

FIGURE 1-1. ■ Sample time management schedule.

Multiple-choice questions can evaluate your knowledge of facts, as well as your ability to apply that knowledge within a client care scenario. Each question will consist of a stem and answer choices. Read each question completely in order to understand what is being asked. Then read each of the choices. Try to eliminate one or more of the choices. Examine each choice to see if anything is incorrect within the answer itself. Watch out for choices that are correct and accurate on their own, but that do not answer the question as it is written. See Box 1-1 ■ for an example.

19 Multiple-choice questions can test **knowledge**, **comprehension**, **application**, and ability to **analyze**. Table 1-1 provides examples and comparisons of each type.

20 Questions that include choices such as "all of the above" or "none of the above" have been eliminated from the NCLEX-PN® examination. However, some textbooks have them as study questions, and some instructors may test with them. A choice of this type can be confirmed or eliminated easily. If you have identified one choice as being correct, then you can eliminate "none of the above." If you can identify one choice that is incorrect, then "all of the above" can also be eliminated. If you can identify at least two answers as correct, then the question qualifies as an "all of the above" answer.

21 If you are able to narrow your choice to two options, don't spend too much time deciding between them. More likely than not, your first impression is correct. Once you have identified your choice, don't go back and change it unless you later figure out the correct response with absolute certainty.

22 Answering the study questions at the end of each chapter and in the student workbook will help you improve your ability to select correct answers in objective tests.

23 Most questions on the NCLEX-PN® exam are standard multiple choice, but some new types of questions are being added. The NCLEX-PN® exam is discussed in more detail in Chapter 37.

24 Several techniques are useful in calling information to mind during a test. For example, by using visualization, you may be able to picture something the instructor wrote on the board during a lecture. You may be able to "see" in your mind a poster or handout that was used during a class presentation. With some practice, you may be able to visualize a word or a passage that you read in the textbook.

ANSWERING ESSAY, SHORT-ANSWER, AND CALCULATION QUESTIONS

25 Answers to essay, short-answer, and calculation questions will need to be extracted from your memory. Read the question carefully to determine what is being asked. Some students find it helpful to develop a brief outline before beginning an essay question. Check with the instructor to see if this can be written on the test paper or if you are permitted to use an additional sheet. The outline can help you organize your thoughts and can serve as a checkpoint that all important information was included. Usually, a number of key introductory words appear in essay questions (Table 1-2 ■). Look for these words, and do only what is required of you. Many low grades are caused by ignoring these key words.

26 Calculation questions are particularly troubling for many students who have convinced themselves that they cannot do math. Although math may be difficult, it is a necessary skill for a nurse. With extra practice, calculations are possible to learn. Several methods are used to do calculations.

27 It is important to show your work on calculations. If you are unable to arrive at the correct answer, your instructor can review your work, and will be able to tell you where you went wrong. Memorizing formulas and frequently used conversions will make calculations on tests and in the clinical area much easier.

BOX 1-1

Example of a Multiple-Choice Question

Which of the following men was responsible for the reduction of maternal death related to infection transmitted by way of unwashed hands?

1. Joseph Lister
2. Louis Pasteur
3. Ignaz Semmelweis
4. Karl Crede

Although all four people were involved in prevention of infection and/or disease, the correct answer is 3. Ignaz Semmelweis was the person who discovered that puerperal fever was related to examination of mothers during the intra- and postpartum periods by doctors who had not washed their hands after performing autopsies.

TABLE 1-1

Test Questions and Levels of Learning

LEVEL	INFORMATION REQUIRED	EXAMPLE	RATIONALE
Knowledge question	Requires recall of information. To answer a knowledge question, you need to commit facts to memory. Knowledge questions expect you to know terminology, specific facts, trends, sequences, classifications, categories, criteria, structures, principles, generalizations, and/or theories.	What does the abbreviation BRP mean? a. bathe daily b. bedrush pt c. blood pressure reading d. bathroom privileges	To answer this question correctly, you have to know the meaning of the abbreviation BRP (bathroom privileges answer d).
Comprehension question	Requires you to understand information. To answer a comprehension question, not only must you commit facts to memory, but it is essential that you be able to translate, interpret, and determine the implications of the information. You demonstrate understanding when you translate or paraphrase information, interpret or summarize information, or determine the implications, consequences, corollaries, or effects of information. Comprehension questions expect you not only to know but also to understand the information being tested. You do not necessarily have to relate it to other material or see its fullest implications.	To evaluate the therapeutic effect of a cathartic, the nurse should assess the client for: a. increased urinary output. b. a decrease in anxiety. c. a bowel movement. d. pain relief.	To answer this question, you not only have to know that a cathartic is a potent laxative that stimulates the bowel, but that the increase in peristalsis will result in a bowel movement (answer c).
Application question	Requires you to utilize knowledge. To answer an application question, you must take remembered and comprehended concepts and apply them to concrete situations. The abstractions may be theories, technical principles, rules of procedures, generalizations, or ideas that have to be applied in a **scenario**. Application questions test your ability to use information in a new situation.	An elderly client's skin looks dry, thin, and fragile. When providing back care, the nurse should: a. apply a moisturizing body lotion. b. wash back with soap and water. c. massage back using short kneading strokes. d. leave excess lubricant on the client's skin.	To answer this question, you must know that dry, thin, fragile skin is common in the elderly and that moisturizing lotion helps the skin to retain water and become more supple. When presented with this scenario, you have to apply your knowledge concerning developmental changes in the elderly and the benefits of using moisturizing lotion (answer a).
Analysis question	Requires you to interpret a variety of data and recognize the commonalities, differences, and interrelationships among present ideas. Analysis questions make assumptions that you know, understand, and can apply information. Now you must identify, examine, dissect, evaluate, or investigate the organization, systematic arrangement, or structure of the information presented in the question. This type of question tests your analytical ability.	A client who is undergoing cancer **chemotherapy** says to the nurse, "This is no way to live." Which of the following responses uses reflective technique? a. "Tell me more about what you are thinking." b. "You sound discouraged today." c. "Life is not worth living?" d. "What are you saying?"	To answer this question, you must understand the communication techniques of reflection, clarification, and paraphrasing. You must also analyze the statements and identify which techniques are represented. This question requires you to understand, interpret, and differentiate information to know that the correct answer is c.

TABLE 1-2

Key Words in Essay Exams

KEY WORD	EXPLANATION
Compare	To point out similarities and differences
Contrast	To point out differences only
Define	Several connotations: (1) to give the meaning of, (2) to explain or describe essential qualities, (3) to place it in the class to which it belongs and set it off from other items in the same class
Describe	Enumerate (list) the special features of the topic Show how the topic is different from similar or related items Give an account of, tell about, and give a word picture of
Discuss	Present various sides or points, talk over, consider the different sides; a discussion is usually longer than an explanation of the same subject
Explain	Make plain or clear, interpret, tell "how" to do
Identify	Show recognition
Illustrate	Describe in narrative form using "word pictures" to provide examples
Justify	Provide supporting data for opinions or actions
List or name	Present a group of names or items in a category
Outline	Give information systematically in headings and subheadings
Summarize	Present in condensed form; give main points briefly

Participating in Clinical Experiences

28 A major part of your learning will occur during your clinical experiences. You will be assigned to assist with the care of one or more clients in a healthcare setting. This experience is extremely valuable in preparing you for the profession you have chosen. You will find that observing signs and symptoms of an illness firsthand is far more impressive than reading about them.

29 At first you will care for just one client, with assistance from other healthcare workers as needed. As you progress through your course of study, you will be assigned more responsibility and more clients. The clients you care for will have more complex illnesses and needs. When you study and learn about performing skills and signs to watch for, you are learning what you need to know to be a safe healthcare practitioner.

30 As a student, your responsibilities in preparing for clinical experience include:

- Ensuring that you understand what you read and how to apply it to the care of real clients
- Practicing skills repeatedly so that you know exactly what to do when called on to perform those skills quickly and efficiently in the clinical setting
- Researching information about an assigned client's medical diagnosis, nursing diagnoses, problems, and needs so that you are prepared and can anticipate what could happen as you care for that client
- Asking for help when you are not sure how to proceed, but proceeding when you are sure of what you need to do
- Reporting any and all deviations from baseline that you observe while caring for clients (You may not realize the significance of your observation, especially early in the program, but other healthcare professionals will know what actions to take.)
- Taking advantage of all learning opportunities in the clinical setting. If a procedure is being done, ask if you can observe, even though the client may not be assigned to you. Spend any "downtime" during your clinical experience observing, assisting, or listening to healthcare staff.

Overview of Nursing History

31 To fully appreciate your position as a contemporary practical/vocational nurse, you need to understand a bit about the history of nursing. Many women and men have been influential in developing nursing into the profession it is today.

NIGHTINGALE (1820–1910)

32 Florence Nightingale's contributions to nursing are well documented. Her achievements in improving the standards for the care of war casualties in Crimea earned her the title "Lady with

Figure 1-2 ■ Considered to be the founder of modern nursing, Florence Nightingale (1820–1910) was influential in developing nursing education, practice, and **administration.** Her 1859 **publication** *Notes on Nursing: What It Is, and What It Is Not* was intended for all women. ***(Source:*** © Bettmann/CORBIS. Reprinted with permission.)

the Lamp" (Figure 1-2 ■). Her efforts in reforming hospitals and in producing and implementing public health policies also made her an accomplished political nurse. She was the first nurse to exert political pressure on government. She is also recognized as nursing's first scientist-theorist for her work *Notes on Nursing: What It Is, and What It Is Not.*

33 When she returned from Crimea, a grateful English public gave Nightingale an honorarium of £4,500. She used this money to establish the Nightingale Training School for Nurses in 1860. At St. Thomas Hospital in London, England, she taught her straightforward requirements.

34 Nightingale believed that nursing education should develop both the intellect and character of the nurse. She gave students a solid background in science to understand the theory behind their care. To develop character, by increasing their understanding of human ethics and morals, she assigned readings in the humanities. She believed that nurses should never stop learning. To her nurses she wrote, "[Nursing] is a field of which one may safely say: there is no end in what we may be learning everyday" (Schuyler, 1992). The school served as a model for other training schools. Its graduates traveled to other countries to manage hospitals and to institute training programs for nurses.

35 Nightingale's vision of nursing, which included public health and health promotion roles for nurses, was only partially addressed in the early days. The focus first was on developing the profession within hospitals. Although Miss Nightingale died in 1910, her influence continues in nursing today.

BARTON (1821–1912)

36 Clara Barton (Figure 1-3 ■) was a schoolteacher who volunteered as a nurse during the American Civil War. Her responsibility was to organize the nursing services. Barton is noted for her role in establishing the American Red Cross, which linked with the International Red Cross when the United States Congress ratified the Treaty of Geneva (Geneva Convention). In 1882, Barton persuaded Congress to ratify this treaty so that the Red Cross could perform humanitarian efforts in times of peace.

WALD (1867–1940)

37 Lillian Wald (Figure 1-4 ■) is considered the founder of public health nursing. Wald and Mary Brewster were the first to offer trained nursing services to the poor in the New York slums. They founded the Henry Street Settlement, and Visiting Nurse Service, which provided nursing and social services, and also organized educational and cultural activities. Soon after the founding of the Henry Street Settlement, school nursing was established as an adjunct to visiting nursing.

Figure 1-3 ■ Clara Barton (1821–1912) organized the American Red Cross, which linked with the International Red Cross when the U.S. Congress ratified the Geneva **Convention** in 1882. (***Source:*** © Bettmann/CORBIS. Reprinted with permission.)

Figure 1-4 ■ Lillian Wald (1867–1940) **founded** the Henry Street Settlement and Visiting Nurse Service (circa 1893), which provided nursing and social services and organized educational and **cultural** activities. She is considered to be the founder of public health nursing. (***Source:*** University of Iowa, College of Nursing, Iowa City, IA.)

DOCK (1858–1956)

38 Lavinia L. Dock (Figure 1-5 ■) was a feminist, as well as a prolific writer, political activist, suffragist, and friend of Wald. She participated in protest movements for women's rights that resulted in the 1920 passage of the 19th Amendment to the U.S. Constitution, which granted women the right to vote. In addition, Dock campaigned for legislation to allow nurses rather than physicians to control their profession. In 1893, Dock, Mary Adelaide Nutting, and Isabel Hampton Robb founded the American Society of Superintendents of Training Schools for Nurses of the United States and Canada. This was a precursor to the current National League for Nursing (NLN).

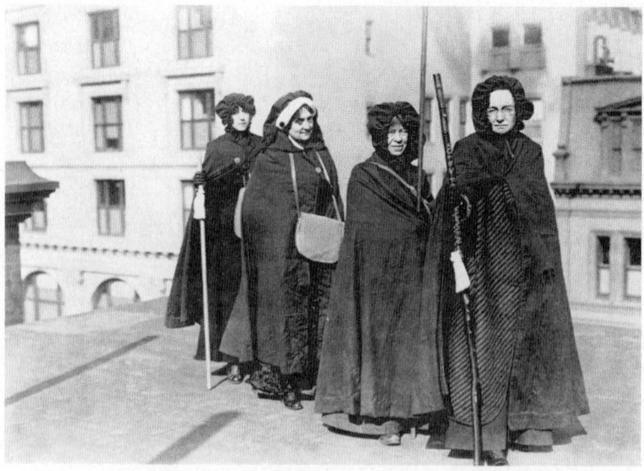

FIGURE 1-5 ■ Nursing leader and suffragist Lavinia L. Dock (1858–1956) was active in the protest movement for women's rights that resulted in the 1920 U.S. **constitutional amendment** allowing women to vote. (***Source:*** Courtesy of Millbank Memorial Library, Teachers' College, Columbia University. Reprinted with permission.)

MALE NURSES IN HISTORY

39 Women were not the sole providers of nursing services. The first nursing school in the world was started in India in about 250 B.C. Only men were considered to be "pure" enough to fulfill the role of nurse at that time. In Jesus's parable in the New Testament, the good Samaritan paid an innkeeper to provide care for the injured man. Paying a man to provide nursing care was fairly common. During the Crusades, several orders of knights provided nursing care to their sick and injured comrades and also built hospitals. The organization and management of their hospitals set a standard for the administration of hospitals throughout Europe at that time. St. Camillus de Lellis started out as a soldier and later turned to nursing. He started the sign of the Red Cross and developed the first ambulance service. Friar Juan de Mena was shipwrecked off the south Texas coast in 1554. He is the first identified nurse in what would become the United States. James Derham, a black slave who worked as a nurse in New Orleans in the late 1700s, saved the money he earned to purchase his freedom. Later, he studied medicine and became a well-respected physician in Philadelphia. During the Civil War, both sides had military men who cared for the sick and wounded.

40 In 1876, only three years after the first U.S. nurse received her diploma from New England Hospital for Women and Children, the Alexian brothers opened their first hospital in the United States and a school to educate men in nursing.

41 During the years from the Civil War to the Korean War, men were not permitted to serve as nurses in the military. Today, men have resumed their historical place in the profession. As the history of nursing continues to be written, men and women will work side by side (Figure 1-6 ■).

HISTORY OF LPNS/LVNS

42 The first training for practical nurses was at the Young Women's Christian Association (YWCA) in New York City in 1892. The following year this

FIGURE 1-6 ■ Modern male nurses work side by side with their female **colleagues** to provide care to hospitalized clients.

became the Ballard School. The program of study was 3 months long, and the participants studied special techniques for caring for the sick as well as a variety of homemaking techniques. Much of the care during this time was done in the client's home, making the licensed practical nurse (LPN) a home health or visiting nurse. Eleven years later, a second school, the Thompson Practical Nursing School, was established.

43 In 1914, the state legislature in Mississippi passed the first laws governing the practice of practical nurses. Other states were slow to follow. By 1940, only six states had passed such laws. In 1955, the state board test pool of the NLN Education Committee established the procedures for testing graduates of approved practical/vocational education programs in all states. Graduates who passed the examination became LPNs or, in California and Texas, licensed vocational nurses (LVNs). Each state set its own passing score.

44 Today, a graduate of an approved LPN/LVN training program is eligible to take the National Council Licensure Examination for Practical Nursing (NCLEX-PN®). The examination is computerized, with a "pass" score that is standardized throughout the United States. All states have licensing laws. *Interstate endorsement* (reciprocity between states) exists. This means that an LPN/LVN from one state can apply for licensure in another state without retesting. It is the responsibility of the individual nurse to contact the board of nursing in the jurisdiction where he or she wishes to work. The nurse must apply for licensure and for information regarding the scope of practice within that state. Table 1-3 ■ lists important events in the history of practical/vocational nursing.

Practical/Vocational Nursing Today

OUR CUSTOMERS

45 The "customers" we serve in nursing today are sometimes called consumers, sometimes patients, and sometimes clients. A consumer is an individual, a group of people, or a community that uses a service or commodity. People who use healthcare products or services are consumers of health care. A patient is a person who is waiting for or undergoing medical treatment and care. The word *patient* comes from a Latin word meaning "to suffer" or "to bear." Traditionally, the person receiving health care has been called a patient. People become patients when they seek assistance because of illness. Some nurses believe that the word *patient* implies passive acceptance of the decisions and care of health professionals. Because nurses interact with family, friends, and healthy people as well as those who are ill, nurses increasingly refer to recipients of health care as *clients*.

46 A client is a person who engages the advice or services of someone who is qualified to provide the service. Therefore, a client is a collaborator, a person who is also responsible for his or her own health. The health status of a client is the responsibility of the individual in collaboration with health professionals. In this book, *client* is the preferred term, although ***consumer*** and *patient* may be used in some instances.

OUR PURPOSE

47 Nurses provide care for individuals, families, and communities. The scope of nursing practice involves four areas: promoting health and wellness, preventing illness, restoring health, and caring for the dying.

PROMOTING HEALTH AND WELLNESS

48 Wellness is a state of well-being. It means engaging in attitudes and behavior that enhance the quality of life and maximize personal potential. Nurses promote wellness in individuals and groups who are healthy or ill. Nurses may hold blood

TABLE 1-3

Important Historical Events for LPNs/LVNs

DATE	EVENT	IMPORTANCE
1893	Ballard School at YMCA, Brooklyn, New York	First formal training for practical nurses.
1914	Mississippi legislature passed license laws for practical nurses	First laws passed to govern the practice of practical nurses.
1917	Smith-Hughes Act	Provided federal funding for vocationally oriented schools of practical nursing.
1918	Third school established	Even with new schools and federal assistance, the need for nurses could not be met because of the demand created by the war and epidemics.
1941	The Association of Practical Nurse Schools was founded; the name was changed to National Association for Practical Nurse Education (NAPNE) in 1942	Standards for practical nurse education were established.
1944	U.S. Department of Education commissioned an intensive study differentiating tasks of the practical nurse	The outcome of the study differentiated tasks performed by the practical nurse from those performed by the registered nurse. State boards of nursing established tasks that could be performed by both groups.
1945	New York established mandatory licensure for practical nurses	The first state to require licensure; by 1955 all other states had followed suit.
1949	The National Federation of Licensed Practical Nurses (NFLPN) was founded by Lillian Kuster; the name was changed to the National Association for Licensed Practical Nurse Education and Services in 1959	The discipline now had an official organization with membership limited to LPNs/LVNs.
1955	All states passed licensing laws for practical/vocational nurses	Practice of nursing by licensed practical nursing was regulated in all states.
1961	The National League of Nursing established a Department of Practical Nursing	Through this department, schools of practical nursing could be accredited by the NLN.
1965	American Nurses Association published a position paper that influenced attitudes about practical/vocational nursing	The paper clearly defined the two levels of nursing: registered nursing and technical nursing. The exclusion of the term *practical/vocational nurse* necessitated that the LPN/LVN prove his or her worth to provide valuable nursing interventions under the direction of a registered nurse.
1994	Computerized NCLEX-PN® examination available to graduates of practical/vocational nursing programs in all states	Allowed for more availability of test dates and interstate endorsement of licensure.

pressure clinics, teach about healthy lifestyles, give talks about drug and alcohol abuse, and instruct about safety in the home and workplace. Nurses who work in public health, community clinics, mental health facilities, and in occupational health settings promote health and wellness.

PREVENTING ILLNESS

49 Illness may be defined as the highly individualized response a person has to a disease. The goal of illness prevention programs is to maintain optimal health by preventing disease. Nurses in physician's offices or health clinics administer

immunizations, provide prenatal and infant care, and teach about the prevention of sexually transmitted infections.

RESTORING HEALTH

50 Restoring health means focusing on the ill client from early detection of disease through the recovery period. Nurses in acute care and rehabilitation facilities perform all of the following:

- Provide direct care to the ill person, such as administering medications, assisting with activities of daily living, and performing specific procedures and treatments.
- Perform diagnostic and assessment procedures, such as measuring blood pressure and examining feces for occult blood.
- Consult with other healthcare professionals about client problems.
- Teach clients about recovery activities, such as exercises that will hasten recovery after a stroke.
- Rehabilitate clients to their optimal functional level following physical or mental illness, injury, or chemical addiction.

CARING FOR THE DYING

51 This area of nursing practice involves comforting and caring for people of all ages who are dying. It includes helping clients live as comfortably as possible until death and helping clients' support persons cope with death. Nurses carry out these activities in homes, hospitals, and extended care facilities. Some agencies, called hospices, are specifically designed for this purpose.

OUR STANDARDS

52 Nurse practice acts, or legal acts for professional nursing practice, regulate the practice of nursing in the United States and Canada. Each state in the United States and each province in Canada has its own act.

53 Although practice acts may differ in various jurisdictions, they all have a common purpose: to protect the public. The title of *nurse* can legally be used *only* by an individual who is licensed as a registered nurse or a licensed practical or vocational nurse.

54 During your nursing education program, you will develop, clarify, and internalize professional values. The National Federation of Licensed Practical Nurses Inc. has identified specific standards (Box 1-2 ■). LPNs/LVNs in all areas of practice should adhere to these standards.

OUR WORK SETTINGS

55 In the past, the acute care hospital was the major practice setting open to most nurses. Today the LPN/LVN works in hospitals, clients' homes, community agencies, ambulatory clinics, health maintenance organizations, and skilled nursing facilities. See also Chapter 38 for a description of opportunities available to the LPN/LVN.

56 LPNs/LVNs work under their own license under direct supervision of a physician or a registered nurse. LPNs/LVNs may be involved in clinical planning meetings because of their expertise, but they are required to do this less than other licensed healthcare providers. Their primary duty is to deliver care to the client.

Professional Organizations for LPN/LVN Students and Graduates

57 When a professional organization is in place to oversee the operation of a group, it becomes a profession rather than an occupation. Several organizations oversee the profession of practical/vocational nursing.

NATIONAL ASSOCIATION FOR PRACTICAL NURSE EDUCATION AND SERVICE

58 The National Association for Practical Nurse Education and Service (NAPNES) was established in 1941. This was the first national organization for the practical/vocational level of nursing. NAPNES was responsible for the accreditation of LPN/LVN education programs from 1945 until 1984. Students can join this organization, and NAPNES publishes a journal called *The Journal of Practical Nursing.*

NATIONAL LEAGUE FOR NURSING

59 The National League for Nursing, formed in 1952, is an organization of both individuals and agencies. In 1961, the NLN established the

BOX 1-2

Nursing Practice Standards for the Licensed Practical/Vocational Nurse

Education

The licensed practical/vocational nurse:

1. Shall complete a formal education program in practical nursing approved by the appropriate nursing authority in a state.
2. Shall successfully pass the National Council Licensure Examination for Practical Nurses.
3. Shall participate in initial orientation within the employing institution.

Legal/Ethical Status

The licensed practical/vocational nurse:

1. Shall hold a current license to practice nursing as an LP/VN in accordance with the law of the state wherein employed.
2. Shall know the scope of nursing practice authorized by the Nursing Practice Act in the state wherein employed.
3. Shall have a personal commitment to fulfill the legal responsibilities inherent in good nursing practice.
4. Shall take responsible actions in situations wherein there is unprofessional conduct by a peer or other health care provider.
5. Shall recognize and commit to meet the ethical and moral obligations of the practice of nursing.
6. Shall not accept or perform professional responsibilities that the individual knows (s)he is not competent to perform.

Practice

The licensed practical/vocational nurse:

1. Shall accept assigned responsibilities as an accountable member of the health care team.
2. Shall function within the limits of educational preparation and experience, as related to the assigned duties.
3. Shall function with other members of the health care team in promoting and maintaining health, preventing disease and disability, caring for and rehabilitating individuals who are experiencing an altered health state, and contributing to the ultimate quality of life until death.
4. Shall know and utilize the nursing process in planning, implementing, and evaluating health services and nursing care for the individual patient or group.
   a. Planning: The planning of nursing includes:
      1. Assessment of health status of the individual patient, the family, and community groups
      2. Analysis of the information gained from assessment
      3. Identification of health goals
   b. Implementation: The plan for nursing care is put into practice to achieve the stated goals and includes:
      1. Observing, recording, and reporting significant changes that require intervention or different goals
      2. Applying nursing knowledge and skills to promote and maintain health, to prevent disease and disability, and to optimize functional capabilities of an individual patient
      3. Assisting the patient and family with activities of daily living and encouraging self-care as appropriate
      4. Carrying out therapeutic regimens and protocols prescribed by an RN, physician, or other persons authorized by state law
   c. Evaluation: The plan for nursing care and its implementations are evaluated to measure the progress toward the stated goals and will include appropriate persons and/or groups to determine:
      1. The relevancy of current goals in relation to the progress of the individual patient
      2. The involvement of the recipients of care in the evaluation process
      3. The quality of the nursing action in the implementation of the plan
      4. A reordering of priorities or new goal setting in the care plan
      5. Shall participate in peer review and other evaluation processes.
      6. Shall participate in the development of policies concerning the health and nursing needs of society and in the roles and functions of the LP/VN.

Continuing Education

The licensed practical/vocational nurse:

1. Shall be responsible for maintaining the highest possible level of professional competence at all times.
2. Shall periodically reassess career goals and select continuing education activities that will help to achieve these goals.
3. Shall take advantage of continuing education opportunities that will lead to personal growth and professional development.
4. Shall seek and participate in continuing education activities that are approved for credit by appropriate organizations, such as the NFLPN.

(continued)

Specialized Nursing Practice

The licensed practical/vocational nurse:

1. Shall have had at least one year's experience in nursing at the staff level.
2. Shall present personal qualifications that are indicative of potential abilities for practice in the chosen specialized nursing area.
3. Shall present evidence of completion of a program or course that is approved by an appropriate agency to provide the knowledge and skills necessary for effective nursing services in the specialized field.
4. Shall meet all of the standards of practice as set forth in this document.

Source: National Federation of Licensed Practical Nurses, Inc.

Council for Practical Nursing Programs. This arm of the organization assumed responsibility for promoting the interests of LPNs/LVNs in the NLN. All of these organizations provide continuing education opportunities and publish literature of interest to the LPN/LVN.

NATIONAL FEDERATION OF LICENSED PRACTICAL NURSES

60 In 1949, Lillian Custer founded the National Federation of Licensed Practical Nurses (NFLPN). This organization is considered to be the official membership organization for LPNs and LVNs. Affiliate memberships are also available for those interested in the work of NFLPN but who are not LPNs/LVNs.

61 NFLPN welcomes LVN/LPN students as members. NFLPN provides leadership for nearly 1 million licensed practical and vocational nurses employed in the United States. It also fosters high standards of practical/vocational nursing education and practice so that the best nursing care will be available to every client.

62 The NFLPN serves as the central source of information on what is new and changing in practical/vocational nursing education and practice on the local, state, and national level. The organization is a three-tiered concept of local, state, and national enrollment. By participating in local, state, and national meetings and conferences, the practical/vocational nursing student can learn firsthand how a professional organization works to maintain the professional status of the membership. NFLPN also encourages continuing education and publishes a quarterly magazine, *Practical Nursing Today.* Through relationships with the National Council of State Boards of Nursing and the U.S. Congress, the NFLPN enables policy makers to better understand the role of practical/vocational nursing in the nation's healthcare delivery system (NFLPN, 2003).

Student Organizations

HEALTH OCCUPATIONS STUDENTS OF AMERICA (HOSA)

63 HOSA is a nationally recognized technical career student organization, which was founded in 1976. HOSA provides a unique program of leadership and team-building development, motivation, and recognition experience. HOSA is an instructional tool integrated into the health careers classroom by the instructor. It is *intracurricular* (occurring within the framework of the school curriculum). It reinforces technical skills and supports service to the community. HOSA helps to develop the "total person." The national organization is made up of health occupations students from 42 affiliated states and Puerto Rico. HOSA's membership is made up of secondary, postsecondary, and collegiate students. Healthcare professionals, alumni, and business and industry members are welcome. There is also an associate membership category for students who are interested in health careers but who are not enrolled in a program. Through participation, the LPN/LVN student can network with other health career students. Involvement in a student organization demonstrates to students the benefits of participating in professional organizations once they have graduated.

Reading Comprehension Check

As you answer the questions below, try to label the question type. The first example is done for you.

1. As used in the sentence, "This text is designed to help you recognize and overcome those challenges as well as to appreciate the rewards," the word *overcome* means
   a. surrender.
   (b.) rise above.
   c. fall down.
   d. struggle.

   Question Type: Vocabulary in Context

2. "In some states, they are part of high schools. In others, they are in community college settings, vocational training centers, or private schools" (p. 400). The term *vocational* could be replaced with
   a. fractional.
   b. unprofessional.
   c. congressional.
   d. occupational.

   Question Type: ____________________

3. In the sentence, "Some students find it helpful to make up their own study questions; they anticipate what instructors might ask by using information from class notes," a synonym for the word *anticipate* is
   a. misunderstand.
   b. predict.
   c. miscalculate.
   d. underestimate.

   Question Type: ____________________

4. As used in the sentence, "It may have been a long time since you studied a subject that really mattered to you, or you may have recently been in school and studied with serious commitment," an antonym for the word *commitment* is
   a. dedication.
   b. obligation.
   c. indifference.
   d. promise.

   Question Type: ____________________

5. The main idea of the chapter is that
   a. pursuing nursing as a career is a poor choice.
   b. aspiring nursing students should learn about the challenges of the nursing profession to overcome them and succeed.
   c. nursing is not a rewarding career because most graduates almost never find lucrative jobs.
   d. only people from a certain ethnic group can succeed as nurses.

   Question Type: ____________

6. Examples of techniques such as outlining and studying with another group are offered to support the idea that
   a. nursing students are better off studying alone.
   b. students can be easily distracted by others in the study group.
   c. nursing students can use these techniques to study effectively.
   d. outlining will make it even more difficult for students to stay focused.

   Question Type: ____________________

7. Which of the following is *not* one of the suggestions for time management on page 399?
   a. Use a blank calendar or planner for the whole year.
   b. Schedule study time by writing it on the calendar or planner.
   c. Delete due dates, tests, homework, and projects as they are assigned.
   d. Schedule personal time for relaxation and being with other people.

   Question Type: ______________

8. "Bring four or five questions with you to discuss with the group. This can be especially helpful if you are having difficulty understanding certain concepts" (page 399).

   It can be inferred from the above passage that
   a. students cannot join a study group if they bring only two questions.
   b. nursing students are not allowed to ask more than five questions in one session.
   c. asking questions for clarification during a group discussion can enable students to comprehend complex ideas.
   d. students do not have to attend the sessions regularly.

   Question Type: ______

9. "If you are able to narrow your choice to two options, don't spend too much time deciding between them. More likely than not, your first impression is correct. Once you have identified your choice, don't go back and change it unless you later figure out the correct response with absolute certainty" (page 399).

   It can be concluded from the statement that
   a. if students spend much time deciding between two options, they are likely to choose the correct answer.
   b. it is always a good idea to go back and change the answer.
   c. if students second-guess themselves, they are likely to choose the incorrect answer.
   d. more likely than not, the first impression is incorrect.

   Question Type: ______

10. The authors' purpose in writing this chapter is to
    a. deter prospective students from choosing the nursing profession.
    b. convince students that it is extremely difficult to graduate from a nursing program.
    c. discourage students from pursuing nursing as a career.
    d. encourage students to enter the field of nursing.

    Question Type: ______________

11. What is the overall tone of the chapter?
    a. intimidating
    b. informative
    c. sorrowful
    d. malicious

    Question Type: __________

12. Which of the following is *not* a fact?
    a. The first nursing school in the world was started in India in about 250 B.C.

b. Wald and Mary Brewster founded the Henry Street Settlement, and Visiting Nurse Service, which provided nursing and social services, and also organized educational and cultural activities.
c. It is a good idea to break a study session down into segments.
d. Florence Nightingale established the Nightingale Training School for Nurses in 1860.

Question Type: ______________

13. Which of the following statements is an opinion?
    a. Although Nightingale died in 1910, her influence continues in nursing today.
    b. Clara Barton was a schoolteacher who volunteered as a nurse during the American Civil War.
    c. Lavinia Dock participated in protest movements for women's rights that resulted in the 1920 passage of the Nineteenth Amendment to the U.S. Constitution, which granted women the right to vote.
    d. St. Camillus de Lellis started out as a soldier and later turned to nursing.

    Question Type: ______________

14. The overall pattern of organization used in Table 1-2 is
    a. comparison and contrast.
    b. chronological order.
    c. spatial order.
    d. definition.

    Question Type: ______________

15. Which of the following patterns of organization is used in Table 1-3?
    a. comparison and contrast
    b. definition
    c. chronological order
    d. cause and effect

    Question Type: ______________

READING 5

Short Story

MyReadingLab

Visit Chapter 7: Life Science in MyReadingLab to complete the Reading 5 activities.

A Nurse's Story

Pre-Reading Questions

Discuss the following questions with your classmates, or consider them independently.

1. In your opinion, what qualities do you think one must possess to be a good nurse? Be specific.
2. Do you think that registered nurses are well compensated for their humanistic services? What, in your opinion, is a decent salary for a full-time nurse?
3. Some people believe that nurses play an even more important role than a physician in helping the patient recover. Do you agree with this position? Why, or why not?

A Nurse's Story (An Excerpt)

By Peter Baida

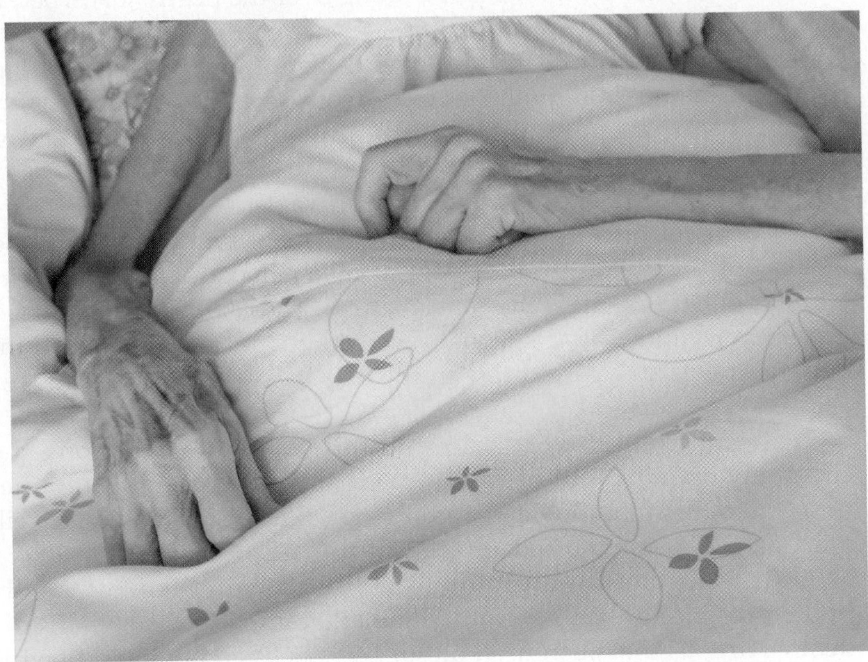

1 The pain in Mary McDonald's bones is not the old pain that she knows well, but a new pain. Sitting in her room in the Booth-Tiessler Geriatric Center, on the third floor, in the bulky chair by the window, Mary tries to measure this pain. She sits motionless, with a grave expression on her face, while the cheerless gray sky on the other side of the window slowly fades toward evening.

2 Mary McDonald knows what this pain comes from. It comes from a cancer that began in her colon and then spread to her liver and now has moved into her bones. Mary McDonald has been a nurse for forty years, she has retained the full use of her faculties, and she understands perfectly where this pain comes from and what it means.

3 "Union?" Eunice Barnacle says. "What do I want with a union?"

4 "Miss Barnacle," Mary McDonald says, looking at her from the chair by the window, "do you think you're paid what you're worth?"

5 Miss Barnacle is a lean, sharp-featured black woman in her middle twenties, with a straight nose, small teeth, wary eyes, and a straightforward manner, who joined the staff at Booth-Tiessler about a month ago. "This place can't afford to pay me what I'm worth," she says.

6 "That's certainly what they want you to believe, Miss Barnacle. May I ask a **nosy** question?"

7 "I suppose."

nosy
always trying to find out private information about someone or something

8 "What do they pay you, Miss Barnacle?"

9 "That's my business."

10 "Eight-fifty per hour. Is that about right, Miss Barnacle?"

11 Miss Barnacle, in her white uniform, turns pale. She has paused with her hand on the doorknob, looking over the neatly made bed to the chair where Mary McDonald is sitting. Pearl gray light falls on a walker near the chair. Mary McDonald's hands are closed in her lap, over a green-and-gold quilt. Her face is solemn.

12 "Do you think this place *knows* what you're worth, Miss Barnacle?"

13 A good death. That's what everyone wants.

14 Mary McDonald still remembers, from her first year as a nurse, well over forty years ago, a little old woman named Ida Peterson, with a tumor in her neck near the carotid artery. The call bell at the nurses' station rang, and Mary McDonald walked down the hall, opened the door, and was struck squarely in the face by something warm, wet, and red.

15 Blood from a ruptured artery gushed out of Mrs. Peterson's tracheotomy opening, out of an ulcerated site on her neck, out of her nose, out of her mouth. Mary was stunned. She saw blood on the ceiling, on the floor, on the bed, on the walls.

16 Mrs. Peterson had wanted to die a peaceful, dignified death, in the presence of her husband. She had wanted to die a "natural" death. Now, as the life poured out of her, she lifted her hand to wipe her nose and mouth. With wide eyes, she looked at the blood on her hand.

17 Ida Peterson had wanted a natural death, in the presence of her husband, and she was getting one, in the presence of Mary McDonald, a nurse she had known for five minutes.

18 Mrs. Peterson's blue, terrified eyes looked into Mary McDonald's eyes for the full fifteen minutes it took her to bleed to death. Her hand gripped Mary's hand. Mary did nothing. Her orders were to allow Mrs. Peterson to die a natural death.

19 Mary had never before seen an arterial bleed. She still remembers the splash of blood on her face when she stepped into Mrs. Peterson's room. She still remembers how long it took Mrs. Peterson to die. You wouldn't think that a little woman could have so much blood in her.

20 "They tell me you were some good nurse," Eunice Barnacle says, taking Mary's blood pressure.

21 "I'm still a good nurse," Mary McDonald says.

22 "They tell me you helped start the nurses' union, over at the hospital."

23 "Who tells you?"

24 "Mrs. Pierce."

25 "Ah."

26 "Mrs. Pierce says those were the days."

27 "Maybe they were."

28 Eunice loosens the blood pressure cup from Mary's arm. "Mrs. McDonald?"

29 "Yes?"

30 "That union—" Eunice hesitates, looking at the floor.

31 "What about it?" Mary says.

32 "You think it helped you?"

33 Booth's Landing is an **unpretentious** town with a population of nearly nine thousand, located among gently rolling hills on the east side of the Hudson River, fifty miles north of New York City. In every generation, for as long as anyone can remember, the Booths and the Tiesslers have been the town's leading families. The Booth family descends from the town's founder, Josiah Booth, a merchant of the Revolutionary War period whom local historians describe as a miniature version of John Jacob Astor. The Tiessler family descends from Klaus Tiessler, an immigrant from Heidelberg who in 1851 founded a factory that makes silverware.

unpretentious simple, honest

34 "A nice town," people who live in Booth's Landing say. "A nice place to bring up a family." That's how Mary McDonald has always felt, and that's what she has always said when people ask her about the place.

35 In every generation, for as long as anyone can remember, one member of the Booth family has run the town's bank, and one member of the Tiessler family has run the silverware factory. The town also supports one movie theater, two sporting goods stores, two opticians, three auto repair shops, one synagogue, and nine churches. Most of the people who die in Booth's Landing were born there. Many have died with Mary McDonald holding their hands.

36 Oh, not so many, Mary thinks, pursing her lips. Not that she has kept count. Why would anyone keep count?

37 You can do worse than to live and die in a place like Booth's Landing. The air is fresh. The streets are clean and safe. The leading families have paid steady attention to their civic and **philanthropic** responsibilities. If you're sick in Booth's Landing, you go to the Booth-Tiessler Community Hospital. If you want to see live entertainment, you buy tickets for the latest show at the Booth-Tiessler Center for the Performing Arts. If you can no longer take care of yourself, you arrange to have yourself deposited in the Booth-Tiessler Geriatric Center.

philanthropic a philanthropic person or institution gives money to people who are poor or who need money in order to do something good or useful

38 At the Booth-Tiessler Community College, nearly fifty years ago, Mary McDonald fulfilled the requirements for her nursing degree. Now, sitting by her window on the third floor in the Geriatric Center, looking over the cherry tree in the yard below toward the river, with the odor of overcooked turnips floating up from the kitchen on the first floor, she finds her mind **drifting** over her life, back and forth, here and there, like a bird that hops from place to place on a tree with many branches.

drifting moving along

Reading with a Critical Eye

1. At the beginning of the story, Baida tells us that Mary knows the old pain well and is beginning to understand the new pain. In your opinion, what do you think her new pain means?
2. Mary asks Miss Barnacle, "Do you think you're paid what you're worth?" Why does she ask Miss Barnacle the question, and how do you think a person's worth is measured?
3. Why does Miss Barnacle turn pale when Mary tells her that she is paid $8.50 an hour? Be specific.
4. The author tells us, "A good death. That's what everyone wants." Discuss this statement with your classmates and give specific examples to either support or refute it.
5. The story ends with the sentence, " . . . she finds her mind drifting over her life, back and forth, here and there, like a bird that hops from place to place on a tree with many branches." Discuss what the bird and the tree with many branches symbolize. Be sure to give specific reasons to support your answer.

Reading Comprehension Check

1. As used in the sentence, "She sits motionless, with a grave expression on her face, while the cheerless gray sky on the other side of the window slowly fades toward evening, " the word *grave* means
   a. unimportant. c. serious.
   b. insignificant. d. trivial.
2. In the sentence, "Mary McDonald has been a nurse for forty years, she has retained the full use of her faculties, and she understands perfectly where this pain comes from and what it means," the word *retained* can be replaced with
   a. preserved. c. discarded.
   b. wasted. d. decimated.
3. "Miss Barnacle is a lean, sharp-featured black woman in her middle twenties, with a straight nose, small teeth, wary eyes, and a straightforward manner, who joined the staff at Booth-Tiessler about a month ago."
   The word *lean* in the above sentence means
   a. obese. c. thin.
   b. overweight. d. emaciated.
4. The overall tone of the opening paragraph is
   a. amusing. c. cheerful.
   b. grim. d. humorous.

5. "'Miss Barnacle,' Mary McDonald says, looking at her from the chair by the window, 'do you think you're paid what you're worth?'"

   Which of the following conclusions can be drawn from Mary McDonald's question?
   a. Miss Barnacle is an overpaid employee.
   b. Miss Barnacle's compensation is more than she deserves.
   c. Miss Barnacle is completely satisfied with her salary.
   d. Miss Barnacle is an underpaid employee.
6. When Mary McDonald tells Miss Barnacle that she most probably earns $8.50 an hour, Miss Barnacle turns pale. It can be inferred that
   a. Miss Barnacle makes at least twice as much.
   b. Miss Barnacle is embarrassed that Mary McDonald knows her actual salary.
   c. Miss Barnacle is excited that Mary McDonald does not know the truth.
   d. Mary McDonald is completely mistaken about Miss Barnacle's compensation.
7. Which of the following is *not* a fact?
   a. Mrs. Ida Peterson had a tumor in her neck near the carotid artery.
   b. Mrs. Ida Peterson wanted to die a dignified death in the absence of her husband.
   c. Mrs. Ida Peterson looked into Mary McDonald's eyes for fifteen minutes before she died.
   d. Mary McDonald's orders were to allow Mrs. Ida Peterson to die a natural death.
8. Which of the following is an opinion?
   a. Approximately nine thousand people live in Booth's Landing.
   b. Klaus Tiessler was an immigrant from Heidelberg who founded a silverware factory in Booth's Landing in 1851.
   c. Booth's Landing is a nice place to raise children.
   d. Booth's Landing is located on the east side of the Hudson River, fifty miles north of New York City.
9. The details in paragraph 37 are offered to support the main point that
   a. it is unwise to raise children in a place like Booth's Landing.
   b. Booth's Landing is a nice place to bring up a family.
   c. senior citizens are not required to make a deposit to their checking accounts.
   d. Booth's Landing is a better place for singles.
10. For the concluding paragraph, the author uses an organizational pattern that
    a. defines technical terms in the field of nursing.
    b. explains the reasons for Mary McDonald's decision to become a nurse.
    c. looks at Mary McDonald's life in chronological order.
    d. contrasts Mary McDonald and Miss Barnacle.

Contemporary Issues in the Discipline

Dr. Hawa Abdi and her daughters (including Dr. Deqo Mohamed) work in Somalia, where they have treated and provided refuge for thousands of over 90,000 women and children displaced by Somalia's civil war. In addition to being an OB/GYN, Dr. Abdi is also a lawyer. She opened her first Somalian clinic in 1983; today she and her daughters run a hospital, a school, and a refugee camp (now called the Hawa Abdi Village) with little help from charities, many of whom consider Somalia too dangerous to navigate.

READING 6

Lecture /Interview (TED Talk)

MyReadingLab

Visit Chapter 7: Life Science in MyReadingLab to complete the Reading 6 activities.

Mother and Daughter Doctor-Heroes

Pre-Reading Activity

Before reading the following transcript of Dr. Hawa Abdi's and her daughter Dr. Deqo Mohamed's speech, you can watch the talk itself here: www.ted.com/talks/mother_and_daughter_doctor_heroes_hawa_abdi_deqo_mohamed (Courtesy of TED). As you listen to the video presentation, take notes. (See the note-taking activity on p.190 for some pointers.)

After reading the transcript, you will answer some open-ended questions about some of the issues the doctors raise in their speech. Finally, you will formulate questions for the two doctors about issues pertinent to medicine or nursing and answer them from their perspective.

Hawa Abdi + Deqo Mohamed: Mother and Daughter Doctor-Heroes

December 2010

1 **Hawa Abdi:** Many people—20 years for Somalia—[were] fighting. So there was no job, no food. Children, most of them, became very malnourished, like this.

2 **Deqo Mohamed:** So as you know, always in a civil war, the ones affected most [are] the women and children. So our patients are women and children. And they are in our backyard. It's our home. We welcome them. That's the camp that we have in now 90,000 people, where 75 percent of them are women and children.

3 **Pat Mitchell:** And this is your hospital. This is the inside.

4 **HA:** We are doing C-sections and different operations because people need some help. There is no government to protect them.

5 **DM:** Every morning we have about 400 patients, maybe more or less. But sometimes we are only five doctors and 16 nurses, and we are physically getting exhausted to see all of them. But we take the severe ones, and we reschedule the other ones the next day. It is very tough. And as you can see, it's the women who are carrying the children; it's the women who come into the hospitals; it's the women [are] building the houses. That's their house. And we have a school. This is our bright—we opened [in the] last two years [an] elementary school where we have 850 children, and the majority are women and girls. *(Applause)*

6 **PM:** And the doctors have some very big rules about who can get treated at the clinic. Would you explain the rules for admission?

7 **HA:** The people who are coming to us, we are welcoming. We are sharing with them whatever we have. But there are only two rules. First rule: there is no clan distinguished and political division in Somali society. [Whomever] makes those things we throw out. The second: no man can beat his wife. If he beat, we will put [him] in jail, and we will call the eldest people. Until they identify this case, we'll never release him. That's our two rules. *(Applause)* The other thing that I have realized, that the woman is the most strong person all over the world. Because the last 20 years, the Somali woman has stood up. They were the leaders, and we are the leaders of our community and the hope of our future generations. We are not just the helpless and the victims of the civil war. We can reconcile. We can do everything. *(Applause)*

8 **DM:** As my mother said, we are the future hope, and the men are only killing in Somalia. So we came up with these two rules. In a camp with 90,000 people, you have to come up with some rules or there is going to be some fights. So there is no clan division, and no man can beat his wife. And we have a little storage room where we converted a jail. So if you beat your wife, you're going to be there. *(Applause)* So empowering the women and giving the opportunity—we are there for them. They are not alone for this.

9 **PM:** You're running a medical clinic. It brought much, much needed medical care to people who wouldn't get it. You're also running a civil society. You've created your own rules, in which women and children are getting a different sense of security. Talk to me about your decision, Dr. Abdi, and your decision, Dr. Mohamed, to work together—for you to become a doctor and to work with your mother in these circumstances.

10 **HA:** My age—because I was born in 1947—we were having, at that time, government, law and order. But one day, I went to the hospital—my mother was sick—and I saw the hospital, how they [were] treating the doctors, how they [are] committed to help the sick people. I admired them, and I decided to become a doctor. My mother died, unfortunately, when I was 12 years [old]. Then my father allowed me to proceed [with] my hope. My mother died in [a] gynecology complication, so I decided to become a gynecology specialist. That's why I became a doctor. So Dr. Deqo has to explain.

11 **DM:** For me, my mother was preparing [me] when I was a child to become a doctor, but I really didn't want to. Maybe I should become an historian, or maybe a reporter. I loved it, but it didn't work. When the war broke out—civil war—I saw how my mother was helping and how she really needed the help, and how the care is essential to the woman to be a woman doctor in Somalia and help the women and children. And I thought, maybe I can be a reporter and doctor gynecologist. *(Laughter)* So I went to Russia, and my mother also, [during the] time of [the] Soviet Union. So some of our character, maybe we will come with a strong Soviet background of training. So that's how I decided [to do] the same. My sister was different. She's here. She's also a doctor. She graduated in Russia also. *(Applause)* And to go back and to work with our mother is just what we saw in the civil war—when I was 16, and my sister was 11, when the civil war broke out. So it was the need and the people we saw in the early '90s—that's what made us go back and work for them.

12 **PM:** So what is the biggest challenge working, mother and daughter, in such dangerous and sometimes scary situations?

13 **HA:** Yes, I was working in a tough situation, very dangerous. And when I saw the people who needed me, I was staying with them to help, because I [could] do something for them. Most people fled abroad. But I remained with those people, and I was trying to do something—[any] little thing I [could] do. I succeeded in my place. Now my place is 90,000 people who are respecting each other, who are not fighting. But we try to stand on our feet, to do something, little things, we can for our people. And I'm thankful for my daughters. When they come to me, they help me to treat the people, to help. They do everything for them. They have done what I desire to do for them.

14 **PM:** What's the best part of working with your mother, and the most challenging part for you?

15 **DM:** She's very tough; it's most challenging. She always expects us to do more. And really when you think [you] cannot do it, she will push you, and I can do it. That's the best part. She shows us, trains us how to do and how to be better [people] and how to do long hours in surgery—300 patients per day, 10, 20 surgeries, and still you have to manage the camp—that's how she trains us. It is not like beautiful offices here, 20 patients, you're tired. You see 300 patients, 20 surgeries and 90,000 people to manage.

16 **PM:** But you do it for good reasons. *(Applause)* Wait. Wait.

17 **HA:** Thank you.

18 **DM:** Thank you. *(Applause)*

19 **HA:** Thank you very much.

20 **DM:** Thank you very much.

Reading with a Critical Eye

1. Dr. Hawa Abdi mentions that the civil war in Somalia went on for 20 years. Why do you think the civil war lasted so long in Somalia? Be specific.
2. Dr. Deqo Mohamed notes that in a civil war, women and children are affected most. Why is it that even though usually men fight and kill each other in a civil war, women and children suffer most?
3. Rather than considering Somalian women helpless victims of the civil war, Dr. Hawa Abdi claims that a woman is the strongest person in the world. Do you concur with her strong statement? Give specific examples to support your answer.
4. Despite the advanced technology in medical science, it is unusual for doctors in the United States to perform 20 surgeries per day and see 300 patients. How, in your opinion, do Drs. Hawa Abdi and Deqo Mohamed manage to do that every day with extremely limited resources in Somalia?

Imagined Interview: If you had the opportunity to interview Drs. Hawa Abdi and Deqo Mohamed in person, what would you ask them? With a partner, compose three questions for them.

Question 1. ______________________________

Question 2. ______________________________

Question 3. ______________________________

Interview Challenge: In a group, ask two students to play Drs. Hawa Abdi and Deqo Mohamed. These students should carefully consider the doctors' views, outlined clearly in the TED Talk, and try to answer the questions from their perspective on health care.

Chapter Recap

Now that you have made it through a full chapter focusing on Nursing, let's review the chapter's reading content, skill focus, and vocabulary to gain a better understanding of what you have learned.

Recap Activity 1: A Quick Glance

In 60 seconds, write brief answers to the following two questions. You may wish to share your answers with your classmates or with your instructor.

1. What is one thing you learned from this chapter?

____

____

____

____

____

2. What was your favorite reading in the chapter? Explain.

____

____

____

____

____

Now discuss what you wrote in a small group. Do not read what you wrote. Paraphrase yourself!

Recap Activity 2: Summary Writing

Choose your favorite reading from this chapter and write a summary containing the main idea and some major details. Keep in mind that the key to summary writing is to convey the author's ideas accurately, but to relay this information in your own words. Last but not least, be sure to include reminder phrases and appropriate transitions.

Recap Activity 3: Internet Research on a Theme of Interest

Think about the choice you just made in Activity 2 concerning which reading in the chapter was your favorite.

What was the theme of your chosen reading?

Theme = ____

Using a search engine such as Google or Bing, go online and locate a quality reading on the same theme as your favorite chapter reading.

Write a three- to five-sentence summary of the reading that you found from your Internet research. Be sure to include the author's most important points in your summary.

Title of Reading	*Article Source*	*Summary of the Reading (in your own words)*

Recap Activity 4: Reinforcing the Skill

Working with a partner, read the following paragraph. Then discuss what strategies you can use to recognize the pattern of organization. It is important for you to understand that you are not being asked to recognize the pattern of organization. Instead, your task is to discuss with your peer the strategies you can use to determine the pattern of organization—that is, discuss with your partner how you will recognize the overall pattern of organization of the following passage.

> Most tests given in nursing programs will be objective, multiple-choice tests. These are the same types of questions used on the NCLEX-PN® exam. Multiple-choice questions can evaluate your knowledge of facts, as well as your ability to apply that knowledge within a client care scenario. Each question will consist of a stem and answer choices. Read each question completely in order to understand what is being asked. Then read each of the choices. Try to eliminate one or more of the choices. Examine each choice to see if anything is incorrect within the answer itself. Watch out for choices that are correct and accurate on their own, but that do not answer the question as it is written.

What strategies can you use to recognize the pattern of organization of the passage above?

Strategy 1: ______________________________

Strategy 2: ______________________________

Recap Activity 5: Recycling Vocabulary

With a partner, locate the following discipline-specific vocabulary items, review them in context, and try to define the terms without using a dictionary. The first example is done for you.

Word and Context Location	*Sentence Containing the Word*	*Meaning in This Context*
illiteracy p. 344, example 10	She notes that nurses should be aware of potential barriers to communication such as **illiteracy** or the patient experiencing stress from learning of a new diagnosis.	Inability to read and write
diverse p. 347, para. 7	Nurses who work with a **diverse** population could consider seeking out diversity training.	
profession p. 355, question 7	To attract students from other disciplines, nursing schools are putting new emphasis on second bachelor's degrees that can be completed in about a year and are introducing master's degrees meant to bring non-nurses into the **profession.**	
urgent p. 353, para. 18	This qualified him to work at an **urgent** care office where he could perform administrative and clinical duties like taking medical histories and recording vital signs.	
addiction p. 387, para. 1	New research suggests as many as 10 to 20 percent of nurses and nursing students may have substance abuse and **addiction** problems, this even as a severe nursing shortage threatens medical care delivery across the globe.	
intervention p. 388, para. 4	Providing early **intervention** and assistance is essential to help nurses and nursing students to recover from an addictive disorder.	
ethnic p. 398, para. 4	Your classmates may represent a variety of life experiences, educational backgrounds, and **ethnic**/cultural influences.	
symptoms p. 402, para. 28	You will find that observing signs and **symptoms** of an illness firsthand is far more impressive than reading about them.	

Word and Context Location	*Sentence Containing the Word*	*Meaning in This Context*
geriatric p. 413, para. 2	Sitting in her room in the Booth-Tiessler **Geriatric** Center, on the third floor, in the bulky chair by the window, Mary tries to measure this pain.	______________________
colon p. 413, para. 2	It comes from a cancer that began in her **colon** and then spread to her liver and now has moved into her bones.	______________________

Further Explorations

Books

1. *Chicken Soup for the Nurse's Soul: 101 Stories to Celebrate, Honor and Inspire the Nursing Profession* by Jack Canfield, Mark Victor Hansen, Nancy Mitchell-Autio, and LeAnn Thieman. HCI. This collection offers inspiring true stories of nurses making sacrifices in their everyday, life-impacting work.
2. *A Cup of Comfort for Nurses: Stories of Caring and Compassion,* Colleen Sell, Editor. Adams Media. This book shares the stories of more than fifty dedicated nurses who provide care to people selflessly but who are underappreciated.

Movies

1. *Miss Evers' Boys* (1997). Based on a true story, this movie tells a gripping tale of medical research conducted on humans in Alabama. The protagonist, devoted Nurse Eunice Evers (played by Alfre Woodard), is faced with a dilemma when government funding is withdrawn.
2. *Nursing Diaries* (2006). In this three-episode series produced by CBS, the real-life experience of nurses at Massachusetts General Hospital is followed. Each episode shows the challenges nurses face in their work.

Internet Sites

1. www.aacn.nche.edu/Media/NewsReleases/06Survey.htm
   This American Association of Colleges of Nursing Web site provides useful information on choosing a nursing program in the United States. If you are seriously considering pursuing a nursing career, this is a helpful site for you.
2. http://allnurses.com/
   Nurses from all over the world find a nursing community here and learn, communicate, and network.

Study TIP

Patterns of Organization across Academic Disciplines

Overview

As you take college courses, it will be important for you to understand that textbooks are organized using specific patterns of organization particular to the academic discipline. Identifying discipline-specific patterns of organization will enable you to understand the author's approach and how information is organized in each chapter. For example, if you are reading a nursing textbook, you will notice that most information is factual, and the two most common patterns of organization are cause and effect and problem–solution.

A great majority of the academic areas covered in this book fall into the categories of social science (education, criminal justice, psychology, and political science), life and physical science (Health, Environmental Science, and Nursing), and business (business and e-commerce). The table shown here lists patterns of organization corresponding to these three academic areas.

You will notice that disciplines such as psychology, criminal justice, and political science fall within the academic area of social science. Textbooks in each of these disciplines use ***listing***, comparison and contrast, and cause and effect patterns of organization. In the academic area of life and physical science, disciplines such as nursing, environmental science, and health rely on ***process, cause-and-effect, and comparison-and-contrast patterns of organization.*** Finally, in the academic area of business, the disciplines of business and Internet marketing use ***definition, illustration,*** comparison-and-contrast, and classification patterns of organization to impart discipline-specific knowledge to the students.

Table 7-1 Discipline-specific Patterns of Organization

Academic Area	*Disciplines*	*Patterns of Organization*
Social Science	Psychology Criminal Justice Political Science	Listing Comparison and Contrast Cause and Effect
Life and Physical Science	Nursing Environmental Science Health	Process Cause and Effect Problem–Solution
Business	Business E-Commerce	Definition Illustration/Examples Problem–Solution Classification

The next table makes this point clear. It shows how each pattern of organization is used in a particular discipline. Notice that the left column shows a specific pattern of organization, and the right column lists discipline-specific examples. For example, the discipline of Political Science may use the comparison and contrast pattern of organization to describe the similarities and differences between different forms of government such as democracy and communism. Likewise, the discipline of psychology also may incorporate the comparison and contrast pattern of organization to delineate the outcome of two types of counseling. Study Table 7-2 to familiarize yourself with the types of patterns of organization that are typical of specific disciplines.

Table 7-2 Patterns of Organization and Discipline-specific Examples

Pattern of Organization	*Discipline-specific Examples*
Comparison and Contrast	1. Political Science—comparison of different forms of government 2. Criminal Justice—discussion of different types of prison systems 3. Psychology—comparing the effects of two different counseling strategies
Cause and Effect	1. Environmental Science—the debilitating effects of human activity on the environment 2. Criminal Justice—a violation of law and sentencing 3. Health—consuming fast food and obesity-related illnesses 4. Nursing—treatment and the patient's health 5. Psychology—parenting and the child's behavior 6. Political Science—the presidential debate and voters choosing a candidate
Listing	1. Psychology—various signs of stress 2. Criminal Justice—using forensic science for different purposes 3. Political Science—law enforcement in different social situations
Process	1. Nursing—how to take a patient's temperature 2. Environmental Science—how a species evolves under certain conditions 3. Health—various stages of weight loss
Problem–Solution	1. Nursing—dealing with an uncooperative patient 2. Environmental Science—deforestation's effect on biodiversity 3. Business—improving the sales of an unsuccessful product 4. E-Commerce—increasing site traffic by attracting consumers
Definition	1. Business—different definitions of entrepreneurship 2. Criminal Justice—defining terms in the specific context of a law, or an offense
Illustration	1. E-Commerce—a portal and examples of its services and resources 2. Health—examples of the debilitating effects of obesity
Classification	1. Business—different categories of businesses from multinational conglomerates to small businesses 2. E-Commerce—Business sites and different categories such as business-to-business, business-to-consumer

Learning Implications

Familiarizing yourself with the specific patterns of organization that various disciplines incorporate will help you read the textbooks with relative ease and success. You will be able to understand the author's purpose and to follow the lectures easily. Once you understand that the discipline you are studying relies on the cause and effect patterns of organization, you will understand that a phenomenon is caused by a single factor or several factors. Similarly, learning that studying certain disciplines such as environmental science and health require you to focus on a problem and find a solution will enable you to complete the assignments more accurately.

PSYCHOLOGY Nature Versus Nurture

8

"Everything that irritates us about others can lead us to an understanding of ourselves."

CARL JUNG

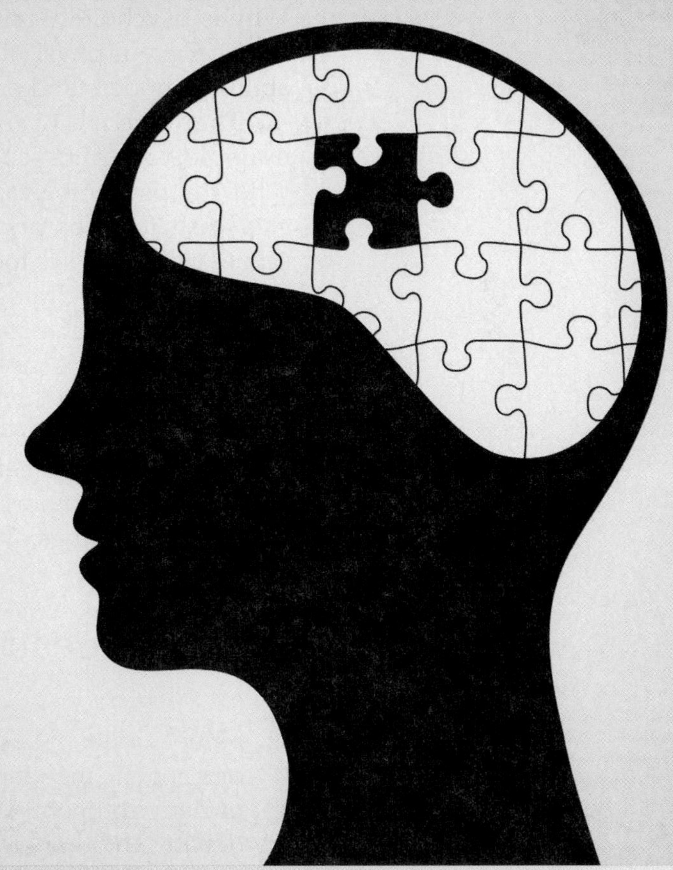

Learning Objectives

AFTER READING THIS CHAPTER, YOU SHOULD BE ABLE TO:

1. Identify foundational knowledge about the discipline of psychology.
2. Recognize and evaluate an author's argument.
3. Use a reading journal.
4. Identify and assess evidence for an author's claim.

INTRODUCTION TO THE FIELD OF PSYCHOLOGY

Psychology is formally defined as the scientific study of the behavior of individuals and their mental processes. Many psychologists seek answers to such fundamental questions as: What is human nature? and Why do we behave the way we do? They study such phenomena as cognition, perception, emotion, personality, and interpersonal relationships. Why is psychology relevant to our daily lives? Psychological research focuses on our physical and mental health, our personal growth, and our ability to understand one another, all topics that regularly impact us.

There are many subdivisions within the field of psychology. For example, clinical psychologists focus on understanding, preventing, and relieving psychologically based distress or dysfunction; cognitive psychologists focus on perception, memory, judgement, and reasoning; and school psychologists focus on students' behavior in educational settings. Each area of psychology offers the opportunity to undertake research and apply research-based findings in a real-world setting.

This chapter focuses primarily on issues related to the "nature versus nurture" debate, which frames many research questions in the field of psychology. How similar are identical twins who were separated at birth? Why do people lie? How much of an effect does TV violence have on children's behavior? These are some of the topics that are explored in the chapter readings.

Preview Questions

1. Some people believe that human behavior is largely determined by our genetic makeup, while others claim that we are the products of our environment. Where do you stand on the nature versus nurture debate? In other words, how much of human nature do you think is genetically determined, and how much of it do you think is shaped by environmental factors such as parenting, education, and so on?
2. A famous psychologist, John Gray, wrote a book entitled *Men Are from Mars, Women Are from Venus*. His central point was that men and women think and behave as if they are from different planets. If you think this is true, first discuss in what ways men and women behave differently. Then offer some explanations to account for these differences.
3. Many studies have focused on identical twins separated at birth and raised far away from each other by different parents. Most of these studies found remarkable similarities between the twins. Do you think this is just a coincidence, or is there a reasonable explanation for these similarities?

4. Most people believe that children learn their first language mainly through imitation; that is, they learn simply by listening and repeating. Yet, research indicates that young children all around the globe learn their first language without getting explicit instructions from their parents or teachers. How do we explain children acquiring a language so effortlessly? How do we explain the fact that adults struggle with mastering a second language while young children pick up second languages with relative ease?
5. Humans have inhabited the planet earth for thousands of years. Yet, we have not learned how to coexist in peace and harmony. Do you believe that violence is a natural part of our behavior? In other words, is conflict built into our psychological makeup?

Writing on The Wall

After you have discussed the preview questions with your classmates, post your responses to two of them on your class blog, which we refer to as The Wall. Review others' postings and respond to at least two of your classmates' posts that grab your interest. Remember the guidelines for blogging and commenting etiquette (see p. 15)! If your class is not using a shared blog, your instructor may ask you to record your individual or collective responses to the preview questions in another form.

EXERCISE 8.1 Interpreting a Cartoon

Reverse Psychology

Examine the cartoon shown above and in pairs answer the following questions.

1. What is amusing about this cartoon?
2. In your opinion, what message is the cartoonist trying to convey to the reader?

Discipline-specific Vocabulary: Understand Key Terms in Psychology

One of the most efficient ways to acquire academic vocabulary is to study key terms that are thematically connected. As you begin your college-level studies, it is critical that you internalize vocabulary terms that relate to the academic disciplines that make up most 100-level content courses. For example, a student taking an Introduction to Psychology course should be able to apply such terms as *analysis, stimuli,* and *therapeutic* in both spoken and written forms.

EXERCISE 8.2 Brainstorming Vocabulary

Directions: What associated words come to mind when you think of the world of psychology? Work with a partner and write down as many related words as you can think of in a period of five minutes.

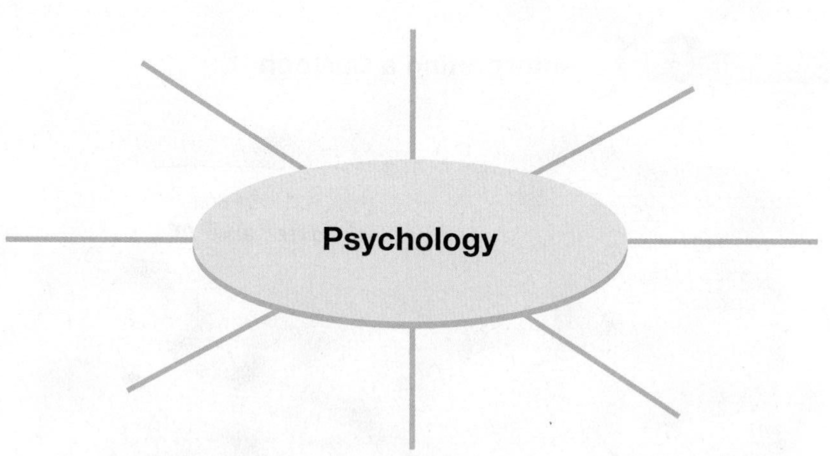

Fishing for Synonyms and Antonyms

In your written work, you will often need to use synonyms and antonyms (see p. 24 to review these terms) in order to paraphrase statements or claims made by writers.

EXERCISE 8.3 Determining Synonyms and Antonyms from Context

Directions: Read the following ten (10) discipline-specific words culled from the readings in this chapter and shown in the context of the sentences in which they appeared. In the space provided after each sentence, write a synonym or antonym for the highlighted term, as directed.

Discipline-specific Word Bank for Psychology

analysis	**behavior**	**correlation**	**human nature**
insight	**traumatic**	**motivation**	**self-esteem**
therapeutic	**genetics**		

1. "At about this time Freud began a new project, his own self-**analysis**, which he pursued by analyzing his dreams."
   A synonym for *analysis* is ________.
2. "Another study looked into the brains of people who qualify as *pathological liars*—these are individuals who lie with sufficient regularity that the **behavior** is considered abnormal."
   A synonym for *behavior* is ____________.
3. "Freedman in his research paper acknowledges a kind of **correlation**: the more violence children watch, the more aggressive they become. But he emphasizes that that finding does not equate to a causal relationship."
   An antonym for *correlation* is __________.
4. "What is **human nature**? Psychology answers this question by looking at processes that occur within individuals as well as forces that arise within the physical and social environment."
   A synonym for *human nature* is ______________________________
   ________________.
5. "Even so, psychologists draw broadly from the **insights** of other scholars."
   An antonym for *insight* is ________.
6. "Freud learned of a hysterical patient who a colleague had treated successfully by hypnotizing her and then tracing her symptoms back to **traumatic** events she had experienced at her father's deathbed."
   A synonym for *traumatic* is ______________.

7. "If you've ever had a job you didn't like, you probably know a lot about what it means to suffer from a lack of **motivation**."
   An antonym for *motivation* is ____________.
8. "Some factors operate within the individual, such as genetic makeup, **motivation**, intelligence level, or **self-esteem**. These inner determinants tell something special about the organism."
   A synonym for *self-esteem* is ________________.
9. "By the turn of the century, Freud had developed his **therapeutic** technique."
   An antonym for *therapeutic* is _______.
10. "Twins really do force us to question what is it that makes each of us who we are. Since meeting Elyse, it is undeniable that **genetics** play a huge role—probably more than 50 percent."
    A synonym for *genetic* is ______.

EXERCISE 8.4 Matching Terms with Definitions

Match the word in Column A with the definition in Column B. Put the letter representing the correct definition in the space preceding each term.

Column A	Column B
Word	**Definition**
1. _____ analysis	a. actions by which an organism adjusts to its environment
2. _____ traumatic	b. the relationship between two variables
3. _____ human nature	c. biological, emotional, or social impulses that activate and direct behavior
4. _____ self-esteem	d. curative
5. _____ genetics	e. the study of the inheritance of physical and psychological traits from ancestors
6. _____ correlation	f. general psychological characteristics, feelings, and behavioral traits of humankind
7. _____ behavior	g. the ability to see clearly and intuitively into the nature of a complex person, situation, or subject
8. _____ therapeutic	h. detailed examination
9. _____ motivation	i. psychologically painful
10. _____ insight	j. confidence; self-regard

EXERCISE 8.5 Choosing the Right Word

In the following sentences, fill in the blanks with a word from the terminology bank that makes the sentence grammatically correct and meaningful.

behavior	therapeutic	correlation	human nature	traumatic
insight	motivation	genetics	self-esteem	analysis

1. The school psychologist realized that the failing student lacked ________ to do his work.
2. At night, the woman would relive the _______ episodes of her difficult childhood.
3. A detailed ______ of Jennifer's behavior revealed that she was extremely depressed.
4. Recent studies have shown that ______ plays a much larger role in our chances of getting certain diseases than we had previously thought.
5. Studies have shown a strong ________ between smoking and lung cancer.
6. The tendency toward jealousy and violence may be part of our __________.
7. Some experts attribute differences between boys and girls to learned _______.
8. The shy student in the back of the classroom suffers from low ________.
9. The war veteran found his discussions with his counselor to be very ________
10. The veteran psychologist shared his years of _____ into the workings of the human mind with his young students.

In-Class Survey on Gender Roles

To explore stereotypes, ask two classmates, one male and one female, to complete these sentences with the first thought that comes to their mind. Please take notes as they respond to your questions. Use a separate sheet of paper, if needed. The goal is to compare the differences in the two respondents' answers. Orally report your findings to the class.

Question	Respondent 1	Respondent 2
The most difficult emotion for a man to display is …		
The most difficult emotion for a woman to display is …		
Women tend to be better than men at …		
Men tend to be better than women at …		
Men get depressed about …		
Women get depressed about …		
Men are most likely to compete over …		
Women are most likely to compete over …		

READING 1

Textbook

MyReadingLab

Visit Chapter 8: Psychology in MyReadingLab to complete the Reading 1 activities.

Why and How Do People Lie?

Pre-Reading Questions

Discuss the following questions with a partner:

1. Have you ever told a "white lie"? Under what circumstances do you think it is OK to tell a white lie?
2. Why are some people habitual liars?
3. How can you tell if someone is lying or telling you the truth?

Why and How Do People Lie?

By Richard J. Gerrig and Philip G. Zimbardo[1]

Psychology in Your Life

1 In this **section** on language use, we have emphasized that people aspire to be cooperative conversationalists. For example, we suggested that people follow the principle, "Try to make your contribution one that is true." However, we know that people often fall away from this standard. When people were asked to keep diaries of the lies they told, most averaged one or two a day (DePaulo et al., 2003). But why do people lie? When the lies are relatively mild, more people lie for psychological reasons (e.g., they wish to spare themselves embarrassment)

[1] From Richard J. Gerrig and Philip G. Zimbardo, *Psychology and Life,* Discovering Psychology Edition, 18th Ed., p. 249. © 2009. Printed and electronically reproduced by permission of Pearson Education, Inc., Upper Saddle River, New Jersey.

than for personal advantage (e.g., they wish to avoid an unpleasant chore). However, when lies become more serious, the motives for lying **shift** in the direction of personal advantage. In one study, participants were asked to reveal the most serious lie that they had ever told (DePaulo et al., 2004). People quite frequently committed serious lies to conceal affairs or other forbidden forms of social contact. People felt that they were entitled to cheat on their partners and lied in service to that sense of entitlement. Thus the lies worked for personal advantage.

2 Let's focus on the mental **processes** that people use to lie. Should it be easier or harder to tell a lie than to tell the truth? The answer is: It depends (DePaulo et al., 2003). Suppose you are asked, "What did you do last night?" If you choose to lie spontaneously, it might be harder for you to formulate a lie than to tell the truth. However, if you have prepared your lie in advance—because you anticipate the awkward question—you might produce your lie with great fluidity. Still, lies and truths differ from each other in some consistent ways. A study that reviewed the literature on the content of lies reported that liars provide fewer details in their accounts than do people who are telling the truth (DePaulo et al., 2003). In addition, liars' accounts were consistently less plausible and less fluent than truthful accounts.

plausible believable, credible

3 These results suggest that speakers may engage different mental processes to produce their lies. To test this hypothesis, researchers have begun to analyze patterns of brain activity that underlie truth-telling and lying. In one study, participants were asked to lie or tell the truth about their participation in an incident in which a gun was fired in a hospital (Mohamed et al., 2006). To make the experience of lying as real as possible, participants in the *guilty* condition actually fired a starter pistol (loaded with blanks) in the testing room. Participants in both the *guilty* and *not-guilty* conditions answered a series of questions while undergoing fMRI scans. Participants in the guilty condition received instructions to lie about their role in the incident. The fMRI scans revealed that several areas of the brain were more active for lying than for truth-telling. For example, brain regions responsible for planning and emotion were harder at work when participants prepared their lies.

4 Another study looked into the brains of people who qualify as *pathological liars*—these are individuals who lie with sufficient regularity that the **behavior** is considered **abnormal** (by the types of *DSM-IV* criteria we describe in Chapter 14). The overall structure of brains of the pathological liars were compared using MRI to the brains of matched controls (Yang et al., 2005). Those brain comparisons revealed consistent differences in the prefrontal cortex. The pathological liars, for example, had more of the type of brain tissue that allows neurons to communicate with each other. Prefrontal cortex is a region of the brain that plays an important role in planning—suggesting that the pathological liars are particularly well equipped to plan their lies. These results, however, leave open the question of cause and effect: Did pathological liars start life with brains of this type (which, perhaps, caused or allowed them to lie frequently) or did frequent lying change their brains?

Reading with a Critical Eye

In a small group, discuss the following reflection questions, which will guide you toward a deeper understanding of the reading.

1. At the beginning of the text, we read about a research finding showing that when a group of people were asked to keep diaries of their lies, most averaged one or two lies a day. Is this result surprising to you? Why, or why not?
2. Research indicates that when people lie mildly, they more often do so for psychological reasons than for personal advantage. What is the difference between lying for psychological reasons and lying for personal advantage?
3. According to the reading, is it easier to tell a lie or to tell the truth? What factors determine the answer to this question?
4. What question remains unanswered in the last lines of the article?
5. If you were to design a scientific study related to the phenomenon of lying, what aspects of lying would you want to learn more about? Explain.

Reading Comprehension Check

1. In the first sentence of the reading, the word *aspire* means
   a. sweat.
   b. aim.
   c. decline.
   d. translate.
2. What is the topic of this reading passage?
   a. people
   b. lying to your family
   c. factors related to the act of lying
   d. confessions about lying
3. What is the main idea of the second paragraph?
   a. People produce lies with great fluidity.
   b. It is always easier to lie.
   c. It is easier to tell the truth.
   d. It is sometimes easier to tell a lie than to tell the truth, depending on the situation.
4. A study reported that liars provide fewer details in their accounts than do people who are telling the truth. Is this a statement of fact or opinion?
   a. fact
   b. opinion
   c. neither fact nor opinion
   d. none of the above
5. Brain regions responsible for planning and emotion are mentioned as
   a. truth tellers.
   b. dormant during the lying process.
   c. more active when people are preparing to lie.
   d. unresponsive.

6. A pathological liar is someone who
   a. lies occasionally.
   b. tells dangerous lies.
   c. lies regularly.
   d. has an occasional lapse.
7. What is the main idea of the final paragraph?
   a. The prefrontal cortex plays an important role in planning.
   b. Pathological liars' brain structures differ from the norm.
   c. pathological liars
   d. none of the above
8. The term *well equipped* in the final paragraph could be replaced by
   a. ready.
   b. unprepared.
   c. distinct.
   d. irrelevant.
9. What is the author's tone in this reading passage?
   a. emotional
   b. objective
   c. optimistic
   d. angry
10. What is the author's purpose in writing this article?
   a. to entertain
   b. to persuade
   c. to dissuade
   d. to inform

MyReadingLab

Visit Chapter 8: Psychology in MyReadingLab to complete the Reading 2 activities.

READING 2

Online Article (Radio Source)

'Identical Strangers' Explore Nature Vs. Nurture

Pre-Reading Questions

Answer the following questions before exploring the text:

1. Have you ever known any identical twins? If yes, did they have similar personalities?
2. In your view, how are identical twins different from the rest of us? Do identical twins have a deeper relationship than most siblings do?
3. What can scientists learn from the close study of identical twins?

'Identical Strangers' Explore Nature Vs. Nurture

By Joe Richman of Radio Diaries
October 25, 2007[2]

1 What is it that makes us who we really are: our life experiences or our DNA? Paula Bernstein and Elyse Schein were both born in New

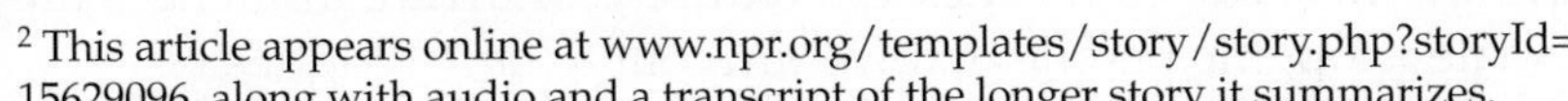

[2] This article appears online at www.npr.org/templates/story/story.php?storyId=15629096, along with audio and a transcript of the longer story it summarizes.

York City. Both women were adopted as infants and **raised** by loving families. They met for the first time when they were 35 years old and found they were "identical strangers."

2 Unknowingly, Bernstein and Schein had been part of a secret research project in the 1960s and '70s that separated identical twins as infants and followed their development in a one-of-a-kind experiment to **assess** the influence of nature vs. nurture in child development. Now, the twins, authors of a new memoir called *Identical Strangers*, are trying to uncover the truth about the study.

"I Have a Twin"

3 In 2004, Paula Bernstein received a phone call from an employee of Louise Wise Services, the agency where she had been adopted. The message: She had a twin who was looking for her. The woman told Bernstein her twin's name. "And I thought, I have a twin, and her name is Elyse Schein," Bernstein says.

4 Schein, who was living in Paris at the time, had been trying to find information about her birth mother when she learned from the adoption agency that she had a twin sister. The two women met for the first time at a cafe in New York City—and stayed through lunch and dinner, talking. "We had 35 years to catch up on. How do you start asking somebody, 'What have you been up to since we shared a womb together?' Where do you start?" Bernstein says.

Separated at Adoption

5 Soon after the sisters were reunited, Schein told Bernstein what she had found out about why they were separated: They were part of a study on nature vs. nurture. It was the only study of its kind on twins separated from infancy. Neither parents nor children knew the real subject of the study—or that the children had been separated from their identical twin.

6 "When the families adopted these children, they were told that their child was already part of an ongoing child study. But of course, they neglected to tell them the key element of the study, which is that it was child development among twins **raised** in different homes," Bernstein says.

A "Practically Perfect" Study

7 Peter Neubauer, a child **psychiatrist**, and Viola Bernard, a child psychologist and consultant to the Louise Wise agency, headed up the study. Lawrence Perlman, a research assistant on the study from 1968 to 1969, says Bernard had a strong belief that twins should be raised separately. "That twins were often dressed the same and treated exactly the same, she felt, interfered with their independent psychological development," Perlman says.

8 Lawrence Wright is the author of *Twins*, a book about twin studies. "Since the beginning of science, twins have offered a unique opportunity to study to what extent nature vs. nurture influences the way we develop, the people that we turn out to be," Wright says.

9 Wright notes that the Neubauer study differs from all other twin studies in that it followed the twins from infancy. "From a scientific point of view, it's beautiful. It's practically the perfect study. But this study would never happen today," Wright says.

Finding the True Story

10 The study ended in 1980, and a year later, the state of New York began requiring adoption agencies to keep siblings together. At that point, Bernstein says, Neubauer realized that public opinion would be so against the study that he decided not to publish it. The results of the study have been sealed until 2066 and given to an archive at Yale University. "It's kind of disturbing to think that all this material about us is in some file cabinet somewhere. And really for ourselves, we had to figure out what the true story was," Bernstein says. The sisters attempted to reach Neubauer, a distinguished and internationally renowned psychiatrist who serves on the board of the Freud Archives. Initially, he refused to speak to them.

No Remorse, No Apology

11 Eventually, he granted the women an unofficial interview—no taping or videotaping allowed. Bernstein says she had hoped Neubauer would apologize for separating the twins. Instead, he showed no remorse and offered no apology.

12 Neubauer has rarely spoken about the study. But in the mid-1990s, he did talk about it with Wright, the author of *Twins*. "[Neubauer] insisted that at the time, it was a matter of scientific **consensus** that twins were better off separated at birth and raised separately," Wright says. "I never found anything in the literature to support that."

13 The author also says Neubauer was "unapologetic" about the study, even though he admits that the project raised **ethical** questions about whether one has a right to or should separate identical twins. "It is very difficult to answer. It is for these reasons that these studies don't take place," Neubauer told Wright. Wright says that no such study will ever be done again—nor should it. But he acknowledges that it would be very interesting to learn what this study has to teach us.

"Different People with Different Life Histories"

14 As for Bernstein and Schein, getting to know each other has raised its own questions. "Twins really do force us to question what is it that makes each of us who we are. Since meeting Elyse, it is undeniable that genetics play a huge role—probably more than 50 percent," Bernstein says. "It's not just our taste in music or books; it goes beyond that. In her, I see the same basic personality. And yet, eventually we had to realize that we're different people with different life histories."

15 As much as she thinks the researchers did the wrong thing by separating the twins, Bernstein says she can't imagine a life growing up with her twin sister. "That life never happened. And it is sad, that as close as we are now, there is no way we can ever compensate for those 35 years," Bernstein says.

16 "With me and Paula, it is hard to see where we are going to go. It's really uncharted territory," Schein says. "But I really love her and I can't imagine my life without her." Neubauer declined to be interviewed for this story. Of the 13 children involved in his study, three sets of twins and one set of triplets have discovered one another. The other four subjects of the study still do not know they have identical twins.

Paula Bernstein (left) and Elyse Schein were reunited in 2004, when they were 35.

Reading with a Critical Eye

In a small group, discuss the following reflection questions, which will guide you toward a deeper understanding of the reading.

1. What was the goal of the secret research project that separated the two identical twins, Paula and Elyse?
2. Do you think this type of research project is ethical? Explain your viewpoint.
3. Paula said: "We had 35 years to catch up on. How do you start asking somebody, 'What have you been up to since we shared a womb together?' Where do you start?" What is Paula's point? Paraphrase this quotation.

4. What was Viola Bernard's (a child psychologist involved in the study) opinion on how identical twins should be raised? Do you agree? Explain.
5. What does Elyse say about her relationship with her identical twin sister near the end of the article? In your opinion, is this a happy or sad story? Explain.

Reading Comprehension Check

1. What is the topic of this article?
   a. research
   b. identical twins separated at birth
   c. It is best for identical twins to grow up together.
   d. identical twins
2. How did Paula find out that she had an identical twin sister?
   a. from her birth mother
   b. Her twin sister called.
   c. She received a phone call from the adoption agency.
   d. from the research project team
3. Why does Lawrence Wright, the author of a book on twins, say that a study like this "would never happen today"?
   a. It is too expensive to run.
   b. The adoption agencies wouldn't want to see the twins separated.
   c. Scientists already know enough about identical twins.
   d. This type of scientific study is considered unethical and wouldn't be permitted.
4. Neubauer, the lead scientist in the research study on twins, claimed that it was a matter of scientific consensus that twins were better off separated at birth and raised separately. Neubauer's claim is
   a. an opinion.
   b. a statement of fact.
   c. both fact and opinion.
   d. neither fact nor opinion.
5. After getting to know her twin sister, what is Paula Bernstein's view on the nature vs. nurture question in relation to twins?
   a. Genetics determines everything.
   b. The environment you grow up in determines who you are.
   c. She believes that genetics can explain about half of the picture.
   d. She is unclear on big questions relating to the nature of identical twins.
6. What are some examples given of ways in which the identical twins are similar?
   a. their taste in music
   b. their taste in books
   c. both a and b
   d. the men they date

7. Paula says: "And it is sad, that as close as we are now, there is no way we can ever compensate for those 35 years." The word *compensate* could be replaced by
   a. sell.
   b. make up for.
   c. hide away.
   d. object to.
8. How many of the thirteen original children involved in the research study know of the existence of their twin?
   a. about two-thirds
   b. none
   c. All of them have been informed.
   d. This information is not offered in the article.
9. What is the author's tone in this reading passage?
   a. angry
   b. objective
   c. sad
   d. confused
10. What is the main idea of the reading?
    a. Twins should never be separated at birth.
    b. Paula is thankful to have finally been introduced to her twin sister.
    c. Scientists do experiments to test theories related to nature vs. nurture.
    d. Two identical twins who were separated at birth were reunited as adults.

BIOGRAPHICAL PROFILE

Sigmund Freud

Courtesy of the Library of Congress

Sigmund Freud is considered the father of psychoanalysis. His revolutionary work marked the beginning of the modern age in psychology by providing the first explanation of the inner mental forces determining human behavior.

Sigmund Freud was born in 1856, in Freiberg, Moravia. Sigmund was the first child of his twice-widowed father's third marriage. He grew up in an atypical family structure, his mother halfway in age between himself and his father. When Sigmund was four, the family moved to Vienna, the capital city of the Austro-Hungarian monarchy. Freud would live in Vienna until the year before his death. Freud was raised in poor conditions, the housing was cramped and the family had to move often. By the time he was ten, Sigmund's family had grown and he had five sisters and one brother.

Freud was a superior student and passed his final examination at the top of his class, qualifying to enter the University of Vienna at the age of seventeen. His parents had recognized his academic gift from an early age, and although they had only four bedrooms for eight people, Sigmund had his own room throughout his school days. Freud received his doctor of medicine degree at the age of twenty-four. He fell in love and wanted to marry, but the low salary of a young scientist could not support a wife and family. Step by step, Sigmund built his career and was able to marry his fiancée four years later. Freud had six children, one of whom, his daughter Anna, became a world-famous psychologist herself.

During the last part of his medical residency, Freud received some money to pursue his neurological studies abroad. He spent four months at a clinic in Paris. Here, Freud first became interested in the phenomena of hysteria, cases in which a person complains of physical symptoms without a medical cause. He soon devoted his efforts to the treatment of hysterical patients with the help of hypnosis. Freud learned of a hysterical patient who a colleague had treated successfully by hypnotizing her and then tracing her symptoms back to traumatic events she had experienced at her father's deathbed. Freud's experiments with hypnosis led him to coauthor a groundbreaking work, *Studies on Hysteria* (1895).

At about this time, Freud began a new project, his own self-**analysis**, which he pursued by analyzing his dreams. The result of these studies was another important publication, *The Interpretation of Dreams* (1901). By the turn of the century, Freud had developed his **therapeutic** technique, dropping the use of hypnosis and shifting to the more effective and more widely applicable method of "free association." Beginning in 1902, Freud gathered a small group of interested colleagues on Wednesday evenings for presentations of psychoanalytic papers and discussion. This was the beginning of the psychoanalytic movement. The first International Psychoanalytic Congress was held in Salzburg in 1908.

Freud spent his last year in London, England, after having been evacuated from Nazi-controlled Vienna, and died on September 23, 1939. While many of Freud's theories have been criticized by contemporary psychologists, the influence of his scientific investigations is limitless.

Some Questions for Group Discussion

1. We learn that Freud grew up in a large family in cramped quarters. How might this experience have influenced his later work in the field of psychology?
2. Much of Freud's early work focused on the treatment of hysteria through the technique of hypnosis. Do you believe hypnosis is a legitimate method of treatment? What purposes does hypnosis serve?
3. One of Freud's groundbreaking works was *The Interpretation of Dreams* (1901). Freud believed we can learn much about ourselves through the analysis of our dreams. Do you agree that our dreams are meaningful? Explain.

Biographical Internet Research

Find out about another historical figure in Psychology online, selecting one from the following list, and share a biographical profile with your classmates:

- Dr. Laura Schlessinger
- Dr. Phil
- Howard Gardner
- Anna Freud

SKILL FOCUS: Argument

Imagine you read the following claim in a newspaper or magazine article:

"Women live longer than men because they talk much more."

With a partner, answer the following questions about the above claim.

1. Would you believe the author's argument simply because you saw it in writing?
2. Would you be more likely to believe it if you learned that the person who said it was an expert? Explain.
3. What kind of proof or evidence would make such a claim more credible to you?

As we discussed in our focus on fact versus opinion in Chapter 6, critical thinkers do not believe everything they read. Anyone can offer an argument, or a position on an issue, but a good reader, like a judge in a courtroom, will evaluate the strength of an argument based on the quality of the evidence given and on the logical reasoning used to support the claim. Note that when we discuss an author's argument, we are not referring to the more common definition of *argument* as a verbal dispute or disagreement, but as an author's opinion on an issue.

Recognizing an Author's Argument

Before you can evaluate the strength of an argument, you must first identify the issue being discussed and the author's position on the issue. Look at the example paragraph below.

Example

The new generation of parents are less likely to spank their kids than those of thirty or fifty years ago. Nowadays, at least in American culture, physical punishment of children is often viewed more as a sign of parental impatience than a sign of parental attentiveness.

What is the topic/issue being discussed? What argument is the author (a pediatrician) trying to make?

The issue under discussion is whether or not parents should spank their children. But if you said that the author's argument is that parents should not spank their children you are assuming an opinion the author clearly did not express.

The author's argument is that today's parents are less accepting of spanking kids than older generations used to be. There is no mention of this pediatrician's personal feeling about hitting kids. It may very well be the case that this pediatrician is discussing the change in societal views on spanking in order to build an argument that hitting your kids is wrong, but you would have to read more to find out if this is the direction the author is going.

It is important not to get distracted by your own personal view on an issue when trying to recognize an author's argument. A reader might feel strongly about a topic, let's say, that it is perfectly fine to spank kids, and misread the argument an author is putting forth.

Another helpful hint is to consider the identity of the author in relation to his or her position on an issue. So, for example, a corporate executive with Coca-Cola might be more likely to argue in favor of maintaining soda in vending machines than a school principal would. The TV producer of a horror show is more likely to make an argument in support of permitting violence on TV than would a concerned parent of three young children.

PRACTICING THE SKILL: IDENTIFYING ARGUMENTS

After each of the following passages, determine both the topic and the argument put forth by the writer.

Passage 1

If you've spent time with older adults, you've probably heard them make casual claims like, "My brain just doesn't work as well as it used to work." Researchers have believed for a long time that older brains function differently from younger brains. However, as brain-imaging techniques have become more available as research tools, an understanding of those changes has grown. Images of the brain at work reveal consistent differences in patterns of brain activity over the adult years.

(Excerpted from the text Psychology and Life, *Richard J. Gerrig and Philip G. Zimbardo, Discovering Psychology Edition, 18th ed. Boston: Pearson Allyn and Bacon, 2009,* p. 320.*)*

What is the topic?

____

What is the author's argument?

____

Passage 2

How do you decide when and what you should eat? To answer this question, first think about the impact of culture. For example, people in the United States typically eat three daily meals at set times; the timing of those meals relies more on social norms than on body cues. Moreover, people often choose what to eat based on social or cultural norms. Would you say "yes" if you were offered a free lobster dinner? Your answer might depend on whether you were an observant Jew (in which case you would say "no"), or a vegetarian (in which case your answer would still depend on whether you are the type of vegetarian who eats seafood).

(From *Psychology and Life,* p. 355)

What is the topic?

____

What is the author's argument?

____

Passage 3

Why are some people happier than others? You might think this question has an easy answer: Aren't some people happier than others because better things happen to them? That's true, in part, but you might be surprised to learn that genetics has a large impact on how happy people are as they make their way through life.

(From *Psychology and Life,* p. 388)

1. What is the topic?

____

2. What is the author's argument?

____

Passage 4

I'm not surprised that adults find children today to be spoiled—but I don't think this is a new phenomenon either. I think it's unfair to fault one single generation of such an old, historically common parent-child dynamic. The way I see it, in one fashion or another, we are all spoiled, but in different ways. Our society is such that everyone feels entitled, even parents.

(from Mandela Gardner in an online blog, Seattlepi.com)

What is the topic?

____

What is the author's argument?

____

Evaluating the Strength of an Author's Argument

Once you have identified the topic being discussed and determined the author's argument, then you may consider how credible, or believable, the author's claim is. Remember, if the author's purpose is to persuade the reader of his or her general theory, opinion, or way of thinking, it is the author's responsibility to make a convincing case for the ideas put forth. It is the reader's responsibility to critically evaluate any arguments presented by the writer and to determine whether or not the author has made a strong case in support of his or her views.

Identify the Types of Support the Author Presents

Pay attention to how the author backs up his or her argument(s). The following is a short list of types of support authors make use of to back up an idea or claim.

Support for Arguments

1. **Fact-based. As discussed in Chapter 6, facts are "testable."**
   a. **Research results.** A writer might mention his or her or another researcher's study.
   b. **Statistics.** Using numerical data taken from survey work or other research models
   c. **Factual examples from the real world.** Citing reference facts (For example, "China is the most populous country in the world.")
   d. **Case studies.** Research focusing on formal observation
2. **Experiential-based. Support coming from experience.**
   a. **Logical reasoning.** An argument can grow from logical assumptions (For example, "If you take their bottles away while they are drinking, most babies will cry.")
   b. **Observations.** Many arguments are based on what we have seen and then analyzed (For example, "Once most five-year-olds realize that they are passing an ice cream shop, they are not going to let their parents go on without first demanding an ice cream.")
   c. **Expert viewpoints.** (For example, "There is a consensus among leading experts that hypnosis plays a critical role in the identification of criminal suspects.")

Consider Whether the Support Is Relevant

Sometimes an author will back up an argument with support that is not relevant to the point they are trying to make; that is, the support does not relate to their claim. Consider the following example.

Example

Clearly, the best way to deal with an alcohol problem is to see an addiction counselor.

Now, you might very well hold the same opinion as the author, but an argument should not be considered well supported simply because you agree with it! The author might back up his or her claim by adding, "Studies have shown that the majority of addiction counselors have dealt with alcohol-related issues." What is the connection between the fact that most addiction counselors often work with alcohol abusers *and* the claim that seeing an addiction counselor is the best solution? If you can't find a connection, that's because there isn't any! Don't be fooled by weak reasoning.

Make a Final Evaluation: Is the Argument Logical and Believable?

To be believable, the author's argument must be based on logic or relevant evidence. If an author's argument seems shaky, spend a little more time with it and try to pinpoint what it is in the argument that you are skeptical about.

- Is the support not relevant to the claim?
- Is the author trying to persuade you with emotional argumentation that is not backed up by facts?
- Does the argument go against something you already know to be true about the topic/issue?

Whatever the case, don't be too shy to challenge arguments you come across in newspaper and magazine editorials and articles, textbook readings, nonfiction books, and other reading sources. Ask questions about what others say to be true, and check up on the "facts" they use to strengthen their claims.

PRACTICING THE SKILL: EVALUATING ARGUMENTS

Read and evaluate these five passages, all on the topic of "bullies."

Passage 1

A bully can turn something like going to the bus stop or recess into a nightmare for kids. Bullying can leave deep emotional scars that last for life. And in extreme situations, it can culminate in violent threats, property damage, or someone getting seriously hurt.

If your child is being bullied, there are ways to help him or her cope with it on a day-to-day basis *and* lessen its lasting impact. And even if bullying isn't an issue in your house right now, it's important to discuss it so your kids will be prepared if it does happen.

(from *Kids Health,* http://kidshealth.org/parent/emotions/behavior/bullies.html. June 2007)

Argument: ____________________

Support Type for Argument: ____________________

Strength of Argument (your judgment from 1 to 5, with 5 being the highest): ____________________

Justification for Your Evaluation: ____________________

____

Passage 2

There are all kinds of reasons why young people bully others, either occasionally or often. Do any of these sound familiar to you?

- Because I see others doing it
- Because it's what you do if you want to hang out with the right crowd
- Because it makes me feel stronger, smarter, or better than the person I'm bullying
- Because it's one of the best ways to keep others from bullying me

Whatever the reason, bullying is something we all need to think about. Whether we've done it ourselves . . . or whether friends or other people we know are doing it . . . we all need to recognize that bullying has a terrible effect on the lives of young people. It may not be happening to you today, but it could tomorrow. Working together, we can make the lives of young people better.[3]

Argument: ____________________

Support Type for Argument: ____________________

Strength of Argument (your judgment from 1 to 5): ____________________

Justification for Your Evaluation: ____________________

____

Passage 3

Bullies are usually people who are just as uncomfortable as you are. Usually it's hard for them to make friends and the only way to get to know other people is by bullying them. Don't worry if you are being bullied, there are a lot of things you can do. You can talk to your parents and tell them what is going on. You could also go and talk to your teacher; your teacher is there to help you with your problems. You could also try to talk to the kid, maybe the bully didn't even realize that he (or she) was hurting you.[4]

[3] (from "Why Do Kids Bully?" U.S. Department of Health and Human Services, Health Resources and Services Administration, http://stopbullyingnow.hrsa.gov/kids/why-kids-bully.aspx)

[4] (from Danielle, a blogger on pbskids.org. © It's My Life, http://pbskids.org/itsmylife)

Argument: ______________________________

Argument: ______________________________

Support Type for Argument: ______________________________

Strength of Argument (your judgment from 1 to 5): ______________

Justification for Your Evaluation: ______________________________

____

____

Passage 4

There aren't any real bullies. Bullies are just a figment of a young person's imagination. They are kids sitting next to you who are bigger and stronger. They are neighborhood kids who might scare you from time to time. The media has pushed this idea of bullies into our heads, but life is how it has always been. Kids simply like to play around and get physical sometimes.

Argument: ______________________________

Support Type for Argument: ______________________________

____

Strength of Argument (your judgment from 1 to 5, with 5 being the highest): ______________________________

Justification for Your Evaluation: ______________________________

____

Passage 5

All bullies should be given meds for hyperactive behavior. One study reported that 80 percent of those identified as neighborhood bullies suffer from ADD (attention deficit disorder). If we recognize these kids not as simply evil and aggressive, but as children who need medical attention, we can better solve the problem and keep our own children safe.

Argument: ______________________________

Support Type for Argument: ______________________________

____

Strength of Argument (your judgment from 1 to 5, with 5 being the highest): ______________________________

Justification for Your Evaluation: ______________________________

____

____

The following reading will allow you to apply the skills learned in this chapter.

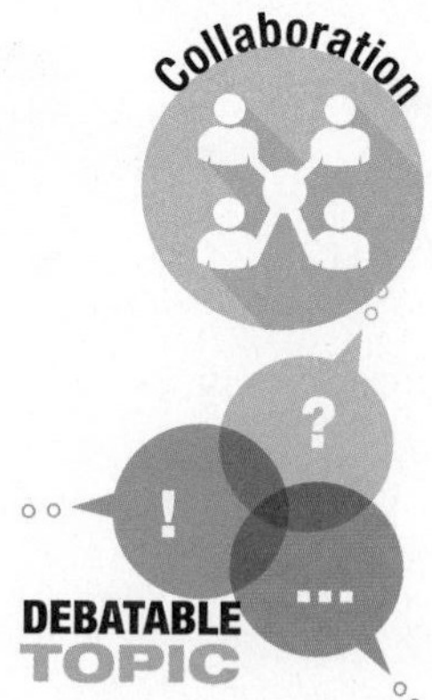

Recommended Debate Topic: Can television be blamed for people's bad behavior?

Brainstorm other debate topics related to psychology with your peers, and present your ideas to your instructor for approval.

Your suggested debate topics:

a. ____________________

b. ____________________

c. ____________________

The following articles will help prepare you for the debate because each takes a pro or con position on the debate topic.

READING 3A

(Pro) Online Editorial

MyReadingLab

Visit Chapter 8: Psychology in MyReadingLab to complete the Reading 3A activities.

No Debate: TV Violence Harms Kids

Pre-Reading Questions

Answer the following questions before exploring the text:

1. Why are violent TV shows so popular with young people?
2. Are violent youth naturally violent, or does their environment make them so? Explain.
3. If all TV violence were banned and all shows depicted only peaceful scenes, would youth violence disappear or at least decrease dramatically?

As you read the article, consider how many arguments are offered, and the kinds of support given to back up these arguments. Highlight each argument you locate.

No Debate: TV Violence Harms Kids

By **Linda S. Mintle, PhD, http://DrLindaHelps.com**

1 TV violence is harmful to kids. Practice these seven **strategies** to protect your kids.

2 TV violence is harmful to kids. The American Psychological Association's Task Force on Television and Society published a 1992 report stating there is a link between TV violence and aggression. We don't need more studies. We need **media** to pay attention to the reams of data we already have available on TV violence.

3 Television violence has three **major** effects on children:

1. Increases in aggression. Studies of preschoolers who watched violent cartoons and other violent shows compared to children who didn't showed these differences: more arguing, disobeying of rules, uncompleted tasks and more **impulsivity**. Furthermore, Leonard Eron, Ph.D. from the University of Illinois, found that elementary age kids who watched lots of hours of TV were more aggressive as teenagers.

impulsivity
acting without thinking or planning

2. Kids are more fearful of the world. This is simply common sense but backed by research. George Gerbner, Ph.D. at the University of Pennslyvania, found that kids' TV shows contain about 20 acts of violence each hour. Watching these violent acts influence kids to view the world as a fearful place.

3. Kids are less sensitive to others. Watching violence makes you less bothered by it. And kids who watch violence are slower to get help for someone in trouble.

4 Knowing this, what can you as a parent do about TV violence?

- Be **aware** of research findings and make every effort to monitor your child's viewing habits.
- Limit the number of hours your child watches, i.e., limit **exposure**.
- Watch one episode of every program. This way you'll know the type and frequency of violence shown.
- Talk about what he/she sees. Ask what motivated the person to act violently and what were the effects of violent behavior on others?
- Turn off the TV or ban specific shows. This is not an extreme act considering what **exposure** does to kids.
- Encourage alternatives to TV viewing, preferably not violent video games or movies that have similar negative effects.
- Find programs that demonstrate healthy behavior and positive moral values.

5 Obviously, doing the above means you have to be involved in your child's life and take time to monitor and supervise media. Time is usually a parent's worst enemy, but the sacrifice is worth it.

6 You should also talk to other parents about what studies tell us. Many parents are simply unaware of the negative effects violent media have on their children and do not want to intentionally harm them. Point out the facts. The more we all know, the more we can do to curb violence in our society.

Reading Comprehension Check

1. The author believes we need more

a. studies.
b. media attention.
c. both a and b
d. psychologists.

2. Preschoolers watching violent TV programs showed all of the following behaviors except
   a. excessive sleeping.
   b. disobeying rules.
   c. more impulsivity.
   d. more arguing.
3. In the sentence, "Make every effort to **monitor** your child's viewing habits," the word *monitor* could be replaced by
   a. ignore.
   b. neglect.
   c. keep track of.
   d. disrupt.
4. What is the author's tone in this reading passage?
   a. frustrated
   b. objective
   c. contented
   d. instructive
5. What is the main idea of the reading?
   a. The only solution to this societal problem is to turn off the television.
   b. Close monitoring and helpful strategies can protect children from the harmful effects of TV violence.
   c. Research suggests that kids are more fearful of the world if they watch violent programming.
   d. Watching too much television will lower one's cognitive ability to make rational choices.
6. What are a few arguments Dr. Mintle makes about TV and violence?
   - Argument: ____________________
   - Argument: ____________________
   - Argument: ____________________
7. What types of evidence does she use to support her claims?
   - Support Type: ____________________
   - Support Type: ________
   - Support Type: ____________________

READING 3B

(Con) Journal Article

MyReadingLab

Visit Chapter 8: Psychology in MyReadingLab to complete the Reading 3B activities.

TV Violence Doesn't Lead to Aggressive Kids, Study Says

Pre-Reading Questions

With a partner, answer the theme-related questions below:

1. Do you believe it is possible that some children are born naturally aggressive? Explain.
2. What are some possible factors that might lead a child to behavioral problems in school?

3. How much do people change from childhood to adulthood? Do you believe that most aggressive children grow up to be aggressive adults? Explain.

As you did with the first reading, highlight each argument you come across as you read.

TV Violence Doesn't Lead to Aggressive Kids, Study Says

By **Joan Oleck, *School Library Journal***
May 23, 2007

1 Violent television does not lead to violent children, says a new **research** paper from the Media Institute, countering a recent, much-heralded report from the **Federal** Communications Commission (FCC) stating that the opposite is true.

2 "Television Violence and Aggression: Setting the Record Straight," **refutes** an April FCC report that called for laws to curb certain television content for children.

refutes
proves that a statement or idea is not correct or fair

3 "The debate is not over," writes Jonathan Freedman, author of the paper and a professor of psychology at the University of Toronto, who also criticizes both the American Academy of Pediatrics and the American Psychological Association for wrongly characterizing previous studies of TV's effects on children. The pediatrics group in particular, he says, used "wildly inaccurate figures" in its studies.

4 "I don't think this kind of television affects children's aggression at all," Freedman, who has been studying children and television for two decades, told *SLJ*. "Some kids may get very excited and look like they're more aggressive because they're very excited. But if they watch some nonviolent program, whatever that means, plus some very active lively program, they'll probably behave the same way."

5 Citing the many studies examining the effect of violence on children, Freedman in his research paper acknowledges a kind of correlation: the more violence children watch, the more aggressive they become. But he emphasizes that that finding does not equate to a causal relationship.

6 "The most likely explanation of the relationship is that some children are more aggressive in general than others and that the more aggressive children prefer violent television, watch and play more aggressive games, and act more aggressively themselves," Freedman writes.

correlation
a relationship between two ideas, facts, and so on, especially when one may be the cause of the other

7 "The evidence is not overwhelming" for a causal link, says the paper, released by the Arlington, VA-based nonprofit research foundation, which specializes in media issues. "Instead it provides no good reason to believe that television violence causes aggression, much less serious violence."

Reading Comprehension Check

1. Why does Jonathan Friedman criticize the American Academy of Pediatrics and the American Psychological Association?
   a. because each institution believes that the debate on TV violence is not over
   b. for using accurate statistics in their publications
   c. for providing misinformation on TV's effects on young children
   d. both b and c
2. "The pediatrics group in particular, he says, used '**wildly** inaccurate figures.'"

   The word *wildly* as used in the above sentence could be replaced with
   a. grossly.
   b. uncontrollable.
   c. hidden.
   d. reasonably.
3. Friedman argues that if kids watch lively, nonviolent programs,
   a. they will act more calmly.
   b. they will behave in a similar fashion.
   c. this would be recommended.
   d. the wild kids will begin to change their behavior.
4. What is the author's tone in this reading passage?
   a. pessimistic
   b. persuasive
   c. enthusiastic
   d. informational
5. What is the main idea of the reading?
   a. It is not the quality, but the quantity of TV programming that has a long-term effect on children's behavior.
   b. The question of whether TV programming has any effect on the behavior of young children has been clearly answered.
   c. Parents need to consider the type of TV programming their children watch.
   d. New research suggests that it is a myth that violent TV programming causes violent behavior in young children.
6. What argument does Joan Oleck report about TV and violence?
   - Argument: ______________________________
   ____
7. What types of evidence does she use to support her claims?
   - Support Type: ______________________________
   - Support Type: ______________________________
   ____

Inventory of Support/Evidence Offered:

Which of the following types of support did the authors make use of to support their arguments in the two above readings? Check off the support types you saw in the articles. Compare with a partner.

Types of Support for Argumentation

1. Factual examples
2. Statistics
3. Mention of a study or a report
4. Experiential examples
5. Logical reasoning
6. Opinion-based (emotional)

Reading with a Critical Eye

In a small group, discuss the following reflection questions, which will guide you toward a deeper understanding of the reading.

1. In paragraph 2 of the first reading, Dr. Mintle writes: "We don't need more studies" of the relationship between TV violence and aggressive behavior. Why does she say this? Isn't more research always helpful?
2. What three major effects does TV violence have on children, according to Dr. Mintle? Do you disagree with each of her arguments? Explain.
3. Dr. Mintle offers some advice on how parents can deal with the problem of TV violence. Which of her points do you feel is the most convincing? Explain.
4. In the second article, Dr. Jonathan Freedman is doubtful that TV violence is the cause of violent behavior. What is Freedman's main idea on the subject?
5. After reading both articles on the topic, which reading was more convincing? Why?

From Reading to Writing: Keeping Double-Entry Reading Journals

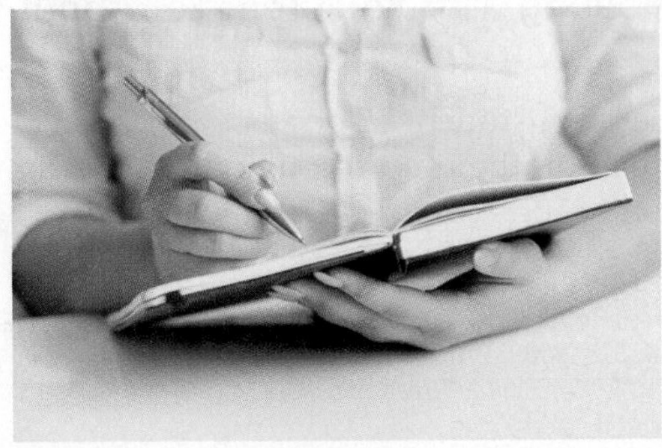

The more you actively engage with a reading, the more likely you are to connect with it, understand it fully, and enjoy it. One way to interact with the texts you read is by keeping a "reading journal." A reading journal is basically a space to share your thoughts, ask questions, and respond to ideas and points you find particularly interesting about a text you are reading. Reading journals work very well with extended reading material, such as novels and nonfiction books, and textbooks as well. In this section, we will discuss a number of ways you can work with a reading journal.

Reading Journals as a Set of Personal Reactions/ Responses to Reading

When you read, it is natural to have a variety of responses to the ideas in the text. You may agree or disagree with a point made, an example mentioned may remind you of something that happened to you, or you may find a quote you connect with emotionally.

It is useful when responding to text to keep a "double-entry" journal; that is, consistently use the left page of the notebook for one purpose and the right page for another. In the example below, the left side is used to copy a section of a text that the reader found interesting, and the right side is the personal reaction. You may remember this unit's first reading, "Why and How Do People Lie?"

Double-Entry Journal Example

Text	Reaction
"Let's focus on the mental processes that people use to lie. Should it be easier or harder for people to tell a lie than to tell the truth?"[5]	I think it is definitely easier to lie. Sometimes I think that telling the truth will get me into more trouble. At the same time I feel bad when I am dishonest.

Who is the audience for your reading journal? Mainly, you are. Keeping a reading journal gives you an opportunity to have a conversation with the text. Sometimes, instructors will collect journals weekly and may serve as another "audience" for your journal responses.

Reading Journals as a Way of Both Responding to Text and Communicating with Your Teacher About What You Are Reading

In the example below, a student responds to a section of a reading (from the article you read on the reunited twins) on the right side, and the teacher subsequently adds comments on the left side.

[5] *From Richard J. Gerrig and Philip G. Zimbardo,* Psychology and Life, *Discovering Psychology Edition, 18th Ed., pp. 4–8. © 2009. Printed and electronically reproduced by permission of Pearson Education, Inc., Upper Saddle River, New Jersey.*

Teacher Response

Yes, it is intriguing to think about how they were separated at such an early age. They share so much genetically, but really don't know each other. They have plenty of catching up to do!

Student Journal Entry

(From *Read to Succeed,* Chap. 8, p. 440) "We had 35 years to catch up on. How do you start asking somebody, 'What have you been up to since we shared a womb together?' Where do you start?" Bernstein says."

I thought this was funny the way she mentions that she has not really been in touch with her sister since they were inside their mother's womb. It makes me wonder if it will be possible for the twins to be close again.

Reading Journals as a Way to Ask Questions About Confusing Concepts or Difficult Terminology

Why hide from what you do not completely understand? It may be helpful to make note in your reading journal of some confusing points in the text. If your instructor will be looking at it, this gives you a chance to have some of your questions answered. You can also make use of your reading journal in class by asking about some of the points you raised while preparing the journal entry at home. See the example below from our textbook application reading (beginning on page 460). On the right is the student's response, and on the left is the instructor's response.

Teacher Response

Good question. I think the writer is trying to make the point that it is the goal of psychologists in making professional **observations** to consider both their personal **insight** based on knowledge of the field together with what they have learned from past research. The example of the master detective is a good one.

Student Question/Concern

I am not sure I understand the section on p. 463 about well-trained psychologists and their role in making observations. It was a little confusing.

Careers in Psychology

Working in small groups, discuss some careers one can pursue after obtaining a degree in Psychology. You may wish to do some research on the Internet to find other careers related to the field of Psychology. In the space below, write down the job title and responsibilities. The first example is done for you. Be sure to share your findings with your peers.

Job Title	*Responsibilities*
1. *VA Psychologist*	*Clinical work with war veterans, teach coping skills, guide veterans toward reintegration into civilian life.*
2.	
3.	
4.	
5.	

Practicing Reader Response

The final reading of this chapter (on p. 467) is the transcript from a TED Talk by a comedian and mental health activist. Reread it carefully, and write a paragraph reaction to what you have read. You can ask questions or share your personal feelings about the reading. Your instructor may ask you to write your response in a double-entry reading journal notebook.

Textbook Application

Read the following selection from the introductory chapter of the textbook *Psychology and Life*, and try to correctly answer the multiple-choice questions that follow. As you read, it may be helpful to highlight key points.

READING 4

Textbook Reading

MyReadingLab

Visit Chapter 8: Psychology in MyReadingLab to complete the Reading 4 activities.

What Makes Psychology Unique?[6]

by Richard J. Gerrig and Philip G. Zimbardo

1 To appreciate the uniqueness and unity of psychology, you must consider the way psychologists define the field and the goals they bring to their research and applications. By the end of the book, we hope you will think like a psychologist. In this first section, we'll give you a strong idea of what that might mean.

Definitions

2 Many psychologists seek answers to this fundamental question: What is **human nature?** Psychology answers this question by looking at processes that occur within individuals as well as forces that arise within the physical and social environment. In this light, we formally define psychology as the scientific study of the behavior of individuals and their mental processes. Let's explore the critical parts of this definition: *scientific, behavior,* ***individual,*** and *mental.*

3 The scientific aspect of psychology requires that psychological conclusions be based on evidence collected according to the principles of the scientific method. The scientific method consists of a set of orderly steps used to analyze and solve problems. This method uses objectively collected information as the factual basis for drawing conclusions. We will elaborate on the features of the scientific method

[6] From Richard J. Gerrig and Philip G. Zimbardo, *Psychology and Life*, Discovering Psychology Edition, 19th ed., pp. 4–8.

Most psychological study focuses on individuals—usually human ones, but sometimes those of other species. What aspects of your own life would you like psychologists to study?

more fully in Chapter 2, when we consider how psychologists conduct their research.

4 Behavior is the means by which organisms adjust to their environment. Behavior is action. The subject matter of psychology largely consists of the observable behavior of humans and other species of animals. Smiling, crying, running, hitting, talking, and touching are some obvious examples of behavior you can observe. Psychologists examine what the individual does and how the individual goes about doing it within a given behavioral setting and in the broader social or cultural context.

5 The subject of psychological analysis is most often an ***individual***—a newborn infant, a teenage athlete, a college student adjusting to life in a dormitory, a man facing a midlife career change, or a woman coping with the stress of her husband's deterioration from Alzheimer's disease. However, the subject might also be a chimpanzee learning to use symbols to communicate, a white rat navigating a maze, or a sea slug responding to a danger signal. An individual might be studied in its natural habitat or in the controlled conditions of a research laboratory.

6 Many researchers in psychology also recognize that they cannot understand human actions without also understanding ***mental** processes,* the workings of the human mind. Much human activity takes place as private, internal events—thinking, planning, reasoning, creating, and dreaming. Many psychologists believe that mental processes represent the most important aspect of psychological inquiry. As you shall soon see, psychological investigators have devised ingenious techniques to study mental events and processes—to make these private experiences public.

7 The combination of these concerns defines psychology as a unique field. Within the *social*

sciences, psychologists focus largely on behavior in individuals, whereas sociologists study the behavior of people in groups or institutions, and anthropologists focus on the broader context of behavior in different cultures. Even so, psychologists draw broadly from the insights of other scholars. Psychologists share many interests with researchers in *biological sciences,* especially with those who study brain processes and the biochemical bases of behavior. As part of the emerging area of *cognitive science,* psychologists' questions about how the human mind works are related to research and theory in computer science, artificial intelligence, and applied mathematics. As a *health science*—with links to medicine, education, law, and **environmental** studies—psychology seeks to improve the quality of each individual's and the collective's well-being.

8 Although the remarkable breadth and depth of modern psychology are a source of delight to those who become psychologists, these same attributes make the field a challenge to the student exploring it for the first time. There is so much more to the study of psychology than you might expect initially—and, because of that, there will also be much of value that you can take away from this introduction to psychology. The best way to learn about the field is to learn to share psychologists' goals. Let's consider those goals.

The Goals of Psychology

9 The goals of the psychologist conducting basic research are to describe, explain, predict, and control behavior. These goals form the basis of the psychological enterprise. What is involved in trying to achieve each of them?

10 **Describing What Happens** The first task in psychology is to make accurate observations about behavior. Psychologists typically refer to such observations as their ***data*** (*data* is the plural, *datum* the singular). Behavioral data are reports of observations about the behavior of organisms and the conditions under which the behavior occurs. When researchers undertake data collection, they must choose an appropriate *level of **analysis*** and devise measures of behavior that ensure *objectivity*.

11 In order to investigate an individual's behavior, researchers may use different *levels of **analysis***—from the broadest, most global level down to the most minute, specific level. Suppose, for example, you were trying to describe a painting you saw at a museum (see Figure 1.1 ■). At a global level, you might describe it by title, *Bathers,* and by artist, Georges Seurat. At a more specific level, you might recount features of the painting: Some people are sunning themselves on a riverbank while others are enjoying the water, and so on. At a very specific level, you might describe the technique Seurat used—tiny points of paint—to create the scene. The description at each level would answer different questions about the painting.

FIGURE 1.1 ■ Levels of Analysis
Suppose you wanted a friend to meet you in front of this painting. How would you describe it? Suppose your friend wanted to make an exact copy of the painting. How would you describe it?

12 Different levels of psychological description also address different questions. At the broadest level of psychological analysis, researchers investigate the behavior of the whole person within complex social and cultural contexts. At this level, researchers might study cross-cultural differences in violence, the origins of prejudice, and the consequences of mental illness. At the next level, psychologists focus on narrower, finer units of behavior, such as speed of reaction to a stop light, eye movements during reading, and grammatical errors made by children acquiring language. Researchers can study even smaller units of behavior. They might work to discover the biological bases of behavior by identifying the places in the brain where different types of memories are stored, the biochemical changes that occur during learning, and the sensory paths responsible for vision or hearing. Each level of analysis yields information essential to the final

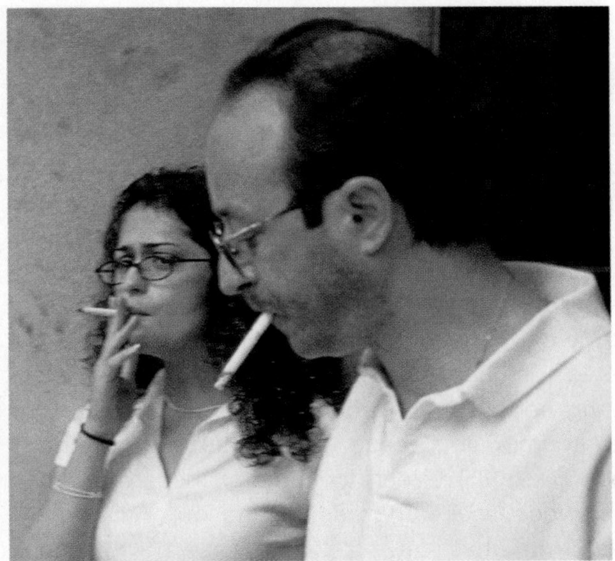

What causes people to smoke? Can psychologists create conditions under which people will be less likely to engage in this behavior?

composite portrait of human nature that psychologists hope ultimately to develop.

13 However tight or broad the focus of the observation, psychologists strive to describe behavior *objectively.* Collecting the facts as they exist, and not as the researcher expects or hopes them to be, is of utmost importance. Because every observer brings to each observation his or her *subjective* point of view—biases, prejudices, and expectations—it is essential to prevent these personal factors from creeping in and distorting the data. As you will see in the next chapter, psychological researchers have developed a variety of techniques to maintain objectivity.

14 **Explaining What Happens** Whereas *descriptions* must stick to perceivable information, *explanations* deliberately go beyond what can be observed. In many areas of psychology, the central goal is to find regular patterns in behavioral and mental processes. Psychologists want to discover *how* behavior works. Why do you laugh at situations that differ from your expectations of what is coming next? What conditions could lead someone to attempt suicide or commit rape?

15 Explanations in psychology usually recognize that most behavior is influenced by a combination of factors. Some factors operate within the individual, such as genetic makeup, **motivation,** intelligence level, or **self-esteem.** These inner determinants tell something special about the organism. Other factors, however, operate externally. Suppose, for example, that a child tries to please a teacher in order to win a prize or that a motorist trapped in a traffic jam becomes frustrated and hostile. These behaviors are largely influenced by events outside the person. When psychologists seek to explain behavior, they almost always consider both types of explanations. Suppose, for example, psychologists want to explain why some people start smoking. Researchers might examine the possibility that some individuals are particularly prone to risk taking (an internal explanation) or that some individuals experience a lot of peer pressure (an external explanation)—or that both a disposition toward risk taking and situational peer pressure are necessary (a combined explanation).

16 Often a psychologist's goal is to explain a wide variety of behavior in terms of one underlying cause. Consider a situation in which your teacher says that to earn a good grade, each student must participate regularly in class discussions. Your roommate, who is always well prepared for class, never raises his hand to answer questions or volunteer information. The teacher chides him for being unmotivated and assumes he is not bright. That same roommate also goes to parties but never asks anyone to dance, doesn't openly defend his point of view when it is challenged by someone less informed, and rarely engages in small talk at the dinner table. What is your diagnosis? What underlying cause might

A psychological prediction

Psychology in Your Life

Can Psychology Help Find Me a Career?

If you've ever had a job you didn't like, you probably know a lot about what it means to suffer from a lack of motivation: You can hardly stand the idea of reporting to work; every minute seems like an hour. An important part of having a successful career is finding a work setting that provides the types of challenges and rewards that fit your motivational needs. It probably will not surprise you that researchers have studied the match between vocations and people's individual personalities, values, and needs.

To remain motivated for career success, you would like to have a job that suits your interests and serves **goals** that you consider worthwhile. A widely used test for measuring vocational interests is the *Strong Interest Inventory,* which was originated in 1927 by psychologist **Edward Strong.** To construct the test, Strong first asked groups of men in different occupations to answer **items** about activities they liked or disliked. Then the answers given by those who were successful in particular occupations were compared with the responses of men in general to create a scale. Subsequent versions of the test, including a 2004 update, have added scales relevant to women and to newer occupations. The Strong Interest Inventory is quite successful at relating people's likes and dislikes to appropriate occupations (Hansen & Dik, 2005). If you take this test, a vocational counselor could tell you what types of jobs are typically held by people with interests such as yours because these are the jobs that are likely to appeal to you.

Suppose you have gotten this sort of advice about what career to **pursue.** How do you **select** a particular company to join—and how does that company select you? Researchers in *personnel psychology* have focused a good deal of attention on the concept of *person–organization fit*—the goal is to maximize the compatibility between people and the organizations that employ them (Dineen et al., 2002; Van Vianen, 2000). One research project has focused on the match between people's personalities and the "culture" of organizations. Consider the personality factor called Agreeableness, which encodes a continuum from "sympathetic and kind" to "cold and quarrelsome" (see Chapter 13). Consider, also, a continuum of organizational cultures from those that are supportive and team oriented to those that are aggressive and outcome oriented. Do you see how these dimensions line up? Research suggests that job seekers who score high on Agreeableness will prefer organizations that are culturally supportive and team oriented (Judge & Cable, 1997). Research of this type suggests why it is not just your own motivational states that matter for career success: The extent to which your preferences for achieving goals match the organization's preferences matters as well.

So, what career path will keep you motivated for success? As with so many of life's dilemmas, psychologists have carried out **research** that can help you make this important decision.

account for this range of behavior? How about *shyness?* Like many other people who suffer from intense feelings of shyness, your roommate is unable to behave in desired ways (Zimbardo & Radl, 1999). We can use the concept of shyness to explain the full pattern of your roommate's behavior.

17 To forge such causal explanations, researchers must often engage in a creative process of examining a diverse collection of data. Master detective Sherlock Holmes drew shrewd conclusions from scraps of evidence. In a similar fashion, every researcher must use an informed imagination, which creatively *synthesizes* what is known and what is not yet known. A well-trained psychologist can explain observations by using her or his insight into the human experience along with the facts previous researchers have uncovered about the phenomenon in question. Much psychological research attempts to determine which of several explanations most accurately accounts for a given behavioral pattern.

18 **Predicting What Will Happen** Predictions in psychology are statements about the likelihood that a certain behavior will occur or that a given relationship will be found. Often an accurate explanation of the causes underlying some form of behavior will allow a researcher to make accurate predictions about future behavior. Thus, if we believe your roommate to be shy, we could confidently predict that he would be uncomfortable when asked to have a conversation with a stranger. When different explanations are put forward to account for some behavior or relationship, they are usually judged by how well they can make accurate and comprehensive predictions. If your roommate was to blossom in contact with a stranger, we would be forced to rethink our diagnosis.

19 **Controlling What Happens** For many psychologists, control is the central, most powerful goal. Control means making behavior happen or not happen—starting it, maintaining it, stopping it, and influencing its form, strength, or rate of occurrence. A causal explanation of behavior is convincing if it can create conditions under which the behavior can be controlled.

20 Just as observations must be made objectively, scientific predictions must be worded precisely enough to enable them to be tested and then rejected if the evidence does not support them. Suppose, for example, a researcher predicts that the presence of a stranger will reliably cause human and monkey babies, beyond a certain age, to respond with signs of anxiety. We might want to bring more precision to this prediction by examining the dimension of "stranger." Would fewer signs of anxiety appear in a human or a monkey baby if the stranger were also a baby rather than an adult, or if the stranger were of the same species rather than of a different one? To improve future predictions, a researcher would create systematic variations in environmental conditions and observe their influence on the baby's response.

Reading Comprehension Check

1. Smiling, crying, running, hitting, and talking are mentioned as examples of

a. signals.
b. disguised behavior.
c. observable behavior.
d. movement.

Question Type ________________

2. *Mental processes* is defined as

a. psychological analysis.
b. human actions.
c. the workings of the human mind.
d. both b and c

Question Type ________________

3. Is the following a fact or opinion? "Mental processes represent the most important aspect of psychological inquiry."

a. an opinion
b. a fact
c. both fact and opinion
d. neither fact or opinion

Question Type ________________

4. Sociology and anthropology are mentioned

a. as fields of social science with different foci than psychology.
b. as similar fields.

c. as more related to biological sciences.
d. as examples within the field of psychology.

Question Type ____________

5. The word *emerging*, in the sentence, "As part of the emerging area of cognitive science" (p. 462), means
a. deflated.
b. rising.
c. stagnant.
d. neutral.

Question Type ____________

6. The example of describing a painting is used to illustrate the concept of
a. varying levels of analysis.
b. equal analysis.
c. individual perspective.
d. questioning.

Question Type ____________

7. Which of the following from the passage can be classified as an author's argument?
a. Often a psychologist's goal is to explain a wide variety of behavior in terms of one underlying cause.
b. Your roommate never raises his hand.
c. Predictions are statements about the likelihood that a certain behavior will occur.
d. all of the above

Question Type ____________

8. What kind of support is offered for the author's claim that "scientific predictions must be worded precisely enough to enable them to be tested"?
a. emotional examples
b. factual examples
c. both emotional and factual examples
d. Not enough information is given to answer the question.

Question Type ____________

9. Which pattern of organization is used in the following passage, taken from the second paragraph of the section Psychology in Your Life? "To construct the test, Strong first asked groups of men in different occupations to answer items about activities they liked and disliked. Then the answers given by those who were successful in particular occupations were compared with the responses of men in general to create a scale."
a. definition and example
b. compare/contrast
c. listing
d. chronological order

Question Type ____________

10. What is the author's tone throughout this textbook chapter?
a. optimistic
b. mostly objective
c. sarcastic
d. condescending

Question Type ____________

Contemporary Issues in the Discipline

Ruby Wax is a comedian who has battled depression throughout her career. Once private about her struggle, Wax now integrates comedy into her work as a mental health advocate—and advocacy into her work as a comic and performer. She produced the stand-up comedy show *Losing It*, and recently established a social network, *The Black Dog Tribe*, which provides a supportive network for people coping with depression.

MyReadingLab

Visit Chapter 8: Psychology in MyReadingLab to complete the Reading 5 activities.

READING 5

Lecture (TED Talk)

What's So Funny about Mental Illness?

Pre-Reading Activity

Before reading the following transcript of Ruby Wax's TED Talk, you can watch the speech itself here: http://www.ted.com/talks/ruby_wax_what_s_so_funny_about_mental_illness?language=en (Courtesy of TED). As you listen to the video presentation, take notes. (See the note-taking activity on p. 190 for some pointers.) After reading the transcript, you will answer some open-ended questions about some of the issues raised in the speech. Finally, you will formulate questions for Ms. Wax about issues pertinent to psychology and mental illness and answer them from her perspective.

What's So Funny about Mental Illness?

By Ruby Wax

June 2012

Transcript courtesy of TED © TED Conferences, LLC

1 One in four people suffer from some sort of mental illness, so if it was one, two, three, four, it's you, sir. You. Yeah. *(Laughter)* With the weird teeth. And you next to him. *(Laughter)* You know who you are. Actually, that whole row isn't right. *(Laughter)* That's not good. Hi. Yeah. Real bad. Don't even look at me. *(Laughter)*

2 I am one of the one in four. Thank you. I think I inherit it from my mother, who, used to crawl around the house on all fours. She had two sponges in her hand, and then she had two tied to her knees. My mother was completely absorbent. *(Laughter)* And she would crawl

around behind me going, "Who brings footprints into a building?!" So that was kind of a clue that things weren't right. So before I start, I would like to thank the makers of Lamotrigine, Sertraline, and Reboxetine, because without those few simple chemicals, I would not be vertical today.

3 So how did it start? My mental illness—well, I'm not even going to talk about my mental illness. What am I going to talk about? Okay. I always dreamt that, when I had my final breakdown, it would be because I had a deep Kafkaesque existentialist revelation, or that maybe Cate Blanchett would play me and she would win an Oscar for it. *(Laughter)* But that's not what happened. I had my breakdown during my daughter's sports day. There were all the parents sitting in a parking lot eating food out of the back of their car—only the English—eating their sausages. They loved their sausages. *(Laughter)* Lord and Lady Rigor Mortis were nibbling on the tarmac, and then the gun went off and all the girlies started running, and all the mummies went, "Run! Run Chlamydia! Run!" *(Laughter)* "Run like the wind, Veruca! Run!" And all the girlies, girlies running, running, running, everybody except for my daughter, who was just standing at the starting line, just waving, because she didn't know she was supposed to run. So I took to my bed for about a month, and when I woke up I found I was institutionalized, and when I saw the other inmates, I realized that I had found my people, my tribe. *(Laughter)* Because they became my only friends, they became my friends, because very few people that I knew—Well, I wasn't sent a lot of cards or flowers. I mean, if I had had a broken leg or I was with child I would have been inundated, but all I got was a couple phone calls telling me to perk up. Perk up. Because I didn't think of that. *(Laughter) (Applause)*

4 Because, you know, the one thing, one thing that you get with this disease, this one comes with a package, is you get a real sense of shame, because your friends go, "Oh come on, show me the lump, show me the x-rays," and of course you've got nothing to show, so you're, like, really disgusted with yourself because you're thinking, "I'm not being carpet-bombed. I don't live in a township." So you start to hear these abusive voices, but you don't hear one abusive voice, you hear about a thousand—100,000 abusive voices, like if the Devil had Tourette's, that's what it would sound like. But we all know in here, you know, there is no Devil, there are no voices in your head. You know that when you have those abusive voices, all those little neurons get together and in that little gap you get a real toxic "I want to kill myself" kind of chemical, and if you have that over and over again on a loop tape, you might have yourself depression. Oh, and that's not even the tip of the iceberg. If you get a little baby, and you abuse it verbally, its little brain sends out chemicals that are so destructive that the little part of its brain that can tell good from bad just doesn't grow, so you might have yourself a homegrown psychotic. If a soldier sees his friend blown up, his brain goes into such high alarm that he can't

actually put the experience into words, so he just feels the horror over and over again.

5 So here's my question. My question is, how come when people have mental damage, it's always an active imagination? How come every other organ in your body can get sick and you get sympathy, except the brain?

6 I'd like to talk a little bit more about the brain, because I know you like that here at TED, so if you just give me a minute here, okay. Okay, let me just say, there's some good news. There is some good news. First of all, let me say, we've come a long, long way. We started off as a teeny, teeny little one-celled amoeba, tiny, just sticking onto a rock, and now, voila, the brain. Here we go. *(Laughter)* This little baby has a lot of horsepower. It comes completely conscious. It's got state-of-the-art lobes. We've got the occipital lobe so we can actually see the world. We got the temporal lobe so we can actually hear the world. Here we've got a little bit of long-term memory, so, you know that night you want to forget, when you got really drunk? Bye-bye! Gone. *(Laughter)* So actually, it's filled with 100 billion neurons just zizzing away, electrically transmitting information, zizzing, zizzing. I'm going to give you a little side view here. I don't know if you can get that here. *(Laughter)* So, zizzing away, and so—*(Laughter)*—And for every one—I know, I drew this myself. Thank you. For every one single neuron, you can actually have from 10,000 to 100,000 different connections or dendrites or whatever you want to call it, and every time you learn something, or you have an experience, that bush grows, you know, that bush of information. Can you imagine, every human being is carrying that equipment, even Paris Hilton? *(Laughter)* Go figure.

7 But I got a little bad news for you folks. I got some bad news. This isn't for the one in four. This is for the four in four. We are not equipped for the 21st century. Evolution did not prepare us for this. We just don't have the bandwidth, and for people who say, oh, they're having a nice day, they're perfectly fine, they're more insane than the rest of us. Because I'll show you where there might be a few glitches in evolution. Okay, let me just explain this to you. When we were ancient man—*(Laughter)*—millions of years ago, and we suddenly felt threatened by a predator, okay?—*(Laughter)*—we would—Thank you. I drew these myself. *(Laughter)* Thank you very much. Thank you. Thank you. *(Applause)* Thank you. Anyway, we would fill up with our own adrenaline and our own cortisol, and then we'd kill or be killed, we'd eat or we'd be eaten, and then suddenly we'd de-fuel, and we'd go back to normal. Okay. So the problem is, nowadays, with modern man—*(Laughter)*—when we feel in danger, we still fill up with our own chemical but because we can't kill traffic wardens—*(Laughter)*—or eat estate agents, the fuel just stays in our body over and over, so

we're in a constant state of alarm, a constant state. And here's another thing that happened. About 150,000 years ago, when language came online, we started to put words to this constant emergency, so it wasn't just, "Oh my God, there's a saber-toothed tiger," which could be, it was suddenly, "Oh my God, I didn't send the email. Oh my God, my thighs are too fat. Oh my God, everybody can see I'm stupid. I didn't get invited to the Christmas party!" So you've got this nagging loop tape that goes over and over again that drives you insane, so, you see what the problem is? What once made you safe now drives you insane. I'm sorry to be the bearer of bad news, but somebody has to be. Your pets are happier than you are. *(Laughter) (Applause)* So kitty cat, meow, happy happy happy, human beings, screwed. *(Laughter)* Completely and utterly—so, screwed.

8 But my point is, if we don't talk about this stuff, and we don't learn how to deal with our lives, it's not going to be one in four. It's going to be four in four who are really, really going to get ill in the upstairs department. And while we're at it, can we please stop the stigma? Thank you. *(Applause)* Thank you.

Reading with a Critical Eye

In a small group, discuss the following reflection questions, which will guide you toward a deeper understanding of the reading.

1. What do we learn about Ruby Wax's mother? How do you think this affected her career choice?
2. What is Wax implying when she discusses her friends comments—"Oh come on, show me the lump, show me the x-rays"?
3. What question does Wax ask about mental illness (para. 5)? What is your reaction to her question?
4. What good news and bad news does the speaker offer in paragraphs six and seven?
5. What is the idea behind Ruby. Wax's closing comments?

Imagined Interview: If you had the opportunity to interview Ruby Wax in person, what would you ask her? With a partner, compose three questions for her.

Question 1. ______________________________

Question 2. ______________________________

Question 3. ______________________________

Interview Challenge: In a group, ask one student to play Ms. Wax. This student should carefully consider Ruby Wax's views, outlined clearly in the TED Talk, and try to answer the questions from Wax's perspective on mental illness.

Chapter Recap

Now that you have made it through a full chapter focusing on the field of psychology, let's review the chapter reading content, skill focus, and vocabulary to gain a better understanding of what we have learned.

Recap Activity 1: A Quick Glance

In 60 seconds, answer the following two questions:

1. What is one thing you learned from this chapter?

____

____

____

____

____

____

2. What was your favorite reading in the chapter? Explain.

____

____

____

____

____

____

Now discuss what you wrote in a small group. Do not read what you wrote. Paraphrase yourself!

Recap Activity 2: Summary Writing

Choose your favorite reading from this chapter and write a summary containing the main idea and some major details. Keep in mind that the key to summary writing is to convey the author's ideas accurately, but to relay this information in your own words. Last but not least, be sure to include reminder phrases and appropriate transitions.

Recap Activity 3: Internet Research on a Theme of Interest

Think about the choice you just made in Activity 2 concerning which reading in the chapter was your favorite.

What was the theme of your chosen reading?

Theme = ____

Search online and locate a quality reading on the same theme as your favorite chapter reading. Write a three- to five-sentence summary of the reading that you found from your research.

Title of Reading	*Article Source*	*Summary of the Reading (in your own words)*

Recap Activity 4: Reinforcing the Skill

Reread the paragraphs below from Reading Selection 3B: "TV Violence Doesn't Lead to Aggressive Kids, Study Says." After reading, discuss with a partner: What plan of action can be used to best identify the arguments offered in the reading?

> "The debate is not over," writes Jonathan Freedman, author of the paper and a professor of psychology at the University of Toronto, who also criticizes both the American Academy of Pediatrics and the American Psychological Association for wrongly characterizing previous studies of TV's effects on children. The pediatrics group in particular, he says, used "wildly inaccurate figures" in its studies.
>
> "I don't think this kind of television affects children's aggression at all," Freedman, who has been studying children and television for two decades, told *SLJ*. "Some kids may get very excited and look like they're more aggressive because they're very excited. But if they watch some nonviolent program, whatever that means, plus some very active lively program, they'll probably behave the same way."

How can you clearly identify arguments contained in the passage you have just read?

Strategy 1: ____

Strategy 2: ____

Recap Activity 5: Recycling Vocabulary

With a partner, locate the following vocabulary terms, review them in context, and try to define the terms without using a dictionary. Make sure to underline the vocabulary term used in the sentence. The first example is done for you.

Word and Context Location	*Sentence Containing the Word*	*Meaning in This Context*
conceal, p. 437, para. 1	People quite frequently committed serious lies to **conceal** affairs or other forbidden forms of social contact.	hide
traumatic, p. 445, para. 1	"… and then tracing her symptoms back to traumatic events she had experienced at her father's deathbed."	____________
neglected, p. 440, para. 6	"But of course, they neglected to tell them the key element of the study."	____________
insight, p. 462, para. 7	"Even so, psychologists draw broadly from the insights of other scholars …"	____________
correlation, p. 443, example. 3	"… Freedman in his research paper acknowledges a kind of correlation: the more violence children watch, the more aggressive they become."	____________
citing, p. 455, para. 5	Citing the many studies examining the effect of violence on children, Freedman in his research paper acknowledges a kind of correlation …	____________
self-esteem, p. 463, para. 3	Some factors operate within the individual, such as genetic makeup, motivation, intelligence level, or self-esteem.	____________
therapeutic, p. 445, para. 2	By the turn of the century, Freud had developed his therapeutic technique, dropping the use of hypnosis and shifting to the more effective and more widely applicable method of "free association."	____________

Further Explorations

Books

1. *Reviving Ophelia: Saving the Selves of Adolescent Girls* by Mary Pipher. New York: Ballantine Books, 1994. A thought-provoking collection of case studies, anecdotes, and educated commentary concerning the problems faced by today's female youth.
2. *Killing Freud: Twentieth Century Culture and the Death of Psychoanalysis* by Todd Dufresne. Continuum Pub. Group, New York, 2003. This nonfiction book takes the reader on a journey through the twentieth century, tracing the work and influence of one if its greatest icons.
3. *The Curious Incident of the Dog in the Night-Time* by Mark Haddon. New York: Doubleday, 2003. The narrator of this novel is a 15-year-old autistic boy.

Movies

1. *Still Alice* (2014). Directed by Richard Glatzer. A linguistics professor and her family find their bonds tested when she is diagnosed with Alzheimer's Disease. This film stars Julianne Moore and Alec Baldwin.
2. *Thirteen Conversations About One Thing* (2001). Directed by Jill Sprecher. This film taps into many issues about perspective and context. The movie examines how one event becomes interrelated and life changing in many people's lives.
3. *A Beautiful Mind* (2001). Directed by Ron Howard. A biopic of the rise of John Forbes Nash, Jr., a math prodigy able to solve problems that baffled the greatest of minds. The movie explores how he overcame years of suffering through schizophrenia to win the Nobel Prize.

Internet Sites

1. *Encyclopedia of Psychology* www.psychology.org/
   Links to Web sites on a variety of psychology topics such as environment, behavior, relationships, organizations, publications, and more.
2. *Go Ask Alice* www.goaskalice.columbia.edu/index.html
   This is the health question-and-answer Internet site produced by Alice, Columbia University's Health Education Program. The site lets you find health information via a search.
3. *Mental Help Net* http://mentalhelp.net
   Contains information on depression and personality disorders and their treatments.

Finding Evidence in the Text

Overview

When reading, you are expected to compare the ideas discussed in a given text with your knowledge and experience of the world. One of the challenges in doing critical reading is being able to separate your own opinions, assumptions, and life experiences from those expressed by the author. So, for example, if you are evaluating an essay on the death penalty in which the author argues against it, you cannot judge the article as weakly reasoned simply because you happen to hold the opposite viewpoint. At the same time, if you agree with the author that the death penalty is wrong, in discussing the merits of the author's support for his or her arguments you cannot bring in your own supporting points to back up the author's arguments. You have to find evidence for any claims made by the author in the original text itself.

In Chapter 8, we discussed the process of first recognizing what issue(s) the reading is focusing on and then identifying the author's argument(s). Evidence in support of an argument usually directly follows it. Factual evidence, or proof, comes in many forms. Some forms of evidence are statistical information, logically reasoned statements, or references to past research.

Highlighting both arguments and any evidence offered in support of them can be very helpful while reading. You can draw an arrow connecting highlighted arguments and supporting evidence, and label them accordingly. If you cannot find evidence for a claim made by the author, skim through the text again. It is easy to miss some details when you are doing a first read.

Challenge Activity

Reread the article "Why and How Do People Lie?" on page 436. Use a highlighter to highlight both the arguments mentioned in the text and the evidence cited in support of these claims. Using a pen, draw arrows connecting arguments and evidence, and label them. When you are finished, compare how the text now looks with that of a colleague's.

Learning Implications

The ability to find evidence in a text is a valuable skill, and not just for lawyers. Whether you are reviewing class readings for an exam, taking a multiple-choice test, or doing research for an assigned paper, building a habit of physically locating evidence within a reading passage will make it much easier to follow both the major and minor ideas contained in the text.

BUSINESS Entrepreneurship

9

"A business is successful to the extent that it provides a product or service that contributes to happiness in all of its forms."
MIHALY CSIKSZENTMIHALYI

Learning Objectives

AFTER READING THIS CHAPTER, YOU SHOULD BE ABLE TO:

1. Identify the fundamentals of business
2. Recognize an author's bias
3. Compose a business letter

INTRODUCTION TO THE DISCIPLINE OF BUSINESS

When we come across the word *business*, we think of multinational American corporations such as Exxon Mobil, Microsoft, IBM, and so forth. However, there are other businesses that may not be as successful as the aforementioned companies. These are relatively smaller businesses such as Kmart, Trader Joe's, and Target. There are yet other businesses that are much smaller, such as a local supermarket or a chain of restaurants. Finally, there are family-owned businesses that do not have the financial resources nor the management skills to expand nationwide. These businesses would include a local pizzeria, a small grocery store, or a florist in your neighborhood.

Regardless of their size, resources, annual revenue, or the kinds of products and services they offer, these businesses have one thing in common—they all offer either products or services to earn profits. All of these businesses try to keep their **overhead** as low as possible and maximize profits. There are inherent risks involved in running a business. For example, a company's profits may be much lower than its expenses. In this case, the company employs various strategies to stay afloat. The company may seek additional funding from venture capitalists, it may try to find a buyer who might be interested in acquiring the company, it may restructure the company, laying off many employees to keep the overhead low, or it may fire management and hire new people to run the company. If everything fails, then the company is forced to file for bankruptcy.

This chapter introduces the discipline of business to you. The articles in this chapter revolve around several aspects of business. The readings address topics such as the role of intercultural awareness in China and the United States doing business with each other, China's government finally allowing Apple to sell new models of the iPhone to the Chinese after raising serious concerns about security issues, and a Russian immigrant turned entrepreneur who runs a successful business in New York City. You will also read an excerpt of a famous American novel entitled *The Adventures of Tom Sawyer*. After you finish this chapter, you will have an understanding of how the United States and China conduct business and why more and more entrepreneurs keep pursuing the American Dream of becoming financially self-sufficient.

Preview Questions

The following questions are all related to the chapter focus area of business. Share your views in small group discussions.

1. Many people believe that there is "no heart in business." This brings up the debate as to whether business and ethics can coexist. Express your opinion on this topic and share some examples based on your personal experience.
2. Millions of Americans share the dream of starting a business. Do you believe that working for yourself offers a better life than working for a company or an organization? Discuss the advantages and disadvantages of entrepreneurship as opposed to simply being an employee.
3. Many American companies install security backdoors in the products they sell in foreign countries such as China, Japan, and India, and allow U.S. agencies such as the National Security Agency and the Federal Bureau of Investigation to access users' data. In your opinion, is this practice ethical? If not, why do you think U.S. agencies are interested in collecting information about users around the world? Explain.
4. Some people are concerned that the United States of America is losing its edge as a world economic leader. They worry that rising powers such as China and the European Union (EU) are a threat to America's supremacy as a leader in science and technology. Discuss what the United States must do to maintain its leadership in the world.
5. Read Csikszentmihalyi's quote at the beginning of the chapter and discuss whether the primary goal of business should be to enhance the quality of life for all. Name a few socially responsible companies that are working toward this goal. Can you think of some whose attitudes are heartless? Do you think that envisioning a world where all businesses contribute to our overall happiness is far-fetched? Explain.

Writing on The Wall

After you have discussed the preview questions with your classmates, post your responses to two of them on your class blog, which we refer to as The Wall. Review others' postings and respond to at least two of your classmates' posts that grab your interest. Remember the guidelines for blogging and commenting etiquette (see Chapter 1, p. 15)! If your class is not using a shared blog, your instructor may ask you to record your individual or collective responses to the preview questions in another form.

EXERCISE 9.1 Interpreting a Cartoon

Working in pairs, examine the cartoon below and answer the following questions.

1. What is so amusing about this cartoon?
2. In your opinion, what is the cartoonist's intended message to the reader?

"We found someone overseas who can drink coffee and talk about sports all day for a fraction of what we're paying you."

Discipline-specific Vocabulary: Understand Key Terms in Business

It is critical for a student majoring in business to internalize vocabulary terms that relate to the discipline. For example, a student taking an Introduction to Business course should be able to apply such terms as *entrepreneur*, *corporation*, and *innovation* in both spoken and written forms. In this chapter, you will have the opportunity to interact with some of these key terms in context.

EXERCISE 9.2 Brainstorming Vocabulary

Directions: What associated words come to mind when you think of the world of business? Work with a partner and write down as many related words as you can think of in a period of five minutes.

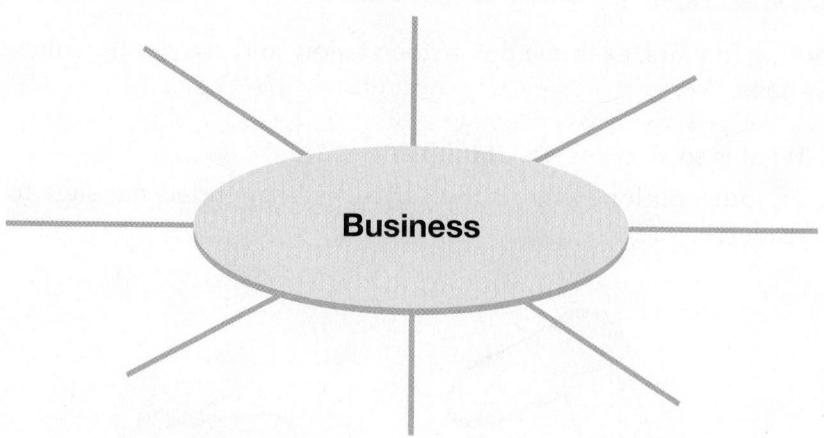

Fishing for Synonyms and Antonyms

As you know, understanding how to work with synonyms and antonyms is a useful skill, especially when you are writing a summary of a text and trying to paraphrase some of the key ideas and pieces of information contained in the original source. To help avoid plagiarism, you'll need to paraphrase the main points of the original text and use synonyms and antonyms.

EXERCISE 9.3 Determining Synonyms and Antonyms from Context

Directions: Read the following ten (10) discipline-specific words culled from the readings in this chapter and shown in the context of the sentences in which they appeared.

Discipline-specific Word Bank for Business

executives	**product**	**negotiation**	**capital**
investing	**global**	**bankrupted**	**attain**
consumers	**innovations**		

In the space provided after each sentence, write a synonym or antonym for the highlighted terms, as directed.

1. "ConAgra hired Carla Kearns, founder of TLI-The Mandarin School, based in Toronto, to provide its **executives** with intercultural business training in China."

   A synonym for *executives* is _____________.

2. "They may be **investing** money in the trip, but not something just as vital: time."

   An antonym for *investing* is ___________.

3. "The iPhone 6 and 6 Plus were released on Sept 19 in the United States and elsewhere, but regulatory delay meant Chinese **consumers** had to wait."

   An antonym for *consumers* is ___________.

4. "Rushed schedules leave no time for skillful **negotiation** and can offend Chinese, who want to build trust and develop relationships, or guanxi, often by socializing over dinners and drinks."

   An antonym for *negotiation* is ________________.

5. "More work meant more income, which provided her with **capital** to complete the store and buy out her partners."

   A synonym for *capital* is ___________.

6. "I work tirelessly to create proper patterns, proper fittings just so I can feel good about the **product** I put out."

   A synonym for *product* is ___________.

7. "What made this gas crisis unusual was that it was the result of an unusual confluence of supply, demand, and **global** forces."

   An antonym for *global* is ___________.

8. "They create most new **innovations** and provide a vast range of opportunities for new businesses, which serve as their suppliers."

   An antonym for *innovations* is ______________.

9. "If he hadn't run out of whitewash he would have **bankrupted** every boy in the village."

   A synonym for *bankrupted* is _____________.

10. "Namely, that in order to make a man or a boy covet a thing, it is only necessary to make the thing difficult to **attain**."

    A synonym for *attain* is ___________.

EXERCISE 9.4 Matching Terms with Definitions

Match the word in Column A with the definition in Column B. Put the letter representing the correct definition in the space preceding each term.

Column A	Column B
Word	**Definition**
1. ____ product	a. insolvent, without money
2. ____ executives	b. committing money for a financial return

Column A		Column B
Word		**Definition**
3. _____ innovation		c. involving the entire world
4. _____ capital		d. people who purchase goods and services
5. _____ bankrupted		e. people who manage other people in a company
6. _____ negotiation		f. something that is made to be sold
7. _____ attain		g. a new idea or device
8. _____ consumers		h. accumulated possessions
9. _____ investing		i. a discussion between people to reach an agreement
10. _____ global		j. to reach, accomplish

EXERCISE 9.5 Choosing the Right Word

In each of the following sentences, **fill in the blank** with a word from the terminology bank below that makes the sentence grammatical and meaningful.

executives	investing	consumers	negotiation	capital
product	global	innovation	bankrupted	attain

1. If he hadn't run out of whitewash he would have ____________ every boy in the village.
2. Starbucks is ____________ a substantial amount of money in marketing in major cities of China, to promote the consumption of coffee among the Chinese people.
3. The popular television network's ____________ decided not to air the controversial show that seemed to have encouraged racial discrimination.
4. CEOs of multinational corporations have to fly overseas quite frequently to meet with their clients and business partners for ____________.
5. Big corporations spend millions of dollars on research and development, using modern technology to launch new products in the ____________ marketplace.
6. Customers welcomed the launch of Apple's much-awaited iWatch, a new ____________, with a great deal of enthusiasm, and most stores ran out of it within a few hours.

7. Stiff competition among businesses makes technology obsolete rather quickly, and most companies are facing the pressures of constant change and ____________ to stay ahead of their competitors.
8. The company's strong management is dedicated to raising ____________ to expand its business overseas.
9. Namely, that in order to make a man or a boy covet a thing, it is only necessary to make the thing difficult to ____________.
10. ____________ were clamoring for the company's revolutionary product so much that it had to employ many workers to keep up with the unprecedented demand.

MyReadingLab

Visit Chapter 9: Business in MyReadingLab to complete the Reading 1 activities.

READING 1

Newspaper Article

East Meets West, but It Takes Some Practice

Pre-Reading Questions

Discuss the following questions in small groups before reading the article:

1. The concept of culture varies from culture to culture. In your opinion, what considerations should an American corporation make in doing business with a Chinese corporation? You will need to have some knowledge of American and Chinese cultural values to answer this question.
2. The United States is an individualistic society, whereas China is collective. What barriers might there be for an American corporation doing business in China? Similarly, what obstacles may a Chinese corporation face selling its products and services in the United States? Explain.
3. Since there are significant differences in the cultural values of the United States and China, what do you think these countries need to do to avoid cultural missteps and communication breakdowns when doing business with each other? Be specific.

East Meets West, but It Takes Some Practice

By **Dan Levin, the *New York Times*,**
December 21, 2010

1 When ConAgra Foods came to China five years ago, the company had high hopes and big worries. Previously, the company entered the Japanese market and repeatedly ran into obstacles like communication breakdowns, cultural missteps and missed deadlines.

2 While those wrinkles were eventually straightened out, ConAgra knew it could not afford to make the same mistake in China. Intent on finding a guide who could shorten the cultural distance, Julie Williams, who was then the company's human resources manager responsible for international organization, hired Carla Kearns, founder of TLI-The Mandarin School, based in Toronto, to provide its executives with intercultural business training.

3 Ms. Kearns teaches companies to understand the fundamental values that Western and Chinese cultures see differently and that if ignored can wreak havoc on their bottom line. They include concepts of time, hierarchy, individualism, personal relationships and saving face.

4 Western executives flying into China for a week of back-to-back meetings but getting nowhere with their Chinese business partners? They may be investing money in the trip, but not something just as vital: time. Rushed schedules leave no time for skillful negotiation and can offend Chinese, who want to build trust and develop relationships, or guanxi, often by socializing over dinners and drinks.

5 Another pitfall is when Westerners lay all the problems on the table, while Chinese will only address two at any given meeting because criticism or blame will make them look bad in front of their peers.

6 Western executives assuming their business practices are successful if their Chinese employees don't object? Think again. Chinese are taught to obey authority and are often loath to disagree with their bosses.

7 The huge influx of foreign companies in China in recent years has spawned a burgeoning industry of cultural communication and innovation consultants paid to train Westerners and Chinese in each other's languages, management styles and corporate cultures. Any cultural trainer worth his salt will start off by saying that the etiquette most novice professionals in China know about, like exchanging business cards with both hands and correct seating arrangements at banquets, may get you in the boardroom door, but to seal the deal—and see profits—requires a significantly more nuanced approach.

8 Ms. Kearns charges corporations about $5,000 for a day of training for 5 to 100 people and speaks to both Westerners and Chinese, focusing on the "core gut reactions" each audience has when facing cultural obstacles at the office.

9 Part therapist, motivational speaker and management consultant, Ms. Kearns, who has worked across East Asia, begins by telling clients like ConAgra to leave their Western assumptions at home.

10 "I'm able to explain these cultural issues to Westerners because I've been through that frustration, too," she said. "So many times I see Westerners go to China and see something different than what happens in North America, and it becomes this judgment and condemnation."

11 At ConAgra, Ms. Williams was losing patience with the company's Chinese recruiters, who were having problems finding prospective managers for Con Agra's China-based tomato-product factories but were unable, or unwilling, to explain why. "We were thinking, 'There are a billion people in China; so how difficult can it be to get the right people?"' she recalled.

12 As a result of the training, Ms. Williams realized that finding Chinese who can fit in at a Western multinational corporation requires a different strategy and more time, something Western companies have little patience for with their "time is money" outlook.

13 "My aha moment came when I realized I was telling our Chinese recruiter to look for North American skills, not Chinese skills," she said. "Once I knew to speak in her cultural language we recruited the right people a lot faster."

14 When the Chinese sportswear company Li Ning began to think about expanding abroad, the company sent its executives to a Chinese intercultural trainer at the suggestion of Feng Jingwen, the company's administration director.

15 She cited a prime example of how the two cultures operate differently regarding the value of "face": "When we're at a meeting, a foreign friend might point out all four problems while Chinese may only discuss two problems to save face for their colleagues," she said. "Now we know not to judge other cultures, since they think and act differently than we do."

16 Jim Leininger, who works for the global human resource consulting company Towers Watson, offers training that can improve what he calls the "global mind-set" of companies both Western and Chinese. As the head of his company's employee engagement business in China, he helps workers streamline their ambitions and abilities in a global market or supply chain.

17 According to Mr. Leininger, there are more than 10,000 Chinese companies operating abroad and more than 200,000 foreign companies in China—a landscape ripe for a clash of cultures that requires dexterity and clarity to overcome. His consulting services can cost 200,000 renminbi, or $30,000, for a series of sessions in which he teaches executives different cultural leadership styles and problem-solving skills.

18 Being told that things are done differently in China rarely soothes Western nerves when it comes to the bottom line. In China, he says, Western businesses are frequently frustrated when their instructions are not followed by Chinese employees, who are in turn annoyed because they feel the foreigners are trying to make them do things a foreign way.

19 To improve communication dynamics, Mr. Leininger sets up "active listening" scenarios during training sessions for his clients to learn how to handle each culture's reactions, so conflicts do not boil over.

20 "If the first thing a Chinese says is, 'Don't be mad,' that will just infuriate a Westerner even more," he says, explaining that Chinese often avoid confrontation by telling their superior what they think he or she wants to hear even if it is not true, while Westerners want to know their boss cares and be part of finding a solution.

21 "Today a local person working for a multinational has to be able to engage with many cultures around the world, and we need to prepare them for that," said Mr. Leininger. As the Chinese government has made a major push toward nurturing domestic innovation, Westerners are doing their part to teach Chinese how to think differently—and creatively. Yoav Chernitz, the chief of the China branch of the information technology training company John Bryce, has developed an innovation training program to help technology companies like Microsoft, China Mobile and PetroChina "find creative solutions" for their engineers.

22 Mr. Chernitz sees many of China's difficulties with Western thinking, whether it be in programming or office politics, coming from the country's rigid education system that is geared to rote learning and obedience to authority—dynamics that often leave Chinese ill prepared to deal with more individualistic Western colleagues and thinking, as the Chinese say, "around corners."

23 John Bryce uses cultural communication techniques to teach creative thinking skills, which can be applied to programming and design through role play, workshops and technological simulations. In one workshop, for example, engineers are presented with deliberately flawed programs and must think through and design their own fixes "rather than go on the Internet and trying to Google something," said Mr. Chernitz.

24 Tamara Brodinsky takes a similar approach when teaching graphic design students at the Raffles Design Institute in Shanghai. In class she often moves chairs around to remove distance between herself, the authority, and the students, to increase collaboration. Following an assignment to create a brand identity for a fictional airline catering to pregnant women, she broke the class down into small role play groups, knowing that public critique is a "foreign" concept that makes Chinese lose face.

25 "In China they can't divide the work from themselves, so criticism hurts their feelings," said Ms. Brodinsky. "So I give them ways to suggest improvements without it sounding like a personal attack."

26 Ultimately, this training gives the students the power to change their cultural attitudes, which they take with them into the professional world.

27 "Once Chinese thought they had to work for a foreign company and learn English to succeed," she said. "But now just learning English isn't enough. They have to develop their talents to compete globally, and that takes training."

Reading with a Critical Eye

1. Most U.S. corporations sell their products all over the world. However, they do not do their due diligence to learn about the languages and cultures of the countries where they do business. In your opinion, why don't these corporations improve their cross-cultural awareness? Be specific.
2. When ConAgra Foods entered the Japanese market, what went wrong, and why did the U.S. corporation hire Carla Kearns, founder of TLI – The Mandarin School?
3. The article states, "Ms. Kearns teaches companies to understand the fundamental values that Western and Chinese cultures see differently and that if ignored can wreak havoc on their bottom line." Discuss what this means.
4. Why is it that while Westerners like to discuss everything at a meeting, Chinese will only address two issues at a given time? Refer to the article to answer this question.
5. In Mr. Chernitz's opinion, why are Chinese ill prepared to deal with individualistic Western colleagues and thinking? Use specific examples to support your answer.

Reading Comprehension Check

1. As used in the sentence, "Previously, the company entered the Japanese market and repeatedly ran into **obstacles** like communication breakdowns, cultural missteps and missed deadlines," in paragraph 1, the word *obstacles* most closely means
   a. openings.
   b. pathways.
   c. hurdles.
   d. entrances.
2. In the sentence, "While those **wrinkles** were eventually straightened out, ConAgra knew it could not afford to make the same mistake in China," the meaning of the word *wrinkles* in this context is
   a. Chinese culture.
   b. communication breakdowns.
   c. intercultural sensitivity.
   d. cross-cultural awareness.
3. Which of the following sentences is the best statement of the main idea of the article?
   a. Most U.S. companies doing business in China need training to avoid cultural missteps.
   b. It is not important for U.S. multinational companies to learn about Chinese culture.
   c. Ms. Kearns helps all U.S. companies avoid cultural misunderstandings by offering a workshop.
   d. Western and Chinese cultures see the fundamental concepts of time and hierarchy differently.

4. The examples of concepts of time, hierarchy, individualism, personal relationships, and saving face are offered to support the idea that
   a. they are insignificant for U.S. companies doing business in China.
   b. they are significant for U.S. companies doing business in China.
   c. Western and Chinese cultures see them in the same light.
   d. Western executives flying into China are familiar with the concepts.
5. Western executives flying into China for a series of business meetings invest all of the following in the trip, *except*
   a. hotel suites.
   b. time.
   c. food.
   d. airfare.
6. "Another pitfall is when Westerners lay all the problems on the table, while Chinese will only address two at any given meeting because criticism or blame will make them look bad in front of their peers."

   A logical conclusion that can be drawn from the above statement is that
   a. Westerners should urge their Chinese business partners to focus on all the issues in one meeting.
   b. when negotiating with their Chinese counterparts, it may be prudent for the Westerners to focus on the two most important issues at a given meeting.
   c. when negotiating with their Chinese counterparts, it may be wise for the Western executives to discuss all the issues at a given meeting.
   d. Chinese executives negotiating with Western executives expect them to only discuss two important issues at a given meeting.
7. All of the following statements are facts *except*
   a. ConAgra Foods ran into cultural obstacles when it entered the Japanese market.
   b. ConAgra Foods hired Ms. Carla Kearns for intercultural business training.
   c. Western executives assume their business practices are successful if their Chinese employees do not object.
   d. Ms. Kearns teaches companies to understand the differences between Western and Chinese cultures.
8. The author's primary purpose is to
   a. entertain.
   b. inform.
   c. persuade.
   d. convince.
9. The overall tone of the article is
   a. objective.
   b. sentimental.
   c. concerned.
   d. melancholic.
10. Throughout the article, which type of support is offered for the author's claim that Western executives doing business in China need to learn about fundamental Chinese cultural values to avoid communication breakdowns, cultural missteps, and missed deadlines?
    a. emotional
    b. objective
    c. irrelevant
    d. sentimental

MyReadingLab

Visit Chapter 9: Business in MyReadingLab to complete the Reading 2 activities.

READING 2

Online Article

China OKs iPhone 6 Sale After Apple Addresses Security Concerns

Pre-Reading Questions

In a small group of classmates, discuss the following questions:

1. Most U.S. agencies access users' data from around the world. Do you think this common practice is ethical, and do you believe this practice may be a concern for some countries? Think of specific countries that might object to U.S. companies collecting data from their users.
2. In your opinion, why do U.S. companies such as Apple and Facebook collect data from users around the world? Discuss the primary purpose for which these companies access users' data.
3. China recently passed the United States as Apple's biggest iPhone market. In your opinion, what social, political, and economic factors may facilitate or impede the iPhone's growth in China? Be specific.

China OKs iPhone 6 Sale After Apple Addresses Security Concerns

By **Paul Carsten**

1 The iPhone 6 will be sold in China from Oct 17, after rigorous regulator scrutiny led to Apple Inc. (AAPL.O) reassuring the Chinese government that the smartphones did not have security "backdoors" through which U.S. agencies can access users' data.

2 Apple won approval to sell the phones after also addressing risks of personal information leaks related to the operating system's diagnostic tools, China's Ministry of Industry and Information Technology (MIIT) said on its website on Tuesday.

3 The iPhone 6 and 6 Plus were released on Sept 19 in the United States and elsewhere, but regulatory delay meant Chinese consumers had to wait. The initial lack of a China launch date caught analysts by surprise because of Apple's repeated comments about the importance of the world's biggest smartphone market.

4 Apple and other American technology companies have been subject to greater scrutiny in China after former U.S. National Security Agency contractor Edward Snowden last year revealed spying and surveillance campaigns, including programs that obtained private data through U.S. technology firms.

5 In July, Chinese state media accused Apple of providing user data to U.S. agencies and called for 'severe punishment.' Apple responded by publicly denying the existence of backdoors.

6 The notice of approval for the iPhone 6 could potentially mark the ministry's first for a specific smartphone, suggesting Apple is subject to more scrutiny than its peers in a year in which the U.S. tech giant will release a new phone on all three of China's major mobile networks for the first time.

7 The MIIT said it conducted "rigorous security testing" on the iPhone 6 and held talks with Apple on the issue, and that Apple shared with the ministry materials related to the potential security issues.

8 One of the concerns the MIIT raised was over a third party's ability to take control of a computer that had been given trusted access to the phone by a user. They also queried Apple on the ability of staff repairing iPhones to access user data through background services.

9 Apple told the MIIT it had adopted new security measures in its latest smartphone operating system, iOS 8, and promised that it had never installed backdoors into its products or services to allow access for any government agency in any country, the MIIT said.

10 Apple earlier this month was hiring a head of law enforcement in Beijing to deal with user data requests from China's government, after it last month began storing private data on Chinese soil for the first time.

1.27 Billion Subscribers

11 With regulatory approval from the world's largest smartphone market, analysts expect the iPhone 6 and 6 Plus to sell well in China, where many people prefer phones with larger screens.

12 The phone will be made available on all three of China's state-owned wireless carriers: China Mobile Ltd (0941.HK), China Unicom Hong Kong Ltd (0762.HK) and China Telecom Corp Ltd (0728.HK). Together, the three had more than 1.27 billion mobile subscribers in August.

13 "iPhone 6 and iPhone 6 Plus customers will have access to high-speed mobile networks from China Mobile, China Telecom and China Unicom," Apple Chief Executive Tim Cook said in a press release on Tuesday.

14 The iPhone 6 will be available in gold, silver and gray with a suggested retail price of 5,288 yuan* ($860.16) for the cheapest model with 16GB of storage. The iPhone 6 Plus, in the same colors, will be 6,088 yuan ($990.29) for the cheapest model, also with 16GB of storage. The most expensive iPhone 6 Plus with 128GB storage will be 7,788 yuan ($1,266.82).

15 The phones will also be available online and by reservation from Apple stores.

16 Apple sold a record 10 million iPhone 6 handsets in the first weekend after their launch, which excluded China. Last year, the U.S. tech firm sold 9 million iPhone 5S and 5C models in 11 countries, including China, in the same period.

17 The Cupertino, California-based company said iPhone sales in China grew 50 percent during April–June from a year earlier, effectively salvaging an otherwise lackluster quarter. The strong sales came despite signs that Chinese consumers were waiting for the next-generation iPhone 6, analysts said.

* 1 US dollar = 6.1477 Chinese yuan

(Additional reporting by Beijing Newsroom; Editing by Miral Fahmy and Christopher Cushing)

Reading with a Critical Eye

1. Why did the Chinese government scrutinize the iPhone rigorously before approving its sale in China? What did Apple have to do to win the Chinese government's approval?
2. According to the article, China is the world's biggest smartphone market. Apple's iPhone sales generate revenue for the Chinese government also. Despite this, the Chinese government delayed the launch of the iPhone 6, foregoing potential revenue. What, in your opinion, is more important than money to the Chinese government when allowing foreign companies to do business in China?
3. Why did China threaten to punish Apple and other American companies severely? Refer to the text to answer this question.
4. Why is it that while many American companies do business in China and sell their products and services, Apple is subject to more scrutiny by the Chinese government? Be specific.
5. What might be the consequences if China allowed Apple to collect users' data? In other words, why is China so concerned about Apple and other American companies installing backdoors into their products and services? You may consider former U.S. National Security Agency contractor Edward Snowden's example to answer the question.

Reading Comprehension Check

1. "The iPhone 6 will be sold in China from Oct 17, after rigorous regulator scrutiny led to Apple Inc. (AAPL.O) reassuring the Chinese government that the smartphones did not have security 'backdoors' through which U.S. agencies can access users' data."

   In the sentence above, the word *scrutiny* most closely means

   a. approval. c. examination.
   b. countenance. d. lenience.

2. "The iPhone 6 will be sold in China from Oct 17, after rigorous regulator scrutiny led to Apple Inc (AAPL.O) reassuring the Chinese government that the smartphones did not have security 'backdoors' through which U.S. agencies can **access** users' data."

In the passage above, the meaning of the word *access* is
a. ignore. c. relay.
b. protect. d. retrieve.

3. The main idea of the article is that
a. U.S. corporations have stopped accessing Chinese users' data.
b. China is seriously concerned about U.S. companies accessing its users' data.
c. Apple has promised China that it will not allow U.S. companies access to its backdoors.
d. China has promised U.S. agencies to have security backdoors to access its users' data.

4. "The iPhone 6 will be sold in China from Oct 17, after rigorous regulator scrutiny led to Apple Inc (AAPL.O) reassuring the Chinese government that the smartphones did not have security 'backdoors' through which U.S. agencies can access users' data."
In the passage above, China is
a. biased against Apple and U.S. agencies.
b. biased in favor of Apple and U.S. agencies.
c. completely unbiased against Apple and U.S. agencies.
d. biased in favor of the U.S. government.

5. "Apple won approval to sell the phones after also addressing risks of personal information leaks related to the operating system's diagnostic tools, China's Ministry of Industry and Information Technology (MIIT) said on its website on Tuesday."
In the passage above, the author is
a. biased against Apple. c. biased against China.
b. biased in favor of Apple. d. completely unbiased.

6. "Apple and other American technology companies have been subject to greater scrutiny in China after former U.S. National Security Agency contractor Edward Snowden last year revealed spying and surveillance campaigns, including programs that obtained private data through U.S. technology firms."

Given the focus of Snowden's accusations, one may be led to believe that he is
a. completely unbiased.
b. biased in favor of American companies.
c. biased against the U.S. government.
d. biased in favor of U.S. politicians.

7. "The MIIT said it conducted 'rigorous security testing' on the iPhone 6 and held talks with Apple on the issue, and that Apple shared with the ministry materials related to the potential security issues."

The passage above implies that it may be the case that the Chinese government
a. is biased against Apple.
b. is totally unbiased.
c. is biased in favor of Apple.
d. is biased against Apple's iPhone 6.

8. "One of the concerns the MIIT raised was over a third party's ability to take control of a computer that had been given trusted access to the phone by a user. They also queried Apple on the ability of staff repairing iPhones to access user data through background services."

   In the passage above, China's Ministry of Industry and Information Technology
   a. is unbiased against Apple staff.
   b. is biased in favor of Apple staff.
   c. is biased against Apple staff.
   d. is biased in favor of a third party.

9. "Apple earlier this month was hiring a head of law enforcement in Beijing to deal with user data requests from China's government, after it last month began storing private data on Chinese soil for the first time."

   Given that Apple hired a Chinese head of law enforcement, it may be the case that this official
   a. is biased in favor of the Chinese government.
   b. is biased in favor of Apple.
   c. is biased against the Chinese government.
   d. is completely unbiased against China.

10. "With regulatory approval from the world's largest smartphone market, analysts expect the iPhone 6 and 6 Plus to sell well in China, where many people prefer phones with larger screens."

    According to the passage above, the Chinese are
    a. biased against smartphones with larger screens.
    b. biased against the iPhone 6 and 6 Plus.
    c. biased in favor of smartphones with smaller screens.
    d. biased in favor of smartphones with larger screens.

BIOGRAPHICAL PROFILE

Oprah Winfrey

Oprah Gail Winfrey, more popularly known as Oprah, is a famous American television host, business tycoon, and philanthropist. She has received many honorary awards for her much-acclaimed internationally syndicated talk show, *The Oprah Winfrey Show*. In addition to being a popular talk show host, Winfrey is also a book critic, an Academy Award–nominated actress, and a magazine publisher. She has been ranked the wealthiest African American of the twenty-first century, the only black billionaire for three consecutive years, and the most philanthropic African American who ever lived. Some people believe that she is the most influential woman in the world.

Winfrey was born on January 29, 1954, in rural Mississippi. A child born out of wedlock and raised in a Milwaukee neighborhood, she was raped at the age of 9 and gave birth to a son at the age of 14. The son died in his infancy, and she went to live with her father in Tennessee. It was there that she landed a job in radio at the age of 19. She never looked back since then, and after working as a talk show host in Chicago for a while, she finally founded her own **production** company and became syndicated globally.

Winfrey's meteoric rise to stardom did not happen overnight. She moved to Chicago in 1983 to host a morning talk show, *AM Chicago*. After she took over the talk show, it went from last place to the highest-rated talk show in Chicago. Such was her popularity as the talk show host that the show was renamed *The Oprah Winfrey Show*. On her twentieth anniversary show, Winfrey told her audience that the famous movie critic Roger Ebert had encouraged her to sign a contact with King World. Ebert had rightly predicted that Winfrey's show would generate 40 times as much revenue as his show. According to *Time* magazine, "Few people would have bet on Oprah Winfrey's swift rise to host of the most popular talk show on TV. In a field dominated by white males, she is a black female of ample bulk. As interviewers go, she is no match for, say, Phil Donahue . . . . What she lacks in journalistic toughness, she makes up for in plainspoken curiosity, robust humor and above all, empathy. Guests with sad stories to tell are apt to rouse a tear in Oprah's eye . . . . They, in turn, often find themselves revealing things they would not imagine telling anyone, much less a national TV audience. It is the talk show as a group therapy session."

Oprah's Angel Network, founded in 1998, encourages people around the world to help the poor. The Network provides grants to nonprofit **organizations** and undertakes projects all over the world to alleviate poverty and improve the lives of the underprivileged. Her network has raised $51 million for the cause so far. She personally covers all costs associated with the charitable projects. She has been listed by *Businessweek* as one of America's 50 most generous philanthropists. Throughout her illustrious career, she has donated an estimated $303 million. She donated $10 million to support the Hurricane Katrina victims in New Orleans. Winfrey has helped 250 African American men get a college education. She received the first Bob Hope Humanitarian Award at the 2002 Emmy Awards for her services to television and film.

Some Questions for Group Discussion

1. Oprah Winfrey had an extremely difficult childhood and grew up in abject poverty. Still she persevered in her professional goals and became a talk show host at the age of 19. Discuss what inspired her to become a businesswoman and philanthropist.
2. As an African American woman, Winfrey had to work hard to climb up the ladder of success. Nevertheless, she overcame all the barriers with diligence and persistence and became extremely rich. Discuss the reasons for her phenomenal success.
3. There are more than 200 billionaires in the United States of America. Yet, not all of them are philanthropists. Winfrey is one of few billionaires who donate generously. Discuss why most of the billionaires keep their enormous wealth to themselves and do not share it with the poor and hungry.

Biographical Internet Research

Do research on the Internet and select a successful entrepreneur from the list below of individuals who have amassed wealth and have donated substantial amounts of money for a noble cause. Be prepared to share their biographical profiles with your classmates.

- Bill Gates
- Chris Gardner
- John D. Rockefeller
- George Soros
- Warren Buffett

SKILL FOCUS: The Author's Bias

You can tell an author's attitude toward the chosen subject matter by paying attention to his or her word choice. The author may have a bias for or against the subject. This opinionated view of the subject may be positive or negative. By recognizing the author's positive or negative attitude toward the subject, you can determine whether the author has a bias for or against the topic.

Sometimes the author does *not* have a positive or a negative attitude toward the topic. In this case, the writing is considered unbiased, without being subjective at all. An unbiased author simply presents opposing viewpoints without challenging or defending a particular view. In unbiased writing, the tone is usually neutral, objective, and straightforward.

To determine the author's bias accurately, pay attention to the following details:

- Does the author use mostly positive language to discuss the subject?
- Does the author use mostly negative language to discuss the subject?
- Does the author simply present both positive and negative aspects of the topic?
- Does the author present facts or opinions?

In addition, you can do the following to get a clue to the author's bias: (1) find the author's topic and main idea; (2) see if the author's attitude toward the subject is positive or negative; consider if the author has taken a subjective, one-sided approach; (3) find opinions expressed in biased writing. If you are unable to find either a positive or negative attitude toward the subject, then you can safely conclude that the writing is unbiased.

Determining Bias

Let's examine two examples to understand how to determine if the author has a bias—and, if so, what it is.

Example 1

The production of tangible goods once dominated most economic systems, but today information resources play a major role. Businesses rely on market forecasts, on the specialized knowledge of people, and on economic data for much of their work. After AOL acquired Time Warner, the new business was initially called AOL Time Warner. But marketing research information suggested that people saw the new name as being confusing and **unwieldy**. Hence, the firm's name was eventually shortened back to simply Time Warner.

unwieldy
bulky, unmanageable

Further, much of what the firm does results either in the creation of new information or the repackaging of existing information for new users. Time Warner produces few tangible products. Instead, America Online provides online services for millions of subscribers who pay monthly access fees. Time Warner Entertainment produces movies and television programming. Turner Broadcasting System, a subsidiary, gathers information about world events and then transmits it to **consumers** over its Cable News Network (CNN). Essentially, then, Time Warner is in the information business.

(Ricky W. Griffin and Ronald J. Ebert, Business, *8th ed. Upper Saddle River, NJ: Pearson Prentice Hall, 2006, p. 10)*

Let's start with the topic and main idea.

Topic: Information resources

Main idea: Information resources play a major role in most economic systems nowadays.

Now let's see if the author sounds positive or negative toward the subject. You will notice that the author refrains from giving an opinion and chooses to remain objective. The above passage, therefore, is an example of unbiased language.

Example 2

McDonald's has become an international icon of the fast-food industry. With 30,000 restaurants in 121 countries, the Golden Arches have become as recognizable to foreign consumers as the shape of a Coca-Cola bottle. Yet in recent years, McDonald's seems to have lost its competitive edge both at home and abroad. In the United States, for example, the company's menu is seen as unhealthy, its stores are outdated, and its customer service skills seem to be slipping. McDonald's no longer leads in technology, with rivals inventing new processing and cooking technologies. The firm's traditional markets, children and young men, are spending less on food while markets McDonald's does not target, notably women and older consumers, spend more. Profits have dropped and Starbucks has replaced McDonald's as the food industry success story.

(Business, *p. 31)*

Topic: McDonald's

Main idea: McDonald's is losing its competitive edge both at home and abroad.

If you read the passage carefully, you will notice that the author uses negative adjectives such as *outdated* and *unhealthy* to describe McDonald's. It is reasonable to conclude that the author is biased against McDonald's.

PRACTICING THE SKILL: DETERMINING BIAS

Now that you have looked at one example of unbiased writing and another of the author's bias, read the following passages carefully and answer the questions that follow.

Passage 1

Inflation occurs when widespread price increases occur throughout an economic system. How does it threaten stability? Inflation occurs when the amount of money injected into an economy outstrips the increase in actual output. When this happens, people will have more money to spend, but there will still be the same quantity of products available for them to buy. As they compete with one another to buy available products, prices go up. Before long, high prices will erase the increase in the amount of money injected into the economy. Purchasing power, therefore, declines.

(Business, *p. 35)*

1. What is the topic?

____

2. What is the main idea?

____

____

3. What is the author's attitude toward the topic?

____

Passage 2

When Starbucks opens new stores in small towns, it threatens locally owned cafes and contributes to the loss of the local flavor of Main Streets across America. Big chains like Starbucks homogenize our lives and leave us wondering what makes my town look any different from other towns. The time is now to support our local businesses and to protest big chain takeovers of our communities.

1. What is the topic?

   ____

2. What is the main idea?

   ____

3. What is the author's attitude toward the topic?

   ____

Passage 3

Two of Enron's notorious plans were code-named Death Star and Ricochet. With Death Star, Enron took advantage of the payouts through which the state managed its power grid. Essentially, California paid as much as $750 per megawatt hour to persuade providers not to ship power on overburdened power lines, especially those running north to south. To create the illusion of congestion on these lines, Enron began overbooking shipments and scheduling power transmissions that it had no intention of making. In each case, it then collected money from the state for changing plans that it never meant to carry out.

(*Business*, p. 11)

1. What is the topic?

   ____

2. What is the main idea?

   ____

3. What is the author's attitude toward the topic?

   ____

Passage 4

Outsourcing does not threaten American jobs whatsoever. On the contrary, outsourcing leads to the creation of more high-quality jobs in the United States. This is because the great majority of jobs that are outsourced have been relatively low-skill in nature. Athletic shoes are produced in factories in Southeast Asia, while the shoe companies' corporate jobs remain in the United States. With higher production abroad, more corporate managers and supervisors are needed at home.

1. What is the topic?

____

2. What is the main idea?

____

3. What is the author's attitude toward the topic?

____

Passage 5

More and more, credit card companies are taking advantage of their clients by adding additional small fees to monthly credit card bills. For example, many clients unknowingly sign on for such services as "credit protector" or "travel advantages" programs, and then see these fees add up over time. When clients realize that they are paying for these unwanted services and try to cancel them, the companies make the cancellation process multi-stepped and tedious to discourage clients from discontinuing these high-profit add-ons.

1. What is the topic?

____

2. What is the main idea?

____

____

3. What is the author's attitude toward the topic?

____

____

Now that you have practiced identifying the author's bias, let's practice reading full-length articles to recognize the author's attitude toward the subject.

Recommended Debate Topic: Outsourcing takes jobs away from the American people and hurts the U.S. economy.

Discuss debatable topics related to business with your classmates and instructor for the debate activity.

Your suggested debate topics:

a. ______________________________

b. ______________________________

c. ______________________________

MyReadingLab

Visit Chapter 9: Business in MyReadingLab to complete the Reading 3 activities.

READING 3

Online Article

How She Does It—Anya Ponorovskaya

Pre-Reading Questions

Discuss the following questions with a small group of your classmates:

1. Do you know someone who came to the United States as an immigrant and made the American dream come true? Tell what this person did to become successful.
2. Most immigrants come to the United States with extremely limited financial resources. Yet, some of them manage to pursue their dreams despite the adverse circumstances. Discuss the driving force behind these people that helps them persevere in their goals.
3. Some people believe that it is better to have a stable job with benefits. Others think that the rewards of entrepreneurship are worth taking the risk of starting one's own business. In your opinion, what are the advantages and disadvantages of working for an employer compared to starting a business? Would you rather work for an employer or be an entrepreneur? Give specific reasons for your choice.

How She Does It—Anya Ponorovskaya

***By* Michele Zipp, www.workingmother.com**

1 She's a single mom who arrived in America a Russian refugee. She vacations with her ex and his girlfriend. And her preferred method of transportation is her bicycle. Who is this **eclectic** woman? Anya Ponorovskaya, a one-woman entrepreneurial powerhouse!

eclectic
including a mixture of many different things or people

2 Anya's mom was just twenty-four years old when she left Leningrad with her two young kids. "I cannot imagine having the life she'd had and always be so positive the way she is." Anya shares. "She survived living in a communist country with two kids . . . and all the while maintained a positive outlook on life. She had no mother to help her the way I have her—no assistance at all. She arrived in a totally new world . . . so brave."

Check out Anya's designs and learn more about her boutiques at www.anyaponorovskaya.com.

dilapidated
old, broken, and in very bad condition

rolled up her sleeves
got ready for a challenging task

3 Eventually, Anya put herself through design school at FIT by bartending and running a start-up real estate company (which to this day still exists). In a record month, she was able to put away $30,000 from these two jobs! We're doing the math and are seriously impressed.

Her love of fashion took her to Florence, Italy's Poly Moda design school, where she completed her studies and began to embark on the greatest "job" of her life—being a mom. Dimitri Maxim-Ilya Joseph Williot was born to her and her then boyfriend. Anya couldn't decide on one name so gave him four, though she often calls her now-nine-and-a-half-year-old Dima.

4 When she returned to NY in 2003, she joined some partners and signed the lease on a small, **dilapidated** storefront in New York's NoLita neighborhood to open a women's boutique, selling clothes and accessories that look great on women for work and play. It would be called GirlCat. Having very little money left, she **rolled up her sleeves** and did all renovations herself. She even hauled sheetrock across town—scavenged from a lumberyard around the corner from her son's school. Neighbors were so impressed they hired her to renovate their lofts in the neighboring SoHo neighborhood. More work meant more income, which provided her with **capital** to complete the store and buy out her partners. "Opening a store and believing in its success with a three-and-a-half-year-old son was terrifying. Deciding not to buy a cup of coffee in the morning so that Dima could have a slice of pizza for dinner was my reality at the time of the opening of my first store," she confesses.

hauled
carried or pulled something heavy

5 (She and Dima's father were no longer together.) Those were difficult times, but Anya knew she couldn't work for anyone else. "I needed my own hours. I felt I had no choice—I couldn't do 9 to 5."

6 "I was cutting wood to make shelves, and Dima knows mommy is going to get a store! He said, 'Mommy is that where the bread and cheese will go?' For him, a store meant one thing only—food." Food it did bring them, but in a different way than Dima expected. The store took off, and a second location with the same intent was opened in a substantially larger space, yet it was equally in need of repair. Once again Anya got to work. And in her free time, she worked on designing her line of women's wear, which she debuted in her third boutique that opened in 2007—this time in Brooklyn's Boerum Hill neighborhood.

7 "A single mother will always succeed because she really has no choice," Anya said. Her son is the reason she takes **risks** because without them, there is often no payoff. But she admits that taking on all their responsibilities as a single mom wasn't without some fear. She says that she had to grow up fast and assume responsibility not just for Dima, but her employees. "Every action I take reflects on another human," she tells us.

8 "I feel a huge responsibility to protect my son," she says. Being a working mom helps her achieve that, and she relishes in the fact that her business not only helps her provide for her own family, but for her employees. "It fills me with an enormous sense of satisfaction that there are 10 people paying rent, paying taxes, and living based on something I created. I feel like I am positively impacting my immediate **community**—decreasing unemployment. It feels great that I **built something from the ground up** that provides for people with a job they like."

built something from ground up
started something challenging from the beginning, with little resources

9 "My goal is to keep my family happy so I must keep myself happy. Don't go against your own grain or punish yourself. It is so easy to feel a tremendous amount of guilt as a mother, but the only thing you can really do is make sure that you are happy and following your heart.

10 "In return your children will feel the rewards of that. As a mother you never feel like you can do enough, but you must accept yourself so that your children can."

11 Dima's dad is a part of his life—both their lives. "I have a great relationship with his father and his father's girlfriend. We have keys to each other's places, we eat together, we vacation together. Dima feels like he has a complete family. All it takes is to let go of anger. This is the hardest thing to do but also the most rewarding. Dima feels like he has a really big family. He has asked me, 'why do people need to get married?'"

12 Anya's life/work balance is **intertwined**. When she's not bicycling around town with him (an accessory Anya is rarely without), Dima's at school weekdays and at grandma's house two days a week—she's teaching him Russian. And he's with his dad on weekends. He also spends time at GirlCat. "I try to **create** something fun for him while I am working—choosing fabrics for my designs, painting prints and patterns for my customized linings. It goes like this: 'Honey, I want a cherry blossom print. Can you incorporate these colors?'"

intertwined
twisted together or closely related

13 As far as her designs, the female body is what inspires her. Her clothes are **impeccably** tailored and incredibly flattering for all body types. "I love love love love when my customers are thankful for the pieces I create," she tells us. "When I hear 'for my body it's very hard to find a good fit' and they walk away thrilled with my clothes there is nothing better. I work tirelessly to create proper patterns, proper fittings just so I can feel good about the product I put out. My repeat customers are my best indication of success. There was a woman who posted a testimonial on yelp.com and I have never met her but her words have been so significant in making me believe in myself. She probably still has no idea how grateful I am for her words."

impeccably
completely perfect and impossible to criticize

14 Anya is working to expand her eponymous line to include handbags and footwear to create a core collection that is "season-less, ageless, and flattering to a **range** of body types."

15 But it's Dima who inspires her and advises her. "Recently he said 'I don't like that on you. Actually, I don't like the last four dresses you made. I like simple shapes, no prints.' It's funny because it was a total affirmation on my instincts. He keeps me on my toes. If I tell him I need something, he makes sure I find it. He contributes to everything I do. If I need a skirt, he goes with me and hunts one down. He doesn't let me get **sidetracked**! He's always been that way.

16 "One day, I was talking about increasing sales to my salesgirls and all the things we should do. Dima was there and all of a sudden he jumped up and said 'I have an idea!' He ran into the street and yelled 'Who wants to buy my mommy's dresses? At the best prices

sidetracked
forced to stop doing or saying something by being made interested in something else

ever?' I told him, 'Dima this isn't a flea market!'" But it made her and her salesgirls think: maybe a flea market isn't such a bad idea.

17 Dima's future certainly seems headed for work in a creative field. Anya tells us that he wants to be an inventor. And it's his mom who he looks up to. "I inspire him because he sees I don't give up and he knows that I'm a tough mommy. When he had a hard time recently and overcame it, he was very proud of himself. He told me, 'You teach me not to give up.'"

Reading with a Critical Eye

1. We learn from the article that Anya arrived in the United States as a Russian refugee. Discuss how she became an entrepreneurial powerhouse. Be specific as you explain the reasons for her remarkable success.
2. Just like her mother, Anya keeps a positive outlook on life. Do you think parents can pass on their positive attitude to their children? How about a negative attitude?
3. Anya went to design school at FIT and worked two jobs simultaneously. Later, she went to Italy to study design further. Tell how it is possible for a person to keep the passion for a profession alive while enduring the hardships of life. Give specific examples to support your answer.
4. Anya knew that she could not work for anyone else, and that is why she started her business. Do you think that some people are born to be entrepreneurs, and that most people are better off working 9 to 5 jobs? Why, or why not?
5. Some people argue that business and ethics cannot coexist. Based on the article, do you think Anya is doing business in an ethical way? Use specific examples from the article to support your answer.

Reading Comprehension Check

1. It can be inferred from paragraph 2 of the reading that
   a. Anya's mom has lots of friends.
   b. Anya doesn't get along with her mom.
   c. Anya's mom struggled before coming to the United States.
   d. having two children is perfect for all families.
2. Anya moved to Italy
   a. as a political refugee.
   b. to get out of New York.
   c. because her mom was there.
   d. to attend a design school.
3. The word *scavenged*, in paragraph 4, "She even hauled sheetrock across town—scavenged from a lumber yard," means
   a. searched through discarded material.
   b. stolen.

c. borrowed.
d. disintegrated.

4. In paragraph 4, the detail of Anya sacrificing her morning cup of coffee in order to buy her son a slice of pizza for dinner is offered to make the point that
   a. Anya would give up eating for her son.
   b. starting your own business as a single mom involves struggle.
   c. saving money is the key to owning a small business.
   d. Anya's son was pressuring her.

5. If Anya shows a bias in her view of business models, it is
   a. in favor of innovative small businesses.
   b. in favor of large-scale homogenous businesses.
   c. against creative enterprises.
   d. against American-owned companies.

6. Anya states, "Every action I take reflects on another human" (para. 7). She makes this point in discussing
   a. her relationship with her son.
   b. her relationship with her employees.
   c. both a and b
   d. her relationship with her boss.

7. "Being a working mom helps her achieve that, and she relishes in the fact that her business not only helps her provide for her own family, but for her employees" (para. 8). In this sentence, the word *relishes* could be replaced by
   a. feels disgusted by.
   b. keeps calm.
   c. feels great pleasure.
   d. loses control.

8. The example of the woman who posted a testimonial on yelp.com (para. 13) is offered to show
   a. how satisfied customers help Anya believe in herself and her work.
   b. the unpredictable nature of business.
   c. that success is not all that it seems.
   d. you can never trust your own judgment.

9. The author's tone in this article is
   a. deflated.
   b. deeply emotional.
   c. mysterious.
   d. optimistic.

10. The main idea of the reading is that
    a. with inspiration and determination, Anya was able to find success as a businesswoman in America.
    b. Anya's son inspires her.
    c. political refugees all have the motivation to succeed in their new lives.
    d. one should try to maintain contact with their ex-husbands and ex-wives.

From Reading to Writing: Writing a Cover Letter

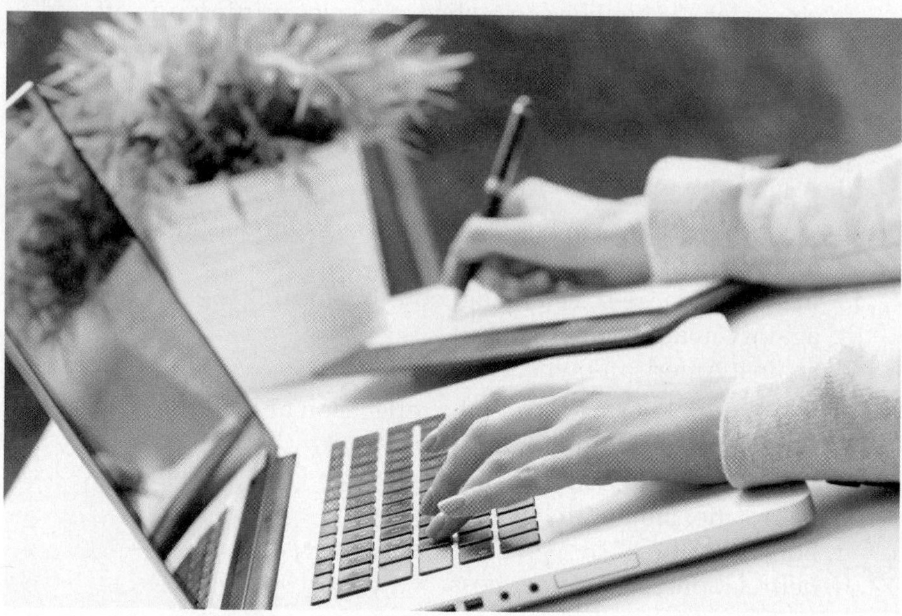

As you begin your academic career, you may also be seeking employment to support yourself economically and to gain experience in the working world. Finding a quality job is not an easy task. The job market is competitive, and you will need to invest a lot of time in putting together an impressive cover letter, as well as a solid resume.

What is a cover letter?

To be considered for almost any position, you will need to write a letter of application. Your cover letter introduces you, explains your purpose for writing, highlights a few of your experiences or skills, and requests an opportunity to meet personally with the potential employer.

You should take great care to write an effective letter because first impressions count and this letter is your introduction to an employer. Keep in mind that the letter not only tells of your accomplishments but also reveals how effectively you can communicate.

The appropriate content, format, and tone for application letters depend on the position being applied for. Therefore, you will want to ask several people who have had experience in obtaining jobs or in hiring in your field to critique a draft of your letter and to offer suggestions for revision.

Advice for Organizing an Impressive Cover Letter

- Try to limit your letter to a single page. Get to the point!

- Consider the employer's needs and how they match up with your skills. Emphasize those skills that will attract your potential employer.
- Take every opportunity to present your work, academic and extracurricular experiences in a positive light. If you were in a club, include this. If you took part in a workshop, include that. Build these achievements into your resume and include them in your cover letter.
- Tailor your letter to each job opportunity. Do not simply send out the same cover letter to every job you apply for!
- Demonstrate some knowledge of the organization to which you are applying. Do your research. Employers are impressed when you have done your homework.
- Write in a clear, formal style. Avoid slang. Be sure to convey confidence and a positive spirit, coupled with respect and professionalism.
- Organize each of your points in a logical sequence; Focus each paragraph around a main point.

Getting Started: Organizing Your Cover Letter

While there are many ways to organize a cover letter, the following guidelines may just work for you.

Opening Paragraph

- Clearly state why you are writing
- Establish a point of contact) did you hear about this opening in an ad or did a particular person suggest you apply?)
- Give a brief idea of who you are ("I'm a sophomore majoring in psychology at the University of Texas")

Paragraph(s) 2-(3)

- Share some of the highlights from your enclosed resume.
- Mention points that are likely to be critical for the position you are seeking.
- Demonstrate how your education and experience match the requirements of the given position.
- Explain how you could contribute to the organization in meaningful ways.

Closing Paragraph

- Focus on action. Make a polite request for an interview.
- Point out what supplementary material is being sent (your resume) and offer to provide additional, supporting documents (a portfolio; a writing sample, etc..)
- Thank the reader for taking the time to read your application letter and indicate that you are greatly looking forward to hearing from them.

A Sample Cover Letter

Dear University of Connecticut Campus Writing Center,

I am writing to you in response to your ad for a writing tutor in the campus newspaper. Professor James in the English Department recommended that I apply for this position, as she believes that I have the necessary skills needed for this job. I am a sophomore majoring in English literature and currently have a GPA of 3.4

As I read the detailed job description for this position, I realized that my professional skills and experience match up quite well. I have had a lot of experience interacting with other students through my volunteer work for our freshman orientations and my involvement in the campus chess club. I have published a number of my own pieces of writing in the campus newspaper and on an online blog called Leapfrog. Furthermore, as requested in the job description, I have a flexible study schedule, which will allow me to work in the writing center three days a week.

I greatly enjoy studying English literature. I took part in an Honor's Course with Professor Harris in which I had the opportunity to work with members of the local prison population on literacy skills. I have also taken classes in journalism and poetry. My strong study skills are reflected in my high GPA. I believe that I can guide more vulnerable students toward building their study skills and progressing in the field of writing.

Once again, I believe my experience and writing skills make me the perfect candidate for this tutoring position in the Campus Writing Center. Please feel free to contact me, by phone or by email, to set up an interview at your earliest convenience. I look forward to hearing from you.

Sincerely,

Nicole Sanders

Your Turn: Compose a Winning Cover Letter

Write a convincing cover letter for a job you would actually be interested in obtaining. You can first check the classifieds online for jobs of interest, or simply consider a job that you already know about.

When you are finished composing your cover letter, spend some time editing and then submit it to your professor for review.

Feedback Form

When you finish writing your cover letter, ask a classmate to read it and answer the questions on this form. You will also read your peer's cover letter and evaluate it. By reviewing your peer's writing, you will learn to read with a critical eye and provide constructive feedback. Your valuable suggestions will enable your peer to make the necessary revisions to get the message across to the intended reader in a precise and clear manner. While it is important that you provide critical comments on your peer's writing, it is also useful to give feedback in a constructive way. Avoid being overly critical and suggest ways to make the letter more effective. Read the following questions carefully before you read your peer's cover letter.

Writer name ______________________________

Reviewer name ______________________________

1. **Does the letter address the employer appropriately? How does the letter begin?**

____

____

____

2. **Does the opening paragraph clearly state the writer's reason for writing, and establish a point of contact?**

____

____

____

3. **Does the writer demonstrate how his/her education and experience match the requirements of the given position?**

____

____

____

4. **Does the closing paragraph make an interview request, point out supplementary material being sent, and thank the employer for reading the letter?**

____

____

____

5. **Do you think the cover letter's length is sufficient? Explain**

____

____

____

6. **Is the writer's language appropriate for a cover letter? What formal terms are used in the letter?**

7. **Does the writer provide a detailed description of their qualifications for the job? Do you think the employer will be impressed with the writer's qualifications? Explain**

8. **Does the writer use polite language? Is the letter too formal, informal, or casual? Explain**

9. **Is the language used in the letter clear and straight to the point?**

Textbook Application

Read the following chapter from an introductory textbook on Business. As you know, this reading exercise gives you an opportunity to practice reading authentic text. Read the chapter carefully and answer the multiple-choice questions that follow.

READING 4

Textbook Reading

MyReadingLab

Visit Chapter 9: Business in MyReadingLab to complete the Reading 4 activities.

from *Understanding the U.S. Business System*

What Goes Up Continues to Go Up

1 The sign in front of a Florida Shell gasoline station summed it up nicely: The "prices" for the three grades of gasoline sold at the station were listed as "An arm," "A leg," and "Your firstborn." While the sign no doubt led to a few smiles from motorists, its sentiments were far from a laughing matter. Indeed, in mid-2004 retail gasoline prices in the United States were at an all-time high, exceeding $2 per gallon in most places. But while

gasoline prices have often fluctuated up and down, the upward price spiral in 2004 left consumers, government officials, and business leaders struggling to find answers.

2 What made this gas crisis unusual was that it was the result of an unusual confluence of **supply, demand,** and global forces. In the past, for instance, gas prices generally increased only when the supply was reduced. For example, an Arab embargo on petroleum exports to the United States in 1971 led to major price jumps. But these higher prices spurred new exploration, and as new oil fields came online, prices eventually dropped again. Subsequent supply disruptions due to political problems in Venezuela, Nigeria, and Iraq have also contributed to reduced supplies and hence higher prices at different times.

3 But the circumstances underlying the 2004 increases were much more complex. First of all, the supply of domestically produced gasoline in the United States has dropped steadily since 1972. This has been due to the facts that domestic oil fields have been nearly exhausted at the same time that new sources were being identified in many other parts of the world. Hence, global supplies have been increasing at a rate that has more than offset the declines in domestic production. As a result, the United States has been relying more and more on foreign producers.

4 Second, demand for gasoline in the United States has continued to rise. A growing population, the increased popularity of gas-guzzling SUVs and other big vehicles, and strong demand for other products (plastics, for instance) that require petroleum as a raw material have all contributed to increased demand. For example, in 2002 the United States consumed 7,191 million barrels of oil. This total was greater than the combined consumption of Germany, Russia, China, and Japan. As prices escalated, fears grew that there could be major economic damage. In the words of one expert, "Higher energy costs flow into every nook and cranny of the economy."

5 The final piece of the puzzle, surprisingly enough, was a surging global economy. As nation after nation started to recover from the global downturn that had slowed economic growth, the demand for oil and gasoline also surged. More people were buying cars, and petroleum refiners worked around the clock to help meet the unprecedented demand for gasoline. China, in particular, has become a major consumer of petroleum.

6 So, rather than weak supplies, it was strong global demand that was propelling the price increases that swept the country. And these price increases were leading to a wide array of consequences. For one thing, automobile manufacturers stepped up their commitment to making more fuel-efficient cars. Refiners posted record profits. And even local police officers were kept busy combating a surge in gasoline theft.

The Meaning of "Business"

business
organization that provides goods or services to earn profits

profits
difference between a business's revenues and its expenses

7 What do you think of when you hear the word "*business*"? Does it conjure images of successful corporations such as Shell Oil and IBM? Or of less successful companies like Enron and Kmart? Are you reminded of smaller firms, such as your local supermarket or favorite restaurant? Or do you think of even smaller family-owned operations, such as the car-repair shop around the corner, your neighborhood pizzeria, or the florist down the street?

8 All these organizations are businesses—organizations that provide goods or services that are then sold to earn profits. Indeed, the prospect of earning profits—the difference between a business's revenues and **expenses**—is what encourages people to open and expand businesses. After all, profits reward owners for risking their money and time. The legitimate right to pursue profits distinguishes a business from those organizations, such as most universities, hospitals, and government agencies, which run in much the same way but which generally don't seek profits.

9 **Consumer Choice and Consumer Demand** In a capitalistic system, then, businesses exist to earn profits for owners; an owner is likewise free to set up a new business, grow that business, sell it to other owners, or even shut it down. But consumers also have freedom of choice. In choosing how to pursue profits, businesses must take into account what consumers want and/or need. No matter how efficient a business is, it won't survive if there is no demand for its goods or services. Neither a snowblower shop in Florida nor a beach-umbrella store in Alaska is likely to do very well.

10 **Opportunity and Enterprise** But if enterprising businesspeople can identify either unmet consumer needs or better ways of satisfying consumer needs, they can be successful. In other words, someone who can spot a promising opportunity and then develop a good plan for capitalizing on it can succeed. The opportunity always involves goods or services that consumers need and/or want—especially if no one else is supplying them or if existing businesses are doing so inefficiently or incompletely.

11 **Quality of Life** Businesses produce most of the goods and services we consume, and they **employ** most working people. They create most new **innovations** and provide a vast range of opportunities for new businesses, which serve as their suppliers. A healthy business climate also contributes directly to the quality of life and standard of living of people in a society. New forms of technology, service businesses, and international opportunities promise to keep production, consumption, and employment growing indefinitely. Business profits enhance the personal **incomes** of millions of owners and **stockholders**, and business taxes help to support governments at all levels. Many businesses support charities and provide community **leadership**. Of course, some businesses also harm the environment, and their decision makers sometimes resort to unacceptable practices for their own personal benefit.

12 In this chapter, we first trace the history of U.S. business. We then examine economic systems around the world. Once you understand the

[1]Define the nature of U.S. *business* and identify its main goals and functions.

"Your Honor, my client pleads guilty to an overzealous but well-intentioned pursuit of the profit motive."

differences among them, you will better appreciate the workings of the U.S. system. We also investigate the concepts of demand and supply and their role in private enterprise.

The Evolution of Business in the United States

13 The landscape of U.S. business has evolved dramatically since the nation's founding. A look at the history of U.S. business shows an evolution from small sole proprietorships to today's intricate corporate structures and an evolving perspective on business accountability. It also sets the stage for better understanding how our business system works.

THE FACTORY SYSTEM AND THE INDUSTRIAL REVOLUTION

14 With the coming of the Industrial Revolution in the middle of the eighteenth century, manufacturing was changed dramatically by advances in technology and by the development of the factory system. Replacing hundreds of cottage workers who had turned out one item at a time, the

Industrial Revolution **major** mid-eighteenth-century change in production characterized by a **shift** to the factory system, mass production, and the specialization of **labor**

[2]Trace the history of business in the United States and the changing view of business accountability.

factory system brought together in one place the materials and workers required to produce items in large quantities and the new machines needed for mass production.

15 The factory system also reduced duplication of equipment and allowed firms to buy raw materials at better prices by buying in large lots. Even more important, it encouraged specialization of labor. Mass production replaced a system of highly skilled craftspeople who performed all the different tasks required to make a single item. Instead, a series of semiskilled workers, each trained to perform only one task and aided by specialized equipment, greatly increased output.

LAISSEZ-FAIRE AND THE ENTREPRENEURIAL ERA

16 Despite problems during the nineteenth century, the U.S. banking system began freeing businesses from European capital markets. In addition, improvements in transportation—steamboat navigation on major rivers and the development of railroads—soon made it economical to move products to distant markets.

17 Another key feature of the times was the rise on a grand scale of the entrepreneur. Like businesses in many other nations, U.S. business embraced the philosophy of *laissez-faire*—the idea that the government should not interfere in the economy. Rather, it should let business run without regulation and according to its own "natural" laws.

18 Risk taking and entrepreneurship became hallmarks of aggressive practices that created some of the biggest companies in the country and, ultimately, the world. During the last half of the 1800s, for instance, Andrew Carnegie founded U.S. Steel and Andrew Mellon created the Aluminum Company of America (Alcoa). J. P. Morgan's Morgan Guarantee and Trust came to dominate the U.S. financial system, and John D. Rockefeller's Standard Oil controlled—in fact, monopolized—the petroleum industry. But these entrepreneurs all too often saw themselves as being accountable to no one.

19 The growth of these businesses increased the national standard of living and made the United States a world power. But the economic power of such firms made it difficult, if not impossible, for competitors to enter their markets. Complete market control became a watchword in many industries, with major corporations opting to collude rather than compete. Price fixing and other forms of market manipulation became business as usual, with captains of industry often behaving as robber barons. Reacting against unethical practices and the unregulated struggle for dominance, critics called for corrective action and, ultimately, for antitrust laws and the breakup of monopolies. Specifically, society began to demand greater accountability from big businesses—accountability to function in ways that did not trample on the rights of others.

20 Among other important laws, the Sherman Antitrust Act of 1890 and the Clayton Act of 1914 were passed specifically to limit the control that a single business could gain over a market. Other laws sought to regulate a variety of employment and advertising practices, and still

others regulated the ways in which businesses could handle their financial affairs. This antitrust legislation was the basis for the U.S. government's recent lawsuit against Microsoft Corporation. (Appendix I gives more information about the legal environment of U.S. business, much of which is rooted in this era.)

THE PRODUCTION ERA

21 The concepts of specialization and mass production were further refined in the early twentieth century, when many experts sought to focus management's attention on the production process. Relying on the advice of efficiency experts, managers began to further boost output by scientifically studying jobs and defining the "one best way" to perform those jobs. Dubbed *scientific management* by its advocates in the early 1900s, this model of management paved the way for a new era of business.

22 This new production era began to emerge in 1913 when Henry Ford introduced the moving assembly line. Ford's focus was on manufacturing efficiency: By adopting fixed workstations, increasing task specialization, using the concepts of scientific management, and moving the work to the worker, Ford dramatically increased productivity and lowered prices. And in so doing, he made the automobile affordable for the average person.

production era
period during the early twentieth century in which U.S. business focused primarily on improving productivity and manufacturing efficiency

23 Unfortunately, both the growth of corporations and improved assembly-line output came at the expense of worker freedom. The dominance of big firms made it harder for individuals to go into business for themselves, and in some cases employer-run company towns gave people little freedom of choice, either in selecting an employer or in choosing what products to buy. Business accountability was again called into question, and new pressures emerged for balance.

24 This need for accountability and balance led to changes in how both the government and workers related to business. For instance, the production era witnessed the rise of labor unions and the advent of collective bargaining (see Chapter 8). In addition, the Great Depression of the 1930s and World War II prompted the government to intervene in the economic system on an unprecedented scale. Today, economists and politicians often refer to business, government, and labor as the three countervailing powers in U.S. society. Although all are big and all are strong, each is limited by the power of the other two.

THE MARKETING ERA

25 After World War II, the demand for consumer goods that had been frustrated by wartime shortages fueled new economic growth in the United States. Despite brief recessions, the 1950s and 1960s were prosperous. Production continued to increase, technology to advance, and the standard of living to rise. During this era, a new philosophy of business came of age: the marketing concept. Previously, businesses had been production and sales oriented. They tended to produce what other businesses produced, what they thought

customers wanted, or simply what owners wanted to produce. Henry Ford, for example, supposedly said that his customers could buy his cars in whatever color they wanted—as long as it was black!

marketing concept idea that a business must focus on identifying and satisfying consumer wants in order to be profitable

26 According to the marketing concept, however, business starts with the customer. Producers start by determining what customers want and then provide it. Successful practitioners of the marketing concept include such companies as Procter & Gamble (P&G) and Anheuser-Busch. Such firms let consumers choose what best suits their needs by offering an array of products within a given market (toothpaste or beer, for example). Moreover, they also rely heavily on marketing and advertising to help shape consumer awareness, preferences, and tastes. Perspectives on business accountability also changed with the advent of the marketing concept, with central issues being truth-in-advertising, advertising directed at children, and so forth.

THE GLOBAL ERA

27 The 1980s saw the continuation of technological advances in production, computer technology, information systems, and communications capabilities. They also witnessed the emergence of a truly global economy. U.S. consumers now drive cars made in Japan, wear sweaters made in Italy, and listen to CD players made in South Korea. Elsewhere around the world, people drive Fords, drink Pepsi, wear Levi's, use Dell computers, and watch Disney movies and television shows.

28 As we will see in **Chapter** 5, globalization is a fact of life for most businesses today. Improved communication and transportation, in addition to more efficient international methods for financing, producing, distributing, and marketing products and services, have combined to open distant marketplaces to businesses as never before.

29 Admittedly, many U.S. businesses have been hurt by foreign competition. Many others, however, have profited from new foreign markets. International competition has also forced many U.S. businesses to work harder to cut costs, increase efficiency, and improve quality. From an accountability perspective, key issues associated with globalization include worker rights in offshore production facilities and balancing the costs and benefits of outsourcing. We explore a variety of important trends, opportunities, and challenges in the new global era throughout this book.

THE INFORMATION ERA

30 The turn of the century has been accompanied by what might be called the *information era,* fueled largely by the Internet. Internet usage in North America grew from about 100 users per 1,000 people in 1995 to more than 750 users per 1,000 by 2005. The growth rate in Western Europe, however, has been even faster and is becoming increasingly significant in the Asia Pacific region as well. How has the growth of the Internet affected business? For one thing, it has given a dramatic boost to trade in all sectors of the economy, especially services. If the Internet makes it easier

for all trade to grow, this is particularly true for trade in services on an international scale.

31 The Internet has also helped to level the playing field, at least to some extent, between larger and smaller enterprises, regardless of their products. In the past, a substantial investment was needed to enter some industries and to expand into foreign markets. Now, however, a small business in central Missouri, southern Italy, eastern Malaysia, or northern Brazil can set up a Web site and compete with much larger businesses located around the world. And finally, the Internet holds considerable potential as an effective and efficient networking mechanism. So-called business-to-business networks, for instance, can link firms with suppliers, customers, and strategic partners in ways that make it faster and easier for everyone to do business. The emergence of the information era also continues to define such accountability issues as rights to privacy.

Reading Comprehension Check

As you answer the questions below, try to label the question type. The first example is done for you.

1. As used in the sentence, "What made this gas crisis unusual was that it was the result of an unusual confluence of supply, demand, and global forces" (p. 509, para. 2), the word *confluence* means
   a. divergence.
   (b.) collection.
   c. branching out.
   d. separate forces.

   Question Type: *Vocabulary in Context*

2. "Subsequent supply disruptions due to political problems in Venezuela, Nigeria, and Iraq have also contributed to reduced supplies and hence higher prices at different times" (p. 509, para. 2).

   The term *disruptions* could be replaced with

   a. improvements.
   b. refinements.
   c. continuity.
   d. interruptions.

   Question Type: ________________

3. In the sentence, "This has been due to the facts that domestic oil fields have been nearly exhausted at the same time that new sources were being identified in many other parts of the world" (p. 509, para. 3), a synonym for the word *exhausted* is

   a. replenished completely.
   b. used up completely.
   c. replaced completely.
   d. improved completely.

   Question Type: ________________

4. The main idea of the chapter is that

   a. different types of global economic systems affect the landscape of U.S. business.
   b. U.S. businesses have evolved dramatically since the nation was founded.
   c. competition plays little or no role in the U.S. economic system.
   d. demand and supply do not affect resource distribution in the United States.

   Question Type: ________________

5. Examples of different eras in U.S. business such as the Industrial Revolution, the entrepreneurial era, the production era, the marketing era, and so forth are offered to support the idea that

   a. the nature of U.S. business has not changed significantly since the country was founded.
   b. the Industrial Revolution was a consequence of the marketing era.
   c. the landscape of U.S. business has changed significantly since the nation's founding.
   d. the entrepreneurial era and the marketing era happened simultaneously.

   Question Type: ________________

6. Which of the following is *not* mentioned as an era in the evolution of business in the United States?

   a. the global era
   b. the information era
   c. the demand and supply era
   d. the entrepreneurial era

   Question Type: ________________

7. "After World War II, the demand for consumer goods that had been frustrated by wartime shortages fueled new economic growth in the United States" (p. 516, para. 25).

   It can be inferred from the above passage that

   a. after World War II, the economy was extremely sluggish in the United States.
   b. in the aftermath of World War II, the U.S. economy plummeted.

c. there was little or no economic growth in the United States during World War II.
d. the demand for consumer goods faded after World War II.

Question Type: ________

8. "How has the growth of the Internet affected business? For one thing, it has given a dramatic boost to trade in all sectors of the economy, especially services. If the Internet makes it easier for all trade to grow, this is particularly true for trade in services on an international scale" (p. 515, para. 30).

A logical conclusion that can be drawn from the above statement is that

a. the growth of the Internet has given a boost to trade in services only in the United States.
b. the growth of the Internet has negatively impacted trade in services.
c. since the advent of the Internet, trade in products has not been as robust as trade in services.
d. trade in products has far surpassed trade in services.

Question Type: ________

9. The authors' primary purpose in this chapter is to
a. persuade the reader to found a small business in the United States.
b. convince students that they should conduct business with businesses in Europe and Asia.
c. deter the reader from pursuing a career in business.
d. educate the reader on the evolution of business in the United States.

Question Type: ______________

10. The overall tone of the chapter is
a. intimidating.
b. objective.
c. sorrowful.
d. concerned.

Question Type: ___________

11. Which of the following is *not* a fact?
a. In mid-2004, gasoline prices were at an all-time high in the United States.
b. In 2002, the American people consumed 7,191 million barrels of oil.
c. Most universities, hospitals, and government agencies do not seek profits.
d. The supply of domestically produced gasoline has dropped steadily in the United States since 1972.

Question Type: ______________

12. Which of the following is *not* an opinion?
a. Most U.S. corporations did business unethically during the entrepreneurial era.
b. Henry Ford introduced the moving assembly line in 1913.

c. Andrew Carnegie, J. P. Morgan, and John Rockefeller were immoral businessmen.
d. Technological advances in production and computer technology have made a negative impact on globalization.

Question Type: ____________

13. The overall pattern of organization of the section entitled What Goes Up Continues to Go Up (p. 508) is
a. listing.
b. classification.
c. cause and effect.
d. comparison and contrast.

Question Type: ____________

14. Which statement does *not* offer support for the author's claim that "As nation after nation started to recover from the global downturn that had slowed economic growth, the demand for oil and gasoline also surged"?
a. China became a major consumer of petroleum.
b. More people were buying cars all over the world.
c. Weak supplies propelled the price increases in the United States.
d. Petroleum refiners worked long hours to meet the demand for gasoline.

Question Type: ________

15. "Admittedly, many U.S. businesses have been hurt by foreign competition. Many others, however, have profited from new foreign markets. International competition has also forced many U.S. businesses to work harder to cut costs, increase efficiency, and improve quality. From an accountability perspective, key issues associated with globalization include worker rights in offshore production facilities and balancing the costs and benefits of outsourcing."

In this passage, the author expresses a bias in favor of
a. emerging foreign markets.
b. U.S. businesses.
c. international competition.
d. globalization.

Question Type: ____________

READING 5

Novel Excerpt

MyReadingLab

Visit Chapter 9: Business in MyReadingLab to complete the Reading 5 activities.

Tom Sawyer Whitewashing the Fence

Pre-Reading Questions

1. Can you think of any work duties that you absolutely would never want to do? What particular qualities of these tasks do you find unappealing?
2. Do good negotiating skills involve some level of trickery? Explain.

3. In the following excerpt from *The Adventures of Tom Sawyer*, you will read about how young Tom fools his friends in business. Do you think there is a certain age where one gains a business sense, or do you think some people are born with business skills? Explain your answer.

Tom Sawyer Whitewashes the Fence

From *The Adventures of Tom Sawyer*, by Mark Twain

1 Saturday morning was come, and all the summer world was bright and fresh, and brimming with life. There was a song in every heart; and if the heart was young the music issued at the lips. There was cheer in every face and a spring in every step. The locust-trees were in bloom and the fragrance of the blossoms filled the air. Cardiff Hill, beyond the village and above it, was green with vegetation and it lay just far enough away to seem a Delectable Land, dreamy, reposeful, and inviting.

2 Tom appeared on the sidewalk with a bucket of whitewash and a long-handled brush. He surveyed the fence, and all gladness left him and a deep melancholy settled down upon his spirit. Thirty yards of board fence nine feet high. Life to him seemed hollow, and existence but a burden. Sighing, he dipped his brush and passed it along the topmost plank; repeated the operation; did it again; compared the insignificant whitewashed streak with the far-reaching continent of unwhitewashed fence, and sat down on a tree-box discouraged. Jim came skipping out at the gate with a tin pail, and singing Buffalo Gals. Bringing water from the town pump had always been hateful work in Tom's eyes, before, but now it did not strike him so. He remembered that there was company at the pump. White, mulatto, and negro boys and girls were always there waiting their turns, resting, trading playthings, quarrelling, fighting, skylarking. And he remembered that although the pump was only a hundred and fifty yards off, Jim never got back with a bucket of water under an hour – and even then somebody generally had to go after him. Tom said:

3 "Say, Jim, I'll fetch the water if you'll whitewash some."

4 Jim shook his head and said:

5 "Can't, Mars Tom. Ole missis, she tole me I got to go an' git dis water an' not stop foolin' roun' wid anybody. She say she spec' Mars Tom gwine to ax me to whitewash, an' so she tole me go 'long an' 'tend to my own business – she 'lowed *she'd* 'tend to de whitewashin'."

6 "Oh, never you mind what she said, Jim. That's the way she always talks. Gimme the bucket – I won't be gone only a a minute. *She* won't ever know."

7 "Oh, I dasn't, Mars Tom. Ole missis she'd take an' tar de head off'n me. 'Deed she would."

8 "She! She never licks anybody – whacks 'em over the head with her thimble – and who cares for that, I'd like to know. She talks awful,

but talk don't hurt – anyways it don't if she don't cry. Jim, I'll give you a marvel. I'll give you a white alley!"

9 Jim began to waver.

10 "White alley, Jim! And it's a bully taw."

11 "My! Dat's a mighty gay marvel, I tell you! But Mars Tom I's powerful 'fraid ole missis – "

12 "And besides, if you will I'll show you my sore toe."

13 Jim was only human – this attraction was too much for him. He put down his pail, took the white alley, and bent over the toe with absorbing interest while the bandage was being unwound. In another moment he was flying down the street with his pail and a tingling rear, Tom was whitewashing with vigor, and Aunt Polly was retiring from the field with a slipper in her hand and triumph in her eye. But Tom's energy did not last. He began to think of the fun he had planned for this day, and his sorrows multiplied. Soon the free boys would come tripping along on all sorts of delicious expeditions, and they would make a world of fun of him for having to work – the very thought of it burnt him like fire. He got out his worldly wealth and examined it – bits of toys, marbles, and trash; enough to buy an exchange of *work*, maybe, but not half enough to buy so much as half an hour of pure freedom. So he returned his straitened means to his pocket, and gave up the idea of trying to buy the boys. At this dark and hopeless moment an inspiration burst upon him! Nothing less than a great, magnificent inspiration.

14 He took up his brush and went tranquilly to work. Ben Rogers hove in sight presently – the very boy, of all boys, whose ridicule he had been dreading. Ben's gait was the hop-skip-and-jump – proof enough that his heart was light and his anticipations high. He was eating an apple, and giving a long, melodious whoop, at intervals, followed by a deep-toned ding-dong-dong, ding-dong-dong, for he was personating a steamboat. As he drew near, he slackened speed, took the middle of the street, leaned far over to star-board and rounded to ponderously and with laborious pomp and circumstance – for he was personating the Big Missouri, and considered himself to be drawing nine feet of water. He was boat and captain and engine-bells combined, so he had to imagine himself standing on his own hurricane-deck giving the orders and executing them:

15 "Stop her, sir! Ting-a-ling-ling!" The headway ran almost out, and he drew up slowly toward the sidewalk.

16 "Ship up to back! Ting-a-ling-ling!" His arms straightened and stiffened down his sides.

17 "Set her back on the stabboard! Ting-a-ling-ling! Chow! ch-chow-wow! Chow!" His right hand, meantime, describing stately circles – for it was representing a forty-foot wheel.

18 "Let her go back on the labboard! Ting-a-ling-ling! Chow-ch-chow-chow!" The left hand began to describe circles.

19 "Stop the stabboard! Ting-a-ling-ling! Stop the labboard! Come ahead on the stabboard! Stop her! Let your outside turn over slow! Ting-a-ling-ling! Chow-ow-ow! Get out that head-line! *Lively* now! Come – out with your spring-line – what're you about there! Take a turn round that stump with the bight of it! Stand by that stage, now – let her go! Done with the engines, sir! Ting-a-ling-ling! *Sh't! s'h't! sh't!*" (trying the gauge-cocks).

20 Tom went on whitewashing – paid no attention to the steam-boat. Ben stared a moment and then said: "Hi- *yi* ! You're up a stump, ain't you!"

21 No answer. Tom surveyed his last touch with the eye of an artist, then he gave his brush another gentle sweep and surveyed the result, as before. Ben ranged up alongside of him. Tom's mouth watered for the apple, but he stuck to his work. Ben said:

22 "Hello, old chap, you got to work, hey?"

23 Tom wheeled suddenly and said:

24 "Why, it's you, Ben! I warn't noticing."

25 "Say – *I'm* going in a-swimming, *I* am. Don't you wish you could? But of course you'd druther *work* – wouldn't you? Course you would!"

26 Tom contemplated the boy a bit, and said:

27 "What do you call work?"

28 "Why, ain't *that* work?"

29 Tom resumed his whitewashing, and answered carelessly:

30 "Well, maybe it is, and maybe it ain't. All I know, is, it suits Tom Sawyer."

31 "Oh come, now, you don't mean to let on that you like it?"

32 The brush continued to move.

33 "Like it? Well, I don't see why I oughtn't to like it. Does a boy get a chance to whitewash a fence every day?"

34 That put the thing in a new light. Ben stopped nibbling his apple. Tom swept his brush daintily back and forth – stepped back to note the effect – added a touch here and there – criticised the effect again – Ben watching every move and getting more and more interested, more and more absorbed. Presently he said:

35 "Say, Tom, let *me* whitewash a little."

36 Tom considered, was about to consent; but he altered his mind:

37 "No – no – I reckon it wouldn't hardly do, Ben. You see, Aunt Polly's awful particular about this fence – right here on the street, you know – but if it was the back fence I wouldn't mind and *she* wouldn't. Yes, she's awful particular about this fence; it's got to be done very careful; I reckon there ain't one boy in a thousand, maybe two thousand, that can do it the way it's got to be done."

38 "No – is that so? Oh come, now – lemme, just try. Only just a little – I'd let you, if *you* was me, Tom."

39 "Ben, I'd like to, honest injun; but Aunt Polly – well, Jim wanted to do it, but she wouldn't let him; Sid wanted to do it, and she wouldn't let Sid. Now don't you see how I'm fixed? If you was to tackle this fence and anything was to happen to it – "

40 "Oh, shucks, I'll be just as careful. Now lemme try. Say – I'll give you the core of my apple."

41 "Well, here – No, Ben, now don't. I'm afeard – "

42 "I'll give you *all* of it!"

43 Tom gave up the brush with reluctance in his face, but alacrity in his heart. And while the late steamer Big Missouri worked and sweated in the sun, the retired artist sat on a barrel in the shade close by, dangled his legs, munched his apple, and planned the slaughter of more innocents. There was no lack of material; boys happened along every little while; they came to jeer, but remained to whitewash. By the time Ben was fagged out, Tom had traded the next chance to Billy Fisher for a kite, in good repair; and when *he* played out, Johnny Miller bought in for a dead rat and a string to swing it with – and so on, and so on, hour after hour. And when the middle of the afternoon came, from being a poor poverty-stricken boy in the morning, Tom was literally rolling in wealth. He had besides the things before mentioned, twelve marbles,part of a jews-harp, a piece of blue bottle-glass to look through, a spool cannon, a key that wouldn't unlock anything, a fragment of chalk, a glass stopper of a decanter, a tin soldier, a couple of tadpoles, six fire-crackers, a kitten with only one eye, a brass door-knob, a dog-collar – but no dog – the handle of a knife, four pieces of orange-peel, and a dilapidated old window sash.

bankrupted
insolvent; without money

44 He had had a nice, good, idle time all the while – plenty of company – and the fence had three coats of whitewash on it! If he hadn't run out of whitewash he would have **bankrupted** every boy in the village.

attain
to reach; accomplish

45 Tom said to himself that it was not such a hollow world, after all. He had discovered a great law of human action, without knowing it – namely, that in order to make a man or a boy covet a thing, it is only necessary to make the thing difficult to **attain**. If he had been a great and wise philosopher, like the writer of this book, he would now have comprehended that Work consists of whatever a body is *obliged* to do, and that Play consists of whatever a body is not obliged to do. And this would help him to understand why constructing artificial flowers or performing on a tread-mill is work, while rolling ten-pins or climbing Mont Blanc is only amusement. There are wealthy gentlemen in England who drive four-horse passenger-coaches twenty or thirty miles on a daily line, in the summer, because the privilege costs them considerable money; but if they were offered wages for the service, that would turn it into work and then they would resign.

46 The boy mused awhile over the substantial change which had taken place in his worldly circumstances, and then wended toward headquarters to report.

Reading with a Critical Eye

1. Twain writes of Tom, "At this dark and hopeless moment an inspiration burst upon him! Nothing less than a great, magnificent inspiration." What vision of business success does Tom have?
2. What are Tom's selling points to attract Ben to his plan?
3. Tom is successful in tricking the neighborhood kids, but cannot put one by Jim, the slave boy. What is Mark Twain's underlying message in portraying Jim the way he did?
4. "He had discovered a great law of human action, without knowing it – namely, that in order to make a man or a boy covet a thing, it is only necessary to make the thing difficult to **attain**." Paraphrase the above sentence.
5. In your opinion, are Tom's business tactics ethical or not? Defend your position on this.

Reading Comprehension Check

1. What excuse does Jim use to get out of Tom's trap to get him to paint the fence?
   a. He wanted to whitewash the fence when non one else could see him doing it.
   b. He had been warned by his overseer that he needed to fetch the water and not get involved in other business.
   c. He could only do Tom's work if Tom offered him a valuable prize, which Tom could not afford.
   d. Jim made the point that slaves were not allowed to touch private property.
2. How does Tom convince Ben that whitewashing the fence is something special?
   a. He offers Ben a high price to do the work for him.
   b. He reminds Ben that Jim had wanted to do it but had lost the opportunity due to his fear of getting in trouble.
   c. Tom makes it sound like whitewashing a fence is a unique task, and only for those with a particular talent.
   d. He shows Ben that the task of painting this long fence would take him years to do on his own.
3. "Soon the free boys would come tripping along on all sorts of delicious **expeditions**, and they would make a world of fun of him for having to work."

   In the above sentence, the word *expedition* could be replaced by _______.
   a. adventures
   b. chores
   c. experts
   d. hiking trips

4. Tom was able to obtain all of the following prizes as a trade off for 'allowing' the local boys to paint the fence EXCEPT for ____________.
   a. a kite
   b. a dead rat
   c. a baseball
   d. twelve marbles
5. From what we learn about Tom in this passage, he could best be described as ____________________.
   a. hard-working and philosophical
   b. honest and kind
   c. lazy and foolish
   d. clever and manipulative
6. "Tom gave up the brush with reluctance in his face, but **alacrity** in his heart."

   In the above sentence, a synonym for the word *alacrity* is ___________.
   a. fear
   b. readiness
   c. bitterness
   d. resentment
7. What is the tone of the story excerpt?
   a. serious
   b. dark and pessimistic
   c. nostalgic
   d. light and playful
8. "Johnny Miller bought in for a dead rat and a string to swing it with – and so on, and so on, hour after hour."

   The above sentence is __________
   a. a statement of fact mixed with opinion.
   b. an opinion
   c. a statement of fact
   d. Neither a fact nor an opinion.
9. What is the main idea of the passage?
   a. Children can be very tricky, and should be watched very carefully.
   b. Tom used the power of illusion to convince his friends that his ugly task was actually a treasure.
   c. Tom had certain business skills, which he put to work to get others to do Jim's job.
   d. Painting a fence is hard work that no one in their right mind would want to do.
10. Tom Sawyer, the protagonist of the story, would most likely agree with which statement below?
    a. You would be wise to follow the instructions of your superiors.
    b. Sometimes you can use your brain to get yourself out of tough spots.
    c. It always pays to be one hundred percent honest.
    d. Fooling your friends will eventually leave you in the poor house.

Contemporary Issues in the Discipline

Lisa Gansky is the founder and CEO of Kodak Gallery (formerly Ofoto), GNN, and other well known Internet companies. She is also a committed environmentalist devoted to launching sustainable ventures; she serves as a Director of the Latin American environmental foundation Dos Margaritas. Gansky is the author of *The Mesh: Why the Future of Business Is Sharing* and the mind behind the Mesh Directory (http://meshing.it).

MyReadingLab

Visit Chapter 9: Business in MyReadingLab to complete the Reading 6 activities.

READING 6

Lecture (TED Talk)

The Future of Business Is the "Mesh"

Pre-Reading Activity

Before reading the following transcript of Lisa Gansky's TED Talk, you can watch the speech itself: http://www.ted.com/talks/lisa_gansky_the_future_of_business_is_the_mesh?language=en (Courtesy of TED).

As you listen to the video presentation, take notes. (See the note-taking activity on p. 190 for some pointers.) After reading the transcript, you will answer some open-ended questions about some of the issues raised in her speech. Finally, you will formulate questions for Lisa Gansky about issues pertinent to business and answer them from her perspective.

The Future of Business Is the "Mesh"

By Lisa Gansky
January 2011
Transcript courtesy of TED © TED CONFERENCES, LLC

1 I'm speaking to you about what I call the "mesh." It's essentially a fundamental shift in our relationship with stuff, with the things in our lives. And it's starting to look at — not always and not for everything — but in certain moments of time, access to certain kinds of goods and service will trump ownership of them. And so it's the pursuit of better things, easily shared. And we come from a long tradition of sharing. We've shared transportation. We've shared wine and food and other sorts of fabulous experiences in coffee bars in Amsterdam. We've also shared other sorts of entertainment — sports arenas, public parks,concert halls, libraries, universities. All these things are share-platforms, but sharing ultimately starts and ends with what I refer to as the "mother of all share-platforms."

2 And as I think about the mesh and I think about, well, what's driving it, how come it's happening now, I think there's a number of vectors that I want to give you as background. One is the recession — that the recession has caused us to rethink our relationship with the things in our lives relative to the value — so starting to align the value with the true cost. Secondly, population growth and density into cities. More people, smaller spaces, less stuff. Climate change: we're trying to reduce the stress in our personal lives and in our communities and on the planet. Also, there's been this recent distrust of big brands, global big brands, in a bunch of different industries, and that's created an opening. Research is showing here, in the States, and in Canada and Western Europe, that most of us are much more open to local companies, or brands that maybe we haven't heard of. Whereas before, we went with the big brands that we were sure we trusted. And last is that we're more connected now to more people on the planet than ever before —except for if you're sitting next to someone. *(Laughter)*

3 The other thing that's worth considering is that we've made a huge investment over decades and decades, and tens of billions of dollars have gone into this investment that now is our inheritance. It's a physical infrastructure that allows us to get from point A to point B and move things that way. It's also — Web and mobile allow us to be connected and create all kinds of platforms and systems, and the investment of those technologies and that infrastructure is really our inheritance. It allows us to engage in really new and interesting ways.

4 And so for me, a mesh company, the "classic" mesh company, brings together these three things: our ability to connect to each other — most of us are walking around with these mobile devices that are GPS-enabled and Web-enabled — allows us to find each other and find things in time and space. And third is that physical things are readable on a map — so restaurants, a variety of venues, but also with GPS and other technology like RFID and it continues to expand beyond that, we can also track things that are moving, like a car, a

taxicab, a transit system, a box that's moving through time and space. And so that sets up for making access to get goods and services more convenient and less costly in many cases than owning them.

5 For example, I want to use Zipcar. How many people here have experienced car-sharing or bike-sharing? Wow, that's great. Okay, thank you. Basically Zipcar is the largest car-sharing company in the world. They did not invent car-sharing. Car-sharing was actually invented in Europe. One of the founders went to Switzerland, saw it implemented someplace, said, "Wow, that looks really cool. I think we can do that in Cambridge," brought it to Cambridge and they started — two women — Robin Chase being the other person who started it. Zipcar got some really important things right. First, they really understood that a brand is a voice and a product is a souvenir. And so they were very clever about the way that they packaged car-sharing. They made it sexy. They made it fresh. They made it aspirational. If you were a member of the club, when you're a member of a club, you're a Zipster. The cars they picked didn't look like ex-cop cars that were hollowed out or something. They picked these sexy cars. They targeted to universities. They made sure that the demographic for who they were targeting and the car was all matching. It was a very nice experience, and the cars were clean and reliable, and it all worked.

6 And so from a branding perspective, they got a lot right. But they understood fundamentally that they are not a car company. They understand that they are an information company. Because when we buy a car we go to the dealer once, we have an interaction, and we're chow — usually as quickly as possible. But when you're sharing a car and you have a car-share service, you might use an E.V. to commute, you get a truck because you're doing a home project. When you pick your aunt up at the airport, you get a sedan. And you're going to the mountains to ski, you get different accessories put on the car for doing that sort of thing. Meanwhile, these guys are sitting back, collecting all sorts of data about our behavior and how we interact with the service. And so it's not only an option for them, but I believe it's an imperative for Zipcar and other mesh companies to actually just wow us, to be like a concierge service. Because we give them so much information, and they are entitled to really see how it is that we're moving. They're in really good shape to anticipate what we're going to want next.

7 And so what percent of the day do you think the average person uses a car? What percentage of the time? Any guesses? Those are really very good. I was imagining it was like 20 percent when I first started. The number across the U.S. and Western Europe is eight percent. And so basically even if you think it's 10 percent, 90 percent of the time, something that costs us a lot of money — personally, and also we organize our cities around it and all sorts of things — 90 percent of the time it's sitting around. So for this reason, I think one of the other themes with the mesh is essentially that, if we squeeze hard on things that we've thrown away, there's a lot of value in those things. What set up with Zipcar — Zipcar started in 2000.

8 In the last year, 2010, two car companies started, one that's in the U.K. called WhipCar, and the other one, RelayRides, in the U.S. They're

both peer-to-peer car-sharing services, because the two things that really work for car-sharing is, one, the car has to be available, and two, it's within one or two blocks of where you stand. Well the car that's one or two blocks from your home or your office is probably your neighbor's car, and it's probably also available. So people have created this business. Zipcar started a decade earlier, in 2000. It took them six years to get 1,000 cars in service. WhipCar, which started April of last year, it took them six months to get 1,000 cars in the service. So, really interesting. People are making anywhere between 200 and 700 dollars a month letting their neighbors use their car when they're not using it. So it's like vacation rentals for cars. Since I'm here — and I hope some people in the audience are in the car business — *(Laughter)* — I'm thinking that, coming from the technology side of things — we saw cable-ready TVs and WiFi-ready Notebooks — it would be really great if, any minute now, you guys could start rolling share-ready cars off. Because it just creates more flexibility. It allows us as owners to have other options. And I think we're going there anyway.

9 The opportunity and the challenge with mesh businesses — and those are businesses like Zipcar or Netflix that are full mesh businesses, or other ones where you have a lot of the car companies, car manufacturers, who are beginning to offer their own car-share services as well as a second flanker brand,or as really a test, I think — is to make sharing irresistible. We have experiences in our lives, certainly, when sharing has been irresistible. It's just, how do we make that recurrent and scale it? We know also, because we're connected in social networks, that it's easy to create delight in one little place. It's contagious because we're all connected to each other. So if I have a terrific experience and I tweet it, or I tell five people standing next to me, news travels. The opposite, as we know, is also true, often more true.

10 So here we have LudoTruck, which is in L.A., doing the things that gourmet food trucks do, and they've gathered quite a following. In general, and maybe, again, it's because I'm a tech entrepreneur, I look at things as platforms. Platforms are invitations. So creating Craigslist or iTunes and the iPhone developer network, there are all these networks — Facebook as well. These platforms invite all sorts of developers and all sorts of people to come with their ideas and their opportunity to create and target an application for a particular audience. And honestly, it's full of surprises. Because I don't think any of us in this room could have predicted the sorts of applications that have happened at Facebook, around Facebook, for example, two years ago, when Mark announced that they were going to go with a platform.

11 So in this way, I think that cities are platforms, and certainly Detroit is a platform. The invitation of bringing makers and artists and entrepreneurs — it really helps stimulate this fiery creativity and helps a city to thrive. It's inviting participation, and cities have, historically, invited all sorts of participation. Now we're saying that there's other options as well. So, for example, city departments can open up transit data. Google has made available transit data API. And so there's about

seven or eight cities already in the U.S. that have provided the transit data, and different developers are building applications. So I was having a coffee in Portland, and half-of-a-latte in and the little board in the cafe all of a sudden starts showing me that the next bus is coming in three minutes and the train is coming in 16 minutes. And so it's reliable, real data that's right in my face, where I am, so I can finish the latte.

12 There's this fabulous opportunity we have across the U.S. now: about 21 percent of vacant commercial and industrial space. That space is not vital. The areas around it lack vitality and vibrancy and engagement. There's this thing — how many people here have heard of pop-up stores or pop-up shops? Oh, great. So I'm a big fan of this. And this is a very mesh-y thing. Essentially, there are all sorts of restaurants in Oakland, near where I live. There's a pop-up general store every three weeks, and they do a fantastic job of making a very social event happening for foodies. Super fun, and it happens in a very transitional neighborhood. Subsequent to that, after it's been going for about a year now, they actually started to lease and create and extend. An area that was edgy-artsy is now starting to become much cooler and engage a lot more people. So this is an example. The Crafty Fox is this woman who's into crafts, and she does these pop-up crafts fairs around London. But these sorts of things are happening in many different environments. From my perspective, one of the things pop-up stores do is create perishability and urgency. It creates two of the favorite words of any businessperson: sold out. And the opportunity to really focus trust and attention is a wonderful thing.

13 So a lot of what we see in the mesh, and a lot of what we have in the platform that we built allows us to define, refine and scale. It allows us to test things as an entrepreneur, to go to market, to be in conversation with people, listen, refine something and go back. It's very cost-effective, and it's very mesh-y. The infrastructure enables that.

14 In closing, and as we're moving towards the end, I just also want to encourage — and I'm willing to share my failures as well, though not from the stage. *(Laughter)* I would just like to say that one of the big things, when we look at waste and when we look at ways that we can really be generous and contribute to each other, but also move to create a better economic situation and a better environmental situation, is by sharing failures. And one quick example is Velib, in 2007, came forward in Paris with a very bold proposition, a very big bike-sharing service. They made a lot of mistakes. They had some number of big successes. But they were very transparent, or they had to be, in the way that they exposed what worked and didn't work. And so B.C. in Barcelona and B-cycle and Boris Bikes in London — no one has had to repeat the version 1.0 screw-ups and expensive learning exercises that happened in Paris. So the opportunity when we're connected is also to share failures and successes.

15 We're at the very beginning of something that, what we're seeing and the way that mesh companies are coming forward, is inviting, it's engaging, but it's very early. I have a website — it's a directory — and it started with about 1,200 companies, and in the last two-and-a-half

months it's up to about 3,300 companies. And it grows on a very regular daily basis. But it's very much at the beginning.

16 So I just want to welcome all of you onto the ride. And thank you very much. *(Applause)*

Reading with a Critical Eye

1. Do you agree with Lisa Gansky that "sharing ultimately starts and ends with what I refer to as the 'mother of all share-platforms'? Even if you agree, explain what she means by that.
2. What are some of the vectors, according to Gansky, that are making us reconsider our relationship with the important things in our lives? What other vectors can you think of that possibly cause us to rethink our relationship with them? Give specific examples to support your answer.
3. Gansky mentions that the "classic" mesh company brings three things together. What are they, and how do they affect our lives? Be specific.
4. Why does Gansky mention businesses like Zipcar and Netflix? What lessons can we learn from these companies about doing business?

Imagined Interview: If you had the opportunity to interview Lisa Gansky in person, what would you ask her? With a partner, compose three questions for her.

Question 1. ______________________________

Question 2. ______________________________

Question 3. ______________________________

Interview Challenge: In a group, ask a student to play Lisa Gansky. This student should carefully consider Gansky's views, outlined clearly in the TED Talk, and try to answer the questions from her perspective on business.

Chapter Recap

Now that you have made it through a full chapter focusing on business, let's review the chapter's reading content, skill focus, and vocabulary to gain a better understanding of what you have learned.

Recap Activity 1: A Quick Glance

In 60 seconds, write brief answers to the following two questions. You may wish to share your answers with your classmates or with your instructor.

1. What is one thing you learned from this chapter?

____

____

____

____

____

____

2. What was your favorite reading in the chapter? Explain.

____

____

____

____

____

____

Now discuss what you wrote in a small group. Do not read what you wrote. Paraphrase yourself!

Recap Activity 2: Summary Writing

Choose your favorite reading from this chapter and write a summary containing the main idea and some major details. Keep in mind that the key to summary writing is to convey the author's ideas accurately, but to relay this information in your own words. Last but not least, be sure to include reminder phrases and appropriate transitions.

Recap Activity 3: Internet Research on a Theme of Interest

Think about the choice you just made in Activity 2 concerning which reading in the chapter was your favorite.

What was the theme of your chosen reading?

Theme = ____

Using a search engine such as *Google* or *Bing*, go online and locate a quality reading on the same theme as your favorite chapter reading. Write a three- to five-sentence summary of the reading that you found from your Internet research. Be sure to include the author's most important points in your summary.

Title of Reading	*Article Source*	*Summary of the Reading (in your own words)*

Recap Activity 4: Reinforcing the Skill

Working with a partner, read the following paragraph. Then discuss what strategies you can use to recognize the author's bias. It is important for you to understand that you are not being asked to recognize the author's bias. Instead, your task is to discuss with your peer the strategies that you can use to determine the author's bias. That is, discuss with your partner how you will recognize the author's bias in the following passage.

Oprah Gail Winfrey, more popularly known as Oprah, is a famous American television host, business tycoon, and philanthropist. She has received many honorary awards for her much-acclaimed internationally syndicated talk show, *The Oprah Winfrey Show*. In addition to being a popular talk show host, Winfrey is also a book critic, an Academy Award–nominated actress, and a magazine publisher. She has been ranked the richest African American of the twenty-first century, the only black billionaire for three consecutive years, and the most philanthropic African American who ever lived. Some people believe that she is the most influential woman in the world.

What strategies can you use to recognize the author's bias in the passage above?

Strategy 1: ____

Strategy 2: ____

Recap Activity 5: Recycling Vocabulary

With a partner, locate the following vocabulary items, review them in context, and try to define the terms without using a dictionary. Make sure to underline the vocabulary term used in the sentence. The first example is done for you.

Word and Context Location	*Sentence Containing the Word*	*Meaning in This Context*
pitfall, p. 484, para. 5	Another pitfall is when Westerners lay all the problems on the table, while Chinese will only address two at any given meeting because criticism or blame will make them look bad in front of their peers.	A problem that is not obvious at first
influx, p. 484, para. 7	The huge influx of foreign companies in China in recent years has spawned a burgeoning industry of cultural communication and innovation consultants paid to train Westerners and Chinese in each other's languages, management styles and corporate cultures.	____________________ ____________________
approval, p. 489, para. 2	Apple won approval to sell the phones after also addressing risks of personal information leaks related to the operating system's diagnostic tools, China's Ministry of Industry and Information Technology (MIIT) said on its website on Tuesday.	____________________

Word and Context Location	*Sentence Containing the Word*	*Meaning in This Context*
launch, p. 489, para. 3	Apple sold a record 10 million iPhone 6 handsets in the first weekend after their launch, which excluded China.	______________
start-up, p. 499, para. 3	Eventually, Anya put herself through design school at FIT by bartending and running a start-up real estate company (which to this day still exists).	______________
capital, p. 500, para. 4	More work meant more income, which provided her with capital to complete the store and buy out her partners.	______________
fluctuated, p. 509, para. 1	But while gasoline prices have often fluctuated up and down, the upward price spiral in 2004 left consumers, government officials, and business leaders struggling to find answers.	______________
crisis, p. 509, para. 2	What made this gas crisis unusual was that it was the result of an unusual confluence of supply, demand, and global forces.	______________ ______________
consumption, p. 509, para. 4	This total was greater than the combined consumption of Germany, Russia, China, and Japan.	______________ ______________
contemplated, p. 520	Tom contemplated the boy a bit, and said: What do you call work?	______________
substantial, p. 522	The boy mused awhile over the substantial change which had taken place in his worldly circumstances.	______________ ______________

Further Explorations

Books

1. *The Tipping Point* by Malcolm Gladwell. Back Bay Books, 2002. Citing many successful examples from the business world, Gladwell argues in his popular book that little changes can have big effects on human behavior.
2. *Business @ the Speed of Thought: Succeeding in the Digital Economy* by Bill Gates. Business Plus, 2009. In this book, Gates provides a twelve-step program for companies that want to do business in the next millennium. He claims that how companies gather and disseminate information will determine their success or failure.

Movies

1. *The Social Network* (2010). Directed by David Fincher. Based on the true story of Mark Zuckerberg, founder of Facebook, this witty movie is an interesting account of how a small company founded by Zuckerberg during his Harvard days became a global phenomenon with more than 500 million users.

2. *The Pursuit of Happyness* (2006). Directed by Gabriele Muccino. Inspired by the true story of Chris Gardner, a successful and wealthy Chicago businessman and philanthropist, this heartwarming movie shows how diligent, hard-working people can make their dreams come true.

Internet Sites

1. www.executivelibrary.com
   Executives from U.S. corporations such as Boeing, Intel, Microsoft, and the New York Stock Exchange (NYSE) visit this Web site for the best business information sources. It has a public library that contains most of the visible and useful business sites.
2. www.investors.com
   This Web site is the online edition of the *Investor's Business Daily*, founded by the American entrepreneur Bill O'Neil. Here, you can read business news and analyst reports, and learn about promising U.S. and foreign businesses.

Discipline Focus: Negotiating with International Business Partners

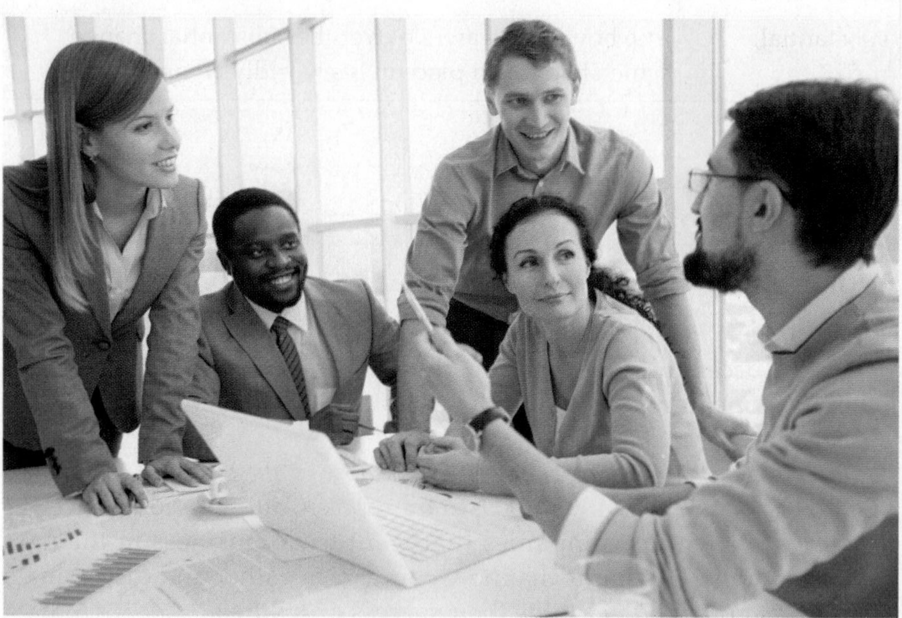

American businesses import products from many countries and export products and services all over the world. Signing a contract to finalize a deal with an international business partner requires negotiation skills. Keep in mind that negotiation is a complex process, which involves a gamut of factors that are culturally determined. What is appropriate and inappropriate in a business meeting depends on where the business meeting is taking place. Being aware of the contrasting cultural values of the country where you are negotiating a business deal can help you avoid confrontation and succeed in getting a signed contract. The following table shows how negotiation is viewed in the North American culture and in other cultures.

Contrasting Cultural Values				
Time	Time is money. Meetings must start and end on time.	Meetings may not start on time. It is considered normal if a business meeting does not start promptly.	It is important to establish friendship before a business meeting begins.	People and relationships are more important than time.
Decision	The individual makes her/his own decision and is responsible for it.	The individual makes her/his own decision and is usually responsible for it.	The individual makes a decision after consulting with friends and coworkers.	The individual makes a decision only after the group or her/his supervisor agrees with it.
Promise	Not delivering on a promise can be serious.	Making a promise and not keeping it can be excused.	Making a promise is equated with delivering on the promise and is understood that way.	Making a promise is often considered politeness and is not to be taken seriously.
Task	Only one task is to be performed in a linear manner.	Several things can happen at the same time during a business meeting.	Several tasks can be accomplished simultaneously.	Frequent interruptions during a business meeting are normal.
Truth	Always tell the truth no matter what.	Truth depends on time and situation.	Graciousness is more important than being truthful.	It is more important to save face than to tell the truth.
Discussion	Discussions are necessary to clarify things.	Discussions are good and necessary.	Discussions tend to be long and intense.	Discussions are brief. Speaking too much can be viewed as a sign of arrogance, thus, the Persian saying, "God gave us two ears, but only one mouth."

(Continued)

Contrasting Cultural Values (cont.)				
Conflicts	It is important to resolve a conflict in a face-to-face conversation.	Conflicts are handled indirectly first.	A mediator is usually involved to resolve a conflict.	Harmony is of utmost importance when resolving a conflict. A mediator is involved in conflict and resolution.
Physical Distance	Two people talking stand at least two and one-half feet apart from each other.	Two people conversing with each other stand two feet apart from each other.	Two people of the same gender talking stand eighteen inches apart from each other.	Two people talking stand at least three to four feet apart from each other.
Eye Contact	It is important to make direct eye contact with the listener.	It is important to make direct eye contact with the listener.	Eyes are lowered or averted to show respect.	Eyes are lowered as a sign of respect.
Contract	Signing a contract is closing a business deal.	A contract is a means of closing a deal.	A contract is seen as an agreement, which can be changed if the situation changes.	A contract is a means of establishing a relationship. The contract can be revised if the situation changes in the future.
Introduction	The two parties shake hands and introduce themselves verbally.	The two parties may shake hands and introduce themselves verbally.	The two parties may embrace and kiss each other on the cheek, especially if they have met before.	Instead of introducing themselves verbally, it is common for the two parties to first exchange business cards, especially Japan.
Communication	Communication is direct. It is important to state exactly what one means, and a direct response is expected.	Communication may be indirect. The meaning is expressed more through emotion than words.	Saying "yes" means that the message is understood, not that the speaker agrees with the business counterpart.	Saying "maybe" is a polite way to say "no."

Learning Styles

Overview

Your academic success will largely depend on how you learn new bits and pieces of information. Keep in mind that learning styles differ from individual to individual. Those who are auditorily dependent must hear information in the form of a lecture, for example, to learn the content. In contrast, others who are visually dependent need to see information on the blackboard, or on posters, or projection screens, or in the textbook. Social learners like to interact with their peers, raising and responding to pertinent questions. On the other hand, independent learners would rather study alone. They set their academic goals and are self-motivated. Spatial learners have the ability to visualize how things are situated in space. Verbal learners, however, lack this ability and rely on verbal skills to learn a new subject matter.

Those who prefer to deal with tangible objects are called *applied learners,* and those who prefer to work with concepts and ideas are called *conceptual learners.* In addition, *creative learners* are not afraid to make mistakes and take risks. They are imaginative and learn through investigation and discovery. Last but not least, *pragmatic learners* are conformists. They find it easy to learn when things are logical and systematic. Some students are good at answering multiple-choice questions, but they have difficulty writing in prose form. Others find it relatively easy to write an academic essay, but they dread the idea of taking a test consisting of multiple-choice questions. It will be important for you to discover how you learn best so that you can optimize learning.

ConAgra hired Carla Kearns, founder of TLI-The Mandarin School, based in Toronto, to provide its executives with intercultural business training in China.

Students often complain that their professors never explain to them how to learn discipline-specific material. However, professors are aware of the fact that different students have different learning styles. For this reason, they do not explain how to learn the material best. If you take into account that students have different learning styles, you will realize that it is impossible for the professor to recommend one learning technique that works for all students. Depending on your learning style, your approach to learning new information should be based on how you learn well.

You may have more than one learning style, but you will need to determine what you do really well. Do you find it cumbersome to listen to a lecture and take notes at the same time? Or do you feel at ease simply copying information down from the blackboard and then revisiting your notes at home for further reflection and analysis? Do you read maps easily or with great difficulty? Do you find certain academic tasks easier than others?

Perhaps you can make a list of the academic tasks that you have no difficulty performing and those you find troublesome.

Implications for Your Learning

The sooner you determine what your learning style is, the better able you will be to succeed in college. It should be noted, though, that just as people change over time, your learning style might also change. It is also possible that you have more than one learning style. Knowing how you learn best will help you understand why you find certain aspects of a course troublesome or easy. Once you know your weaknesses and strengths in learning, you can adapt to different teaching styles. Finally, it is always a good idea to speak to the professor about the course requirements, your learning styles, and your professor's expectations so that you can get the most out of the course and perform well.

Challenge Activity

Some people learn by visualizing the concept; that is, they are visually dependent. Others learn by listening to lectures or audiotapes, meaning they are auditorily dependent. Yet others learn by making a list of new ideas or by taking notes. Depending on people's learning styles, they learn differently. If you want to know how you learn best, go to the following site and complete the questionnaire: www.vark-learn.com/english/page.asp?p=questionnaire

POLITICAL SCIENCE
American Government

"It is rather for us to be here dedicated to the great task remaining before us . . . and that government of the people, by the people, for the people, shall not perish from the earth."

ABRAHAM LINCOLN

Learning Objectives

AFTER READING THIS CHAPTER, YOU SHOULD BE ABLE TO:

1. Identify key fundamentals about the U.S. political system
2. Synthesize skills to navigate your way through a text
3. Compose an argument to a political representative about a community concern

INTRODUCTION TO THE DISCIPLINE OF POLITICAL SCIENCE

The United States has witnessed changing perceptions of political science in the twenty-first century as a result of recent wars and terrorist attacks. In the past, people thought that politics was exclusively for the politicians, and that political science as a discipline had little or no bearing on people's lives. However, terrorist threats to America's national security, U.S. relations with oil-producing countries, and violent crimes committed in countries around the world have caused students, activists, and intellectuals to take politics seriously. Many people who took no interest in political involvement, thinking it was for the government to deal with political matters, are now playing an active role in the governmental process. It may be the case that the American people are dissatisfied with America's foreign policy, or that they are concerned about their beloved country's image in the world, or that they are afraid of another terrorist attack. Perhaps they are following politics more closely because of anger, fear, insecurity, and controversial issues that concern them. Whatever the reason, political scientists are obviously pleased with the resurgence of interest in politics among the American people and claim that politics determine and influence economics and education.

In this chapter, you will become familiar with political science as a discipline. The articles included in this chapter relate to issues of immigration, racial discrimination, democracy, and other aspects of government. As you read the articles carefully, you will understand how politics is intricately woven into the fabric of society.

Preview Questions

With a small group of your classmates, discuss the following questions:

1. In his famous Gettysburg Address, U.S. President Abraham Lincoln said, "It is rather for us to be here dedicated to the great task remaining before us . . . and that government of the people, by the people, for the people, shall not perish from the earth." Do you believe that this is true of America today? Do you believe that every citizen in the country has political power? Explain. Can you think of another country in the world where Lincoln's vision of democracy is more or less realized?
2. Many people seem to have little or no interest in political involvement, arguing that it is for the government to worry about political matters. Others believe that a true democracy can thrive only when its citizens play an active role in the governmental process. Where do you stand on the issue of political involvement? Do you keep yourself abreast of local and national politics?

3. Despite the fact that U.S. citizens 18 and older are eligible to vote, the reality is that only 52 percent of eligible voters actually exercise their right to vote. Discuss what factors might keep the rest of the voters from participating in the electoral process. Given these factors, what would motivate nonvoters to turn out at the polls?
4. According to the law, only U.S.-born citizens have the right to run for the presidency, and naturalized citizens are excluded from this privilege. In your opinion, should immigrant political figures such as Arnold Schwarzenegger be allowed to become the president of the United States of America?
5. In the United States, we often speak of the virtues of a democratic form of government—that is, a system where political representatives are chosen by citizens of the country. Is democracy always the best system of governance? Are there any shortcomings to the concept of democracy? Can you think of other forms of government that may be superior to democracy?

Writing on The Wall

After you have discussed the preview questions with your classmates, post your responses to two of them on your class blog, which we refer to as The Wall. Review others' postings and respond to at least two of your classmates' posts that grab your interest. Remember the guidelines for blogging and commenting etiquette (see p. 15)! If your class is not using a shared blog, your instructor may ask you to record your individual or collective responses to the preview questions in another form.

EXERCISE 10.1 Interpreting a Cartoon

"You can't take the Ethics course-you're a Political Science major."

Working in pairs, examine the cartoon in above and answer the following questions.

1. What is humorous about this cartoon?
2. In your opinion, what is the cartoonist's intended message for the reader?

Discipline-specific Vocabulary: Understand Key Terms in Political Science

One of the most efficient ways to acquire academic vocabulary is to study key terms that are thematically connected. As you begin your college-level studies, it is critical that you internalize vocabulary terms that relate to the academic disciplines that make up most 100-level content courses. For example, a student taking an introductory political science course should be able to apply such terms as *constitution*, *amendment*, and *governance* in both spoken and written forms.

EXERCISE 10.2 Brainstorming Vocabulary

Directions: What associated words come to mind when you think of the world of political science? Work with a partner and write down as many related words as you can think of in a period of five minutes.

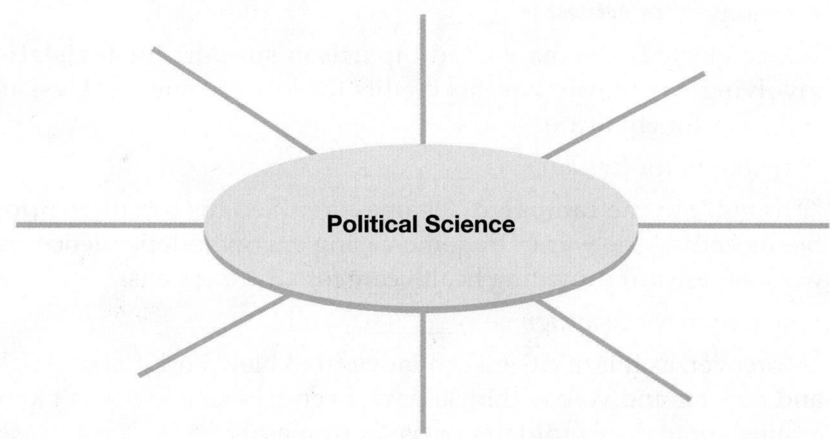

Fishing for Synonyms and Antonyms

A **synonym** is a word used to express a similar meaning to another word. An **antonym** is a word that conveys the opposite meaning of another word. Understanding how to work with synonyms and antonyms is a useful skill, especially when you are writing a summary of a text and trying to paraphrase some of the key ideas and pieces of information contained in the original source. To avoid plagiarism, you cannot simply copy the same terms you see in the text; one useful technique is to make selective use of synonyms and antonyms.

EXERCISE 10.3 Determining Synonyms and Antonyms from Context

Directions: Read the following ten (10) discipline-specific words culled from the readings in this chapter and shown in the context of the sentences in which they appeared. In the space provided after each sentence, write a synonym or antonym for the highlighted term, as directed.

Discipline-specific Word Bank for Political Science

activist	**constitutional**	**candidate**
legislation	**representation**	**suffrage**
campaign	**pluralism**	**authority**
conflict resolution		

1. "U.S. relations with oil-producing countries, and violent crimes committed in countries around the world have caused students, **activists**, and intellectuals to take politics seriously."

   A synonym for *activist* is ________.
2. "Once elected, Obama gained bipartisan support for **legislation** involving health care law, tax credits for low-income workers, and subsidies for childcare."

   A synonym for *legislation* is _____.
3. "Throughout the **campaign**, Obama identified his top three priorities as ending the war in Iraq, increasing energy independence, and working toward providing health care for all Americans."

   A synonym for *campaign* is ________.
4. "Moreover, as it is, a citizen can move from New York to Los Angles and register and vote within 30 days, even if he or she doesn't know a thing about the **candidates** or ballot proposals."

   A synonym for *candidate* is _________.
5. "Non-citizen voting is the suffrage movement of our time."

   An antonym for *suffrage is* ________________.
6. "No sooner was the U.S. Constitution ratified than Americans demanded and received the Bill of Rights: 10 **constitutional** amendments that safeguard basic rights."

   A synonym for *constitutional* is ______.

7. "Unless those people would relinquish the right of **Representation** in the Legislature, a right inestimable to them and formidable to tyrants only."

   An antonym for *representation* is ______.

8. "The American self-image has always harnessed a creative tension between **pluralism** and assimilation."

   A synonym for *pluralism* is ________.

9. "Is this really a legitimate reason for adults in **authority** positions to force a 13-year-old girl to submit to a humiliating strip search?"

   An antonym for *authority* is ____________.

10. "While universities are trying to devise courses in **conflict resolution**, and governments are trying to stop skirmishes at borders, we are surrounded by violence."

    A synonym for *conflict resolution* is ______________.

EXERCISE 10.4 Matching Terms with Definitions

Match the word in Column A with the definition in Column B. Put the letter representing the correct definition in the space preceding each term.

Column A **Word**	Column B **Definition**
1. ___ campaign	a. right of being represented by delegates having a voice in legislation or government
2. ___ constitutional	b. a piece of law
3. ___ candidate	c. someone who takes direct action to achieve a political goal
4. ___ suffrage	d. the act of finding a peaceful solution
5. ___ representation	e. the right to control, command, or determine
6. ___ authority	f. the right to vote
7. ___ activist	g. someone running for political office
8. ___ pluralism	h. a competition to gain political office
9. ___ legislation	i. in accordance with the constitution of a government
10. ___ conflict resolution	j. condition in which many cultures coexist within a society and maintain their cultural differences

EXERCISE 10.5 Choosing the Right Word

In each of the following sentences, **fill in the blank** with a word from the terminology bank that makes the sentence grammatically correct and meaningful.

activist	constitutional	authority	representation	conflict resolution
legislation	suffrage	pluralism	campaign	candidate

1. The accused used his __________ right to not speak to anyone but his attorney.
2. Women activists worked for decades to gain ______ for women.
3. An environmental _____ tied himself to a tree to protest the logging industry's deforestation.
4. The United States has been criticized for abusing their _______ as a world super-power.
5. The United Nations wants all warring countries to seek ______ ________.
6. Some presidential ________ raise hundreds of millions of dollars to support their campaign.
7. The senate passed new job-training _______ after a sustained fight on the Senate floor.
8. Immigrants without citizenship have no political ___________ at all.
9. The presidential _________ includes lots of TV advertising, media hype, and a group of televised debates.
10. In the United States, we can see _______ at work with people from many religious and cultural backgrounds sharing in the political process.

Create Your Own Survey with a Political Focus

Throughout the text, you have been asked a number of times to conduct an in-class or field survey, working with questions related to the academic focus of the chapter. In Chapter 3 on nutrition, you asked respondents about their dietary habits. In Chapter 4, the survey was on personal connections to environmental issues. Chapter 6 offered a survey on attitudes on issues related to crime. Finally, Chapter 8 on psychology included a survey exploring stereotypes on gender roles.

As this is the final chapter and you now have had some experience with surveying, this time it is your turn to organize an interesting survey with a political focus, and then to administer your survey to at least two respondents.

Some Tips

- Focus your survey around a particular issue. Some examples are immigrant rights, women in politics, support for a particular candidate, gun control, and so forth.
- Try to steer away from issues that will make respondents feel uncomfortable. Some topics—abortion, for example—are very controversial and may result in some respondents not wanting to take part in your survey.
- Do not ask for respondents' names, and make sure that you let respondents know that the survey is anonymous and that the results will in no way be connected to personal identities.
- You may need to make use of a separate piece of paper to organize your survey.

Survey Worksheet

Question	*Respondent 1*	*Respondent 2*
1.		
2.		
3.		
4.		

Post-Survey Discussion: Share the results and analysis of your survey work with the class!

MyReadingLab

Visit Chapter 10: Political Science in MyReadingLab to complete the Reading 1 activities.

READING 1

Government Document

The Declaration of Independence: The Want, Will, and Hopes of the People

Pre-Reading Questions

With a classmate, answer these questions before reading the selection.

1. One of the oft-quoted claims of the Declaration of Independence, a political document written by America's founders, is that "all men are created equal." Do you believe this claim to be true? Do you think that in most countries government policy is guided by this principle?
2. According to the Declaration of Independence, all people have the "unalienable rights" to life, liberty, and happiness. However, there

are certain groups of people who firmly believe that these virtues should pertain to a privileged few. If you were to speak to one of these groups, how would you convince them that liberty and happiness are for all?

3. At the time the Declaration of Independence was written, most of the nation's founders themselves owned slaves, not practicing what they preached. Knowing this fact about the writers, how much faith can we put into the authenticity of their egalitarian principles? Might slave owning be justified given the historical context of the times? (Slave ownership was a common practice among the wealthy in the late eighteenth century.)

The Declaration of Independence: The Want, Will, and Hopes of the People

In Congress, July 4, 1776

The Unanimous Declaration of the Thirteen United States of America

1 When in the Course of human events it becomes necessary for one people to dissolve the political bands which have connected them with another and to assume among the powers of the earth, the separate and equal station to which the Laws of Nature and of Nature's God entitle them, a decent respect to the opinions of mankind requires that they should declare the causes which impel them to the separation.

self-evident clearly true and needing no proof

2 We hold these truths to be **self-evident**, that all men are created equal, that they are endowed by their Creator with certain unalienable Rights, that among these are Life, Liberty and the pursuit of Happiness.—That to secure these rights, Governments are instituted among Men, deriving their just powers from the consent of the governed.—That whenever any Form of Government becomes destructive of these ends, it is the Right of the People to alter or to abolish it, and to institute new Government, laying its foundation on such principles and organizing its powers in such form, as to them shall seem most likely to effect their Safety and Happiness. Prudence, indeed, will dictate that Governments long established should not be changed for light and transient causes; and accordingly all experience hath shewn that mankind are more disposed to suffer, while evils are sufferable than to right themselves by abolishing the forms to which they are accustomed. But when a long train of abuses and usurpations, pursuing invariably the same Object evinces a design to reduce them under absolute Despotism, it is their right, it is their duty, to throw off such Government, and to provide new Guards for their future security.—Such has been the patient sufferance of these Colonies; and such is now the necessity which constrains them to alter their former Systems of Government. The history of the present King of Great Britain is a history of repeated injuries and **usurpations**, all having in direct

usurpations wrongful seizure or exercise of authority

object the establishment of an absolute Tyranny over these States. To prove this, let Facts be submitted to a candid world.

3 He has refused his Assent to Laws, the most wholesome and necessary for the public good.

4 He has forbidden his Governors to pass Laws of immediate and pressing importance, unless suspended in their operation till his Assent should be obtained; and when so suspended, he has utterly neglected to attend to them.

5 He has refused to pass other Laws for the accommodation of large districts of people, unless those people would **relinquish** the right of **Representation** in the Legislature, a right inestimable to them and formidable to tyrants only.

relinquish
give up your position, power, rights, and so forth

6 He has called together legislative bodies at places unusual, uncomfortable, and distant from the depository of their Public Records, for the sole purpose of fatiguing them into compliance with his measures.

7 He has dissolved Representative Houses repeatedly, for opposing with manly firmness his invasions on the rights of the people.

8 He has refused for a long time, after such dissolutions, to cause others to be elected, whereby the Legislative Powers, incapable of Annihilation, have returned to the People at large for their exercise; the State remaining in the mean time exposed to all the dangers of invasion from without, and convulsions within.

9 He has endeavoured to prevent the population of these States; for that purpose obstructing the Laws for Naturalization of Foreigners; refusing to pass others to encourage their migrations hither, and raising the conditions of new Appropriations of Lands.

10 He has obstructed the Administration of Justice by refusing his Assent to Laws for establishing Judiciary Powers.

11 He has made Judges dependent on his Will alone for the tenure of their offices, and the amount and payment of their salaries.

12 He has erected a multitude of New Offices, and sent hither swarms of Officers to harass our people and eat out their substance.

13 He has kept among us, in times of peace, Standing Armies without the **Consent** of our legislatures.

14 He has affected to render the Military independent of and superior to the Civil Power.

15 He has combined with others to subject us to a jurisdiction foreign to our constitution, and unacknowledged by our laws; giving his Assent to their Acts of pretended Legislation:

16 For quartering large bodies of armed troops among us:

17 For protecting them, by a mock Trial from punishment for any Murders which they should commit on the Inhabitants of these States:

18 For cutting off our Trade with all parts of the world:

19 For imposing Taxes on us without our Consent:

20 For depriving us in many cases, of the benefit of Trial by Jury:

21 For transporting us beyond Seas to be tried for pretended offences:

abolishing
officially ending a law, system, and so forth

22 For **abolishing** the free System of English Laws in a neighbouring Province, establishing therein an Arbitrary government, and enlarging its Boundaries so as to render it at once an example and fit instrument for introducing the same absolute rule into these Colonies.

23 For taking away our Charters, abolishing our most valuable Laws and altering fundamentally the Forms of our Governments:

24 For suspending our own Legislatures, and declaring themselves invested with power to legislate for us in all cases whatsoever.

abdicated
refused to continue being responsible for something

25 He has **abdicated** Government here, by declaring us out of his Protection and waging War against us.

plundered
stole money or property from a place while fighting in a war

26 He has **plundered** our seas, ravaged our coasts, burnt our towns, and destroyed the lives of our people.

27 He is at this time transporting large Armies of foreign Mercenaries to compleat the works of death, desolation, and tyranny, already begun with circumstances of Cruelty & Perfidy scarcely paralleled in the most barbarous ages, and totally unworthy the Head of a civilized nation.

28 He has constrained our fellow Citizens taken Captive on the high Seas to bear Arms against their Country, to become the executioners of their friends and Brethren, or to fall themselves by their Hands.

29 He has excited domestic insurrections amongst us, and has endeavoured to bring on the inhabitants of our frontiers, the merciless Indian Savages whose known rule of warfare, is an undistinguished destruction of all ages, sexes and conditions.

redress
correction or reformation

30 In every stage of these Oppressions We have Petitioned for **Redress** in the most humble terms: Our repeated Petitions have been answered only by repeated injury. A Prince, whose character is thus marked by every act which may define a Tyrant, is unfit to be the ruler of a free people.

magnanimity
the quality of being forgiving

consanguinity
relationship by blood

31 Nor have We been wanting in attentions to our British brethren. We have warned them from time to time of attempts by their legislature to extend an unwarrantable jurisdiction over us. We have reminded them of the circumstances of our emigration and settlement here. We have appealed to their native justice and **magnanimity**, and we have conjured them by the ties of our common kindred to disavow these usurpations, which would inevitably interrupt our connections and correspondence. They too have been deaf to the voice of justice and of **consanguinity**. We must, therefore, acquiesce in the necessity, which denounces our Separation, and hold them, as we hold the rest of mankind, Enemies in War, in Peace Friends.

32 We, therefore, the Representatives of the United States of America, in General Congress, Assembled, appealing to the Supreme Judge of the world for the rectitude of our intentions, do, in the Name, and by Authority of the good People of these Colonies, solemnly publish and declare, That these united Colonies are, and of Right ought to be Free and Independent States, that they are Absolved from all Allegiance to the British Crown, and that all political connection between them and the State of Great Britain, is and ought to be totally dissolved;

and that as Free and Independent States, they have full Power to levy War, conclude Peace, contract Alliances, establish Commerce, and to do all other Acts and Things which Independent States may of right do.—And for the support of this Declaration, with a firm reliance on the protection of Divine Providence, we mutually pledge to each other our Lives, our Fortunes, and our sacred Honor.

Reading with a Critical Eye

In a small group, discuss the following reflection questions, which will guide you toward a deeper understanding of the reading.

1. In paragraph 2, we read, "That whenever any Form of Government becomes destructive of these ends, it is the Right of the People to alter or to abolish it, and to institute new Government . . ."

   What would be an accurate paraphrase of the above statement?
2. "The history of the present King of Great Britain is a history of repeated injuries and usurpations, all having in direct object the establishment of an absolute Tyranny over these States." The above statement, from paragraph 2, is full of anger. From your knowledge of history, why were the colonial leaders so infuriated with the King of England?
3. "A Prince, whose character is thus marked by every act which may define a Tyrant, is unfit to be the ruler of a free people" (para. 30).

   What would be an accurate paraphrase of the above statement?
4. In the final section, the writers of the document make their declaration loud and clear. "We . . . solemnly publish and declare, That these united Colonies are, and of Right ought to be Free and Independent States . . ." (para. 32). In your view, did the colonists truly have the right to make such a bold break with their mother government back in England? Share your reasoning.
5. Try to imagine the reaction of the British rulers upon reading this declaration. What do you think was their first reaction?

Reading Comprehension Check

1. "When in the Course of human events it becomes necessary for one people to dissolve the political bands which have connected them with another and to assume among the powers of the earth, the separate and equal station to which the Laws of Nature and of Nature's God entitle them, a decent respect to the opinions of mankind requires that they should declare the causes which impel them to the separation."

   In the above sentence, the word *impel* means

   a. cause to move away from.
   b. cause to move backward.
   c. cause to move forward.
   d. cause to move downward.

2. The main idea of the Declaration of Independence is that
   a. every person's right to life, freedom, and happiness is alienable.
   b. it is morally right to deprive some people of liberty and happiness.
   c. only a special group of people have the right to liberty and happiness.
   d. the right to life, liberty, and happiness is unalienable.
3. The facts related to the king of Great Britain are presented to prove the main point that
   a. he was a generous and just king.
   b. he was a tyrant.
   c. he was a kind king.
   d. he was a lenient king.
4. "But when a long train of abuses and usurpations, pursuing invariably the same Object evinces a design to reduce them under absolute Despotism, it is their right, it is their duty, to throw off such Government, and to provide new Guards for their future security."

   It can be inferred from the above statement that
   a. people have the right to fight the government to defend their country.
   b. people should unquestionably surrender to despotism.
   c. citizens of a country must not rise against the government.
   d. people ought to accept abuses without ever complaining.
5. The primary purpose of the Declaration of Independence is
   a. to criticize the king of Great Britain.
   b. to persuade the readers to declare freedom from the despotic king of Great Britain.
   c. to describe the king of Great Britain in detail.
   d. to define the meaning of despotism.
6. The overall tone of the Declaration of Independence is
   a. humorous.
   b. reverent.
   c. neutral.
   d. inspirational.
7. The overall pattern of organization of the Declaration of Independence is
   a. classification.
   b. cause and effect.
   c. generalization and example.
   d. spatial order.
8. Which of the following sentences is a statement of fact?
   a. "We hold these truths to be self-evident, that all men are created equal."
   b. ". . . men are endowed by their Creator with certain unalienable Rights."
   c. "He has kept among us, in times of peace, Standing Armies without the Consent of our legislatures."
   d. ". . . among these rights are Life, Liberty and the pursuit of Happiness."

9. Which sentence is a statement of opinion?
   a. "He has plundered our seas, ravaged our coasts, burnt our towns, and destroyed the lives of our people."
   b. "He has dissolved Representative Houses repeatedly, for opposing with manly firmness his invasions on the rights of the people."
   c. "He has refused to pass other Laws for the accommodation of large districts of people, unless those people would relinquish the right of Representation in the Legislature, a right inestimable to them and formidable to tyrants only."
   d. "In every stage of these Oppressions We have Petitioned for Redress in the most humble terms."
10. "We, therefore, the Representatives of the United States of America, in General Congress, Assembled, appealing to the Supreme Judge of the world for the rectitude of our intentions, do, in the Name, and by Authority of the good People of these Colonies, solemnly publish and declare, That these united Colonies are, and of Right ought to be Free and Independent States, that they are Absolved from all Allegiance to the British Crown, and that all political connection between them and the State of Great Britain, is and ought to be totally dissolved; and that as Free and Independent States, they have full Power to levy War, conclude Peace, contract Alliances, establish Commerce, and to do all other Acts and Things which Independent States may of right do."

    In this passage, the author is in favor of
   a. immediately submitting to all allegiance to the British Crown.
   b. declaring independence from the State of Great Britain.
   c. obeying the king of Great Britain unconditionally.
   d. developing strategies to cooperate with the king of Great Britain.

MyReadingLab

Visit Chapter 10: Political Science in MyReadingLab to complete the Reading 2 activities.

READING 2

Newspaper Editorial

Give Non-Citizens the Right to Vote. It's Only Fair

Pre-Reading Questions

Discuss the following questions in small groups before reading the article:

1. U.S. law stipulates that one must be a citizen in order to be eligible to vote. In your opinion, why do you think the U.S. government has excluded lawful immigrants from this privilege?

2. Permanent U.S. residents argue that they are no different from U.S. citizens in that they work hard, contribute to society, and pay state and federal taxes. They believe that they are being treated like second-class citizens in their lack of political representation. Do you think that these legal immigrants have a valid concern? Why, or why not?
3. Some argue that a true democracy is only conceivable when no one is excluded from the electoral process. Yet, in the United States, certain people such as convicted felons, prisoners, illegal immigrants, permanent residents, and citizens without proper documentation are denied the right to vote. Can a true democracy exist when a country's citizens and noncitizens are discriminated against in this manner? Explain.

Give Non-Citizens the Right to Vote. It's Only Fair

By Ron Hayduk
***Los Angeles Times*, December 22, 2014**

1 The contemporary immigrant rights movement has commanded attention through civil disobedience, student walkouts and intensive lobbying. But there's another tactic—increasing immigrant clout by allowing all noncitizens to vote—that also deserves serious consideration.

2 Many Americans understandably question why immigrants should be able to vote before they become U.S. citizens. They know citizenship is required for federal elections, and they attested to their status when they registered. But what most don't know is that the right to vote in this country has never been intrinsically tied to citizenship. And even now, in a few jurisdictions and on some issues, noncitizens have a limited right to vote.

3 As it turns out, voting by noncitizens is as old as the Republic. From 1776 until 1926 in 40 states and federal territories, residents who weren't citizens could vote in local, state, and sometimes federal elections. They also have held public office; Indiana and Louisiana elected noncitizen aldermen and coroners, for example. In a country where "no taxation without representation" was the rallying cry for revolution, and where government theoretically rests "on the consent of the governed," allowing all residents to vote only makes sense.

4 Today, immigrants here legally and illegally work in every sector of the economy. They own homes and businesses, attend colleges and send children to schools. They pay billions in taxes each year, and make countless social and cultural contributions to their communities. They are subject to all the laws that govern citizens, serve in the

military and even die defending the U.S. But most are without formal political voice.

5 Their numbers are staggering. According to the U.S. Census Bureau, more than 22 million adults in the U.S. are barred from voting because they lack U.S. citizenship. In some districts—and in some whole cities and towns—noncitizens make up 25% to 50% of voting-age residents. In Los Angeles they make up more than a third of the voting-age population; in New York City, they are 22% of adults. Such levels of political exclusion approximate the exclusion of women prior to 1920, African Americans before the Voting Rights Act of 1965 and 18-year-olds prior to 1971.

6 Sadly, America knows all too well what can occur when groups don't have a formal political voice: discriminatory public policy and private practices—in employment, housing, education, healthcare, welfare and criminal justice. Noncitizens suffer social and economic inequities, in part, because policymakers can ignore their interests. The vote is a proven mechanism to keep government responsive and accountable to all.

7 But why don't they just become citizens? Most immigrants want to, but the average time it takes for the naturalization process is eight years and sometimes longer. That's a long time to go without a vote. Besides, many who are here legally are barred from pursuing citizenship by the terms of their visas; they are students or green card holders who are nonetheless members of their community who deserve a voice in its policies. And of course, those who are here illegally, who overstayed a visa or never had one have no practical pathway to citizenship.

8 But do noncitizens possess sufficient knowledge of our political system to vote responsibly? If political knowledge was a criteria for voting, many U.S. citizens would be out of luck, as public surveys regularly show. Moreover, as it is, a citizen can move from New York to Los Angles and register and vote within 30 days, even if he or she doesn't know a thing about the candidates or ballot proposals. So why should literacy tests or restrictive residency requirements be able to disenfranchise noncitizen voters?

9 There are now a handful of U.S. jurisdictions where noncitizens have a right to vote in some elections. In six towns in Maryland since the 1990s, all residents (except felons serving sentences or those judged mentally incompetent by a court) can vote in local elections. Chicago permits all noncitizen parents of schoolchildren to vote in school district elections. In California, all parents can participate in "parent trigger" votes to change the administration of their children's schools.

10 Next year, the New York City Council will take up a bill—which has broad political support—that would allow noncitizens lawfully residing in the U.S. to vote in local elections. In March, Burlington, Vt., voters will decide on a similar ballot proposition to let legal

permanent residents vote in local elections. The District of Columbia has a similar bill pending.

11 The right to vote helps keep our democracy inclusive and fair, and resident voting is the next logical step toward creating a truly universal franchise. It is what America's past and future as an immigrant nation requires. Noncitizen voting is the **suffrage** movement of our time.

Reading with a Critical Eye

In a small group, discuss the following reflection questions, which will guide you toward a deeper understanding of the reading.

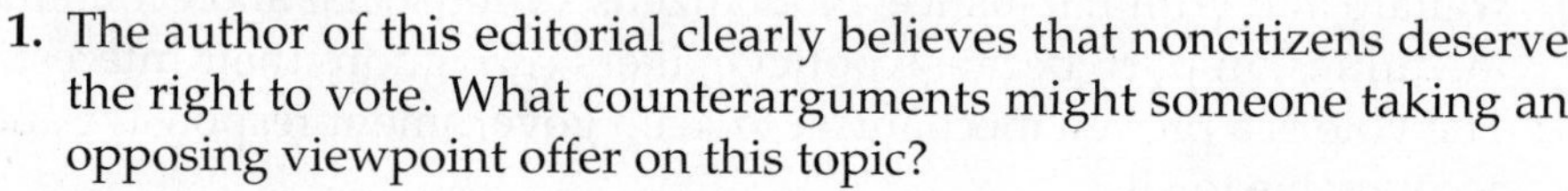

1. The author of this editorial clearly believes that noncitizens deserve the right to vote. What counterarguments might someone taking an opposing viewpoint offer on this topic?
2. In paragraph 6, the author writes, "Noncitizens suffer social and economic inequities, in part, because policymakers can ignore their interests." In your opinion, do you think politicians ignore the needs of noncitizens in America? Explain your ideas.
3. The author poses the question that if voting rights are so important, why don't noncitizens just get their citizenship? What barriers stand in the way of the path to citizenship?
4. How does the author respond to the argument that noncitizens do not have sufficient knowledge of America's political system to take part in it?
5. What is your personal view on the topic of noncitizen voting rights?

Reading Comprehension Check

1. In the sentence, "But there's another tactic—increasing immigrant **clout** by allowing all noncitizens to vote—that also deserves serious consideration," the word *clout* could be replaced with
   a. positivity.
   b. influence.
   c. parity.
   d. legality.
2. What point is the author trying to make when he gives the statistics (para. 3) about voting rights from 1776 to 1926?
   a. Noncitizen voting rights have been a reality for much of American history.
   b. Noncitizens do not pay fair taxes.
   c. In only a handful of states do noncitizens have the right to vote in state and federal elections.
   d. All immigrants—both legal and nonlegal—have voted throughout American history.

3. In the second paragraph, in the sentence, "But what most don't know is that the right to vote in this country has never been **intrinsically** tied to citizenship," a synonym for the term *intrinsically* is
   a. hypocritically.
   b. inversely.
   c. naturally.
   d. inconsistently.
4. Which is *not* mentioned as a consequence a group suffers when they are denied a political voice?
   a. employment discrimination
   b. housing discrimination
   c. shopping bias
   d. unfair treatment under the criminal justice system
5. It can be inferred that the author
   a. holds a neutral view on the issue of immigrant rights.
   b. is against the idea of letting more immigrants into the United States.
   c. has mixed feelings about the power of democratic voting.
   d. believes that voting rights are an essential element of a democratic system.
6. Why does the author make reference to the exclusion of women prior to 1920, African Americans before the Voting Rights Act, and 18-year-olds before 1971?
   a. Immigrants contribute, but they cause security concerns.
   b. Each of these groups was unfairly denied the right to vote in the past as noncitizens are today.
   c. These groups have always enjoyed the rights granted to U.S. citizens.
   d. History is not on the side of immigrants.
7. What does the author want to illustrate by mentioning Maryland, Chicago, and California in paragraph 9?
   a. to show the perils of allowing noncitizens to take part in the political system
   b. These are all areas where there is a high percentage of immigrants.
   c. There are some exceptions to the barring of noncitizens from voting.
   d. The judicial system holds a lot of sway in determining whether noncitizens should have voting rights.
8. What is the author's purpose in writing this piece?
   a. to entertain
   b. to persuade readers to support his ideas about immigrant voting rights
   c. to inform readers about a political issue
   d. to inform readers about the history of immigrants
9. What is the author implying when he writes, "Noncitizen voting is the suffrage movement of our time" in the last sentence of the editorial?
   a. All movements share the same goals.
   b. He is pessimistic about the prospects for social change.

c. This issue is as important today as women's suffrage was a hundred years ago.
d. Noncitizen voting is an issue of the past.

10. Which of the following statements would the author be most likely to support?
a. If more Americans speak out, noncitizen voting can become a reality.
b. It will take at least one hundred years before the victory of noncitizen voting rights is sealed.
c. Permitting noncitizen voting will involve endless paperwork and confuse existing voters.
d. More studies need to be done to determine whether noncitizens are truly worthy of the vote.

READING 3

Novel (Satire)

MyReadingLab

Visit Chapter 10: Political Science in MyReadingLab to complete the Reading 3 activities.

Animal Farm

Pre-Reading Questions

Animal Farm is considered to be one of the greatest political novels of the twentieth century. In this scene at the beginning of the novel, Major, a 12-year-old pig and animal leader, makes a speech in the barn to the other animals of an English farm. Before reading the excerpt, discuss the following questions with a group of your classmates:

1. When politicians speak passionately about their ideals, do you usually believe them? Why, or why not?
2. What is the difference between patriotism and jingoism? In your view, what is a true patriot?
3. In your opinion, if a group of people is being exploited and generally treated unfairly by the government, do you think they have the right to protest and plan a revolution? Explain.

Animal Farm (An excerpt)

By George Orwell
1946

1 All the animals were now present except Moses, the tame raven, who slept on a perch behind the back door. When Major saw that they had all made themselves comfortable and were waiting attentively, he cleared his throat and began:

2 "Comrades, you have heard already about the strange dream that I had last night. But I will come to the dream later. I have something else to say first. I do not think, comrades, that I shall be with you for many months longer, and before I die, I feel it my duty to pass on to you such wisdom as I have acquired. I have had a long life, I have had much time for thought as I lay alone in my stall, and I think I may say that I understand the nature of life on this earth as well as any animal now living. It is about this that I wish to speak to you.

3 "Now, comrades, what is the nature of this life of ours? Let us face it: our lives are miserable, laborious, and short. We are born, we are given just so much food as will keep the breath in our bodies, and those of us who are **capable** of it are forced to work to the last atom of our strength; and the very instant that our usefulness has come to an end we are slaughtered with hideous cruelty. No animal in England knows the meaning of happiness or leisure after he is a year old. No animal in England is free. The life of an animal is misery and slavery: that is the plain truth.

capable
having power and ability

4 "But is this simply part of the order of nature? Is it because this land of ours is so poor that it cannot afford a decent life to those who dwell upon it? No, comrades, a thousand times no! The soil of England is fertile, its climate is good, it is capable of affording food in abundance to an enormously greater number of animals than now inhabit it. This single farm of ours would support a dozen horses, twenty cows, hundreds of sheep—and all of them living in a comfort and a dignity that are now almost beyond our imagining. Why then do we continue in this miserable condition? Because nearly the whole of the produce of our labour is stolen from us by human beings. There, comrades, is the answer to all our problems. It is summed up in a single word—Man. Man is the only real enemy we have. Remove Man from the scene, and the root cause of hunger and overwork is abolished for ever.

5 "Man is the only creature that consumes without producing. He does not give milk, he does not lay eggs, he is too weak to pull the plough, he cannot run fast enough to catch rabbits. Yet he is lord of all the animals. He sets them to work, he gives back to them the bare minimum that will prevent them from starving, and the rest he keeps for himself. Our labour tills the soil, our dung fertilises it, and yet there is not one of us that owns more than his bare skin. You cows that I see before me, how many thousands of gallons of milk have you given during this last year? And what has happened to that milk which should have been breeding up sturdy calves? Every drop of it has gone down the throats of our enemies. And you hens, how many eggs have you laid in this last year, and how many of those eggs ever hatched into chickens? The rest have all gone to market to bring in money for Jones and his men. And you, Clover, where are those four foals you bore, who should have been the support and pleasure of your old age? Each was sold at a year old—you will never see one of them again. In return for your four confinements and all your labour in the fields, what have you ever had except your bare rations and a stall?

6 "And even the miserable lives we lead are not allowed to reach their natural span. For myself I do not grumble, for I am one of the lucky ones. I am twelve years old and have had over four hundred children. Such is the natural life of a pig. But no animal escapes the cruel knife in the end. You young porkers who are sitting in front of me, every one of you will scream your lives out at the block within a year. To that horror we all must come—cows, pigs, hens, sheep, everyone. Even the horses and the dogs have no better fate. You, Boxer, the very day that those great muscles of yours lose their power, Jones will sell you to the **knacker** who will cut your throat and boil you down for the foxhounds. As for the dogs, when they grow old and toothless, Jones ties a brick round their necks and drowns them in the nearest pond.

knacker
a person who buys animal carcasses for slaughter

7 "Is it not crystal clear, then, comrades, that all the evils of this life of ours spring from the tyranny of human beings? Only get rid of Man, and the produce of our labour would be our own. Almost overnight we could become rich and free. What then must we do? Why, work night and day, body and soul, for the overthrow of the human race! That is my message to you, comrades: Rebellion! I do not know when that Rebellion will come. It might be in a week or in a hundred years, but I know, as sure as my feet, that sooner or later justice will be done. Fix your eyes on that, comrades, throughout the short remainder of your lives! And above all, pass on this message of mine to those who come after you, so that future generations shall carry on the struggle until it is victorious.

8 "And remember, comrades, your resolution should never **falter**. No argument must lead you astray. Never listen when they tell you that Man and the animals have a common interest, that the prosperity of the one is the prosperity of the others. It is all lies. Man serves the interests of no creature except himself. And among us animals let there be perfect unity, perfect comradeship in the struggle. All men are enemies. All animals are comrades."

resolution
determination

falter
to hesitate or waver in action

9 At this moment there was a tremendous uproar. While Major was speaking four large rats had crept out of their holes and were sitting on their hindquarters, listening to him. The dogs had suddenly caught sight of them, and it was only by a swift dash for their holes that the rats saved their 1ives. Major raised his trotter for silence.

10 "Comrades," he said, "Here is a point that must be settled. The wild creatures, such as rats and rabbits—are they our friends or our enemies? Let us put it to the vote. I propose this question to the meeting: Are rats comrades?"

11 The vote was taken at once, and it was agreed by an overwhelming majority that rats were comrades. There were only four dissentients, the three dogs and the cat, who was afterwards discovered to have voted on both sides. Major continued:

12 "I have little more to say. I merely repeat, remember always your duty of enmity towards Man and all his ways. Whatever goes upon two legs is an enemy. Whatever goes upon four legs, or has wings, is a friend. And remember also that in fighting against Man, we must not come to

resemble him. Even when you have conquered him, do not adopt his vices. No animal must ever live in a house, or sleep in a bed, or wear clothes, or drink alcohol, or smoke tobacco, or touch money, or engage in trade. All the habits of Man are evil. And, above all, no animal must ever tyrannize over his own kind. Weak or strong, clever or simple, we are all brothers. No animal must ever kill any other animal. All animals are equal."

Reading with a Critical Eye

In a small group, discuss the following reflection questions, which will guide you toward a deeper understanding of the reading.

1. Major states that he has something important to tell his comrades. Why do you think giving this speech was so important to him?
2. Major describes the hard life of farm animals (para. 3): "Let us face it: our lives are miserable, laborious, and short. We are born, we are given just so much food as will keep the breath in our bodies, and those of us who are capable of it are forced to work to the last atom of our strength; and the very instant that our usefulness has come to an end we are slaughtered with hideous cruelty."

   Do you think his description is accurate? Explain.
3. Major criticizes humans in paragraph 5: "Man is the only creature that consumes without producing. He does not give milk, he does not lay eggs, he is too weak to pull the plough, he cannot run fast enough to catch rabbits. Yet he is lord of all the animals." How would you paraphrase his main point?
4. In Major's call to rebellion (para. 7: "Only get rid of Man, and the produce of our labour would be our own. Almost overnight we could become rich and free. What then must we do? Why, work night and day, body and soul, for the overthrow of the human race! That is my message to you, comrades: Rebellion!"), what political point is the author, George Orwell, trying to make about the state of the human world we live in?
5. "Weak or strong, clever or simple, we are all brothers. No animal must ever kill any other animal. All animals are equal."

   What type of political system do the last lines of Major's speech bring to mind? Can such a system work in the world? Explain.

Reading Comprehension Check

1. In the introduction to his speech, what does Major say he is going to speak about first?

   a. his dream
   b. his old age
   c. the nature of life
   d. the barn story

2. What does Major say about the life of an animal?
   a. It is mostly happy.
   b. It is miserable.
   c. It is life where enough good food is offered.
   d. both a and c
3. When Major says, "No animal in England is free," we can infer that the author's intention was to
   a. send a critical message on the cruelty of zoos.
   b. slaughter the pigs.
   c. focus the reader's attention on the issue of human slavery.
   d. compare the lives of pigs, horses, and other animals.
4. What does Major mean when he says, "Man is the only creature that consumes without producing"?
   a. Man takes without making an effort.
   b. Man only knows how to work.
   c. Man is lazy and therefore has no power.
   d. Animals are to blame.
5. What is Major's ultimate purpose in making this speech?
   a. debate
   b. rebellion
   c. escape
   d. compromise
6. When Major asks, "Are rats comrades?", we can infer that Orwell, the writer, is asking which of these political questions?
   a. Does power bring some groups to exclude other groups?
   b. Are humans better than animals?
   c. Are all men created equal?
   d. both a and c
7. To whom is Major referring when he says, "Even when you have conquered him, do not adopt his vices"?
   a. humans
   b. pigs
   c. power
   d. animals
8. Which "evil of man" is *not* mentioned in Major's speech?
   a. drinking alcohol
   b. wearing clothes
   c. listening to music
   d. smoking tobacco
9. In the last line of this excerpt, Major says, "All animals are equal." Considering what we know about power relations between groups of people, what can we expect will happen to this animal ideal?
   a. It will prosper and a truly egalitarian society will result.
   b. The animals will learn how to accept each other.
   c. It will fall apart because some animals will want to dominate other animals.
   d. none of the above
10. What is the tone of this excerpt?
   a. pessimistic
   b. angry, yet inspired
   c. objective
   d. nostalgic

BIOGRAPHICAL PROFILE

Barack Hussein Obama

Barack Obama made history in 2008 when he became the first African American elected to the presidency. Barack Hussein Obama was born on August 4, 1961, in Honolulu, Hawaii, to Barack Obama Sr., a Kenyan, and Ann Dunham, a white American from Kansas. His parents met at the University of Hawaii where his father was a foreign student. They separated when Obama was just 2 and later divorced. Obama's father returned to Kenya and saw his son only once more before dying in a car accident in 1982.

Obama was always a very strong student, graduating from Columbia University with a degree in political science, and later going on to receive a law degree from Harvard University. While at Harvard, Obama served as the first black president of the *Harvard Law Review.*

Between his time at Columbia and Harvard, Obama moved to Chicago and worked as a community organizer for three years, from 1985 to 1988. He worked for a community organization called the Developing Communities Project. Some of his accomplishments with the DCP included helping to set up a job training program, a college preparatory tutoring program, and a tenants' rights organization.

After receiving his law degree, Obama taught constitutional law at the University of Chicago Law School from 1992 until 2004. In 1993, he joined Davis, Miner, Barnhill & Galland, a twelve-attorney law firm specializing in civil rights **litigation** and neighborhood economic development.

Obama's political rise began when he was elected to the Illinois Senate in 1996. Once elected, Obama gained bipartisan support for legislation involving healthcare law, tax credits for low-income workers, and **subsidies** for childcare. Obama won reelection to the Illinois Senate in 1998 and again in 2002. In 2000, however, he lost a Democratic primary run for the U.S. House of Representatives.

A great moment in Obama's political career was when he was asked to write and deliver the keynote address for the 2004 Democratic National Convention in Boston, Massachusetts. Drawing examples from U.S. history, Obama criticized partisan politics and asked Americans to find unity in diversity. "There is not a liberal America and a conservative America; there's the United States of America."

Six months later, he was sworn in as a U.S. senator on January 4, 2005. He served proudly in his role as Illinois senator for two years, and in February 2007, he announced his candidacy for president of the United States. Throughout the campaign, Obama identified his top three priorities as ending the war in Iraq, increasing energy independence, and working toward providing health care for all Americans. In what would become one of the most dramatic presidential primary races in U.S. history, Obama battled Senator Hillary Clinton for the Democratic ticket; he emerged victorious in the end. He then battled Senator John McCain for the presidency and was elected president on November 4, 2008.

As president, Obama focused on health care reform, immigration reform, and on measures to stimulate the U.S. economy. In 2012, he won reelection against his Republican opponent, Mitt Romney.

Obama met his wife Michelle, a fellow lawyer, in 1989 when he was employed as a summer associate at a Chicago law firm. They married in 1992 and have two daughters.

Some Questions for Group Discussion

1. Many people believe that to be a candidate for president of the United States you have to be born into a rich family. Yet, Obama came from a humble background, raised mostly by his mother and grandmother. What made the difference in Obama's rise to the top?
2. The media uses the label African American when discussing Barack Obama. Yet, his mother was a white American. Why do you think the media focuses more on Obama's black ancestry? Do you think this is fair and accurate? Explain.
3. At the 2004 Democratic National Convention in Boston, Obama urged the American people to reconcile their political differences and unite. Discuss what forces unite and divide citizens of a country.

Biographical Internet Research

Do research on the Internet and find out about another historical figure in political science, chosen from the list below. Share a biographical profile with your classmates.

- Niccolò Machiavelli
- Thomas Jefferson
- Mao Zedong
- Sarah Palin
- Shirley Chisholm

SKILL FOCUS: Combined Skills

So far, you have focused on one reading skill in each chapter. By now, you have learned reading skills such as vocabulary in context, main idea, supporting details, making inferences, purpose and tone, fact and opinion, argument, patterns of organization, and author's bias. You have also practiced answering multiple-choice questions after each of the readings. You may have noticed that some reading comprehension questions refer to a "particular point" in the article, and that others are related to the "overall meaning" of the article. Particular-point questions test reading skills such as vocabulary in context, supporting details, fact and opinion, and making inferences. On the other hand, overall-meaning questions focus on the entire article instead of referring to just a specific part of the text. Overall-meaning questions focus on the main idea, author's purpose, and tone.

It is important to note that while you have focused on only one skill in each chapter, most standardized reading tests require you to read a full-length article and answer multiple-choice questions including *both* particular-point and overall-meaning questions. It is, therefore, necessary for you to master combined skills so that you can readily identify whether you need to focus on a particular point of the text or whether you should look at the overall meaning of the text.

When we read, we usually do so holistically—that is, we take the whole of the reading into consideration and do not consider just one aspect of the passage. It may be useful for the purposes of skill review, however, to map out key aspects of a reading as a way of entering and connecting to a text.

Read the following section of an article about the American identity, and review the reading map that follows.

Example

Melting Pot or Salad Bowl?

harnessed
directed or captured the force of something

The American self-image has always **harnessed** a creative tension between **pluralism** and assimilation. On the one hand, immigrants traditionally have been expected to immerse themselves in the American "melting pot," a metaphor popularized by the playwright Israel Zangwill's 1908 drama *The Melting Pot*, in which one character declares:

> *Understand that America is God's Crucible, the great Melting-Pot where all the races of Europe are melting and reforming! A fig for your feuds and vendettas! Germans and Frenchmen, Irishmen and Englishmen, Jews and Russians—into the Crucible with you all! God is making the American.*

Nor were Zangwill's sentiments new ones. As far back as 1782, J. Hector St. John de Crèvecoeur, a French immigrant and keen observer of American life, described his new compatriots as:

. . . a mixture of English, Scotch, Irish, French, Dutch, Germans, and Swedes. . . . What, then, is the American, this new man? He is neither an European nor the descendant of an European; hence that strange mixture of blood, which you will find in no other country. I could point out to you a family whose grandfather was an Englishman, whose wife was Dutch, whose son married a French woman, and whose present four sons have now four wives of different nations. He is an American . . . leaving behind him all his ancient prejudices and manners . . .

The melting pot, however, has always existed alongside a competing model, in which each successive immigrant group retains a measure of its distinctiveness and enriches the American whole. In 1918 the public intellectual Randolph Bourne called for a "trans-national America." The original English colonists, Bourne argued, "did not come to be assimilated in an American melting pot. . . . They came to get freedom to live as they wanted to . . . to make their fortune in a new land." Later immigrants, he continued, had not been melted down into some kind of "tasteless, colorless" **homogeneous** Americanism but rather added their distinct contributions to the greater whole.

homogeneous consisting of parts or members that are all the same

The balance between the melting pot and transnational ideals varies with time and circumstance, with neither model achieving complete dominance. Unquestionably, though, Americans have internalized a self-portrait that spans a spectrum of races, creeds, and colors. Consider the popular motion pictures depicting American troops in action during the second World War. It became a Hollywood cliché that every platoon included a farm boy from Iowa, a Brooklyn Jew, a Polish millworker from Chicago, an Appalachian woodsman, and other diverse examples of mid-20th century American manhood. They strain at first to overcome their differences, but by film's end all have bonded—as Americans. Real life could be more complicated, and not least because the African-American soldier would have served in a segregated unit. Regardless, these films depict an American identity that Americans believed in—or wanted to.[1]

Reading Map	
Main Idea	The American identity has always been defined by a compromise between assimilation and pluralism.
An Argument	"The balance between the melting pot and transnational ideals varies with time and circumstance."
Supporting Detail *(for argument)*	The popular movies of World War II always contained a diverse group of American soldiers.
A Fact	In 1918 the public intellectual Randolph Bourne called for a "trans-national America."

[1] From "American Identity: Ideas, Not Ethnicity," by Michael J. Friedman, www.america.gov/st/diversity-english/2008/February/20080307154033ebyessedo0.5349237.html, February 13, 2008

An Opinion	"Understand that America is God's Crucible, the great Melting-Pot where all the races of Europe are melting and reforming."
Author's Tone	Straightforward and unemotional
Author's Purpose	To inform
(An example of) *A Pattern of Organization*	Cause and effect Cause: Hollywood wanted to portray an image of a united America. Effect: By the end of most WWII war films, all the different types of Americans were bonded.
An Inference	We can infer that life for African American soldiers in WWII was a great struggle, beyond the given fact that they were segregated.

Now that you have had a chance to see a reading passage mapped out, read another section from the same article and practice mapping by skill area.

PRACTICING THE SKILL: COMBINING SKILLS

Passage

Individualism and Tolerance

If American identity embraces all kinds of people, it also affords them a vast menu of opportunities to make and remake themselves. Americans historically have scorned efforts to trade on "accidents of birth," such as great inherited wealth or social status. Article I of the U.S. Constitution bars the government from granting any title of nobility, and those who cultivate an air of superiority toward their fellow Americans are commonly disparaged for **"putting on airs,"** or worse.

putting on airs
acting superior or snobbish

Americans instead respect the "self-made" man or woman, especially where he or she has overcome great obstacles to success. The late 19th-century American writer Horatio Alger, deemed by the *Encyclopedia Britannica* perhaps the most socially influential American writer of his generation, captured this **ethos** in his many rags-to-riches stories, in which poor shoeshine boys or other street urchins would rise, by dint of their ambition, talent, and fortitude, to wealth and fame.

ethos
moral element

In the United States, individuals craft their own definitions of success. It might be financial wealth—and many are the college dropouts working in their parents' garage in hopes of creating the next Google, Microsoft, or Apple Computer. Others might prize the joys of the sporting arena, of creating fine music or art, or of raising a loving family at home. Because Americans spurn limits, their national identity is not—cannot be—bounded by the color of one's skin, by one's parentage, by which house of worship one attends.

Americans hold differing political beliefs, embrace (often wildly) divergent lifestyles, and insist upon broad individual freedoms, but they do so with a remarkable degree of mutual tolerance. One key is their representative form of government: No citizen agrees with every U.S. government decision; all know they can reverse those policies by persuading their fellow citizens to vote for change at the next election.

Another key is the powerful guarantees that protect the rights of all Americans from government overreaching. No sooner was the U.S. Constitution ratified than Americans demanded and received the Bill of Rights: 10 constitutional amendments that safeguard basic rights.

There simply is no one picture of a "typical" American. From the powdered-wigged Founding Fathers to the multiracial golf champion Tiger Woods, Americans share a common identity grounded in the freedom—consistent always with respecting the freedom of others—to live as they choose. The results can bemuse, intrigue, and inspire. Cambodia's biggest hip-hop star, born on a Cambodian farm, lives in southern California. (He goes by the name "praCh.") Walt Whitman, the closest Americans have produced to a national poet, would not have been surprised. "I am large," Whitman wrote of his nation, "I contain **multitudes**."

multitudes
a great number

Reading Map	
Main Idea	
An Argument	
Supporting Detail *(for argument)*	
A Fact	
An Opinion	
Author's Tone	
Author's Purpose	
(An example of) ***A Pattern of Organization (exemplification)***	
An Inference	

Now that you have reviewed and practiced the combined skills, read the following full-length article and answer the multiple-choice questions that follow.

Recommended Debate Topic: Should U.S. permanent residents be allowed to vote?

Discuss controversial topics related to Political Science with your classmates and instructor for the debate activity.

Your suggested debate topics:

a. ______________________________

b. ______________________________

c. ______________________________

READING 4

Online Magazine Article

MyReadingLab

Visit Chapter 10: Political Science in MyReadingLab to complete the Reading 4 activities.

Should the Voting Age Be Lowered?

Pre-Reading Questions

In small groups, consider the following questions before focusing on the following blog reading.

1. Why do you think so many young people show little interest in politics? What factors play a role in youth apathy?
2. What can be done to encourage more young people to participate in the electoral process?
3. In the United States, a citizen must be eighteen or older to be eligible to vote. Is this a fair minimum age? Should the voting requirement be lowered, or should it be made higher? Explain.

Should the Voting Age Be Lowered?

By Timothy Noah, www.slate.com
November 7, 2000

1 Today, as voters flocked to the polls, one group was staging demonstrations around the country to protest its exclusion from the electoral process. That group was children. You probably think Chatterbox is kidding. He isn't. "Lower the Vote" protests were planned for Election Day in 14 states, including California, Texas, Florida, and Massachusetts. According to its Web page,

> *Lower the Vote is a partnership of various youth rights organizations and independent organizers all committed to lowering the voting age in the United States of America. We believe that the current voting age denies millions of deserving U.S. citizens the fundamental right to vote and should be lowered.*

Young people are tired of being treated like second-class citizens in America. They are tired of facing oppression at the hand [of] adult American society. They are tired of unconstitutional age restrictions. They are tired of being stereotyped by the media as violent, lazy, stupid and apathetic. Above all else, young people want to be a partner in the political process. They want the right to vote, to have a voice in the American democratic process.

2 Obviously, the first question you want answered is, "How far do they want to lower it?" Apparently there isn't much **unanimity** about this within the youth rights movement (whose constituent groups include the National Youth Rights Association; the Youth Rights Action League; Americans for a Society Free from Age Restrictions, or ASFAR; the Association for Children's Suffrage; and YouthSpeak). John Anderson, the 1980 independent presidential candidate, who is currently teaching constitutional law at Nova Southeastern University in Fort Lauderdale, Fla., has been pushing to lower the voting age for several years. Reached today by phone, he told Chatterbox:

unanimity everyone being of one mind

Given the abilities of young people I think to get a driver's license and to operate motor vehicles and otherwise begin to assume some of the responsibilities that you normally put in the category of being adults, I think that it's not unreasonable to contemplate that we would lower it to 16.

3 The Cambridge, Mass., City Council plans to hold a hearing on Nov. 16 in which it will consider lowering the voting age to 16 for city council and school committee races; if the measure clears the city council, it will be forwarded to the Statehouse as a home-rule petition. But others in the movement consider enfranchisement at 16 to be too restrictive. Vita Wallace, then aged 16, advocated eliminating the age limit *entirely* in a 1991 article for *The Nation*:

What I suggest is that children be allowed to grow into their own right to vote at whatever rate suits them individually . . . As for the ability to read and write, that should never be used as a criterion for eligibility, since we have already learned from painful past experience that literacy tests can be manipulated to insure discrimination. In any case, very few illiterates vote, and probably very few children would want to vote as long as they couldn't read or write . . . . I think I would not have voted until I was 8 or 9, but perhaps if I had known I could vote I would have taken an interest sooner.

4 This sentiment was echoed in a 1997 *Brown Daily Herald* interview with Anthony Fotenos, founder of the Association for Children's Suffrage. Fotenos said that although the ideal constituency would be 10 to 18, toddlers should be eligible, too.

5 Among the many reasons Chatterbox can think of *against* lowering the voting age even to 16 is that voters at the low end of the youth spectrum rarely exercise their rights now. In 1971, out of **deference** to the powerful argument that 18-year-olds were old enough to die in Vietnam, the 26th Amendment lowered the voting age from 21. (Ironically, the author of that amendment, Sen. Jennings Randolph of West Virginia, lived to the ripe old age of 96.) What did America's youth do

deference respect

spawned
made something happen or start to exist

with this newfound right? As little as possible! The failure of young folks to vote has **spawned** a small nonprofit industry aimed at getting them interested, and the embarrassing quadrennial ritual of having presidential candidates answer inappropriate or irrelevant "youth-oriented" questions on MTV. At the risk of sounding peevish, Chatterbox thinks that if young people want more of the vote, they will first have to finish what's on their plate.

6 Alex Koroknay-Palicz, president of the National Youth Rights Association, disagrees. Chatterbox caught up with Koroknay-Palicz, a fuzzy-bearded 19-year-old who attends American University, early this evening in D.C.'s Franklin Park. He and five other protesters were standing at the foot of a statue of Cmdr. John Barry, father of the American Navy, and waving magic-markered posterboard signs that said things like "Lower the Voting Age" and "Democracy = Voting." Korknay-Palicz argued to Chatterbox that lowering the voting age would stimulate greater participation among those over 18. "The fact that people have been denied the right to vote for the first 18 years of their lives has given them a sense of powerlessness when it comes to voting and civic participation," he said. If the voting age were lowered, it would help them establish "good voting habits for the rest of their lives."

7 But the makeup of Korknay-Palicz's ragtag group of protesters called into serious question whether the under-18 set even *wanted* the vote. There were only six of them. (They said there had been about a dozen before I got there. According to Korknay-Palicz, the National Youth Rights Association has about 400 members nationwide.) Of the six, five were already 18, hence able to vote *now*. (All five did so today.) The sixth was a stocky and somewhat charismatic fellow in a black T-shirt named Jason Gerber. "I operate a small business. Why am I not allowed to vote?" he bellowed into a megaphone as rush-hour commuters sped by. But even Jason (who attends Montgomery College and, had he been enfranchised today, would have voted for Libertarian candidate Harry Browne) really doesn't have much to complain about. He's 17. He'll be able to vote within a year!

8 Anyway, to establish the sort of lifelong habit that Korknay-Palicz is talking about, you'd have to start voting a lot earlier than 16. In order to assess the fitness of the under-16 crowd to make decisions that would affect the broad polity, Chatterbox posed a few questions to his 7-year-old son, Willie:

Do you think you should be able to vote?

Yes.

Do you think you should be able to go to bed whenever you want?

No.

If you could choose dinner every night, what would it be?

Pasta.

Do you think you should be able to drive a car?

No.

What can Chatterbox say? He's a very levelheaded child. But he still shouldn't be allowed to vote.

Reading with a Critical Eye

In a small group, discuss the following reflection questions, which will guide you toward a deeper understanding of the reading.

1. On the Chatterbox blog excerpt, in support of lowering the voting age, we read: "Young people are tired of being treated like second-class citizens in America. They are tired of facing oppression at the hand [of] adult American society. They are tired of unconstitutional age restrictions. They are tired of being stereotyped by the media as violent, lazy, stupid and apathetic. Above all else, young people want to be a partner in the political process. They want the right to vote, to have a voice in the American democratic process." Do you think most young people share this desire, or, as is argued in the first reading, they simply don't care about the political world?
2. Vita Wallace argues that, "children be allowed to grow into their own right to vote at whatever rate suits them individually." Paraphrase his point, and share your view on his idea.
3. Korknay-Palicz states that "The fact that people have been denied the right to vote for the first 18 years of their lives has given them a sense of powerlessness when it comes to voting and civic participation." What is your reaction to this provocative argument? Do minors in America feel "powerless"?
4. In paragraph 5, we read some arguments made against lowering the voting age. Which, if any, of these arguments is convincing to you?
5. One interesting point that comes up in the blog post is that many under-eighteen-year-old citizens may not choose to vote, if given this freedom. How do you think most minors will respond to the option of voting?

Reading Comprehension Check

1. The word *flocked,* in the first sentence of the reading, means
   a. denied.
   b. ran away from.
   c. went to a place in large numbers.
   d. panicked.
2. What is the tone in the first few paragraphs of the reading, where the voice of the Lower the Vote organization is heard?
   a. humorous
   b. objective
   c. contented
   d. angry and determined

3. According to John Anderson, the 1980 independent presidential candidate, to what age should the voting age be lowered?
   a. 16
   b. 17
   c. 18
   d. 9
4. What argument is offered in opposition to lowering the voting age?
   a. Young people cannot drive.
   b. Young people who are currently eligible to vote often do not do so.
   c. Young people are enthusiastic about politics.
   d. none of the above
5. What is the message behind Chatterbox interviewing his seven-year-old son at the end of the piece?
   a. There is no message.
   b. Even little kids should have this right.
   c. The thought of allowing young, immature kids to vote is ridiculous.
   d. Young people have sophisticated knowledge of the political world.

From Reading to Writing: Writing to a Political Representative

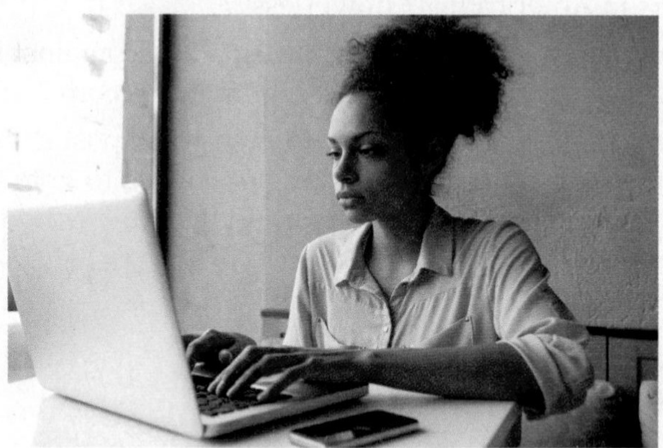

Overview

In representative democracies, the voters elect representatives to act as legislators, and, as such, to voice and protect their general interest. When a member of a community has a concern he or she would like to raise, that person has the right to contact his or her local representative, whether it be a city council member, state senator, mayor, or house representative. Voters, of course, can also contact politicians in higher offices, such as their governor or the president, but local representatives are more likely to respond to community concerns. It will only take you a minute to find your local representative's e-mail contact information online.

There are a few important points to keep in mind when e-mailing a political representative:

- Try to write your letter in a formal voice.

  Begin your letter respectfully with "Dear Councilwoman Green," or "Dear Mayor Jones." Choose more formal vocabulary in the body of your letter. Avoid colloquial usage terms such as "gonna" or "wanna" and so forth. For example, "I'm gonna explain what I wanna do for our community" becomes "I am going to explain what I want to do for our community." Choice of language goes a long way in getting political representatives to pay attention to the concerns you are expressing.
- In the first sentence, offer some context by making clear what your connection is to the issue you are addressing.

  Introduce your identity in relation to the issue at hand. If you are a college student writing about the lack of financial aid funding coming from the state, begin your letter by saying, "I am a junior at Smith and Smith College and . . ." If you are a teacher and want to voice your opinion on how overcrowded your classrooms have become, you might begin your letter with "I am a fifth-grade teacher at Central Elementary and . . ."
- Get to the point. Be clear and straightforward.

  Politicians and their staff are busy people with many community members competing for their attention. Keep your letter short and focused. Introduce your relation to the issue, briefly describe the problem or community concern, and clearly express what actions you think your representative should take to improve the situation. Do not digress from the issue at hand by discussing your life story or by sharing your feelings about the particular politician's political problems. This would only serve to distract your reader from the real concerns you would like to see addressed.

An Example Letter to a Representative

Dear Councilwoman Rogers,

I am a freshman at Dandelion Community College and I am writing to you about the strict parking rules in the residential area just outside the campus. I have gotten two tickets already for parking on nearby residential streets around 5:40 PM, where the parking signs state that you can only park after 6:00 PM. I know there are many other students like me who drive to college after working all day and need to park before 6:00 in order to make to it class on time.

The problem is that there is nowhere else around to park. The campus parking lot is always full that late in the day and there are no public parking lots in the area. I have already addressed this issue to my campus dean, but I think there is a lot you can do to alleviate the situation. First, you should consider changing the parking rules within three blocks of the campus, so that students can park legally on the street at any hour of the day. Another possible solution would be to build a modest-sized public parking lot somewhere within walking distance of the campus.

Thank you, Councilwoman Rogers, for considering my concerns. I look forward to hearing from you soon about this matter.

Sincerely,
Jane Doe

Assignment: Writing a Letter to Send to a Local Representative

Before doing any writing for a letter you can later send, spend a few minutes with a classmate, making a list of complaints/concerns you have about your community.

Choose one community concern to be the focus of your letter. Consider to whom you would like to address this concern, for example, a community board member, a state representative, the mayor, or other public representative. Make sure you know the name of the political representative to whom you are writing.

Concern/Issue:

Name and title of political representative:

Write a letter addressing a community concern and send it via e-mail or post. You should be able to locate political representatives' e-mail and office addresses easily through an Internet search. We hope you will receive a prompt response to your letter. Good luck!

Careers in Political Science

Working in small groups, discuss careers one can pursue after obtaining a degree in Political Science. You may wish to do some research on the Internet to find other careers related to the field of Political Science. In the space below, write down the job title and responsibilities. The first example is done for you. Be sure to share your findings with your peers.

Job Title	*Responsibilities*
1. Immigration Attorney	Guiding immigrants through the process of obtaining permanent residency and citizenship. Representing immigrants in deportation proceedings.
2.	
3.	
4.	
5.	

Textbook Application

Read the following chapter from an introductory book on political science. As you know, this reading exercise will give you an opportunity to practice reading and answering multiple-choice questions based on authentic text. You are likely to come across this type of text when you take mainstream courses in college.

MyReadingLab

Visit Chapter 10: Political Science in MyReadingLab to complete the Reading 5 activities.

READING 5

Textbook Excerpt

from Understanding the Political World: A Comparative Introduction to Political Science, 12/e

by James N. Danziger and Charles Anthony Smith

1 Imagine you have a 13-year-old sister in eighth grade. She has quite the day at school: The vice principal comes into her math class unexpectedly and asks her to bring her backpack and accompany him to his office. In his office, she sees a planner, a knife, a lighter, and some white pills on his desk. The vice principal lectures her about the importance of telling the truth, then asks which of the items belong to her. She tells him that she had lent the planner to another girl a few days earlier, but that the other items are not hers. The vice principal responds that the other girl has reported your sister for giving her the pills, which students are not allowed to possess at school.

2 The vice principal asks if he can look through your sister's backpack, and she agrees. A female secretary enters the office and searches the backpack. Your sister is then told to follow the secretary to the nurse's office, where she is asked to remove her jacket, socks, and shoes. She follows their directions. They next ask her to take off her pants and shirt, and again she follows their directions. These clothes are searched, and when nothing incriminating is found, they order your sister to stand up, pull her bra away from her body and shake it, then pull her underwear loose and shake it. No pills drop out when she complies. She is allowed to put her clothes back on and sit outside the principal's office for several hours. Finally, she is sent back to class.

3 What do you think of the events just described? Is this situation *political*? Do the actions of the vice principal seem appropriate? What about the actions of the school's secretary and nurse? Did your sister do the right thing by complying with each of their requests? Did she have a choice? What would you do in a similar situation?

4 Of course, this did not happen to your little sister (if you have one), but it did happen to 13-year-old Savana Redding of Safford,

Arizona, in 2003. Here are some additional facts in this case. This public school has a responsibility to ensure the safety and health of all of its students. The previous year, a student nearly died from drugs taken without permission at the school. The school district has a zero-tolerance policy for all drugs—no student is allowed to possess any drugs at school, whether over-the-counter, prescription, or illegal. The vice principal acted on information from another girl who reported that Savana had given her pills that day. It was not really a "strip search" because Savana never took off her underwear. All of these conditions seem to justify the actions that occurred.

5 However, there are valid points on the other side of the issue. The Fourth Amendment to the U.S. Constitution seems to protect Savana from this type of search unless significant evidence indicates that something illegal is occurring (probable cause). The vice principal's actions were taken based on questionable information from another girl who was already in trouble for possessing the pills. And the search occurred despite Savana's claim that she had no pills, without parental approval, and before any further investigation of the situation was attempted. Then there is common sense: the pills are merely extra-strength ibuprofen (painkillers). Is this really a legitimate reason for adults in authority positions to force a 13-year-old girl to submit to a humiliating strip search?

6 Savana's mother was outraged. With the assistance of a lawyer from the American Civil Liberties Union (ACLU), she sued the school officials on the grounds that they had subjected her daughter to an 'unreasonable search.' Savana's lawyer argued that, while a search of her backpack might be reasonable, a strip search was not, given the flimsy evidence of guilt and the minimal threat associated with ibuprofen. The school district's officials responded that the vice principal's actions were justified and consistent with numerous court cases that uphold the rights and responsibilities of schools to prevent dangerous behavior among their students, including searches for drugs or weapons.

7 Initially, a judge in Tucson ruled in favor of the actions by the school officials; however, on appeal, the circuit court reversed the decision by the narrowest of margins (6–5). The court concluded that the strip search of an eighth grader, while looking for prescription drugs, was a violation of her constitutional rights, and it held that the family could sue the school for damages. The school's lawyer then appealed the case to the U.S. Supreme Court. In 2009, the court's majority (8–1) held that the search of Savana was unconstitutional. The majority reasoned that the particular drugs suspected in this case were not sufficiently threatening to justify the search. However, the court did not allow the family to sue school officials, leaving open the question of how it might rule if school officials suspected a student of possessing something more dangerous than ibuprofen.

8 **Toward a Definition of Politics**

The first step in our journey toward a better understanding of the political world is to establish what we mean by politics. The Savana Redding search captures some of the crucial themes related to politics:

- Politics is the competition among individuals and groups pursuing their own interests.
- Politics is the exercise of power and influence to allocate things that are valued.
- Politics is the determination of who gets what, when, and how.
- Politic is the resolution of conflict.

9 All of these definitions share the central idea that politics is the process through which power and influence are used in the promotion of certain values and interests. Competing values and interests are clearly at the heart of the search of Savana Redding. The values that guide a zero-tolerance policy regarding drugs at the school are balanced against values that protect a student against an illegal search. Other groups might have a stake in this conflict, as did the ACLU, which intervened to promote its views about individual liberty, and the courts, which asserted their responsibility to interpret the laws.

10 As individuals, groups, and governmental actors make decisions about what is good or bad for society, and as they try to implement their decisions, politics occurs. Every individual holds an array of preferred values and interests, and that individual cares more about some of those values than others. What values is each individual willing to promote or yield on? If the values of different individuals come into conflict, whose values and rights should prevail? And, if people cannot work out their conflicting values privately through discussion and compromise, must the government intervene? How does the government exercise its power to resolve the conflict? Who benefits and who is burdened by the policies of the government? These are all *political* questions.

Reading Comprehension Check

1. As used in the second paragraph, "These clothes are searched, and when nothing **incriminating** is found, they order your sister to stand up," the word *incriminating* could be replaced with
   a. impulsive.
   b. advantageous.
   c. implicating.
   d. beneficial.
   Question Type: ____________________
2. "Did your sister do the right thing by **complying** with each of their requests?" (para. 3)
   The word *complying* could be replaced with
   a. obeying.
   b. protesting.
   c. plummeting.
   d. denying.
   Question Type: ____________________

3. In the sentence, "However, there are **valid** points on the other side of the issue" (para. 5), a synonym for the word *valid* is
   a. illogical.
   b. acceptable.
   c. weakened.
   d. dramatic.
   Question Type: ____________________

4. The main idea of the reading is that
   a. people should not concern themselves with political issues.
   b. only political leaders need to understand how politics works.
   c. politics is a game you cannot win, and this is clearly demonstrated through the case of Savana Redding.
   d. the case of Savana Redding demonstrates how politics is a process through which power and influence are used in the promotion of certain values and interests.
   Question Type: ____________

5. What was the school's rationale for why they were so strict with Savana?
   a. She had been caught many times with pills.
   b. The school has a zero-tolerance policy for student possession of any types of drugs.
   c. Another girl had said that Savana was in possession of illegal drugs.
   d. Savana's mom had tried to sue the school for damages.
   Question Type: ____________________

6. According to the author, which two values were in opposition in the Savana Redding case?
   a. freedom of press versus freedom of privacy
   b. individual protection versus democratic principles
   c. values guiding a zero-tolerance policy regarding drugs against values that protect a student against an illegal search
   d. values of the state versus values of the individual
   Question Type: ____________________

7. "The Savana Redding search captures some of the crucial themes related to politics."

   Which of the following can we conclude about the author from the above statement?
   a. Political science has mostly to do with issues related to criminal justice.
   b. The economic systems determine politics.
   c. The author believes that this case was not handled well.
   d. The author chose to highlight the Savana Redding case to exemplify critical themes in politics.
   Question Type: ____________________

8. The author's primary purpose in writing this section is to
   a. persuade the reader not to be concerned with political issues.
   b. inform the reader that only political scientists should be concerned with political science.
   c. convince the reader that politics matters in our everyday lives.
   d. explain to the reader that politics is not intimately connected to economics.
   Question Type: ____________________

9. The overall tone of the reading is
   a. humorous.
   b. sad.
   c. serious.
   d. pessimistic.

   Question Type: ________________

10. Reread this section and then choose the best answer to complete the sentence that follows:

    The Savana Redding search captures some of the crucial themes related to politics:

    - Politics is the competition between individuals and groups pursuing their own interests.
    - Politics is the exercise of power and influence to allocate things that are valued.
    - Politics is the determination of who gets what, when, and how.
    - Politics is the resolution of conflict.

11. The author's overall pattern of organization
    a. offers information chronologically.
    b. lists some themes connected to the term *politics*.
    c. compares and contrasts the different roles politics play in our lives.
    d. shows the causes and effects of political thinking.

    Question Type: ______________________

Contemporary Issues in the Discipline

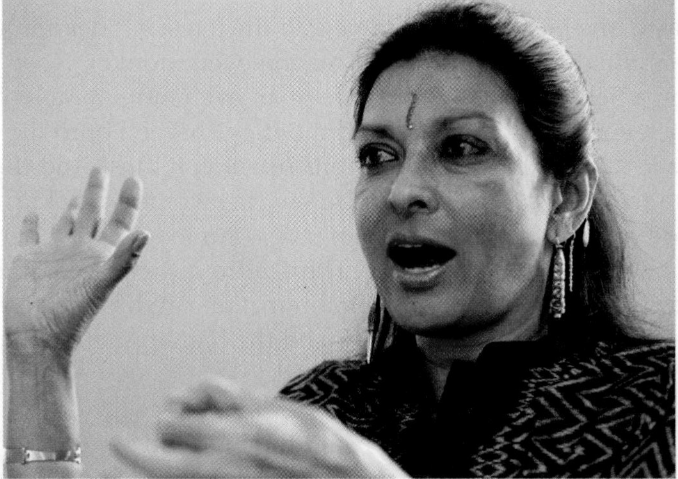

Mallika Sarabhai is an activist, choreographer, dancer, actor, publisher, and writer who leads the Darpana Dance Company. She is the founder of a Gujarati television production company producing activist programming, and she serves as the head of a book publishing company, Mapin. Sarabhai has run for office in her district, Gandhinagar, in India, and despite not winning the election, she continues to champion social justice and advocate for the rights of all people from all castes in India.

READING 6

Lecture (TED Talk)

MyReadingLab

Visit Chapter 10: Political Science in MyReadingLab to complete the Reading 6 activities.

Dance to Change the World

Pre-Reading Activity

Before reading the following transcript of Ms. Sarabhai's Ted Talk, you can watch the speech itself here: **www.ted.com/talks/mallika_sarabhai?language=en** (Courtesy of TED).

As you listen to the video presentation, take notes. (See the note-taking activity on p. 190 for some pointers.) After reading the transcript, you will answer some open-ended questions about some of the issues raised in her speech. Finally, you will formulate questions for Ms. Sarabhai about issues pertinent to political science and answer them from her perspective.

Dance to Change the World

By Mallika Sarabhai

November 2009

Transcript courtesy of TED © TED CONFERENCES, LLC

1 One day a one-eyed monkey came into the forest. Under a tree she saw a woman meditating furiously. The one-eyed monkey recognized the woman, a Sekhri. She was the wife of an even more famous Brahmin. To watch her better, the one-eyed monkey climbed onto the tree. Just then, with a loud bang, the heavens opened. *(Claps)* And the god Indra jumped into the clearing. Indra saw the woman, a Sekhri. Ah-hah. The woman paid him no heed. So, Indra, attracted, threw her onto the floor, and proceeded to rape her. Then Indra disappeared. *(Clap! Clap!)* And the woman's husband, the Brahmin, appeared. He realized at once what had happened. So, he petitioned the higher gods so that he may have justice. So, the god Vishnu arrived.

2 "Are there any witnesses?"

"Just a one-eyed monkey," said the Brahmin.

Now, the one-eyed monkey really wanted for the woman, a Sekhri, to get justice, so she retold events exactly as they had happened. Vishnu gave his judgment.

"The god Indra has sinned, in that he has sinned against . . . a Brahmin. May he be called to wash away his sins."

3 So, Indra arrived, and performed the sacrifice of the horse. And so it transpired that a horse was killed, a god was made sin-free, a Brahmin's ego was appeased, a woman . . . was ruined, and a one-eyed monkey was left . . . very confused at what we humans call justice.

4 In India there is a rape every three minutes. In India, only 25 percent of rapes come to a police station, and of these 25 percent that come to a police station, convictions are only in four percent of the cases. That's a lot of women who don't get justice. And it's not only about women. Look around you, look at your own countries. There is a certain pattern in who gets charged with crimes. If you're in Australia, it's mostly aboriginals who are in jail. If you're in India, it's either Muslims or Adivasis, or tribals, the Naxalites. If you're in the U.S., it's mostly the blacks. There is a trend here. And the Brahmins and the gods, like in my story, always get to tell their truth as The Truth. So, have we all become one-eyed—two-eyed instead of one-eyed—monkeys? Have we stopped seeing injustice?

5 Good morning. *(Applause)* You know, I have told this story close to 550 times, in audiences in 40 countries, to school students, to black-tie dinners at the Smithsonian, and so on and so forth, and every time it hits something. Now, if I were to go into the same crowd and say, "I want to lecture you about justice and injustice," they would say, "Thank you very much, we have other things to do." And that is the astonishing power of art.

6 Art can go through where other things can't. You can't have barriers, because it breaks through your prejudices, breaks through everything that you have as your mask, that says, "I am this, I am that, I am that." No. It breaks through those. And it reaches somewhere where other things don't. And in a world where attitudes are so difficult to change, we need a language that reaches through.

7 Hitler knew it; he used Wagner to make all the Nazis feel wonderful and Aryan. And Mr. Berlusconi knows it, as he sits atop this huge empire of media and television and so on and so forth. And all of the wonderful creative minds who are in all the advertising agencies, and who help corporate sell us things we absolutely don't require, they also know the power of the arts.

8 For me it came very early. When I was a young child, my mother, who was a choreographer, came upon a phenomenon that worried her. It was a phenomenon where young brides were committing suicide in rural Gujarat, because they were being forced to bring more and more money for their in-laws' families. And she created a dance piece, which then Prime Minister Nehru saw. He came to talk to her and said, "What is this about?" She told him and he set out the first inquiry into what today we call Dowry Dance. Imagine a dance piece for the first inquiry into something that even today kills thousands of women.

9 Many years later, when I was working with the director Peter Brook in *The Mahabharata* playing this feisty feminine feminist called Draupadi, I had similar experiences. Big fat black mamas in the Bronx used to come and say, "Hey girl, that's it!" And then these trendy young things in the Sorbonne would say, "Madame Draupadi, on n'est pas feministe, mais ça? Ça!" And then aboriginal women in

Africa would come and say, "This is it!" And I thought, "This is what we need, as a language."

10 We had somebody from public health. And Devdutt also mentioned public health. Well, millions of people around the world die of waterborne disease every year. And that's because there is no clean water to drink, or in countries like India, people don't know that they need to soap their hands after defecation. So, what do they do? They drink the water they know is dirty, they get cholera, they get diarrhea, they get jaundice and they die. And governments have not been able to provide clean water. They try and build it. They try and build pipelines; it doesn't happen. And the MNCs give them machines that they cannot afford. So what do you do? Do you let them die?

11 Well, somebody had a great idea. And it was a simple idea. It was an idea that could not profit anybody but would help health in every field. Most houses in Asia and India have a cotton garment. And it was discovered, and WHO endorses this, that a clean cotton garment folded eight times over, can reduce bacteria up to 80 percent from water sieved through. So, why aren't governments blaring this on television? Why isn't it on every poster across the third world? Because there is no profit in it. Because nobody can get a kickback. But it still needs to get to people. And here is one of the ways we get it to people.

12 *[Video]* Woman: Then get me one of those fancy water purifiers.

Man: You know how expensive those are. I have a solution that requires neither machine, nor wood, nor cooking gas.

Woman: What solution?

Man: Listen, go fetch that cotton sari you have.

Boy: Grand-dad, tell me the solution please.

Man: I will tell all of you. Just wait.

Woman: Here father. (Man: Is it clean?) Woman: Yes, of course.

Man: Then do as I tell you. Fold the sari into eight folds.

Woman: All right, father.

Man: And you, you count that she does it right. (Boy: All right, grand-dad.)

Man: One, two, three, four folds we make. All the germs from the water we take.

Chorus: One, two, three, four folds we make. All the germs from the water we take. Five, six, seven, eight folds we make. Our drinking water safe we make. Five, six, seven, eight folds we make. Our drinking water safe we make.

Woman: Here, father, your eight-times folded cotton sari.

Man: So this is the cotton sari. And through this we will have clean water.

(Applause)

13 I think it's safe to say that all of us here are deeply concerned about the escalating violence in our daily lives. While universities are trying to devise courses in conflict resolution, and governments are

trying to stop skirmishes at borders, we are surrounded by violence, whether it's road rage, or whether it's domestic violence, whether it's a teacher beating up a student and killing her because she hasn't done her homework, it's everywhere. So, why are we not doing something to actually attend to that problem on a day-to-day basis?

14 What are we doing to try and make children and young people realize that violence is something that we indulge in, that we can stop, and that there are other ways of actually taking violence, taking anger, taking frustrations into different things that do not harm other people? Well, here is one such way.

15 *(Video) (Laughs)* You are peaceful people. Your parents were peaceful people. Your grandparents were peaceful people. So much peace in one place? How could it be otherwise?

(Music)

16 But, what if . . . Yes. What if . . . One little gene in you has been trying to get through? From your beginnings in Africa, through each generation, maybe passed on to you, in your creation. It's a secret urge, hiding deep in you. And if it's in you, then it's in me, too. Oh, dear.

17 It's what made you smack your baby brother, stamp on a cockroach, scratch your mother. It's the feeling that wells up from deep inside, when your husband comes home drunk and you wanna tan his hide. Want to kill that cyclist on the way to work, and string up your cousin 'cause she's such a jerk. Oh, dear. And as for outsiders, white, black or brown, tar and feather them, and whip them out of town.

18 It's that little gene. It's small and it's mean. Too small for detection, it's your built-in protection. Adrenaline, kill. It'll give you the will. Yes, you'd better face it 'cause you can't displace it. You're V-I-O-L-E-N-T. Cause you're either a victim, or on top, like me.

19 Goodbye, Abraham Lincoln. Goodbye, Mahatma Gandhi. Goodbye, Martin Luther King. Hello, gangs from this neighborhood killing gangs from that neighborhood. Hello governments of rich countries selling arms to governments of poor countries who can't even afford to give them food. Hello civilization. Hello, twenty-first century. Look what we've . . . look what they've done. *(Applause)*

20 Mainstream art, cinema, has been used across the world to talk about social issues. A few years ago we had a film called *Rang De Basanti*, which suddenly spawned thousands of young people wanting to volunteer for social change. In Venezuela, one of the most popular soap operas has a heroine called Crystal. And when, onscreen, Crystal got breast cancer, 75,000 more young women went to have mammographies done. And of course, *The Vagina Monologues* we know about. And there are stand-up comics who are talking about racial issues, about ethnic issues.

21 So, why is it, that if we think that we all agree that we need a better world, we need a more just world, why is it that we are not using the one language that has consistently showed us that we can break down barriers, that we can reach people? What I need to say to the planners of the world, the governments, the strategists is, "You have treated the arts as the cherry on the cake. It needs to be the yeast." Because, any future planning, if 2048 is when we want to get there, unless the arts are put with the scientists, with the economists, with all those who prepare for the future, badly, we're not going to get there. And unless this is actually internalized, it won't happen.

22 So, what is it that we require? What is it that we need? We need to break down our vision of what planners are, of what the correct way of a path is. And to say all these years of trying to make a better world, and we have failed. There are more people being raped. There are more wars. There are more people dying of simple things. So, something has got to give. And that is what I want. Can I have my last audio track please?

23 Once there was a princess who whistled beautifully. *(Whistling)* Her father the king said, "Don't whistle." Her mother the queen said, "Hai, don't whistle." But the princess continued whistling. *(Whistling)* The years went by and the princess grew up into a beautiful young woman, who whistled even more beautifully. *(Whistling)* Her father the king said, "Who will marry a whistling princess?" Her mother the queen said, "Who will marry a whistling princess?"

24 But the king had an idea. He announced a Swayamvara. He invited all the princes to come and defeat his daughter at whistling. "Whoever defeats my daughter shall have half my kingdom and her hand in marriage!" Soon the palace filled with princes whistling. *(Whistling)* Some whistled badly. Some whistled well. But nobody could defeat the princess.

25 "Now what shall we do?" said the king. "Now what shall we do?" said the queen. But the princess said, "Father, Mother, don't worry. I have an idea. I am going to go to each of these young men and I am going to ask them if they defeated correctly. And if somebody answers, that shall be my wish."

26 So she went up to each and said, "Do you accept that I have defeated you?" And they said, "Me? Defeated by a woman? No way, that's impossible! No no no no no! That's not possible." Till finally one prince said, "Princess, I accept, you have defeated me." "Uh-huh, . . ." she said. "Father, mother, this man shall be my wife." *(Whistling)*

27 Thank you. *(Applause)*

Reading with a Critical Eye

In a small group, discuss the following reflection questions, which will guide you toward a deeper understanding of the reading.

1. What point is Ms. Sarabhai trying to make by beginning her presentation with the story of the one-eyed monkey?
2. What is Ms. Sarabhai's view on the power of art?
3. How did Ms. Sarabhai's mother inspire her?
4. Ms. Sarabhai speaks of a "violence gene." "It's that little gene. It's small and it's mean. Too small for detection, it's your built-in protection." Do you agree with her idea that we all contain the seed of violence within us? If yes, how can we best contain this violent tendency?
5. What is the implied message of the last line of the story about the whistling princess? "Father, mother, this man shall be my wife."

Imagined Interview: If you had the opportunity to interview Mallika Sarabhai in person, what would you ask her? With a partner, compose three questions for her.

Question 1. ____________________

Question 2. ____________________

Question 3. ____________________

Interview Challenge: In a group, ask one student to play Ms. Sarabhai. This student should carefully consider Mallika Sarabhai's views, outlined clearly in the TED Talk, and try to answer the questions from Sarabhai's perspective on the power of art to inspire social change.

Chapter Recap

Now that you have made it through a full chapter focusing on the field of Political Science, let's review the chapter reading content, skill focus, and vocabulary to gain a better understanding of what we have learned.

Recap Activity 1: A Quick Glance

In 60 seconds, answer the following two questions:

1. What is one thing you learned from this chapter?

____

____

____

____

____

____

2. What is your favorite reading in the chapter? Explain.

____

____

____

____

____

____

Collaboration

Now discuss what you wrote in a small group. Do not read what you wrote. Paraphrase yourself!

Recap Activity 2: Reinforcing the Content

Which reading in this chapter did you find the most interesting/valuable, and why?

____

____

____

____

____

____

Share your choice with your class partners.

Recap Activity 3: Internet Research on a Theme of Interest

Think about the choice you just made in Activity 2 concerning which reading in the chapter was your favorite.

What was the theme of your chosen reading?

Theme = ______________________________

Using a search engine, such as Google, go online and locate a quality reading on the same theme as your favorite chapter reading. Write a three- to five-sentence summary of the reading that you found from your Internet research.

Title of Reading	*Article Source*	*Summary of the Reading (in your own words)*

Recap Activity 4: Reinforcing the Skill

Reread the following questions from the comprehension check from Reading 2: Give Non-Citizens the Right to Vote. It's Only Fair (p. 553). After examining the questions, discuss with a partner: What plan of action can be used to best identify the question type for each?

> **Question 1:** In the sentence, "But there's another tactic—increasing immigrant **clout** by allowing all noncitizens to vote—that also deserves serious consideration," the word *clout* could be replaced with ____________.
> **Question 2:** What point is the author trying to make when he gives the statistics (para. 3) about voting rights from 1776 to 1926?
> **Question 3:** In the second paragraph, in the sentence, "But what most don't know is that the right to vote in this country has never been **intrinsically** tied to citizenship," a synonym for the term *intrinsically* is ____________.

How can you clearly identify the question types for each of the three questions listed?

Strategy 1: ______________________________

Strategy 2: ______________________________

Recap Activity 5: Recycling Vocabulary

activist	**constitutional**	**authority**
legislation	**representation**	
pluralism	**candidate**	

With a partner, locate these vocabulary terms, review them in context, and try to define the terms without using a dictionary. Make sure to underline the vocabulary term used in the sentence. The first example is done for you.

Word and context location	*Sentence containing the word*	*Meaning in this context*
authority (p. 550, para 32)	. . . and by <u>Authority</u> of the good People of these Colonies.	**power and recognition**
campaign (p. 563)	More recently, she made a run for the Lok Sabha, campaigning on a platform of social responsibility, and focusing on the problems of average people in India regardless of caste or language.	______________
candidate (p. 569, para 2)	John Anderson, the 1980 independent presidential candidate, is currently teaching constitutional law at Nova Southeastern University.	______________

legislation (p. 563)	"Once elected, Obama gained bipartisan support for legislation involving healthcare law, tax credits for low-income workers, and subsidies for childcare."	______________
abolish (p. 548, para 2)	"... while evils are sufferable than to right themselves by abolishing the forms to which they are accustomed."	______________
lobbying (p. 554, para 1)	"... The contemporary immigrant rights movement has commanded attention through civil disobedience, student walkouts and intensive lobbying."	______________
representation (p. 549 , para 5)	"He has refused to pass other Laws for the accommodation of large districts of people, unless those people would relinquish the right of Representation in the Legislature."	______________
tyrannize (p. 561, para 1)	"And, above all, no animal must ever tyrannize over his own kind."	______________

Further Explorations

Books

1. *Long Walk to Freedom: The Autobiography of Nelson Mandela*. Holt McDougal, 2000. In this autobiography, secretly written in prison on Robben Island over a period of twenty-seven years, the South African President Nelson Mandela describes his struggle for freedom from the apartheid regime. He discusses how he persevered under trying circumstances with his indomitable spirit.
2. *Animal Farm* by George Orwell. 1st World Library–Literary Society, 1946. A classic political allegory in which Orwell uses animal characters in order to draw the reader away from the world of current events into a fantasy space where the reader can grasp ideas and principles more clearly. At the same time, Orwell personifies the animals so that they symbolize real historical figures. An eye-opening, humorous, somewhat dark view of what power does to people.

Movies

1. *The Adjustment Bureau* (2011). Directed by George Rolfi. Dark-horse Senate candidate David Norris (played by Matt Damon) watches his campaign crash and burn just before election night thanks to an extraordinarily tame-seeming secret from his past. This is a top-notch political thriller also starring Emily Blunt.

2. *The Contender* (2000). Directed by Rod Lurie. The vice president has died while in office. The president wants to leave a legacy of having put a woman in the office of vice president. Senator Laine Hanson gets his nomination, but information and disinformation about her past surfaces that threatens to throw off her confirmation.

Internet Sites

1. www.uscis.gov/portal/site/uscis
   This is the U.S. Citizenship and Immigration Services Web site, where you can find information about visiting the United States either temporarily or permanently, passing the new naturalization exam, filling out immigration forms, and applying for permanent residence.
2. www.un.org/
   The United Nations' official Web site. Learn about UN issues around the globe. Find statistical information about all the countries of the world. Read in detail about how this world-governing body functions.
3. www.independent.co.uk/news/world/politics/
   The Independent is a British publication that is trusted for its breaking news on world politics. Here, you can read stories of a host of political issues affecting the world.

Study TIP

Improving Reading Fluency

Overview

To improve reading fluency, it is important for you to know what fluent readers do. Fluent readers read rapidly for comprehension, recognize words rapidly and automatically, draw on a very large vocabulary, integrate text information with their own knowledge base, recognize the purpose for reading, comprehend the text as necessary, shift purpose to read strategically, constantly monitor their own comprehension of the text, recognize and repair misunderstanding, and read critically to evaluate information. They employ a wide range of strategies such as skimming and scanning (see Chapter 2 for details), annotations, highlighting the text, and so forth.

If your goal is to become a fluent reader, then you will need to build a large vocabulary that is readily accessible, have a range of reading strategies at your disposal for successful comprehension, become a strategic reader by framing questions as you read, and avail yourself of every opportunity to read so that you can develop fluency and automaticity. Diversify your reading experiences by exposing yourself to different genres of reading such as short stories, magazine articles, novels, poems, and editorials.

It is recommended that before you read the text you explore key vocabulary, answer any pre-reading questions, and reflect on previous texts in connection with the new text. While you read, you can make an outline or write a summary of the original text. You can also examine the author's attitude toward the topic, determine sources of difficulty so that you can ask your professor or peers for clarification, and make predictions as to what will happen next. After you finish reading, you can complete a graphic organizer—a diagram, a picture, or a graph that enables you to organize information in a way that is easy to see and remember—based on text information, answer comprehension questions, and connect the content to your personal experiences.

Keep in mind that fluent readers preview a text, make predictions as to what will happen next in the text, summarize, learn new words from context and through the analysis of word formation, use context throughout to maintain understanding, recognize how the text is organized, formulate appropriate questions about the text, and repair miscomprehension.

Remember that reading fluency development involves rapid and automatic word recognition, the ability to recognize basic grammatical information, and the combination of word meanings and structural information.

Implications for Your Reading

Developing fluency has several implications for your reading. By improving your reading fluency, you will be able to search for information, comprehend a text rather quickly, learn new information, and synthesize and evaluate information. Since you will be taking many courses in college and will have several reading assignments to complete, it is imperative that you develop reading fluency by employing effective reading strategies.

Text Credits

Chapter 1

Pacesetter English: an Overview by Robert Scholes Preamble, http://www.brown.edu/Departments/MCM/people/scholes/PacesetterEnglishOverview.html

Baldwin, Amy; Brian Tietje and Paul G. Stoltz; The College Experience, Compact 2/e. ISBN 978-0-321-98003-8. From pp 17–20

Chapter 2

Aristotle (384–322 BC) Greek Philosopher

Michelle Lefort, "Learning and Teaching a Two-Way Calle in Boston," From USA Today, December 20, 2005. Copyright © 2005 Gannett-USA Today. All rights reserved. Used by permission and protected under the Copyright Laws of the United States. The printing, copying, redistribution, or retransmission of this content without express written permission is prohibited.

Hannah Boyd, Education.com (2008), Hannah Boyd, "The Lowdown on Single-Sex Education." Article reprinted with permission from Education.com

Johnson, James, et al., *Foundations of American Education*, 14th ed., © 2008. Printed and electronically reproduced by permission of Pearson Education, Inc., Upper Saddle River, New Jersey.

Gootman, Elisa. "Undercount of Violence in Schools," from *The New York Times*, September 20, 2007. Text; 910 total words out of 910 in context as originally published.

Singh, Neha and Kin Mai Aung. "A Free Rise for Bullies." from *The New York Times*, September 23, 2007. Text; 910 words out of 910, in context as originally published

Medina, Jennifer. "Recruitment by Military in Schools Is Criticized," from *The New York Times*, September 7, 2007; Text, 562 total words out of 562, in context as originally published.

From The New York Times, July 17, 2007. © 2007 *The New York Times*. All rights reserved. Used by permission and protected by the Copyright Laws of the United States. The printing,copying, redistribution, or retransmission of this Content without express written permission is prohibited.

NEA Today May 2004, "Should We Reward Good Grades with Money and Prizes?" *NEA Today*, May 2004, p. 39. Reprinted by permission of the National Education Association

TED Conferences, LLC

Chapter 3

Lindlahr, Victor. *You Are What You Eat*. (New York: National Nutrition Society, 1940)

Food Pyramid, National Institute of Health, United States Department of Health and Human Services.

Thompson, Janice; Manore, Melinda. *Nutrition: An Applied Approach*, 4th Ed., © 2015. Reprinted and Electronically reproduced by permission of Pearson Education, Inc., New York, NY.

"Fresh Produce, The Downside," from *The New York Times*; 12/1/2003; Text; 470 total words out of 470, in context as originally published.

Elliott, Stuart. "Telling Dieters A Pill Works Only If They Work, Too," from *The New York Times*; 5/9/2007; Text; 1,060 total words out of 1,060, in context as originally published.

From Marian Burros, "Eating Well: Is Organic Food Provably Better?" From *The New York Times*, July 16, 2003. © 2003 *The New York Times*. All rights reserved. Used by permission and protected by the Copyright Laws of the United States. The printing, copying, redistribution, or retransmission of this Content without express written permission is prohibited. www.nytimes.com

O'Neill, John. "Mothers' Minds and Babies' Bellies," from *The New York Times*; 4/8/2003; Text; 324 total words out of 324, in context as originally published.

Thompson, Janice J.; Manore, Melinda. *Nutrition: An Applied Approach*, 4th Ed., © 2015. Reprinted and Electronically reproduced by permission of Pearson Education, Inc., New York, NY.

Emily Bazelon, *The New York Times* May 6, 2007, Emily Bazelon, "Fat Chance." From *The New York Times*, May 6, 2007. © 2007 *The New York Times*. All rights reserved. Used by permission and protected by the Copyright Laws of the United States. The printing, copying, redistribution, or retransmission of this Content without express written permission is prohibited.

Reynolds, Gretchen. "How Weight Training Can Help You Keep the Weight Off," *The New York Times*, 1/28/15. © 2015. All rights reserved. Used by permission and protected by the Copyright Laws of the United States. The printing, copying, redistribution, ore re-transmission of this Content without express written permission is prohibited.

Taubes, Gary. What If It's All Been a Big Fat Lie? *NYT* 7/7/02.

From *The New York Times*, May 4, 2006. © 2006 *The New York Times*. All rights reserved. Used by permission and protected by the Copyright Laws of the United States. The printing, copying, redistribution, or retransmission of this Content without express written permission is prohibited.

Jonathan Panter, "My Soda, My Choice." Letter to the Editor, *New York Times*, May 15, 2006. © 2006 Reprinted by permission of the author.

Amanda Pressner Kreuser, "The 9 Most Common Kitchen Mistakes Even Healthy Women Make...and Why They're Robbing Your food Nutrients." *Shape magazine*. © Reprinted by permission of the author.

Chapter 4

Senator John Kerry, *Forgein Policy Speech*, Georgetown University, Washington, DC January 23, 2003

From Teresa Audesirk, Gerald Audesirk, and Bruce E. Byers, *Biology: Life on Earth*, 8th Edition, © 2008. Printed and electronically reproduced by permission of Pearson Education, Inc., Upper Saddle River, New Jersey.

Butt, Maggie, "Meltwater." Copyright © 2008 by Maggie Butt. Reprinted by permission of Maggie Butt. From *Feeling the Pressure: Poetry and science of climate change*, ed. Paul Munden. Berne, Switzerland: British Council, 2008.

"Ocean Life Faces Mass Extinction, Broad Study Says, from *The New York Times*, 1/16/15 © 2015 *The New York Times*. All rights reserved. Used by permission and protected under the Copyright Laws of the United States. The printing, copying, redistribution, or re-transmission of this Content without express written permission is prohibited.

From *The New York Times*, April 12, 2007. © 2007 *The New York Times*. All rights reserved. Used by permission and protected by the Copyright Laws of the United States. The printing, copying, redistribution, or retransmission of this Content without express written permission is prohibited.

Environmental Protection Agency. Climate Change –What You Can Do: At Home. 07/21/2015. http://www.epa.gov/climatechange/wycd/home.html

Christy, John R., "My Nobel Moment." Reprinted from *The Wall Street Journal*, November 1, 2007. © 2007 Reprinted by permission of the author.

McGough, Roger, "Give and Take," by Roger McGough (copyright © Roger MCGough 2002) from Good Enough to Eat is reprinted by permission of United Agents (www.unitedagents.co.uk) on behalf of Roger McGough.

Chapter 5

Bill Gates, Business @The Speed of Thought, © Bill Gates 1999 (New York: Warner Books, Inc. 1999)

Cox, Barbara G., and Koelzer, William, *Internet Marketing* (NetEffect Series), 1st ed., © 2004. Printed and electronically reproduced by permission of Pearson Education, Inc., Upper Saddle River, New Jersey.

Fawzy, Lara; Dworski, Lucas, *Emerging Business Online: Global Markets and the Power of B2B Internet Marketing*, 1st Ed., © 2011. Reprinted and Electronically reproduced by permission of Pearson Education, Inc., New York, NY.

From *The New York Times*, August 5, 2007. © 2007 *The New York Times*. All rights reserved. Used by permission and protected by the Copyright Laws of the United States. The printing, copying, redistribution, or retransmission of this Content without express written permission is prohibited. www.nytimes.com

Neagle, Colin. UN report highlights massive Internet gender gap. Network World. Sep 24, 2013.

Graham, Jefferson, "Got a Search Engine Question? Ask Mr. Sullivan," From *USA Today*, August 1, 2006. Copyright © 2006 Gannett-USA Today. All rights reserved. Used by permission and protected under the Copyright laws of the United States. the printing, copying, redistribution, or retransmission of this Content without express written permission is prohibited.

Jimmy Chuang. "Baidu CEO Robin Li Becomes China's Richest Man," *WantChinaTimes*, March 11, 2011.

Chapter 6

Sir William Blackstone, *Commentaries on the Laws of England*, 1st ed. © Sir William Blackstone (Oxford: Clarendon Press, 1765)

Sharon Smith, Shooting to Kill on the Border. Counter Punch, May 23, 2006, http://www.counterpunch.org/2006/05/23/shooting-to-kill-on-the-border/

Weiss, Rick, "Push for DNA Registry Could Affect All," *The Washington Post*, June 4, 2006

Kevin Johnson, "Inmates Go to Court to Seek Right to Use Internet," *USA Today*, November 23, 2006

The 2007 National Justice Survey: Tackling Crime and Public Confidence, http://www.justice.gc.ca/eng/rp-pr/csj-sje/jsp-sjp/rr07_4/a.html. Adaptation of Appendix A - questionnaire, Department of Justice, Canada, 2007. Reproduced with permission of the Department of Justice, Canada, 2015

From *The New York Times*, November 25, 2007. © 2007 *The New York Times*. All rights reserved. Used by permission and protected by the Copyright Laws of the United States. The printing, copying, redistribution, or retransmission of this Content without express written permission is prohibited.

Pauline Arrillaga, "Schizophrenic Teen Looks for Justice After Murder," April 16, 2006. Used with permission of The Associated Press. Copyright © 2015. All rights reserved.

Joe Cordill, From "Parents Share Blame for Crime Stats," Letter to the Editor, July 2006. http://blogs.usatoday.com/oped/2006/07/parents_share_b.html. Reprinted by permission of the author.

Excerpt(s) from *The Other Wes Moore: One Name, Two Fates* by Wes Moore, copyright © 2010 by Wes Moore. Used by permission of Spiegel & Grau, an imprint of Random House, a division of Penguin Random House LLC. All rights reserved.

Blow, Charles M. "Library Visit, Then Held At Gunpoint," from *The New York Times*; 1/26/2015; Text; 871 total words out of 871, in context as originally published.

Chapter 7

Val Saintsbury Quoted in Sue Heacock, Inspiring the Inspirational: Words of Hope from Nurses to Nurses, © Sue Heacock 2008, (Published by Author House, 2008)

Ramont, Roberta Pavy, and Niedringhaus, Dee, *Excerpts from Fundamental Nursing Care*, 2nd ed., © 2008. Printed and electronically reproduced by permission of Pearson Education, Inc., Upper Saddle River, New Jersey.

Krischke, Megan M., "Engaging Patients in Dialogue: A Partnership," Nursezone.com, August 26, 2011. © 2011 AMN Healthcare. Inc. Reprint and audio used with permission.

Simon, Cecilia Capuzzi. "45, Male And Now A Nurse," from *The New York Times*; 11/7/2010; Text; 1,247 total words out of 1,247, in context as originally published.

Nauert, Rick, "New Approach Addresses Substance Abuse Among Nurses," PsychCentral.com, January 27, 2011.Copyright © 2015 Psych Central.com. all rights reserved. Reprinted with permission.

National Federation of Licensed Practical Nurses, Inc. Copyright © 1991.

From A Nurse's Story by Peter Baida. Reprinted by permission of International Creative Management, Inc. Copyright © 2001 by Peter Baida.

Chapter 8

Carl Jung and Aniela Jaffe, translated by Richard and Clara Winston, *Memories, Dreams, Reflections* (New York: Pantheon Books, 1963)

Gerrig, Richard J., and Zimbardo, Philip G., *Psychology and Life, Discovering Psychology Edition*, 18th ed., © 2009. Printed and electronically reproduced by permission of Pearson Education, Inc., Upper Saddle River, New Jersey.

Helping Kids Deal With Bullies, Kids Health, The Nemours Foundation, June 2007

© It'sMyLife,http://pbskids.org/itsmylife

"Why Do Kids Bully?" U.S. Department of Health and Human Services, Health Resources and Services Administration,http://stopbullyingnow.hrsa.gov/kids/why-kids-bully.aspx

Excerpt from 'Identical Strangers' Explore Nature vs. Nuture' by Joe Richman and Radio Diaries, originally broadcast on NPR's All Things Considered. To hear the entire documentary visit radiodiaries.org or subscribe to the Radio Diaries Podcast. Used by permission of Radio Diaries.

Mandela Gardner, From an online blog, http://seattlepi.nwsource.com/health/252423_condor19.html. Reprinted by permission of Seattle Post-Intelliger.

Mintle, Linda S., "No Debate: TV Violence Harms Kids," www.drlindahelps.com. Reprinted by permission of Linda S. Mintle. Dr Linda Helps © 2009

Oleck, Joan, "TV Violence Doesn't Lead to Aggressive Kids, Study Says," *School Library Journal*, May 23, 2007. Used with permission of School Library Journal. Copyright © 2015. All rights reserved.

TED Conferences, LLC

Chapter 9

Mihaly Csikszentmihalyi, *Good Business: Leadership, Flow and the Making of Meaning*, © Mihaly Csikszentmihalyi 2003 (New York: Penguin Books, 2003)

Richard Zoglin, "Lady with a Calling", *Time Magazine*, June 24, 2001, http://content.time.com/time/magazine/article/0,9171,149830,00.html

Griffin, Ricky W.; Ebert, Ronald J., *Business*, 8th Ed., © 2006. Reprinted and Electronically reproduced by permission of Pearson Education, Inc., New York, NY.

Levin, Dan. "East Meets West, But It Takes Some Practice," from *The New York Times*; 12/22/2010; Text; 1,367 total words out of 1,367, in context as originally published.

Carsten, Paul. "China OKs iPhone 6 Sale After Apple Addresses Security Concerns." From reuters.com, 9/30/14. © 2014 reuters.com. All rights reserved. Used by permission and protected by the Copyright Laws of the United States. The printing, copying, redistribution, ore re-transmission of this Content without express written permission is prohibited.

Michele Zipp, "Designer Anya Ponorovskaya," from Working Mother, 8/8/2013 Copyright © 2013 Bonnier Corp. All rights reserved. Used by permission and protected under the Copyright Laws of the United States. The printing, copying, redistribution, or retransmission of this Content without express written permission is prohibited.

Twain, Mark, *Tom Sawyer*, © Mark Twain 1876 (London: Chatto and Windus, Piccadilly).

Chapter 10

Abraham Lincoln, *The Gettysburg Address*, Gettysburg, PA, November 19, 1863.

The Declaration of Independence, July 4, 1776, The United States Congress

Ron Hayduk, Op-Ed: "Give Non-citizens the Right to Vote? It's Only Fair," *LA Times*, December 22, 2014. Copyright 2014. Reprinted by permission of the author.

Excerpt from *Animal Farm* by George Orwell, copyright 1946 by Harcourt, Inc. and renewed 1974 by Sonia Orwell, reprinted by permission of the publisher.

Melting Pot or Salad Bowl? from "American Identity: Ideas, Not Ethnicity," by Michael J. Friedman, http://www.america.gov/st/diversity-english/2008/February/20080307154033ebyessedo0.5349237.html, February 13, 2008

J. Hector St. John, *Letters From An American Farmer 1782* (London: Davies and Davis 1782)

Noah, Timothy, "Should the Voting Age Be Lowered?" From *Slate*, November 7, 2007. Copyright 2007 The Slate Group. All rights reserved. Used by permission and protected by the Copyright Laws of the United States. The printing, copying, redistribution, or retransmission of this Content without express written permission is prohibited.

Danziger, James N.; Smith, Charles A.; *Understanding the Political World*, 12th Ed. 2016, pp. 1–3. Reprinted and Electronically reproduced by permission of Pearson Education, Inc, New York, NY.

Photo Credits

P. 1 Lakov Kalinin/Fotolia; P. 3 Helder Almeida/Shutterstock; P. 3 Darrin Henry/Shutterstock; P. 8 Sam Spiro/Fotolia; P. 14 Zerophoto/Fotolia; P. 21 Michaeljung/Fotolia; P. 22 AntonioDiaz/Fotolia; P. 23 Randy Glasbergen; P. 28 imaginando/Fotolia; P. 32 Michaeljung/Fotolia; P. 36 Stew Milne/AP Images; P. 58 bst2012/Fotolia; P. 60 Rido/Fotolia; P. 62 Kolett/Fotolia; P. 66 Peter Brooker/Presselect/Alamy; P. 77 Monkey Business Images/Shutterstock; P. 21 Michaeljung/Fotolia; P. 22 AntonioDiaz/Fotolia; P. 23 Randy Glasbergen; P. 28 imaginando/Fotolia; P. 32 Michaeljung/Fotolia; P. 36 Stew Milne/AP Images; P. 58 bst2012/Fotolia; P. 60 Rido/Fotolia; P. 62 Kolett/Fotolia; P. 66 Peter Brooker/Presselect/Alamy; P. 77 Monkey Business Images/Shutterstock; P. 79 Gennadiy Poznyakov/Fotolia; P. 80 Gennadiy Poznyakov/Fotolia; P. 81 Fran/CartoonStock; P. 92 Tim Boyle/Bloomberg/Getty Images; P. 97 SolisImages/Fotolia; P. 102 LOIC VENANCE/AFP/Getty Images; P. 113 Tunedin/Fotolia; P. 119 Jillchen/Fotolia; P. 130 Ematon/Fotolia; P. 130 Dorling Kindersley ltd/Alamy; P. 131 Monkey Business Images/Shutterstock; P. 135 Christina Horsten/dpa/Alamy; P. 148 Monkey Business Images/Shutterstock; P. 152 Axily/Fotolia; P. 154 Tom Toles/The Washington Post/Universal Uclick; P. 159 Marco De Swart/AFP/Getty Images; P. 164 Pixavril/Fotolia; P. 169 ASSOCIATED PRESS; P. 183 ImageBROKER/SuperStock; P. 194 Pearson Education, Inc.; P. 196 Accent Alaska.com/Alamy; P. 197 Vanessa Miles/Alamy; P. 198 NHPA/SuperStock; P. 200 Valery Rizzo/Alamy; P. 212 Monkey Business Images/Shutterstock; P. 216 Monkey Business/Fotolia; P. 218 Matt Buck; P. 223 Ducdao/Fotolia; P. 230 Shutterpix/123RF; P. 235 Martin Magunia/ullstein bild/Getty Images; P. 242 Google, Inc; P. 247 Q/Fotolia; P. 252 LuciaP/Fotolia; P. 265 Nicole Craine/Getty Images; P. 277 Monkey Business Images/Shutterstock; P. 278 Aijohn784/Fotolia; P. 280 CartoonStock Ltd.; P. 286 Clerkenwell/Getty Images; P. 290 Victor Zastol'skiy/Fotolia; P. 301 Afplive/Newscom; P. 308 Tinx/Fotolia; P. 323 ZUMA Press/Alamy; P. 337 Monkey Business Images/Shutterstock; P. 339 Giorgiomtb/Fotolia; P. 341 Richard Sly/CartoonStock Ltd.; P. 346 Godfer/Fotolia; P. 347 Tyler Olson/Fotolia; P. 356 Georgios Kollidas/Fotolia; P. 357 Leonid Shtandel/Fotolia; P. 386 Fotomaximum/Fotolia; P. 391 Bacho Foto/Fotolia; P. 397 Minerva Studio/Fotolia; P. 403 Georgios Kollidas/Fotolia; P. 403 Brady-Handy Studio/Bettmann/Corbis; P. 404 Everett

Collection Historical/Alamy; P. 404 Bain News Service/Corbis; P. 405 Monkey Business Images/Shutterstock; P. 413 Nielskliim/Fotolia; P. 418 Michelle Shephard/Toronto Star/Getty Images; P. 426 Monkey Business Images/Shutterstock; P. 429 Mrhighsky/Fotolia; P. 430 Jiris/Fotolia; P. 431 Nick Kim/CartoonStock Ltd.; P. 442 Elena Seibert; P. 444 Sigmund Freud Archives Publication may be restricted. For information see (http.//w.w.w.loc.gov//rr/print/res/118_freu.html); P. 457 Rostislav Sedlacek/Fotolia; P. 461 Myrleen Ferguson Cate/PhotoEdit; P. 461 Tony Savino/The Image Works; P. 461 JCREATION/Shutterstock; P. 461 Michael Schwarz/The Image Works ; P. 462 National Gallery, London/Art Resource; P. 463 Jeff Greenberg/PhotoEdit; P. 463 Pearson Education, Inc.; P. 467 Tony Charnock/Alamy; P. 475 Monkey Business Images/Shutterstock; P. 476 Rawpixel/Fotolia; P. 479 Randy Glasbergen; P. 493 Newscom; P. 504 Sepy/Fotolia; P. 509 Corbis; P. 511 Joseph Mirachi/CartoonStock Ltd.; P. 515 Ritz Sino/The New York Times/Redux Pictures; P. 525 Lisa Gansky; P. 534 Pressmaster/Fotolia; P. 537 Monkey Business Images/Shutterstock; P. 537 Hill Street Studios/Blend Images/Alamy; P. 538 Alex Pin/Fotolia; P. 540 Nobilior/Fotolia; P. 542 Marty Bucella/CartoonStock Ltd.; P. 553 Rawpixel/Fotolia; P. 563 Pete Souza/Public Domain; P. 572 Mimagephotos/Fotolia; P. 579 Yonhap News/Newscom; P. 590 Monkey Business Images/Shutterstock.

Index